Cultural Reception, Translation and Transformation
from Medieval to Modern Italy
Essays in Honour of Martin McLaughlin

LEGENDA

LEGENDA is the Modern Humanities Research Association's book imprint for new research in the Humanities. Founded in 1995 by Malcolm Bowie and others within the University of Oxford, Legenda has always been a collaborative publishing enterprise, directly governed by scholars. The Modern Humanities Research Association (MHRA) joined this collaboration in 1998, became half-owner in 2004, in partnership with Maney Publishing and then Routledge, and has since 2016 been sole owner. Titles range from medieval texts to contemporary cinema and form a widely comparative view of the modern humanities, including works on Arabic, Catalan, English, French, German, Greek, Italian, Portuguese, Russian, Spanish, and Yiddish literature. Editorial boards and committees of more than 60 leading academic specialists work in collaboration with bodies such as the Society for French Studies, the British Comparative Literature Association and the Association of Hispanists of Great Britain & Ireland.

The MHRA encourages and promotes advanced study and research in the field of the modern humanities, especially modern European languages and literature, including English, and also cinema. It aims to break down the barriers between scholars working in different disciplines and to maintain the unity of humanistic scholarship. The Association fulfils this purpose through the publication of journals, bibliographies, monographs, critical editions, and the MHRA Style Guide, and by making grants in support of research. Membership is open to all who work in the Humanities, whether independent or in a University post, and the participation of younger colleagues entering the field is especially welcomed.

ALSO PUBLISHED BY THE ASSOCIATION

Critical Texts
Tudor and Stuart Translations • *New Translations* • *European Translations*
MHRA Library of Medieval Welsh Literature

MHRA Bibliographies
Publications of the Modern Humanities Research Association

The Annual Bibliography of English Language & Literature
Austrian Studies
Modern Language Review
Portuguese Studies
The Slavonic and East European Review
Working Papers in the Humanities
The Yearbook of English Studies

www.mhra.org.uk
www.legendabooks.com

EDITORIAL BOARD

Chair: Professor Jonathan Long (University of Durham)
For *Germanic Literatures*: Ritchie Robertson (University of Oxford)
For *Italian Perspectives*: Simon Gilson (University of Warwick)
For *Moving Image*: Emma Wilson (University of Cambridge)
For *Research Monographs in French Studies*:
Diana Knight (University of Nottingham)
For *Selected Essays*: Susan Harrow (University of Bristol)
For *Studies in Comparative Literature*: Duncan Large
(British Centre for Literary Translation, University of East Anglia)
For *Studies in Hispanic and Lusophone Cultures*:
Trevor Dadson (Queen Mary, University of London)
For *Studies in Yiddish*: Gennady Estraikh (New York University)
For *Transcript*: Matthew Reynolds (University of Oxford)

Managing Editor
Dr Graham Nelson
41 Wellington Square, Oxford OX1 2JF, UK

www.legendabooks.com

Cultural Reception, Translation and Transformation from Medieval to Modern Italy

Essays in Honour of Martin McLaughlin

Edited by Guido Bonsaver,
Brian Richardson and Giuseppe Stellardi

Modern Humanities Research Association
2017

Published by Legenda
an imprint of the Modern Humanities Research Association
Salisbury House, Station Road, Cambridge CB1 2LA

ISBN 978-1-78188-469-0 (HB)
ISBN 978-1-78188-470-6 (PB)

First published 2017

All rights reserved. No part of this publication may be reproduced or disseminated or transmitted in any form or by any means, electronic, mechanical, photocopying, recording or otherwise, or stored in any retrieval system, or otherwise used in any manner whatsoever without written permission of the copyright owner, except in accordance with the provisions of the Copyright, Designs and Patents Act 1988, or under the terms of a licence permitting restricted copying issued in the UK by the Copyright Licensing Agency Ltd, Saffron House, 6–10 Kirby Street, London EC1N 8TS, England, or in the USA by the Copyright Clearance Center, 222 Rosewood Drive, Danvers MA 01923. Application for the written permission of the copyright owner to reproduce any part of this publication must be made by email to legenda@mhra.org.uk.

Disclaimer: Statements of fact and opinion contained in this book are those of the author and not of the editors or the Modern Humanities Research Association. The publisher makes no representation, express or implied, in respect of the accuracy of the material in this book and cannot accept any legal responsibility or liability for any errors or omissions that may be made.

Trademark notice: Product or corporate names may be trademarks or registered trademarks, and are used only for identification and explanation without intent to infringe.

© Modern Humanities Research Association 2017

Copy-Editor: Dr Susan Wharton

CONTENTS

	Notes on Contributors	ix
	List of Figures	xv
	Introduction	xvii
	Bibliography of Publications by Martin McLaughlin	xxviii
1	'Io mi rivolgo indietro a ciascun passo' (*Rvf* 15. 1): Petrarch, the *fabula* of Eurydice and Orpheus and the Structure of the Canzoniere ZYGMUNT G. BARAŃSKI	1
2	Boccaccio's 'spirante turbo': An Intertextual Defence of Tolerance ELISABETTA TARANTINO	25
3	Beyond Borghini: The Oxford Manuscript of Sacchetti's *novelle* and their New Critical Edition MICHELANGELO ZACCARELLO	40
4	Why Retranslate the Classics? Griselda in French from the Renaissance to the Twentieth Century LINDA LOUIE, MAIRI MCLAUGHLIN AND DIANA THOW	52
5	La raffigurazione del potere nell'*Orlando furioso* MARCO DORIGATTI	69
6	Intricate Intertextuality: Lucan's Wood in Ariosto and Tasso ELENA LOMBARDI	84
7	Improvising Lyric Verse in the Renaissance: Contexts, Sources and Composition BRIAN RICHARDSON	97
8	Piero Vettori and France RICHARD COOPER	117
9	From Shadows towards Light: Transformations of Allegorical Journeys in Dialogue II of Giordano Bruno's *Cena de le ceneri* HILARY GATTI	136
10	Sebastiano Serlio: *giudizio, mescolanza, invenzione* FRANCESCO PAOLO FIORE	150
11	Giacomo Leoni: Unsung Intermediary between Alberti and Palladio JOHN WOODHOUSE	158
12	Repurposing Renaissance Literature for Language Learning: Giuseppe Baretti's *An Introduction to the Italian Language* (1755) VILMA DE GASPERIN	173
13	Goldoni and Gozzi: Disquisition on a Statue that Walks JOSEPH FARRELL	188

14 *Romantic, romantico, romanzesco*: An Aspect of Walter Scott's Reception in Italy
DAVID ROBEY   199

15 Hypatia of Alexandria, Pagan or Christian? Propaganda Wars between John Toland's *Hypatia* of 1720 and Diodata Saluzzo's *Ipazia* of 1827
LETIZIA PANIZZA   215

16 John Dickson Batten's Illustrations to the *Inferno*
PETER HAINSWORTH   239

17 Turns of Chance: Modern Luck and Italian Modernism (Marinetti, Montale, Pirandello)
ROBERT S. C. GORDON   257

18 Johnny's Epic Resistance: Classical Echoes in Fenoglio's *Il partigiano Johnny*
ROSALBA BIASINI   272

19 Una questioncella privata: su un racconto inedito di Italo Calvino
MARIO BARENGHI   287

20 Calvino's *Il barone rampante* and Leopardi's *Elogio degli uccelli*
EMANUELA TANDELLO COOPER   299

21 Transformations in the *giallo*: Italo Calvino's Metafictional Anti-Detective Novel *Se una notte d'inverno un viaggiatore* (1979)
HELEN ANDERSON   315

22 'Senti 'n po', a Gregori Pècche...': Shavelson's *It Started in Naples* and Fellini's *La dolce vita* between Italian and U.S. Culture
GUIDO BONSAVER   331

23 Diffracting Dante's *Paradiso* with Pasolini and Morante: Transformation, Identity and the Form of Desire
MANUELE GRAGNOLATI   352

24 'Poetry is not eggs': Luigi Meneghello on Italian and Foreign Poetry, Translation and 'Transplants'
DIEGO ZANCANI   367

25 'Double trouble': Giampaolo Pansa's *Il sangue dei vinti* from Novel to Film
PHILIP COOKE   383

26 Controtendenze narrative novecentesche: *La Storia Romanzo* di Elsa Morante
FRANCA PELLEGRINI   395

27 Fragments of (Urban) Space and (Human) Time: Gadda's Poetics (with Baudelaire and Benjamin)
GIUSEPPE STELLARDI   410

28 Il mistero dei due anelli: una postilla sopra la natura del discorso letterario, da Virgilio a Calvino
NICOLA GARDINI   424

A Note on Legenda   435

Index   437

NOTES ON CONTRIBUTORS

Helen Anderson completed a DPhil in 2010 at St Anne's College, Oxford, under the supervision of Martin McLaughlin. Her thesis offered the first comparative analysis of the experimental historical and detective novels of Italo Calvino, Luigi Malerba and Laura Mancinelli. Helen worked as Heath Harrison teaching fellow at the Faculty of Medieval and Modern Languages in the University of Oxford during her doctoral studies. She joined a top five global contract research organization in 2010 and now leads its life-sciences translation and linguistic validation group.

Zygmunt G. Barański is Serena Professor of Italian Emeritus, University of Cambridge, and Notre Dame Professor of Dante & Italian Studies, University of Notre Dame. Among his books are *'Luce nuova, sole nuovo': saggi sul rinnovamento culturale in Dante* (1996); *Pasolini Old and New: Surveys and Studies* (1999); *Dante e i segni* (2000); *'Chiosar con altro testo': leggere Dante nel Trecento* (2001); *Cambridge Companion to Modern Italian Culture* (with Rebecca West, 2001); *Petrarch and Dante* (with Theodore J. Cachey Jr, 2009); *Dante in Context* (with Lino Pertile, 2015). Between 1981 and 2008 he was senior editor of *The Italianist*, and he is currently editor of *Le tre corone*.

Mario Barenghi teaches Contemporary Italian Literature at Milan University, Bicocca. His interests concern literary theory, memoirs, Manzoni and various twentieth-century authors, particularly Calvino (*Italo Calvino, le linee e i margini*, 2007; *Calvino*, 2009). His most recent publications are: *Perché crediamo a Primo Levi? / Why Do We Believe Primo Levi?* (2013) and *Che cosa possiamo fare con il fuoco? Letteratura e altri ambienti* (2013), with which he started a discussion on the role of the poetic word in bio-cultural evolution. He contributes to the annual periodical *Tirature* and the online journal *Doppiozero*.

Rosalba Biasini graduated in Lettere Classiche (L'Aquila, 2004). She holds an MA in Translation Studies (Manchester, 2005) and a Master ITALS (Ca' Foscari, Venezia, 2013). She completed a DPhil in Italian (Oxford, 2010) under Martin McLaughlin's supervision on the presence of the epic mode in Fenoglio's *Il partigiano Johnny*. She is currently Lecturer in Italian at the University of Liverpool where she teaches Italian language and culture. Her research interests range from the literature of the Resistance to the use of translation in foreign language acquisition.

Guido Bonsaver is Professor of Italian Cultural History at Oxford and a Fellow of Pembroke College. He is currently working on the reciprocal influence of Italian and U.S. culture. His principal publications are *Il mondo scritto di Italo Calvino* (1995), *Elio Vittorini* (2000), *Censorship and Literature in Fascist Italy* (2007), *Vita e* *omicidio di Gaetano Pilati* (2010) and *Mussolini censore* (2013). He also co-edited, with Robert Gordon, *Culture, Censorship and the State in Twentieth-Century Italy* (2005); with Martin McLaughlin and Franca Pellegrini, *Sinergie narrative: cinema e letteratura nell'Italia contemporanea* (2008); and with Emma Bond and Federico Faloppa, *Destination Italy: Representing Migration in Contemporary Media and Narrative* (2015).

Philip Cooke is Professor of Italian History and Culture at the University of Strathclyde (Glasgow). His research centres on the long-term impact of the Italian Resistance movement and on twentieth-century Italian social and cultural history. His publications range from analyses of literary texts (*Fenoglio's Binoculars, Johnny's Eyes*, 2000), to social/protest movements (*Luglio 1960: Tambroni e la repressione fallita*, 2000) and Italian partisan exiles living clandestinely in Czechoslovakia (various articles). His most recent books are *The Legacy of the Italian Resistance* (2011), *Ending Terrorism in Italy* (2012, co-authored with Anna Cento Bull) and *European Resistance in the Second World War* (2013, co-edited with Ben H. Shepherd).

Richard Cooper is Professor of French at the University of Oxford and a Fellow of Brasenose College. He works on relations between France and Italy in the Renaissance. His principal publications are *Rabelais et l'Italie* (1991); *Litteræ in tempore belli: études sur les relations littéraires italo-françaises pendant les guerres d'Italie* (1997); *Roman Antiquities in Renaissance France (1515–65)* (2013); and editions of Maurice Scève, *The Entry of Henri II into Lyon, September 1548* (1997); Jean du Bellay, *Poemata*, with Geneviève Demerson (2007); Marguerite de Navarre, *Chrétiens et mondains, poèmes épars* (2007); and *Histoire et ancienne cronique de Gerard d'Euphrate, duc de Bourgogne* (2012).

Vilma De Gasperin is Senior Instructor in Italian at the Faculty of Medieval and Modern Languages in the University of Oxford and Lecturer in Italian at Exeter College and Somerville College, Oxford. She holds a degree in Modern Languages from the University of Padua, a DPhil in Italian Literature and an MLitt in History of the Italian Language from the University of Oxford. She has published *Loss and the Other in the Visionary Work of Anna Maria Ortese* (2014), and essays on Ortese, Vivian Lamarque, Giuseppe Baretti and Benvenuto Italiano. She has edited *'Ciò che potea la lingua nostra': Lectures and Essays in Memory of Clara Florio Cooper* (2011).

Marco Dorigatti graduated from Florence and then obtained a doctorate from the University of Oxford, where he is now a lecturer in Italian literature at St Hilda's College. He has edited digital texts for the Oxford Text Archive and he has published studies on Boiardo, Ariosto and the chivalric literature of the Renaissance, and also on the modern period (Deledda, Aleramo, Dessì) and on cinema (Bergman and Antonioni). He is above all a philologist, and he published the first critical edition of Ariosto's *Orlando furioso secondo la princeps del 1516* (2006), which received the High Patronage of the President of the Italian Republic.

Joseph Farrell is Professor Emeritus in Italian of the University of Strathclyde. He has written widely on Italian, especially Sicilian, culture and theatre history, and is author of *Leonardo Sciascia*, *Dario Fo and Franca Rame: Harlequins of the Revolution*, and *Sicily: A Cultural History*. He has translated many books from Italian, co-edited with Paolo Puppa the *History of Italian Theatre*, and has edited volumes of essays on Goldoni, Fo, Primo Levi, Carlo Levi and Betti. He has produced editions in English of plays by Fo, Pirandello and Goldoni, and interview-books with Franca Rame and Dacia Maraini. He has translated three film scripts by Giuseppe Tornatore.

Francesco Paolo Fiore retired as Professor of the History of Architecture at the University of Rome 'La Sapienza'. He has edited and contributed to *Francesco di Giorgio architetto* (with Manfredo Tafuri, 1993); Sebastiano Serlio, *Architettura civile: trattati manoscritti VI, VII e VIII dai codici di Monaco e Vienna* (1994); *Storia dell'architettura italiana: Il Quattrocento* (1998); *L'architettura militare di Venezia in terraferma e in Adriatico fra XVI e XVII secolo* (2014). He is the author of *Leon Battista Alberti* (2012). He was twice Visiting Professor at Harvard University, president of the Comitato Nazionale per il VI centenario della nascita di Leon Battista Alberti (2004) and Isaiah Berlin Visiting Scholar at Oxford (2007–08).

Nicola Gardini is Professor of Italian and Comparative Literature at the University of Oxford. His main research areas are the Renaissance, the classical legacy and comparative literature. Among his publications are *Rinascimento* (2010), *Per una biblioteca indispensabile* (2011), *Lacuna* (2014), *Tradurre è un bacio* (2015) and *Viva il latino* (2017). His most recent novels are *Le parole perdute di Amelia Lynd* (2012, Premio Viareggio 2012 and Zerilli Marimò Prize 2012), *Fauci* (2013) and *La vita non vissuta* (Feltrinelli, 2015). *Le parole perdute di Amelia Lynd* has also appeared in America (*Lost Words*, translated by Michael Moore, 2016).

Hilary Gatti started teaching English at the State University of Milan, and retired as associate Professor in the Philosophy Faculty of the University of Rome 'La Sapienza'. She has been an Honorary Fellow of University College, London, a member of the Institute of Advanced Study in Princeton and an Honorary Fellow of the University of Auckland. Her publications include *The Renaissance Drama of Knowledge*, *Giordano Bruno and Renaissance Science*, *Essays on Giordano Bruno* and *Ideas of Liberty in Early Modern Europe: From Machiavelli to Milton*. A festschrift in her honour, edited by Martin McLaughlin, Ingrid Rowland and Elisabetta Tarantino, was published in 2015 by Legenda.

Robert S. C. Gordon is Serena Professor of Italian and Fellow of Gonville and Caius College, Cambridge. He was Lecturer in Italian and Fellow of Pembroke College, Oxford, from 1990 to 1997. His research centres on modern Italian literature, cinema and cultural history. He is the author of *Pasolini: Forms of Subjectivity* (1996); *Primo Levi's Ordinary Virtues: From Testimony to Ethics* (2001); *Introduction to Twentieth-Century Italian Literature: A Difficult Modernity* (2005); *Bicycle Thieves* (2008); *'Sfacciata fortuna': la Shoah e il caso* (2010); and *The Holocaust in Italian Culture, 1944–2010* (2012).

Manuele Gragnolati is Professor of Medieval Italian Literature at the University of Paris-Sorbonne. From 1999 to 2003 he taught at Dartmouth College and from 2003 to 2015 at Oxford University, where he was Professor of Italian Literature. His publications include a dozen co-edited volumes and the monographs *Experiencing the Afterlife: Souls and Body in Dante and Medieval Culture* (2005) and *Amor che* *move: linguaggio del corpo e forma del desiderio in Dante, Pasolini e Morante* (2013). He is Associate Director at the ICI Berlin Institute for Cultural Inquiry and Senior Research Fellow at Somerville College, Oxford.

Peter Hainsworth is an Emeritus Fellow of Lady Margaret Hall, Oxford. After lectureships at the universities of Hull and Kent, he taught at Oxford until retiring in 2003. As well as *Petrarch the Poet* (1986), he has written widely on other Italian authors, medieval and modern. He co-edited with David Robey *The Oxford Companion to Italian Literature* (2002) and co-authored with him a *Very Short Introduction to Italian Literature* (2012) and *Dante: A Very Short Introduction* (2015). He has recently published two volumes of translations: *The Essential Petrarch* (2012) and *Tales from the Decameron* (2015).

Elena Lombardi is Associate Professor of Italian Studies at Oxford and a Fellow of Balliol College. She is the author of two books, *The Syntax of Desire: Language and Love in Augustine, the Modistae and Dante* (2007), and *The Wings of the Doves: Love and Desire in Dante and Medieval Culture* (2012), and has published articles on the Sicilian School, Guido Cavalcanti, Dante, D'Annunzio and De Sica. Her current research focuses on the theme of reading and the material culture of the book in the times of Dante.

Linda Louie is a doctoral student in Romance Languages and Literatures, emphasis French, at the University of California, Berkeley. She is currently working on her dissertation, *Repatriating Romance in Renaissance France*, which looks at translation and pseudo-philology in Renaissance French romance and epic. She specializes in French, Italian and Spanish literature and translation studies; other research interests include translation and foreign language pedagogy; history of the book; and science and literature.

Mairi McLaughlin is an Associate Professor of French and an Affiliated Member of the Linguistics Department and the Department of Italian Studies at the University of California, Berkeley. She specializes in French/Romance Linguistics and Translation Studies. Her book *Syntactic Borrowing in Contemporary French: A Linguistic Analysis of News Translation* was published in 2011. She has published in journals such as *French Studies*, *The Italianist* and *Perspectives: Studies in Translatology*. She is working on two major projects: a book on the origins and evolution of the language of the French press (1631–1789) and an edition of the *Journal de la langue françoise* (1784–95).

Letizia Panizza is a research fellow in Italian at Royal Holloway University of London. She has published widely on humanism and women's writing. She is the editor of *Women in Italian Renaissance Culture and Society* (2000) and coeditor of *A History of Women's Writing in Italy* (2000), of *Lucian of Samosata vivus et redivivus* (2007), and, with Martin McLaughlin, of *Petrarch in Britain: Interpreters, Imitators, and Translators over 700 Years* (2007). She wrote the introduction to Lucrezia Marinella's *The Nobility and Excellence of Women and the Defects and Vices of Men* (1999), and she edited and translated Arcangela Tarabotti's *Paternal Tyranny* (2004).

Franca Pellegrini teaches literature and Latin in the Liceo Copernico, Prato. She took her DPhil in the University of Oxford and taught there as a Lettore of the Ministero degli Affari Esteri. Her publications include the *Censimento del carteggio di Vincenzio Borghini* (1993) and *Il Carteggio di Vincenzio Borghini 1541–1552* (2001), *La tempesta originale: la vita in poesia di Alda Merini* (2006), *Il romanzo nazional-regionale nella letteratura italiana contemporanea* (2014). With Elisabetta Tarantino she edited *Il romanzo contemporaneo: voci italiane* (2006) and with Martin McLaughlin and Guido Bonsaver she co-edited *Sinergie narrative: cinema e letteratura nell'Italia contemporanea* (2008).

Brian Richardson is Emeritus Professor of Italian Language at the University of Leeds. His publications include *Print Culture in Renaissance Italy: The Editor and the Vernacular Text, 1470–1600* (1994), *Printing, Writers and Readers in Renaissance Italy* (1999), *Manuscript Culture in Renaissance Italy* (2009), an edition of Giovan Francesco Fortunio's *Regole grammaticali della volgar lingua* (2001) and works arising from the project Oral Culture, Manuscript and Print in Early Modern Italy, 1450–1700, funded by the European Research Council from 2011 to 2015.

David Robey was Lecturer in Italian at Oxford, then Professor of Italian at the universities of Manchester and Reading. Chair of the Society for Italian Studies from 1998 to 2003, he is currently Digital Humanities Consultant at the Oxford e-Research Centre. His publications include *Sound and Structure in Dante's 'Divine Comedy'* (2000), now extended to include the major narrative poems of the Italian Renaissance in an on-line analytical database. With Peter Hainsworth he was joint editor of the *Oxford Companion to Italian Literature* and joint author of *Italian Literature: A Very Short Introduction* (2012) and *Dante: A Very Short Introduction* (2015).

Giuseppe Stellardi studied in Pavia and Paris and worked in Cape Town and Lancaster, before joining the University of Oxford. His main research areas lie in modern Italian literature, but he is also interested in literary theory and continental philosophy. He has written on Dossi, Tarchetti, Michelstaedter, Svevo, Gadda, Moravia, Eco, Morante; also on Deconstruction (Derrida), on *Pensiero debole* (Vattimo) and on metaphor. He has published a book on metaphor in Derrida and Heidegger, and one on the work of Carlo Emilio Gadda, as well as a translation into English of Carlo Michelstaedter's *La persuasione e la rettorica*. He is currently working on temporality in twentieth-century Italian literature.

Emanuela Tandello Cooper teaches at Oxford, and is a Student of Christ Church. She has worked extensively on Amelia Rosselli, as well as on Pirandello and Svevo, and on poetry in dialect. She has published *Amelia Rosselli: la fanciulla e l'infinito* (2007) and co-edited the Meridiano Mondadori edition of Amelia Rosselli, *L'opera poetica* (2012), of which she also wrote the preface; she has introduced, edited and translated Rosselli's sonnet sequence in English, *October Elizabethans* (2015). With Giuseppe Stellardi, she has edited *Italo Svevo and his Legacy for the Third Millennium* (2014). She is currently working on Leopardi.

Elisabetta Tarantino studied English literature at postgraduate level in Strasbourg and Rome, and then taught in Italian departments in the UK. She is currently an honorary research fellow of the Faculty of Medieval and Modern Languages, University of Oxford. She has published on both English and Italian literature. She specializes in early modern English drama and intertextuality. One of her latest publications is a volume co-edited with Martin McLaughlin and Ingrid Rowland, *Authority, Innovation and Early Modern Epistemology: Essays in Honour of Hilary Gatti* (2015).

Diana Thow is a doctoral student in Comparative Literature at the University of California, Berkeley. She specializes in Italian, English and French literature as well as translation studies. Her dissertation is entitled '*La prova del fuoco*': *Lyric Translation and Poetic Innovation in English, Italian, and French Postwar Poetry*. Her work as a translator includes an English translation and annotation of Amelia Rosselli's *Impromptu* (2014) and a translation of Elisa Biagini's *The Guest in the Wood* (2013) which won the Best Translated Book Award in 2014.

John Woodhouse is Emeritus Fiat-Serena Professor of Italian Studies at Oxford, and Emeritus Fellow of Magdalen College. From his reappraisal of Calvino's trilogy in 1968 to his present efforts to vindicate the true architectural aims and merits of Giacomo Leoni, his researches have sought to unearth new, even subversive views: Borghini's opinions on Florentine family histories and Renaissance linguistic controversies, reinterpretations of court diplomacy and a reassessment of Castiglione's *Courtier*, the vast, intriguing, but largely misguided Dantesque correspondence of Gabriele Rossetti, an objective view of Gabriele D'Annunzio's life and work, and accounts of the capture of Fiume, witnessed by Santi Ceccherini and Giuseppe Sovera.

Michelangelo Zaccarello taught in Dublin and Oxford, and is now Professor of Italian Philology in the University of Verona. Among his publications are editions of the *Sonetti del Burchiello* (2000 and 2004) and of Franco Sacchetti's *Le Trecento Novelle* (2014), *Reperta: indagini recuperi ritrovamenti di letteratura italiana antica* (2008) and *Alcune questioni di metodo nella critica dei testi volgari* (2012). He has co-edited *Dante in Oxford* (2011, with Martin McLaughlin and Tristan Kay), *Language and Style in Dante* (2013, with John C. Barnes) and a special issue of *Dante Studies* on *Dante e i Malaspina* (2008, with H. Wayne Storey).

Diego Zancani is an Emeritus Fellow of Balliol College, and Emeritus Professor of Italian at Oxford University, where he taught for over twenty years, after working in the universities of Reading, Liverpool and Kent at Canterbury. He was twice Visiting Professor at Harvard University, and in Italian universities where he was also a member of ministerial research evaluation committees. His publications range from fifteenth-century court literature to late Renaissance popular culture, history of the language and history of food. He has also written extensively on modern and contemporary literature, most recently on Meneghello.

LIST OF FIGURES

FIG. 5.1. Bartolomeo Veneto (attribuito a), *Ritratto di Ippolito d'Este* (ca. 1508–10), olio su tavola, 60,5 × 48,5 cm, Vienna, Dorotheum, presso cui il dipinto fu battuto all'asta il 17 ottobre 2012

FIG. 5.2. Raffaello Sanzio, *Ritratto del cardinale Ippolito d'Este* (ca. 1504–05), olio su tavola, 54 × 39 cm, Budapest, Szépművészeti Múzeum

FIG. 16.1. The Centaur Nessus Carries Dante across the River of Blood

FIG. 16.2. The Meeting with Homer, Horace, Ovid and Lucan

FIG. 16.3. Beatrice Watches from Paradise

FIG. 16.4. Paolo and Francesca

FIG. 16.5. The Devils Fallen in the Pitch

FIG. 16.6. Minos, the Judge of Hell

FIG. 16.7. Geryon Carries Virgil and Dante down to Malebolge

FIG. 16.8. Virgil and Dante Climb out of the Sixth Pit of Malebolge

FIG. 16.9. Antaeus

FIG. 22.1. *It Started in Naples*. Set photo: Mike (Clark Gable) teaches Nando (Marietto Angeletti) how to prepare and eat a hamburger. (Courtesy of Margaret Herrick Library.)

FIG. 22.2. *It Started in Naples*. Set photo: Mike (Clark Gable) tries to squeeze into the Fiat car of his lawyer (Vittorio De Sica) and his assistant (Giovanni Filidoro). (Courtesy of Margaret Herrick Library.)

FIG. 22.3. *La dolce vita*. Film still: the prostitute and her pimp wait for Maddalena and Marcello to reappear whilst standing next to Maddalena's Cadillac. (Courtesy of Cineteca di Bologna.)

FIG. 22.4. *It Started in Naples*. Set photo: Lucia (Sophia Loren) sings *Tu vuo' fa' l'americano* accompanied by guitarist Renzo (Paolo Carlini). (Courtesy of Margaret Herrick Library.)

FIG. 22.5. *La dolce vita*. Film still: Adriano (Adriano Celentano) singing *Ready Teddy* the moment before he slips and falls to the ground. Sylvia (Anita Ekberg) and Frankie (Alain Dijon) are visible to the right. (Courtesy of Cineteca di Bologna.)

FIG. 24.1. Gerard Manley Hopkins' sonnet 'I wake and feel the fell of dark, not day', translated by Luigi Meneghello into Vicentino dialect, with numerous autograph additions, to be compared with the published text in *Trapianti: dall'inglese al vicentino* (Milan: Rizzoli, 2002), p. 23. (Courtesy of the Centro di ricerca sulla tradizione manoscritta di autori moderni e contemporanei, University of Pavia.)

INTRODUCTION

Guido Bonsaver, Brian Richardson and Giuseppe Stellardi

Martin McLaughlin was born on 4 December 1950 in Glasgow, where he grew up in a large, happy family of eight brothers and sisters. He studied Classics at the University of Glasgow from 1968 to 1973. His own interest in all things Italian can be traced back to this period: it was then that he met his future wife Cathy, who was herself a student of Italian. Indeed, he first travelled to Italy in 1970 to visit Cathy at a time when he spoke not a word of Italian. Martin and Cathy were married in 1974 and both went on to have careers involving Italian: Martin as an academic and Cathy as a schoolteacher. They have one daughter, Mairi, who shares her parents' love of languages and is also an academic.

After graduating from Glasgow, Martin received a Snell Fellowship to study at Balliol College, Oxford, where he obtained a BA in Classics and Italian with first-class Honours (1975). This was when he first became interested in Humanism and Renaissance studies and he began a DPhil the following year, also at Balliol; under the supervision of Cecil Grayson, Martin wrote a thesis on 'Imitation in Literary Theory and Practice in Italy, 1400–1530' (1983).

Martin's first post was as a lecturer in the Italian Department of the University of Edinburgh, where he taught between 1977 and 1990. He then moved back to Oxford to become University Lecturer in Italian at Oxford and Student of Christ Church. In 2001, he was elected to the Agnelli-Serena Chair of Italian Studies at Oxford and became a Fellow of Magdalen College. From his time at Edinburgh onwards, Martin was a very active member of the academic community, and not only in the pursuit of academic goals: colleagues and students report seeing him perform, with enthusiasm, in the Italian Play at Edinburgh and play football, equally enthusiastically, at Christ Church.

Martin's research interests range from classical literatures, to the Renaissance, to modern and contemporary literature, and his undergraduate teaching and graduate supervision cover an equally impressive variety of authors and topics, from Dante, Petrarch and Vernacular Humanism to Verga, Vittorini, Pavese, Fenoglio, Calvino, Eco, Tabucchi and beyond, including travel literature and translation studies. The long list of his publications contains a host of ground-breaking books, edited volumes, articles and book chapters on a wide range of topics that have attracted his curiosity and study over the course of the past four decades, as well as outstanding translations of Calvino and Eco.

At the heart of Martin's scholarship in the period from the fourteenth to the sixteenth century lies his equal mastery of Latin and vernacular cultures and of the interactions between them. His foundational and much-cited study of *Literary Imitation in the Italian Renaissance* (1995) rewrote the map of literary criticism in the period before the rediscovery of Aristotle's *Poetics* from the 1530s onwards. It showed that the debates on imitation from the time of Dante to that of Bembo had been seriously underestimated in terms of their significance for literary and linguistic practices in both languages. Martin's investigations into literary imitation, understood in a broad sense, have always stressed its creative aspects, and have brought them to light through meticulous and perceptive readings of the texts concerned, set out with the utmost clarity and without jargon. His studies of Renaissance translations, from Latin to the vernacular or vice versa, have demonstrated how the process was often akin to rewriting, for reasons connected with the different readerships that were being addressed. Martin has had a special interest in the many Latin versions of individual stories from Boccaccio's *Decameron* created between the Trecento and the early Cinquecento by authors such as Petrarch, Neri de' Nerli, Beroaldo and Bandello. He has studied several of the 'autotraduzioni' of Leon Battista Alberti, identifying the general tendencies that underlie them: those of the *De pictura*, written first in the vernacular and then in a fuller Latin version, and of two of the *Intercenales*, *Uxoria* and *Naufragus*, translated in the other direction. In his research on translations and also in his work on original texts, Martin has illuminated the practices of intertextuality in Renaissance literature. He stressed in the introduction to *Literary Imitation* that he was interested not only in the theories and polemics surrounding imitation, but also in '"rhetorical imitation", that is to say, the process whereby one writer consciously or unconsciously borrows from another text, and that borrowing effects a significant intertextual echo'. Thus, for example, Martin's analysis of Beroaldo's version of the story of Tito and Gisippo in the *Decameron* shows that, far from lacking in inventiveness, it 'is rich in Apuleian (and other) resonances, and these subtexts or intertexts shimmer beneath the surface of the translation'. This essay leads to a conclusion with wide implications: 'Beroaldo wants us to read Boccaccio's famous novella in the way we should read all classic tales, with many classical parallels and contrasts lurking below the surface, reminding us that literature comes as much from what we read as from what we experience'. On the other hand, Martin's study of Alberti's *Naufragus* (2012) reveals how the Latin original is very rich in intertextual allusions, while the vernacular reworking is less precise and learned in nature. His essay on Poliziano's *Stanze* (2000) explores the scholar-poet's taste for intertextuality, seen as an aspect of his 'postmodern poetics' together with features such as eclecticism (a trait that Poliziano praised in Alberti's writing) and avoidance of narration. Significantly, *intertextus*, as a noun, was a neologism favoured by Poliziano and his circle. This rich and striking essay is just one of many demonstrations of Martin's rare ability to combine a cogent overview of a complex question with a penetrating and original analysis of details that illuminate the whole.

Martin's work on cultural transfer across different periods has, in particular, deepened our understanding of the influence of Ciceronian rhetoric in the Renaissance. He has investigated Petrarch's attitude towards the Latin author, which lay between 'adulation and critical distance'. A fascinating close reading of a group of ten poems from Petrarch's *Canzoniere* (2007) brings out the poet's attention to the tonal and auditory effects of his verse, to the contrasting qualities of melodiousness (*sonoritas*) and harshness (the *raucum*), and points to the roots of Petrarch's practice in rhetorical works of Cicero's that are found in a manuscript owned and annotated by Petrarch. Alberti, an anti-Ciceronian in terms of the debates on imitation, subtly points out that even Cicero, in the course of his lifetime, could be 'sui dissimilior' ('quite unlike himself'). The essay just mentioned on Petrarch's vernacular poetry provides another example of Martin's sparing but fertile use, in his Renaissance scholarship, of perceptions from the modern era, in this case when he notes that, in these poems 'che chiudono bene', Petrarch displayed an artisanal skill of a kind to which Calvino aspired. The modern reception of Renaissance authors has been examined in essays on biographical studies of Petrarch in Britain between 1775 and 1850 (2007) and more recently on Calvino's literary 'thefts' from Ariosto's *Orlando furioso* (2013). Martin is also attentive to combinations of political and cultural factors that may affect an author's reception. His survey of the reading and translation of the works of Julius Caesar in Italy from Dante to Machiavelli (2009) shows how Caesar — statesman, soldier and author — was much studied because of his relevance to the debate on monarchy and republicanism, to humanism, in which the Italians were remarkably competent pioneers, and to European warfare, in which they were in contrast remarkably unsuccessful. The plays of Terence, an essay of 2015 suggests, were used in contrasting ways in the comedies of Alberti and Machiavelli. While both these authors were indebted to the content and language of the classical models, Machiavelli blended borrowed elements into the shocking immorality associated with his political treatises, as if saying 'welcome to the modern world!'.

As is already apparent, the Renaissance authors whom Martin has studied most closely have been Petrarch, a writer 'between two ages, between two languages' as the title of one of his essays puts it (2007), and especially Alberti. His interest in Alberti is not surprising for a scholar who studied with Grayson, but it reflects and is shaped by Martin's own exceptional dual expertise in the two principal literary languages of the Italian Renaissance, by his breadth of scholarship and by his versatility. He has done much to promote the understanding of the humanistic and scientific writings of Alberti ('perfettamente a suo agio in entrambe le lingue', as he observes), and he has elucidated the intellectual ideals that shaped them. Martin's approach, as he explains in the introduction to his recent collection of essays on Alberti (2016), has been 'sempre quello di cercare di spiegare ciò che l'Alberti scriveva tramite quello che leggeva'. His British Academy Italian Lecture of 2009 demonstrated how Alberti steered the humanist movement in a direction not envisaged by Petrarch as its founder, shifting it 'towards the vernacular, the humorous and the technical'. Just as importantly, Martin has led the way towards a fresh appreciation of Alberti's personality and tastes, including his pragmatic spirit, his work ethic, his inventiveness, his wit, his anti-elitism, his cult of friendship, his *iocunditas* and his love of *varietas*. These are qualities with which Martin reveals an evident affinity and sympathy, as anyone who knows him will imagine.

Beyond and in parallel with his interest in the Italian Renaissance, Martin has developed an equally ground-breaking expertise in modern Italian literature and its translation into English. This has been happening under the sign of one of Italy's greatest authors, Italo Calvino (1929–1985). Martin's interest in Calvino dates back to his Edinburgh years: his first scholarly contribution was published in 1982, dedicated to the meta-literary thread already present in Calvino's early work in the 1950s. Martin's sophisticated skills in detecting the complex patterns — thematic and intertextual — of an author's work is a trait he brought from his Renaissance work to the moderns and it very much defines the original core of many of his contributions to Calvino studies. Other essays followed, dedicated to the state of Calvino's papers (1989), his relation with Jorge Luis Borges (1996), with Joseph Conrad (2002), with Marco Polo's *Il milione* (2008) and, as mentioned, with Ariosto. Something similar can be said of his monograph dedicated to the entire oeuvre of Calvino, published in 1998. The book is a model of clarity in its discussion of the biographical and literary trajectory of one of the most innovative fiction writers of his generation. At the same time, Martin's painstaking attention to stylistic features, intertextual traces and historical reconstruction makes it a book that is both a still unsurpassed introduction to Calvino for English readers and a most innovative analysis of the 'diachronic evolution of the texts'.

The year Martin published his monograph coincided with his first translation of Calvino's work. Up until the 1990s two names had been mainly involved in the publication of this author's fiction in English: Archibald Colquhoun in Britain and William Weaver in the USA. In an almost symbolic 'passaggio del testimone', Martin complemented Colquhoun's 1956 translation of Calvino's early novel *Il sentiero dei nidi di ragno* with the careful translation of all the changes that — almost surreptitiously — Calvino had inserted since the first edition of 1947, and re-inserting a number of passages that had been censored in the British edition, 'deemed unsuitable for the sexual and political climate of the 1950s'. Soon after, Martin was asked to work on the translation of a collection of Calvino's literary essays published in English with the title *Why Read the Classics?*, published by Cape in 1999. This translation won the prestigious John Florio Prize for best translation in 1999–2000 and established Martin's reputation in the field. In the following years Martin continued to alternate between the translation of Calvino's fiction and essay writing. Together with another renowned translator and John Florio Prize winner, Tim Parks, Martin completed the translation of all of Calvino's *Cosmicomics*, whose first edition had been translated by Weaver. On the non-fictional front, the most challenging work was the translation of a wide selection of Calvino's correspondence. Many of Martin's friends and colleagues remember having the odd conversation or receiving the odd email from him concerning a minute reference to Italian culture or to an Italian expression which he had come across in the correspondence. His commitment towards detecting and reproducing every possible semantic detail was equal to his capacity to imitate (in the Classical sense he knows so well) the clarity and precision of Calvino's prose style. The result is a 600-page tome, which will be extremely useful to generations of English-speaking scholars approaching Calvino from outside the restricted circles of Italian studies. Martin also translated a collection of literary essays by Umberto Eco and a small gem of Italian travel writing, *L'isola delle tartarughe* by Sergio Ghione, charting the journey of an Italian scientist to one of the most remote corners of British sovereignty.

If Calvino has been a recurrent presence in Martin's scholarly work on contemporary Italian literature, other authors have been studied from time to time. Umberto Eco's non-fiction work was not only translated but also discussed in search of a definition of the author's own literary canon. Once again, Martin's keen eye for the philological genesis and history of literary works has allowed him to shed light on the development of a number of contemporary works: from his study of two versions of Ignazio Silone's *Fontamara* to the prose style and structures of Andrea De Carlo's novels, to the careful unpicking of intertextual threads in the narrative of Antonio Tabucchi, whose postmodernist stance 'invita il lettore a non accettare la realtà di superficie, ma ad interrogarla'. Finally, Martin's interest in the dialogue between the written and the visual arts found its way into the co-editing of two collections of essays, both deriving from well-attended conferences. The first concentrated on the visual element in Calvino's work, whereas the second opened up a wide-ranging discussion on the narrative synergies between contemporary literature and cinema.

It almost goes without saying that Martin's scholarly work on modern Italian literature found an equally important outlet in his teaching career, at Edinburgh first and then at Oxford. There is hardly any major nineteenth- or twentieth-century Italian author who has not been the subject of one of Martin's series of lectures: from Manzoni and Verga to Pavese, Vittorini, Fenoglio and obviously his beloved Calvino. His Oxford lectures on the latter have been so successful amongst undergraduates that, unbeknown to him, the Faculty library found itself forced to increase, year after year, the available number of copies of his Calvino monograph. With thirteen copies now held in the Taylor Institution plus another fifteen in college libraries, Martin's book is easily the most popular critical study by an Italianist at Oxford.

No less significant than Martin's research and translation has been his contribution to the running of academic periodicals and monograph series. He was successively editor of the *Bulletin of the Society for Italian Studies*; reviews editor of *Italian Studies*; Italian editor of the *Modern Language Review* (1994–2001) and then its general editor (2002–03), efficiently and calmly seeing the journal through a difficult transition in its production while maintaining its high standards of scholarship; guest editor of *Renaissance Studies*; chair of the Legenda imprint (on which Graham Nelson adds a note elsewhere in this volume) and a member of the OUP Monographs Committee. He has also been a member of many other advisory boards of journals and publishers.

In recent years, Martin has held visiting posts at the University of Malta, at Monash University in Melbourne and at the University of Notre Dame in Indiana. He has given many invited lectures and keynote speeches in the UK, Europe, North America and Australia.

Martin has taken a very significant part in University administration at Oxford, in particular as Chair of the Italian Sub-Faculty, Vice-Chair and subsequently Director for Research of the Faculty of Medieval and Modern Languages, and

Director of the European Humanities Research Centre, as well as Chair of Reviews of Master courses.

His involvement in the life of the profession led to his election as Chair of the national Society for Italian Studies and his expertise, fairness and wisdom made him an ideal panel member in two cycles of research assessment in the UK, as well as in the equivalent Italian exercise (ANVUR).

He has collected numerous honours and awards as well as the John Florio Prize already mentioned. He was appointed 'Commendatore dell'Ordine della Stella della Solidarietà Italiana' by the President of Italy in 2008. He was elected President of the Modern Humanities Research Association in 2015, and he is an Honorary Life Member of this association.

Above and beyond all the success that his career has brought him, what Martin really values and enjoys about his work is the interaction with colleagues and students. Among the people who were important influences in the various stages of his life, a few stand out: Peter Brand, his first head of department and mentor at Edinburgh, for his dedication to work and infectious enthusiasm; Lino Pertile, from whom he learnt the rigour of scholarship and intellectual discourse; his predecessor in the Oxford chair of Italian, John Woodhouse, who has remained a close friend and advisor after his retirement; and Italo Calvino's widow, Chichita, with whom he developed a great friendship through years of studying and translating the works of the writer.

Martin is incredibly modest about his own achievements but tirelessly interested in other people's research; he is renowned for his generosity and always willing to give his time to offer advice and to share knowledge and ideas. This has led to an intense involvement with the wider community, be it by chairing the Oxford Italian Association, participating in summer outreach programmes and visits to schools, or being active in the FIAT bursary programme.

Martin's love of all things Italian extends well beyond Dante, Alberti and Calvino to a love of Italian food, wine and culture. If Martin could, he would spend every holiday in Italy. His day starts with characteristic efficiency by clearing his inbox but it always ends with a good thirty minutes spent reading the sports pages of *La Repubblica*, and keeping track of the ups and downs of the team that he has supported all his life, Celtic Football Club.

When the editors planned this tribute to Martin's career, they invited contributors to write on any topic within a group of themes that are central to his scholarly interests: reception, translation and transformation in Italian culture. The resulting collection of essays has proved to be as multifaceted as Martin's own interests, ranging as it does from Trecento literature to contemporary culture.

Zyg Barański opens the volume with an essay that examines Petrarch's recourse to the myth of Orpheus in his Canzoniere and his 'deconstruction' of it to serve his own ends, both in fashioning his lyric collection and as part of his sustained criticism of Dante. Petrarch grants Orpheus a prominent position in connection with his major artistic and ideological concerns, and hence he forges suggestive links between himself and his mythological predecessor. Elisabetta Tarantino notes the links between the phrase with which Boccaccio describes the blast of his detractors' criticism in the *Decameron*, 'spirante turbo', a passage in Dante's *Inferno* and another in Lucan's *Pharsalia*, and she argues that a metaphorical interpretation of Lucan's passage can be used to illustrate Boccaccio's ethical stance. Michelangelo Zaccarello gives an account of the manuscript of Sacchetti's *Le Trecento novelle* that he identified in the library of Wadham College, Oxford, and he evaluates its contribution to the textual reconstruction of what is the most important narrative collection of the Trecento after Boccaccio's masterpiece.

The next group of essays takes us into the full Renaissance period. Linda Louie, Mairi McLaughlin and Diana Thow analyse three translations or retranslations into French, respectively from the sixteenth, eighteenth and twentieth centuries, of Boccaccio's tale of Griselda (*Decameron*, x. 10), whose humanist Latin versions have been studied by Martin. The notion of fidelity is a central concern both in translation studies and in the Griselda tale, and these case studies are used to explore the hypothesis that retranslations are always more faithful to the source text than is the first translation. Marco Dorigatti compares the depiction of figures of power in Ariosto's *Orlando furioso*, on two levels: the external level of the world contemporary to the author and the internal level of literary fiction, inherited from predecessors such as Boiardo. The two levels are not independent of each other: real characters can take on features from the world of chivalry, while the Christian knights, who are subject to a strong centrifugal force, can take on the role of captains or condottieri. The theme of intertextuality returns in the essay by Elena Lombardi, which traces the intricate way in which Lucan's 'dark wood' in *Pharsalia* III is employed in the *Furioso* and in Tasso's *Gerusalemme liberata*, and how other intertexts from Virgil, Ovid and Dante interact in these two receiving texts. The figure of the emblem, a new Renaissance vogue, helps to conceptualize some of the intricacies of Renaissance intertextuality in issues of inscription, memory, property and circulation. Brian Richardson discusses evidence for the improvisation, or semi-improvisation, of lyric verse, associated most closely with social gatherings but sometimes arguably also created in the course of correspondence, and he considers the extent to which improvisers may have used imitation in the course of composition. Richard Cooper's subject is the many French connections of Pier Vettori, the leading Italian humanist scholar of the Cinquecento. Vettori's mostly unpublished correspondence illustrates his relations with a host of members of the Republic of Letters in France, including Florentine exiles, French humanists and the printers in Lyon and Paris with whom he chose to publish some of his new works. Hilary Gatti's essay examines the second dialogue of Giordano Bruno's *La cena de le ceneri*, and in particular the remarkably colourful and dramatic account of the night-time journey that took Bruno and his party from Salisbury Court in London to the rooms of Fulke Greville in Whitehall where the *Cena* is set. The dialogue offers much more than a historical account, and Gatti's contribution provides an analysis of the night-time journey, with its multiple literary memories, that characterizes it as an intimate part of Bruno's progress towards the new dawn of an infinite cosmology.

Two essays on architecture, concerning respectively the sixteenth and the early eighteenth century, relate to one aspect of Martin's work on Alberti. Francesco Paolo Fiore examines Sebastiano Serlio's discussions of the orders in his extensive treatise on architecture, of which six books and a further *Extraordinario* book were printed between 1537 and 1575 in Venice, France and Germany, with two further books remaining in manuscript. The innovative relationship between text and illustrations in the printed volumes makes it difficult to identify Serlio's general rules of architecture, and Fiore sheds new light on the author's concepts of the good architect's judgement, his combination (*mescolanza*) of different styles, and his *invenzione*, this last being the fruit of *commodità* and *decoro*. While Serlio applied Italian architectural practices to châteaux in France, Giacomo or James Leoni helped to introduce the ideas of Alberti and Palladio into England. John Woodhouse reassesses the impact of this highly industrious 'Anglicized Venetian', responsible for the first English translations of Alberti's *De re aedificatoria* (another retranslation, from Bartoli's Italian version) and Palladio's *Quattro libri dell'architettura*, and the designer of country houses such as Lyme Park in Cheshire and Clandon Park in Surrey.

Moving forward in time, Vilma De Gasperin discusses the 'repurposing' of Italian literature in Britain in the mid-eighteenth century as a means of learning the language rather than as an end to itself, focusing in particular on Giuseppe Baretti's 1755 anthology *An Introduction to the Italian Language* and considering his choice of authors and his manipulation of literary texts for language-learning purposes. A different aspect of Baretti's work is mentioned in Joseph Farrell's contribution. In his *Account of the Manner and Customs of Italy*, Baretti presents a eulogy of the work of Carlo Gozzi and an attack on the theatre of Carlo Goldoni. The clash between the two playwrights and their views of innovation and tradition is apparent in their differing views of the role of fantasy in theatre, Goldoni spurning it and Gozzi embracing it.

The early Ottocento debate on Romantic literature is indirectly at the centre of David Robey's contribution. His essay concentrates on the fortune of the expressions 'romantic' and 'romance' in their linguistic and cultural journey from the novels of Walter Scott to their Italian translations (often indebted to French ones). By tracing the rendering of those two words in Italian editions, from the first translation of *Waverley* in 1822 to Carlo Rusconi's of 1847, Robey shows the extent to which the controversial identity of 'romantico' and 'romanzesco' in the Italian context proved slightly distracting and disrupting to Italian translators. An unexpected parallel between Scott and Leopardi concludes this factually rich analysis of a key moment in Italy's literary history. Letizia Panizza's essay, too, concerns the historical novel in this period. She shows how Diodata Saluzzo's narrative poem *Ipazia*, published in 1827, aimed to turn the tables on a work of a century earlier by John Toland, a 'godless' author who had portrayed the philosopher Hypatia of Alexandria as pagan rather than Christian. Saluzzo, a staunch Catholic and a correspondent of Manzoni's, was intending to write a 'romanzo istorico e filosofico'; but although she had poetic talent, she was, as Panizza shows, no historian and no philosopher.

Peter Hainsworth discusses the illustrations to the *Inferno* by John Dickson Batten (1860–1932), the originals of which are now in Lady Margaret Hall library. These offer interesting and in many ways arresting interpretations of Dante, and deserve to be much better known than they are. They were done primarily to accompany a revised version of the translation of the *Inferno* (into Spenserian stanzas) by George Musgrave, originally published in 1893, and then — with the illustrations — in 1932.

The development of early twentieth-century Italian literature is examined by Robert Gordon through an original thematic approach devoted to the idea of chance and luck. This allows him to trace unexpected parallels between authors rarely compared to each other such as Filippo Tommaso Marinetti, Eugenio Montale and Luigi Pirandello. Beyond their ideological differences, what they are shown to have in common is a tendency towards reformulating the concept of luck at a time when nineteenth-century positivist certainties crumble and provide space for the fragile structures of a new vision of modernity.

Rosalba Biasini sets out to investigate the presence of the epic mode in Beppe Fenoglio's unfinished masterpiece *Il partigiano Johnny* and, notably, how the writer activates a web of intertextual links between his text and other works related to the epic genre. Through the analyses of such references what emerges is Fenoglio's intention of offering an enriched, but not rhetorical representation of the Resistance, whilst at the same time asserting the role of tragedy as a timeless (albeit historically configured) aspect of the human condition.

Fenoglio's work is still present in the following essay but only as a model of the partisan novel, to which another author aspired. The doubts and uncertainties of Italo Calvino's early work are tackled by Mario Barenghi in an essay dedicated to an unpublished short story written in 1946. In analysing *'Flirt' prima di battersi*, Barenghi's philological eye successfully retraces Calvino's attempts to control the awkward mixture of sentimentalism and morality which characterizes this early attempt. The second of the three essays dedicated to Calvino takes us to the 1950s and more precisely to *Il barone rampante*. Here Emanuela Tandello Cooper offers a fresh re-reading of the novel and an appreciation of the threads that link it to Giacomo Leopardi, one of Calvino's most revered Italian authors. The *operetta morale Elogio degli uccelli* provides the starting point, but Tandello explores the comparison in further depth, showing the extent of Calvino's literary debt to Leopardi. The third Calvinian contribution is Helen Anderson's essay on *Se una notte d'inverno un viaggiatore*. Her aim is to examine Calvino's sophisticated questioning of conventional crime fiction as it takes shape in both the novel's frame story and in the ten *incipits*. Anderson's formal reading shows the multilayered complexity of Calvino's novel to be ordered by a metafictional rewriting of the *giallo* that lays bare the mechanics of narrative and reveals the dazzling potential of literature.

The theme of cultural encounters is approached by Guido Bonsaver in his study of the film representation of the meeting of U.S. and Italian culture in the late 1950s. His selection of a Hollywood blockbuster — Melville Shavelson's *It Started in Naples*, starring Sophia Loren and Clark Gable — and an Italian auteur film, Federico Fellini's *La dolce vita*, allows him to study the peculiarities of each production and at the same time note similar preoccupations that, in Fellini's case, go back to two 1948 scripts on a similar theme. Cinema is also at the centre of another essay, this time by Philip Cooke, and devoted to the film adaptation of Resistance novels. The first half of the essay provides a very useful overview of the reception on the big screen of various Resistance books — with Viganò's *L'Agnese va a morire* as the most successful example, and with the telling absence of Calvino's *Il sentiero dei nidi di ragno*. In the second half, Cooke concentrates on a recent and most controversial novel and film adaptation: Giampaolo Pansa's *Il sangue dei vinti* (2003) whose homonymous film version opened the 2008 Rome Film Festival (in its first edition under the mayorship of former neofascist Gianni Alemanno).

Manuele Gragnolati's paper, inspired by Donna Haraway's concept of 'diffractive reading', explores a constellation of texts by Dante and two twentieth-century authors, Pasolini and Morante, who have confronted Dante, either directly or obliquely, from a queer and feminine/feminist position. In particular, the paper is interested in both testing the diffractive method of reading and exploring how Dante's concept of heavenly experience corresponds to a paradoxical coexistence of continuity and radical change with respect to earthly selfhood.

Luigi Meneghello ironically dismissed himself as a failed poet, but poetry is at the centre of Diego Zancani's essay on the author. In fact, through his careful examination of Meneghello's published and unpublished writings, Zancani brings to light Meneghello's intense interest and practice in poetic language, from the sardonic revisiting of his own early lyrical compositions to his sometime scathing, sometime enraptured, but always lucid discussions of other poetic works, in Italian and in English, many of which he translated with great skill into his own native Veneto.

Franca Pellegrini follows the trail of the heated debate that followed the 1974 publication of Elsa Morante's *La Storia Romanzo*, looking at the impact of the novel both in the immediate context of its reception and in the longer-term evolution of its critical assessment. An initial and almost uniform rejection (dictated by both aesthetic and ideological objections) gives place to a more nuanced appreciation twenty years later, when critics identified the book as a kind of new start for the genre of the novel, and an anticipation of the resurrection of the historical narrative in the 1980s.

Giuseppe Stellardi proposes a comparative, transnational, decentralizing and destabilizing reading of Gadda's *L'Adalgisa*, by first debunking the notion that Gadda's work may be subsumed and normalized under one of the available labels (modernism, post-modernism, expressionism) and then exploring hidden references and unsuspected resonances (in this case with Baudelaire and Benjamin); the suggestion is that literary affinities and influences do not always work according to established interpretative schemes.

In the final essay Nicola Gardini, taking as his starting point his own book *Lacuna*, meditates on the relationship between speech and silence, presence and absence, void and totality, truth and falsehood in the literary text; his choice of examples, including (in addition to Proust) Virgil, Ariosto and Calvino, also works very well as an appropriate, final reminder of Martin's breadth of interests.

The editors are very grateful to all the contributors for their generous collaboration in putting this volume together. They regret that reasons of space prevented them from inviting contributions from a greater number of the many colleagues and students who have worked with Martin over the years. For invaluable practical assistance and advice, they would also like to thank most warmly Cathy McLaughlin, Mairi McLaughlin, Graham Nelson, Elisabetta Tarantino and Susan Wharton.

BIBLIOGRAPHY OF PUBLICATIONS BY MARTIN MCLAUGHLIN

Books

1. *Literary Imitation in the Italian Renaissance: The Theory and Practice of Literary Imitation in Italy from Dante to Bembo* (Oxford: Clarendon Press, 1995)
2. *Italo Calvino* (Edinburgh: Edinburgh University Press, 1998)
3. *Leon Battista Alberti: la vita, l'umanesimo, le opere letterarie* (Florence: Olschki, 2016)
4. *Leon Battista Alberti: Writer and Humanist* (Princeton, NJ: Princeton University Press [forthcoming])

Editions of Primary Works

1. Leon Battista Alberti, *Autobiographical Writings*, I Tatti Renaissance Library (Cambridge, MA: Harvard University Press [forthcoming])

Edited Volumes

1. *Leopardi: A Scottis Quair*, co-ed. with R. D. S. Jack and C. Whyte (Edinburgh: Edinburgh University Press, 1987)
2. *Britain and Italy from Romanticism to Modernism* (Oxford: Legenda, 2000)
3. *Petrarch in Britain: Interpreters, Imitators and Translators over 700 Years*, co-ed. with Letizia Panizza (Oxford: Oxford University Press, 2007; Proceedings of the British Academy, 146)
4. *Italy's Three Crowns: Reading Dante, Petrarch, and Boccaccio*, co-ed. with Zygmunt G. Barański (Oxford: Bodleian Library, 2007)
5. *Image, Eye and Art in Calvino: Writing Visibility*, co-ed. with Birgitte Grundtvig and Lene Waage Petersen (London: Legenda, 2007)
6. *Biographies and Autobiographies in Modern Italy*, co-ed. with Peter Hainsworth (London: Legenda, 2007)
7. *Sinergie narrative: cinema e letteratura nell'Italia contemporanea*, co-ed. with Guido Bonsaver and Franca Pellegrini (Florence: Cesati, 2008)
8. *Dante the Lyric and Ethical Poet. Dante lirico e etico*, co-ed. with Zygmunt G. Barański (London: Legenda, 2010)
9. *Dante in Oxford: The Paget Toynbee Lectures*, co-ed. with Tristan Kay and Michelangelo Zaccarello (London: Legenda, 2011)
10. *Authority, Innovation and Early Modern Epistemology: Essays in Honour of Hilary Gatti*, co-ed. with Ingrid D. Rowland and Elisabetta Tarantino (London: Legenda, 2015)
11. *Machiavelli's* Prince: *Traditions, Text and Translations*, co-ed. with Nicola Gardini (Rome: Viella, 2017)

Translations

1. ITALO CALVINO, *The Path to the Spiders' Nests*, co-trans. with Archibald Colquhoun (London: Jonathan Cape, 1998)

2. Italo Calvino, *Why Read the Classics?* (London: Jonathan Cape, 1999) (winner of the John Florio Prize for translation in 1999–2000)
3. Italo Calvino, Introduction to *Fantastic Tales* (London: Penguin, 2001), pp. vii-xvii
4. Sergio Ghione, *Turtle Island: A Journey to Britain's Oddest Colony* (London: Allen Lane, 2002)
5. Italo Calvino, *Hermit in Paris: Autobiographical Writings* (London: Cape, 2003)
6. Umberto Eco, *On Literature* (London: Secker and Warburg, 2005)
7. Italo Calvino, 'Waiting for Death in a Hotel', *New Yorker*, 12 June 2006, pp. 104–10
8. Italo Calvino, *The Complete Cosmicomics*, co-trans. with Tim Parks and William Weaver (London: Penguin, 2009)
9. Italo Calvino, *Into the War* (London: Penguin, 2011)
10. Italo Calvino, *Collection of Sand* (London: Penguin, 2013)
11. Italo Calvino, *Letters 1941–1985*, selected by Michael Wood (Princeton, NJ: Princeton University Press, 2013)

Chapters in Books

1. 'Biographical Introduction' to *Leopardi: A Scottis Quair*, ed. by R. D. S. Jack, M. L. McLaughlin and C. Whyte (Edinburgh: Edinburgh University Press, 1987), pp. 1–4
2. 'Histories of Literature in the Quattrocento', in *The Languages of Literature in Renaissance Italy*, ed. by P. Hainsworth and others (Oxford: Clarendon Press, 1988), pp. 63–80
3. 'Petrarch's Rewriting of the *Decameron*, X.10', in *Renaissance and Other Studies: Essays Presented to Peter M. Brown*, ed. by Eileen A. Millar (Glasgow: Glasgow University Press, 1988), pp. 42–59
4. 'Calvino's Library: Labyrinth or Laboratory', in *Italian Storytellers*, ed. by Eric Haywood and Cormac Ó Cuilleanáin (Dublin: Irish Academic Press, 1989), pp. 263–87
5. 'Andrea De Carlo: The Surface of Consciousness', in *The New Italian Novel*, ed. by Zygmunt G. Barański and Lino Pertile (Edinburgh: Edinburgh University Press, 1993), pp. 75–88
6. 'Humanism and Italian Literature', in *The Cambridge Companion to Renaissance Humanism*, ed. by Jill Kraye (Cambridge: Cambridge University Press, 1996), pp. 224–45
7. 'Borges e Calvino: la letteratura e l'intelletto', in *Borges, Calvino, la literatura (El coloquio en la isla): coloquio internacional*, 2 vols (Madrid: Espiral Hispano-Americana, 1996), I, 85–103
8. 'The Discovery of Classical Texts', in *Atlas of Medieval Europe*, ed. by Angus Mackay and David Ditchburn (London: Routledge, 1997), pp. 239–41
9. 'The Rock and the Vine: Pier della Vigna, Dante, and the Imagery of Empire', in *Dante and Governance*, ed. by John Woodhouse (Oxford: Clarendon Press, 1997), pp. 121–36
10. 'Note to the 1998 Translation', in Italo Calvino, *The Path to the Spiders' Nests*, trans. by Archibald Colquhoun, rev. by Martin McLaughlin (London: Jonathan Cape, 1998), pp. 1–5
11. 'Italo Calvino, 1985–95: romanzi, racconti e la fondazione di uno stile', in *Italo Calvino: nuevas visiones*, ed. by María J. Calvo Montoro and Franco Ricci (Cuenca: Ediciones de la Universidad de Castilla-La Mancha, 1997), pp. 99–117
12. 'El humanismo y la literatura italiana', in *Introducción al humanismo renacentista*, ed. by Jill Kraye and Carlos Clavería (Cambridge and Madrid: Cambridge University Press, 1998), pp. 269–94
13. '*La speculazione edilizia*: natura e storia in un racconto "difficile"', in *Italo Calvino: A Writer for the Next Millennium*, ed. by Giorgio Bertone (Alessandria: Edizioni dell'Orso, 1998), pp. 204–20
14. 'Translator's Introduction', in Italo Calvino, *Why Read the Classics?*, trans. by Martin McLaughlin (London: Jonathan Cape, 1999), pp. vii-x

15. 'The Centrality of Dante', introductory chapter to *Britain and Italy from Romanticism to Modernism* (Oxford: Legenda, 2000), pp. 1–12
16. 'Poliziano's *Stanze*: Post-Modern Poetics in a Proto-Renaissance Poem', in *Italy in Crisis: 1494*, ed. by Jane E. Everson and Diego Zancani (Oxford: Legenda, 2000), pp. 129–51
17. 'Biography and Autobiography in the Italian Renaissance', in *Mapping Lives: The Uses of Biography*, ed. by Peter France and William St Clair (London: British Academy, 2002), pp. 37–65
18. 'Le città visibili di Calvino', in *La visione dell'invisibile: saggi e materiali su 'Le città invisibili' di Italo Calvino*, ed. by Mario Barenghi, Gianni Canova and Bruno Falcetto (Milan: Mondadori, 2002), pp. 42–61
19. 'Calvino saggista: anglofilia letteraria e creatività', in *Italo Calvino Newyorkese*, ed. by Anna Botta and Domenico Scarpa (Cava de' Tirreni: Avagliano, 2002), pp. 41–66
20. 'Literature and Science in Leon Battista Alberti's *De re aedificatoria*', in *Science and Literature in Italian Culture: From Dante to Calvino. A Festschrift for Patrick Boyde*, ed. by Simon Gilson and Pierpaolo Antonello (Oxford: Legenda, 2004), pp. 94–114
21. 'Latin and Vernacular from Dante to the Age of Lorenzo (1321–c. 1500)', in *The Cambridge History of Literary Criticism*, vol. II: *The Middle Ages*, ed. by Alastair Minnis and Ian Johnson (Cambridge: Cambridge University Press, 2005), pp. 612–25
22. 'Humanist Criticism of Latin and Vernacular Prose', in *The Cambridge History of Literary Criticism*, vol. II: *The Middle Ages*, ed. by Alastair Minnis and Ian Johnson (Cambridge: Cambridge University Press, 2005), pp. 648–65
23. 'La *Selva Caledonia* tra guerrieri e poeti: la Scozia nell'immaginario italiano dal medioevo al Romanticismo', in *Scrittori italiani in Inghilterra*, ed. by Gianni Oliva (Naples: Edizioni Scientifiche Italiane, 2004), pp. 7–26
24. 'Introduction' to Dante Alighieri, *The Divine Comedy: Inferno*, trans. by J. G. Nichols (London: Hesperus, 2005), pp. xi–xv
25. 'Bilinguismo e strategie retoriche nel *De Pictura* dell'Alberti', in *Leon Battista Alberti teorico delle arti e gli impegni civili del 'De Re Aedificatoria'*, ed. by Arturo Calzona, Francesco Paolo Fiore, Alberto Tenenti and Cesare Vasoli (Florence: Olschki, 2007), pp. 203–23
26. 'Tradizione letteraria e originalità del pensiero nel *De Re Aedificatoria* dell'Alberti', in *Leon Battista Alberti teorico delle arti e gli impegni civili del 'De Re Aedificatoria'*, ed. by Arturo Calzona, Francesco Paolo Fiore, Alberto Tenenti and Cesare Vasoli (Florence: Olschki, 2007), pp. 451–69
27. 'Intertestualità e struttura nella narrativa di Antonio Tabucchi: da *Il gioco del rovescio* a *Sostiene Pereira*', in *Il romanzo contemporaneo: voci italiane*, ed. by Franca Pellegrini and Elisabetta Tarantino (Leicester: Troubador, 2006), pp. 29–42
28. 'Struttura e "sonoritas" in Petrarca ("Rvf" 151–60)', in *Il Canzoniere: lettura micro e macrotestuale*, ed. by Michelangelo Picone (Ravenna: Longo, 2007), pp. 361–82
29. 'Calvino's Rewriting of Marco Polo: From the 1960 Screenplay to *Invisible Cities*', in *Marco Polo and the Encounter of East and West*, ed. by Suzanne Conklin Akbari and Amilcare A. Iannucci (Toronto: Toronto University Press, 2008), pp. 182–200
30. 'Alberti e le opere retoriche di Cicerone', in *Leon Battista Alberti e la tradizione: per lo 'smontaggio' dei mosaici albertiani*, ed. by Roberto Cardini and Mariangela Regoliosi (Florence: Polistampa, 2008), pp. 177–206
31. 'Introduction' to Italo Calvino, *The Complete Cosmicomics* (Harmondsworth: Penguin, 2009), pp. vii–xxiv (paperback published April 2010)
32. 'Empire, Eloquence and Military Genius: Renaissance Italy', in *A Companion to Julius Caesar*, ed. by Miriam Griffin (Chichester: Wiley-Blackwell, 2009), pp. 335–55
33. 'Alberti and the Classical Canon', in *Italy and the Classical Tradition: Language, Thought and Poetry 1300–1600*, ed. by Carlo Caruso and Andrew Laird (London: Duckworth, 2009), pp. 73–100

34. 'I Preraffaelliti e la letteratura italiana', in *I Preraffaelliti: il sogno del Quattrocento italiano da Beato Angelico a Perugino, da Rossetti a Burne-Jones*, ed. by Colin Harrison, Christopher Newall and Claudio Spadoni (Milan: Silvana, 2010), pp. 30–37
35. 'Frederick Rolfe, Baron Corvo: un eccentrico alla ricerca dell'altrove', in *Personaggi stravaganti a Venezia tra '800 e '900* (Venice: Antiga, 2010), pp. 141–59
36. 'Scrivere la Liguria: paesaggio e mondo nelle opere di Calvino', in *Scrittori liguri verso il terzo millennio. International Seminar, La Spezia, 18 giugno 2009*, ed. by Daniela Rapattoni (Pisa and Rome: Serra, 2010), pp. 57–63
37. 'The Pre-Raphaelites and Italian Literature', in *The Pre-Raphaelites and Italy*, ed. by Colin Harrison and Christopher Newell (Oxford: Ashmolean Museum, 2010), pp. 22–35
38. 'Pessimismo stoico e cultura classica nel *Theogenius* dell'Alberti', in *Leon Battista Alberti: actes du Congrès International 'Gli Este e l'Alberti: tempo e misura' (Ferrara, 29. XI–3. XII. 2004)*, ed. by Francesco Furlan and Gianni Venturi, 2 vols (= *Schifanoia*, 30–31) (Pisa and Rome: Serra, 2010), I, 131–43
39. 'Really Reading Calvino in English Translation?', in *'Ciò che potea la lingua nostra': Lectures and Essays in Memory of Clara Florio Cooper*, ed. by Vilma De Gasperin, *The Italianist*, 30 (2010), Special Supplement, pp. 203–20
40. 'Alberti traduttore di se stesso: *Uxoria* e *Naufragus*', in *Autotraduzione: teoria ed esempi fra Italia e Spagna (e oltre)*, ed. by Marcial Rubio Árquez and Nicola D'Antuono (Milan: LED, 2012), pp. 77–106
41. 'Unité thématique et structurelle dans le *De familia* d'Alberti', in *'Les Livres de la famille' d'Alberti: sources, sens et influence*, ed. by Michel Paoli and others (Paris: Garnier, 2013), pp. 177–203
42. 'Calvino, Eco e il canone della letteratura mondiale', in *Tra Eco e Calvino: relazioni rizomatiche. Atti del convegno 'Eco and Calvino: Rhizomatic Relationships', University of Toronto, 13–14 April 2012*, ed. by Rocco Capozzi (Milan: EncycloMedia, 2013), pp. 41–67
43. 'Petrarch and Cicero: Adulation and Critical Distance', in *Brill's Companions to Classical Reception: Cicero*, ed. by William H. F. Altman (Leiden and Boston: Brill, 2015), pp. 19–38
44. 'The Recovery of Terence in Renaissance Italy: From Alberti to Machiavelli', in *The Reinvention of Theatre in Sixteenth-Century Europe*, ed. by T. F. Earle and Catarino Fouto (London: Legenda, 2015), pp. 115–39
45. 'Alberti's *Musca*: Humour, Ethics and the Challenge to Classical Models', in *Authority, Innovation and Early Modern Epistemology: Essays in Honour of Hilary Gatti*, ed. by Martin McLaughlin, Ingrid D. Rowland and Elisabetta Tarantino (London: Legenda, 2015), pp. 8–24
46. 'Shakespeare in Calvino tra la saggistica e le opere creative', in *La scatola a sorpresa: studi e poesie per Maria Antonietta Grignani*, ed. by Giada Mattarucco, Margherita Quaglino, Carla Riccardi and Silvana Tamiozzo Goldmann (Florence: Cesati, 2016), pp. 87–95
47. 'La *Storia del Ciceronianismo*, centotrenta anni dopo', in *La filologia classica e umanistica di Remigio Sabbadini*, ed. by Fabio Stok and Paola Tomè (Pisa: ETS, 2016), pp. 189-200

Journal Articles

1. 'Life and Literature in Calvino's Early Works', *Journal of the Association of Teachers of Italian*, 35 (1982), 49–59
2. 'Continuity and Innovation in Calvino's *Palomar*', *Bulletin of the Society for Italian Studies*, 17 (1984), 43–49
3. 'Imagery in the Two Versions of Silone's *Fontamara*', *Journal of the Association of Teachers of Italian*, 47 (1986), 33–42

4. 'Humanist Concepts of Renaissance and Middle Ages in the Tre and Quattrocento', *Renaissance Studies*, 2 (1988), 131–42
5. 'Vetrina: Il "Fondo Italo Calvino"', *Autografo*, VI.17 (1989), 93–103
6. 'The Genesis of Calvino's *La speculazione edilizia*', *Italian Studies*, 48 (1993), 71–85
7. 'Calvino's Visible Cities', in *The Image of the City*, special issue of *Romance Studies*, 22 (1993), 67–82
8. 'Words and Silence: Calvino Criticism 1985–1995', *Romance Studies*, 28 (1996), 79–105
9. 'Tasso's Epic Style: Changes in Theory and Changes in Practice', *Journal of the Institute of Romance Studies*, 5 (1997), 23–46 (jointly with David Robey)
10. 'Il carteggio Calvino–de' Giorgi: problemi di datazione', *Autografo*, XIV.36 (1998), 13–32
11. 'Calvino e Conrad: dalla tesi di laurea alle *Lezioni americane*', *Italian Studies*, 57 (2002), 113–32 (jointly with Arianna Scicutella)
12. 'Introduction' (jointly with David Rundle), *Renaissance Studies*, 17.1 (March 2003), 1–8
13. 'Colori e paesaggi negli *Amori difficili*', *Nuova prosa*, 42 (2005), 165–90
14. 'Lightness and Multiplicity: The Origin and Development of Calvino's Poetics', in *Italo Calvino: Lightness and Multiplicity/Leggerezza e molteplicità*, special issue ed. by Rocco Capozzi, *Biblioteca di Rivista di Studi Italiani*, 21.1 (2003), 42–58
15. 'Humanist Rewriting and Translation: The Latin *Griselda* from Petrarch to Neri de' Nerli', *Hvmanistica*, 1.1 (2006), 23–40
16. 'L'ambigua freschezza dell'*Orlando Furioso* del 1516', *Italianistica*, 37.3 (2008), 159–66
17. '*Titi Romani Historia*: nowela o Tytusie i Gisippie w lacinskim przecladzie Mattea Bandello (1509)', *Odrodzenie ii Reformacja w Polsce*, 53 (2010), 167–96
18. 'Alberti and the Redirection of Renaissance Humanism', *Proceedings of the British Academy: 2009 Lectures*, 167 (2010), 25–59
19. 'Alberti's *Canis*: Structure and Sources in the Portrait of the Artist as a Renaissance Dog', *Albertiana*, 14 (2011), 55–83
20. '"C'è un furto con scasso in ogni vera lettura": Calvino's Thefts from Ariosto', *Parole Rubate/Purloined Letters*, 7 (June 2013), 139–63 <http://www.parolerubate.unipr.it>
21. 'From Lepidus to Leon Battista Alberti: Naming, Renaming and Anonymizing the Self in Quattrocento Italy', *Romance Studies*, 31.3–4 (November 2013), 152–66
22. 'Da Lepidus a Leon Battista Alberti: metamorfosi onomastiche e anonimizzazioni nell'Italia del Quattrocento', *Albertiana*, 16 (2013), 5–26
23. 'Boccaccio between Apuleius and Cicero: Bandello's Latin Version of *Decameron*, X.8 (1509)', *Humanistica*, 8.1 (2013), 71–82
24. 'Introduction' to *Ideology, Censorship and Translation across Genres: Past and Present*, special issue of *Perspectives: Studies in Translatology*, 24.1 (2016), 1–6 (issue co-written and edited with Javier Muñoz Basols) <http://dx.doi.org/10.1080/0907676X.2016.1095579)>
25. '*Renascens ad superos Cicero*: Ciceronian and Anti-Ciceronian Styles in the Italian Renaissance', in *The Afterlife of Cicero*, ed. by Gesine Manuwald, BICS Supplement 135 (London, 2016), pp. 67–81

CHAPTER 1

'Io mi rivolgo indietro a ciascun passo' (*Rvf* 15. 1): Petrarch, the *fabula* of Eurydice and Orpheus and the Structure of the Canzoniere

Zygmunt G. Barański

> Please don't you ever die,
> You ever die,
> You ever die.
> (The Felice Brothers, 'Radio Song')[1]

1. 'Come Euridice Orpheo sua'

Since the 1990s, a growing number of scholars has begun to recognize the significance of the myth of Orpheus as a structuring and ideological motif in Part II of the *Rerum vulgarium fragmenta*.[2] They generally concur that, drawing on the canonical accounts of the 'Threicius vates' (Thracian poet; *Met.* XI. 2) in Virgil's *Georgics* and Ovid's *Metamorphoses*,[3] Petrarch established meaningful correspondences between his and Orpheus's reactions to the deaths of their respective beloveds, and hence, by extension, between Laura and Eurydice. As a matter of fact, several common elements unite the anguished stories of the two bereaved lovers: the untimely demise of both women, the natural settings that the poets inhabit, their obsessive weeping, the shift in poetic style occasioned by their tragedies, their appeals to a higher power, and the irreversibility of their loss (in Orpheus's case after Eurydice's 'second death'). What is surprising, therefore, is not that Petrarch should have had recourse to the *fabula*, but that his readers should have been so slow to acknowledge its presence and function in the Canzoniere.[4] Indeed, the poet's keen propensity to illuminate and ennoble his experiences, whether autobiographical or fictional, by equating them to classical mythology ought to have served,[5] long before it actually did, as a trustworthy spur to seek out the *Fragmenta*'s Orphic reverberations.

Anyhow, in the *Parte in morte*, Petrarch explicitly drew attention to similarities between his and Orpheus's tragic circumstances:

> Or avess'io un sí pietoso stile
> che Laura mia potesse tôrre a Morte,
> come Euridice Orpheo sua senza rime,
> ch'i' viverei anchor piú che mai lieto! (332. 49–52)[6]

The double sestina 'Mia benigna fortuna e 'l viver lieto', especially in its ninth stanza, brings to a climax and seeming close Petrarch's recourse to the myth in Part II. For the only time in the Canzoniere, and with fitting refinement, the poem openly unites Orpheus and Eurydice, intimately placing their names next to each other in a manner that never occurs in Virgil or in Ovid. Indeed, Petrarch's syntax and wording most precisely recall those of another of his favourite *auctores*, Boethius, in his short reworking of the myth: 'Orpheus Eurydicen suam' (*Cons.* III. met. 12. 50).[7] At the same time, the poet only very occasionally drew on Boethius's account. I suspect that this was because the heavily allegorized character of the *metrum* restricted the story's connotative possibilities. (As ought to become clear during the course of this chapter, what Petrarch found so appealing and useful about the fable was its semantic and narrative malleability.) Even if Petrarch carefully distinguished himself from Ovid, he structurally followed the Latin poet's example. The couple's concluding syntactic 'reconciliation' in the Canzoniere alludes to their eternal reunion 'beneath the earth' at the end of Ovid's two-part account of their tormented love story: 'hic modo coniunctis spatiantur passibus ambo | [...] | Eurydicenque suam iam tuto respicit Orpheus' (here they now both walk side by side [...] and Orpheus now safely looks back at his Eurydice; *Met.* XI. 61, 64, and 66). In truth, one cannot but wonder whether the poet's decision to pen that 'variante strana', the sestina 'doppia o raddoppiata' (Bettarini, p. 1465), may not owe something to Ovid's exceptional 'doubling' of the myth across two books. As Orpheus and Eurydice take their leave in the *Fragmenta*, so Boethius bleeds into Ovid and both flow into Virgil — 'Eurydicenque suam iam luce sub ipsa' (his Eurydice now on the brink of light; *Georg.* IV. 490) — in keeping with Petrarch's ideas on *imitatio* that Martin has masterfully illustrated.[8] And there is more. Thanks to the subtlety of his composition, Petrarch concurrently refers to different moments and inflexions of the myth — first small proof of that malleability of which I have already made mention. While in Virgil and Boethius the phrase 'his Eurydice' melancholically confirms her 'second death', the event that marks the beginning of Orpheus's desperate weeping, in Ovid, as we have just seen, it touchingly crowns the lovers' everlasting companionship in death. The ambivalence captures well Petrarch's state at this juncture of the Canzoniere. He bemoans Laura's passing, but he is also increasingly confident that he will soon join 'Laura mia' — the unique coupling of beloved's name and possessive clearly calques the tradition's *Euridicen sua*[9] — in Paradise (ll. 2 and 14) and not 'beneath the earth' (ll. 2 and 4), where only her mortal remains lie 'scattered' (l. 7), as sonnet 333, 'Ite, rime dolenti, al duro sasso', that may be read as a 'Christianized' Orphic coda to stanza nine of the preceding sestina, memorably affirms.[10] Petrarch points to similarities between his condition and Orpheus's, while at the same time stressing that their experiences are also fundamentally different. In addition, if, on the one hand, the poet's avowed hope for an effective 'pietoso stile' highlights Orpheus's key role in Part II as the section's ideal elegiac model — a role that raises the perplexing question how in practice Petrarch might 'imitate' the vanished 'vatis Apollinei vocalia [...] ora' (the melodious mouth of Apollo's poet; *Met.* XI. 8)[11] — , on the other, the nature of the poet-prophet's artistic accomplishment is moot. In fact, he did not actually succeed in 'taking [Eurydice] away from Death'. His victory was brief and transitory; his defeat definitive. Ultimately, Orpheus's unrepeatable fleeting achievement is less an emblem of the power of poetic song than a bitter affirmation of its powerlessness in the face of *Morte* — a view Petrarch regularly affirms in the Canzoniere's later stages. Thus, in the opening of stanza nine, poetry's agonizing failure is memorably captured in the mood of the verbs, the 'congiuntivo ottavio che scivola nel periodo ipotetico dell'irrealtà',[12] that confirms the vanity of the poet's aspiration: 'S'esser non pò' (332. 53). Orpheus, for Petrarch, is beginning to look as if he may actually be an ambiguous artistic and existential model. Indeed, I should like to go a bit further. Unlike what most other scholars maintain,[13] and as I shall endeavour to document here, I do not believe that, in the Canzoniere, Orpheus and Eurydice can be tidily superimposed onto Francesco and Laura. Their purpose in the *Fragmenta* is much more nuanced and complex.

I shall have more to say about Petrarch's presentation of the myth's shortcomings in due course. For the moment, I wish to continue to explore the ways in which Part II of the *Rvf* is overtly placed under the sign of Orpheus and Eurydice.

After a sequence of fifty-two sonnets (271–322), the metrical monotonalism is broken by the *canzone delle visioni*, 'Standomi un giorno solo a la fenestra' (323). *Rvf* 323 is usefully placed alongside 332, since, together, they serve as 'grandiosi testi-guida' (Vecchi Galli, p. 1104) especially with respect to Part II. As befits the canzone's striking entry into the make-up of the Canzoniere, it has summatic functions. The components comprising the six visions — a 'fera [...] | con fronte humana' (ll. 4–5; possibly a doe), a boat (with ties to Ulysses), a laurel tree, a fountain, a phoenix, and Eurydice — are 'legate alla mitografia poetica petrarchesca dopo la morte di Laura e dopo l'avvio del *Fragmentorum liber*', whereby 'i miti classici, ormai "criptati", [sono] fusi in un compiuto sistema autoreferenziale' (Vecce, pp. 227–28). It is immediately striking that, by bringing the visionary sequence to a close, of the symbols, only Eurydice, and by implication Orpheus, mirrors her actual position in the mythological development of the *Fragmenta*. She is further privileged by being the only human being with whom Laura is associated.[14] Even the laurel appears to play a subordinate part to Eurydice, evocatively signalling the vitality of Orphic elements in Part II; and this is confirmed by the fact that, beyond their common concern with 'lo scacco della poesia, l'incapacità di questo strumento, che il poeta umanista aveva creduto divino, a fare fronte alla morte',[15] what first and foremost unites the two 'guiding texts' is, of course, the myth of Orpheus and Eurydice. Indeed, it is not simply the only myth treated in the canzone to return in the sestina, but, more tellingly, it is also the sole myth present in the latter.

Although the 'canzone of the visions' mentions neither lover by name, the scene evoked in the sixth stanza unambiguously calques Eurydice's physical death in Ovid, as Giovanni Gesualdo had already recognized in the sixteenth century:[16]

> Alfin vid'io per entro i fiori et l'erba
> pensosa ir sí leggiadra et bella donna,
> [...]
> punta poi nel tallon d'un picciol angue (ll. 61–62 and 69)

and compare:

> [...] nam nupta per herbas
> dum nova naiadum turba comitata vagatur,
> occidit in talum serpentis dente recepto

> [for while the newly wedded bride wandered through the grass accompanied by a crowd of Naiads, she was struck down, having received a serpent's bite on her ankle.] (*Met.* x. 8–10)

As in 332, Petrarch adroitly sketches the vignette so that it encapsulates Eurydice's two deaths and integrates both his principal Orphic sources.[17] There is no question that the description of the demise of the 'beautiful woman' has its roots in the *Metamorphoses*. The *Georgics*' dark and disturbing account of her death is strikingly different in tone:

> illa quidem, dum te [Aristaeus] fugeret per flumina praeceps,
> immanem ante pedes hydrum moritura puella
> servantem ripas alta non vidit in herba

> [She, to escape you, in headlong flight along the river, did not see in the tall grass before her feet, doomed girl, the monstrous water-serpent that guarded the banks.] (*Georg.* IV. 457–59)

It is not difficult to appreciate why Petrarch would have felt that Virgil's lines jarred with the elegant melodiousness and refined mannerism of the ninth stanza. At the same time, however, the portrayal of the woman's 'parti supreme' that 'eran avolte d'una nebbia oscura' (ll. 67–68) is Virgilian in origin. Rather than recall the portent of Marcellus's death — 'sed nox atra caput tristi cicumvolat umbra' (but night's black shadow flies mournfully around his head; *Aen.* VI. 866) — , as scholars have claimed since Gesualdo's annotation (fol. CCCXLIV[r]), its more likely and appropriate source is to be found in Eurydice's 'live' depiction of her second descent into the afterlife — 'feror ingenti circumdata nocte' (I'm taken away wrapped around by huge night; *Georg.* IV. 497) — combined with the image evoking her disappearance: 'ceu fumus in auras | commixtus tenuis' (like smoke intermingled with rarified air; *Georg.* IV. 499–500),[18] a line which may also have exercised some passing influence on 'sí texta, ch'oro et neve parea inseme' (l. 66).[19] As in 332, Petrarch stresses the myth's ambiguities, pointing not so much to similarities between his and Laura's circumstances and those of Orpheus and Eurydice, but to the fact that, in a Christian universe, the beloved's death is not the doomed tragedy of the ancients. Nothing underlines this better than the manner of the passing of the 'bella donna' — 'lieta si dipartio, nonché secura' (l. 71) — when compared to Eurydice's desperate departure: 'invalidasque tibi tendens, heu! non tua, palmas' (stretching out towards you feeble hands, alas, no longer yours; *Georg.* IV. 498; but see the full account 491–502, as well as *Met.* X. 57–63). Instead of cruel, unfeeling pagan deities, the shadow of a loving and salvific God spreads out over the close of the canzone's final stanza and its congedo.[20] Petrarch, like Orpheus, cannot but weep for his loss ('Ahi, nulla, altro che pianto, al mondo dura!'; l. 72); however, unlike Orpheus, he can also hope that, once dead, not only will he be reunited with his beloved but that their relationship will also be enriched: 'Queste sei visïoni al signor mio | àn fatto un dolce di morir desio' (ll. 74–75).

Rvf 323 and 332 form a perfectly calibrated and harmoniously complementary Orphic diptych that discernibly illustrates the myth's key guiding functions in the Canzoniere's *Parte in morte*. In fact, the poems stand in balanced yet sharp contrast to the two direct references to Orpheus in Part I: 'perché d'Orpheo leggendo et d'Amphïone | se non ti meravigli' (28. 68–69) and 'Ché d'Omero dignissima et d'Orpheo, | o del pastor ch'anchor Mantova honora' (187. 9–10). Both allusions, unlike those in Part II, are highly conventional. They recall in a compressed manner Orpheus's extraordinary poetic talents: in 28 the marvellous effects of his song on nature, which were generally interpreted as an *integumentum* of the civilizing power of poetry, and in 187 his exemplary status as an 'authoritative' (elegiac) poet, the equal in his *stilus* of Homer and Virgil. Both representations are long-established commonplaces for which no precise antecedent can be established.[21] In measured opposition to the two earlier evocations, Petrarch's subjective reworking of the tale and rewriting of his sources, as well as the crucial introduction of Eurydice, underscore the transformation that the *fabula* undergoes in Part II. From cultural cliché, Orpheus is converted into one of the Canzoniere's key personalized mythic tropes that control the collection's structure, development, and meaning. At the same time, the fact that Orpheus is introduced into the first of the *Fragmenta*'s political canzoni and into one of its principal statements on Petrarch's relationship to the poetic tradition hints that even in Part I, and regardless of the general critical insensitivity to this section's Orphic reverberations, the *vates* may have functions that are not entirely negligible.

2. 'Vox forte sequetur Orphea'

It is in fact possible to reconstruct on reasonably solid foundations the process whereby Orpheus and Eurydice became key to the Canzoniere's organizational logic. The evidence unambiguously indicates that Petrarch came to appreciate their value for systematizing his vernacular lyric 'book' only during its last evolutionary stages.[22] The first of the Orphic poems that can be located with certainty as part of the anthology is 28, which, as the internal historical references indicate, Petrarch composed in late 1333 or early 1334,[23] and which appears in the *forma Chigi*, the first of the forms of the *rime sparse* for which we have definitive manuscript proof, and which was assembled between 1359–63. At this stage, Orpheus is essentially a one-off and isolated allusion. He appears in a guise, that of the civic poet, which, while appropriate for a canzone on the crusades, never returns again in the Canzoniere. Indeed, the *vates* is not even connected to Petrarch but to the poem's anonymous dedicatee. The situation begins to change somewhat with the *forma di Giovanni* of Vaticano latino 3195 that was copied between 1366–67 and incorporates 187,[24] whose reference to Orpheus is of course connected to Petrarch and Laura. Consequent to this second allusion, a first, albeit slight and not especially cogent, Orphic intratextual system is created in the collection. At this stage, although the

Canzoniere was clearly divided into two halves, the *Parte in morte*, constituted by 264–318, did not have distinct and programmed Orphic characteristics (and see below, section 3).

Things change, possibly between 1371–72, if one accepts the existence of the *forma Malatesta*, when both 323 and 332 enter into the universe of the *Fragmenta*.[25] I would like to suggest, however, that it is feasible that Petrarch grasped the potential of the myth, especially its Eurydicean dimension, a few years earlier. In the *Codice degli abbozzi* (Vat. Lat. 3196, fol. 2^v), the poet transcribed stanzas 3–6 and the congedo of 323, which he prefaced with the following annotation: '1368 octobris 13, veneris, ante matutinum. Ne labatur contuli ad cedulam plusquam triennio hic inclusa[m] [that contained stanzas 1 and 2], et eodem die, inter primam facem et concubium, transcripsi in alia papiro quibusdam et cetera' (1368 October 13, Friday, before morning. So that this was not lost, I juxtaposed what is written here below to a sheet that had been inserted here for more than three years, and on the same day, between when it grew dark and the dead of night, I transcribed everything onto another sheet, making some changes).[26] Despite its concision, the phrase 'ne labatur', as Rosanna Bettarini helpfully elucidates, 'sembra alludere a una labescenza mentale e a un progetto che precipita dalla mente' (p. 1409). Consequently, one cannot but wonder whether Petrarch's sudden insight concerned the potential of the Orpheus myth, especially when due prominence was granted to Eurydice, to capture the existential, spiritual, and poetic prerogatives of Part II.[27] Indeed, the fact that Eurydice should constitute the canzone's culmination would appear to support this hypothesis; as would the stanza's formal construction. Unlike the other symbols, the poet delays revealing the mythic identity of the 'bella donna' until the final line of the first sirma: 'punta poi nel tallon d'un picciol angue', when, at the point of death, her Eurydicean traits are finally unveiled. Furthermore, by witholding her name, Petrarch ensures that we focus not so much on the character, but on those aspects of her story that he deems noteworthy for his collection. Equally, the strategy allows him to refigure 'his' Orpheus — no longer simply a great poet as in Part I but also the man beset by misfortune — , while leaving no doubt about the crucial significance of Eurydice's entry into the Canzoniere.[28]

Unfortunately, we are unable to date 332, and so cannot conjecture about its possible compositional ties to 323. On the other hand, however, when considered in Orphic terms, it is not difficult to appreciate the reasons for the sestina's inclusion in the *Fragmenta*, especially once 323 had entered into the collection's system. In addition to fashioning, together with the *canzone delle visioni*, an elegant and meaningful contrastive balance between the Canzoniere's two parts that signals and grants substance to Orpheus and Eurydice's prominence within the collection, sestina 332, as we have seen, climactically unites the names of the doomed lovers in a manner that further distinguishes the *vates* from his commonplace one-dimensional appearance in Part I. Likewise, by concentrating on Orpheus's otherworldly singing, Petrarch amplified the remit of the story that he had begun to evoke in 323's final stanza, while forging a clear link not just between Laura and Eurydice but also between himself and the bereaved poet. Emphasizing the myth's forceful resonance in the Canzoniere, the *sestina doppia* thus brings to a final and cogent fulfilment the intuition of 13 October 1368, when Eurydice and Orpheus entered so decisively into Vat. Lat. 3196. Indeed, I suspect that it was not only Ovid's double redaction of the myth that inspired Petrarch to invent the sestina's unusual form, but also Eurydice's 'double death' — 'quo se rapta bis coniuge ferret?' (where could he turn, twice robbed of his wife?; *Georg.* IV. 504); and 'iterum moriens' (dying a second time) and 'gemina nece coniugis' (by his wife's double death; *Met.* X. 60 and 64) — , which, as we saw, is delicately intimated in both 323 and 332: 'et doppiando 'l dolor, doppia lo stile' (332. 39).

The structural and ideological consequence of the *fabula* of Orpheus and Eurydice in the *Rvf* is beyond question. Yet, it is also important to recognize that, albeit in a lesser key, approximately twenty years before he began work on the post-Giovanni sections of Vat. Lat. 3195, Petrarch had already begun to test the myth's effectiveness as an organizing trope. The Canzoniere's Orphic intuition had sprung from deep roots.

Towards the middle of the century, Petrarch composed two Latin poems — the eclogue *Parthenias* (*Buc. carm.* I; 1346–47) and the first of the Horatian *epystolae* to the musician Floriano da Rimini (*Ep.* III. 15; 1352) — whose organization is substantially controlled by the myth. Indeed, Orpheus frames each text, exerting a major sway on their development and content. This strategy is quite explicit in the *epystola*. The poem opens with the *vates*' name, conventionally rehearses the miraculous effects of his song on nature, and recalls his glorious lineage — 'Orpheus Euxinios solitus vel carmine fluctus | Vel Tracum mulcere feras, truncosque sequentes, | Clarus avis proavisque fuit' (Orpheus, who used to calm with his song the waves of the Black Sea and the beasts of Thrace and the trees that followed him, was illustrious thanks to his ancestors; ll. 1–3) — before returning to the extraordinary power of his art in the *explicit*: 'tum currere quercus | Saxaque mota sono, blandosque videbimus ursos' (then we will see the oak trees run, the rocks move, and the bears become tamed; ll. 34–35).[29] The myth's framing functions, in keeping with what I deem to be the eclogue's greater consequence and sophistication (see below), are more subtly introduced into *Parthenias*. Silvius-Petrarch's final speech ends on a note of modest Orphic hope: 'vox forte sequetur | Orphea, promeritum [of Scipio Africanus] modulabor harundine parva' (perhaps an Orpheus-like voice will follow, I will play on a small flute to celebrate him; ll. 122–23). On the surface, the poem's *incipit* appears to have no ties to Orpheus. Intertextually, however, the opening lines owe considerable debts to the myth, and in particular to *Georgics* IV's treatment of the events surrounding Eurydice's 'second death':

> *Silvius* Monice, [...] solus
> [...]
> Ast ego dumosos colles silvasque perrero
> Infelix! Quis fata neget diversa gemellis?
>
> [...]
>
> *Monicus* Silvi, quid quereris? Cunctorum vera laborum
> Ipse tibi causa es. Quis te per devia cogit?
> Quis vel inaccessum tanto sudore cacumen
> Montis adire iubet, vel per deserta vagari?

[*Silvius*: Oh Monicus, alone [...] while I, wretch that I am, wander over hills full of thorn-bushes and through forests. Who could ever deny the different fates of two brothers? [...] *Monicus*: Oh Silvius, why do you complain? You yourself are the cause of all your travails. Who forces you to go to out-of-the-way places? Who makes you reach with so much sweat the inaccessible peak of a mountain, or wander deserted places?] (ll. 1, 3–4 and 6–9)

There are several points of contact, especially if one recalls Petrarch's imitative predilection creatively to rework his sources (McLaughlin, pp. 26–32). Silvius's lines 1 and 3 are a variation on 'solus Hyperboreas glacies Tanaimque nivalem | arvaque Riphaeis numquam viduata pruinis | lustrabat' (alone he wandered the icy North, snowy Tanais and fields that are never free of Riphaean frost; *Georg.* IV. 517–19); while line 4 recalls 'illa "quis et me" inquit "miseram et te perdidit, Orpheu, | quis [...]?' (she said, 'what is this that has lost my wretched self and you, oh Orpheus, what?'; ll. 494–95) combined with 'a miseram Eurydicen!' (ah wretched Eurydice; l. 526) and 'miserabilis Orpheus' (wretched Orpheus; l. 454). In the *Georgics*, the latter designation is immediately followed in the next verse by the interjection 'ni fata resistant' (unless the fates oppose it; l. 455) that exercises some pull on the remainder of line 4. More generally, Petrarch replays Virgil's anaphoric repetition of questions beginning in *Quis* in verses 4, 7, and 8, as well as the older poet's recourse to exclamation. In his turn, Monicus, who stands for Petrarch's brother Gherardo, merges Virgilian and Ovidian elements with the heavily moralizing interpretations of Orpheus's error that had their origins in commentaries to Boethius's *Consolation*.[30] Specifically, lines 6–9 fuse Virgil's 'victusque animi respexit. ibi omnis | effusus labor' (and his resolve overwhelmed, he looked back. In that moment all his effort was squandered; ll. 491–92) and 'rupe sub aëria deserti ad Strymonis undam | flevisse' (beneath a high rock, by the wave of deserted Strymon he wept; ll. 508–09) with Ovid's 'esse deos Erebi crudeles questus, in altam | se recipit Rhodopen pulsumque aquilonibus Haemum' (after having complained that the gods of the underworld were cruel, he retreated to lofty Thrace and to Haemus buffeted by north winds; *Met.* X. 76–77) — all quotations that refer to Orpheus's 'mad' (*Georg.* IV. 488) behaviour that first led to, and then followed on from, Eurydice's 'second death'.

The Orphic patina of *Parthenias*'s opening exchange is certainly striking. At the same time, as with *Ep.* III. 15, it is the reasons why Petrarch may have resorted to the myth, as well as its subsequent unfolding during the course of each poem, that deserve especial attention, not least if these also help us better appreciate the *fabula*'s function in the Canzoniere. As is well known, the introductory eclogue of the *Bucolicum carmen*, via the dialogue between Petrarch and his brother Gherardo, assesses the merits of two ways of life, the active and the contemplative, and of two types of literature, classical and classicizing secular poetry as against Biblical verse, specifically the Psalms. The discussion seemingly ends in an impasse, with both brothers remaining firm in their contrasting opinions regarding life and literature. But what role might Orpheus, long-associated with harmony, play in this drama of brotherly intransigence? Although Orphic allusions recur throughout the eclogue, these are principally concentrated in the second part of Silvius's poetic autobiography and self-justification (ll. 29–45) and in Monicus's sharp response to his brother (ll. 46–49), namely, *Parthenias*'s key section, not simply because in it Petrarch speaks of himself as a poet, but also because it includes ideological legitimation for the brothers' respective positions. Indeed, Petrarch forcefully signals the importance of the 'Rhodopeius [...] heros' (Thracian hero; *Met.* x. 50) for his self-portrait by unusually following his source in Ovid with greater precision than usual; and this more than once. Silvius's melodramatic conclusion — 'Si fata viam [...] negarit, | Stat, germane, mori' (If the fates will deny the way, it is better, oh brother, that I die; ll. 44–45) — repeats Orpheus's valiant altruistic declaration: 'quodsi fata negant veniam pro coniuge, certum est | nolle redire mihi: leto gaudete duorum' (For if the fates deny this favour to my wife, it is certain that I will not return: enjoy the death of two people; x. 38–39). Equally, as occurs with Orpheus's 'flebile lingua murmurat' (tongue mournfully murmuring) to which 'respondent flebile ripae' (the riverbanks mournfully respond; xi. 52–53) so 'arentes respondent undique cautes' to Petrarch's 'song' (from every side the arid rocks respond; ll. 34–35). Around these two quotations, the poet distributes an array of Orphic motifs. Silvius mentions following his poetic masters but without losing contact with them (l. 29), as well as poetry's impact on the environment (ll. 30–31, 34–35, and 41–42), and the fluctuating nature of his existence — 'Sic eo, sic redeo' (Thus I go, thus I return; l. 40) — , which succinctly captures the logic of events culminating in Eurydice's 'second death'. As he would do in the *Parte in morte* of the *Fragmenta*, Petrarch filters his poetic and human experiences through those of Orpheus, who, together with Homer and Virgil, is presented as one of his three seminal literary models.[31] Yet, in the Canzoniere, as we saw, while extolling the *vates*, the poet also highlights the limits of his predecessor's verse. Similarly, in the eclogue, returning to his opening Orphic gambit (ll. 6–9), Monicus stresses the error of his brother's exclusive dedication to secular poetry, once more implying parallels between Silvius's conduct and Orpheus's looking back at Eurydice, an unconscionable action (*Georg.* IV. 491) that both marked the start of the bard's unrelieved suffering and erratic behaviour, and resulted in the beloved being confined for eternity in Hell:

> O! si forte queas durum hoc transcendere limen.
> Quid refugis? Turpesque casas et tuta pavescis
> Otia? Quid frontem obducis? Nemo ante coactus
> Nostra petit; plures redeunt a limine frustra.
>
> [Oh, if by chance I could cross the hard threshold. Why do you flee? Why do you fear the base houses and calm leisures? Why do you furrow your brow? Nobody is made to seek our caves.] (ll. 46–49)[32]

The danger to which Silvius is exposing his immortal soul in Monicus's warning is obvious, although for the moment he leaves his brother's admonition unheeded. Subsequently, as I hope to have clarified above, in Part II of the *Rvf*, Petrarch accepts Gherardo's criticism and will acknowledge the error of the hero's (and by extension of his own earlier) exaggerated faith in poetry, especially when this is considered *sub specie aeternitatis*.

The basic Orphic characteristics of the second section of the Canzoniere, namely, the myth's key structural functions and the *vates*' status as a great yet flawed poetic and existential model, are thus already evident in the proemial poem of the *Bucolicum carmen*. In addition, the eclogue appears to reveal that what attracted Petrarch to the myth was its semantic and symbolic flexibility: first, its 'reversibility', the way in which elements from the myth can be assigned different, even contrasting, values (Orpheus's singing and the act of following as having both positive and negative connotations), and second, its 'universalism', the manner in which Eurydice's and Orpheus's experiences can be simultaneously embodied by a single character and are not gender-specific (Silvius who commits an error reminiscent of Orpheus's, but who concurrently, like Eurydice, faces the dire consequences of the misstep). These elements too would become constants in Petrarch's treatment of the *fabula* in the *Fragmenta*. Crucially, however, what is still missing is proper recognition of Eurydice's importance. It will be canzone 323, of course, that finally acknowledges her indispensable status in the story.[33] Indeed, I wonder whether my hypothesis regarding Petrarch's intuition of 13 October can be refined further. The insight may have involved an understanding not so much of the *fabula*'s ideological and creative efficacy — *Parthenias* offers proof that Petrarch was well aware of this by the late 1340s —, but of Eurydice's rich and decisive potential.

By diverting to the Canzoniere, I have failed adequately to address Orpheus's status in the eclogue. On the one hand, I had begun to establish his significance as an emblem, together with Homer and Virgil, of the allure, success, and spectacular potential of secular poetry at its best, as well as his aptness to serve as an ideal for Petrarch to imitate. To put it simply, as far as Silvius is concerned, Orpheus legitimates his choice of life and art.[34] On the other, however, Monicus highlights the myth's pitfalls and ambiguities, and goes on to propose and celebrate an alternative literary and existential model, David the psalmist (ll. 53–58, 70–71, and 91–109). Scholars correctly read the brothers' claims in antithetical terms. In addition, they generally also maintain that, in *Parthenias*, Petrarch asserted the autonomy of the greatest poets and their achievements, and, in contrast to other contemporary intellectuals, most notably Dante and Mussato, denied that meaningful contacts might exist between theology and poetry, thereby also criticizing the connected notion of the *poeta-theologus*.[35] The presence of Orpheus in the eclogue, however, calls these latter interpretations into question. Unlike Homer and Virgil, whose poetic achievements the fourteenth century largely deemed beyond reproach, Orpheus, for all his artistic prowess, did raise questions about the efficacy of poetry,[36] as Monicus avers. Equally, in the late Middle Ages, if there was one poet who more than any other embodied the figure of the *poeta-theologus*, that poet was Orpheus, who praised the gods and civilized humanity.[37] Moreover, it is interesting that, in *Parthenias*, David too is presented as having Orphic attributes: 'Semper habet lacrimas et pectore raucus anelat' (He always has tears and draws hoarse breaths from his breast; l. 74) and 'Omnia [riverbanks and seashores] iam resonant pastoris carmina nostri' (all now resound with the songs of our shepherd; l. 109). In itself, the association between the two singers, since it was widely present in medieval culture (Friedman, pp. 148–55, 188–89), is little more than a commonplace; in terms of the first eclogue, however, it further blurs the distinction, but without obliterating it, between theology and poetry. By dexterously insinuating Orpheus as his poem's controlling mechanism, Petrarch undermined the intransigence of both brothers, and furthermore introduced a third position that recognized both the achievements and limitations of secular poetry, as well as its points of contact with the sacred.[38] While placing the emphasis on profane literature, the 'Orphic' idea of poetry that emerges from *Parthenias* is one of possible and useful contacts between secular and religious writers that does not unbalance or overwhelm either tradition. In terms of mid-Trecento poetics, Petrarch's nuanced view of poetry constitutes a compromise between the claims of those who insisted on literature's glorious self-sufficiency and the contentions of those who were intent on excessively 'theologizing' it. It is the type of compromise, in fact, that will also be apparent in Part II of the *Fragmenta*, where Petrarch increasingly leavens his distinctly secular lyric poetry with Christian intertexts and values, a process that reaches a climax with 'Vergine bella'. My reading is actually not that dissimilar from the explanation that Petrarch offers as his framework for interpreting *Parthenias* in *Familiaris* x. 4. 1–2:

> theologie quidem minime adversa poetica est. Miraris? parum abest quin dicam theologiam poeticam esse de Deo: Cristum modo leonem modo agnum modo vermem dici, quid nisi poeticum est? mille talia in Scripturis Sacris invenies que persequi longum est. Quid vero aliud parabole Salvatoris in Evangelio sonant, nisi sermonem a sensibus alienum sive, ut uno verbo exprimam, alieniloquium, quam allegoriam usitatiori vocabulo nuncupamus? Atqui ex huiusce sermonis genere poetica omnis intexta est. Sed subiectum aliud. Quis negat? illic de Deo atque divinis, hic de diis hominibusque tractatur, unde et apud Aristotilem primos theologizantes poetas legimus.
>
> [in fact poetry is barely in opposition to theology. Are you surprised? I might almost say that theology is God's poetry: when Christ is called a lion or a lamb or a worm, what is it if not poetry? You will find thousands of such cases in Sacred Scripture that are too many to treat here. In truth what else do the Saviour's parables in the Gospel resound if not a discourse different from its customary meaning or, to put it simply, other speech, which in everyday language we term allegory? Nevertheless all poetry is woven from this type of discourse. But its subject is different. Who'd deny it? The first discourse treats God and divine things, the other gods and men, so that even in Aristotle we read that the first theologians were poets.][39]

Petrarch indicates the points of contact between theology and poetry, while also clearly discriminating between them; although it is suggestive that, albeit to different degrees, a divine dimension, as well as similarities in style, characterizes both. Yet nowhere in its exegesis does the letter refer to Orpheus. The omission cannot but be deliberate. Now that Petrarch himself is openly clarifying the poem's meaning — the task that the *vates* performs allusively in the weave of the eclogue — his presence is predictably redundant.

In cultural terms, *Bucolicum carmen* I effects a valid compromise on a matter of significant intellectual concern. Yet, if read 'autobiographically', it is doubtful whether the eclogue displays a similar conciliatory equilibrium with respect to the poet's personal engagement with poetry. Petrarch confusingly associates himself with both Silvius and Orpheus. He is caught between the shepherd's intransigent pursuit of self-satisfying poetic glory and the hard lessons regarding poetry's shortcomings taught by the bard's harsh experiences. Importantly, both alternatives are present in the myth: the former in Orpheus's wondrous authority over his earthly and otherworldly surroundings, the latter in Orpheus's loss of the almost regained Eurydice. It is indicative that, in lines 29–47, Silvius should stress the bard's triumphs, while Monicus his failures, although, more revealingly, both also allude to the contrary experience.[40] Petrarch's personal dilemma is all here: his inability to resolve in his own life tensions that, at a purely intellectual and external level, he was able to reconcile satisfactorily. As occurs time and again in his oeuvre, the poet presents himself trapped between the two possibilities — a predicament whose implications Monicus pithily summarizes in the eclogue's closing line: 'I sospes, variosque vie circumspice casus' (Go safely, and look out for the journey's many dangers; l. 124). In Orphic terms, Petrarch is incapable of accepting and usefully integrating the myth's full implications. His Orpheus is a poet who is 'sundered' from his own history. Yet, when, towards the end of his life, in Part II of the Canzoniere, Petrarch returned to the *vates* to help him make sense of Laura's death, it was because he had finally begun to acquire a clear and balanced appreciation of the fabled poet's successes and failures — an acquisition that was largely due to the recovery of Eurydice that first and foremost represented a belated acceptance of Orpheus's limitations. It was the coming together of all these factors, I would like to think, that most likely constituted the stuff of Petrarch's sudden intuition.

Before returning definitively and conclusively to the *Fragmenta*, I need to say something about the Horatian *epystola* to Floriano. The poem lacks the layered complexity of *Parthenias*. As a political *satyra*, it aims to make its polemical points rather more directly.[41] Nevertheless, its recourse to the *vates* is anything but uninteresting. Behind the veil of hyperbolically praising the addressee as a modern-day Orpheus (compare *Ep.* III. 16. 1–2; *Sen.* XI. 5. 1) and pleading with him to abandon the corrupt environment in which he resides — surroundings that are largely described in mythological terms —, Petrarch launches yet another scathing attack on the papal court at Avignon. His condemnation of the present, as is evident from the opening allusion to Orpheus, is achieved in part through a starkly unfavourable comparison with classical antiquity. As in *Rvf* 28, another political poem, the bard is exclusively evoked as a great civic poet whose song morally improves its listeners. Yet, even he would be unable to affect and improve the 'monstrous' Avignonese clergy (compare *De remediis* I. 24. 10), an affirmation that contrastively alludes to Orpheus mesmerizing even the most fearsome horrors of Hades (*Georg.* IV. 481–84 and *Met.* X. 40–47):

> Nisi quod modo surda canenti
> Monstra parit tellus; redeat licet ille, nec iram
> Nec luxum frenare queat, victusque tenaci
> Cedet avaritiae.

[Except that now the earth brings forth monsters that are deaf to the singer;

even if he [Orpheus] were to return, he would not be able to curb their wrath
and debauchery, and overcome by stubborn greed he will withdraw.] (ll. 6–9)

As Petrarch muses about Orpheus's return from the dead, the hero metamorphoses into Eurydice, underlining again her occasional 'exploitable' status for much of the poet's career.[42] More significantly, the bard also rehearses her 'second death'. Orpheus's defeat in a hypothetical present is associated with his murder at the hands of the savage Bacchantes, the myth's horrific climax, that Ovid describes in detail (*Met.* XI. 1–60), but which, in his œuvre, Petrarch never directly remembers. Orpheus, 'overcome by deaf and stubborn greed',[43] relives the women's unrelenting attack (ll. 13–14), their insensitivity to his song, and his cruel death: 'in illo tempore primum | inrita dicentem nec quicquam voce moventem | sacrilegae perimunt' (then for the first time he spoke without effect and his voice did not move any of them, the impious women killed him; ll. 39–41; and compare ll. 15–18). Indeed, the clergy's 'bloody hands' ('dextrasque cruentas', *Ep.* III. 15. 13) explicitly calque those of the Maenads who 'cruentatis vertuntur in Orphea dextris' (with their bloody hands they turn on Orpheus; *Met.* XI. 23).

Although, during the remainder of the *epystola* and before its *explicit*, Orphic elements occasionally reappear (ll. 12, 18–21, 23, 29), Petrarch relies on a very different source to depict the curia's perversions:

> Semiviros per prata boves, perque atria cernas
> Semiboves errare viros. Non unus opacam
> Minotaurus habet perplexi tramitis aulam;
> Plurima permixtae caecaeque libidinis extant
> Signa per infames partus sobolemque nefandam
> Et natos furor exagitat, rabiesque famesque
> Dira, nec immites cessant a sanguine fauces.
> Nec septena virum, sed iam millena vorantur
> Corpora iustorum; nec solae urgentur Athenae,
> Sed cupidis totus laceratur dentibus orbis.

[You see half-men wander through the fields like bulls and half-bulls through the houses like men. Not only is the Minotaur found in the dark hall of the unintelligible labyrinth; many signs of intermingled and blind lust are visible, the result of disreputable births and abominable progeny, and fury torments the offspring, and anger and dreadful hunger, and their savage jaws never cease from craving blood. Not seven men, but now thousands of bodies of the just are devoured; nor is Athens alone oppressed, but the whole world is torn to pieces by greedy teeth.] (*Ep.* III. 15. 23–32)

We are back in Dante's Hell. At first sight, Avignon, the home of the blood-crazed Minotaur and *semiviri*, appears to have been transformed into the circle of violence. Yet, express intertextual links with *Inferno* XII are hard to find. Instead, while undeniably evoking the region of 'la riviera del sangue in la qual bolle | qual che per vïolenza in altrui noccia' (ll. 47–48),[44] Petrarch increases the infernal intensity of his Hell-on-earth by deftly combining a series of interconnected Dantean passages drawn from different parts of the the first canticle. *Inferno* XXV — canto of thieves, abominations, and sexually inflected perverse transformations (compare *Ep.* III. 15.

26–27) — provides the key to the *epystola*'s Dantean intertextual system:

> Per tutt' i cerchi de lo 'nferno scuri
> non vidi spirto in Dio tanto superbo [Vanni Fucci],
> non quel che cadde a Tebe giù da' muri.
> El si fuggì che non parlò più verbo;
> E io vidi un centauro pien di rabbia.
> (ll. 13–17; and compare *Ep.* III. 15. 28)

Dante's passage yokes together *Inferno* XII, XIV, and XXV, namely, violence by introducing Cacus the centaur, blasphemy through the figure of Capaneus, and thievery — a potently apt *permixtum* (*Ep.* III. 15. 26) that captures and condemns the clergy's principal sins. Indeed, the latter two *canti* provide the sources for some elements in Petrarch's description. Thus, 'fuor che la tua [Capaneus's] rabbia | sarebbe al tuo furor dolor compito' (*Inf.* XIV. 65–66) anticipates 'Et natos furor exagitat, rabiesque famesque' (and fury torments the offspring, and anger and dreadful hunger; *Ep.* III. 15. 28);[45] while 'nec immites cessant a sanguine fauces' (their savage jaws never cease from craving blood; *Ep.* III. 15. 29) fuses 'di sangue fece spesse volte laco' with 'onde cessar le sue opere biece' (*Inf.* XXV. 27 and 31). In addition, at least one other, 'extraneous', Dantean intertext is present in the mix: 'cagne, bramose [...] | miser li denti, | e quel dilaceraro' (*Inf.* XIII. 125 and 127–28) which returns in line 32, 'Sed cupidis totus laceratur dentibus orbis' (but the whole world is torn to pieces by greedy teeth). As in *Parthenias*, Petrarch brings Orpheus and Dante together in a move that he repeats elsewhere. I shall very soon briefly address the coupling of the two great poets. At this point, I simply wish to note that, while Orpheus is presented in all his glory as he seduces the natural and the other world, Dante is reduced to the poet of *monstra*;[46] and it is of course in the footsteps of Orpheus the civilizer that Petrarch the political poet follows, cherrypicking Dante along the way.

3. 'Bella donna punta poi nel tallon'

The poems that I have discussed so far document both the pliability of the *fabula* of Orpheus and Eurydice and Petrarch's formal, narrative, and ideological skill at exploiting the myth's possibilities. Especially in *Parthenias* the poet displayed its organizational, cultural, and semantic potential. However, as we have begun to recognize, it is in Part II of the Canzoniere that Petrarch most fully develops the story and adapts it to his personal needs and preoccupations. I do not have the space here to trace the myth's imposing advancement and rich elaboration in the later reworkings of the second half of the *Fragmenta* (never mind its far from inconsequential presence in the *Parte in vita*). At most I can allude to a few large-scale elements that help confirm its importance in the lyric collection; and it is precisely the *fabula*'s significance — its range and adaptability — that Petrarch scholarship has either almost entirely ignored or minimized.

Let us begin with some numbers. I have recognized Orphic elements, that range from generalized allusions, such as the theme of looking back, to more specific suggestions, such as nature's lament that involves trees, rivers, birds, and to precise evocations — thus, among the birds, 'Quel rosignuol' (311. 1) is the vernacular progeny of Virgil's distraught 'philomela' (*Georg.* IV. 511; and compare ll. 511–15 to ll. 1–5) — in thirty-five poems from Part I and in just about half the lyrics, fifty-one out of 103, in Part II. The poems are: in Part I, 1, 10, 15, 23, 28, 49, 50, 51, 53, 54, 58, 59, 93, 97, 99, 110, 123, 125, 129, 130, 135, 143, 152, 156, 170, 180, 187, 188, 190, 195, 203, 212, 222, 237, 239; and in Part II, 264, 265, 267, 268, 269, 270, 271, 273, 275, 276, 277, 278, 279, 281, 282, 283, 286, 288, 290, 291, 292, 294, 296, 297, 298, 301, 302, 304, 305, 306, 310, 311, 316, 318, 320, 323, 324, 325, 332, 333, 334, 336, 342, 346, 347, 349, 353, 357, 358, 359, 366. Simply in themselves, the statistics are eye-catching and confirm the myth's weight in the *Fragmenta*. They are even more impressive when placed against Peter Hainsworth's '51 poems in which allusions are made to Daphne or to the laurel in a readily recognizable manner'.[47] I am not trying to suggest that Orpheus and Eurydice are more significant than Apollo and Daphne or that the two doomed lovers trump all the Canzoniere's other myths. I am simply underscoring their vitality and persistence in the collection; indeed, a first inkling of their import can come from the fact that, before Petrarch, Orpheus is not named in the Occitan and Italian lyric tradition, something which the poet is very likely to have known and which confirms the highly personalized character of the myth in the *Rvf*.[48]

I am thus tempted to wonder whether Petrarch's Canzoniere may not in fact be the great overlooked Orphic text of the Western tradition,[49] with Part II as its apogee. Petrarch immediately imprints the tragic lovers onto the section: sixteen of the first twenty poems — the exceptions are 266, 272, 274, 280 — include elements drawn from the myth, and this sudden Orphic outpouring is all the more visible given that the close of Part I is devoid of references to the myth. The last allusions are strategically located in a sestina, 'Non à tanti animali il mar fra l'onde' (237), that does not appear in the Canzoniere until the Malatesta form, namely, the version, as we saw, that definitively marks the entry of Orpheus and Eurydice as key players in the collection. By accumulating a range of motifs that specify its programmed Orphic function, the sestina both anticipates the myth's dominant presence in the *Parte in morte* and emphasizes its disappearance in 238–63: 'né tanti augelli albergan per li boschi' (l. 4) calques the simile of the souls flocking to listen to Orpheus, 'quam multa in foliis avium se milia condunt' (as many as the thousands of birds that shelter among the leaves; *Georg.* IV. 473); variations on Virgil's 'te [Eurydice] veniente die, te decedente canebat' (he sang about you as the day approached, about you as it departed; l. 466) appear several times (ll. 12, 14, 20); woods are affected by the poet's sad condition (ll. 11 and 24); and he finds himself alone in wild places (ll. 9, 12, 15, 25–26, 37–38 and compare *Georg.* IV. 507–09 and 517–19). In focusing on the Malatesta form, I should not like to create the impression that, before it, Part II was bereft of references to the myth. The opposite is in fact the case. Twenty-one out of the twenty-nine Correggio poems (264–92) assigned to the *Parte in morte* embrace Orphic elements; while, in the Chigi (264–304), the numbers are twenty-eight out of forty-one and, in Giovanni (264–318), thirty-four from fifty-five. Petrarch had long appreciated the relevance of the *fabula* when representing himself as a bereaved poet-lover, not least because he had already seriously engaged with it elsewhere. What was missing in his treatment until the inclusion of 323 and 332, but also 237, was an articulated structural and ideological Orphic system that could grant coherence to the disparate manifestations of the myth in the individual poems. I believe, as I have already stated, that this move to formal symmetry and intellectual orderliness was the result of the intuition of 13 October 1368 — an intuition which, for the first time, revealed to Petrarch the capacity of Eurydice to exert the necessary shaping function on the second part of his collection. As a result, for him, the myth became no longer simply that of Orpheus, but of Orpheus and Eurydice. Indeed, to put it more accurately, it became the *fabula* of Eurydice and Orpheus.[50]

I am keenly aware that I am dealing with complex matters in a cursory and unsatisfactory manner. Substantial research needs to be done before we can begin to understand the processes whereby the myth became ever more crucial for the construction of the *Fragmenta*.[51] As with this study as whole, I am simply mapping out a few co-ordinates that might offer some directions to an in-depth investigation. Many issues would need to be taken into consideration. As I have adumbrated, attention would first need to be given to the Orphic make-up of individual forms of the Canzoniere and their interrelationship, in particular to the processes whereby the myth entered into their systems, which would also entail, wherever possible, as in the case of 323, an assessment of the different phases of the Orphic construction of individual poems. For instance, the relative weight, prominence, and intratextual import of elements drawn from the myth in 'I' vo pensando, et nel penser m'assale' (264), the first poem of Part II, cannot but vary between versions: in the *forma Chigi* they play a secondary role, while in the post-Malatesta forms they help to introduce major structural and ideological concerns.[52] Furthermore, the potential sources — from Horace to Servius and from Statius to Claudian — of Petrarch's knowledge of the myth need to be evaluated much more efficiently and widely than I have been able to do here. In particular, much more can be said about the likely impact on the poet of the hermeneutic tradition. The myth's flexibility is at the core of its medieval reception, not least because its protagonists, like Petrarch and Laura in the Canzoniere, can represent both positive and negative values, as well as much else that comes between these two poles.[53] It is the commentators that stress the rapprochement in the *fabula* between art and ethics, vice and virtue, *sapientia* and *eloquentia* — all concerns that also haunt the Canzoniere. Finally, and it is the aspect of the medieval engagement with the myth that I find most suggestive for Petrarch, exegetes consistently read it in expressly Christian terms.[54] Indeed, I believe that such interpretations aided the poet in his endeavour to integrate secular and religious elements in Part II. A couple of examples ought to suffice. Scholars normally cite Job 30. 31 — 'versa est in luctum cithara mea et organum meum in vocem flentium' (my harp is turned to mourning and my organ into the voice of those that cry) — as the source for

> Or sia qui fine al mio amoroso canto:
> Secca è la vena de l'usato ingegno,
> Et la cetera mia rivolta in pianto. (292. 12–14)

However, the reference is also Orphic: from the lyre, to abandoning a former style, and to finding a new poetic register to express sorrow. What makes the sonnet's close so powerfully apposite, especially as a declaration of the *Parte in morte*'s poetics, is the manner in which it no longer posits, unlike for much of the Canzoniere, the Christian and the classical as contrasting alternatives but presents them as coming together to illuminate the poet-mourner's condition, while also offering him models to imitate in his effort to give voice to his predicament. *Mutatis mutandis*, the commentators had recognized in the story of Orpheus and Eurydice elements that could neatly dovetail with Christian situations, from the Fall[55] to Christ's salvific power, thereby serving to legitimate the myth's Christianizing overtones in the Canzoniere.[56] As a result, Laura-Orpheus may lead Petrarch-Eurydice-the human 'soul' to Heaven:

> Ché, come i miei pensier' dietro a lei vanno,
> cosí leve, expedita et lieta l'alma
> la segua, et io sia fuor di tanto affanno. (278. 9–11)

The tercet successfully captures the myth's potent and valuable adaptability in the *Fragmenta*. Throughout Part II, as I have indicated, its details are moved back and forth between Petrarch and Laura depending on the context of individual poems. Furthermore, to appreciate Petrarch's reworking of his Orphic borrowings, it is necessary, as 323 establishes, to recognize the functions of both lovers in the *fabula*. Indeed, if Eurydice's original attributes, as in sonnet 278, are now reassigned to a male character, this is no longer a mark of her inconsequentiality, as in *Epystola* III. 15, but of her indispensable vitality and uniqueness. Indeed, since elsewhere in the Canzoniere she is regularly linked to Laura, Eurydice is not simply the saved soul but, Christologically, also the means by which that same soul achieves salvation. The myth's subtle complexity in the Canzoniere is neatly captured, if far from resolved, in its paradoxes.

4. In conclusion: *Ille*

As far as I am aware, in the medieval tradition Eurydice was never linked to Christ. This new connotation originates with Petrarch. Indeed, however much the Middle Ages may have acknowledged the myth's malleability, Petrarch energetically and deliberately 'deconstructed' it to serve his own ends. To put it somewhat differently, he appropriated and personalized the *fabula* and its exegesis, so that its values and circumstances became potentially applicable, whether *per analogiam* or contrastively, to any of the different moments, convolutions and demands of his own story. I posed the question at the outset how Petrarch might imitate a writer whose texts he could never read. The answer, I believe, beyond following him at the general level of adopting the same (elegiac) genre, was by personally and creatively rewriting his story so that it became part of his own narrative of self-presentation. The myth ceases to be part of a common cultural heritage but becomes Petrarchan.[57] With no originary text by Orpheus to deflect attention, the reader's focus is entirely on Petrarch and his poetry, which, as is well known, is not infrequently the poet's goal. As I have noted, Orpheus is put into contact with other authors, who, whether together or individually, allow Petrarch to define his own identity as a poet — and this feature too of Petrarch's Orphism needs to be evaluated properly. As well as the conventional association with *auctores* of the calibre of Homer and Virgil, or with ancient singers such as Amphion and Linus,[58] another poet is regularly associated with Orpheus. That poet, of course, is Dante, 'ill[e] qui in his [vernacular studies] etatem totam posuit' (the one who dedicated his whole life to these), and hence whom Petrarch could never have 'envied' (*Fam.* XXI. 15. 21). This is most certainly not the place even to begin to enter into the tangled thicket of Petrarch's attitude to his predecessor. Suffice it to say that the rapprochement to Orpheus, as in *Epystola* III. 15, and in general to other poets, does Dante few favours. Yet, as has now been definitively established, Petrarch owed much to Dante. For instance, the assigning of Christological qualities to Eurydice-Laura is almost certainly filtered through Dante's sacralizing treatment of Beatrice in the *Vita nova* and in the Earthly Paradise. However, in Part II of the Canzoniere, being placed in Dante's ambit also has negative effects on Orpheus. Time and again, Petrarch challenged Dante's central claim in the *Commedia* that he had been providentially granted direct knowledge of the other world. By denying the truthfulness of the poem, Petrarch denied too its intellectual claims, one of the key elements on which Dante's Trecento *auctoritas* was being constructed. He thus returned the *Commedia* to the realm of *fictio*, whence, by 'theologizing' it, Dante had striven to distance his masterpiece. Rather more energetically than in *Parthenias*, in the *Fragmenta*, Petrarch repudiated the idea of a transcendental poetry, replacing it with his exquisitely literary fusion of lyric and Scriptural and of classical-secular and Christian. Equally, by insisting on the autobiographical nature of the experiences that he was describing, Petrarch was also implying that, unlike the *Commedia*, the Canzoniere was *historia* and not *fictio*. By denying that the living Dante had been miraculously reunited with the dead Beatrice, Petrarch also rejected that Orpheus had descended to Hades and, however briefly, had spent time with his deceased spouse (Barański, '"Piangendo"', pp. 633–39),[59] hence the reason why, as in 278, the poet regularly reversed the *fabula*'s central situation. In the *Fragmenta*, Eurydice no longer futilely follows Orpheus back to life and damnation; instead Orpheus now beneficially trails Eurydice to death and deliverance. The ancient poet's endeavours are criticized, called into question, and rebuffed. Only the Canzoniere faces up honestly to the loss of a loved one, while also ensuring that poetry's rhetorically refined self-sufficiency is never compromised by its encounter with the transcendent. The greater were Petrarch's debts to a writer, the more likely that that writer would be radically transformed at the poet's hands. Petrarch is intent on making it manifest that, in the last analysis, he did not need Orpheus's 'sí pietoso stile | che Laura mia potesse tôrre a Morte'; and this was not so much because the 'style' was ultimately no more than a consolatory delusion, but because, in the Canzoniere, he had forged his own decidedly 'realistic' and highly effective 'vario stile in ch'io piango et ragiono' (I. 5).[60]

Notes to Chapter 1

1. Track 14, The Felice Brothers, *The Felice Brothers* (Team Love Records, B0012IWHKK, 2008). Martin and I are friends. That we are also colleagues is very much of secondary importance. For me, Martin will always be Martin the family man, the Celtic supporter, the friend with whom to go and have a few pints of real ale, and the aficionado of popular music. Often, when we get together with Cathy and Maggie, we play music and chat. I'm not sure, Martin, whether you know The Felice Brothers, a great roots band from New York's Catskill Mountains, or whether I ever played them for you. If you don't and I didn't, go and check 'em out. They're great. As you can see, they're also very distant *nipotini* of both Orpheus and Petrarch. And, of course, thanks for your friendship. I should also like to thank warmly other friends — Ted Cachey, Unn Falkeid, Peter Hainsworth and Brian Richardson — for their comments on an earlier version of this study.
2. See Giuseppe Mazzotta, 'Orpheus: Rhetoric and Music in Petrarch', in *Forma e parola: studi in memoria di Fredi Chiappelli*, ed. by Dennis J. Dutschke and others (Rome: Bulzoni, 1992), pp. 137–54; Nicola Gardini, 'Un esempio di imitazione virgiliana nel Canzoniere petrarchesco: il mito di Orfeo', *MLN*, 110 (1995), 132–44; Ingrid Rossellini, *Nel trapassar del segno: idoli della mente ed echi della vita nei 'Rerum vulgarium fragmenta'* (Florence: Olschki, 1995), pp. 53–102; Federica Brunori, 'Il mito ovidiano di Orfeo e Euridice nel *Canzoniere* di Petrarca', *Romance Quarterly*, 44 (1997), 233–44; Thérèse Migraine-George, 'Specular Desires: Orpheus and Pygmalion as Aesthetic Paradigms in Petrarch's *Rime sparse*', *Comparative Literature Studies*, 36 (1999), 226–46; Maria Elisa Raja, 'Per Euridice (nel Trecento)', in her *Il dolce immaginar: miti e figure della poesia trecentesca* (Piacenza: Vicolo del Pavone, 2005), pp. 97–120; Zygmunt G. Barański, '"Piangendo e cantando" con Orfeo (e con Dante): strutture emotive e strutture poetiche in *Rvf* 281–90', in *Il Canzoniere: lettura micro e macrotestuale*, ed. by Michelangelo Picone (Ravenna: Longo, 2007), pp. 617–40 (pp. 637–39); Francesco Giusti, 'Le parole di Orfeo: Dante, Petrarca, Leopardi, e gli archetipi di un genere', *Italian Studies*, 64 (2009), 56–76 (pp. 64–68), and *Canzonieri in morte: per un'etica poetica del lutto* (L'Aquila: Textus, 2015), pp. 92–100. For a reliable overview of the myth in Petrarch's oeuvre, see Luca Marcozzi, *La biblioteca di Febo: mitologie e allegoria in Petrarca* (Florence: Cesati, 2002), pp. 219–33.
3. *Georg.* IV. 453–527 and *Met.* X. 1–154 and XI. 1–66. The *Georgics* are quoted from Virgil, *Eclogues. Georgics. Aeneid I-VI*, trans. by H. Rushton Fairclough, rev. by G. P. Goold (Cambridge, MA: Harvard University Press, 1999), while the *Metamorphoses* are quoted from Ovid, *Metamorphoses*, trans. by Frank Justus Miller, 2nd edn, 2 vols (Cambridge, MA: Harvard University Press, 1984). All translations are my own. My aim in translating is accuracy and not elegance.
4. In truth, the myth's status in the Canzoniere continues to remain largely unacknowledged as evidenced by the notes to recent editions of the collection (Fenzi, Dotti, Santagata, Bettarini, Stroppa, Vecchi Galli). Bettarini's commentary is the most sensitive to the *fabula*, and see her *Lacrime e inchiostro nel Canzoniere di Petrarca* (Bologna: CLUEB, 1998), pp. 10–14, 19–20.
5. See in particular Luca Marcozzi, 'Petrarca lettore di Ovidio', in *Testimoni del vero: su alcuni libri in biblioteche d'autore*, ed. by Emilio Russo (= *Studi (e testi) italiani*, 6 (2000)), pp. 57–106; Marcozzi, *Biblioteca*; Carlo Vecce, 'Francesco Petrarca. La rinascita degli dèi antichi', in *Il mito nella letteratura italiana*, ed. by Pietro Gibellini (Brescia: Morcelliana, 2003-), I: *Dal Medioevo al Rinascimento*, ed. by Gian Carlo Alessio (2008), pp. 177–228. See also Anne-Marie Telesinski, 'Pétrarque, le poète des métamorphoses', 2 vols (unpublished doctoral thesis, University of Paris 3, 2014), who discusses Orpheus and Eurydice at I, 17–18, 240, 246, 262–64, 266, 271–72.
6. The Canzoniere is quoted from Francesco Petrarca, *Canzoniere: 'Rerum vulgarium fragmenta'*, ed. by Rosanna Bettarini, 2 vols (Turin: Einaudi, 2005); henceforth Bettarini.
7. The *Consolatio Philosophiae* is quoted from Boethius, *The Theological Tractates*, trans. by S. J. Tester and others, 2nd edn (Cambridge, MA: Harvard University Press, 1973).
8. See Martin L. McLaughlin, *Literary Imitation in the Italian Renaissance* (Oxford: Clarendon Press, 1995), pp. 22–48.
9. Laura is very rarely named in the *Fragmenta* (239. 8 and 23; 291. 4; see also 225. 10). Petrarch

names Eurydice on five other occasions in his œuvre: *Africa* VI. 56; *Secretum* III. 146; *Sen.* IX. 1. 7; XV. 3. 1; *Tr. Cupid.* IV. 13.
10. Appropriately, the sonnet reverses several Orphic motifs connected to Eurydice's 'second death': the beloved's otherworldly abode is not a 'loco oscuro et basso' (l. 4) as in the myth; it is the male lover who follows his beloved (l. 8); and his journey will successfully end not in an earthly but in an otherworldly reunion (ll. 13–14). See below on the myth's Christian interpretations.
11. I return to this question below; see pp. 17–18.
12. Francesco Petrarca, *Canzoniere*, ed. by Paola Vecchi Galli, 2nd edn (Milan: Rizzoli, 2013), p. 1111; henceforth Vecchi Galli. On the issue of Orpheus and 'irreality', see below, subsection 4.
13. See, for instance, Brunori, p. 240; Gardini, pp. 135, 138, and 141–43; Marcozzi, p. 227; Migraine-George, pp. 226–27; Raja, pp. 97 and 99, but see also 107 and 113; Rossellini, pp. 69–71, 100. See also Loredana Chines, '"Doppi" del Petrarca: Perseo, Orfeo, Pigmalione', in her *'Di selva in selva ratto mi trasformo': identità e metamorfosi della parola petrarchesca* (Rome: Carocci, 2010), pp. 31–41.
14. In a similar vein, Maria Elisa Raja notes: 'Nella serie dei sonetti precedenti [317–21] la canzone "delle visioni" manca soltanto la figura di Euridice, cosicché la sua presenza nell'ultima stanza della canzone 323 diviene ancora più significativa, perché inattesa e inedita' (p. 107).
15. Marco Santagata, 'Il lutto dell'umanista', in his *Amate e amanti: figure della lirica amorosa fra Dante e Petrarca* (Bologna: il Mulino, 1999), pp. 195–221 (p. 211).
16. *Il Petrarcha colla spositione di Misser Giovanni Andrea Gesualdo* (Venice: Giovann' Antonio di Nicolini & fratelli da Sabbio, 1533), fol. CCCXLIV[r].
17. Rather too often scholars have unhelpfully overemphasized one source over the other. In some instances, they have entirely ignored one of the two intertexts (customarily the *Georgics*).
18. See Fredi Chiappelli, *Studi sul linguaggio del Petrarca: la Canzone delle visioni* (Florence: Olschki, 1971), p. 167.
19. Petrarch is also recalling his own distillation in *Laurea occidens* (1348 and revised several times until 1366) of the long list of poets presented in Ovid's *Epistula ex Ponto* IV. 16: 'Vultus densissima nubes | Texerat ambiguos' (A very dense cloud had covered the uncertain faces; *Buc. carm.* X. 191–92). The *Bucolicum carmen* is cited from Francesco Petrarca, *Il Bucolicum carmen e i suoi commenti inediti*, ed. by Antonio Avena (Bologna: Forni, 1969).
20. 'The story of Orpheus weaves through the double sestina, but there is no indication of his losing Eurydice for the second and last time. His myth recalled through the positive exempla connotes eternity triumphant over ending, loss, and closure': Marianne Shapiro, *The Hieroglyph of Time: The Petrarchan Sestina* (Minneapolis: University of Minnesota Press, 1980), p. 139. Santagata ('Lutto', pp. 219–20) has written well on the Christian character of the final version of the canzone. See also Raja, p. 105, as well as pp. 108–17 that examine the poem's Scriptural substratum. For a different interpretation, see Michelangelo Picone, 'Morte e temporanea rinascita dei miti dell'eros (*Rvf* 321–30)', in *Canzoniere*, ed. by Picone, pp. 701–23 (pp. 721–22).
21. See Virgil, *Ecl.* IV. 55–57; Horace, *Ars poetica* 391–96 and *Odes* III. 11. 13–24; Quintilian, *Instit. orat.* I. 9. 9; Augustine, *De civ. Dei* XVIII. 37; Boethius, *Cons.* III. met. 12. 7–9; Isidore, *Etym.* III. 22. 8–9; For medieval expressions of these views, see the examples cited in Zygmunt G. Barański, 'Notes on Dante and the Myth of Orpheus', in *Dante mito e poesia*, ed. by Michelangelo Picone and Tatiana Crivelli (Florence: Cesati, 1999), pp. 133–62 (pp. 139, 143–46). Petrarch made regular recourse to both topoi: *Africa* V. 675–78; *Buc. carm.* II. 75 and 110; *Contra medicum* I. 153; *De vita solitaria* II. 12. 3; *Ep.* III. 35. *Fam.* I. 9. 7; VIII. 10. 25; *Tr. Cupid.* IV. 91–93. On Orpheus in the Middle Ages, see Klaus Heitmann, 'Orpheus im Mittelalter', *Archiv für Kulturgeschichte*, 45 (1963), 253–94; John Block Friedman, *Orpheus in the Middle Ages* (Syracuse, NY: Syracuse University Press, 2000; original edn Cambridge, MA: Harvard University Press, 1970); Eleanor Irwin, 'The Songs of Orpheus and the New Song of Christ', in *Orpheus: The Metamorphoses of a Myth*, ed. by John Warden (Toronto: University of Toronto Press, 1982), pp. 51–62; Patricia Vicari, '*Sparagmos*: Orpheus among the Christians', in *Orpheus*, ed. by Warden, pp. 63–83; Elizabeth A. Newby, *A Portrait of the Artist: The Legends of Orpheus and their Use in Medieval and Renaissance Aesthetics* (New York: Garland, 1987).
22. While I generally concur with those who have warned against placing too much weight on

the conjectured forms of the *Fragmenta*, it is also the case that, over many years, Petrarch did 'make' and 'remake' the collection of his vernacular *nugae*. Consequently, any assessment of the Canzoniere and its evolution must needs take this obsessive revising into consideration even when the evidence for a particular form is circumstantial. In what follows I shall concentrate as much as possible, although not exclusively, on the documented forms of the *Rvf*. On the formation of the collection, see in particular Ernest Hatch Wilkins, *The Making of the 'Canzoniere' and Other Petrarchan Studies* (Rome: Edizioni di Storia e Letteratura, 1951); Marco Santagata, *I frammenti dell'anima: storia e racconto nel Canzoniere di Petrarca* (Bologna: il Mulino, 1992).

23. Canzone 28 does not contain Petrarch's earliest extant reference to Orpheus. It is anticipated, possibly by a matter of weeks, by another political poem, 'Ursa peregrinis modo' — 'Orpheus [...], dum flectere Tartara credit, | squalidus in ripa Cereris sine munere sedit' (Orpheus, while he believes he can move the underworld, sits filthy on the shore without Ceres' gift; ll. 35–36) — which was composed between Autumn and Winter 1333; see Giuseppe Billanovich, 'Un carme ignoto del Petrarca', *Studi petrarcheschi*, n.s., 5 (1988), 101–26 (p. 110); the poem is printed on pp. 118–25.

24. The sonnet cannot be dated with any degree of certainty; however, see Vincenzo Fera, 'I sonetti CLXXXVI e CLXXXVII', *Lectura Petrarce*, 7 (1987), 219–43 (pp. 221–23).

25. Wilkins claims that Petrarch 'copied No. 323 [into 3195] within the period October 13–31, 1368' (p. 142). The canzone would thus have entered into the second of Wilkins' Pre-Malatesta forms ('Probably September-October, 1368'; p. 173); see also Francesco Petrarca, *Canzoniere*, ed. by Marco Santagata, 4th edn (Milan: Mondadori, 2010), pp. 1244–45. Sestina 332 belongs to Wilkins' third Pre-Malatesta form ('Probably May-December 1369') and was copied after 27 June (pp. 174–75).

26. *Il codice Vaticano latino 3196*, ed. by Laura Paolino, in Francesco Petrarca, *Trionfi, Rime estravaganti, Codice degli abbozzi*, ed. by Vinicio Pacca and Laura Paolino, 2nd edn (Milan: Mondadori, 2000), pp. 755–889 (p. 792).

27. The question also arises whether a relationship might exist between the Orphic intuition and the fact that 'la decisione di collocare al centro del libro la morte di Laura [...] sopravvenne tardi, se non all'ultima ora': Santagata, *Frammenti*, p. 306.

28. Further evidence of Petrarch's effort to establish the importance of the myth for Part II emerges if the sixth stanza is compared to its earlier drafts. Rather than conceal his sources as was his avowed custom, the poet makes these more explicit. In line 62, he eliminated the adjective 'sola' applied to the 'bella donna' since, in Virgil (*Georg.* IV. 517), the epithet is associated with Orpheus; in line 68, he substituted 'coperte' with 'avolte', since the latter translates 'circumdata' (*Georg.* IV. 497), an alteration that appears to confirm the *Georgics* and not the *Aeneid* as the primary source for the verse (see p. 4 above); finally and most tellingly, he eliminated his original line 71 ('in terra cadde ove star pur sicura') and replaced it with "lieta si dipartio, nonché secura' which stresses the moment of the woman's final departure that is key both to the myth and to the Canzoniere. All quotations are from *Il codice*, p. 789. On Petrarch's reworking of the canzone, see Bettarini, *Lacrime*, pp. 113–36; Chiappelli, who dedicates a whole chapter to 'La strofa di Euridice', pp. 139–83.

29. The lines primarily draw on Ovid (*Met.* X. 89, 143–44, and XI. 1–2, 44–48, and 54), although the influence of *Cons.* III. met. 12. 8–9 and of *Georg.* IV. 510 is also recognizable. The *Epystole* are quoted from Francesco Petrarca, *Poëmata minora quae extant omnia*, ed. by Domenico Rossetti, 3 vols (Milan: Societas Typographica Classicorum Italiae Scriptorum, 1829–34); *Ep.* III. 15 may be read at II, 112–15, where it is numbered 14.

30. In line with Boethius's admonition in the *metrum*'s *explicit* ('Nam qui Tartareum in specus | Victus lumina flexerit, | Quidquid praecipuum trahit | perdit, dum videt infernos'; For he who overwhelmed should turn his eyes towards the Tartarean cave, he loses whatever superiority he has achieved, when he looks at those below; ll. 55–58), his commentators explained Orpheus's descent to Hades and subsequent despair as signifying the allure of and dedication to *temporalia*; see Friedman, pp. 98–114. Surprisingly, not least in light of Petrarch's friendship with Pierre Bersuire, author of the influential *Metamorphosis Ovidiana*, which offers a heavily Christianized

interpretation of the story of Orpheus and Eurydice, several scholars have denied the impact of the exegetical tradition on the poet's view of the myth. For further examples of Petrarch's indebtedness to the medieval reception of the *fabula*, see subsection 3.

31. In an important study, Albert Russell Ascoli has demonstrated that, intertextually, in *Parthenias*, Petrarch is critical of Dante as a poetic *auctoritas* by censuring his exchange of eclogues with Giovanni del Virgilio: 'Blinding the Cyclops: Petrarch after Dante', in *Petrarch and Dante: Anti-Dantism, Metaphysics, Tradition*, ed. by Zygmunt G. Barański and Theodore J. Cachey, Jr (Notre Dame: University of Notre Dame Press, 2009), pp. 114–73.
32. Monicus's response integrates and refashions (in particular contrastively: the 'tranquillity' of the monastery as against the horrors of Hades) *Georg.* IV. 467–69, 500, 502–03 and *Met.* X. 13, 29, 32–35, 55, 72.
33. It was not uncommon for Eurydice to be marginalized in the myth's medieval reception; see Friedman, pp. 99–100, 113.
34. Petrarch's embracing of Orpheus as a poetic model is further developed in *Laurea occidens*, the first version of which has been dated to 1348. The *vates* is not just given special prominence in the long catalogue of ancient writers (ll. 147–56), but, suggestively, of all the poets he had previously mentioned, Petrarch chose to close the eclogue in an Orphic key that, differently from *Parthenias*, began to give prominence to Laura-Eurydice, as well as to Petrarch-Orpheus, and that anticipates one of the woman's key functions in Part II: 'Vestigia [*lauri sacrae*] suplex | consequere, atque precare aditum, verbisque caveto | Invidiam conflare dejs' (Follow beseeching the tracks [of the sacred laurel], and beg that you be allowed to draw close, but beware not to enflame the envy of the gods with your words; ll. 407–09).
35. Ascoli; Aldo S. Bernardo, 'Petrarch's Attitude toward Dante', *PMLA*, 70 (1955), 488–517 (pp. 501–06); Thomas M. Greene, 'Petrarch *Viator*', in his *The Vulnerable Text: Essays on Renaissance Literature* (New York: Columbia University Press, 1986), pp. 18–45 (pp. 22–23); Giuseppe Mazzotta, 'Humanism and Monastic Spirituality', in his *The Worlds of Petrarch* (Durham, NC and London: Duke University Press, 1993), pp. 147–66 (pp. 153–58).
36. See in particular Augustine, *Contra Faustum* XIII. 15; Boethius, *Cons.* III. met. 12. 14–17; John Scot Eriugena, *Annotationes in Marcianum*, ed. by Cora E. Lutz (Cambridge, MA: Medieval Academy of America, 1939), pp. 192–93; Remigius of Auxerre, *Commentum in Martianum*, ed. by Cara E. Lutz, 2 vols (Leiden: Brill, 1962–65), p. 310. See also J. Keith Atkinson, 'Orpheus, vates threicus et la transgression', in *Le metamorfosi di Orfeo*, ed. by Anna Maria Babbi (Verona: Fiorini, 1999), pp. 83–102.
37. See Quintilian, *Instit. orat.* I. 10. 9; Augustine, *De civ. Dei* XVIII. 14 and 37 (and see Petrarch, *Contra medicum* III. 197); Thomas Aquinas, *Comm. De anima* I. 12 and *Comm. Metaph.* I. 3. See also Friedman, pp. 100, 112, 120–21, 130–31, 157.
38. 'It is clear that Petrarch [...] was aware that both Monicus and Silvius represented extremes. What he is declaring is, in effect, that the true poet lies somewhere between these extremes' (Bernardo, p. 505). I believe that Bernardo's basic insight continues to be valid; however, the presence of Orpheus in the eclogue complicates the idea that Petrarch was attempting to mediate between extremes.
39. Francesco Petrarca, *Le Familiari*, ed. by Vittorio Rossi amd Umberto Bosco, 4 vols (Florence: Sansoni, 1933–47), II, 301.
40. See for instance, Silvius: l. 34 and compare *Met.* I. 53; Monicus: l. 46 and compare *Georg.* IV. 467–69.
41. On *satyra* see at least Charles A. van Rooy, *Studies in Classical Satire and Related Literary Theory* (Leiden: Brill, 1965); Udo Kindermann, *Satyra: Die Theorie der Satire im Mittellateinischen. Vorstudie zu einer Gattungsgeschichte* (Nuremberg: Hans Carl, 1978); Ben Parsons, '"A Riotous Spray of Words": Rethinking the Medieval Theory of Satire', *Exemplaria*, 21 (2009), 105–28. What is striking about Petrarch's satirical style is his recourse to allegory and its rhetorical refinement, both attributes that medieval definitions of the genre presented as antithetical to the *stilus*.
42. Later in the poem, Eurydice is once more absorbed into other figures: 'senes, Stygiaque datum sit valle reverti' (if the ancients were permitted to return from the Stygian valley; l. 12).

43. Suggestively, *victus* recalls both Orpheus's last success and his greatest failure. The 'lapis' (stone) thrown by one of the Cicones 'concentu victus vocisque lyraeque est' (is vanquished by the harmony of song and lyre; *Met.* XI. 10–11). However, the past participle also appears, when, 'on the very verge of light', Orpheus 'immemor heu! victusque animi respexit' (forgetful alas! and his resolve overwhelmed, he looked back; *Georg.* IV. 490–91). Petrarch's knowing manipulation of his sources is impressive.
44. All quotations from and references to the *Commedia* are taken from Dante Alighieri, *La Commedia secondo l'antica vulgata*, ed. by Giorgio Petrocchi, 2nd edn, 4 vols (Florence: Le Lettere, 1994).
45. The line also depends on the lion's 'rabbiosa fame' (*Inf.* I. 47). In addition, Petrarch's 'septena virum' (l. 30) may relate to Dante's 'sette regi | ch'assiser Tebe' (*Inf.* XIV. 68–69), although seven is also associated with Orpheus (*Georg.* IV. 507 and *Met.* X. 73). Equally, *furor* is the term that Eurydice uses to describe her husband's looking back: 'Orpheu, | quis tantus furor' (Oh Orpheus, what frenzy; *Georg.* IV. 494–95).
46. See Zygmunt G. Barański, 'Petrarch, Dante, Cavalcanti', in *Petrarch and Dante*, ed. by Barański and Cachey, pp. 50–113 (pp. 85–87).
47. Peter R. J. Hainsworth, 'The Myth of Daphne in the *Rerum vulgarium fragmenta*', *Italian Studies*, 34 (1979), 28–44 (p. 29). The comparison between the figures of my friend and former teacher and mine can only be approximate, since it is just about certain that we arrived at our totals employing different criteria — something that Peter confirmed when he read an earlier draft of this study. Nevertheless, despite its inadequacies, the comparison is instructive. Furthermore, sixteen of our poems (23, 28, 51, 129, 180, 188, 190, 195, 269, 270, 291, 318, 323, 325, 333, 359) contain both Daphneic and Orphic elements, which raises the question of the interrelationship between two of the great foundational myths of the *Fragmenta*. Not dissimilarly, it would be worth investigating the extent to which Ovidian myths associated with Orpheus (for instance, Cyparissus) or recounted by the bard (say, Pygmalion) in *Met.* X ought to be considered as Orphic. The serious study of Orpheus in Petrarch is very much in its infancy.
48. See Valeria Bertolucci Pizzorusso, 'Orfeo "englouti" nelle letterature romanze dei secc. XII e XIII: prime attestazioni', in *Le metamorfosi*, ed. by Babbi, pp. 135–54 (pp. 138–40).
49. It is conspicuous that neither Friedman nor Charles Segal, *Orpheus: The Myth of the Poet* (Baltimore and London: Johns Hopkins University Press, 1989) in their generally excellent books refer to Petrarch.
50. Petrarch's position recalls 'the Fulgentian approach to the myth which makes Eurydice the equal of or the superior to Orpheus' (Friedman, p. 113; and see also pp. 89–90).
51. For the moment, see Brunori.
52. Just in the opening stanza, Petrarch introduces wandering, weeping, self-pity, divine indifference to his appeals, and outstretched arms (ll. 14–15 and compare *Met.* X. 58). The canzone as a whole, but especially in its last two stanzas, is dependent on moralizing Boethian interpretations of the myth (ll. 103, 111–12).
53. 'Between the extremes of Christ and sinner are other figures with whom the hero of this legend can be compared' (Friedman, p. 130). See also Michel Zink, 'Le poète désacralisé: Orphée médiéval et l'*Ovide moralisé*', in *Le metamorfosi*, ed. by Babbi, pp. 15–27.
54. See Friedman, pp. 38–85, 125–28; 130; 147–55; Penelope B. R. Doob, *Nebuchadnezzar's Children: Conventions of Madness in Middle English Literature* (New Haven and London: Yale University Press, 1974), pp. 173–74, 181–84; Irwin; Vicari; Maria Tabaglio, 'La cristianizzazione del mito di Orfeo', in *Le metamorfosi*, ed. by Babbi, pp. 65–82.
55. See Sara Sturm-Maddox, 'Petrarch's Serpent in the Grass: The Fall as Subtext in the *Rime sparse*', *Journal of Medieval and Renaissance Studies*, 13 (1983), 213–26, esp. pp. 216–17; see also Friedman, pp. 122, 125, and 127.
56. In his *Metamorphosis Ovidiana moraliter explanata* (Paris: in aedibus Ascensianis et sub Pelicano, 1509), Pierre Bersuire offers an especially suggestive interpretation of Orpheus as a Christian penitent — 'Solus enim timor infernalis supplicii facit de vitiis poenitere & et sic facit uxorem per gratiam rehaberi [...] ipsam uxorem scilicet animam recuperatam' (Only the fear of infernal suffering made him repent his sins and thereby he regained his wife through grace [...] his wife

namely the recovered soul; fol. LXXIII^r) — that dovetails neatly with interpretations of Part II as 'penitential' (see Santagata, *Frammenti*, p. 305).

57. 'La lirica petrarchesca si comporta insomma, [...] con grande libertà: scopre che il mito non esiste una volta per sempre, con una veste immutabile, ma è sempre di chi lo riscrive e lo reinterpreta; ed è questa, in fondo, la più alta innovazione che Petrarca apporta all'uso lirico del mito: la possibilità non solo di *usare* e di *interpretare* il materiale mitologico, ma in assoluto di *riscriverlo*, anche contaminando passi diversi' (Marcozzi, 'Petrarca lettore', p. 104, italics in original; and see also *Biblioteca*, p. 104).

58. See *Ep.* II. 10. 231–33; *Fam.* XXIV. 12. 22 and 44. Although Petrarch recognized Orpheus's marvellous attainments as fictional (*Contra medicum* I. 153), like all his contemporaries, he accepted his historical reality; see Barański, 'Notes'.

59. See also Peter Hainsworth, *Petrarch the Poet: An Introduction to the 'Rerum vulgarium fragmenta'* (London and New York: Routledge, 1988), p. 169.

60. In addition to the passages already cited, Petrarch directly referred to Orpheus in *Fam.* XII. 9. 5; *Sen.* X. 4, where he confuses him with Morpheus.

CHAPTER 2

Boccaccio's 'spirante turbo': An Intertextual Defence of Tolerance

Elisabetta Tarantino

This essay explores the relationship linking three passages in Lucan, Dante and Boccaccio. It seeks to establish that there is an actual intertextual connection among the three passages, but also, and especially, it shows how a metaphorical interpretation of Lucan's passage could be used to illustrate the ethical stance of Boccaccio's *Decameron*. In fact, the main purpose of this chapter is to rehearse once again the wonderfully *moral* operation that is the *Decameron*.

1. Three Sandstorms

I will first set out the passages in question, highlighting the keywords to which I will refer in my discussion below. The first passage is a bravura piece in Lucan's *De bello civili* (or *Pharsalia*, the title that will mostly be used for brevity in this chapter). In the author's characteristically naturalistic style, it depicts a sandstorm experienced by Cato's soldiers in the Libyan desert. I quote the original Latin from a modern edition, followed by a fourteenth-century *volgarizzamento*:

>   nam litore sicco,
> quam pelago, Syrtis violentius excipit Austrum,
> et terrae magis ille nocens. non montibus ortum
> adversis frangit Libye scopulisque repulsum   450
> dissipat et liquidas e *turbine* solvit in auras,
> nec ruit in silvas annosaque robora torquens
> lassatur: patet omne solum, liberque meatu
> Aeoliam rabiem totis exercet harenis,
> et non imbriferam contorto pulvere nubem   455
> in flexum violentus agit: pars plurima terrae
> tollitur et numquam resoluto vortice pendet.
> regna videt pauper Nasamon errantia vento
> discussasque domos, volitantque a culmine raptae
> detecto Garamante casae. non altius ignis   460
> rapta vehit; quantumque licet consurgere fumo
> et violare diem, tantus tenet aera pulvis.
> tum quoque Romanum solito violentior agmen
> aggreditur, nullisque potest consistere miles
> instabilis, raptis etiam quas calcat, harenis.   465

> concuteret terras orbemque a sede moveret,
> si solida Libye compage et pondere duro
> clauderet exesis Austrum scopulosa cavernis;
> sed, quia mobilibus facilis *turbatur* harenis,
> nusquam luctando stabilis manet, imaque tellus   470
> stat, quia summa fugit.
> (Lucan, *De bello civili*, IX. 447–71)[1]

> Però che Syrtis riceve più crudelmente nel seccho lito lo vento Austro ch'ella non fae nel mare, e quelgli, più nocente alla terra, non ronpe il nascimento ne' contraposti monti di Libia, e cacciato dalli scolgli, e' disfà sé, e con *discorrevole turbamento* si risolve ne' venti Auri, e non ruina nelle selve, e tormentante l'antiche quercie non si allassa: tutta la terra gli è aperta, e libero nel discorrimento, aopera la rabbia d'Eulo per tutte l'arene, e crudele non mena nebbia portante piova mescolata nella gettata polvere; grande parte della terra èe tolta, e mai non pende nel risoluto monte. Lo povero Nasamon vede i regni erranti al vento e le case disfatte, e le case tolte dal colmingno volano, scoperto lo Garamante. Lo fuocho non porta più alto le cose tolte; quanto ch'elgli voli in alto col fummo e corrompa il die, tanta èe la polvere che tiene l'aria.
>
> Allora lo vento Austro, molto più crudele che no era usato, assalisce la schiera de' Romani, e niuno cavaliere puote stare fermo, e tremante per l'arene che quasi erano tolte, etiandio quelle ch'elgli scalpita. Elgli farebbe crollare le terre e rimuoverebbe il mondo dalla sua sedia, se lla scopulosa Libia lo rinchiudesse nelle scostate caverne col saldo congiungimento e col duro peso; ma però che *agevolmente si turba* nelle mobili harene, mai non sta fermo combattendo, e la terra di sotto sta, però che quella ch'è di sopra fugge.[2]

The ninth book of the *Pharsalia* is explicitly recalled at the beginning of *Inferno*, XIV,[3] as well as in *Inferno*, XXIV–XXV (including the famous challenge, 'Taccia Lucano [...]', XXV. 94). Dante may, therefore, also have had in mind the specific passage quoted above when depicting the whirlwind of lamentable sounds that greets him in the *antinferno*, where he sees the group of souls that the critical tradition calls the *ignavi*:

> Quivi sospiri, pianti e alti guai
>   risonavan per l'aere sanza stelle,
>   per ch'io al cominciar ne lagrimai.
> Diverse lingue, orribili favelle,
>   parole di dolore, accenti d'ira,
>   voci alte e fioche, e suon di man con elle
> facevano un tumulto, il qual s'aggira
>   sempre in quell'aura sanza tempo tinta,
>   *come la rena quando turbo spira*.
> (*Inferno*, III. 22–30)

In turn, this passage by Dante is recalled in the Prologue to the Fourth Day of the *Decameron*, where Boccaccio is defending himself, and his *novelle*, from the accusation of levity and obscenity:

> E volendo per questa volta assai aver risposto, dico che dall'aiuto di Dio e dal vostro, gentilissime donne, nel quale io spero, armato, e di buona pazienza,

con esso procederò avanti, dando le spalle a questo vento e lasciandol soffiar: per ciò che io non veggo che di me altro possa avvenire che quello che della minuta polvere avviene, la quale, *spirante turbo*, o egli di terra non la muove, o se la muove la porta in alto e spesse volte sopra le teste degli uomini, sopra le corone dei re e degl'imperadori, e talvolta sopra gli alti palagi e sopra le eccelse torri la lascia; delle quali se ella cade, più giù andar non può che il luogo onde levata fu. (IV. Intr. 40)[4]

In this case, because of the presence of the direct lexical echo 'spirante turbo', there is no doubt that Boccaccio was borrowing this image from the passage in *Inferno*, III.

2. Metaphor and Allusion in the Three Passages: Correspondences and Polarities

A characteristic of the intertextual complex created by these passages is that in all three cases the meteorological metaphor is stretched out across the whole piece, as corresponding passages at the other end of the whole of the *Pharsalia* in Lucan's case, of *Inferno*, III, and of the Introduction to Day IV in the *Decameron* can be linked back to the ones listed above. This creates a framing effect, and emphasises the significance of the theme that we are exploring in this chapter, which is conveyed through the joint deployment of metaphor and allusion.

2.1. Earth, Wind and Fire in 'De bello civili', I and IX

Less than a quarter of the way into the first book of his *De bello civili*, or *Pharsalia*, Lucan introduces his negative hero, Julius Caesar, whose ambition would spark off the civil war that is the subject of his poem:

> qualiter expressum ventis per nubila fulmen
> aetheris impulsi sonitu mundique fragore
> emicuit rupitque diem populosque paventes
> terruit obliqua praestringens lumina flamma:
> in sua templa furit, nullaque exire vetante
> materia magnamque cadens magnamque revertens
> dat stragem late sparsosque recolligit ignes.
> (Lucan, *De bello civili*, I. 151–57)

> Sì come la saetta mandata da' venti per li nuvili risprendeo col suono della costretta aria e con l'ardore del mondo, e tolse il die e spaventoe li tementi popoli, costringente i lumi con torta fiamma, va furiosa contra ' suoi tempî, e niuna materia vietantela d'uscire, cadente e ritornante, dàe grande abbattimento e raccolgle gli sparti fuochi ampiamente. (p. 5)

The main link between this passage, which depicts a storm complete with thunder and lightning, and the sandstorm in *Pharsalia*, IX is the similar geophysical dynamics of obstruction and release, which in this case are the cause of both thunder (affecting the element of air) and lightning (when the process is applied to fire): see the mentions of the sound of compacted air ('aetheris impulsi', l. 152) and the absence of obstructing matter ('nullaque exire vetante | materia', ll. 155–56). Thus, in both *Pharsalia*, I and *Pharsalia*, IX the more solid element (earth) is described as failing to constrict the more volatile ones (air and/or fire).⁵ There is an important formal difference, in that the meteorological phenomenon in the earlier passage is a metaphor for Caesar's destructive action, while in the later one it is an actual event taking place within the story. In fact, in the passage from *Pharsalia*, IX too it is possible to read the dynamics between the wind, the earth and the sand in a metaphorical sense: the wind is given some leeway as it is allowed to drive the superficial sand up in whirlwinds, and in this way the fundamental layers of the earth remain stable and unmoved. Given the theme of the work as a whole, that of civil war, and the openly metaphorical character of the similar passage in Book I, it is not too far-fetched to read this passage as a metaphor illustrating how one could and should handle the presence of dissension or anything negative, down to evil itself, within the human consortium. The main aim is to prevent the overall upheaval of the affected system, as that caused by civil war to the Roman state.⁶ (It goes without saying that this applies only to legitimate and desirable systems, the ones that we would definitely wish to preserve, like free civil society.) The recipe is very simple: give vent, allow certain things to follow an unruly course, like the sand in Lucan's passage, in order that core values, represented by the mass of the earth, may be preserved in all their solidity.

In what follows, I discuss how a reading of the Lucanian passage along these lines is relevant to both Dante and Boccaccio.

2.2. *Dante and Lucan*

The intertextual relationship between *Inferno*, III. 22–30 and *Pharsalia*, IX is not as obvious as the other link that we are exploring here, that between Dante's text and its recollection in Boccaccio. Out of the commentaries listed in the Dartmouth Dante Project database for this passage in the *Commedia*, *Pharsalia*, IX is cited only by Niccolò Tommaseo, as one in a series of classical antecedents.⁷ There may well be a variety of textual influences at play here, with a conflation of Biblical and classical sources that is not untypical of the *Commedia*.⁸ Accordingly, Giorgio Padoan (1967) adduces Hosea 13. 3: 'erunt [...] sicut pulvis turbine raptus ex area [et sicut fumus de fumario]', while Francesco Mazzoni (1965–85) mentions Psalms 34. 5: 'Tamquam pulvis ante faciem venti'.

However, as I have argued elsewhere, in the *Commedia* the term 'rena', which is found at *Inferno*, III. 30 and in eight other *loci* of the *Inferno* only, tends to have negative connotations, in a way that is intrinsically related to Dante's appreciation of specific imitative series linking together some of his key classical authors: Virgil, Ovid and Lucan.⁹ In my reading, Dante's 'rena' borrows an association with violence and strife from its classical antecedents. Lucan's depiction of Roman internecine wars as they are played out in the African desert is a key element in determining this Dantean *topos*, which the Christian poet additionally links to the struggle of the human soul against evil. Therefore, while acknowledging the relevance of the Biblical parallels mentioned above, it is in my view significant that the 'pulvis' from both those instances is replaced here by 'rena'.¹⁰

The relationship between *Inferno*, III. 22–30 and *Pharsalia*, IX appears strengthened when we consider the wider intertextual networks in which these passages participate: first of all, the passages that figure as a counterweight to these in either work, as mentioned at the end of section 1 above; then, other passages in Dante that appear linked to this *turbo* complex.

If we consider the passage from *Pharsalia*, I quoted in section 2.1 with Dante in mind, we can gather several pieces of intertextual evidence that help connect the Auster (South Wind)/*turbo* episode from *Pharsalia*, IX to Dante's *turbo* metaphor in *Inferno*, III.

Gregorio Di Siena's commentary (1867) quotes a line from a little further down in this same episode, 'quo fertis mea signa, viri?' (*De bello civili*, I. 191; 'ove portate le mie insegne', p. 6), in relation to the punishment of the *ignavi* in *Inferno*, III, who run incessantly in a circle following a flag ('insegna', l. 52) as *contrappasso* for their refusal to consistently follow a cause in life.[11] Overall Lucan's depiction of Caesar in this book of the *Pharsalia* is an important intertext in Dante, as is abundantly indicated, for instance, in commentaries on *Paradiso*, VI, where Dante follows Lucan's account closely in his excursus on the history of Rome. To the indications commonly provided by critics we should add that the description of Julius Caesar as destructive lightning in *Pharsalia*, I. 151–57 is probably at the basis of *Paradiso*, VI. 70, on how Caesar 'scese folgorando a Iuba'.

Moreover, this passage from *Pharsalia*, I connects directly with *Inferno*, III in at least two ways. One is the occurrence of the words 'lumina flamma' at the end of l. 154: these words also feature in the expression used by Virgil for Charon's eyes in *Aeneid*, VI. 300 ('stant lumina flamma') and are taken up by Dante in his own description of the same character.[12]

The second, more important way in which this passage relates to the intertextual network that we are examining here has already been mentioned above, and consists in the similar dynamics of a volatile element failing to be obstructed by a more solid one. This applies not only to a comparison between the two *Pharsalia* passages discussed in section 2.1, but also to relevant passages in *Inferno*, III. In fact, with a polarity already observed in the *Pharsalia*, the *turbo* passage that introduces the *ignavi* episode is reprised in the final lines of the same canto (where it also serves as a ploy not to recount Dante's actual crossing of the Acheron):

> Finito questo, la buia campagna
>   tremò sì forte, che de lo spavento
>   la mente di sudore ancor mi bagna.
> La terra lagrimosa diede vento,
>   che balenò una luce vermiglia
>   la qual mi vinse ciascun sentimento;
> e caddi come l'uom che 'l sonno piglia.
>   (*Inferno*, III. 130–36)

In this passage we have both an earthquake, believed to be caused by the earth giving the wind free rein: 'La terra lagrimosa diede vento'; and some kind of lightning: 'balenò una luce vermiglia', as in the passage from *Pharsalia*, I, where this phenomenon is linked to a similar lack of obstruction towards the element of fire.

What we also have in this passage is an important additional connecting element with another, nearby episode that prominently features a whirlwind: that of the *lussuriosi* in Canto v.

In fact, it seems that Dante went out of his way to create parallels between his two locations either side of limbo: he has Virgil speak exactly the same formula in waving aside the objections of the creatures guarding access to either place, Charon and Minos: 'vuolsi così colà dove si puote | ciò che si vuole, e più non dimandare' (*Inferno*, III. 95–96 and v. 23–24); he describes the two places in almost identical terms — 'Quivi sospiri, pianti e alti guai' (*Inferno*, III. 22) and 'quivi le strida, il compianto, il lamento' (*Inferno*, v. 35); and both cantos end with Dante the pilgrim falling into a swoon. Thus, through his intertextual strategies Dante is establishing a connection between the sins of *ignavia* and *lussuria*. The rationale for this may not be entirely obvious, but will become apparent if we retrace the poet's intertextual trail a little further.

I referred above to other passages where Dante demonstrates an awareness of the *turbo* episode from *Pharsalia*, IX. The first in order of importance for our discussion is from the first of his 'Rime per la donna Pietra':

> Levasi de la rena d'Etiopia
>   lo vento peregrin che l'aere turba,
>   per la spera del sol ch'ora la scalda;
> e passa il mare, onde conduce copia
>   di nebbia tal, che, s'altro non la sturba,
>   questo emisperio chiude tutto e salda;
> e poi si solve, e cade in bianca falda
>   di fredda neve ed in noiosa pioggia,
>   onde l'aere s'attrista tutto e piagne
>   (*Rime*, C. 14–22)

Here the influence of Lucan's *turbo*, which can be seen especially in the first two lines, seems to have merged by the end of the passage with another Auster passage, from Virgil's *Georgics*, III. 278–79: 'unde nigerrimus Auster | nascitur et pluvio contristat frigore caelum' ('whence up-springs | Black Auster, that glooms heaven with rainy cold').[13] This book of the *Georgics* refers to the terrible effects of sexual passion, particularly in diverting and abating the kind of fervour that should be directed towards heroic deeds. Thus this text (together with Lucan's *Pharsalia*) may be at the root of Dante's association of the Auster with evil and sinfulness. Most crucially, for our present purposes, it explains his linking of the *ignavi*, who displayed a marked lack of heroism, with the *lussuriosi*.

Traces of this connection are found in another passage relevant to our discussion, *Purgatorio*, XXXI. 70–73, where Dante describes his mortification at Beatrice's rebukes:

> Con men di resistenza si dibarba
>   robusto cerro, o vero al nostral vento
>   o vero a quel de la terra di Iarba,
> ch'io non levai al suo comando il mento.

This passage is interesting in several respects. First of all, it confirms that Dante had the *Pharsalia* in mind whenever he mentioned the African wind: in the first book of the *De bello civili*, Lucan's positive but flawed hero Pompey is famously compared to a great oak — see here the 'robusto cerro' at line 71 (though Dante may have been thinking precisely of how Pompey in Lucan's depiction was no longer a particularly 'robust' opponent).[14] Secondly, it confirms the association of that wind with the *lussuriosi*, since 'Iarba' was the suitor of Dido, whom Dante places among this group in *Inferno*, V. A further important element is the fact that soon after these lines (at ll. 88–90) Dante faints for the third time in the *Commedia*. Interestingly, though, while cantos III and V of the *Inferno* both end with Dante's swoon, at *Purgatorio*, XXXI. 91 he comes round again and the canto continues for another 54 lines with a series of ceremonies that prepare him for the next step in his journey. The passage thus becomes an obvious symbol of Dante's recovery from sin, enacted not least through his intertextual recollection of the beginning of his painful journey, as represented by the two cantos either side of the entrance to Hell.

Finally, by mentioning the idea of 'resistenza' at line 70 in this passage, in connection with the (African) wind, Dante shows that he was in fact aware of the central node in Lucan's text as we have described it in section 2.1, that is, the idea of allowing some leeway as a means to avoid overall destruction. This is interesting specifically because, at least in the passages that we have identified as directly connected with Lucan's *turbo* episode, Dante does not seem to follow this up (contrary to what we will observe in Boccaccio). This may have something to do with the fact that in many respects Dante and Lucan are at opposite ends of the ideological spectrum. In fact, Dante sometimes seems unaware of, or to be deliberately ignoring, certain aspects of Lucan's naturalistic and anti-Caesarist positions that go counter to his own view of the world.[15]

This can be seen most clearly in a passage from Dante's *Monarchia* that is important for our discussion because it refers explicitly to Lucan's *turbo* episode:

> Quod autem pro Romano Imperio perficiendo miracula Deus portenderit, illustrium auctorum testimoniis comprobatur. Nam sub Numa Pompilio, secundo Romanorum rege, ritu gentilium sacrificante, ancile de celo in urbem Deo electam delapsum fuisse Livius in prima parte testatur. Cuius miraculi Lucanus in nono Farsalie meminit incredibilem vim austri, quam Libia patitur, ibi describens; ait enim:
>
> > Sic illa profecto
> > sacrifico cecidere Nume, que lecta iuventus
> > patricia cervice movet: spoliaverat auster
> > aut boreas populos ancilia nostra ferentes.
> > (*Monarchia*, II. 4. 5–6)

[That God performed miracles so that the Roman empire might be supreme is confirmed by the testimony of illustrious authors. For Livy tells in the first part of his work that in the time of Numa Pompilius, the second king of the Romans, a shield fell from heaven into God's chosen city as [the king] was sacrificing according to the pagan rite. Lucan recalls this miracle in the ninth book of the *Pharsalia* where he describes the incredible force of the South wind to which Libya is exposed; for he says:

> No doubt the shields,
> Which chosen youths bore on patrician necks,
> Fell before Numa as he sacrificed;
> The South wind or the North had robbed their bearers
> Of shields which now are ours.][16]

Dante quotes here *Pharsalia*, IX. 477–80, that is, an episode that follows closely our main *turbo* passage. However, as noted by commentators, he takes at face value a story that in Lucan's intention illustrated the credulity of those who see some miraculous intervention in what are in fact purely natural phenomena (there is a similar undertone in the reference to the 'populos paventes' terrorized by thunder in the *Pharsalia*, I passage quoted in section 2.1). The episode featuring Numa Pompilius is in fact assimilated by Lucan to what is happening in the Libyan desert, as the high wind sends soldiers' helmets and weapons flying until they rain down on some bewildered tribe far away:

> illud in extrema forsan longeque remota
> prodigium tellure fuit, delapsaque caelo
> arma timent gentes hominumque erepta lacertis
> a superis demissa putant.
> (*De bello civili*, IX. 474–77)

> Forse che quello fue grande meravilglia nelle terre rimosse e da lungi, e le genti temono l'armi gittate dal cielo, e pensano che quelle che sono tolte dalle braccia delli uomini siano mandate dall'iddiei di sopra. (p. 173)

While this is not the place to discuss Dante's views on statecraft, it is not surprising that he would be unreceptive towards the political advantages of 'giving vent'. However, on a poetic level, he not only keenly appropriated Lucan's negative metaphor of the Auster: he also responded to the rhetorical and affective possibilities offered by the image of the *turbo*.

This is something of which our *volgarizzatore* is also obviously aware. He recognized the ready opportunity for pathetic fallacy offered by the correspondence between the noun *turbo, -inis* (compare *Pharsalia*, IX. 451) and the verb *turbo*, which in *Pharsalia*, IX. 469 is applied in the passive to the effect of the wind on the territory of Libya through its easily displaced sand: 'mobilibus facilis *turbatur* harenis'. Thus, although he gives the wind its proper name of 'Auster', he makes sure he maintains a version of this very effective lexeme in exactly the same position as in the original: his wind first 'con *discorrevole turbamento* si risolve ne' venti Auri' and then '*agevolmente si turba* nelle mobili harene' (p. 173). In *Inferno*, III Dante does not play with the verb *turbare* explicitly in the same way. However, he does so implicitly, by accompanying each manifestation of the *turbo* wind in the *Commedia* (*Inferno*, III and V, and *Purgatorio*, XXXI) with a corresponding physical effect, the swoon, that only in the first of these three cantos is caused directly by a (linked) meteorological manifestation: in the other two it is purely the exteriorization or 'venting' of an internal emotional state. It is again through an intertextual link that we can make this meaning explicit, namely by comparing Dante's fainting out of pity at the end of *Inferno*, V:

> Mentre che l'uno spirto questo disse,
> l'altro piangea sì, che di pietade
> io venni men così com'io morisse;
> e caddi come corpo morto cade
> (*Inferno*, v. 139–42)

with the reference in the *Vita nuova* to 'li occhi di quella pietosa | che si *turbava* de' nostri martiri' (XXXVIII. 10). Something similar happens at the beginning of *Purgatorio*, where Cato — the hero of Lucan's sandstorm episode — describes his new imperviousness to human and sexual love with the phrase 'più *muover* non mi può' (*Purgatorio*, I. 89), which exploits the parallel affective metaphor offered by the verb *muovere*, as already found in Lucan's 'mobil(es) haren(ae)', or 'mobili harene', in *Pharsalia*, IX. 469.[17]

2.3. Boccaccio and Lucan (via Dante)

The relationship between *Inferno*, III. 22–30 and Boccaccio's self-defence in IV. Intr. 40 is both obvious and widely recorded in editions of the *Decameron*. In addition, Bernardino Daniello's commentary (1547–68) mentions Boccaccio's passage in the note on *Inferno*, III. 30. It is also worth pointing out that the Introduction to Day IV contains the only explicit mention of Dante in the *Decameron*.[18]

On the other hand, the network of intertextual links described in section 2.2 makes it likely not only that there was an actual connection between the sandstorm passages in Lucan and Dante, but also that Boccaccio would have recognized it. It should be said straightaway that Boccaccio does not mention Lucan in his commentary on Dante's *turbo* passage, part of his *esposizioni* on the first half of the *Inferno* written in 1373–75: in the *esposizione litterale* for *Inferno*, III. 30 Boccaccio gives a strictly scientific report, referring to the second book of Aristotle's *Meteorology*.[19] However, he discusses and refers to Lucan several times in commenting on the fourth canto of the *Inferno* (where the author of the *Pharsalia* appears among the great Latin poets fêted by Dante in Limbo), and in the ninth, quoting first hand from *Pharsalia*, VI in relation to Allecto and Erichtho,[20] and from *Pharsalia*, IX. 624–26 about Medusa. Lucan is also included (alongside Dante himself) in Boccaccio's version of Dante's 'bella scola' in the *Filocolo*, the Life of Petrarch, and the *Amorosa visione*.[21] On the whole there is no doubt that for Boccaccio, as for Dante, Lucan was an author to be reckoned with.[22]

Indeed, it is possible to add a Lucanian element to the tendency towards metaliterary reflection that has already been highlighted as a constant in Boccaccio's use of Dante.[23] At the end of his *Teseida* Boccaccio hails his own book as the first military epic in the vernacular, in words that famously refer back to *De vulgari eloquentia*, II. 2. 10, where Dante states that 'Arma vero nullum latium adhuc invenio poetasse':[24] Lucan would have been one of the classical antecedents for such a work, next to the perhaps more obvious Virgil and Statius. Also, in his *esposizione litterale* on *Inferno* IV. 90, Boccaccio mentions how Lucan had been denied the 'laurea' by the Roman Senate for 'non avere nella sua opera tenuto stilo poetico, ma più tosto di storiografo metrico'; this despite the fact that Lucan's work shows 'maravigliosa eccellenzia d'ingegno' (lesson XIII). Furthermore, in his lesson III, on *Inferno* I, Boccaccio had made an impassioned defence of poetry against its detractors, referring to the Roman *lauro* and how it made poets as worthy as 'Africano [...] Pompeo [...] Ottaviano', that is, as worthy as the Roman heroes who had been sung, respectively, by Petrarch (who famously was awarded the *lauro* in Rome), Lucan,[25] and Virgil (as Boccaccio himself reminds us later in this peroration). These instances, then, highlight a tendency in Boccaccio to link together a defence of literature, Lucan and Dante (though in the example we have just seen it is Petrarch to whom he is paying a huge compliment, by including him not only among but at the head of this implicit list of great Latin poets).

The *turbo* passage in *Decameron*, IV. Intr. would then be part of this defence-of-literature-Dante-Lucan complex. Thus, whether or not we accept that an actual link exists between the *turbo* passages in Lucan and Boccaccio, via Dante, comparing these three passages can help us give 'a local habitation and a name' to aspects and themes that are undoubtedly there, regardless of their affiliation.

In Boccaccio, the *turbo* metaphor is used to illustrate his own Stoicism and imperviousness in the face of the harsh criticism that had been voiced against his *novelle*, which had obviously already begun to circulate.[26] As in the case of both Lucan and Dante, this metaphor runs throughout the piece in question, in this case the Introduction to the Fourth Day of the *Decameron*, since Boccaccio's 'spirante turbo' in IV. Intr. 40 picks up from the first paragraph of the same Introduction, a passage that is itself characterized by a strong Dantean aura:

> Carissime donne, sì per le parole de' savi uomini udite e sì per le cose da me molte volte e vedute e lette, estimava io che lo 'mpetuoso vento e ardente della 'nvidia non dovesse percuotere se non l'alte torri o le più levate cime degli alberi: ma io mi truovo della mia estimazione ingannato. Per ciò che, fuggendo io e sempre essendomi di fuggire ingegnato il fiero impeto di questo rabbioso spirito, non solamente pe' piani ma ancora per le profondissime valli mi sono ingegnato d'andare; il che assai manifesto può apparire a chi le presenti novellette riguarda, le quali non solamente in fiorentin volgare e in prosa scritte per me sono e senza titolo, ma ancora in istilo umilissimo e rimesso quanto il più si possono. Né per tutto ciò l'essere da cotal vento fieramente scrollato, anzi presso che diradicato e tutto da' morsi della 'nvidia esser lacerato, non ho potuto cessare; per che assai manifestamente posso comprendere quello esser vero che sogliono i savi dire, che sola la miseria è senza invidia nelle cose presenti. (IV. Intr. 2–4)[27]

Near the end of the Introduction to Day IV, in the passage already quoted in section I above, Boccaccio announces that his strategy for dealing with this malevolent whirlwind is to turn his back on it and just let it blow:

> per ciò che io non veggo che di me altro possa avvenire che quello che della minuta polvere avviene, la quale, spirante turbo, o egli di terra non la muove, o se la muove la porta in alto [...] se ella cade, più giù andar non può che il luogo onde levata fu. (IV. Intr. 40)

The tenor of this metaphor is in fact rather different from what we have identified in Lucan's passage. The dust here stands for Boccaccio himself and his work: they cannot be hurt by their detractors because they start from such a lowly place (in literary terms, he has chosen a humble rather than a lofty genre) that the wind of criticism can only, if anything, bring them more fame, but cannot cause the loss of an exalted position to which they never lay claim in the first place.

From a formal point of view, however, Boccaccio's passage reproduces the vehicle of Lucan's metaphor quite closely, including two elements that are not found in Dante. The first is the mention of part of the sand being borne aloft, as in *Pharsalia*, IX. 460–62: Dante's sand is simply being tossed around. The second element that aligns Boccaccio directly with Lucan is the contrast between two alternative kinds of behaviour: being carried up in a whirlwind or remaining unmoved. This in itself is an indication of the different slant that Boccaccio gives to this passage. As in Dante, we have lost the unmoved earth. But while in Dante this is still the implicit positive term of comparison to the negative constituted by the sinners, in Boccaccio the focus is entirely on the fate of the dust itself, which is not at all predetermined and not necessarily negative: the dust, to which the Dantean passage has given human connotations that are only implicit in Lucan, in Boccaccio is itself given the chance to remain stoically unmoved, or it can be tossed high (and low). Boccaccio's 'stoical' sand is indeed closer to Lucan's passage than Dante's whirlwind; and while the whole idea of Dante's whirlwind is that it is a form of punishment, Boccaccio also takes up from Lucan the focus on the *limitation* of harm.

However, what is interesting about Boccaccio's *turbo* simile is that, while it reproduces the contrast we found in Lucan between mobility and immobility, adding to the former a distinctly positive sense of resilience, its direct use, as we have seen, does not channel the same metaphoric warning against the dangers of an unyielding, immovable system, or the corresponding recommendation to allow some latitude, to 'give vent'. On the other hand, this is precisely the subject of the Introduction to Day IV, which is framed between the two turbulent-wind passages, and is also especially relevant to Boccaccio's *Decameron* as a whole.

It is probable that the wider Dantean context analysed in section 2.2 also played a role. Indeed, since one of the main themes of the Introduction to Day IV, and of the *Decameron* in general, is the irrepressibility of the sexual instinct (and of human impulses in general), the 'physical' whirlwind of the *lussuriosi* canto is likely to have been in Boccaccio's mind as much as the metaphorical one from Inferno, III that he directly recalls in IV. Intr. 40.[28] However, the concept of the *ignavi* is also highly relevant to what Boccaccio is trying to do in the *Decameron*, and for the same reason that led Dante to establish such insistent intertextual links between the two passages. For Boccaccio, tolerance for human impulses and the avoidance of conflict are equally desirable, connected states of affairs.[29] Although he would never have put it quite in this way (but that is what intertextuality does: it allows you to 'say' things that you could never have put in so many words), what Dante saw as a negative, Boccaccio saw as a positive.

Critics have often baulked at Boccaccio's book being 'cognominato prencipe Galeotto' (as is stated in both its initial and final epigraph), given that in *Inferno*, V. 137 'Galeotto fu il libro e chi lo scrisse' is a clear indictment of Paolo and Francesca's romantic reading matter as an illicit, and fatal, go-between.[30] But in the perspective of our discussion this makes perfect sense. It is about allowing or indeed facilitating the venting of impulses in such a way that core human values can be preserved. Once again, what Dante meant in a negative sense is here being justified, or even glorified outright.

3. Boccaccio's Intertwined Defence of Human Nature and of Literature

This idea of licence as a necessary corrective is often enacted as well as explicitly defended in the *Decameron*. The juxtaposition of the *novelle* in Day IV (on 'coloro li cui amori ebbero infelice fine') with those in Day V ('di ciò che a alcuno amante, dopo alcuni fieri o sventurati accidenti, felicemente avvenisse') corrects the tragic outcomes of the former. See for instance how the phrase used to express the protagonist's fear in V. 4. 42 — 'Quando Ricciardo il vide, parve che gli fosse il cuore del corpo strappato' — echoes the literal fate of Guiscardo in IV. 1, but in the Day V novella this is just a metaphor, and tragedy is averted thanks to the much more reasonable and tolerant attitude of the father of Ricciardo's beloved compared to Tancredi in Day IV. On the other hand, the constant, fruitful dynamics of rule and transgression that is built into the structure of the book itself is theorized by Emilia as she grants freedom of choice for the Day IX *novelle*, with words that could serve well to illustrate a metaphorical reading of Lucan's sandstorm passage:

> voglio che ciascuno secondo che gli piace ragioni, fermamente tenendo che la varietà delle cose che si diranno non meno graziosa ne fia che l'avere pur d'una parlato; e così avendo fatto, chi appresso di me nel reame verrà, sì come più forti, con maggior sicurtà ne potrà nell'usate leggi ristrignere. (VIII. Concl. 5)

Then there is the frequently mentioned figure of Dioneo, 'licentious' in more senses than one, who with his final novella exceptionally renounces all kinds of 'licence' and conforms to the theme of the last day with what is perhaps the gravest tale of the whole collection. As pointed out by Umberto Bosco in his pioneering study of the *Decameron* as a work of literature, there is a subtle but important link between this character and that of Elissa.[31] With a familiar dynamics, the 'licensed fool' is linked to the only lady in the *brigata* who, 'non senza cagion', is given a regal name — and not just that of any queen: Elissa bears the original name of that Queen of Carthage whose honour had been 'slandered' by Dante (following Virgil) in *Inferno*, V, and restored by Petrarch in his *Triumphus Pudicitie* and by Boccaccio himself in 'De Didone seu Elissa Cartaginiensium regina' (*De mulieribus claris*, XLII).

In fact, as the Galeotto 'incident' shows, and as has already emerged from our discussion of the Lucan-Dante complex in Boccaccio's writings in section 2.3, there is an important metaliterary aspect to all this. In the Introduction to Day IV of the *Decameron* Boccaccio is defending not only himself but also his tales from accusations of fatuity and obscenity. Characteristically, he does so first of all through a story, the meta-novella of Filippo Balducci, which demonstrates both the irrepressibility of Nature and the foolishly pernicious consequences of attempting to go against it. He then goes on to state his belief explicitly: 'gli altri e io, che v'amiamo, [gentilissime donne,] naturalmente operiamo; alle cui leggi, cioè della natura, voler contrastare troppo gran forze bisognano, e spesse volte non solamente invano ma con grandissimo danno del faticante s'adoperano' (IV. Intr. 41). This is what Boccaccio means in IV. Intr. 36, with his impassioned claim that 'queste cose tessendo, né dal monte Parnaso né dalle Muse non mi allontano quanto molti per avventura s'avisano'. His defence of tolerance in life and his defence of licence in literature go hand in hand: in both cases, judgement should be applied 'con ragionevole occhio da intendente persona' ('Conclusione dell'autore', 4).

4. Conclusion

This essay has shown how Lucan, Dante and Boccaccio took the same relatively small descriptive detail, the perturbation caused by the Auster, and applied it through metaphor and allusion to represent the central concern in their respective masterpieces. Difficult as it is to pinpoint the origin of a metaphor, I suspect that this is linked to the Auster's appearance in the third book of Virgil's *Georgics*, with its opposition between a 'positive' and a 'negative' type of fervour. Thus the turbulent Auster becomes a metaphor for political dissension in Lucan, and for sinfulness in Dante. In Boccaccio, as used in the Introduction to the Fourth Day, it refers simply to human envy and malevolent judgement, and their inability to harm him. However, the wider context of the *Decameron* enacts its own version of Lucan's whirlwind-sand dynamics, as it shows how human impulses are guaranteed to cause more trouble when pent up than when judiciously released. Through its intertextual origin, this defence of the 'human' in Boccaccio also turns naturally into a defence of his own art, and of literary fiction in general.

Notes to Chapter 2

1. Quotations from Lucan in this chapter are from *De bello civili*, ed. by D. R. Shackleton Bailey (Stuttgart: Teubner, 1988). I have also used Lucan, *Civil War*, trans. by Susan H. Braund (Oxford: Oxford University Press, 1992). Emphases in quotations are mine throughout.
2. *Volgarizzamento pratese della 'Farsaglia' di Lucano*, ed. by Laura Allegri (Florence: Accademia della Crusca; Gruppo Bibliofili Pratesi 'Aldo Petri', 2008), p. 173. This translation of Lucan's *De bello civili* into the early Italian vernacular is found in MS 1548 in the Biblioteca Riccardiana in Florence. It is attributed to Arrigo Simintendi and believed to date from the fourth decade of the fourteenth century, which means that it is roughly contemporary with the *Decameron*.
3. 'Lo spazzo era una rena arida e spessa, | non d'altra foggia fatta che colei | che fu da' piè di Caton già soppressa.' (*Inferno*, XIV. 13–15) In this chapter I quote from *Le opere di Dante: testo critico della Società Dantesca Italiana*, ed. by Michele Barbi and others, 2nd edn (Florence: Società Dantesca Italiana, 1960).
4. Giovanni Boccaccio, *Decameron*, 2 vols, ed. by Vittore Branca (Turin: Einaudi, 1980). *Decameron* quotations in this chapter are from this edition. Quotations from other works by Boccaccio are from the relevant volume in *Tutte le opere*, ed. by Vittore Branca (Milan: Mondadori, 1964–98).
5. A more central passage in the *Pharsalia* depicts another meteorological phenomenon of compression and release, involving all four elements, where water takes centre stage. This passage features all the main winds with the exclusion of the one with which we are mostly concerned here, the Auster or South Wind. Cf. *De bello civili*, IV. 50–82. (I am grateful to Professor Michael Reeve for pointing out this passage to me, and for several other useful comments on this article.)

6. Cf. Elisabetta Tarantino, '*Fulvae harenae*: The Reception of an Intertextual Complex in Dante's *Inferno*', *Classical Receptions Journal*, 4 (2012), 90–126 (pp. 110–11).
7. Cf. <https://dante.dartmouth.edu> [accessed 22 July 2015]. Niccolò Tommaseo (1837 [edn of 1865]), *Inferno*, III. 28–30: 'Spira: *Aen.* I {83}: *Terras turbine perflant. Georg.* I {327}: *Fretis spirantibus.* Lucan. {9.455–456}: *Umbriferam contorto pulvere nubem In flexum violentus agit.* Orazio, dell'avaro (*Sat.* I, 4): *Per mala praeceps Fertur uti pulvis collectus turbine.*' (Italics as in the original.) All Dante commentaries mentioned in this chapter can be found in the Dante Dartmouth database.
8. Cf. for instance Giuseppe Mazzotta, *Dante, Poet of the Desert: History and Allegory in the Divine Comedy* (Princeton, NJ: Princeton University Press, 1979), esp. pp. 62–65 on the conflation of Lucan and Exodus; and Peter S. Hawkins, *Dante's Testaments: Essays in Scriptural Imagination* (Stanford, CA: Stanford University Press, 1999).
9. Cf. Tarantino, '*Fulvae harenae*'. Dante repeatedly mentions Lucan as part of a roll-call of eminent classical poets: cf. *Vita Nuova*, XXV. 9; *De vulgari eloquentia*, II. 6. 7; *Inferno*, IV. 88–90. On Dante and Lucan in general see, for instance, Edward Moore, *Studies in Dante*, First Series: *Scripture and Classical Authors in Dante* (Oxford: Clarendon Press, 1896), pp. 228–42; Ettore Paratore, 'Lucano e Dante', in his *Antico e nuovo* (Caltanissetta and Rome: Sciascia, 1965), pp. 165–210; Violetta de Angelis, '"... e l'ultimo Lucano"', in *Dante e la 'bella scola' della poesia*, ed. by Amilcare A. Iannucci (Ravenna: Longo, 1993), pp. 145–203.
10. It will be noted that 'pulvis'/'polvere' is found instead in Boccaccio's passage, and also as an alternative to 'harenae'/'(h)arene' in both the original of Lucan's text and in the *volgarizzamento* quoted above.
11. Cf. *ad loc. Inferno*, III. 52.
12. Cf. *Inferno*, III. 99 ('che 'ntorno a li occhi avea di fiamme rote') and 109 ('Caron dimonio, con occhi di bragia'). In fact, Lucan's phrase, 'obliqua praestringens lumina flamma', refers both to *Aeneid*, VI. 300 in its metrical form and, in its meaning, to *Aeneid*, VII. 448–49: 'tum flammea torquens | lumina', which is again applied to the eyes of an 'infernal' being (in this case, the fury Allecto). On how Ovid too may have had a hand in this intertextual complex, see Tarantino, '*Fulvae harenae*', pp. 94–95.
13. For the original Latin quotation I have consulted Virgil, *Georgics*, ed. by R. A. B. Mynors (Oxford: Clarendon Press, 1990); for the translation, *Bucolics, Aeneid, and Georgics of Vergil*, trans. by J. B. Greenough (Boston: Ginn & Co., 1900), available at <http://www.perseus.tufts.edu/> [accessed 3 October 2015].
14. In his version of Dante's 'bella scola', Boccaccio, too, stresses the prominence of Pompey in Lucan's epic poem: 'Lucan seguitava, ne' cui | atti parea ch'ancora la battaglia | di Cesare narrasse e di colui, | Magno Pompeo chiamato, che 'n Tesaglia | perdé il campo; e quasi lagrimando | mostra che di Pompeo ancor li caglia' (*Amorosa visione*, first redaction, V. 19–24). Note how the rhyme scheme alludes to the vernacular title of Lucan's *Farsaglia*.
15. On the possibility nevertheless of viewing certain Lucanian metaphors in a quasi-religious sense, and the relevance of this to Dante, see Tarantino, '*Fulvae harenae*', pp. 106–10.
16. The English translation is from Dante, *Monarchy*, ed. and trans. by Prue Shaw (Cambridge: Cambridge University Press, 1996), p. 38.
17. Dante gives a (rather different) metaphorical interpretation of Cato's relationship with his wife Marcia in *Convivio*, IV. 28. 13–19, in an extended passage based on what is reported by 'quello grande poeta Lucano nel secondo de la sua Farsalia'. Boccaccio too refers to Lucan in commenting on the mention of Marcia in *Inferno* IV. 128.
18. Cf. IV. Intr. 33. On the presence of Dante in the *Decameron*, see Robert Hollander, *Boccaccio's Dante and the Shaping Force of Satire* (Ann Arbor: University of Michigan Press, 1997). See also Guyda Armstrong, 'Boccaccio and Dante', in *The Cambridge Companion to Boccaccio*, ed. by Guyda Armstrong, Rhiannon Daniels, and Stephen J. Milner (Cambridge: Cambridge University Press, 2015), pp. 121–38.
19. For the text of Boccaccio's lessons, or *esposizioni*, on the *Commedia* see the Dante Dartmouth database or *Tutte le opere*, VI.
20. We cannot know whether Boccaccio was aware of this, but there is a certain degree of interplay here between Dante's text, Lucan and *Aeneid*, VII, since Lucan's Erichtho seems to

be intertextually linked to Virgil's Allecto (on which see n. 12 above): see Philip Hardie, *The Epic Successors of Virgil* (Cambridge: Cambridge University Press, 1993), pp. 76–77; Paratore, pp. 171–72.
21. Cf. *Filocolo*, v. 97, and *De vita et moribus Francisci Petracchi*, 6. For the *Amorosa visione*, see n. 14 above. Interestingly, Lucan is not explicitly mentioned in the list of authors with whom Dante is said to have made himself 'familiarissimo' in the first redaction of Boccaccio's *Trattatello in laude di Dante*. On the differences between the versions of this passage in the two redactions of the *Trattatello* see Martin McLaughlin, *Literary Imitation in the Italian Renaissance* (Oxford: Clarendon Press, 1995), p. 55.
22. On Boccaccio and Lucan see Antonio Enzo Quaglio, 'Boccaccio e Lucano: una concordanza e una fonte dal *Filocolo* all'*Amorosa visione*', *Cultura neolatina*, 23 (1963), 153–71, together with Giuseppe Velli, 'Cultura e *imitatio* nel primo Boccaccio', *Annali della Scuola normale superiore di Pisa*, 2nd ser., 37 (1968), 65–93 (especially pp. 76–91), who argues against the idea that the importance of Lucan is significantly reduced in Boccaccio's later works. We also know that Boccaccio owned a manuscript of the *Pharsalia*, which is probably the one extant in Florence, Biblioteca Laurenziana, MS Plut. 35.23, on which see *VI Centenario della morte di Giovanni Boccaccio: mostra di manoscritti, documenti e edizioni*, 2 vols (Florence and Certaldo: Comitato Nazionale onoranze a G. Boccaccio, 1975), I, 148–50 and fig. XXXIV.
23. 'Throughout his writing career, Boccaccio consistently deploys Dantean references at moments of metaliterary reflection: in the authorial frames of his works, when discussing poetic inspiration, the ideal life of the poet, literary languages and genealogies, and the problems of posterity' (Armstrong, p. 136).
24. Cf. *Teseida*, XII. 84. 6–8: 'ma tu, o libro, primo a lor cantare | di Marte fai [hai?] gli affanni sostenuti, | nel volgar lazio più mai non veduti'.
25. See n. 14 above on how Boccaccio saw Pompey as the main subject in the *Pharsalia*.
26. Cf. Branca's note 1 on p. 460, and the bibliography therein.
27. The first sentence of this paragraph in particular has been linked to *Paradiso*, XVII. 133–34: 'Questo tuo grido farà come vento, | che le più alte cime più percuote'. Cf. Vittore Branca's note on this passage, p. 459; and Hollander, *Boccaccio's Dante*, pp. 25 and 59–60. Hollander (p. 60, n. 13) also reports Margherita Frankel's suggestion that an even closer antecedent for this sentence may be found in *Purgatorio*, v. 13–15: 'Vien dietro a me, e lascia dir le genti: | sta come torre ferma che non crolla | già mai la cima per soffiar de' venti'. For references to Dante in relation to the rest of the paragraph, see Branca's notes 2 and 4 on p. 460.
28. The third canto where we have found traces of the Auster, *Purgatorio*, XXXI, part of the Earthly Paradise episode, also belongs to one of the 'key sites in Boccaccio's Dantean intertextual topography' (Armstrong, p. 134).
29. See Chapter V, 'Tolerance', in Robert Hastings, *Nature and Reason in the 'Decameron'* (Manchester: Manchester University Press, 1975), pp. 21–23: 'It is this quality of tolerance that has so often been mistaken for lack of moral principle, or even for incitement to vice. It is in fact neither of these things. Boccaccio's indulgence of human weakness is compounded of sympathy and understanding, based on the realisation of our common humanity' (p. 23).
30. Cf. Chapter IV, 'The Book as *Galeotto*', in Robert Hollander, *Boccaccio's Two Venuses* (New York: Columbia University Press, 1977), pp. 92–116. As Hollander points out, Boccaccio calls Galeotto 'prencipe' also in his exposition on *Inferno*, v.
31. Cf. Umberto Bosco, *Il 'Decameron': saggio* (Rieti: Bibliotheca, 1929), p. 33. See especially the exchange between these two characters in v. Concl.

CHAPTER 3

Beyond Borghini: The Oxford Manuscript of Sacchetti's *novelle* and their New Critical Edition

Michelangelo Zaccarello

Franco Sacchetti's *novelle* are among the undisputed classics of early Italian literature, and their author (born Ragusa di Dalmazia, now Dubrovnik, 1332, died San Miniato al Tedesco, 1400) may be considered Boccaccio's most important follower in the 'golden century' of the Italian literary language.[1] However, their prominent position in literary history and criticism was not accompanied by a proportionate attention to the establishment of their text.[2] Despite a relatively large number of extant manuscripts, Sacchetti's *novelle* have been thus far published by means of an extremely simplified *recensio*, i.e. based on a single source: the first manuscript copy commissioned by the famous rector of the Spedale degl'Innocenti and distinguished philologist Vincenzio Borghini (1515–1580). Datable to around 1570, the Borghini codex (B) is now split into two sections, held by different Florentine libraries (M = Florence, Biblioteca Nazionale Centrale, Magl. VI 112 + L_I = Florence, Biblioteca Medicea Laurenziana, XLII 12), both in a rather precarious state of preservation. For much of the 1570s, B must have been the only source for reading Sacchetti's text and this circumstance led to its rapid deterioration; in order to safeguard the text's survival, Borghini ordered a second copy (L = Florence, Biblioteca Medicea Laurenziana, XLII 11), that survives in far better condition. Often used to fill the textual gaps arising from material loss in B, however, L is usually considered a *codex descriptus* of B, hence not taken into account for the establishment of the critical text. With the latter being essentially based on a single source, it is hardly surprising that all reconstruction attempts have thus far made extensive use of integrations and conjectures.[3]

The textual *status quaestionis* about Sacchetti's *novelle* may be summarized as follows: in the 1950s Franca Brambilla Ageno announced a forthcoming critical edition for Mondadori but published only some preparatory studies (among them those cited in note 3). As a result, the only comprehensive account of the textual transmission of the *Trecento novelle* is the full essay published by Michele Barbi in 1927.[4] Although based on a vast and detailed survey of the textual tradition, Barbi's essay aimed to focus on specific editorial issues and set out some guidelines for future editors: with a main focus on methodology, his conclusions — in favour of the adoption of B as the only reliable source — are thus declaredly cautious and provisional, and accompanied by a hope for future verification. Although based on limited selective collations, however, Barbi's essay was never discussed nor his research continued; subsequent editors referred to it as an undisputed paradigm for any more or less scholarly publication of the *Trecento novelle*, with their textual revision being conducted, for the most part, as a close analysis and discussion of individual passages, occasionally leading to valuable amendments and conjectures. These efforts were mainly interpretative in purpose, and thus limited to problematic passages of the text read in B; more extensive collations have shown unsatisfactory or problematic readings in a far greater number of passages. To quote just one example: despite being elderly, Agnolo di ser Gherardo accepts an invitation to joust with some young men and is almost killed by his own horse. In all editions, Agnolo's wife reprimands him with these words:

— Deh, va' col malanno — disse la moglie –, va' scamata [= 'comb'] la lana, come tu sei uso, e lascia *l'arte* a quelli che la sanno fare. (LXIV. 17)

Quite clearly, Agnolo should go back to his usual *arte*, that of weaving wool, rather than leaving it for something else. Witnessed by several non-Borghini manuscripts, the correct reading is obviously 'lascia *l'arme* a quelli che la sanno fare', 'leave the arms to those who can carry them'. With a typical visual or psychological lapse, the Borghini scribe has inverted two similar nouns ('arme' and 'arte'), but none of the modern editors — including myself — realized the problem until better manuscript sources came to hand.

On a number of occasions, the possibility of collating the *textus receptus* with the new witness alerts us to some possible omissions in the former, not necessarily motivated by a *saut du même au même*: since Ageno's studies, in fact, the Borghini scribes have been described as distracted and inclined toward various types of eye-skip. In *novella* XLI, the Florentines, disappointed with the witty captain Ridolfo da Camerino (second earl of Varano, who died at Tolentino in 1384), banish him from the city, but Ridolfo turns their punishment upside down: 'Fu dipinto a Firenze, quando venne in disgrazia del comune, *impiccato per li piedi*, per fargli vergogna; et essendogli stato detto, disse: — Così si dipingono molti santi. Io sono dunque sì fatto santo' (XLI. 11). Such is the passage in G N, but the italicized words are omitted by B L, and are thus absent from all editions. Needless to say, the detail of his 'hanging by the feet' is crucial: there would be no shame in having one's portrait on the Comune walls, unless the painting is a mocking image. Moreover, Ridolfo's punchline makes little sense without the addition, as saints were usually portrayed during their martyrdom, in a posture similar to that described in the z-text of our own novella.[5] Without such detail, one would hardly understand Ridolfo's following words: 'i Fiorentini m'hanno fatto *impiccare pei piedi* perch'io ho fatto i fatti miei'.[6]

Let us turn back to Barbi's essay. Alongside Borghini's paramount contribution, his collation highlights a large number of macroscopic variants that may be ascribed to a different branch of textual transmission, never identified before. Needless to say, an independent stream of textual transmission may shed much light on the actual reliability of Borghini's text, and reveal possible amendments to it. Such variants, however, were known to Barbi only through the sole witness of a much later codex, known as N.[7] If the latter were deemed a trustworthy representative of an otherwise lost branch of the textual transmission, Sacchetti's editors should take it into account, not just for individual corrections but for the entire *constitutio textus*:

> O le varianti [...] sono genuine, e allora bisogna che accanto alla trascrizione borghiniana s'ammetta *qualche altra tradizione manoscritta indipendente*, che va tenuta nel debito conto non soltanto per quei dati passi ma per tutto il testo; oppure tutti i codici esistenti derivano, come il Gigli credé, dalla copia Borghini, e allora le varianti che offre la stampa o il codice II 1 25 [N] devono tenersi per arbitrarie, o tutt'al più si possono accogliere - se felicemente dedotte dagli elementi che il testo Borghini ci conserva - come correzioni congetturali di manifesti errori incorsi nella tradizione genuina. (Barbi, *Per una nuova edizione*, p. 97; my italics)

It is worth noting that *indipendente* does not mean 'arising from a different origin', since Borghini himself repeatedly reports that he discovered the single source of the *novelle* that had survived till his time; rather, we would be looking at a different, independent transcription of Borghini's lost original, carried out by scribes of a different kind, far more enthusiastic and collaborative with the text. In other words, these *copisti per passione* — according to Vittore Branca's famous definition — would be accountable for the large number of conspicuous variants, some of remarkable quality, listed by Barbi at the end of his essay. Unlike Borghini's detached professionals (who simply left large lacunae, usually marked by a series of dots), these other scribes may have attempted to read their source carefully even in its vanished or damaged parts, without surrendering to its poor legibility; thus, they managed to amend damaged words and/or restore missing parts, with a clear tendency to adjust the readings to their own comprehension. This is the interpretation of such phenomena given by Barbi:

> Per accettare nel testo queste parole in più bisogna credere che un copista, avendo davanti l'originale che ebbe a sua disposizione il Borghini, *sia riuscito in questo punto (guasto e svanito) a leggere qualche cosa che all'amanuense del Borghini, e al Borghini stesso nei suoi riscontri, non venne fatto*. (Barbi, *Per una nuova edizione*, p. 97; my italics).

Barbi often hints at this fascinating possibility in the course of his essay, but eventually abandons it in favour of a severe dismissal of this group of variants, considered the result of an invasive revision — in fact, a rewriting — of the text: 'lezioni così evidentemente arbitrarie da poter noi senza scrupolo attribuire ad arbitrio anche le parole che troviamo aggiunte nella fine della novella CXXXVIII' (*Per una nuova edizione*, p. 116). While such conclusions seem at odds with the textual evidence collected before, it is hardly surprising that Barbi dismissed a manuscript such as N: copied shortly before the publication of Sacchetti's *editio princeps* in 1725,[8] N may well seem to be the result of a period of intense philological study and editorial revision of the *Trecento Novelle*, considered a very important source for both lexicography and general linguistic research on the *buon secolo della lingua*.[9]

Even in the preface to the 1724 edition, the editors highlight a general inclination toward interpolation in Sacchetti's textual transmission, although with a single reference to Lorenzo Gherardini's activity on the text. Although Borghini's text is credited with the maximum degree of accuracy, this *Prefazione* suggests that some 'noteworthy' variants deserve at least to be reported in the edition's margins: 'Solo nella novella 100 vi sono in fine alcuni pochi versi postivi per conclusione, che sono copiati da un ms. *moderno*, che fu del canonico Lorenzo Gherardini, e che non si leggono in quello di S. Lorenzo. Pure, *quando la diversità c'è paruta notabile, l'abbiamo posta in margine*' (*Delle novelle di Franco Sacchetti*, p. 37, my italics). In my edition, such 'pochi versi' are the whole § 7 of the novella, witnessed solely by the non-Borghini stream of textual transmission. Looking at both its language and contents, it certainly deserves a closer look:

> E però conviene che il predicatore sia sì discreto che se predica a una gente in una terra che sieno ricchi per usure, molto gli riprenda in su quello; e se predica ai poveri, gli conforti in su la povertà; s'e' sono maculati di sfrenate concupiscenze, contro a quelle dica; se da storsioni, se da rubarie o da ingiurie, e così d'altri vizi deve fare il simile, acciò che non sia ripreso da uno pover uomo come fu colui.[10]

Maybe damaged or incomplete in the source text, this moral could certainly be exposed to some degree of censorship, especially by Counter-Reformation scribes who had little sympathy for Sacchetti's frequent satire of the clergy. However, Borghini himself must have considered it original, as he corrects his own scribe's work and restores the passage — in his own hand — on the Magliabechiano portion of B.[11]

After no less than eighty years, Barbi's intuition about a separate branch in the textual tradition of Sacchetti's *Trecento Novelle* found further and sounder evidence in a new manuscript witness discovered at Wadham College, University of Oxford, the Codex Guadamensis (G).[12] Before this research, the only prior mention of G is found in H. O. Coxe's catalogue of Oxford college libraries.[13] Rather than using the latter's entry, I here offer a concise description of the manuscript:

> MS on paper, *c.* 1590–1610 (the only date recorded by the MS is 1739, following Richard Warner's ownership signature on [I]^v), 310 × 211 mm, 524 pp. (the original pagination is accurate), of which pp. 76, 436, 447–48, 455, 502–03 are all blank and pp. 456 and 504 are mostly blank. Excellent state of preservation, with the sole exception of some trimming of the outer margins, making it occasionally difficult to read marginalia and — less frequently — page numbers. Owing to the pale brown ink used, writing appears to have vanished in some parts, but remains legible almost everywhere, even without the use of UV light. Of the four watermark types found in the paper, at least two (a pilgrim and the Medici coat of arms: 6 small spheres on a shield) seem to suggest a date between 1590 and 1610, confirmed by a palaeographical examination by Armando Petrucci (Zaccarello, 'Tracce di una tradizione', p. 106 and nn. 3–4). The codex's main hand appears very capable but lacking any aesthetic concern, with a swift cursive script that is often barely intelligible. Later calf binding (possibly added at the time of Richard Warner's purchase, first half of 18th century), gilt spine with the title 'NOVELLE | DI | SACCHETTI || MSS.'.

> Provenance: the personal library of the botanist Richard Warner (1713?–1775), whose *ex libris* and signature are found in the book. Bought in all likelihood during the owner's grand tour in Italy (1734–39), the book was bequeathed to Wadham College library upon Warner's death.

With its witness of the N-version of text, G confirms that such a textual configuration already existed just a few years after Borghini's scribes had completed their transcriptions: its script and watermarks seem to suggest a date between the last decade of the sixteenth century and the very early years of the seventeenth. G can be deemed to prove that Sacchetti's text is witnessed by an alternative textual tradition, by and large contemporary to Borghini's scribes, but seemingly derived from the same witness used by them; of their common exemplar, however, the alternative descent offers a different, complementary image, prompted by a closer, often insightful reading of the source, despite a general inclination toward revision and rewriting of obscure or incomplete passages.

Based on an extensive series of shared lacunae and other common faults, combined with a large number of *lectiones singulares* of the two, I am able to prove that G's text shares with N a common lost ancestor, called z (Zaccarello, 'Tracce di una tradizione', pp. 149–82; *Le Trecento Novelle*, pp. li–lx of the *Introduction*). The z-text stands out for witnessing several passages — often entire sections — that are omitted by the Borghini scribes. In principle, such portions of text should be handled with care, as 'active' scribes would not think twice of adjusting an obscure passage with some additions or even filling blank gaps with text of their own invention.

In fact, there are some *loci* that fall under this kind of suspicion, such as LXXXIX. 8–9, where the conclusion of the Borghini text is concise and makes perfect sense: 'Che diremo che fosse quella ostia da sì devoto cherico sacrata e portata? Io per me non credo che cattivo arbore possa fare buon frutto, e tutto il mondo n'è pieno di tali, che Dio 'l sa tra cui mani è venuto!'. In the z-text (i.e. in G N), the latter section is replaced by a spurious, moralizing addition, with an anticipated punishment for both the impious priest and the blasphemous *garzone*:

> Ma non però questo indegno andò impunito de' suoi errori, perché, tornado a casa e riposto il santissimo nel ciborio, si levò una fierissima tempesta con gragnuola grossissima, la quale passando per lo scoperto tetto diede sopra alla testa all'indegno prete et uccíselo, sì come fece in campagna a colui che coglieva i fichi, il quale rimase anch'egli poco lontano di quivi ucciso dalla tempesta.

In general, such additions always display clear moralistic and/or censoring motivations; moreover, because of both their naïve content and linguistic usage, they are relatively easy to detect (in my critical edition, they are marked by square brackets: see p. 209 for the passage in question). However, a large number of passages are witnessed in a more complete, and often very convincing, form by the z-text, thanks to the scribe's greater participation and understanding, and/or his ability to sharpen his eye on the damaged original that he used as his exemplar.[14] My critical edition lists the most prominent examples found in G N (Table 1, pp. xxv–xxviii), where the Borghini scribes produced a faulty or incomplete text, needless to say reproduced by all current editions. Let us turn to a few cases in point.

The final part of the already cited *novella* XLI ends abruptly in the Borghini text and of course in current editions; but the words uttered by the wise and witty captain Ridolfo da Camerino may be recovered through G N:

> Essendo ripreso da Messer Galeotto ch'egli era vecchio senza figliuoli maschi, e esortato a doversi rimaritare e che teneva certe terre altrui, rispose: — Saccio che ogni cosa ha da ritornare in comune, e però poco m'importa l'aver figliuoli; e tanto più che la roba, che dici che io ho d'altri, sarà di fastidio non a' miei figliuoli ma ad altri che poco mi atterranno; e tu forse sarai uno di quelli, e vedràssi se saprai così bene operare spogliandotene, come sai consigliarmi a lasciargli.

In Ridolfo's words, the opening verb *saccio* (< Lat. SAPIO) is often used by Sacchetti as a recurring feature in imitation of central Italian dialects (e.g. CXXXIV. 9 and CLX. 25), and appears earlier in dialogue by Ridolfo from the same novella XLI (§§ 3 and 5). In the rest of his speech, we found other linguistic features that are original in all likelihood and may hardly be considered a Cinquecento falsification or forgery: the verb *attenere* is used by Sacchetti, in the same early meaning 'to keep a promise or other commitment', also at CXLII. 5 and CLXXXIX. 12: as such, it may be considered consistent with the author's *usus scribendi*, and opposed to later meanings of the same verb.[15] Moreover, the newly supplied portion of Ridolfo's words features a well-known syntactic rule, the Tobler-Mussafia law, according to which the pronoun must cliticize under special clause conditions, i.e. after a conjunction as in 'e vedràssi se saprai'. It is widely known that the Tobler-Mussafia restrictions decline already toward the end of the fifteenth century, and it is extremely rare to see them operate in the Cinquecento, when cliticization becomes essentially unrestricted, or related to special requirements such as rhythm or prosody.[16] Even in the preceding sentence, the extensive damage in the Borghini source has prompted various conjectures, including a particularly prominent integration proposed by Franca Brambilla Ageno and accepted by all following editors: Ridolfo is 'vecchio e senza figliuoli maschi, <o figliuole da> maritare'. Rather than on the acknowledgement of a lacuna, the correction seems to depend upon the difficulty of attributing the verb *maritare* to a man. In early Italian, however, the verb means generally 'to marry' and the *TLIO* database returns many instances attributed to masculine subjects in texts of the thirteenth and fourteenth centuries (Rustico Filippi, Domenico Cavalca etc.).[17] A case in point, for its proximity to both Sacchetti's time and provenance, may be the *Libro del difenditore della pace* (Florence, 1363), where we read: 'Giesù Cristo non fu punto *maritato*, dunque lo stato de' *maritati* elli pare condannare'. To sum up, in its transitive use, the verb means 'to give a husband to a maid', but its absolute (intransitive) use means generally 'to marry', even metaphorically (since the *Ritmo su sant'Alessio*, it may be used for the Church's spiritual marriage with Christ, applicable to both men and women).

Our second example regards the moral of *novella* LXXXIII, i.e. all of § 22. Following the Borghini text, current editions have several lacunae, especially after *signori*, to an extent that it is quite difficult to make sense of what the author is talking about: '[...] e per divertirsi dai negozi più gravi [...] il cervello ottuso e matto a poterle maturamente disserire'. In the *z*-text version, the section reads: 'benché gli uomini sien signori e sapienti, perché spesso hanno malinconie, pare che non si disdica fare simili cose per sollazare la mente e per divertirsi dai negozi più gravi, affinché le materie più importanti non rendano il cervello ottuso e matto a poterle maturamente disserire'. Not only does this version appear plausible for both language and meaning, it adds a detail that seems essential to understand the moral: it is essential that the *signori* are also *sapienti*, because in many of Sacchetti's stories (IV, VI, LXI and so on) aristocrats are just described as capricious and voluble. In the context of the *novella*, they deserve leisure and entertainment to recreate their minds and recover from stress, in order to deal with pressurizing commitments and important decision-making. Here, Sacchetti strikes us once again as a great admirer of Boccaccio, strictly following a topos widely used in his works. A case in point may be the prologue of the *Epistola napoletana* or *Machinta*, addressing the aristocratic dedicatee Francesco de' Bardi: 'E così tu, ancora molto giovinetto, essendo, sì come sentito abbiamo, *da molte varie e noiose faccende or quinci or quindi percosso*, ti dovrai ritrarre, se savio sarai, ad alcuno laudevole trastullo, il quale abbia forza di *recreare alquanto gli spiriti affaticati*'.[18]

In the last of my examples, not only does the *z*-text seem preferable on various accounts such as general meaning and linguistic aspects, it also seems to offer a valid motivation for the innovation found on the Borghini side. At CXLIII. 6–8, Giovanni dell'Innamorato mocks the illegitimate birth of a priest (*piovano*), prompting the latter's indignant reaction. In the new critical edition, the last section reads:

> Il minacciare e il rimbrottare del Piovano fu assai, e stette più coppie d'anni dinanzi che non favellò a l'Innamorato, sfuggendo ancora d'incontrarlo. E l'Innamorato, poco di ciò curandosi, andava dicendo questa novella e nel contado e nella città, e dando gran diletto a molti che lo stavano ad ascoltare.

On the other hand, the shorter version attested by B L, and of course reproduced by modern editors, appears unconvincing on the whole, and shortened — in all likelihood — by a typical *saut du même au même* affecting the words between the first and second occurrence of 'Innamorato' and thus accounting for the omission of a significant detail in the priest's subsequent behaviour: 'sfuggendo ancora d'incontrarlo'. Hence the reading found in all current editions: 'favellò allo Innamorato, *il quale non vi diè nulla*, dicendo questa novella e nel contado'. The Borghini text seems to derive from an early scribal conjecture, where the general meaning was restored by means of an idiom (*non dar nulla* 'to disregard, to pass without notice') which has no other instances in Sacchetti's language; in one passage, on the other hand, the same phrase is not taken phraseologically but literally: (LXXXI. 1) 'il Senese dice che non gli deve dar nulla', i.e. his debt is cancelled.

Let us take a general look at passages that appear more complete in the *z*-text: on top of any issue of reliability that may be associated with individual passages, there is a general factor of paramount importance. It has been said that both B and L are revised — although far from systematically — by Vincenzio Borghini himself: whilst correcting his scribe's work and adding his marginalia, all in his own hand, the Priore adopts the readings attested by G N (*Le Trecento novelle*, pp. xxxxix-xl and Table 4). Since the *z* copy was seemingly transcribed after Borghini's death, such circumstances suggest that Borghini drew such readings from the damaged original that was still in his possession, and which would later originate a different branch of the textual transmission of Sacchetti.

Among the non-Borghini manuscripts (G and N), the former's contribution appears valuable not only in terms of many substantive readings, but also for the faithful reproduction of a number of formal features that are apparently original, at least if compared with Sacchetti's usage in his well-known autograph manuscript.[19] On top of Sacchetti's *rime*, the latter in fact contains extensive parts in prose that offer a valuable point of comparison for the language used in his *novelle* (needless to say, verse sections may not serve this purpose, as they are influenced by factors such as metre, rhyme, literary genre and so forth). In more detail, Sacchetti's *Sposizioni di vangeli* (fols 97^r-145^v, a collection of homilies associated with various days of the liturgical calendar, with a number of narrative *exempla*) and his many *epistole* scattered in the Ashburnham codex offer vast, valuable grounds for linguistic analysis. For brevity's sake, I have focused on a limited range of phonomorphological features that were subject to rapid evolution during Sacchetti's lifetime: owing to massive immigration from rural parts of Tuscany, linguistic change seems particularly rapid in the Florentine vernacular after the mid fourteenth century. As argued in classic studies by Paola Manni and Massimo Palermo, the innovative features were not always promptly adopted in literary writings, because of their geographical or sociolinguistic alterity.[20]

My study of 2012 suggests that Sacchetti, far from the 'discolo e grosso' stereotype of the *novelle*'s prologue, remains loyal to Boccaccio's model and regularly prefers earlier Florentine forms, with innovative ones relegated to a marginal and ultimately negligible presence.[21] Thus, many popularizing features currently read in Sacchetti's *novelle* must be ascribed to scribes working in the Cinquecento, an age in which such features had long been absorbed and assimilated into the city's vernacular. Cases in point are the non-declined possessives (the type *mie figliuoli, la tuo donna, la suo fante*, etc.) that dot Sacchetti's *novelle* in current editions, with A and G that have almost an almost exclusive presence of declined forms.[22] With the Florentine vernacular subject to radical changes during almost two hundred years, however, it is hardly surprising that some linguistic phenomena attested in Sacchetti's autograph are absent from all extant manuscripts of his *novelle*: for the present subjunctive of *dare* and *stare*, for example, Sacchetti used only the original forms of the type *dea*, whilst B L G have the innovative variants *dia, diano* and *stia, stiano*, adopted by the modern standard. Even adopting G as our copy-text and drawing all formal aspects from its usage, a scholarly editor should refrain from extensively 'amending' its language. The edition's rule of thumb was to remove some features that met two basic criteria: they were absent from Sacchetti's autograph, and they had ambiguous attestation in the Cinquecento manuscripts. A case in point is the innovative type of the perfect indicative and imperfect subjunctive of *essere* (the types *fussi, fusti* instead of *fossi, fosti*, forms that co-exist in Florence from the mid-Trecento: Manni, pp.

143–44); whilst in Sacchetti's autograph A only the conservative forms *fosti, fossi* are used, our copy text G inclines toward more modern forms in *fuss-*, found in 364 cases against only 19 occurrences of the original ones.[23] Where possible, adjusting the *novelle*'s language to Sacchetti's own linguistic options marks a definite, albeit limited progress in the textual reconstruction.

There are, however, more significant features of Sacchetti's language that may be retrieved from the newly recovered witness. In the narrative tradition established by Boccaccio, regionalisms could be used deliberately to better the representation of non-Tuscan characters of the *novella*, thus enhancing its realism.[24] As is well known, Sacchetti adopts the same expressive technique, with most examples concerning varieties spoken in central and northern Italy, areas that Franco had often visited as a representative of the Comune of Florence. Although the Borghini codices bear witness to this tendency, there are a number of cases in which the *z*-text offers a better or more articulated and complete representation of the dialect imitated, a circumstance consistent with the better, more attentive understanding and participation highlighted earlier. In *novella* LIX, Gian Galeazzo Visconti, Duke of Milan, punishes a priest who refused to celebrate a poor man's funeral by burying him alive with the dead. In current editions, his first words are: '– *Venite cià*, o messer lo prete, e voi messer lo cherico: è vero quello che costoro dicono?' (§ 3). The *z*-text has a much better imitation of the Milanese: '*Venì za*, messer lo prete'.[25] In the same *novella* LIX, the imitation of the Milanese dialect is far more articulate in the following section, when the Duke reveals his cruel verdict: '– Et io ve lo darò io. Debito vostro è la morte. Dove è il morto? *addugélo za, mettél nella fossa*; pigliate il prete e cacciatel giù! Dove è il cherico? *mettéghel sovra; mo tirè giù la terra!*'. I have highlighted in italics the various parts in which G has a closer, more convincing representation of the original, whereas B L have Tuscanized forms that are found in all modern editions: *adugélo qua, mettetel* and *mettetel su, mo tirà*. It is not only a matter of better imitation of a Northern variety. In the narrative context, it is indispensable to point out that the priest in thrown 'on top of' the dead body that was already in the grave: thus, *mettéghel sovra* 'on top of him' is a substantive variant that had to be adopted in the new edition.[26]

In conclusion: the acquisition of a new witness to the textual reconstruction of a literary work is always an occasion to discuss and redefine the state of its tradition of scholarship; in G's case, the particular nature of the witness — its remarkable difference from the Borghini sources and its better understanding of the original's linguistic and idiomatic peculiarities — lends textual reconstruction greater possibilities: systematically comparing Sacchetti's more mechanical witnesses with an example of 'active' transmission allows a better insight of the passages in questions, and ultimately a more motivated decision about the reading that had to be adopted in the new critical text. Kept in one of the least known of Oxford college libraries, G gives us a good example of the careful consideration with which older library catalogues should be consulted: especially in terms of date and contents, scholars can often expect to find many surprises when directly inspecting the artefacts listed. Of Oxford's many beautiful memories, the opportunities given by its 'minor' or hidden libraries are most notable, especially if combined with the inspiration and advice offered by colleagues and friends like Martin.

Notes to Chapter 3

1. This essay draws upon the conclusions of my introduction to *Le Trecento novelle*, ed. by Michelangelo Zaccarello (Florence: Edizioni del Galluzzo, 2014), pp. vii–ccx. Some preparatory essays will be cited only to clarify specific issues: 'Un nuovo testimone del *Trecentonovelle* di Franco Sacchetti (Oxford, Wadham College, MS A.21.24)', in *Storia della lingua e filologia: per Alfredo Stussi nel suo sessantacinquesimo compleanno* (Florence: Edizioni del Galluzzo, 2004), pp. 177–217, then in my *Reperta: indagini, recuperi, ritrovamenti di letteratura italiana antica* (Verona: Fiorini, 2008), pp. 105–47, quoted here; 'Tracce di una tradizione non borghiniana del *Trecentonovelle*', in *Reperta*, pp. 149–82; 'Il trattamento linguistico rinascimentale delle *Trecento novelle* di Franco Sacchetti e le relative implicazioni nella scelta del testo base', *Medioevo romanzo*, 35.2 (2012), 348–82; 'Schede linguistiche per le *Trecento novelle* di Franco Sacchetti', *Quaderni veneti*, n.s., 2 (2013), *Miscellanea di studi in onore di Gino Belloni*, 161–72. It is worth noting that, following an extensive collation of the main witnesses, the title which appears preferable is *Le Trecento novelle*; the form *Il Trecentonovelle*, used so far in all editions, is likely to represent a later variant, doubtless influenced by *Il Centonovelle*, the title given to Boccaccio's masterpiece in the high Renaissance (see *Le Trecento novelle*, p. xx and nn. 8–9).

2. The main editions of Sacchetti's works are, in alphabetical order: *Il Trecentonovelle*, in *Opere*, ed. by Aldo Borlenghi (Milan: Rizzoli, 1957); *Il Trecentonovelle*, ed. by Emilio Faccioli (Turin: Einaudi, 1970); *Il Trecentonovelle*, ed. by Antonio Lanza (Florence: Sansoni, 1984); *Il Trecentonovelle*, ed. by Ettore Li Gotti (Milan: Bompiani, 1946); *Il Trecentonovelle*, ed. by Valerio Marucci (Rome: Salerno Editrice, 1996); *Il Trecentonovelle*, ed. by Vincenzo Pernicone (Florence: Sansoni, 1946); *Opere*, I. *Il Trecentonovelle*, ed. by Davide Puccini (Turin: UTET, 2004). The edition used previously was that of Ottavio Gigli, *Le novelle di Franco Sacchetti, pubblicate secondo la lezione del codice borghiniano con note inedite di Vincenzio Borghini e Vincenzio Follini*, 2 vols (Florence: Le Monnier, 1860–61, repr. 1888).

3. Some of these essays greatly contributed to the understanding of Sacchetti's language, in its lexical and idiomatic peculiarity: e.g. Franca Brambilla Ageno's review of Aldo Borlenghi's edition, in *Giornale storico della letteratura italiana*, 134 (1957), 368–92, and her full essay 'Per il testo del *Trecentonovelle*', *Studi di filologia italiana*, 16 (1958), 193–274.

4. 'Per una nuova edizione delle novelle del Sacchetti', *Studi di filologia italiana*, 1 (1927), 87–131, later included in *La nuova filologia e l'edizione dei nostri scrittori da Dante a Manzoni* (Florence: Sansoni, 1938; 3rd edn, 1977), pp. 87–124. In this essay, Barbi successfully warned against the shortcomings of the text commonly read in his time, that of Gigli, cited at the end of n. 2.

5. For a full discussion of variants, see my edition of the *Trecento novelle*, 'Introduzione', p. cviii.

6. Further reference to Ridolfo's portrait is found in § 16: 'Non tenendosi quelli del reggimento di Firenze contenti da lui, nella fine della guerra della Chiesa, *lo feciono dipingere come adietro è detto*' (i.e. *senza calze in gamba*, as specified in the following section; my italics in all passages).

7. Florence, Biblioteca Nazionale Centrale, MS II 1 25 (formerly Magl. VI 40), paper, 318–20 × 219–21 mm, first half of the 18th century (although the front flyleaf says otherwise: 'saec. XVII exeuntis'), vellum binding; 615 fols, Sacchetti's text at fols 1^r–581^r (after a blank leaf with the title); fols 582–85 are left blank and an alphabetical index of the *novelle* occupies fols 586^r–615^r (Zaccarello, 'Tracce di una tradizione', pp. 152–53).

8. *Delle novelle di Franco Sacchetti cittadino fiorentino, Parte prima* (Proemio and novelle I-CXLIII); *Parte seconda* (novelle CXLIV-CCXXIII) (Florence: [n.pub.], 1724). Drawn mainly from MS L, through a copy made for the occasion, now Florence, Biblioteca Medicea Laurenziana, Acquisti e Doni 223, the *editio princeps* was edited by Giovanni Gaetano Bottari (1689–1775) and published with the date 'Firenze 1724', although printed in Naples the following year. The edition and its preparatory stages have recently been studied in an essay by Eugenio Salvatore, 'Note linguistiche degli editori settecenteschi nelle novelle di Franco Sacchetti', *Studi di grammatica italiana*, 31–32 (2012–13), 195–222.

9. In the early Settecento, Sacchetti reaches the apex of his literary success: because of the great lexicographical and linguistic interest of his works, many famous intellectuals contributed to their recovery and publication: Anton Maria Biscioni, who wrote the manuscript cited in n. 6 (Salvatore, 'Note linguistiche', pp. 195–96, with a description and bibliography), Giovanni Gaetano Bottari who worked on the printed text, or the *cruscante* Rosso d'Antonio di Piero Martini, scribe of one of the most complete codices of Sacchetti's *Rime*, Florence, Biblioteca Nazionale Centrale, MS Palatino 205, dated 1725–26 (Zaccarello, 'Tracce di una tradizione', p. 153 and n. 8, with bibliography).
10. It is the 'moral' of this novella; see p. 228 of my edition.
11. M, p. 241; the editor of the *editio princeps* had access only to L, hence the note about the particular credit given to 'San Lorenzo' manuscripts: as a result, further collation was possible only for the Laurentian part of B (L_I).
12. Among the smaller and relatively recent colleges of Oxford University, Wadham College is by no means an obvious place to find scarcely known manuscripts: housed in a modern building opened in 1976, and mainly devoted to reference and general study, its library does not have a designated space for special collections. I wish to thank the librarian, Ms Sandra Bailey, for her time and support, e.g. the possibility of using office space for the direct inspection of the Codex Guadamensis.
13. Henry Octavius Coxe, *Catalogus codicum MSS. qui in collegiis aulisque oxoniensibus hodie adservantur / Catalogue of the Manuscripts in the Oxford Colleges*, 2 vols (Oxford: Oxford University Press, 1852; repr. Wakefield: EP Publishing, 1972). The sections devoted to individual colleges have separate pagination: Coxe's description of G is found in the Wadham College section, p. 9. For a more detailed description, see Zaccarello, 'Tracce di una tradizione', pp. 105–06.
14. See the whole of Chapter IV in Zaccarello, *Reperta*, but some similar hypotheses were anticipated in my essay 'Un nuovo testimone del *Trecentonovelle*', pp. 111–15. The latter lists some scribal errors that seem caused by inaccurate reading of an early script, for example the palaeographical error *che* > *de*, i.e. between clusters that appear particularly similar in mercantile script, p. 114). Further research has found more evidence to support this idea, with a number of misreadings — found in various manuscripts — that may be explained by Sacchetti's own *mercantesca* script (*Trecento novelle*, pp. lxxx-lxxxi).
15. For example, the verb's meaning is already different (and often used as a reflexive as in modern Italian: *attenersi* 'to agree, to adhere'), in Ludovico Ariosto, *Orlando furioso*, ed. by Cesare Segre and Santorre Debenedetti (Bologna: Commissione per i testi di Lingua, 1960): XVIII. 116. 3, 'altri, a cui la città più non attenne'; XXVII. 99. 1, 'Il re Agramante volentier s'attenne'.
16. On this well-known phenomenon of early Italian syntax, see for example Angela Marcantonio, 'Alcune considerazioni sulla legge Tobler-Mussafia', in *Problemi di analisi linguistica*, ed. by Pierangiolo Berrettoni (Rome: Cadmo, 1980), pp. 145–66; Antonio Rollo, 'Considerazioni sulla legge Tobler-Mussafia', *Studi di grammatica italiana*, 15 (1993), 5–33; Paola Benincà, 'La sintassi dei clitici complemento nelle lingue romanze medievali', in *La variazione sintattica: studi di dialettologia romanza* (Bologna: il Mulino, 1994), pp. 213–46.
17. Examples are drawn from the database *TLIO: Tesoro della lingua italiana delle Origini*, developed by the Opera del Vocabolario italiano (Accademia della Crusca, Florence). To date, the *TLIO* database includes some 23 million occurrences and is accessible, through the Gattoweb software, at <http://tlio.ovi.cnr.it/TLIO>.
18. Boccaccio's *Epistola*, with a thorough linguistic commentary, may be read in Francesco Sabatini, 'Lingue e letterature volgari in competizione', in *Storia e civiltà della Campania: Il medioevo*, ed. by Giovanni Pugliese Caratelli (Naples: Electa, 1992), pp. 401–31. The dedicatory letter to Francesco de' Bardi is also published in my essay '*Exemplum* e *lusus*: nota sulla dedicatoria alle *Poretane novelle* di Giovanni Sabadino degli Arienti', *Neuphilologische Mitteilungen*, 103 (2002), 63–71 (pp. 70–71, my italics).
19. Florence, Biblioteca Medicea Laurenziana, MS Ashburnham 574 (A). The manuscript contains all of Sacchetti's minor works, with the exception of the *Battaglia delle belle donne di Firenze con le vecchie*, witnessed solely by later manuscripts. Among the many scholarly contributions on the manuscript, it is worth citing the entry in *Mostra di codici romanzi nelle biblioteche fiorentine:*

catalogo della mostra (Firenze, Biblioteca Medicea Laurenziana) (Florence: Sansoni, 1956): L 51 at pp. 49–50 and Plate V; Franco Sacchetti, *Il libro delle Rime*, ed. by Franca Brambilla Ageno (Florence: Olschki; Perth: University of Western Australia, 1990), pp. 1–4; Luisa Battaglia Ricci, 'Tempi e modi di composizione del *Libro delle Rime* di Franco Sacchetti', in *Palazzo Vecchio e dintorni* (Rome: Salerno Editrice, 1990), pp. 109–37.

20. Paola Manni, 'Ricerche sui tratti fonetici e morfologici del fiorentino quattrocentesco', *Studi di grammatica italiana*, 8 (1979), 115–79; Massimo Palermo, 'Sull'evoluzione del fiorentino nel Tre-Quattrocento', *Nuovi annali della Facoltà di Magistero dell'Università di Messina*, 5–12 (1990–92), 131–54. The analysis was carried out through a methodology explained in Zaccarello, 'Il trattamento linguistico rinascimentale', pp. 348–57, which may be summarized as follows: if Sacchetti adopts an innovative feature in his autograph manuscript, the sixteenth-century copies may either accept it or suppress it (the latter is generally the case when the scribe is influenced by Boccaccio's highly conservative usage); if, on the other hand, an innovative phonomorphological feature does not appear in Sacchetti's autograph, but only in later manuscripts, it may be safely attributed to scribal interference. In both cases, the linguistic reliability of both the Borghini text (B, L) and the *z*-text (assessed through G only, since N is copied in the 1700s and its language is subject to later influences) were compared in a chart that demonstrates, by a relatively clear margin, that G offers a more reliable image of the lost original's language, or at least one more compatible with Sacchetti's own usage (p. 378).
21. The only element widely present is the loss of the voiceless labiovelar element *-que* in *qualunche*, *adunche* etc., a feature that had spread from Siena, where it is found from the earliest phases, but also from Prato and Pistoia: see Manni, pp. 130–31.
22. See my 'Il trattamento linguistico rinascimentale', pp. 364–65: the autograph manuscript of Sacchetti has only one certain form of the innovative type, 'i suo cittadini' (fol. 131$^\text{v}$, col. 1).
23. With Borghini codices following the established use of Boccaccio's works, current editions have a majority of original forms: 349 cases as opposed to only 36 of the *fuss-* variants (Zaccarello, 'Il trattamento linguistico rinascimentale', p. 370).
24. Relevant examples may be the Venetian spoken by madonna Lisetta in *Decameron*, IV. 2, or the various Sicilianisms in madonna Iancofiore's words to Salabaetto, VIII. 10; see Alfredo Stussi, 'Scelte linguistiche e connotati regionali nella novella italiana', in *La novella italiana: Atti del convegno di Caprarola (19–24 settembre 1988)* (Rome: Salerno Editrice, 1989), pp. 191–214, then in his *Lingua, dialetto e letteratura* (Turin: Einaudi, 1993), pp 129–53.
25. The same opposition appears in the words uttered by another famous leader of Sacchetti's times, Mastino della Scala, who dismisses one of his courtiers after many years of service: '– Vien cià, va', apparecchia tutte le tue scritture de' fatti miei che ti sono pervenuti alle mani, poi che tu fosti nella corte mia'. Such is the text commonly read, drawn from B (in agreement with L), but G has again a better imitation of the regional adverb: 'Vien za'.
26. The examples cited are drawn from Zaccarello, 'Schede linguistiche', pp. 165–66. This essay offers several other examples, concerning varieties as diverse as Genoese, Umbrian and the dialects of the Marche.

CHAPTER 4

Why Retranslate the Classics? Griselda in French from the Renaissance to the Twentieth Century

Linda Louie, Mairi McLaughlin and Diana Thow

1. Introduction

In this essay, we take Martin McLaughlin's article on humanist Latin versions of Boccaccio's Griselda tale (*Decameron* x. 10) as a starting point to examine three French translations of the same novella.[1] In his article, McLaughlin discusses Petrarch's 1373 and Neri de' Nerli's 1503 Latin translations of the tale both individually and in relation to one another.[2] He argues that, although Nerli's translation is 'much more faithful' than Petrarch's,[3] it is nevertheless 'more than a mere "traduzione": it is in its own way a modest "riscrittura" in its emphasis on Gualtieri's defects and Griselda's virtues, and it is a humanist, classicizing re-writing particularly in its intertextual realignments'.[4] Previous scholarship on Latin translations of *Decameron* x. 10 focused primarily, if not exclusively, on Petrarch's changes to Boccaccio's tone, characterization and narrative sequence. In these three areas, Petrarch's changes are so significant, and Nerli's so minor, that Nerli's translation looks simply — and perhaps uninterestingly — faithful in comparison. But McLaughlin's analytical approach, which focuses primarily on the two translations' style and intertextual references, allows him to take a different perspective on Nerli. In these two areas, comparing the translation choices made by Nerli and Petrarch illuminates the approach of each translator. In part, the stylistic and intertextual differences between Petrarch and Nerli can be explained in terms of the evolution of literary Latin from the fourteenth to sixteenth centuries. However, McLaughlin also argues that the 'classical patina' of Nerli's translation cannot be explained exclusively as a result of such changes, and that his translation possesses its own 'artistic autonomy and coherence'.[5]

The approach that we developed for the present study is directly inspired by McLaughlin's article. Like McLaughlin, we examine translations of the Griselda tale into a single target language, in our case French, and the translations date from different historical periods. We chose to examine three translations, each of which comes from a complete translation of the *Decameron*: a sixteenth-century translation by Antoine Le Maçon,[6] an eighteenth-century translation by Antoine Sabatier de

Castres,[7] and a twentieth-century version by Henri Demeurisse.[8] As scholars have shown, there is a rich tradition of Boccaccio in French, so we selected these three translations on the grounds that there is a genealogical link between them.[9] Both Sabatier and Demeurisse base their versions (to varying degrees) on Le Maçon's 1545 translation. McLaughlin's article was also the inspiration for the methodology used to carry out the textual analysis. We chose to focus on twelve key moments in the tale which McLaughlin examines in his article. Limiting our analysis to these key moments allowed us to compare in detail each translation to the source text and also to compare the translations to each other.

Where this study starts to depart from McLaughlin's approach, and also from the long tradition of literary scholarship on translations of the *Decameron* and the Griselda tale, is in its blending of a more traditional literary studies approach with the tools and techniques of translation studies. In carrying out the analysis of the three French translations, we therefore draw heavily on taxonomies of types of translational change established by translation scholars. There is no space here to offer definitions of each of the different kinds of change we discuss and, in any case, most of the terms are fairly straightforward.[10] Taxonomies of translational changes are not, in fact, incompatible with a literary studies approach and we retain a major interest in the kinds of change which were particularly important for McLaughlin's work. We therefore give special consideration to translational choices which relate to style and intertextuality (which for us primarily concerns relationships between the different retranslations) and we note significant changes to tone, characterization and narrative sequence. Translation studies also forms the theoretical backdrop for this essay. Before we turn to the three French translations of *Decameron* x. 10, we therefore present the three areas that are the most relevant for this study, namely translation history, retranslation and fidelity.

Although there is a long line of scholarship on translations from different historical periods within literary studies, it is only recently that translation history has developed into an important subfield of translation studies. This is evidenced for the target language of this study by the recent publication of histories of translation theory and practice.[11] Despite this proliferation of studies, scholars continue to express concern about the place of translation history within the wider discipline. For example, D'hulst talks of translation history as 'a discipline or subdiscipline that still has to find its way within translation studies'[12] and Long describes research in this field as 'somewhat patchy'.[13] Aside from the question of coverage, the main problem is the lack of an established methodology for translation history.[14] Nevertheless, such concerns are not sufficient to call into question the value of translation history research. The most common theme in reflections on translation history is undoubtedly the idea that we can use the past to understand the present. Gürçağlar writes that '[t]he drive to study the history of translations and translators is inevitably connected to a wish to understand and promote current issues about translations'.[15] It seems to us that this study is most likely to elucidate further current issues surrounding the nature of 'translation' itself. This is mostly due to certain particularities of the Griselda tale and of its translation history which make it the ideal candidate for a study of this type. We can note, among other things, the existence of multiple retranslations dating from different historical periods; the existence of translations alongside both adaptations and rewritings; the instability of the source text caused by the fact that Petrarch's Latin version was used as the source for the earliest French translations of the tale;[16] and the range of different interpretations of the tale's meaning. The present study will let us address two main translation theoretic issues concerning the notion of translation itself: first, retranslation, and second, fidelity.

The phenomenon of retranslation has attracted a great deal of attention since the publication of Antoine Berman's article 'La Retraduction comme espace de la traduction'.[17] For Berman, retranslation results from the paradox that translations, unlike originals, age such that there is never a single definitive translation of a given work.[18] However, there are also what he calls 'great translations' ('grandes traductions'), namely exceptional translations that gain a cultural significance equal to or surpassing the original.[19] 'Great translations' can only ever be retranslations because a literary work must await its *kairos* and this can only come after the work has an established history of reception in the target culture.[20] There are two main strands to research in this area today, both of which are relevant to the present study. The first kind of scholarship is concerned with motivations for retranslations. For example, Pym distinguishes between 'passive retranslations' (those that 'seem to be responding to long-term processes of linguistic or cultural change in the target community') and 'active retranslations' (those that '[tend] to locate causes far closer to the translator, especially in the entourage of patrons, publishers, readers and intercultural politics').[21] Gambier suggests a more granular distinction between passive retranslations that are 'endogenetic' (motivated by linguistic change) and those that are 'exogenetic' (motivated by other changes in target-culture translational 'taste').[22] The second kind of scholarship on retranslation focuses instead on retranslations of a single source text. This kind of work is often framed as a test of the so-called 'retranslation hypothesis' which was derived from Berman's article and posits that first translations tend to assimilate or domesticate the source text to the target culture, while retranslations are more foreignizing.[23] Interestingly, such studies tend to conclude that the retranslation hypothesis does not hold, or, at the very least, they point out the difficulties involved in adequately measuring domestication. In examining three French translations of the closing tale of the *Decameron*, our work is directly concerned with the phenomenon of 'retranslation' and our analysis will shed light on both categories of motivations for retranslation and also on the retranslation hypothesis.

Fidelity, or the degree of proximity between the translated text and its original, is a central issue for the practice, study and theory of translation. However, there is considerable variation in the way that the term is defined and measured in individual studies of specific translations. It is widely acknowledged that fidelity can operate at a range of different levels, such as the formal or functional, and scholars tend to agree that it is an historically relative notion. Despite the difficulties surrounding the notion of fidelity, it is a concept that we have to address directly in the present study, both as a feature that we measure in the analysis and as part of the theoretical context. As explained above, our methodological approach involves paying special attention to the kinds of translational choices in which McLaughlin was interested. However, we do not use fidelity to judge the quality of the various retranslations, since, like McLaughlin, we are not interested in asking 'which is better'; rather, we are seeking 'objective insights'.[24] At a more theoretical level, our study touches on various questions regarding the notion of fidelity and its application in translation studies. There is an interesting thematic link between this theoretical concept and the Griselda tale itself because fidelity is its moral centrepiece. Previous scholars such as McLaughlin have already drawn attention to decisions made by translators of the novella that place extra emphasis on the theme of fidelity.[25] With reference to the French tradition, for example, Campbell has noted that translations of the Griselda tale often emphasize the lesson of fidelity specifically for its female audience.[26] Campbell's article is relevant for our study because it also straddles literary studies and translation theory by building on feminist and queer translation scholarship. Our analysis will therefore also explore fidelity in the light of recent theoretical developments in this area.

2. Le Maçon (1545)

The first translation we examine was carried out by Antoine Le Maçon and his was the first complete French translation of the *Decameron* directly from the Italian.[27] His translation appeared in 1545, in the middle of what Balsamo calls one of two 'moments forts' when there was 'une exceptionnelle floraison de grandes traductions littéraires élaborées à la cour ou pour la cour'.[28] Le Maçon was himself in royal service and he produced his version at the behest of Marguerite de Navarre, to whom the work is dedicated. His translation is best known for its close fidelity to Boccaccio's original and Le Maçon explicitly comments on this feature in his prefatory letter. He explains that throughout the work, he took care 'de ne dire en nostre langue plus ne moins que Bocace à faict en la sienne' (LM, a2^v) and the feedback that he received from both French and Tuscans was that the stories he had translated 'estoient (sinon bien) au moins tresfidelement traduictes' (LM, a2^{r-v}).[29] The preface also sets up the translation as an illustration of good French by linking his work to Marguerite de Navarre's desire that the Tuscans should not think that Boccaccio 'ne peust estre representé en nostre langue, aussi bien qu'il est en la leur' (LM, a2^r), an impression which was presumably created in part by Laurent de Premierfait's earlier translation from Latin.[30] It should also be remembered that Le Maçon's translation has a unique status in the history of French translations of the *Decameron* because, as Rothstein notes, 'it continued to be the basis of the standard French version of the *Decameron* for some 350 years' and, as will be seen in Section 4, it was still the basis of Demeurisse's version published in 1955.[31]

Our analysis of Le Maçon's translation of *Decameron* x. 10 confirms that there is definitely a close relationship between the source and target texts. This is easily illustrated by the following excerpt:

> Griselda, tempo è omai che tu senta frutto della tua lunga pazienzia, e che coloro li quali me hanno reputato crudele e iniquo e bestiale conoscano che ciò che io faceva a antiveduto fine operava, volendoti insegnar d'esser moglie e a loro di saperla tenere (GB, 61) > Greselidis [sic], il est desormais temps que tu sentes le fruict de ta longue pacience: & que ceulx qui mont reputé cruel mauvais & bestial, congnoissent que ce que je faisois, estoit une œuvre preveue: voulant t'enseigner d'estre femme mariée: & à eulx de la scavoir prendre & garder (LM, 251^v).[32]

The close genetic relationship between French and Italian means that the formal proximity of the two texts is manifested at the most superficial level through the many etymological cognates such as 'tempo/temps', 'pazienzia/pacience', 'crudele/cruel' and 'bestiale/bestial', and the sentence structure is essentially the same. Nevertheless, using the tools of translation studies to examine Le Maçon's text revealed that the translation cannot be considered faithful in an absolute sense, even at the formal level. We will show here that the target text differs from the source in certain interesting ways.

Le Maçon's translation contains multiple examples of each of the following type of change: explicitation, 'logisieren', particularization, amplification, reduction, intensification and modulation. However, there does not seem to be any pattern in the way that these translational procedures are applied. This is most easily illustrated by intensification which touches all sorts of aspects of the tale in Le Maçon's version. For example, it augments both Gualtieri's argument against taking a wife but also Griselda's virtues. Gualtieri's argument that 'sieno **spesse volte** le figliuole a' padri e alle madri dissimili' (GB, 7) becomes in French 'si voit on **le plus souvent** les filles ne ressembler à pere ne à mere' (LM, 249^r) and he later admires her 'constanzia' (GB, 33) in Italian but her '**grande** constance' (LM, 250^r) in French. Read together, these examples show that intensification does not introduce any kind of systematic change such as bias toward one character over the other; rather, it just has the effect of slightly emphasizing in all directions at once. The same goes for the other types of change listed above. There is no space to illustrate each type of change separately but we might note a general tendency towards explicitation and towards 'logisieren'. The term 'logisieren' can refer to various types of interpretative acts from unpacking and explaining to intellectualizing.[33] In this case, the 'logisieren' takes place through an explicit structuring of the text. The most obvious example is found in the title where the tale is presented as the 'Nouvelle dixiesme, **& derniere**' (LM, 248^v) but it is also achieved on a handful of other occasions, for example when adverbs and connectors such as 'ainsi' and 'ensuite' are added in translation. As with intensification, these changes bring about a general change whereby the text as a whole is slightly clearer and more structured but they are neither sufficiently frequent nor sufficiently significant to call into question the status of Le Maçon's text as a translation.

We did, however, come across two other types of change which have a bigger impact on the Griselda tale. The first of these is the introduction of synonymic doublets which can be found throughout Le Maçon's translation. Examples include 'parole generali' (GB, 30) which becomes 'parolles generalles & ouvertes' (LM, 250^r);

'viso duro' (GB, 46) turned into 'visaige cruel & courroussé' (LM, 251ʳ), and 'donna' (GB, 8) translated as 'dame & maistresse' (LM, 249ʳ). McLaughlin observes a similar use of doublets in Nerli's version of the Griselda tale which he links to 'Latin's love of synonymic pairings'.³⁴ Le Maçon introduces these doublets for a similar reason. It is both an imitation of Latin style in the vernacular, and also a common feature of Renaissance French translations which can be associated with a need to enrich the French lexis. As in Nerli's Latin version, the consistent use of synonymic pairings in Le Maçon's translation can therefore be considered a stylistic choice which has the effect of altering the patina of the original. As far as we can tell, however, none of the doublets has the effect of introducing an intertextual reference as they can be seen to do in Nerli's version. It seems more appropriate to link the use of doublets to his desire to illustrate the vernacular by demonstrating that French is 'riche, & copieuse' and that anything that can be written in any language can now also be written in French (LM, a2ʳ).

The second set of changes which has a significant effect on Le Maçon's translation concerns references to individuals. We noticed throughout the tale a general de-personalization of individuals and, at times, their relationships. The clearest example concerns Gualtieri who is referred to almost constantly not by his proper name as in Italian but by his title, 'Le Marquis'. This has the effect of emphasizing his role as a leader. Similarly, his relationship with his men becomes less personal in Le Maçon's translation. This is clearly illustrated by the translation of 'tutta la compagnia **sua**' (GB, 15) by simply 'toute la compaignie' (LM, 249ᵛ) and by the frequent use of the term 'subjectz' in French which identifies the men through their hierarchical relationship with the Marquis. A similar change affects references to Griselda's father who is referred to on three occasions by his proper name ('Jehannot') as in Italian ('Giannucolo') but is otherwise referred to as 'ung paysant' (LM, 250ʳ), 'ton pere' (LM, 250ᵛ) and 'le paovre pere' (LM, 251ʳ). The effect of this is either to emphasize his lower status or to privilege his position as Griselda's father. We can therefore point to two general consequences of these different kinds of de-personalization in Le Maçon's translation. First, there is greater emphasis on the social functions of the various individuals and, second, Griselda herself, and to a lesser extent Gualtieri, are brought into greater focus. This analysis is supported by the fact that Griselda remains untouched by this change since Le Maçon calls her 'Griselidis' throughout whereas he reduces the importance of several other figures through textual reduction and de-intensification. Both of these effects can be understood as part of the French tradition of emphasizing Griselda's exemplary status.

It is very clear, therefore, that Le Maçon's translation cannot be considered completely faithful to Boccaccio's original and, in this way, it conforms to what we know generally about sixteenth-century French translation. As Balsamo says of translation from Italian, 'loin de se plier au style, de chercher à rendre les textes avec fidélité, elle adapte, elle joue de l'écart, elle modifie le texte d'origine pour en faire un texte français'.³⁵ Le Maçon's twin aims of producing a faithful translation and illustrating the French language explain why we observe a delicate balance in his work between formal proximity and moments of movement away from the source text. Paradoxically, it is the very clear formal proximity of most of Le Maçon's translation that makes his changes more visible. Messina, comparing de Premierfait's and Le Maçon's translations, describes the results of her analysis of Le Maçon as 'molto meno interessanti' as a result of Le Maçon's scrupulous fidelity.[36] We hope to have shown, as does McLaughlin, that even a faithful translation can demonstrate 'a consistent pattern of small additions and emphases' which are worthy of analysis.[37]

3. Sabatier de Castres (1779)

The translation of the *Decameron* by the cleric, author and critic Antoine Sabatier de Castres has not, to our knowledge, received any significant attention in the literature on Boccaccio in French. Gathercole calls it 'a rejuvenation of the LeMaçon version',[38] but this translation's relationship to Le Maçon's is complex. Its 'Préface de l'éditeur' calls Le Maçon's style 'gothique' and 'barbare' (SdC, i). This linguistic archaism is, according to the preface, a failing of this particular translation rather than of sixteenth-century translations in general; it states that while the language of Amyot's translations remains relevant, Le Maçon's is 'différent & inintelligible' (SdC, ii). It is also argued in the preface that Sabatier's translation improves upon Le Maçon's in its use of 'un style correct, simple, quelquefois élégant & toujours naturel' (SdC, v). On the other hand, the preface praises Le Maçon's fidelity to the original *Decameron,* while criticizing an anonymous 1697 translation printed in Amsterdam for its many omissions: 'il n'a pris que l'*essentiel* des Nouvelles; [...] il a *changé même le plan général de l'Ouvrage*' (SdC: iii, emphasis in original). The preface to Mirabeau's 'traduction libre' of the *Decameron,* published in 1802, affirms (and disparages) the faithfulness of Sabatier's translation: 'En vain M. de C★★ dirat-il que Boccace est un auteur classique, et qu'ainsi sa version doit être littérale et entière.'[39] Mirabeau, by contrast, entirely rewrites many of the cornice sections and removes or replaces several stories. Both Mirabeau and Sabatier's 'Éditeur', then, consider Sabatier to be making a consciously faithful choice in adhering to 'le plan général de l'Ouvrage', while the translations that immediately preceded and followed his did not. Thus in general Sabatier's preface presents the translation as passive, simply updating the language and style for the modern era, although it does admit to being active in one respect: in replacing obscenities with 'des tours & des expressions en usage dans la bonne compagnie', so that women can read the *Decameron* without encountering 'ces mots grossiers qui blessent la délicatesse & font rougir la pudeur' (SdC, vii).

Our analysis finds that Sabatier is indeed referring to Le Maçon's translation in writing his own. To take one example, Sabatier's rendering of the list of wedding guests ('molti suoi amici e parenti e **gran gentili uomini e altri da torno**' (GB, 14) as 'plusieurs de ses amis & de ses parens, & **quelques Gentilhommes d'alentour**' (SdC, 204)) departs from Boccaccio by combining the 'gran gentili uomini' and the 'altri' just as Le Maçon's translation does. Likewise, Sabatier also maintains some of the choices in Le Maçon's translation that reflect Renaissance stylistic conventions, such as Le Maçon's translation of 'donna' with the doublet 'Dame & maîtresse' (SdC, 202). More often, Sabatier adopts parts of Le Maçon's translation while incorporating endogenetic changes, such as modernizing his punctuation, spelling and lexis (for example, he replaces the verb 'querir' (LM, 249^v) with its modern equivalent, 'chercher' (SdC, 204)). Sometimes these modernizations have the effect of further amplifying changes to Boccaccio's text introduced by Le Maçon. For example, describing Gualtieri's reluctance to take a wife, Boccaccio begins: 'La qual cosa a' suoi uomini **non piaccendo**' (GB, 5), which Le Maçon translates as 'Laquelle chose **estant tresdeplaisante** à ses subjectz' (LM, 249^r), including one of his characteristic intensifications. In Sabatier's translation, this phrase becomes '**Cette façon de penser & de vivre** déplaisoit **fort** à ses Sujets' (SdC, 200); he further amplifies Le Maçon's 'tres' to 'fort', while also modernizing the introductory 'relatif de liaison' by specifying the reason for the subjects' displeasure.

These examples demonstrate that Sabatier used Le Maçon's earlier translation, maintaining or lightly modernizing some of his translational changes. However, more striking are the many new translational changes that Sabatier introduces. Many of these, as advertised in the 'Préface de l'éditeur', are stylistic in nature, serving the goal of greater clarity and elegance in French. However, such stylistic changes tend to go hand in hand with more interpretive changes at the levels of tone, characterization and narrative. Sabatier's translation of the very first sentence of the story clearly illustrates this tendency:

> Già è gran tempo, fu tra' marchesi di Sanluzzo il maggior della casa un giovane chiamato Gualtieri, il quale, essendo senza moglie e senza figliuoli, in niuna altra cosa il suo tempo spendeva che in uccellare e in cacciare, né di prender moglie né d'aver figliuoli alcun pensiero avea; di che egli era da reputar molto savio (GB, 4). > Un des plus illustres & des plus célèbres descendans de la Maison de Saluces fut un nommé *Gautier*. Sans femme, sans enfans, & n'ayant aucune envie de se marier ni d'avoir des héritiers, il employoit son tems à la chasse (SdC, 200).

Dividing Boccaccio's long sentence into two is a stylistic change, allowing Sabatier to highlight the parallel phrase 'Sans femme, sans enfans', present in the original but given more emphasis here. Sabatier's description of Gualtieri as not just 'il maggior della casa', but 'Un des plus illustres & des plus célèbres descendens' could likewise be seen as an extension or imitation of the stylistic tendency toward synonymic pairings that we saw in Le Maçon's translation. But Sabatier's omissions are notable in their consistency; here he removes both the introductory phrase ('Già è gran tempo') and Dioneo's wry commentary on Gualtieri's bachelor lifestyle ('di che egli era da reputar molto savio'), both phrases that link the Griselda story itself to the frame narrative. This pattern of redacting the cornice is consistent throughout the translation. The most striking example appears at the end of the story. In the original tale, Dioneo famously undercuts Griselda's exemplary fidelity by saying that Gualtieri deserved 'una che quando, fuor di casa, l'avesse in camiscia cacciata, s'avesse sí a un altro fatto scuotere il pilliccione che riuscito ne fosse una bella roba' (GB, 69). Sabatier's translation omits both Dioneo's vulgar phrasing and the subversively ambiguous ending, summarizing the wife Gualtieri deserves as 'une Femme capable de se venger...' but emphasizing that 'Griselidis fut en tout point un modèle de vertu' (SdC, 227).

In addition to these modifications to the narrative, Sabatier introduces a number of changes related to the story's tone and characterization. This can be seen immediately in his title for the story: he includes the slightly amplified 'logisieren' taken from Le Maçon ('Nouvelle dixiesme, & **derniere**') but also adds a second title of his own that casts Griselda as protagonist and exemplar ('*Griselidis ou la Femme éprouvée*') (SdC, 199). While for Petrarch, Griselda's poverty was linked to her piety, Sabatier avoids referring to her as poor: her first appearance as a 'povera giovinetta' (GB, 9) becomes simply 'une jeune Fille' (SdC, 202), and the description of Griselda's father as 'poverissimo' (GB, 9) is omitted. Perhaps the most consistent and pervasive set of characterization changes is Sabatier's emphasis on the pathos of Griselda's situation, effected in part through the increased villainization of Gualtieri (an interesting counterpoint to Petrarch, whose translational changes make Gualtieri 'almost perfect', as shown by McLaughlin).[40] For instance, when Gualtieri's servant comes to take away her daughter, Griselda's plea to 'non la lasciar per modo che le bestie e gli uccelli la divorino' (GB, 32) becomes 'ne pas laisser **cette innocente victime** exposée à **la rapacité** des animaux **carnassiers** & des oiseaux **de proie**' (SdC, 210). Similarly, when Gualtieri calls Griselda before him to send her away, 'fattalasi venir dinanzi' (GB, 42) becomes 'Il fit venir l'Infortunée qu'il tourmentoit' (SdC, 215). Sabatier emphasizes the uniqueness of Griselda's ability to hold back her tears, amplifying the original's description ('oltre alla natura delle femine' (GB, 44)) to make it 'chose assez **extraordinaire** dans **une** Femme' (SdC, 216). This focus on Griselda's tears recurs at the end of the story. When Gualtieri finally reveals his motivations to Griselda, Sabatier amplifies the pathos of the scene. 'E cosí detto l'abbracciò e basciò: e con lei insieme, la qual d'allegrezza piagnea, levatosi [...]' (GB, 64) is in French 'Il l'embrassa ensuite **tendrement, & recueillit les larmes de joie qui couloient de ses yeux**' (SdC, 225).

With this analysis in mind, we can make some interesting amendments to the way in which Sabatier's translational approach is described in his preface and in Mirabeau's. While Sabatier does indeed retain the cornice narration, we have seen that he consistently minimizes or omits phrases that refer back to the cornice from within the Griselda story (especially in places where Dioneo's narratorial voice is prominent), thereby creating greater stylistic and tonal homogeneity. Although his rendering of the cornice is very faithful compared to those of his fellow eighteenth-century translators, we see that other aspects of his translation can be called unfaithful: he reflects the aesthetic preferences of his time by minimizing the cornice within the story, and modifies the tone and characterization of the source text. His relationship to Le Maçon's translation, furthermore, is more ambiguous than is suggested by Gathercole's description of it as a 'rejuvenation'. Sabatier uses Le Maçon's translation as a resource, but not a source text. He adopts or modernizes numerous aspects of Le Maçon's translation, but introduces many of his own translational changes that well surpass Le Maçon's in scope and directionality.

In making an interpretive intervention in Boccaccio's style, tone, narrative and characterization, Sabatier goes further than a mere stylistic modernization would demand, and much further than the translation's reputation for fidelity (or the preface's professed respect for Boccaccio's status as a classical author) would suggest.

4. Demeurisse (1955)

At the end of her bibliographic account of Boccaccio in French, Gathercole takes the existence of numerous translators of his work in the twentieth century as a sign that 'the present generation continues to value Boccaccio's works very highly'.[41] The third and final translation that we examine here was published in 1955 during a peak in the translation history of the *Decameron* into French; Gathercole cites a total of five (complete and excerpted) translations and adaptations of the *Decameron* published between 1950 and 1964.[42] As was the case for Sabatier's translation, there has been little scholarly attention paid to Demeurisse's version and little is known about the translator. It is clear, however, that this is a somewhat particular version of Boccaccio's work and it might better be understood as a blend of high and low genres, especially as it compares to Jean Bourciez's more scholarly translation that had been published just three years earlier by Garnier.[43] First, Demeurisse's version is not presented as a translation but as a modernization of Le Maçon's translation, which had in fact already been reprinted earlier in the century.[44] Second, its production emphasizes its status as an art object. Its two volumes, with a print run of 2000, were bound beautifully in vellum and adorned with forty erotic watercolours by Pierre Laurent Brénot, a well-known pin-up artist. While there is a long history of illustrations in editions of the *Decameron*, as well as a history of French translations featuring erotic illustrations, this edition appears to be unusual in its highlighting the female characters and narrators of the tales with minimal or no visual context representing other elements of the narrative.[45]

Unsurprisingly, our analysis of Demeurisse's version of *Decameron* x. 10 confirms that there is a direct relationship between his text and Le Maçon's Renaissance translation. In fact, it seems that Le Maçon's translation functions as the source text for Demeurisse and there is no evidence that he consulted the original Italian. The primary examples which are telling in this regard show that Demeurisse adheres to Le Maçon's departures from Boccaccio and there are numerous such examples throughout. To take just one example, in Gualtieri's speech about taking a wife, 'donde argomentate di darlami tal che mi piacerà' (GB, 7) is translated by Le Maçon using an explicitation, '& par tel argument me donner **femme**' (LM, 249ʳ), and he omits the notion of pleasing. Demeurisse does the same: 'et user d'un tel argument pour me donner **une épouse**' (HD, 398). However, it is not just translational procedures such as modulation, explicitation, specification, amplification and reduction which are retained by Demeurisse. He also retains a number of the synonymic doublets that were introduced by Le Maçon. If we return to the passage which we quoted early in Section 2 to illustrate the apparent fidelity of Le Maçon's translation, Demeurisse retains Le Maçon's binomial 'prendre & garder' as 'la choisir et la garder' (HD, 405) instead of something closer to the Italian 'saperla tenere' (GB, 61). He also, like Le Maçon, uses the doublet 'comme dame et maîtresse' (HD, 398) where Boccaccio simply has 'come donna' (GB, 8). Although Demeurisse did not retain all of the doublets which Le Maçon had introduced, we consider the retention of at least some of them to be a notable feature of this version of the *Decameron*. The fact that synonymic doublets are such a well-known feature of Renaissance French style means that their inclusion here suggests a limit to the modernization carried out by Demeurisse.

There is another feature of Demeurisse's version of *Decameron* x. 10 which can be considered specific to the context of retranslation. We conceive of this as a kind of telescopic effect whereby a change introduced by a translator is added to in the retranslation. We saw a similar example in Sabatier's work in Section 3 where 'non piaccendo' in Boccaccio became 'estant **tres**deplaisante' in Le Maçon but was further amplified and intensified as 'déplaisoit **fort**' in the 1779 retranslation. Examples found in Demeurisse's version include Le Maçon's intensification of Gualtieri's words 'e come **dura** vita sia' (GB, 6) as 'combien **malheureuse** est la vie' (LM, 249^r) which is further intensified through amplification by Demeurisse with the addition of an adverb: 'qu'**infiniment malheureuse** est l'existence' (HD, 398). We do not consider intensification or amplification of this kind to be an explicit goal of Demeurisse's version but rather a natural effect of retranslation, because the versions of the *Decameron* produced by Sabatier and by Demeurisse represent such different kinds of retranslation yet both display this same effect. Together, the retention of synonymic doublets and telescopic changes illustrate very clearly the complexity of the relationships that can obtain between a retranslation, an earlier (re)translation and an original source text. The fact that there is a genealogical link between these (re)translations also means that we are obliged to expand the concept of fidelity beyond source and target texts. In the case of Demeurisse, it seems far more important to examine the relationship between his text and Le Maçon's translation than it is to examine its fidelity to Boccaccio's original.

Returning to the textual analysis, it should be clear from the examples cited above that Demeurisse also introduces basic endogenetic changes to modernize Le Maçon's orthography, punctuation, typography, syntax and lexis. This includes, for example, the introduction of diacritics, updating conventions for marking reported speech, and an increased use of definite and indefinite articles. Such changes are to be expected in the case of a typical passive retranslation. However, Demeurisse goes further than this and introduces some changes which cannot be attributed to modernization or retranslation alone. There are a number of changes which appear to be dictated by stylistic or aesthetic concerns but which do not take the retranslation in any one direction. For example, Demeurisse uses particularization to replace frequent and semantically general verbs with more specific items so that 'faire' (LM, 249^r) becomes 'accomplir' (HD, 398) or 'préparer' (HD, 399), and 'dire' (LM, 252^r) becomes 'ajouter' (HD, 406). We might interpret this as a diversification of diction that is in accordance with twentieth-century narrative styles. He also renders certain notions more concrete so that 'voller & chasser' (LM, 249ʳ) becomes 'la chasse au faucon et [...] la poursuite du gibier' (HD, 397) and 'je t'ay picquée de parolles' (LM, 251v) becomes 'je t'ai criblée de paroles insultantes' (HD, 405). Aside from these isolated aesthetic changes, there is also a slight tendency to amplify the pathos of the story at moments when it is already emotionally charged. For instance, Demeurisse introduces adjectives such as 'petite' and 'jeune' when referring to Griselda or to her daughter. The most striking example comes when Griselda is forced to give up her daughter: Le Maçon's 'ne **la** laisse en lieu, ou les bestes ou oyseaulx la peussent devorer' (LM, 250ʳ) becomes in Demeurisse's version 'n'abandonne point **la petite** en un lieu où elle puisse être dévorée par les bêtes ou les oiseaux' (HD, 401). Similarly, like Sabatier, Demeurisse intensifies the poignant reunion between Gualtieri and Griselda by having Gualtieri take Griselda in his arms and cover her with kisses (HD, 405) where Le Maçon uses the more minimal structure 'la baisa, & embrassa' (LM, 252ʳ) which comes straight from the Italian. Although these changes do not add up to the level of changes to style, characterization, tone and narrative introduced by Sabatier, they bear mention here because they prevent us quite definitively from classifying Demeurisse's translation of the Griselda tale as a passive retranslation concerned mostly with linguistic modernization.

Although there was no simple way to describe either Le Maçon's or Sabatier's translation of *Decameron* X. 10, it is particularly difficult to categorize Demeurisse's version. We can be sure that Demeurisse, in contrast to Sabatier, used Le Maçon's translation not just as a resource but as a source. In fact, we might go so far as to say that he is not translating Boccaccio's tale at all but rather Le Maçon's 'great translation'. It is also clear that Demeurisse's version can be considered a retranslation: although he does not limit himself to endogenetic changes, he definitely has not engaged in the kind of rewriting seen in Sabatier's version. But there are other aspects of Demeurisse's Griselda tale which are harder to grasp. In fact, there are a number of unusual blends in this version. At a textual level, the retention of synonymic doublets limits the effects of the dominant trend towards modernization. Brénot's accompanying illustrations are also temporally unanchored, since the women they depict wear boat-neck tops of the 1950s alongside gowns with pointed shoes and caps which are reminiscent of a highly stylized take on the medieval period. The images therefore create an interesting blend of time periods, as well as blending the literary with the pulp tradition. However, this blend is limited since the titillating nature of these images does not mirror a more salacious tone in Demeurisse's translation. This is nowhere more clear than at the end of *Decameron* X. 10. Dioneo's bawdy line, 'l'avesse fuori in camiscia cacciata, s'avesse sí a un altro fatto scuotere il pilliccione che riuscito ne fosse una bella roba' (GB, 69), was translated literally by Le Maçon but, as in Sabatier, actually gets toned down by Demeurisse through an instance of generalization: '[...] aurait accepté **les caresses d'un autre** et su gagner ainsi une belle robe' (HD, 406). In the absence of a translator's introduction, we are left to wonder about the 'skopos', or purpose, of this retranslation and about the role of the images therein. Whatever its intended purpose, and despite its being largely ignored in the secondary literature, Demeurisse's version clearly has the effect of extending the afterlife of Le Maçon's translation in a very vivid way and, as such, it is central to our work on genealogies of (re)translations.

5. Discussion

Although we might use this study to draw attention to the long history and enduring significance of the reception of Boccaccio in French, its principal contribution is to help us to further our understanding of two current issues in translation studies, namely retranslation and fidelity. As we saw in Section 1, one primary concern of current scholarship is to create typologies of motivations for retranslation. Our textual analyses in Sections 2–4, however, called into question neat categorizations of retranslations as either passive (endogenetic and/or exogenetic) or active. On this score, paratext can be misleading. Sabatier's 'Préface de l'éditeur' claims that his translation is passive (both endogenetic and exogenetic), and Demeurisse's translation advertises its endogenetic passivity in its title. However, we have shown that at the textual level, both of these translations are active in many respects. We suggest that all retranslations should be understood as containing moments of activeness and passiveness, and that these moments can productively be distinguished and analysed. In addition, our work has shown that retranslations can be active or passive not just in relation to their source text, but also with respect to previous (re)translations. The same applies to domestication and foreignization which lie at the heart of the retranslation hypothesis; it would be meaningless to use Demeurisse's *Decameron* to test this hypothesis because his is a modernization of Le Maçon's translation and Boccaccio's text is all but irrelevant. Indeed, the very blending and layering which we saw in Demeurisse's version of the Griselda tale indicate that it would also resist any kind of simple categorization as regards the retranslation hypothesis. Our critical stance on traditional categories such as active/passive and foreignizing/domesticating does not mean that they are of no value. Instead, we suggest that they are more revealing when applied locally rather than in any holistic manner.

A similar level of nuance is required when it comes to the even trickier notion of fidelity. Like McLaughlin, we have shown that there is value in reconsidering a reputedly faithful translation. There is no doubt that Le Maçon's Renaissance translation of the *Decameron* is relatively faithful to Boccaccio's original Italian but it is not faithful in an absolute sense. We need to use close textual analysis to track moments and patterns of departure from the source in order to understand the nature of Le Maçon's project and, crucially in the case of a 'great translation', the consequences of those departures for later translations. It seems to us that working on fidelity in the context of retranslation is particularly productive because it draws attention to the complexity of this notion and to the paradoxes which surround it. Retranslation by necessity complicates the status of fidelity by adding a potential second source text into the equation. A retranslation such as Sabatier's triangulates between the original source and a previous ('great') translation, thereby creating a doubled fidelity which alters the typical relationship between the source and the target texts. On the other hand, when the original source drops out of the process, as is the case with Demeurisse, the only kind of fidelity that is relevant is fidelity to the earlier translation. Paradoxically, then, in the context of retranslation, fidelity can entail infidelity.

Comparing these three genealogically linked translations also further underscores the flexibility and historically relative nature of fidelity. Fidelity has been used as a criterion to evaluate French translations of the *Decameron* either positively (in the case of Le Maçon's translation whose long afterlife depends on its fidelity) or negatively (in the case of Sabatier whose translation was criticized by Mirabeau for being too faithful, despite the fact that readers today would no doubt judge it to be the least faithful of the three examined here). Despite its changing meanings, one constant about the term 'fidelity' itself is its discursive power. It is useful to refer here to feminist and queer translation scholarship which highlight the overlap between translational metaphors of fidelity and gender relations, showing that translations have been feminized and considered subordinate to their originals.[46] In this theoretical context, a translator, editor, or scholar's claiming or identifying fidelity can be understood as performative. This allows us to move beyond a more structural approach which favours neat categories towards an approach which recognizes dynamicity, multiplicity and variability. This will draw us to explore in a new light apparent disconnects between the text and the paratext, between the translator's motivation and the translation's reception, and between different translation decisions. By focusing on translations of the story of the (in)famously patient Griselda in our analysis, we have also highlighted the interventions that translators place upon this tale in order to reveal the active decisions that are always present in a work of translation, and our analysis therefore works against the concept of translation as an inactive form of literary production.

This investigation of three French translations of *Decameron* x. 10 was directly inspired by both the methods and content of McLaughlin's article on Latin versions of the same tale. We replicated those aspects of his methodology which we found to be the most promising, including the transhistorical and comparative components, as well as the close textual analysis. We hope to have shown the value of combining literary history and translation studies, both at the theoretical and the methodological levels. We also hope to have made a small contribution to the development of appropriate methods for translation history by showing the value that lies in studying translations that are linked genealogically. It is this approach that led us to examine a translation of the *Decameron* that lies outside the canon, and it is this approach that helped to reveal a literary historical narrative that is not linear. There of course remains much more work to be done on the many other translations, rewritings and adaptations of the Griselda tale in French, not to mention the other 99 tales that make up Boccaccio's masterpiece.[47] In the meantime, we conclude here by returning to the title of our contribution and its obvious intertextual reference to both Italo Calvino's *Perché leggere i classici* and to its English translation by Martin McLaughlin.[48] At the end of his 'Translator's Introduction', McLaughlin suggests adding another definition of what a classic is to the fourteen already provided by Calvino: 'A classic is a work which (like each of Calvino's texts) retains a consciousness of its own modernity without ceasing to be aware of other classic works of the past.'[49] It struck us that by replacing 'classic' with 'retranslation', we would have a very fitting definition of retranslation as conceptualized in the present study: 'A *retranslation* is a work which [...] retains a consciousness of its own modernity without ceasing to be aware of other *(re)translations* of the past.'

Notes to Chapter 4

A note from Mairi McLaughlin: Our contribution to this festschrift is intended to recognize the important contribution made by my father, Martin McLaughlin, to the field of Italian studies and to my own development as a scholar and teacher. Along with my mother, he fostered within me a deep love of language and letters. My father did all the normal things like teaching me to drive but he also taught me to read Virgil and Horace, and I attribute my own proclivity for close reading to nights spent poring over Latin texts with him during my teenage years. I might always have gone on to become a linguist, but it is only because of him that I became interested in translation and have ended up working with graduate students in literary studies like Linda and Diana. I hope that despite his humility, he can be proud of his work reflected here. With the exception of this footnote, the rest of the essay was planned, researched and written jointly by the three co-authors.

1. Martin McLaughlin, 'Humanist Rewriting and Translation: The Latin Griselda from Petrarch to Neri de' Nerli', *Humanistica*, 1.2 (2006), 23–40.
2. To avoid confusion between one of the co-authors of this essay and the Festschrift's dedicatee, any references to Mairi McLaughlin's work will use her full name. Here and throughout, 'McLaughlin' refers only to Martin McLaughlin.
3. McLaughlin, p. 30.
4. Ibid., p. 40.
5. Ibid., p. 40.
6. Antoine Le Maçon, *Le Décaméron de Mesire Jehan Bocace Florentin, Nouvellement traduict d'Italien en Francoys par Maistre Anthoine le Maçon conseiller du Roy & tresorier de lextraordinaire de ses guerres* (Paris: Estienne Rosset, 1545); cited as LM with folio number.
7. Antoine Sabatier de Castres, *Contes de J. Bocace, Traduction nouvelle, enrichie de belles Gravures*, 10 vols (London [Paris]: [n. pub.], 1779); cited as SdC with page numbers referring to Vol. 1 (in the case of the preface) and to Vol. x (in the case of the Griselda story).
8. Henri Demeurisse, *Contes de Boccacce: traduits par Antoine le Maçon et mis en français moderne par Henri Demeurisse*, 2 vols (Paris: Editions du Demi-Jour, 1955); cited as HD with page number.
9. For an overview of French translations of all of Boccaccio's work until the mid-twentieth century, see Patricia M. Gathercole, 'The French Translators of Boccaccio', *Italica*, 46.3 (1969), 300–09.
10. For formal definitions of key terms from translation studies, see Anthony Pym, *Exploring Translation Theories* (London: Routledge, 2010), ch. 2.
11. See Mairi McLaughlin, 'Etat Présent: Translation Studies', *French Studies*, 68.3 (2014), 377–85 (pp. 381–83).
12. Lieven D'hulst, 'Translation History', in *Handbook of Translation Studies*, ed. by Yves Gambier and Luc van Doorslaer (Amsterdam: Benjamins, 2010), pp. 397–405 (p. 403).
13. Lynne Long, 'History and Translation', in *A Companion to Translation Studies*, ed. by Piotr Kuhiwczak and Karin Littau (Clevedon: Multilingual Matters, 2007), pp. 63–76 (p. 75).
14. Theo Hermans, for example, regrets the fact that only one book treats the question of methodology, namely Anthony Pym, *Method in Translation History* (London: Routledge, 1998). See Theo Hermans, 'Introduction: How is Translation Possible?', in *Between Cultures and Texts: Itineraries in Translation History*, ed. by Antoine Chalvin, Anne Lange and Daniele Monticelli (Frankfurt a.M.: Lang, 2011), pp. 11–18 (p. 13).
15. Şehnaz Tahir Gürçağlar, 'Translation History', in *The Routledge Handbook of Translation Studies*, ed. by Carmen Millán and Francesca Bartrina (London: Routledge, 2013), pp. 131–43 (p. 134).

16. Petrarch's Latin version dating from 1373 was the source for the first two prose translations of the tale: a translation attributed to Philippe de Mézières, finished before 1395, and an anonymous translation dating from the mid-fifteenth century. For more information on the early French translations of the Griselda tale, see Marie-Dominique Leclercq, 'L'Histoire de Grisélidis en France: les éditions anciennes', in *Griselda: Metamorfosi di un mito nella società europea, Atti del Convegno internazionale a 80 anni dalla nascita della Società per gli Studi Storici della Provincia di Cuneo*, ed. by Rinaldo Comba and Marco Piccat with Giovanni Coccoluto (Cuneo: Società per gli Studi Storici, Archeologici ed Artistici della Provincia di Cuneo, 2011), pp. 211–39.
17. Antoine Berman, 'La Retraduction comme espace de la traduction,' *Palimpsestes*, 4 (1990), 1–7. For references to recent scholarship, see Mairi McLaughlin, 'État présent', p. 379, n. 17.
18. Berman, p. 1.
19. Ibid., p. 2.
20. Ibid., p. 6.
21. Pym, *Method in Translation History*, pp. 82–83.
22. Yves Gambier, 'La Retraduction: ambiguïtés et défis', in *Autour de la retraduction: perspectives littéraires européennes — avec un texte inédit de Jean-René Ladmiral*, ed. by Enrico Monti and Peter Schnyder (Paris: Orizons, 2011), pp. 49–66 (p. 63).
23. For example see Isabelle Desmidt, '(Re)translation Revisited', *Meta: journal des traducteurs / Meta: Translators' Journal*, 54.4 (2009), 669–83, or Sharon Deane-Cox, *Retranslation: Translation, Literature and Reinterpretation*, Bloomsbury Advances in Translation (London: Bloomsbury, 2014).
24. McLaughlin, p. 23.
25. Ibid., p. 27.
26. See Emma Campbell, 'Sexual Poetics and the Politics of Translation in the Tale of Griselda', *Comparative Literature* 55.3 (2003), 191–216 (p. 194).
27. The first complete French *Decameron* translation by Laurent de Premierfait (1411–14) was based on an intermediary translation into Latin. For a recent critical edition, see Laurent de Premierfait, *Décaméron*, ed. by Giuseppe di Stefano, Bibliothèque du Moyen Français, 3 (Montreal: CERES, 1998).
28. Jean Balsamo, 'Introduction', in *Les Traductions de l'italien en français au XVIe siècle*, ed. by Jean Balsamo, Vito Castiglione Minischetti and Giovanni Dotoli (Fasano: Schena; Paris: Hermann, 2009), pp. 15–64 (p. 21).
29. As in McLaughlin's article, references for all quotations from the translations are given in parentheses in the text alongside the translator's initials. See the notes to Section 1 for full bibliographical details. Quotations from the Italian are accompanied by the initials GB and a section number referring to the same edition used by McLaughlin: Giovanni Boccaccio, *Decameron*, ed. by Vittore Branca, 2 vols (Turin: Einaudi, 1980), II, 1232–48; these section numbers are the same as those used by the Decameron Web <http://www.brown.edu/Departments/Italian_Studies/dweb/texts/> [accessed 1 July 2015]. We noticed a printing error affecting the folio numbers in the two different copies of Le Maçon's translation that we were able to consult. We cite the correct folio numbers here and not the printed numbers, so that *Decameron* x. 10 starts on 248^v and ends on 252^r. A version with corrections in pencil can be seen in the Bodleian Library.
30. Le Maçon implicitly criticizes his predecessor's translation in the prefatory letter (LM, a2^r).
31. Marian Rothstein, 'Translation and the Triumph of French: The Case of the *Decameron*', in *Translation in French and Francophone Literature and Film*, ed. by James Day, French Literature Series, 36 (Amsterdam: Rodopi, 2009), pp. 17–33 (p. 22).
32. The French spelling is modernized minimally as follows: we distinguish between i/j and u/v; represent the tilde as a nasal consonant; and modernize the long s.
33. The term 'logisieren' comes from the following discussion of intellectualization through translation: Jiří Levý, *Die literarische Übersetzung: Theorie einer Kunstgattung*, trans. by Walter Schamschula (Frankfurt a.M.: Athenäum, 1969) p. 117.
34. McLaughlin, p. 33.
35. Balsamo, p. 17.
36. Marguerite Messina, 'Le due prime traduzioni in francese de *Il Decameron*', *Revue romane*, 12 (1977), 39–53 (pp. 48–49).

37. McLaughlin, p. 30.
38. Gathercole, p. 305.
39. Honoré-Gabriel Riquetti, comte de Mirabeau, *Nouvelles de Jean Boccace [...]*, Tome Premier (Paris: L. Duprat, Latellier et Cie, 1802), 'Avis de l'Editeur'.
40. McLaughlin, p. 25.
41. Gathercole, p. 308.
42. Ibid.
43. Jean Bourciez, *Decameron. Le Décaméron* (Paris: Garnier, 1952). The difference between these two translations maps onto a distinction between the two traditions of erotic and scholarly Decameron translations in English since the 1890s. See Cormac Ó Cuilleanáin, 'Translating Boccaccio', in *The Cambridge Companion to Boccaccio*, ed. by Guyda Armstrong, Rhiannon Daniels and Stephen J. Milner (Cambridge: Cambridge University Press, 2015), pp. 203–18 (p. 211). In bringing together the history of French and English translations of Boccaccio, Ó Cuilleanáin also highlights other aspects of Boccaccio translations that these two traditions share.
44. Rothstein, p. 22, n. 6.
45. See, for example, Guyda Armstrong, 'Eroticism *à la française*: Text, Image, and Display in Nineteenth-Century English Translations of Boccaccio's *Decameron*', *Word & Image*, 30.3 (2014), 194–212.
46. For a discussion of feminist translation theory and fidelity, see Rosemary Arrojo, 'Fidelity and the Gendered Translation', *TTR: Traduction, Terminologie, Rédaction*, 7.2 (1994), 147–63.
47. A future study should also address an obvious gap in the current approach whereby variation in the editions used as source texts is not taken into account. This will be particularly difficult in the case of Le Maçon because, as far as we know, the Italian edition that he used has not been established. See, for example, Messina, p. 52.
48. See Italo Calvino, *Perché leggere i classici* (Milan: Mondadori, 1991) and Italo Calvino, *Why Read the Classics*, trans. by Martin McLaughlin (New York: Vintage Books, 2000).
49. Martin McLaughlin, 'Translator's Introduction', in Calvino, *Why Read the Classics*, pp. vii-x (p. x).

CHAPTER 5

La raffigurazione del potere nell'*Orlando furioso*

Marco Dorigatti

L'*Orlando furioso* costituisce un osservatorio privilegiato sull'idea di potere come pure sulle sue multiformi manifestazioni. Il potere, infatti, vi è raffigurato su un doppio piano: quello interno, rappresentato da personaggi appartenenti alla finzione letteraria e che fanno capo alle figure di Carlo Magno da una parte e Agramante dall'altra, e quello esterno, costituito invece da personalità attinte direttamente dall'attualità contemporanea, come vedremo tra breve. Due piani, quello della favola e quello della realtà, che peraltro — e questa è la grande novità del poema ariostesco — non mancano di intersecarsi scambiando le loro prerogative: ecco allora che, all'atto di entrare nel poema ariostesco, i personaggi reali spesso assumono tratti e comportamenti cavallereschi, mentre quelli appartenenti alla sfera propriamente letteraria non di rado alludono a modi e parvenze della realtà storica. Nel *Furioso*, cioè, e in special modo nella versione del 1516, l'autore cerca di far coesistere reale e immaginario in un complesso rapporto osmotico, dove il problema sta semmai nel discernere il punto — di contatto come pure di demarcazione — fra tradizione letteraria e attualità storica, che è quanto si cercherà di fare, cominciando da una perlustrazione del piano esterno.

1. Figure della realtà

Una rassegna delle figure tratte dalla realtà storica deve necessariamente partire da quella che si impone all'attenzione del lettore con maggiore evidenza, ossia dal dedicatario del poema, 'il liberal, magnanimo, sublime, | gran Cardinal dela Chiesa di Roma' (III. 56. 3–4 ABC[1]), al secolo Ippolito I d'Este (1479–1520). Un ritratto tornato alla luce di recente a Vienna, dopo che se ne erano perse le tracce, ci restituisce l'immagine come doveva apparire all'altezza del 1508–1510, indubitabile in forza della presenza, sul retro della tavola, dello stemma cardinalizio che ne comprova l'identità.[2] Ed è, quella che ci viene incontro, un'immagine sorprendente (Fig. 1). Un volto latteo (tipico di un frequentatore della notte) emerge dal fondo scuro della tela e fissa intensamente l'osservatore; ma qui conviene cedere la parola a Marialucia Menegatti:

> Ippolito riserva, almeno in gioventù, una dedizione maniacale al proprio aspetto. Le sue curatissime 'manine' piacciono moltissimo alle disinvolte dami-

Fig. 5.1. Bartolomeo Veneto (attribuito a), *Ritratto di Ippolito d'Este* (ca. 1508–10), olio su tavola, 60,5 × 48,5 cm, Vienna, Dorotheum, presso cui il dipinto fu battuto all'asta il 17 ottobre 2012

gelle estensi, la lunga capigliatura gli attira i rimbrotti di Giulio II che gli intima di accorciare la 'zazzarina', poco confacente a un cardinale, e di smettere di 'far tanto la nympha'.[3]

La ricomparsa del dipinto congiunta alla certezza del soggetto raffigurato ha permesso di pervenire ad un ulteriore accertamento, dal punto di visto artistico anche più rilevante. Si tratta del *Ritratto di giovane* di Raffaello conservato a Budapest e già ritenuto effigie del giovane Pietro Bembo, il quale però — secondo Alessandro Ballarin,[4] cui si deve una più fondata attribuzione — altro non sarebbe che un *Ritratto del cardinale Ippolito d'Este* (Fig. 5.2), che lo coglie in un periodo antecedente (ca. 1504–1505) rispetto all'altro dipinto, più o meno come doveva presentarsi all'Ariosto nel momento in cui questi entrava al suo servizio.

Sennonché, questo temperamento languido e un po' effeminato che traspare dall'arte coeva non è il solo tratto significativo di Ippolito. Occorre infatti tener conto di un altro lato del suo carattere che in certo modo lo completa fornendoci un ritratto più realistico, come già osservava a suo tempo Giuseppe Antonelli:

> Il nostro cardinale amava grandemente lo studio, e Celio Calcagnini ci racconta a questo proposito, che Ippolito passava studiando la maggior parte della notte, e che per qualunque affare importante e pressante che avesse, non ommetteva mai di leggere un qualche libro; ed aggiunge, che ne' suoi viaggi sempre seco trasportava buon numero di volumi.[5]

Né si trattava di letture unicamente ricreative:

> Era Ippolito di vivace e penetrante ingegno, coltivò le matematiche e singolar-mente la geometria, l'aritmetica e la prospettiva, secondoché scrissero il ricordato Calcagnini nell'elogio funebre che recitò nelle di lui sontuose esequie fatte nella nostra cattedrale, e nell'altro che nelle Settime replicò Alessandro Guarini.[6]

Alla lista di interessi si dovrebbe aggiungere perlomeno quello per l'astronomia (testimoniato ancora una volta da Calcagnini) nonché quello per la musica (fu gran collezionista di strumenti musicali e cultore di musica sacra): senza contare che, ogni tanto, sua Eminenza si occupava pure di religione...

È questa l'immagine del cardinale — più complessa e variegata di quella vulgata, seppure mancante ancora di una sintesi complessiva — che presiede alla nascita e alla stesura dell'*Orlando furioso*. Un'immagine fortemente giovanile (accentuata dal fatto che Ippolito ha 4 anni e mezzo meno di Ludovico, suo stipendiato) di un prelato *dandy*, con le 'manine' affusolate (chiaramente visibili nel dipinto di Budapest), dedito alle attività sportive (sua passione era la caccia[7]) come pure culturali e scientifiche, che la storiografia moderna ha cercato di sminuire se non addirittura di rimuovere dal testo ariostesco. Basti per tutti il giudizio di Panizzi, secondo cui 'IPPOLITO was a haughty, cruel, and grasping prelate, who, with an immense fortune, never did any thing for the good of mankind',[8] per non dire per l'autore del *Furioso*. Né si tarda a comprenderne la ragione. Ippolito fu vittima di una *damnatio memoriae* perpetrata dallo stesso Ariosto nelle *Satire* postume al poema (la prima in special modo), sintomo di un profondo *malaise* che però — e qui sta il punto cruciale, non ancora recepito dalla critica — insorge e si palesa soltanto

Fig. 5.2. Raffaello Sanzio, *Ritratto del cardinale Ippolito d'Este* (ca. 1504–05), olio su tavola, 54 × 39 cm, Budapest, Szépművészeti Múzeum

attorno il 1515, allorché il rapporto tra i due effettivamente comincia a deteriorarsi, giungendo ad una e vera propria rottura nell'ottobre del 1517, in seguito al rifiuto del poeta di seguire il cardinale in Ungheria. Se così, pare incongruo o quantomeno anacronistico leggere (sulla scia dei biografi cinquecenteschi) il poema alla luce di questa frattura, che non si manifesta che tardivamente, nelle fasi conclusive della composizione.

L'*Orlando furioso* vide la luce sotto altro segno, che è quello che traspare dall'opera medesima purché, abbandonando un pregiudizio secolare, si sappia ridare credibilità alla voce del poeta. Sta di fatto che la figura — anzi il personaggio — del cardinale Ippolito non è, nell'economia dell'opera, una presenza saltuaria o accessoria, bensì un filo conduttore. Signore per antonomasia, interlocutore del poeta narratore, tacito garante delle sue affermazioni oltre che dedicatario dell'opera, egli è anche un principe che all'occorrenza non esita a calarsi nel ruolo protagonista di difensore della patria minacciata da nemici esterni. In questo senso nessuna impresa può paragonarsi per risonanza ma soprattutto per la sua portata teatrale e propagandistica alla vittoria da lui riportata nella battaglia della Polesella, combattuta sulle rive del Po contro la flotta veneziana il 22 dicembre 1509. '[F]u tale questa vittoria — scriverà Paolo Zerbinati, testimonio oculare — che si può anoverare fra le più memorabile de tutti li seculi, attesa la facilità del vincere et la grandezza dell'armata vinta e la potenza de nemici cioè di una signoria di Venetia formidabile per terra ma più in aqua.'[9] Iperbole a parte, lo Zerbinati non si sbagliava: non solo la vittoria era stata clamorosa ma si doveva ascrivere quasi esclusivamente ad Ippolito. Il lettore moderno sarà magari scettico, ma la conferma arriva nientemeno che dal duca Alfonso, suo fratello, che da Ferrara, dove si trovava in quel mentre, gli inviava il seguente dispaccio: 'Vorei sapere ringratiare vostra signoria et congratularmi con quella di sì proprio et felicissimo successo di sì gloriosa et comodissima victoria.'[10] Ad essa concorreva non soltanto la passione per le arti belliche ma anche per le scienze naturali: il cardinale, infatti, aveva atteso la piena del fiume avvenuta a notte tarda, la quale, innalzando il livello delle acque, aveva portato le imbarcazioni nemiche all'altezza degli argini, rendendole così facili bersagli. Al resto pensò l'artiglieria, fatta scattare al momento più opportuno.[11]

Eppure, non è così che l'Ariosto presenterà il fatto nel poema, e questo per una scelta ben precisa. L'immagine da lui introdotta fin dal terzo canto (e che si riverbera lungo l'intero arco del poema fino ad assurgere a mito) è, rispetto alla storia, diversamente configurata:

> costui *con pochi a piedi e meno in sella*
> veggio uscir mesto, e poi tornar iocondo,
> che quindeci galee mena captive,
> oltra mill'altri legni, alle sue rive.
> (*Fur.*, III. 5. 5–8 ABC)

Qui il ruolo dell'artiglieria viene sottaciuto di proposito e la vittoria presentata come impresa tutta cavalleresca, evidente fin dall'impiego di espressioni tipiche, quali ad esempio '*con pochi a piedi e meno in sella*'. A che cosa mira l'operazione ariostesca? Ecco che nel momento di accogliere il cardinale Ippolito nella compagine del poema —

'fra' più degni Heroi' (I. 4. 1 ABC) che sono in gran parte anche suoi antenati — la vittoria che lo distingue viene mondata di quanto potrebbe inquinarla o sminuirla, massimamente l'uso delle armi da fuoco, già qui, nella prima edizione, sentite come incompatibili con il mondo cavalleresco, quindi con l'opera che il poeta va costruendo. Così facendo, egli conferisce al proprio 'signore' una sorta di 'patente cavalleresca' che lo mette sullo stesso piano degli altri personaggi del poema, gli 'Heroi' appunto; ed è evidente come, con tale espediente, l'Ariosto intenda creare un ponte tra il mondo della favola e quello della realtà.

L'immagine del principe dedicatario raffigurato come prode cavaliere ricorre anche altrove. L'esempio migliore si trova forse nel padiglione di Cassandra che Melissa trasporta da Bisanzio a Parigi in occasione delle nozze di Ruggiero e Bradamente; padiglione — merita ricordare — cui Ariosto alludeva già nel 1509 in una lettera in cui si complimentava col cardinale per la vittoria riportata alla Polesella.[12] Ebbene, nel padiglione, sul quale è ricamata l'infanzia di Ippolito, compare un'ottava che sarà soppressa nella redazione C (ma non in B, nonostante che a quella data il cardinale fosse già morto).[13] Essa mostra la *paideia* del principe 'giovinetto' che si prepara a diventare un cavaliere:

> Qua con molt'arte e con più forza lotta,
> e con robusti giovani s'afferra:
> par ch'abbattuti già n'habbia una frotta,
> e s'apparecchi a poner l'altri in terra.
> Là par ch'egli habbia più d'un'hasta rotta,
> armato in simulacro d'aspra guerra,
> *a piè e a cavallo, con ogni arma destro,*
> di tutti li altri e principe e maestro.
> (*Fur.*, XL. 64 AB; manca C)

'Attraverso la caccia e la lotta corpo a corpo, dunque l'attività ginnica — scrive Gerarda Stimato —, il cardinale è dipinto nell'atto di compiere imprese del tutto simili a quelle degli eroi del poema, ed in particolar modo a quelle del suo avo: Ruggiero'.[14] Per quanto possa sembrare lusinghiera o artefatta, l'immagine del principe guerriero è da ritenersi veritiera. Basti a provarlo la descrizione che del porporato estense traccia l'ambasciatore veneziano a Roma, Marino Giorgi: 'il cardinal di Ferrara [è] più atto alle armi che ad altro; ed è ricco'.[15] Tale caratterizzazione, del resto, è confermata dallo stesso Ariosto in un carme latino (LVII), scritto all'indomani della nomina di Ippolito a vescovo di Ferrara nell'ottobre 1503: 'Quis patre invicto gerit Hercule fortius arma?' ('Chi porta le armi con maggior fierezza d'Ercole, padre invitto?').[16]

Se Ippolito è il prelato che al bisogno non esita ad impugnare le armi e mettersi al posto di comando ('Come vincer si de', ne dimostraste', XIII. 2. 7 AB; XV C), Alfonso — il fratello maggiore che, con lui, forma una diarchia di potere che regge Ferrara — rappresenta, più che un sovrano intrepido o 'invicto', una guida fidata; 'Alfonso è quel che — come l'Ariosto dirà in BC (III. 51. 5–6) — col saper accoppia | [...] la bontà', una presenza rassicurante, specialmente nel momento di pericolo: 's'io vedrò voi, non tremarò alla voce' (XIII. 2. 6 AB; XV C). Ed anche Alfonso, presentandosi sul palcoscenico dell'*Orlando furioso*, tiene in mano la palma di una vittoria cui è legata la sua fama: si tratta della battaglia combattuta nei pressi di Ravenna la domenica di Pasqua (11 aprile 1512) a fianco dell'esercito francese contro le forze ispano-pontificie della Lega Santa voluta da Giulio II. Piccolo il contingente a sua disposizione (appena 300 soldati); ma furono le sue artiglierie, a quel tempo le più avanzate, a determinare la sorte del conflitto. Artiglierie che, beninteso, spariranno puntualmente dal resoconto che ne farà l'Ariosto:

> Costui serà, *col senno e con la lancia*,
> c'havrà nela pinifera campagna
> gloria d'haver l'exercito di Francia
> vincitor fatto contra Iulio e Spagna:
> nuotaranno i destrier sin alla pancia
> nel sangue humano, e i campi di Romagna
> veranno a sepelire il popul manco
> Tedesco, Hispano, Greco, Itàlo e Franco.
> (*Fur.*, III. 55 ABC)

Nel poema, cioè, anche la battaglia di Ravenna (tra le più sanguinose, come riconosce lo stesso Ariosto) si trasforma in vittoria cavalleresca, ottenuta 'col senno e con la lancia', segno che nel *Furioso* il potere, per essere degno di gloria, deve conformarsi ad un ideale cavalleresco. Ciò che stupisce è che, per il poeta, tale ideale non è stato sorpassato dalla storia, non è anacronistico; è un valore vivo.

Se mai vi fosse dubbio, lo dissiperebbe l'altro personaggio storico, colui che più di ogni altro impersona l'ideale del principe cavalleresco: Francesco I, appena salito al trono di Francia, nel 1515. La sua è una comparsa che si profila all'orizzonte *in extremis*, quando la composizione dell'opera sta per giungere a termine, ma che con ciò stesso rivela come l'autore non avesse ancora chiuso i conti con la contemporaneità storica. Francesco non solo compare tardi, ma anche arriva da fuori, d'oltralpe, recante anch'egli una palma (la vittoria conseguita sulla pianura di Marignano il 13–14 settembre 1515), ed è visto non come invasore, bensì un liberatore ('L'anno primier del fortunato regno, | non ferma anchor ben la corona in fronte, passerà l'Alpe [...]', *Fur.*, XXIV. 44. 1–3 AB; XXVI C). Su di lui si addensano le speranze dell'Ariosto che lo mette al centro di un apposito episodio semi-allegorico che inscena la lotta contro un 'Mostro', sotto cui si cela l'avarizia:

> Poi si vedea d'Imperïale alloro
> cinto le chiome *un cavallier* venire
> con tre giovani a par, che i gigli d'oro
> tessuti havean nel lor real vestire [...].
> (*Fur.*, XXIV. 34 AB; XXVI C)

I 'tre giovani' al suo seguito sono Massimiliano d'Austria, Carlo di Borgogna e Enrico d'Inghilterra, ma vi è anche Leone X. Si tratta di un drappello di principi uniti da una causa comune: la sconfitta dell'abominevole 'Mostro' e il trionfo della liberalità. Un sogno umanistico di concordia europea, come è stato osservato da più di un interprete, 'storicamente sfiorante almeno i limiti dell'utopia o dell'idillio',[17] ma che per l'Ariosto, che sa per esperienza quanto la liberalità sia rara, resta un ideale fortemente ambìto, anche a livello personale. La preminenza concessa a Francesco

I rivela anche, *e converso*, l'assenza, nelle prime posizioni (dove ci aspetteremmo di trovarlo), di colui che prima era stato definito 'il liberal [...] | gran Cardinal dela Chiesa di Roma' (III. 56. 3-4 ABC), ossia la sua retrocessione *e silentio*. È il re francese, ora, il capofila nella lotta contro l'avarizia, e la maniera in cui la debella è quella di 'un cavallier' che la combatte con la spada: 'L'un c'havea sin a l'elsa ne la pancia | la spada immersa alla maligna fiera, | Francesco primo, havea scritto, di Francia' (*Fur.*, XXIV. 35. 1-3 AB; XXVI C).

L'Ariosto non è il solo a guardare Francesco I con fiducia. Nel medesimo momento in cui fa questo inserto, nel tardo autunno del 1515, anche il Castiglione nella prima stesura del *Cortegiano* aggiungeva un proemio (indirizzato ad Alfonso Ariosto, l'allora dedicatario) che conteneva un ampio elogio di Francesco I (mirante a ingraziarlo a sé e alla causa urbinate). Tuttavia — e questo ci aiuta a comprendere la diversità con il caso dell'Ariosto –, giunto alla seconda redazione, elaborata tra il '18 e il '21, il Castiglione, pur conservando la dedica ad Alfonso Ariosto, non esiterà ad espungere la porzione encomiastica dedicata al sovrano francese. Così non farà, invece, il cantore del *Furioso*, la cui fedeltà è tanto più commovente se si pensa che nell'elezione imperiale del 1519 perfino il cardinale Ippolito si era dichiarato a favore di Carlo V, inviando a tale proposito Calcagnini a Francoforte. Possono mutare le alleanze nella politica ufficiale estense ('Fan lega hoggi Re, Papi e Imperatori; | diman seran nemici capitali [...]', XL. 13. 3-4 AB; XLIV. 2. 3-4 C), ma l'Ariosto non passerà mai dalla parte filospagnola, nel '21 come pure nel '32.

A farcelo capire è un altro inserto (*Fur.*, XV. 18-36 C; manca AB) aggiunto all'ultima redazione, per quanto si tratti di un brano controverso, che divide l'opinione degli studiosi. La maga Andronica, che assieme a Sofrosina scorta Astolfo di ritorno dal paese di Logistilla, approfitta del lungo viaggio per mostrargli le scoperte geografiche che verranno fatte in tempi di là da venire, in un segmento narrativo che in realtà — o perlomeno in apparenza — è una celebrazione di Carlo V e del suo ruolo provvidenziale, paragonato al ritorno di Astrea, intendasi la Giustizia ('Astrea veggio per lui riposta in seggio, | anzi di morta ritornata viva', XV. 26. 5-6 C), nonostante che in precedenza tale ruolo fosse già stato assegnato ad Alfonso ('Alfonso è quel [...] | ch'al secolo futuro | la gente crederà che sia dal cielo | tornata Astrea dove può il caldo e il gielo', III. 51. 5-8 ABC).

'Veggio la santa croce, e veggio i segni | imperïal nel verde lito eretti' (XV. 23. 1-2 C): così prende avvio il panegirico in onore di Carlo V, con un forte accento religioso, insolito per l'Ariosto che non lo usa mai nei casi che suscitano la sua partecipazione emotiva. Carlo è detto 'il più saggio imperatore e giusto, | che sia stato o sarà mai dopo Augusto' (24. 7-8), e per questo la divina Bontà 'vuol che sotto a questo imperatore | solo un ovile sia, solo un pastore' (26. 7-8), secondo quanto sta scritto nell'apostolo Giovanni (X. 16: 'et fiet unum ovile et unus pastor'). Ma rappresenta la nuova posizione assunta dall'Ariosto all'indomani del convegno di Bologna (novembre 1529), oppure si tratta di un omaggio a Carlo V che in realtà nasconde un che di freddo nei suoi confronti? Come già accennato, i pareri degli interpreti sono discordi su questo punto. Secondo taluni si assisterebbe ad un atto di integrazione ovvero di adesione alla politica imperiale da parte dell'Ariosto: così pensano, ad esempio, Rajna ('È questo uno dei pochi elogi sinceri e propriamente meritati che ci accada di ascoltare nel *Furioso*'),[18] Moretti (che presenta l'avvicinamento alla politica imperiale come rinuncia al sogno di concordia europea accarezzato nella prima edizione),[19] Casadei (secondo cui 'la sconfitta di Francesco [...] ebbe senza alcun dubbio un peso nell'indirizzare l'attenzione del poeta verso il campo imperiale. Ma era soprattutto la grande operazione ideologico-culturale condotta da Carlo e dai suoi consiglieri a trovare disponibile Ariosto, e con lui buona parte dei letterati coevi')[20] e Jossa (che vede nel *Furioso* del '32 'una speranza di restaurazione dell'età dell'oro',[21] ossia 'l'adesione al sogno dell'Impero universale').[22] Questa lettura non pare tuttavia convincente. Anzitutto è da notare che l'Ariosto non sopprime, quindi non ritratta, quanto già scritto, mantenendo pressoché intatto, pur integrandolo, l'impianto ideologico quale si presentava all'altezza di AB: strano a dirsi se, come nella realtà, Carlo V doveva soppiantare Francesco I. Inoltre, il suo elogio è ambiguo. 'En effet — osserva Sangirardi, cui si devono pagine illuminanti su questo argomento — la leçon d'histoire prophétique d'Andronica à Astolfo se termine par un éloge d'Andrea Doria (30. 6–35) d'une vigueur et d'une ampleur même supérieures à celui de Charles-Quint',[23] elogio che pertanto supera, eclissandolo, quello di Carlo V: e basterebbe soltanto questo a mettere in subordine, rispetto ai suoi ministri, colui che è il sovrano. Ma non è tutto. Hempfer ci ricorda che 'François Ier est glorifié aussi dans l'addition de 1532 pour sa victoire sur les Suisses en 1515 à Marignan (O. F., XXXIII. 43)',[24] mentre Segre, forse colui che ha visto più a fondo, afferma che 'quando, sul filo dei ricordi, l'Ariosto allude alla sconfitta di Francesco I nella battaglia di Pavia (1525) e alla vittoria del "sagace Spagnuol", coadiuvato da Francesco e Alfonso d'Ávalos (XXXIII. 51), è chiaro che il suo cuore è tutto dalla parte del re francese':[25] 'A Carlo V, del resto, è evidente che l'Ariosto rinfaccia soprattutto, pur non nominandolo, il sacco di Roma (1527)'.[26]

Manca ancora un particolare a completare il ritratto di Carlo V nel *Furioso*. È un sovrano potente, che regna sopra un 'grande impero', ma non è un *cavaliere*, come invece lo era e lo è ancora, anche nella sconfitta, Francesco I. L'Ariosto gli concede bensì il 'valor' militare, ma non 'la lancia' o altro attributo cavalleresco, prerogativa che, semmai, sembra concedere più volentieri ai suoi capitani.

2. Figure dell'immaginario

Veniamo così alla rappresentazione del potere sul piano interno, costituito da personaggi che appartengono alla finzione letteraria, dove quel che conta eventualmente rilevare è lo scarto tra l'innovazione ariostesca e la tradizione cavalleresca. Il primo ad affacciarsi alla ribalta e ad attirare la nostra attenzione è ovviamente Carlo Magno, 'uno imperator de' più lodati | che mai tenuto al mondo abbiano corte', secondo la caratterizzazione di Rinaldo (*Fur.*, XVI. 33. 5–6 C). Eppure, a proposito di nessun altro personaggio l'opinione degli interpreti ha oscillato tanto come a proposito di Carlo. Egli sembra fungere da specchio in cui si riflette sia il passato che il presente, storico come pure letterario. Se infatti ai commentatori cinquecenteschi pareva di ritrovarvi le sembianze di un re virgiliano (così ad l'esempio Fausto da

Longiano, uno dei primissimi a trattare le fonti del poema: 'Sotto la persona di Carlo Re di Francia è ritratto il Re Latino; sotto Agramante, Turno'),[27] altri non hanno esitato a ravvisarvi l'immagine di un regnante attuale, nella fattispecie Carlo V (Giudicetti);[28] mentre per altri la versione ariostesca del personaggio avrebbe acquistato, non diversamente da Agramante, 'una generica dignità regale nel confronto del poema boiardesco' (Fubini),[29] risultando nondimeno l'uno e l'altro 'tendenzialmente indifferenti al lettore, anche perché non si esimono [...] dal compiere azioni ciniche, spietate' (Giudicetti).[30]

Nel *Furioso*, il ruolo di Carlo appare tutto sommato secondario, se non scontato, specialmente ove si distingua la carica (in quanto rappresentante della massima autorità cristiana) dalla funzione narrativa (la parte effettivamente svolta nel poema). Manca nella sua parabola biografica un gesto paragonabile alla famosa 'guanciata' ovvero guantata con cui, preso dalla rabbia, l'imperatore aveva colpito al volto il nipote Rolando nell'*Entrée d'Espagne* (vv. 11.086–137),[31] o un evento protagonistico equiparabile alla decisione presa da Agramante di invadere la Francia. Il suo è un ruolo complementare, perlopiù di difesa (come si evince particolarmente dall'assedio di Parigi), che si limita a spronare e rincuorare i meno intrepidi o a scongiurare la rovina ('– Dove fuggite turba spaventata? | non è tra voi chi 'l danno suo contempli? [...] — Così Carlo dicea, che d'ira acceso | tanta vergogna non potea patire', XV. 7. 5–6; 8. 5–6 AB; XVII C).

Diversamente dalla sua controparte saracena, raramente Carlo appare di persona alla testa di un esercito ('Trovò tutto il contrario al suo pensiero | in questa parte il Re de' Saracini: | perché in persona il capo de l'Impero | eravi Carlo, e de' suoi paladini', XIII. 8. 3–4 AB; XV C); e così pure raramente, anzi una sola volta, lo vediamo impegnato in un'azione guerriera ('Al fin de le parole urta il destriero, | con l'hasta bassa, al Saracino adosso', XV. 16. 1–2 AB; XVII C), peraltro soltanto accennata. Anche a XXXVIII. 79 C si dice che 'Da l'altra parte fuor di gran ripari | Re Carlo uscì con la sua gente d'arme | con li ordini medesmi e modi pari | che terria se venisse al fatto d'arme' (XXXIV. 79. 1–4 AB; XXXVIII C), ma si tratta di parata cerimoniale. Di certo Carlo non combatte di persona come combatte il suo rivale Agramante. È significativo che nel duello finale di Lipadusa tra i guerrieri non soltanto presenti ma anche combattenti figuri Agramante ma non la sua diretta controparte, che si trova a Parigi. Del resto, a differenza di Agramante — il quale, vale la pena ricordare, ha appena 'vinte e doï anni' secondo il Boiardo (*Inam.*, II. i. 16. 1–2[32]) –, Carlo è un uomo 'vecchio' (VIII. 70. 2 A), e il divario generazionale che li separa spicca ancor più nelle redazioni seriori ('o 'l vecchio Carlo, o 'l giovene Agramante', XXXV. 8. 8 B; XXXIX C), contrapponendo i 'giovenil furori' dell'uno alla stanca saggezza dell'altro. Ciò nonostante, l'età non pare il fattore determinante. Anche Sobrino, nell'altro campo, è vecchio ('D'una vecchiezza valida e robusta' lo dice l'autore a XXXVI. 54. 1–2 AB; XL C): ma di fronte alla possibilità di un combattimento, vale a dire di un atto cavalleresco, questi non si tira indietro malgrado gli anni, e infatti Sobrino prenderà parte nientemeno che al duello di Lipadusa.

Una presenza morale, quindi, quella di Carlo, più che di uomo d'azione; tant'è che poco si sposta da Parigi, ancora una volta in antitesi a quanto fa Agramante che si avventura fin dentro il cuore della Francia per poi ripiegare di nuovo verso l'Africa. Carlo, invece, stabile a Parigi, capitale dell'impero cristiano, non si spinge mai oltre Arli: nel *Furioso* tutta la sua esistenza si svolge nello spazio compreso tra queste due roccaforti.³³ Scarsi gli attributi cavallereschi, come abbiamo visto, ma resta da dire della carenza forse più grave: già Boiardo rimproverava Re Carlo 'perché tiéne ad Amor chiuse le porte | e sol se dete ale bataglie sante' (*Inam.*, II. xviii. 2. 5–6). Così non fa un vero cavaliere secondo Boiardo ('Però ch'Amor [...] dona ardir al cavalier armato', ibid., 3. 1–4), prontamente seguito dall'Ariosto.

Vi sono, è vero, le preghiere, che lo mettono in contatto con Dio e che ne fanno un 'imperator devoto' (XII. 73 AB; XIV C), come vuole una lunga tradizione; preghiere del resto non sempre bene accolte nel *Furioso* perché, se talvolta vengono esaudite (ad esempio a VIII. 70. 1–3 ABC: 'Il sommo Creator gli occhi rivolse | al giusto lamentar del vecchio Carlo, | e con sùbita pioggia il fuoco tolse'), talaltra Dio pare fare orecchi da mercante, ignorarle o fare giusto l'opposto ('Così Fortuna ad Agramante arrise, | ch'un'altra volta a Carlo assedio mise', XXV. 33. 7–8 AB; XXVII C).³⁴

Tra tutte, la preghiera rivolta a Dio alla vigilia della battaglia di Parigi (XII. 69. 6–72 AB; XIV C) rappresenta la sua prova oratoria più sostenuta, sia in termini di estensione (tre ottave e tre versi) che di eloquenza. Già la premessa, però, con il richiamo 'a preti, a frati e bianchi, neri e bigi', accomunati da nient'altro che un gioco cromatico (e letterario), motivo ludico impiegato anche altrove dall'Ariosto, pare negare sul nascere la possibilità di un sentimento religioso vero:

> L'Imperatore, il dì che 'l dì precesse
> de la battaglia, fe' dentro a Parigi
> per tutto celebrare uffici e messe
> a preti, a frati e bianchi, neri e bigi;
> e le genti che dianzi eran confesse,
> e di man tolte all'inimici stygi,
> tutti communicâr, non altrimente
> c'havessero a morire il dì seguente.
> (*Fur.*, XII. 68 AB; XIV C)

Rivolgendosi a Dio nel momento del massimo bisogno, Carlo gli propone un patto, in sostanza di soccorrere il proprio esercito affinché la fede cristiana non debba fare l'ennesima brutta figura (la sconfitta, infatti, non solo ne confermerebbe la cattiva reputazione ma 'li pagani diran che nulla puoi, | che perir lasci i partigiani tuoi', 70. 7–8); facendo appello, cioè, ad un principio utilitaristico di mera convenienza, per cui la vittoria rientrerebbe nell'interesse di Dio, quasi che essa non importasse al supplicante. Ben altro, se lo confrontiamo, il sentimento etico di Agramante (per di più un 'pagano'), il quale, dando un esempio luminoso, rifiuta proprio e anzitutto il principio utilitaristico come base della propria appartenenza religiosa.³⁵

Se per Rajna 'quelle preghiere di Carlo [...] mostrano chiaro quanto Lodovico abbia preso sul serio il soggetto',³⁶ Giudicetti sembra ribadire che

> Già Galileo ('vorrei che Carlo si contentasse di pregare Dio, senza starlo ad annoiare o consigliare'³⁷) aveva rilevato con irritazione la natura didattica dell'implorazione pronunciata dall'imperatore, che cerca di spingere Dio con

un 'tono quasi coercitivo'[38] ad agire in suo favore, non con un'umile richiesta nella quale dovrebbe consistere una domanda a Dio, bensì con argomenti vani e inconvenienti rispetto all'onnipotenza divina.[39]

Difficilmente, pertanto, 'di Carlo si può dire che sia stato restituito addirittura alla sua maestà primitiva', come reputava Rajna.[40] Non ha un rapporto privilegiato con la divinità e neanche spicca per doti cavalleresche. Quanto alla possibilità che possa in qualche modo alludere alla figura o al ruolo di Carlo V, come pretenderebbe qualcuno, è da dubitare se non altro per una semplice considerazione di ordine cronologico: tutta la parte che lo riguarda fu, nella sostanza, composta nel periodo antecedente al 1516, quindi prima dell'ascesa di Carlo V al trono imperiale.

Chi dunque, nell'*Orlando furioso*, tiene le redini del potere nello schieramento cristiano? Carlo di nome e in piccola parte di fatto; ma nella pratica, specialmente man mano che il poema si approssima alla conclusione, sono i paladini a prendere il comando. L'organizzazione dell'esercito imperiale, infatti, prevede un numero imprecisato ma certo cospicuo di uomini 'd'Italia, di Lamagna et Inghilterra, | che tutte son genti di valore, | et hanno i paladin sparsi tra loro | come le gemme in un riccamo d'oro' (*Fur.*, XXXV. 28. 5–8 A; 17 B; XXXIX C). Sono costoro ('le gemme'), dunque, il 'sostegno | del santo Imperio e la maggior colonna' (XL. 36. 1–2 AB; XLIV. 28 C), il punto di forza specialmente nei momenti in cui l'autorità centrale, nella fattispecie Carlo, è latitante.

È Orlando, ad esempio, l'Orlando da poco 'rinsavito', che assume la responsabilità generale per l'assedio e la presa di Biserta (XXXV. 75–76 A; 64–65 B; XXXIX C), e a cui spetta ogni decisione strategica, come stabilire 'Ch'ordine abbian tra lor, come s'assaglia | la gran Biserta, e da che lato e quando' (ibid., 76. 1–2 A; 65 BC). Si tratta di una battaglia marina e allo stesso tempo terrestre, momento determinante al quale però — ed è significativo — Carlo si trova assente. L'assedio è coordinato da Orlando, che ritiene per sé il comando generale delegando parte del potere ad Astolfo, che a sua volta impartisce ordini a Dudone (capo della flotta cristiana) e a Sansonetto (che conduce una propria armata). Astolfo si avvale anche del 'Senapo Imperator de la Etïopia' (XXX. 74. 1 A; 78 B; XXXIII. 102 C), come pure dei Nubi. All'operazione militare partecipano inoltre Oliviero e Brandimarte, ma è Orlando a svolgere mansioni che erano tipiche di Carlo, quali ad esempio rinforzare le difese (cfr. XXXVI. 20. 1–2 AB; XL C). Anche Rinaldo, da parte sua, svolge funzioni prima riservate all'imperatore: a IX. 75 sgg. AB (X. 75 C) passa in rassegna le truppe inglesi e scozzesi, 'mandato da Carlo'; a XIV. 29–38 (XVI C) le divide secondo la necessità e le arringa.

Si assiste, cioè, ad una metamorfosi per cui i principali paladini ovvero 'heroi' — Orlando, Rinaldo, Oliviero, Brandimarte e Astolfo, ma specialmente i primi due — assumono su di sé il ruolo di capitani o condottieri, riflesso della realtà contemporanea e anticipazione del mondo della *Gerusalemme liberata*; sennonché, nel *Furioso* la prodezza del capitano non è mai (o non del tutto) disgiunta dalla cavalleria, valore che per l'Ariosto è irrinunciabile.

Che cosa significa tutto ciò? Significa che sul piano interno, vale a dire al livello della favola, vi sono due forze che agiscono in competizione: una forza centripeta che tende a relegare il potere nell'autorità imperiale, e una forza centrifuga che agisce sui personaggi spingendoli a contrastare l'autorità centrale e a cercare spazi autonomi e individuali, anche perché i grandi assembramenti, tipici della corte e degli eserciti, sono percepiti in antitesi agli atti di cavalleria, per definizione opera del singolo, come faceva osservare Marfisa ai suoi compagni, 'dicendo che lodevole non era | ch'andasser tanti cavallieri insieme' (XVIII. 103. 1–2 AB; XX C). Ora, nell'*Orlando furioso* la forza centripeta è una forza debole, che non riesce a raggiungere i personaggi e ad imporsi in modo decisivo. Ciò spiega perché Carlo non sia nell'Ariosto detentore di un potere vero, come lo era indubbiamente nella primitiva *Chanson de Roland* o nella *Spagna*. Non lo può essere proprio perché, all'estremo opposto, è potente l'altra forza che spinge i personaggi a rivendicare una propria indipendenza, come emerge specialmente dalla parte iniziale e mediana del poema. Qui si assisterebbe, cioè, per usare le parole di Giuseppina Zironi, alla 'rivolta quasi inconsapevole ma fatale dei paladini contro il loro sovrano e, quindi, contro la loro fede. E questa rivolta, divenuta ormai esplicita, prende il sopravvento anche se, in conclusione, rientrerà nel corso della tradizione antica, dominata e redenta'.[41] Dalla tensione fra queste due spinte opposte si creano le condizioni favorevoli alle 'audaci imprese' e alle avventure, da ricercarsi piuttosto a Damasco che a Parigi, ossia in periferia: è questo il punto zero della forza centripeta, lo spazio privilegiato dell'individualità come pure dell'invenzione ariostesca.

Anche per questa ragione la figura di Carlo stenta a farsi portatrice di significati nuovi o allusivi a personaggi storici, legandosi piuttosto ad una consolidata tradizione letteraria che passa per il Pulci e il Boiardo. Senza contare che nel *Furioso*, come abbiamo visto, i rappresentanti del potere, quello vero, sono importati direttamente dal mondo reale e accolti nella favola secondo un piano dell'autore che prevede l'abbattimento del divario tra le due sfere, tra la poesia e la storia.

Notes to Chapter 5

Rappresenta, nella sostanza, la comunicazione tenuta al Sixty-First Annual Meeting of the Renaissance Society of America (RSA), svoltosi a Berlino dal 26 al 28 marzo 2015.

1. Tali sigle denotano le tre stampe originali dell'*Orlando furioso*, e cioè: A = Ferrara, per Giovanni Mazocco dal Bondeno, 1516; B = Ferrara, per Giovanni Battista da la Pigna milanese, 1521; C = Ferrara, per Francesco Rosso da Valenza, 1532. Salvo diversa indicazione, il testo delle diverse redazioni è conforme alle seguenti edizioni: A = *Orlando furioso secondo la princeps del 1516*, a cura di Marco Dorigatti, con la collaborazione di Gerarda Stimato (Firenze: Olschki, 2006); B = *Orlando furioso secondo l'edizione del 1532 con le varianti delle edizioni del 1516 e del 1521*, a cura di Santorre Debenedetti e Cesare Segre (Bologna: Commissione per i Testi di Lingua, 1960); C = *Orlando furioso*, a cura di Cesare Segre, in *Tutte le opere di Ludovico Ariosto*, I (Milano: Mondadori, 1964).
2. Cfr. Marialucia Menegatti, 'Ippolito d'Este e il ritratto di Raffaello a Budapest', in *Storiedellarte: un blog di storici dell'arte*, 20 marzo 2014 <http://storiedellarte.com/2014/03/ippolito-deste-e-il-ritratto-di-raffaello-a-budapest.html> [consultato il 16 maggio 2016].
3. Ibid.
4. Alessandro Ballarin, 'Nota sul Cardinale di Raffaello a Budapest: "Ippolito fa la ninfa"', in *Leonardo a Milano: problemi di leonardismo milanese tra Quattrocento e Cinquecento. Giovanni Antonio Boltraffio prima della pala Casio*, con la collaborazione di Marialucia Menegatti e Barbara Maria Savy, 4 voll. (Verona: Aurora, 2010), II, 990–1000.

5. *Vita del Cardinale Ippolito I. d'Este scritta da un anonimo, con annotazioni*, [a cura di Giuseppe Antonelli] (Milano: Tip. Paolo Ripamonti Carpano, 1843), p. 40.
6. Ibid. Quanto all'elogio funebre di Alessandro Guarini (1486–1556), si allude alla *Funebris oratio in Reveren. et Illustriss. Dominum D. Hippolytum Estensem* [...] *in Cathedrali Templo habita IIII Idus Septembres 1520*, Ferrara ca. 1520.
7. In tale veste, vale a dire nel ruolo di cacciatore, Ippolito figurava già nella *Venatio* di Ercole Strozzi, composta tra il 1594 e il 1500, in cui compariva anche il giovane Ariosto.
8. *Orlando Innamorato di Bojardo, Orlando Furioso di Ariosto, with an Essay on the Romantic Narrative Poetry of the Italians: Memoirs and Notes by Antonio Panizzi*, 9 voll. (Londra: Pickering, 1830–34), VI, *The Life of Ariosto*, p. xi, su cui si veda anche Marco Dorigatti, 'Il manoscritto dell'*Orlando furioso* (1505–1515)', in *L'uno e l'altro Ariosto in Corte e nelle Delizie*, a cura di Gianni Venturi (Firenze: Olschki, 2011), pp. 1–44 (pp. 8–9).
9. Giovanni Maria Zerbinati, *Croniche di Ferrara quali comenzano del anno 1500 sino al 1527*, a cura di Maria Giuseppina Muzzarelli (Ferrara: Deputazione provinciale ferrarese di storia patria, 1989), p. 87.
10. Foglietto accluso ad altra lettera firmata 'Frater Alfonsus dux Ferrariae', 22 dicembre 1509, Modena, Archivio di Stato; cfr. Enrica Guerra, 'L'educazione militare del cardinale Ippolito I d'Este', in *Formare alle professioni: la cultura militare tra passato e presente*, a cura di Monica Ferrari e Filippo Ledda (Milano: Franco Angeli, 2011), pp. 101–15 (p. 114).
11. Ibid., pp. 114–15.
12. Lettera al cardinale Ippolito d'Este, 25 dicembre 1509, in Ludovico Ariosto, *Lettere*, a cura di Angelo Stella, in *Satire, Erbolato, Lettere* (Milano: Mondadori, 1984), n. 5, pp. 138–39.
13. Sulle ragioni della sua soppressione, che ha dato luogo a opinioni divergenti, cfr. almeno Bigi, che parla di particolari 'che potevano sembrare troppo coloriti e realistici' (Emilio Bigi, commento al *Furioso* (Milano: Rusconi, 1982), nota a XLVI. 91. 7), e Casadei, secondo cui il cardinale veniva ritratto 'in un atteggiamento certo avvertito come non conveniente' (Alberto Casadei, *La strategia delle varianti: le correzioni storiche del terzo 'Furioso'* (Lucca: Maria Pacini Fazzi, 1988), p. 75).
14. Gerarda Stimato, 'Il ritratto di "Hippolyto da Este" nel primo *Furioso*: un'ecfrasi problematica', in *Gli dèi a corte: letteratura e immagini nella Ferrara estense*, a cura di Gianni Venturi e Francesca Cappelletti (Firenze: Olschki, 2009), pp. 209–25 (p. 221).
15. Cfr. *Relazioni degli ambasciatori veneti al Senato*, a cura di Eugenio Albèri, 13 voll. (Firenze: Tipografia all'insegna di Clio, 1840–55), ser. II, III, 58.
16. Ludovico Ariosto, *Lirica latina*, in *Opere minori*, a cura di Cesare Segre (Milano e Napoli: Ricciardi, 1954), p. 94.
17. Adriano Seroni, 'L'Ariosto e la Francia in due inserti storici del "Furioso"', *Notiziario culturale italiano*, 15.3 (1974), 43–47 (p. 44).
18. Pio Rajna, *Le fonti dell'Orlando Furioso*, ristampa della seconda edizione 1900 accresciuta d'inediti, a cura di Francesco Mazzoni (Firenze: Sansoni, 1975), p. 261.
19. Walter Moretti, 'Carlo V e i suoi "capitani invitti" nel *Furioso* del 1532', in *Rinascimento meridionale e altri studi in onore di Mario Santoro*, a cura di Maria Cristina Cafisse et al. (Napoli: Società Editrice Napoletana, 1987), pp. 321–31.
20. Casadei, p. 13.
21. Stefano Jossa, *Ariosto* (Bologna: Il Mulino, 2009), p. 122.
22. Ibid., p. 124.
23. Giuseppe Sangirardi, 'L'Arioste et l'Empire: réflexions sur les rédactions du *Roland furieux*', in *Les Poètes de l'Empereur: la cour de Charles-Quint dans le renouveau littéraire du XVIe siècle (1516–1556)*, a cura di Mercedes Blanco e Roland Béhar, e-Spania. Revue interdisciplinaire d'études hispaniques médiévales et modernes, n. 13 (juin 2012), <http://e-spania.revues.org/21345> [consultato il 16 maggio 2016], par. 18 di 26.
24. Klaus W. Hempfer, 'La Mise en fiction de l'histoire dans le *Roland furieux*: les campagnes d'Italie', in *La Naissance du monde et l'invention du poème: mélanges de poétique et d'histoire littéraire du XVIe siècle offerts à Yvonne Bellenger*, a cura di Jean-Claude Ternaux (Paris: Champion, 1998), pp. 219–38 (p. 234).

25. Cesare Segre, 'Imperialismo spagnolo nella traduzione del *Furioso* di Jerónimo de Urrea' [2008], in *Critica e critici* (Torino: Einaudi, 2012), pp. 198–210 (p. 206).
26. Ibid., p. 207, e cfr. *Fur.*, XXXIII. 55 C (manca AB): 'Vedete gli omicidii e le rapine | in ogni parte far Roma dolente; | e con incendi e stupri le divine | e le profane cose ire ugualmente'.
27. Fausto da Longiano, *Paragone di tutti i luoghi, d'istorie, di favole, di nomi proprj, d'Abbattimenti, e d'altre cose, che l'Ariosto per via d'imitazione ha tolto da gli antichi Greci* [...], in Ariosto, *Orlando furioso* (Venezia: Bindoni e Pasini, 1542) (si cita dall'ed. Orlandini (Venezia: Zatta, 1730), c. d*r*).
28. '[N]el corso di geografia impartito da Andronica ad Astolfo s'insinua il paragone implicito tra Carlo Magno e Carlo V, attraverso la cui opera si attuerebbero "gli ordini in ciel eternamente scritti" (XV. 27: v. 2)': Gian Paolo Giudicetti, *Mandricardo e la melanconia: discorsi diretti e sproloqui nell'"Orlando furioso"* (Bruxelles: Lang, 2010), p. 142.
29. Mario Fubini, voce 'Agramante', in *Dizionario Bompiani delle opere e dei personaggi di tutti i tempi e di tutte le letterature* (Milano: Bompiani, 1983), XI, 17.
30. Giudicetti, p. 147.
31. Si veda anche *Li fatti de Spagna: testo settentrionale trecentesco già detto 'Viaggio di Carlo Magno in Ispagna'*, a cura di Ruggero M. Ruggieri (Modena: Società tipografica modenese, 1951), cap. XXX; *La Spagna: poema cavalleresco del secolo XIV*, edito da Michele Catalano, 3 voll. (Bologna: Commissione per i testi di lingua, 1939–40), cantare XIV; *Spagna ferrarese*, a cura di Valentina Gritti e Cristina Montagnani (Novara: Interlinea, 2009), canto XII.
32. Edizione di riferimento: Matteo Maria Boiardo, *Opere: L'Inamoramento de Orlando*, a cura di Antonia Tissoni Benvenuti e Cristina Montagnani, introd. e commento di Antonia Tissoni Benvenuti, 2 voll. (Milano e Napoli: Ricciardi, 1999).
33. Ben diversamente ne *I Narbonesi*, uno degli ultimi romanzi scritti da Andrea da Barberino, in cui il sovrano si spostava 'rapidamente per l'Europa, dalla Calabria alle mura di Saragozza': Gerardo C. A. Ciarambino, *Carlomagno, Gano e Orlando in alcuni romanzi italiani del XIV e XV secolo* (Pisa: Giardini, 1976), p. 112.
34. Noteremo di passaggio che nell'Ariosto Dio e la Fortuna sono spesso intercambiabili, come ci ricorda Ruggiero: 'abbia chi regge il ciel cura del resto, | o la Fortuna, se non tocca a lui' (XX. 57. 3–4 AB; XXII C).
35. Così, infatti, replica all'offerta fattagli da Brandimarte di convertirsi: 'Che a vincere habbia o perdere, o nel regno | tornare antiquo o sempre starne in bando, | in mente sua n'ha Dio fatto disegno, | il qual né veder io posso, né Orlando. | Sia quel che vuol, non potrà ad atto indegno | di Re inchinarmi mai timore; e quando | fussi certo morir, vuo' restar morto, | prima ch'al sangue mio far sì gran torto' (*Fur.*, XXXVII. 44 AB; XLI C).
36. Rajna, p. 240.
37. Cfr. Galileo Galilei, *Scritti letterari*, a cura di Alberto Chiari (Firenze: Le Monnier, 1970), p. 286.
38. Stefano Prandi, 'Premesse umanistiche del *Furioso*: Ariosto, Calcagnini e il silenzio (*O.F.* XIV, 78–97)', *Lettere italiane*, 58.1 (2006), 3–32 (p. 15).
39. Giudicetti, p. 140.
40. Rajna, p. 57.
41. Giuseppina Zironi, voce 'Re Carlo', in *Dizionario Bompiani*, XI, 539–40 (p. 540).

CHAPTER 6

Intricate Intertextuality: Lucan's Wood in Ariosto and Tasso

Elena Lombardi

In this essay, which I intend as a tribute to Martin McLaughlin's essential research on the concepts of *imitatio* and *aemulatio* in the Italian late Middle Ages and Renaissance,[1] I examine one particularly complex specimen of Renaissance intertextuality: the intricate way in which Lucan's 'dark wood' (*Pharsalia* III) is employed in Ariosto's *Orlando furioso* (*Cinque canti* II) and Tasso's *Gerusalemme liberata* (III, XII and XVIII), and the ways in which other intertexts from Virgil, Ovid and Dante interact in the receiving texts. While carrying out a fairly detailed description of such episodes, I shall point out two related issues. On the one hand, this essay will show two different stagings of intertextual relations, one that openly displays its source and playfully acknowledges the existence of multiple versions of a story (Ariosto), and one that clouds and displaces the source through other intertexts, and aims at compounding and confusing the preceding tradition (Tasso). On the other hand, I shall also explore the consequences of 'negative' intertextuality: that is, the relevance of what the rewritings leave out from the original episode. In our case, appropriately, the discarded theme is a taboo (the sacrilege committed by the Roman leader) that resurfaces in unpredictable ways in the receiving texts, showing how the epic-chivalric poem, regenerating itself through intertextuality, accurately, if unconsciously, reflects the preoccupations of its times.

The wood itself can be taken as an image for intertextuality. It is intricate, and, in it, trees are tightly, often indistinguishably, interlocked, obscuring notions of direct and linear relations between objects. The forest is a locus of liveliness, renewal and creativity, but also of errance, uncertainty and fear, illustrating both the excitement of emulation and the 'anxiety' of influence. The woods we shall examine are botanically rich and diverse and thoroughly vital, but also seats of 'unknown' gods and fearful rites.[2] Moreover, such woods must be cut down to provide material to build something new, an image that fits the workings of intertextuality, because it is necessary to apply a certain amount of 'violence' to the original episode in order for the creativity of the rewriting to emerge.[3]

Lucan's Wood: 'Pharsalia', III. 399–452

The *Bellum civile* represents an extravagant chapter in the history of epics. Un-epic is its style, as well as the infamous subject matter — 'bella plus quam civilia' (I.1), the fratricidal war between Caesar and Pompey. Lucan exposes the crisis of the Virgilian model and of the Augustan and imperial political and aesthetic ideals, and distorts the form and content of the classic epic poem, infusing them with horror and the grotesque. As Gian Biagio Conte remarks, Lucan's poem registers the dissolution of the relation between reality and poetry.[4] Although banning the Olympian world of gods and magic from the strict historicity of the narration, Lucan infuses his poem with a sense of awe and of divine horror. Nature and the human being are now the *loci* of dis-humanity and unnaturalness. In the unthinkable cruelty of war, in bodies graphically dismembered, and in places horridly transfigured there resides an inherent evil. The enemy, the monstrous, the unforgiving divinity are now contained within the human world and are epitomized by the dissolution of moral values brought about by the civil war.

These unsettling traits appear also in the episode of the magic wood in Book III, where Lucan recounts the explosion and extension of the civil war to the whole Roman world. After storming Rome, Caesar heads toward the Alps and besieges Marseille. In order to fortify his camp, the leader orders the construction of a wooden palisade, which entails the cutting of a sacred wood, so far untouched ('numquam violatus ab aevo', l. 399) as it was dedicated to the cult of 'barbarian' gods ('barbara ritu sacra deum', l. 403), involving ominous altars, human blood, and statues roughly carved in the trees. The fear of the unknown gods ('quos non nosse deos', l. 417) creates legends, such as roars coming from caves, trees falling and rising again, fires that burn without consuming the wood, and dragons crawling through the trees. While the troops are petrified by the frightful majesty of the place, Caesar grabs a weapon and 'violates' a trunk, taking the blame for the sacrilegious act: 'Credite me fecisse nefas' (l. 437).[5] The crowd, now less afraid of the gods' anger than of Caesar's, starts cutting the wood, while the people of Marseille invoke the revenge of the gods, although Lucan bitterly remarks that 'Servat multos fortuna nocentes, | et tantum miseris irasci numina possunt' (448–49; 'Fortune often guards the guilty, and the gods must reserve their wrath for the unlucky').

The theme of the sacred wood is not recorded in Caesar's *Bellum civile*, where the siege of Marseille is a substantial yet side episode, centred on a six-storey war-tower, which is burnt down by the inhabitants of Marseille and rebuilt by the assailants (which Tasso will adopt in the episode of Clorinda and Argante in canto XII of the *Liberata*).[6] Lucan's text is, in turn, reminiscent of three passages from Virgil's *Aeneid* and one from Ovid's *Metamorphoses*. The passages from the *Aeneid* convey notions of leadership, destructiveness, and fear in connection to deforestation: in Book VI (178–84) Aeneas leads his soldiers in the cutting of a deep wood, in his search for the golden bough and of wood for Misenus's funerary altar. A further deforestation takes place in Book XI (134–38), during the truce proclaimed to bury Pallas: in it, Virgil emphasizes the energy applied to the destruction of the wood. Finally, in Book VIII (349–54), in the context of King Evander's description of Rome's future location, the Capitol is described as a horrid wood, seat of an 'uncertain god' ('quis deus incertum est', l. 352). In addition, the episode of Erysichthon's violation of Ceres's sacred grove from Ovid's *Metamorphoses* (VIII. 741–76) conveys the theme of brute sacrilege, as well as another crucial epic and romance locus, that of the animated and speaking tree, also developed by Virgil in the *Aeneid* (III. 24–63). Moreover, Statius rewrites Virgil's, Ovid's and Lucan's woods in several places of his *Thebaid*.[7] Most notably, in Book VI (84–115) we witness a coming together of Virgil and Lucan: as in the Virgilian episode, wood is needed to build a funeral pyre, and the cutting of the forest does not imply a sacrilege. Statius, however, enhances the hieratic aspect of the wood, which closely recalls Lucan's, in particular for the theme of the dense shade which inspires a sacred horror in the local population, for the lengthy description of the falling of the trees and for the presence of numina in the forest (although Statius's are peaceful Roman gods in contrast to Lucan's barbarian gods). All such passages are also present in the memory of the Renaissance poets when they construct their own wood based on Lucan's, and further themes and intertexts are at play in their works: namely the theme of the chivalric wood as a locus of errance, wandering, and test, the myth of Medea in Ariosto, and the episode of Polydorus from the *Aeneid* (III. 24–63) and its rewriting by Dante (*Inferno*, XIII) in Tasso. Finally, a myriad of shorter intertexts, through multiple and heterogeneous cross-references, construct a complex and flexible signifying structure.

The deeply unsettling qualities of the subject matter, style and content of Lucan's poem, make it a difficult source for Renaissance poets, who use it cautiously and sparingly.[8] When they do employ it, however, as is the case with the Marseille wood, it appears that Lucan's texts questions and unsettles the very foundations of the epic chivalric poem. The main themes of the episode of the Marseille wood are threefold: the unnatural horror of the place, fear deriving from unknown gods, and the *nefas* committed by the leader. The Latin *nefas* is what we would call today a taboo, involving prohibition, magic and desire infringing it. While the first two are maintained and played upon with inventive variations by the Renaissance poets, especially through a massive employment of the theme of magic, the leader's *nefas*, the central theme of this short episode as well as of Lucan's entire poem (the civil war is itself a *nefas* that brings about the dissolution of the entire Roman society), is erased in the Renaissance texts — an elimination superficially due to the fact that it is now the Christian leader who commits it. It is my argument, however, that the repressed theme resurfaces implicitly in the form of a sexual and ideological *nefas* in Ariosto and as genre taboo in Tasso.[9]

Ariosto's 'Cinque canti', II. 101–26

Lucan's wood resurfaces, not by chance, in the most problematic section of the *Orlando furioso*: the *Cinque canti*. Conceived around 1518–19 and revised around 1526 as an extension of the themes of the betrayal in Charles's rank and the praise of Ruggiero, the eponymous hero of the Casa d'Este, to be placed around canto 40, the *Cinque canti* eventually did not fit into either the 1521 or the 1532 edition. The exclusion is traditionally explained by the dissonance between the bitter and dark tone of the *Cinque canti* and the substantial 'luminosity' of the *Furioso*. According to Sergio Zatti, the author of the *Furioso* appears to have lost, in this section, 'la fiducia nell'ordinamento del reale', thus forfeiting two crucial roles: that of controlling director of the *entrelacement* and that of ironic narrator.[10] Lucan's *Pharsalia* is a fitting inspiration for the fragment, recognizably unified and dark, as it deals with the revolt, indeed a civil war, of the Christian people against Charles, as a result of the intrigues of Alcina and the betrayal of Gano di Maganza, a fiction intended to represent and criticize the Protestant schism in Europe.[11] Moreover, Ariosto's *Cinque canti*, like Lucan's *Pharsalia*, abound in negative deities (hate, suspicion, envy, violence), horrid places, monstrous apparitions and the insistence on graphic details.[12] In canto II, while the Christian army, shaken by the revolt, starts dispersing throughout Europe, Charles and the majority of the troops gather at the siege of the rebel city of Prague. In a quasi-translation from Lucan (stanzas 100–02), the material needed to fortify the Franks' position is sought in an impenetrable wood, dwelling place of 'wicked spirits' and a 'troublesome religion' that requires human sacrifices ('dove di sangue uman a Dei non noti | si facean sacrifici empi e voti', 102. 7–8).

Lucan's 'unknown Gods' ('Dei non noti') entice Ariosto into invention, through the grafting of an expansion on the myth of Medea (stanzas 103–12). Ariosto most probably received the consolidated tradition of this complex myth from Ovid's *Metamorphoses* (VII. 402–24), culminating in Medea's flight from Athens after her attempt to have Aegeus kill his son Theseus. Ovid's Medea disappears into an enchanted cloud, a beautiful way of ending this dense episode and handing it over to other writers for further elaboration. Indeed, Ariosto does not miss the opportunity for a brilliant intertextual play, recalling other versions of the myth, and adding his own:

> So ch'alcun scrive che la via non prese,
> quando fuggì dal suo figliastro audace,
> verso Boemia, ma andò nel paese
> che tra i Caspi e l'Oronte e Ircania giace,
> e che 'l nome di Media da lei scese:
> il che a negar non serò pertinace;
> ma dirò ben ch'anco in Boemia venne
> o dopo o allora, e signoria vi tenne.
> (*Cinque canti*, II. 103)

Ariosto presents the workings of intertextuality as multiple and non-exclusive: there is no such thing as one single version of a story, nor any need to disavow or excise other strands of the myth in order to create a new one. The consolidated tradition is for Ariosto a multiple and open structure: the poet acknowledges the other versions ('so ch'alcun scrive'), thus initiating an open game with his educated reader, accepting variations ('il che a negar non sarò pertinace') and underplaying chronology ('o prima o dopo').

Medea is an intricate figure, as she encompasses several and conflicting roles, specifically the helper-maiden, the sorceress, the passionate and grieving lover, the murderer of several people, beginning with her own brother and ending with her own children, the foreigner, most obviously the 'colonized other', the 'horrifying barbarian' (who is stolen, raped, tamed, and fights back by doing 'what no Greek woman' would ever do), but also, in some minor strands of the myth, the colonizer, the (direct or indirect) founder of cities, the wanderer from land to land, who collects enemies everywhere she goes and is always unable to settle.[13] In shaping his own Medea, Ariosto stresses the sorceress, foreigner-colonizer aspect of Medea, the wanderer who gets to the end of her journey becoming the political leader of a new world, although the aspect of the compulsive lover is alluded to ironically and the murderer is lurking about.[14] Interestingly, Ariosto provides a partial closure to the myth of Medea as wanderer, travelling from land to land and from city to city without ever finding a home, by making her settle in Bohemia for several centuries and, after the advent of Christianity, in the wood that Charles's troops destroy.

In Ariosto's account, Medea first installs herself in the wood and, made immortal by Fairies and wise by age, acts like a Machiavellian leader: first she fortifies her location (stanza 105), then patiently waits for the death of her enemies (stanza 106), and finally reflects on how to overcome her only weakness: the tyranny of love. Not suited to chastity, because of Venus's curse, she soon realizes that the root of love's pain lies in the obsessive uniqueness of the object of love (107–09). Once elected queen of the region, she institutes a new religion of sexual freedom ('nuova religion | e disciplina, da ogn'altra differente: | che senza nominar marito e moglie | tutti empian sossopra le sue voglie', 110. 5–8) — an overt allusion to the slanderous tales of immorality that circulated against the reformers and heretical sects of the region of Prague, which ties in with the general subtext of the *Cinque canti*, the global crisis brought about by the Reformation. Medea is indeed presented as the founder of the alleged practices of sexual freedom of the Reformers: 'e quella usanza, ch'ebbe inizio allora, | tra gli Boemi par che duri ancora' (112. 7–8). Six days out of ten Medea's people gather for a sacrilegious mass and an orgy, in which the *nefas* resurfaces in the form of incest: 'venian al nefandissimo complesso; | e meschiarsi le madri coi figliuoli, | con le sorelle i frati accadea spesso' (112. 4–6).

Medea is a fitting character to take upon herself the theme of the *nefas* from Lucan's episode: the murderer of brother and children turns into the instigator of incestuous intercourse of 'madri co' figliuoli' and sisters with brothers. Medea's institutions inspire an authorial intervention in the next stanzas (113–14) in which Ariosto satirically condemns the immorality of contemporary Italian women. The author wishes that Medea in her flight from Athens or Media had come to Italy instead of Bohemia, and installed her custom among Italian women, making them happy, fulfilled and 'fatter' than they are, and reproaching himself for instilling in them the desire to flee to Prague. Thus Ariosto seems to compound his critique of the Reformers within a predictable triptych: foreignness, sexual freedom and women's moral weakness.

After a hasty conclusion of the Medea episode, with the return of the priestess in the wood after the birth of Christ, Ariosto's text joins Lucan's once again. As in Lucan, the soldiers fear that their axes would kill them instead of cutting the wood, and Charles intervenes like a new Caesar, with the only exception that he takes the precaution of having a solemn mass sung before striking the tree. The mass disempowers the demonic forces that are unable to utter more than a couple of roars at the destruction of the wood (stanzas 122–24), while the 'pagans' in Prague, like Lucan's inhabitants of Marseille, both lament and rejoice at the event, hoping in the vengeance of the gods. The stamina with which Charles's troops assault the wood occasions a second authorial intervention recalling the happiness of the feast day of St John under Ercole and Borso d'Este. Political nostalgia storms in for two stanzas (120–21), celebrating the happy times of the early days of the Este family, when every pleasure was still whole ('piacere integro', 120. 4) as opposed to the desolate state of Italian affairs in Ariosto's day:

> Chi si ricorda il dì di san Giovanni,
> che sotto Ercole o Borso era sì allegro?
> che poi veduto non abbian molt'anni,
> come né ancora altro piacere integro,
> di poi che cominciar gli assidui affanni
> dei quali è in tutta Italia ogni core egro:
> parlo del dì che si facea contesa
> di saettar dinanzi alla sua chiesa.
> (*Cinque canti*, II. 120)

The two interpolations into Lucan's text, the Medea episode and the Ferrara episode display some interesting cross-references. Sergio Zatti points out that under the leadership of Medea, nobility and plebs are mingled ('confusamente i nobili e i plebei', III. 4), exactly as under Borso and Ercole ('poi con la nobiltà la plebe mista', 121. 5–6).[15] Moreover, the key word of the episode of Medea is 'piacere', which recurs in every stanza. Pleasure is what guides the 'wise' choice of Medea's sexual policy; and 'piacere integro' is also a feature of 'golden age' Ferrara, regrettably absent from today's Italy. Ariosto's position on Medea and the Reformation is thus more ambivalent than it appeared before. Indeed, Medea's kingdom is both condemned and wished for: together with sexual freedom it brings a strong political leadership, which is absent from Catholic Italy, but emerging in Reformed countries.

With respect to Lucan's text, Ariosto's textual strategy is surgical. In the episode of the wood of Prague in the *Cinque canti*, Lucan's text is dismembered in three *tranches* of quasi-translation (100–02, 118–19, 122–26)[16] and intermingled with three sections (Medea, Italian women, old Ferrara). In the episode of Medea, which takes off from Ovid's cloud and reinvents the traditional myth, the Lucanian *nefas* resurfaces as sexual (Medea's orgies) and ideological (the critique of the Reformed sects). The double *nefas* is then actualized and problematized in the two ambivalent authorial interventions, describing two golden ages (one satirical: the depravity of Italian women, and one idealized: old Ferrara) and lamenting the disgraced state of contemporary Italy in terms of both morality and politics.

Tasso's 'Gerusalemme liberata', III, XIII and XVIII

Like Lucan's, Tasso's poem is poised at the dissolution of the genre. Unlike Lucan, however, Tasso strives, although somewhat unsuccessfully, to preserve the structure and features of the epic poem, now threatened by the irruption of the *romanzesco*, and to uphold in it imposing Christian ideals. Lucan's wood becomes in the *Liberata* an intricate theme, complicated by chivalric and Dantean intertexts, which directs the plot of the second half of the poem. Tasso's wood begins with the end of Lucan's and Ariosto's: it appears 'unproblematically' at the end of canto III, where a crew of carpenters, sent by Goffredo to provide material for the war machines for the siege of Jerusalem, starts cutting, fearlessly and vigorously, the hidden wood of Saron,[17] and they spur each other on to cause 'unusual abuse' on the wood ('L'un l'altro essorta che le piante atterri, | e faccia al bosco inusitati oltraggi', 85. 1–2). The rich wood falls without difficulty, much like Virgil's woods (*Aeneid* VI and XI), and the plot moves on. The 'unusual abuse' is indeed intertextual at this point; it is the erasure of Lucan's horror and Ariosto's magic. Such features are, however, retroactively applied to the wood in the resumption of the episode in canto XIII.

The forest, now dense with horrid trees — showing by day an uncertain and fearful light ('luce incerta e scolorita e mesta', 2. 6) and by night a hellish horror ('notte, nube, caligine ed orrore | che rassembra infernal, che gl'occhi ingombra | di cecità, ch'empie di tema il core', 3. 2–4)[18] is described, as in Lucan, as a cause of fear for the local people, and said to be a meeting place for witches, who, in lines reminiscent of Ariosto's Medea, celebrate sacrilegious sexual rites ('con pompe immonde e sozze | i profani conviti e l'empie nozze', 4. 7–8). This antecedent, 'second-hand', source-related horror and magic is quickly dismissed, by recalling the Franks' bravery in canto III: 'ma i Franchi il violar, perch'ei sol uno | somministrava lor machine eccelse' (5. 3–4). However, the pagan magician Ismeno re-enchants the wood (stanzas 5–12), evoking devils with a complex rite involving human blood, as in Lucan and in Ariosto. Thus, after tearing down Lucan's and Ariosto's woods in canto III, Tasso builds his own on their foundations, reinstating in it the *romanzesco*. When the Crusaders approach the area in need of more material to rebuild the war-tower burnt down by Clorinda, the wood has turned into a composite intertext. In it, other woods converge: the chivalric-Arthurian wood, as a test that each knight needs to undergo and that only one passes, as well as Dante's dark wood, as the place where every character meets and faces his own sin, or weakness, or taboo. Moreover, Tasso embeds at the core of the wood two further arboreal intertexts, already mutually interlocked: the episode of Polydorus from the third book of the *Aeneid* and that of the suicides' wood from Dante's *Inferno*.

First, a crew of carpenters (stanzas 17–18), that so easily deforested the wood before, approaches it, but an unusual fear ('timor novo', 17. 8) is enough to scatter these workers. Second (stanzas 19–22), a bold and strong troop of chosen warriors is sent ('ardita | e forte squadra di guerrieri eletti', 19. 6), who are able to overcome the initial horror, but not a frightening roar that explodes from the wood, itself reminiscent of another passage of Lucan.[19] A 'fearless' man volunteers to go alone, Alcasto, 'uom di temerità stupida e fera' (24. 3) symbolizing brute, bestial force. For him, who has overcome the roar, the wood turns into the representation of a true Dantean hell, complete with flames and a vision of the city of Dis (stanzas 24–30). It is now Tancredi's turn, one of the two truly chosen heroes around whom the plot revolves (stanzas 32–49). Having just killed and buried his beloved Clorinda, Tancredi has little to fear, and indeed neither horror, nor roar and not even the fiery city can stop him, although some uncomfortable bodily sensation (heat and cold) warn the reader that hell is becoming more and more individually tailored. At the same time, the poem is more and more vertiginously playing with itself and with its sources. The poem hints at itself in the fact that Tancredi's memorable bravery ('memorando ardire', 35. 8) leads him to a place shaped like an amphitheatre. Memorability and theatre are the features of one of the key episodes of the poem, the duel between Tancredi and Clorinda (canto XII), during which epic becomes theatrical and turns the spotlight on the stage of a drama worth of remembrance.[20] Here Tancredi's 'memorando ardire' leads him not only on the internal theatre of his guilt, but also on the stage where the intricacies of intertextuality unfold. A cypress stands in the middle, its trunk inscribed with hieroglyphs: 'era di vari segni il tronco impresso, | simili a quei che in vece usò di scritto | l'antico già misterioso Egitto' (38. 6–8). Within the incomprehensible hieroglyphs, Tancredi discovers a sentence written in a language he can understand:

> Fra i segni ignoti alcune note ha scorte
> del sermon di Soria ch'ei ben possede:
> 'O tu che dentro a i chiostri de la morte
> osasti por, guerriero audace, il piede,
> deh! se non sei crudel quanto sei forte,
> deh! non turbar questa secreta sede.
> Perdona a l'alme omai di luce prive:
> non dée guerra co' morti aver chi vive.'
> (*Gerusalemme liberata*, XIII. 39)

Line 7, 'Perdona a l'alme omai di luce prive', is the inscription of the primary intertext of this episode, the theme of the soul trapped in the tree, here carried by the main line cried out by Polydorus after Aeneas strikes his thorn-bush: 'Iam parce sepulto' (*Aeneid*, III. 41). Tasso declares his intertext but also makes it 'illegible', confusing it within a pictographic script and a foreign language. Thus, the source has become an occult 'motto':

> Cosí dicea quel motto. Egli era intento
> de le brevi parole a i sensi occulti:
> fremere intanto udia continuo il vento
> tra le frondi del bosco e tra i virgulti,
> e trarne un suon che flebile concento
> par d'umani sospiri e di singulti,
> e un non so che confuso instilla al core
> di pietà, di spavento e di dolore.
> (*Gerusalemme liberata*, XIII. 40)

And indeed, while Tancredi is puzzled by the reading, the wood (initially Lucan's + Dante's, *Inferno* I) turns from Virgilian (Polydorus) to Dantesque again, this time with a strong echo of the suicides' wood (*Inferno* XIII): not only in the cypress, but in every tree, the souls of both Christian and Pagans fallen at the battle of Jerusalem appear to be imprisoned, and they all begin to sigh, as at the beginning of the Dantean episode. The Virgilian motto, then, here stands not only for the *Aeneid*, but also for a whole genealogy of an epic/chivalric topos, the man-tree, that spans from Virgil's Polydorus to Dante's Pier delle Vigne, to Ariosto's Astolfo, becoming a classic challenge for the epic/chivalric poet. How does Tasso approach this episode, so famous as to be almost trite, rewritten so many times that it seems almost exhausted? He reinvents it by 'killing it'. While other authors (most notably Dante) struggled to emphasize the credibility of their version, Tasso presents it as an act of magic, indeed an act of fiction; no one is actually trapped in the wood. One could even read this further within Tasso's great struggle away from the *romanzesco* in the *Liberata*, and interpret this literary topos itself as an 'evil enchantment', as a lure for the author openly to give in to fiction and magic.[21]

This time the allegedly imprisoned soul is that of Clorinda, androgynous enough to have reinvented in the preceding canto (the sortie of Clorinda and Argante, XII) another mandatory episode, that of Euryalus and Nisus (*Aeneid* IX, which passes more traditionally into the *Furioso* as Cloridano and Medoro in canto XVIII). In the 'theatre of his memory' Tancredi, seized by fear, twice attempts to kill Clorinda but eventually gives up.[22] His defeat stalls the episode, in the wait for the hero truly able to approach the wood and currently lost in Armida's lascivious garden: in canto XVIII Rinaldo, who has now boldly returned to the camp, embodies the Christian and epic virtues needed to destroy the wood (stanzas 1–11). After a night of confession, contrition and forgiveness on the Mount of Olives, a section woven with references to Dante's Purgatory and Petrarchan tones (Rinaldo's 'sin' is, indeed, both Dantean and Petrarchan: 'i folli amori'; 'i giovanili errori', 9. 2, 4), cloaked in a robe as white as the dawn, Rinaldo approaches the wood. Instead of the external and internal horror that drove back the other knights, a magic pastoral awaits him (stanzas 19–25) — a reproduction of Armida's garden, with streams, golden bridges, roses, lilies, dew, nightingales, organs, singing and poetry, indicating that an entire poetic tradition, and one very dear to Tasso, is at stake: romance, lyric, and the pastoral.

At the centre of the garden is a myrtle tree, traditionally the tree of Venus. Carolling around him, the forest nymphs born from the trees (an echo of Ovid's version of the topos of the animated tree), praise his coming and introduce the apparition of Armida (stanzas 26–33). Unable to bend Rinaldo's intention to cut the myrtle, Armida, and with her the whole *romanzesco*, explode like a firework into a grand, and useless, finale: giants, cyclops, earthquake, winds, the whole fantastic apparatus from the Odyssey on — nothing can stop Rinaldo, the now non-wandering knight ('pur mai colpo il cavalier non erra', 27. 5) from cutting down the tree, which reveals itself as a walnut, a tree traditionally linked to witchcraft. Thus, another *nefas* is at stake here: the killing of the *romanzesco* perpetrated by epic. The *selva* itself turns into an epic emblem inscribed in the heart of the poem. It absorbs and annihilates other 'centrifugal' genres, namely theatre, the pastoral, the lyric-Petrarchan tradition, and romance. The wood resumes its natural, 'epic' state, the innate horror of canto III ('al natural suo stato | non d'incanti terribile né lieta | piena d'orror, ma dell'orror innato', 28. 2–4) and Rinaldo comes back as Caesar — not Lucan's Caesar, the leader who commits the *nefas*, though; but Caesar's Caesar, the triumphal leader, proverbially recalled with 'veni, vidi, vici':

> A quel temuto
> bosco n'andai, come imponesti, e 'l vidi:
> vidi, e vinsi gl'incanti; or vadan pure
> le genti là, ché le vie son sicure.
> (*Gerusalemme liberata*, XVIII. 40. 5–8)

In the *Conquistata*, where the episode is substantially the same, there is at this point an interesting, although predictable, variant: 'Andai (lor disse) a quella selva, io vidi, | Vinse la croce ombre maligne ed atre' (*Gerusalemme conquistata*, XXII. 25.3–4).

The image of the inscribed cypress shows that Tasso stages the question of intertextuality 'emblematically.' As Antoine Compagnon explains, the emblem is a quintessential Renaissance sign, deeply implicated with the changes in reading and writing brought about by the printing press.[23] The Renaissance vogue for emblems originated in Italy in the fifteenth century, and is connected to the archaeological curiosity raised by the images on the verso of Roman coins and by the hieroglyphs found on the obelisks in Rome. The emblem is a composite figure, usually made up of title, drawing, explicative epigram (motto) and often a moral explanation, whose signification rests in the coming together of the various parts, especially from the coalescing of drawing (or pictographic script) and motto. The emblem is, in sum, something in the making: each time it is employed, its meaning is different. In the episode of Tancredi, a pictographic script (the hieroglyph), and a motto written in an equally mysterious but more interpretable language, become, in turn, the inscription of the source of the episode. The emblematized 'Iam parce sepulto' no longer has a stable meaning: indeed it has no meaning prior to Tancredi's discovery and attempted interpretation. Turning a well-known, much trodden, literary topos into an inscribed emblem, Tasso seems to underline the serendipity and lack of memory of intertextuality, which exists only in the act of reading itself. It is also worth recalling that the emblem was the favourite sign for printers (such as Manuzio's dolphin and anchor): as such, it is an economic sign, a sign of both property (the printer owns the manuscript and the printed edition) and circulation (he is making it public). The emblematic quotation is thus both a sign of appropriation (of the old text) and dissemination (of the new).

In conclusion, the image of the enchanted wood from Lucan to Ariosto to Tasso can be taken to illustrate the workings of intertextuality itself: each time, the new author, armed with an 'intertextual axe', cuts and rebuilds it, thus operating an intertextual *nefas*, yet one vital to the creativity of the genre. Indeed, intertextuality is the *nefas*, a quite violent, sacrilegious appropriation of another text. However, the authority of the source text is compared to a 'barbarian', unknown divinity, which both establishes and demystifies the taboo. The destruction of the wood is both violent and generative. It is, on the one hand, featured as a violation ('violata' in Lucan; 'violar' in Ariosto), inflicted on a rather passive matter,[24] but also, on the other hand, as a going beyond: Tasso calls it 'inusitato oltraggio', where 'oltraggio' encapsulates both the notion of abuse and beyondness. The source is then transplanted into the next text, with very different outcomes: where Ariosto welcomes the multiplicity and variance of the same story, Tasso appears to 'kill' the textual predecessor in order to bring to the fore his own version.

Notes to Chapter 6

1. Martin McLaughlin, *Literary Imitation in the Italian Renaissance: The Theory and Practice of Literary Imitation in Italy from Dante to Bembo* (Oxford: Clarendon Press, 1995).

2. Although there is no space here for minute textual analysis, just a quick look at the description of four deforestations gives the sense of the magnitude and power of the theme of the cutting of the wood in the epic chivalric poem. These woods are most probably illogical from the botanical point of view, yet symbolically rich. *Aeneid*, VI. 180–82: 'procumbunt piceae, sonat icta securibus ilex | fraxineaeque trabes cuneis et fissile robur | scinditur, aduoluunt ingentis montibus ornos' ('down drop the pitchy pines, and the ilex rings to the stroke of the axe; ashen logs and splintering oak are cleft with wedges, and from the mountains they roll down huge ash trees'). *Aeneid*, XI. 136–38: 'ferro sonat alta bipenni | fraxinus, euertunt actas ad sidera pinus | robora nec cuneis et olentem scindere cedrum | nec plaustris cessant uectare gementibus ornos' ('The lofty ash rings under the two-edged axe; they lay low star-towering pines, and ceaselessly their wedges cleave oak and fragrant cedar, and groaning wagons convey the mountain ash'). Translation from Virgil, *Aeneid,* trans. by H. Rushton Fairclough, rev. by G. P. Goold (Cambridge, MA: Harvard University Press, 1999). *Pharsalia*, III. 440–45: 'procumbunt orni, nodosa inpellitur ilex, | siluaque Dodones et fluctibus aptior alnus | et non plebeios luctus testata cupressus | tum primum posuere comas et fronde carentes | admisere diem, propulsaque robore denso | sustinuit se silua cadens' ('Ash trees were felled, gnarled holmoaks overthrown; Dodona's oak, the alder that suits the sea, the cypress that bears witness to a monarch's grief, all lost their leaves for the first time; robbed of their foliage, they let in the daylight; and the toppling wood, when smitten, supported itself by the close growth of its timber'). Lucan, *The Civil War*, trans. by J. Duff (Cambridge, MA: Harvard University Press, 1952). *Cinque canti*, II. 125: 'Cade l'eccelso pin, cade il funebre | cipresso, cade il venenoso tasso, | cade l'olmo atto a riparar che l'ebre | viti non giaccian sempre a capo basso; | cadono, e fan cadendo le latebre | cedere agli occhi et alle gambe il passo.' *Gerusalemme liberata*, III. 75–76: 'Caggion recise da i pungenti ferri | le sacre palme e i frassini selvaggi, | i funebri cipressi e i pini e i cerri, | l'elci frondose e gli alti abeti e i faggi, | gli olmi mariti, a cui talor s'appoggia | la vite, e con piè torto al ciel se 'n poggia. | Altri i tassi, e le quercie altri percote, | che mille volte rinovàr le chiome, | e mille volte ad ogni incontro immote | l'ire de' venti han rintuzzate e dome; | ed altri impone a le stridenti rote | d'orni e di cedri l'odorate some. | Lascian al suon de l'arme, al vario grido, | e le fère e gli augei la tana e 'l nido.' For the significance of the composition of the chivalric wood, see Sergio Zatti, *L'ombra del Tasso: epica e romanzo nel Cinquecento* (Milan: Mondadori, 1996), p. 53.
3. For deforestation as an image for intertextuality, see Jamie Masters, *Poetry and Civil War in Lucan's 'Bellum civile'* (Cambridge: Cambridge University Press, 1992), pp. 25–28.
4. Gian Biagio Conte, 'Mutamento di funzioni e conservazione del genere', in *Memoria dei poeti e sistema letterario* (Turin: Einaudi, 1971), pp. 77–108 (p. 91).
5. *Pharsalia*, III. 433–37: 'inplicitas magno Caesar torpore cohortes | ut uidit, primus raptam librare bipennem | ausus et aeriam ferro proscindere quercum | effatur merso uiolata in robora ferro | iam nequis uestrum dubitet subuertere siluam | credite me fecisse nefas.' (When Caesar saw that his soldiers were sore hindered and paralysed, he was the first to snatch an axe and swing it, and dared to cleave a towering oak with the steel: driving the blade into the desecrated wood, he cried: 'Believe that I am guilty of sacrilege, and thenceforth none of you need fear to cut down the trees.')
6. See *Bellum civile*, I. 34–36, 56–58 and II. 1–16. Caesar appears only at the beginning of this episode, where he prepares the siege that is afterwards left to his commander Trebonius. Throughout the episode there are several references to the need for wood for earthworks and war machines and to the deforestation of the area around Marseille (see in particular II. 15). For a comparison between the two episodes see Masters, *Poetry and Civil War*, pp. 11–39.
7. For a detailed discussion of such instances see Carole Newlands, 'Statius and Ovid: Transforming the Landscape', *Transactions of the American Philological Association*, 134 (2004), 133–55.
8. On Lucan's fortune see Enrica Malcovati, *Lucano* (Brescia: La Scuola, 1947), pp. 109–29 and 'Sulla fortuna di Lucano' *Atene e Roma*, n.s., 8 (1963), 27–33; and Lao Paoletti, 'La fortuna di Lucano dal Medioevo al Romanticismo', *Atene e Roma*, n.s., 7 (1962), 144–57.
9. On the notion of the resurfacing of a repressed idea in literary texts through intertextuality, see Francesco Orlando, *Per una teoria freudiana della letteratura* (Turin: Einaudi, 1982).

10. Sergio Zatti, 'La frantumazione del mondo cavalleresco', in *L'ombra del Tasso*, pp. 28–58, especially pp. 30–37.
11. David Quint, 'Introduction' to *Cinque canti/Five Cantos*, ed. by David Quint and trans. by Alexander Sheridan (Berkeley: University of California Press, 1996), pp. 2–13.
12. Lanfranco Caretti, 'Storia dei *Cinque canti*', in Ariosto, *Cinque canti*, ed. by Lanfranco Caretti (Turin: Einaudi, 1977), pp. xiv-xv.
13. The story of Medea after her flight from Athens becomes confused. The most common outcome, the one quoted here by Ariosto, is her flight to Asia Minor with Medus, the son she had from Aegeus, who becomes the founder of the region of Media. Other versions of the myth see her returning to her native Colchis with Medus; transported directly in the Elysian Fields where she establishes a relationship with Achilles; and, interestingly, in Italy (where Ariosto, probably not knowing this version of the myth, wishes her presence), where, after teaching the Marubii how to enchant snakes, she is venerated like a goddess under the name of Angizia. See Fritz Graf, 'Medea the Enchantress from Afar: Remarks on a Well-Known Myth', and Nita Krevans, 'Medea as Foundation Heroine', both in *Medea: Essays on Medea in Myth, Literature, Philosophy and Art*, ed. by James J. Clauss and Sarah I. Johnston (Princeton: Princeton University Press, 1997), pp. 21–43 and 71–83. For Medea in the Middle Ages, see Ruth Morse, *Medieval Medea* (New York: Boydell and Brewer, 1998) and Alessandro Ballor, 'Il mito di Giasone e Medea nel Medioevo francese (XII-XIV secolo)', *Studi francesi*, 44 (2000), 455–71.
14. According to Cesare Segre (Ariosto, *Opere minori* (Milan and Naples: Ricciardi, 1954), p. 651), the main source of Ariosto's rewriting of Medea's story is the episode of the Sibarites and Arganora in the third book of the *Mambriano* with reminiscences of the fifth book of Plato's *Republic*, where the theme of the communion of women and wealth is discussed (see in particular *Republic* v, 449A-466D).
15. Zatti, *L'ombra del Tasso*, pp. 54–55. Zatti also notes, interestingly, that Medea's (and the Reformers') politics of sexual freedom, here condemned as incestuous, are similar to those upheld in contemporary utopian and travel literature.
16. In his 'Appunti sulle fonti dei *Cinque Canti*' (in *Esperienze ariostesche* (Pisa: Nistri Lischi, 1966), pp. 97–109), Cesare Segre notes that even in the instances of translation Ariosto's tone is always lighter than Lucan's.
17. As commentators point out, the hidden wood, shown to the Christians by a Syrian, is present in the chronicle of William of Tyre, the historical basis of the *Liberata*.
18. Besides the reference to the hellish quality of the wood, the relevance of the Dantean intertext is evident also from XIII. 3.7: 'né v'entra peregrin, se non smarrito'.
19. The roar emerging from the wood (stanza 21), made up of different terrifying voices, recalls the horrifying voice of Erichtho in *Pharsalia*, VI. 685–93.
20. *Gerusalemme liberata*, XII. 54: 'Degne d'un chiaro sol, degne d'un pieno | teatro, opre sarian sì memorande. | Notte, che nel profondo oscuro seno | chiudesti e ne l'oblio fatto sì grande, | piacciati ch'io ne 'l tragga e 'n bel sereno | a le future età lo spieghi e mande. | Viva la fama loro; e tra lor gloria | splenda del fosco tuo l'alta memoria.'
21. For textual comparisons between Virgil's Polydorus, Dante's Pier delle Vigne and Clorinda, see Laura Scotti, 'Memorie poetiche di Torquato Tasso: la *Commedia* di Dante', *Studi tassiani*, 36 (1988), 129–39. The intriguing way in which this classical topos crosses the epic tradition deserves more time than this essay allows. At least one fact is, however, worth mentioning. In rewriting the episode, each author claims for himself the credibility of it. The way Dante masterfully but somewhat heavy-handedly manages the episode signals the issues and problems related to credibility: he has Virgil himself, the author of the original episode, spurring the pilgrim to tear the branch and then consoling Pier delle Vigne for the broken stump by saying that it was not enough for Dante the pilgrim to trust the text of the *Aeneid* — a fable if compared to the truth of the new Christian world: the pilgrim has to try for himself, tear the branch, see the blood and hear the pain; to rewrite, in sum, the story, claiming its truthfulness as authorized by God. In the new Christian epic, Virgil's narrative is no longer valid, but the reader is called to trust the new Christian writer: 'S'elli avesse potuto creder prima, | rispuose 'l savio mio, | anima lesa, | ciò c'ha veduto pur con la mia rima, | non avrebbe in te la man distesa; | ma

la cosa incredibile mi fece | indurlo ad ovra ch'a me stesso pesa.' (*Inferno*, XIII. 46–51). Indeed Dante seems to exploit the episode to a point of no return. Only Ariosto, through irony and stylistic refinement is able if not to resuscitate it, at least to elegantly mummify it (*Orlando furioso*, VI. 26–54). In Tasso, as we have seen, the intertextual tradition is presented as an act of magic, and evil fiction, which lures the character away from the 'straight path' and the author into the incredibility of the *romanzesco*.

22. It is worth pointing out that the description of the fear of both the workers and Tancredi is patterned on Lucretius's famous characterization of fear as an infantile or dreamlike condition, as in *De rerum natura*, II. 55–58 and III. 87–90.
23. Antoine Compagnon, *La Seconde Main ou le travail de la citation* (Paris: Seuil, 1979), especially pp. 258–70.
24. For the gender implication of deforestation, see Alison Keith, *Engendering Rome: Women in Latin Epic* (Cambridge: Cambridge University Press, 2000), pp. 58–62.

CHAPTER 7

Improvising Lyric Verse in the Renaissance: Contexts, Sources and Composition

Brian Richardson

We have many accounts of cultured poets creating lyric poetry in Renaissance Italy 'all'improvviso' or 'ex tempore', in Latin or in the vernacular. The composition and the circulation of this kind of verse can nevertheless be in some respects difficult to characterize and assess. This essay considers the types of evidence that we have about the circumstances in which it was generated and its reception, together with some possible examples of surviving improvised poetry, under two headings. The first is relatively straightforward: the social gatherings at which poets performed verse extempore, sometimes at the request of others. Such performances elicited both praise and some criticism, as we shall see. The second kind of circumstance involves some speculation on our part, since it entails not oral performance but poetry that may have been invented in the course of writing a letter. I shall then come to the more difficult question of how far the process of improvising lyric verse drew on resources available to the poet in advance, while still manifesting the distinctive quality of spontaneity.

Descriptions of social gatherings can mention the actual or supposed adlibbing of poetry in order to entertain those present or to make a point in a discussion. Such occasions could be relatively formal. Francesco Sansovino attests that Cassandra Fedele (*c.* 1465–1558) improvised at a Venetian banquet: 'Si legge che in uno de' predetti conviti in tempo del Doge Agostino Barbarigo [1486–1501], Cassandra Fedele, giovanetta assai bella, et illustre per molte scienze, cantò su la lira versi latini all'improvisa, con tanta maraviglia de i circonstanti, che ne acquistò gloria per tutta Italia.'[1] The instrument with which Fedele accompanied herself was presumably the lira da braccio. Camillo Querno of Monopoli, known as the Archipoeta, was employed to sit at the table of Pope Leo X and improvise six lines of verse before each course of the meal, a service for which he received nine ducats a month from September 1519.[2] At Leo's court, contests in singing improvised Latin verse were organized at which the pope selected the topic. According to Lilio Gregorio Giraldi's *Dialogi duo de poetis nostrorum temporum*, the Florentine poet Aurelio Lippo Brandolini competed on one such occasion: 'hic utique extemporali facultate etiam insignis, seu prosa seu versu velitis; non multos ante hos dies a Leone X iussus cum

Marone certare in Medicorum Cosmiana sollemnitate, victus cessit' ('This man was especially marked out by his improvisational skills in both prose and verse. Not many days ago he was ordered by Leo X to compete with [Andrea] Marone in the festival of Cosmas and Damian [27 September] celebrated by the Medici, but he came out defeated').[3] Giraldi goes on to give more information on Marone and his victory:

> occurrit Andreas Maro noster Foroiuliensis, quem et Brixiani suum faciunt. Hunc extemporalis facultas commendat adeo ut superioribus his mensibus [...] in Cosmiano Leonis X convivio ceteros qui multi aderant poetas proposita materia, quam referrent ex tempore obmutescere quasi elingues fecerit, inter quos Lippus.
>
> [There comes to mind [...] our own Andrea Marone, from Friuli, whom the Brescians also claim to be one of theirs. He is known for his great power of extempore composition. His skill was shown a few months ago at Leo X's festival of Cosmas and Damian, [...] which was attended by many poets. For when the topic on which the poets had to improvise was given, he struck all the others (including Lippo) dumb, so to speak, as if they were tongueless.][4]

Marone's style of performance is described by Paolo Giovio in the second dialogue of *De viris et foeminis in nostra aetate florentibus*. The poet is driven with such force, writes Giovio, 'ut fortuita et subitariis tractibus ducta multum ante provisa et meditata carmina videantur' ('that his poems, though composed on the spur of the moment and without premeditation, seem the result of long advance planning and prior reflection'). Marone combines huge physical effort with fine artistic control: as he sings, his sweat pours and his veins swell, yet 'eruditae aures tamquam alienae ac intentae omnem impetum profluentium numerorum exactissima ratione moderantur' ('his trained ears, as though not his own, intently and precisely regulate every beat').[5]

Other accounts concern informal events where the topic depended on chance circumstances. Marone was called upon to improvise when among friends, according to the account of Pierio Valeriano in his *De litteratorum infelicitate*:

> Sed nolim [...] Andreae Maronis oblivisci, cuius felicissimam pangendis carminibus extemporalitatem nemo unus aetate nostra non admiratus est. Solitus ille quidem, ut super eo Pierius noster cecinit:
>
> > Mille ex tempore carmina erudita,
> > Quis nil sit lutulentum, inexpolitum,
> > Nil absurdum, et inane, nil hiulcum
>
> emodulari quotiescumque amicorum rogatu invitaretur. Id quod tribus praecipue versuum generibus indifferenter factitare consuerat: sive elegum, sive Phalaecium, seu Saphicum hendecasyllabum deposceres, nihil contatus quod proposuisses argumentum, horum quovis carminis numero concinebat.
>
> [I would not want to forget Andrea Marone, whose happy talent for composing extemporaneous verses gained the universal admiration of our age. For whenever he was called on by his friends, he used to set to rhythm, as our Pierio says in his verses about him,

> thousands of verses extemporaneous,
> learned and polished, and marred by no blemish,
> without gaps, with no rough spots, and nothing extraneous.

> And he used to do this with equal ease in three meters especially: whether you asked for elegiac, or the Phalaecean or Sapphic hendecasyllable, without hesitation he would celebrate whatever subject you had proposed in any one of these meters.][6]

Benvenuto Cellini's autobiography contains an account of a dinner held in Rome around 1524 in which a Spanish student called Diego dressed as a woman. After the meal, 'venne un poco di mirabil musica di voce insieme con instrumenti', sung and played 'con i libri inanzi'; this probably means that the performers used written parts, although the most advanced techniques of *cantus super librum* included improvised counterpoint.[7] A sung improvisation in praise of women was then performed by the poet Aurelio Morani of Ascoli:

> Apresso alla musica, un certo Aurelio Ascolano, che maravigliosamente diceva allo improviso, cominciatosi a lodar le donne con divine e belle parole, in mentre che costui cantava, quelle due donne, che avevano in mezzo quella mia figura, non mai restate di cicalare; che una di loro diceva innel modo che la fece a capitar male, l'altra domandava la mia figura in che modo lei aveva fatto, e chi erano li sua amici, e quanto tempo egli era che l'era arrivata in Roma, e molte di queste cose tale.[8]

Casual meetings of friends seem to be the contexts for the improvisations, accompanied by a lira, of the unidentified 'pretuzzo' described in the *Monte Parnaso* of Filippo Oriolo: he sings 'tante favole',

> Poi d'una cuoca sua lodò 'l bel viso
> con tali e tante sue millantarie,
> ch'ogni un levossi co' un po[co] di riso.[9] (ll. 103–05)

Another context for informal improvisation involving music is revealed in Montaigne's account of his visit to Fano in the spring of 1581. He was struck by the presence in the inns of poets, apparently even from the working classes, who would put together verses that were fitting for those who happened to be present: 'Il se treuve quasi à toutes les hostelleries des rimeurs qui font sur le champ des rimes accommodées aus assistans. Les instrumens sont en toutes le boutiques, jusques aus ravaudeurs des quarrefours des rues.'[10]

Montaigne's description, like those concerning Fedele and Morani (who 'diceva' and 'cantava'), suggests that the improvisation of verse habitually went together with an instrumental accompaniment. Both the vocal line and the accompaniment could have involved a certain amount of improvisation on a basic melodic scheme, and this presented a further challenge. Giorgio Vasari emphasizes vocal rather than verbal improvisation when he writes of Leonardo da Vinci: 'Dette alquanto d'opera alla musica, ma tosto si risolvé a imparare a sonare la lira, come quello che da la natura aveva spirito elevatissimo e pieno di leggiadria, onde sopra quella cantò divinamente all'improviso.'[11] However, a musical accompaniment would above all have assisted the improviser of verse by providing a pattern and a rhythmic structure into which the words had to fit. Nino Pirrotta has suggested that 'easy memorization of the musical strophic unit [...] eventually enabled the performer to concentrate on the improvisation of new texts'.[12]

Like Cellini, Antonfrancesco Grazzini uses both *cantare* and *dire* in his tale of a certain maestro Manente. In the story, this doctor is kidnapped by Lorenzo de' Medici, who was himself in real life a renowned improviser, as punishment for something unspecified that Manente had done to Lorenzo during a session of improvisation: as the character Burchiello says, 'Io me l'indovinai sempre, perché egli ti avessi a fare una burla simile, d'allora in qua, che dicendo seco improvviso a Careggi, tu li facesti quella villania.'[13] When Manente is being kept prisoner in the Benedictine hermitage of Camaldoli, he decides to thank those who look after him by providing different kinds of performance:

> il medico [...] cantava sovente certe canzonette che egli era solito cantare a desco molle in compagnia de' suoi beoni, e diceva qualche volta improvviso. E perché egli aveva bella voce e buona pronunzia, recitava spesso certe stanze di Lorenzo, che nuovamente erano uscite fuora, chiamate *Selve d'Amore*.[14]

It is possible that some of the stanzas of Lorenzo's *Selve* had themselves originated as extemporized individual strambotti or rispetti.[15]

Extemporized verse tended by its nature to be evanescent, and much of it must have gone unrecorded in writing. Some written texts may well have originated in improvisation but not be declared as such. However, we do have some written texts that are explicitly claimed to have been improvised. Some are embedded within narratives. Such accounts may be completely or partly fictitious, intended to create a neat story; but even then, they at least indicate the circumstances in which improvisation may have been used. Aldo Manuzio cites, in his letter of dedication of Plutarch, *Opuscula LXXXXII*, addressed to Iacopo Antiquario in March 1509, a Latin poem in Phalaecean hendecasyllables with which Antiquario had welcomed him to Milan in 1506:

> Libuit hic subiungere hendecasyllabos, quos, cum veni ad te Mediolanum, lusisti extempore prae summo gaudio adventus nostri, ut faciant et hi fidem mutui amoris nostri.
>
> > Aldus venit en, Aldus ecce venit,
> > nostrum sinciput occiputque nostrum,
> > mel, sal, lac quoque corculumque solus,
> > Graios altera et altera Latinos
> > qui apprendendo manu, reduxit omneis
> > in verum modo limitem, superbos
> > victores superans Olympiorum.
> > Nunc, o nunc, iuvenes, ubique in urbe
> > flores spargite: vere nanque primo
> > Aldus venit en, Aldus ecce venit![16]

[Here I want to add the hendecasyllables that you composed extempore when I visited you in Milan, in your great joy at our arrival, so that they, too, may attest our love for one another: 'Aldus has arrived, behold, Aldus has arrived: he who alone is our brain and head, our honey, salt, milk and heart; he who, taking the Greeks with one hand and the Latins with the other, has now brought all of them back to the true path, surpassing the proud victors of the Olympic games. Now, now, young people, strew flowers throughout the city: for in springtime Aldus has arrived, behold, Aldus has arrived.']

Another salutation that may well have been spontaneous is recorded in Cellini's story of the Spaniard Diego, when he recounts that the Sienese sculptor Michelangelo di Bernardino exclaimed these *ottonari* on seeing the student: 'O Angiol bella, o Angiol degna, | tu mi salva, et tu mi segna'.[17] Such brevity must have characterized many improvised verses, and it is found also in a story told by Giraldi apropos of Camillo Querno:

> de hoc memini ex tempore pontificem Leonem ipsum [...] cecinisse:
>> Archipoeta facit versus pro mille poetis,
>> Et pro mille aliis Archipoeta bibit.
>
> [I remember Leo [...] sang the following about him extemporaneously:
>> Archipoeta makes enough verses for a thousand poets –
>> And drinks enough for a thousand others.][18]

Giovio gives a possibly more correct account in which Querno and the pope compose alternately, in a competitive spirit. Querno speaks the first line of this elegiac couplet, but he then hesitates, and Leo adds the pentameter. Querno continues: 'Porrige quod faciat mihi carmina docta Falernum' ('Give me some Falernian wine to make my verses learned'); to which 'Leo repente mutuatus a Virgilio subdiderit: "Hoc etiam enervat debilitatque pedes"' ('Leo added swiftly, borrowing from Virgil: "This, too, weakens and debilitates the feet"').[19]

There may be some substance in Giraldi's narration of how a Latin elegiac couplet was improvised by Flavio Antonio Giraldi as another put-down:

> Audite, quaeso, eius distichon, quod de glorioso quodam poeta [cui Pignius cognomen] se iactante in multorum corona ex tempore fudit.
>> Aesopi veluti variis cornicula plumis
>> Induta inter aves conspiciendus ades.
>
> [Listen, please, to his distich which he spouted extemporaneously on the subject of a boastful poet [called Pignius] who was bragging before a large crowd:
>> Just like Aesop's crow clad in the colored feathers of others,
>> There you stand, a sight to behold among true birds.][20]

In the second half of the sixteenth century, Lodovico Guicciardini includes in his *L'ore di ricreazione* anecdotes that involve more elaborate improvised poems. One is entitled 'La natura dell'uomo essere inconstante e tribolata da varie passioni':

> Trovandosi il magnifico Lorenzo de' Medici, padre di papa Leone e gran poeta, in buona compagnia e divisandosi della natura dell'uomo, chi una cosa e chi un'altra dicea. Onde egli pregato di dirne la sua opinione, la descrisse all'improviso graziatamente in questa guisa, dicendo:
>> Teme, spera, rallegrasi e contrista,
>> ben mille volte il dì nostra natura.

> Spesso il mal la fa lieta e 'l ben l'attrista,
> spera il suo danno e del ben ha paura,
> tanta ha il viver mortal corta la vista.
> Al fin vano è ogni pensier e cura.[21]

However, these lines also form the tercets of Lorenzo's sonnet 'Fortuna, come suol, pur mi dileggia', which has the rubric 'Sonetto fatto per un certo caso che ogni dì si mostrava in mille modi'.[22] If the anecdote is based on fact, was Lorenzo quoting his own verse from memory or did he improvise the lines and reuse them later as part of the sonnet? In favour of the latter hypothesis is the slight 'disconnect' between the argument of the quatrains, on the variability of Fortune, and that of these tercets, on the variability of human nature.

In another of Guicciardini's stories, entitled 'Molesta e odiosa esser la garrulità d'alcuni presuntuosi', the Florentine poet Luigi Alamanni, when in Paris, is said to have improvised a stanza in order to rebuke someone who mocked others:

> Trovandosi messer Luigi Alamanni in Parigi in una onesta compagnia, sopravvenne fra loro un certo Matteo Rigogoli, uomo loquace e che faceva professione di schernire e uccellare le genti. Così cominciando egli con poca grazia a usar quivi con qualcuno de' suoi termini, l'Alamanno aborrendolo, voltatosi alli altri disse leggiadramente all'improvviso questi versi:
>
>> Com'io veggo qualcun che parla molto
>> e piacer prende di schernir altrui,
>> oltr'a che io 'l tengo senza senno e stolto,
>> penso ch'ogn'altro fallo aggia con lui.
>> Sia da pigrizia e codardia involto:
>> dall'ignoranza e da' seguaci suoi,
>> cioè superbia, invidia, ira e menzogna,
>> senza dramma d'onor né di vergogna.[23]

In this instance, too, the verses form part of another poem, Alamanni's romance *Girone il Cortese* (II. 95). Nevertheless, even if the anecdote is invented, it illustrates another aspect of the occasionally agonistic nature of improvisation.

In another case, a poem can be identified as possibly originating in improvisation because it can be linked to a narrative account of an event. Castiglione, in *Il libro del cortegiano*, mentions the performance by Bernardo Accolti, l'Unico Aretino, of a sonnet on the subject of the letter S that the duchess Elisabetta Gonzaga wore on her forehead, probably referring to a scorpion.[24] A sonnet that fits this description, since its key nouns start with an 's', appears separately in a manuscript compilation:

> Consenti, o mar di bellezza e virtute,
> ch'io, servo tuo, sia d'un gran dubbio sciolto,
> se lo S che porti nel candido volto
> significa mio stento, o mia salute,
>
> se dimostra soccorso, o servitute,
> sospetto, o securtà, secreto, o stolto,
> se speme, o strido, se salvo, o sepolto,
> se le catene mie strette, o solute;

>ch'io temo forte che non mostri segno
>de superbia, sospir, severitate,
>stratio, sangue, sudor, suplicio, e sdegno.
>
>Ma se loco ha la pura veritate,
>questo S dimostra con non poco ingegno
>un sol solo in bellezza, e 'n crudeltate.[25]

Another kind of testimony, which can be considered relatively reliable, can come from the rubric with which a poem is transmitted. This is the case with a sonnet by Lorenzo de' Medici, composed in the voice of a male lover but addressed 'to a stone found in a wood':

>Sonetto fatto ex tempore, ad saxum in lucu repertum
>
>>Già fui misero amante, or transformato
>>per la vaghezza di due occhi belli
>>da una ninfa tra verdi arbuscelli,
>>di amante un duro sasso diventato.
>>
>>Se qualche gentil cor quinci è passato,
>>per essemplo di me sia più saggio elli;
>>né facci gli occhi alla ragion ribelli,
>>perché son tesi i lacci in ogni lato.
>>
>>Benché rigida pietra, ancor mi resta
>>tanta pietà, che ammonir posso altrui
>>e farlo saggio col pericol mio.
>>
>>Cauto con gli occhi bassi e con la testa
>>passi di qui chi è come già fui,
>>ché ancora in questi luoghi Amore è dio.
>>   (*Canzoniere*, no. 117)

A miscellaneous manuscript of the Biblioteca Marciana, Venice, Lat. XII 248 (10625), fol. LVII^r, contains a Latin poem whose rubric states that it was written 'ex tempore'; its author is Pietro Antonio Acciaiuoli, a Ferrarese lawyer of the period of Duke Alfonso I.[26]

Marin Sanudo wrote out four poems, two in Latin and two in the vernacular, with rubrics declaring that Aurelio Brandolini had improvised and sung them in Rome in the presence of Venetian ambassadors. The first was a Sapphic ode of eight stanzas, beginning 'Alma, que caelo resides sereno | Virgo', concerning the ambassadors and the health of Pope Innocent VIII. It is introduced with the words: 'Lyppi Florentini ex temporales versus saphica canit clavicimbala Romae anno 1495' ('Extemporized verses of Lippo the Florentine [that] he sings with a Sapphic harpsichord, Rome, 1495'). This rubric presents problems, however, not just because of the confused syntax and the terminology used for the instrument (which has the feminine gender rather than the usual masculine), but also because the date must be earlier: Nella Giannetto has suggested 1485.[27] As in most cases, it is not clear how this poem came to be written down; it could have been reconstructed from memory, by the poet or by listeners. However, we are told that the other poems were transcribed while Brandolini sang.[28] The second, in elegiac couplets (ninety-two lines long), dates from the same period and was composed on a theme set by one of the ambassadors, as its rubric records: 'Rogatus a Bernardo Bembo equiti [sic] legato uti tempora deploraret nostra, prisca autem lauderet, Petro Bembo legati ipsius filio scribente lyra sic cecinit' ('Asked by Bernardo Bembo, knight and ambassador, to lament our times and praise the old ones, he sang thus to the lira, with the ambassador's son Pietro Bembo transcribing'). Pietro was then aged about fifteen. At the outset, the scribe receives a warning:

> Ad Latios veniam prompto nunc carmine versus:
> ipse para calamum, scriptor amice, tuum.
> Non poteris mea verba sequi: velocius ibo,
> non poteris nostros scribere versiculos.

[I shall come now to Latin verses with my song ready: friendly scribe, prepare your pen. You will not be able to follow my words: I shall go faster, you will not be able to write our little verses.]

The record concludes with two strambotti, termed 'rithmi', sung at the request of Pietro Diedo, one of three other Venetian ambassadors, who presumably now wanted some vernacular verse. The first insists on the precedence to be given to Latin over the vernacular, while the second asks listeners to await the performance, carrying on with their business in the meantime:

Cecinerat Latinos versus, iussusque Petro Diedo equiti legato rithmos canere in hunc modum Lyppum [sic] exorsus est:

> Non debbe ananti la ricolta andare,
> o pecti generosi, a la semente;
> non debbe il caro <il> forte buo menare,
> debbeno i tauri andar imantenente.
> Non de' el men degno el degno superare,
> vincer l'indocto el savio intelligente.
> Egli è consiglio humano e divino
> che vadi ananzi al vulgar il latino.
>
> Hor aspectiati, o mie signor, un pocho,
> spazate in questo mezo le facende
> et date agli aspectanti il modo e locho;
> la lyra in questo megio se difende.
> Io mentre che fenisse un altro giocho
> non vo' che qui nissun [h]a mi riprende;
> pur presto le vostre facende spazati [sic],
> in questo mezo un pocho m'aspectate.

Si quos invenisti versus minus bonos id erroris ascribito iis qui Lyppo Florentino ceco canente scriptitarunt.

[He had sung the Latin verses, and at the command of Pietro Diedo, knight and ambassador, Lippo began to sing poems in this manner. [...] If you have found any verses that are less good, ascribe the error to those who wrote while the blind Florentine Lippo was singing.]

Linguistic alterations and errors must indeed have been introduced during transmission (for one thing, the penultimate line has twelve syllables),[29] and the final note suggests that Pietro Bembo was not the only transcriber. Yet the two strambotti, at least, and especially the second with its evident verbal padding and threefold repetition of 'in questo mezzo' or 'megio', have the ring of authentic, unrevised, records of an improvisation.

Judgements on the quality of improvised verse should be seen in the context of the esteem shown for promptness and spontaneity of wit. Pride in the ability to conjure up an apt and pithy comment, is reflected in Alberti's autobiography. The *Vita* ends, in the manner of lives of philosophers by Diogenes Laertius, with many examples of his 'dicta', introduced with the comment: 'Fuerunt qui eius dicta et seria et ridicula complurima colligerent, quae quidem ille ex tempore atque e vestigio celerius ediderit ferme quam praemeditarit' ('Some collected many sayings, both serious and amusing, that he uttered on the spur of the moment and instantly, more swiftly almost than he considered in advance').[30] A similar list is given at the end of Machiavelli's life of Castruccio Castracani, who 'era mirabile nel rispondere o mordere, o acutamente o urbanamente'.[31] A gift for extempore eloquence was widely admired. Cristoforo Landino praised Dante as 'in extemporanea oratione molto eloquente'.[32] Landino counted this among the many talents of Lorenzo de' Medici, while also noting the need to burnish it: 'Eloquentiam vero sive extemporanea sit sive excogitata et a natura copiosam accepit et artificio atque exercitatione illam gravitate iocunditateque illustrem reddidit' ('In truth he both received eloquence — whether extemporary or prepared in advance — in abundance from nature, and rendered it illustrious with skill and practice, with seriousness and enjoyment').[33]

Some Renaissance voices speak with admiration of the nature of extempore verse. Agnolo Poliziano concluded a eulogy of Baccio Ugolini by asking: 'Quid postremo carminibus illis, sive quae ad citharam canit extempore, sive quae per otium componit, dulcius, mundius, limatius, venustius?' ('Finally, what is sweeter, more elegant, more polished, more charming than his poems, whether those he sings extempore to the lira or those he composes at leisure?').[34] Although polish is mentioned here, elsewhere Poliziano writes that Homer's best poems were spontaneous: 'pulcherrima illa carmina [...] illaborata ipsi atque extemporanea fluebant' ('his most beautiful poetry flowed from him without effort and extemporaneously').[35] Elsewhere Poliziano takes a stance against Horace's 'labor limae' (*Ars poetica*, 291), ranking improvisation above excessive polishing: 'saepe usu venit ut scripta nostra nimia cura vel peiora fiant: neque tam lima poliantur quam exterantur' ('often it happens that too much application worsens our writings, and the file does not smooth them as much as it wears them out').[36] Likewise, Raffaele Brandolini, younger brother of Aurelio, goes as far as writing, in a treatise dedicated to Leo X, that an improvised song deserves more credit than one composed with care: 'dico [...] maiorem deinde fidem admirationemque improvisum quam elaboratum poema procul dubio comparare' ('I claim [...] that an extempore song unquestionably merits greater credit and admiration than one carefully composed').[37] Brandolini was of course biased, since he was himself an improviser of Latin verse, but we also have unqualified praise from the more objective Mario Equicola when he writes: 'Di nostri tempi, Bernardo Accolti, unico, per essere in le inventioni beato, in le parole felice, in commovere admirabile, in extemporale dictione non solo de li altri, ma di sé stesso vincitore laudato.'[38]

Paolo Cortese, in 1510, writes of the pleasure to be derived from vernacular improvisation — from Ugolini and Iacopo Corsi in the previous generation, and now from Accolti, the most celebrated living exponent:

> Mirifice etiam voluptas ex his hominibus capi honesta potest qui ex tempore dicuntur plebeio sermone canere solere ad lyram. Quo ex genere, ut nuper B. Ugolinus et Jacobus Corsus in Italia sunt laudari soliti, sic hodie maxime debet Bernardus Accoltus celebrari, qui, quanquam versus ex tempore dicat, ita tamen apte sententiis verba concinna iungit, ut, cum celeritati semper parata sit venia, magis in eo sint laudanda quae fundat quam ignoscendum quod ex tempore et partu repentino dicat, quae sit gignentis ingenii, non dicentis cogitate laus.[39]

> [And an honourable pleasure can be obtained marvellously from these men who are said to sing usually extempore in the vernacular to the lira. In this genre, just as Baccio Ugolini and Iacopo Corsi used recently to be praised, so nowadays Bernardo Accolti deserves to be most greatly celebrated. Although he speaks verses extempore, he joins elegant words to his subject matter so suitably that, since one is always ready to make allowances for rapidity, he is to be praised more greatly for what he pours forth than he is to be forgiven because speaking extempore and on the spur of the moment; this is a ground for praise of a prolific spirit, but not of a thoughtful speaker.]

However, Cortese's comments on Accolti imply that his verse suffered somewhat from being composed rapidly. Lilio Gregorio Giraldi expresses similar reservations even more firmly. He appears to approve of the verses of Flavio Antonio Giraldi mentioned above but, when discussing Battista Mantovano, an improviser in Latin, he states clearly that poetry that seems made up off the cuff is bound to be limited in its nature: 'Laudo institutum piumque propositum, verum extemporalis magis quam poeta maturus' ('I value highly his religious order and the devout purpose of his life, but as a poet I think he produced verses that have an extemporaneous flavor rather than being the product of fully developed skills').[40] With this, one can contrast Giraldi's praise for the Latin verse composed and revised by Iacopo Sannazaro: 'non enim verborum volubilitate fertur, sed limatius quoddam scribendi genus consectatur et lima in dies atterit' ('he is not carried away by too copious a flow of diction; he aims rather for a more polished style of writing. He refines his verse day after day').[41] Indeed, elsewhere Giraldi seems to imply that improvisation was a secondary accomplishment. Of Niccolò Leoniceno he writes: 'in iuvenili sua aetate non modo meditatos argute et docte composuit, sed etiam, ut saepe mihi memorare solitus fuit, ex tempore et impraemeditata carmina cecinit' ('in his youth not only did he produce, after great thought, verses that were learned and well-crafted, but, as he often would say to me, he also composed poems extemporaneously and without any forethought').[42] Andrzei Krzycki (Andreas Critius), the Polish bishop of Plock, 'carmina pangit feliciter, et felicior in oratione soluta; dicit et ex tempore' ('is a felicitous poet, and is even more felicitous in his prose writings; he can also speak extemporaneously').[43]

Lyric poetry could also have been extemporized not for oral performance, but in the course of writing a prose composition, as a spontaneous effusion in a moment of intense feeling. A study of some instances of extempore poetry embedded in eighteenth-century English correspondence has described it as 'verse within prose letters that appears to be composed during the process of writing, that continues the matter of the letter but in a different mode of expression'; it is 'an immediate and integral part of the letter, unlike verse that has merely been inserted'.[44] It is not easy to identify verse found within prose as extemporized, since it might have been composed earlier; but there is a good chance that it is new if it develops what the writer is saying and is not a straightforward quotation. Moreover, the autograph manuscript of the letter, if it survives, may indicate that its composition is continuous, unlike, for instance, letters of Aretino where sonnets follow the signature, or those of Michelangelo in which poems are inserted on the verso or in the margins of a letter.

One possible example of epistolary extempore verse is found in the correspondence of Niccolò Machiavelli. On 4 February 1514, he replied to a letter in which his friend Francesco Vettori, who was in Rome, had recounted how one evening he, Giuliano Brancacci and Filippo Casavecchia were visited by three neighbours: a widow, her daughter aged twenty and her son aged fourteen. The girl proved of great interest to Brancacci, while Casavecchia, typically for him, made a beeline for the boy. Machiavelli, in reply, describes how he imagines the scene in Vettori's house, and at one point he breaks into a tercet describing Casavecchia:

> Volsimi da man destra, e viddi il Casa
> che a quel garzone era più presso al segno,
> in gote un poco, e con la zucca rasa.[45]

It seems certain that these lines had not been composed earlier, but rather that they came into Machiavelli's mind as he was writing his letter, which forms part of a correspondence full of poetry and poetic allusions.[46]

Two letters of the same correspondence open with lines of poetry that are original. Although these verses did not arise from a process of writing that had already begun, as did the tercet of 4 February 1514, they may have been created when the men took up their pens to write the letters. The first case is Vettori's letter of 30 December 1514 (no. 245, p. 485), which begins with an elegiac couplet: 'Ecce iterum mihi bella movet violenta cupido, | compater, ecce iterum torqueor igne novo' ('Behold, my friend, a violent desire is again beginning a war on me; behold, again I am tortured by a new fire'). The lines are not quoted from elsewhere, although the image of love as warfare is inspired by the opening of Ovid's *Remedia amoris*: 'Legerat huius Amor titulum nomenque libelli: | "Bella mihi, video, bella parantur" ait' ('Love read the name and title of this book: "Wars," said he, "wars are in store for me, I perceive"').[47] A month later, on 31 January 1515, Machiavelli outdoes Vettori by opening a letter with a sonnet on his own sufferings in love ('Havea tentato il giovinetto Arciere'). The poem could of course have been composed over a period of time, but Machiavelli insists that it is an integral part of his letter: 'Io non saprei rispondere all'ultima vostra lettera [16 January

1515] della foia con altre parole che mi paressino più a proposito, che con questo sonetto'.[48]

A letter sent by Annibal Caro to Giovanni Gaddi on 13 October 1532 includes a tailed sonnet that might have been inspired during the process of writing the letter. Caro was in the small town of Tolfa, in the hills north of Rome. The sonnet gives a graphic description of this 'deserto', as he describes it at the start of the letter, and it is intended to be passed on to a certain Giovanni Boni, 'che vuol sapere che cosa sia la Tolfa, e non ci manda danari'.[49] A later letter, sent to Francesco Maria Molza on 28 June 1543, contains the cryptic single hendecasyllable 'Che son nimiche de le giovaresche', a line that may have come into Caro's mind apropos of certain 'stregaccie' to whom he is referring.[50] Incidentally, we can see, from all these possible surviving examples, that extempore lyric verse varied in length from a single line to a pair of lines, one or two tercets, a strambotto, a sonnet or a long sequence of verses. However, canzoni and madrigals do not appear to have been improvised, no doubt because they were metrically more complex.

How far was improvisation spontaneous and how far could it draw on resources at the poet's disposal? A show of spontaneity was certainly admired. Girolamo Ruscelli's account of Machiavelli as an improviser of strambotti mentions how Francesco del Nero, Machiavelli's brother-in-law, and others tested his inventiveness as far as possible:

> fra molti s'ha memoria di M. Nicolò Macchiavelli, il quale aprendo qual si voglia poeta Latino, et mettendoselo avanti sopr'una tavola egli sonando la lira veniva improvisamente cantando, et volgarizando, o traducendo quei versi di quel poeta, et facendone stanze d'Ottava Rima, con tanta leggiadria di stile, et con tanta agevolezza serbando i veri modi del tradurre, che il mio M. Francesco del Nero, il quale fu molto suo domestico, mi raccontava in Napoli, che egli con molt'altri in Fiorenza fecero ogni pruova per chiarirsi, che il detto Macchiavelli ciò facesse improvisamente, parendo à ciascuno impossibile, che all'improviso egli potesse far quello, che molti dotti, et di sublime ingegno confessavano, che haverebbono penato a far con qualche convenevole spatio di tempo.[51]

According to an account given in Benedetto Varchi's dialogue *L'Hercolano*, Silvio Antoniano insisted on not choosing his own topic when he improvised 'in su la lira' in Florence in the mid-1550s:

> VARCHI   [...] io per me, se udito non l'havessi, mai non harei creduto che si fussono improvvisamente potuti fare così leggiadri e così sentenziosi versi.
> CONTE   Il tutto sta se sono pensati innanzi, come molti dicono.
> VARCHI   Lasciategli pure dire, che egli non canta mai che non voglia che gli sia dato il tema da altri, et io gliele diedi due volte e amendue, una in terza rima e l'altra in ottava, disse tutto quello che in sulla materia postagli parve a me che dire non solo si dovesse, ma si potesse, con graziosissima maniera e modestissima grazia.[52]

However, we need to recall that the appearance of spontaneity in any activity in early modern Italy did not, indeed was not supposed to, preclude drawing on some resources in order to prepare and support a performance. Castiglione wanted his ideal courtier to seem to exercise all his skills without premeditation, but at the same time he argued that any effective show of improvisation had to be grounded in preparation: 'in ogni cosa che egli abbia da far o dire, se possibil è, sempre venga premeditato e preparato, mostrando però il tutto esser all'improviso' (II. 38, p. 250).

By the late fifteenth century, all well-educated poets would have been familiar with the advice given by Quintilian in the *Institutio oratoria* on the ability to improvise a speech, the 'ex tempore dicendi facultas' (x. 7. 1).[53] The aspiring orator is told that speaking off the cuff requires much preparation and practice, and a good memory. 'Mobilita[s] animi' ('nimbleness of mind', x. 7. 8) is needed but plays a relatively small role. 'Usus quidam inrationalis' ('a sort of irrational knack', x. 7. 11–12) is useful only as long as it is based on reason. The skill has to be developed gradually and is found also among poets (x. 7. 18–19). Improvisation should be grounded in preparatory writing by the orator: 'Scribendum certe numquam est magis quam cum multa dicemus ex tempore' ('Certainly, writing is never more necessary than when we have to improvise a lot', x. 7. 28).

For improvising poets as well as for orators — and for other performers with the word including preachers and actors of the *commedia dell'arte* — a key supporting technique for mental composition was the use or the imitative reworking of ideas and phrases stored in the memory.[54] Giraldi implies that the success of Panfilo Sasso as an improviser depended at least in part on his excellent memory, so good that it worked to the detriment of the quality of his verse:

> Pamphilus etiam Sassius Mutinensis, extemporalis poeta, qui, ut inter loquendum celerrime verba volvit, ita in faciendis versibus promptissimus. [...] Illi memoria paene divina non in poetis modo, sed et in ceteris in omni facultate scriptoribus. Sed ne in eo verissimum illud esse videtur, quod est ab Aristotele proditum, quod qui memoria excellunt plerumque ingenio ac iudicio deficiunt: minus enim omnino Sassio iudicii ac limae.
>
> [Panfilo Sasso, from Modena, is also an improvisational poet, and his speed in composing verses matches the great speed with which he speaks in conversation. [...] He has an almost superhuman memory, not only as far as poets are concerned, but for all other writers in every subject. [...]. But, to be sure, he seems to illustrate the great truth of what Aristotle said, that those who surpass others in the power of their memory are generally deficient in natural talent and judgment. For Sasso completely lacks discrimination and the desire to polish his work.][55]

The repertoire of some of those who had a reputation as improvisers may well have included pieces that had been committed to memory verbatim, though they might have been adapted for different occasions. Benedetto Dei's *Croniche fiorentine*, of the late fifteenth century, includes a list of thirty-eight 'sonetti a mente', which probably means sonnets learned by heart. He lists only their openings (quotations range from one line to up to part of the third line), suggesting that he now held them all in memory.[56] The characters in Castiglione's *Il libro del cortegiano* suspected that the sonnet on the letter S performed by Accolti under the guise of improvisation, mentioned earlier, had been thought out beforehand: 'da molti fu estimato fatto all'improviso, ma, per esser ingenioso e culto più che non parve che comportasse la brevità del tempo, si pensò pur che fosse pensato' (I. 9). Varchi's Conte Ercolani shared such scepticism about how much apparently extempore material was in fact 'pensato' or 'premeditato' ('Il tutto sta se [i versi] sono pensati innanzi'); and on occasion it must have been hard, or even impossible, for listeners to say where a performance belonged on a spectrum ranging from entirely prepared orality to partly or wholly improvised orality.

It is probable that those lyric poets who did improvise combined inventiveness with the use of material that they held in memory, or perhaps texts that they even had before them in writing, as in Ruscelli's account of Machiavelli translating.[57] Although lyric poets did not apparently rely on stock formulae in the same way as did narrative improvisers, it is certain that they were in the habit of adapting source material by other poets and perhaps by themselves. This was part of the art of *imitatio* as taught by Roman rhetoricians, albeit to be used with some caution, as Martin has shown in his classic study.[58] Anyone with a humanistic education was trained not just to memorize texts by canonical Latin authors but also to mark and write down striking phrases and maxims for possible reuse on a suitable occasion.[59] Giovio must have had this in mind when he wrote of Marone's apparently 'multum ante provisa et meditata carmina'. Lorenzo's sonnet on the transformed lover, for example, draws on Petrarch's canzone of the metamorphoses, 'Nel dolce tempo de la prima etade': one can compare 'per essemplo di me sia più saggio elli' (line 6) with 'di ch'io son facto a molta gente exempio' (*Rerum vulgarium fragmenta*, 23. 9), and Lorenzo's lover turned into stone with Petrarch's use of the Ovidian myth of Battus transformed by Mercury ('ed ella [...] fecemi, oimè lasso, | d'un quasi vivo et sbigottito sasso', *RVF*, 23. 78–80). Lorenzo's phrase 'duro sasso' (line 4) is found in Petrarch's description of the metamorphosis of Echo in the *Triumphus Cupidinis*: 'ignuda voce | fecesi, e 'l corpo un duro sasso asciutto' (II. 149–50), and it refers to Laura's tomb in Petrarch's 'Ite, rime dolenti, al duro sasso' (*RVF*, 333. 1). Lorenzo's 'misero amante' (line 1) echoes a phrase of Petrarch's (*RVF*, 87. 10); his 'rigida pietra' (line 9) recalls 'petra [...] rigida' (*RVF*, 51. 7); like Lorenzo's eyes (line 12), Petrarch's are 'bassi' in *RVF*, 306. 7. The improvising performer Cristoforo Fiorentino could reuse his own material with some variation between his lyric and his narrative verse.[60] An example of creative imitation is found in the poem with which Iacopo Antiquario welcomed Aldo to Milan, in which lines 3 and 9 draw on a line from Plautus's *Casina*: 'meum corculum, melculum, verculum'.[61] Similarly, the tercet in Machiavelli's letter to Vettori of 4 February 1514 combines phrases drawn from the opening canto of Dante's *Purgatorio* — 'I' mi volsi a man destra, e puosi mente | a l'altro polo' (I. 22–23) — and from Petrarch's *Triumphus Fame*:

> Volsimi da man manca, e vidi Plato,
> che 'n quella schiera andò più presso al segno
> al qual aggiunge cui dal cielo è dato. (III. 4–6)

Such reminiscences are akin to the verse semiquotations that can be found within prose compositions, with distortions that can sometimes be thought of as intentional adaptations, since they are not necessarily due to errors of memory. A case in Machiavelli's correspondence concerns his letter to Vettori of 31 January 1515. This ends with two lines of verse that Machiavelli uses to remind his friend not to forget him and his political experience if Vettori's brother Paolo were appointed by Leo X as a governor in the Romagna: 'E nel cadere el superbo ghiottone, | e' non dimenticò però Macone'.[62] As Najemy has shown, Machiavelli is drawing here on three stanzas from Luigi Pulci's *Morgante* in which Orlando kills two giants, who die without forgetting another name that begins with the syllable 'Mac':

> e nel cadere il superbo e villano
> divotamente Macon bestemiava. (I. 35. 5–6)
>
> Che pensi tu, ghiotton, gittar quel sasso? (I. 37. 6)
>
> e morto cadde questo badalone,
> e non dimenticò però Macone. (I. 38. 7–8).[63]

A letter of Machiavelli's to Francesco Guicciardini of 19 December 1525 includes this tercet based on Dante's *Paradiso*, VI. 133–35:

> Quattro figlie ebbe, e ciascuna regina,
> della qual cosa al tutto fu cagione
> Romeo, persona umile e peregrina.

The second line of Dante's text, 'Ramondo Beringhiere, e ciò li fece', was replaced, surely not through misremembering (the two other lines are recalled perfectly), but rather because its detail was irrelevant to Machiavelli's discussion of the marriage prospects of his fellow-Florentine's four daughters, and his ironic comparison of his own advisory role to that of Dante's Romeo di Villanova.[64] Such bricolages can be described as a kind of improvisation, and they reflect the ability of improvisers such as Machiavelli to reuse on the spur of the moment, consciously or unconsciously, the stock of source material that they stored in their minds. As literary historians and musicologists have argued, improvisation of text or music normally involved both creativity and the recycling or refashioning of material held in a well-trained memory.[65]

A further underlying technical skill that was common to all vernacular poets of the period, educated and uneducated alike, was the almost instinctive ability to compose a correct hendecasyllable; Luca Zuliani has pointed out that this widespread 'competenza metrica' was largely lost only in the twentieth century.[66]

Some aspects of the improvisation of Latin and vernacular lyric poetry in Renaissance Italy are fairly clear-cut, while others remain in part elusive. We know the names of several renowned improvisers, and another reason for which the genre deserves attention is that they include figures of the stature of Lorenzo de' Medici and Niccolò Machiavelli. We know a fair amount about the social circumstances in which improvisation took place, and about its roles, including that of comment on the behaviour of others, sometimes with a cutting edge. We can see that the skill of improvising verse was admired, even if the results were regarded as inherently ephemeral and were not always taken seriously in terms of quality. We can argue plausibly that improvisation could take place during an act of writing as well as in the course of oral performance.

However, it is harder to evaluate the verse itself. Much of what was performed appears to have gone unrecorded in the written tradition, or at least is not identified as such. Even when we have verse that is described as having been improvised, it may have been altered when written down. And it is not easy to judge how much improvisation went into verse that is embedded within letters. This absence of firm textual evidence means in turn that it is difficult to analyse the methods of composition used by lyric improvisers. Yet we still have enough evidence to see that the alchemy of improvisation depended on a blend of ingredients, on preparation and memory as well as some spontaneous mental agility. While we must admire the remarkable gifts for verbal and musical invention that were displayed by Renaissance improvisers of lyric verse, we should also recognize that their techniques were firmly grounded in skills of composition and adaptation that were developed through reading and study.

Notes to Chapter 7

The research leading to this essay received funding from the European Research Council under the European Union's Seventh Framework Programme (FP7/2007–2013) / ERC Grant Agreement no. 269460. I am very grateful to my research colleague Luca Degl'Innocenti for his suggestions.

1. *Venetia città nobilissima et singolare* (Venice: Giacomo Sansovino, 1581), fol. Bbb2^r. A survey of improvised verse in Italy is Adele Vitagliano, *Storia della poesia estemporanea nella letteratura italiana dalle origini ai nostri giorni* (Rome: Loescher, 1905).
2. Domenico Gnoli, 'I Cosmalia', in *La Roma di Leon X: quadri e studi originali* (Milan: Hoepli, 1938), pp. 108–24 (p. 122).
3. Lilio Gregorio Giraldi, *Modern Poets*, ed. and trans. by John N. Grant (Cambridge, MA: Harvard University Press, 2011), I. 136, pp. 80–81. Dialogue I is set between 1513 and 1515: see p. xxvi.
4. Giraldi, I. 140, pp. 80–83.
5. Paolo Giovio, *Notable Men and Women of Our Time*, ed. and trans. by Kenneth Gouwens (Cambridge, MA: Harvard University Press, 2013), pp. 226–27. Giovio refers to this description in his *Elogia*, LXXII: see *Gli Elogi degli uomini illustri*, ed. by Renzo Meregazzi (Rome: Istituto poligrafico dello Stato, Libreria dello Stato, 1972), pp. 96–97. On these performances, see also Gnoli, pp. 119–20.
6. Julia Haig Gaisser, *Pierio Valeriano on the Ill Fortune of Learned Men: A Renaissance Humanist and his World* (Ann Arbor: University of Michigan Press, 1999), pp. 184–87. Valeriano is quoting from own poem 'De Andreae Maronis extemporalitate ad Dantem III Aligerum'.
7. Philippe Canguilhem, 'Singing upon the Book according to Vicente Lusitano', *Early Music History*, 30 (2011), 55–103 (p. 96).
8. Benvenuto Cellini, *La vita*, ed. by Lorenzo Bellotto (Parma: Guanda, 1996), I. 30, p. 110. On Morani, see the entry by Giuseppe Crimi in the *Dizionario biografico degli Italiani*, 76 (Rome: Istituto della Enciclopedia Italiana, 2012), 499–502.
9. Vittorio Cian, *Un decennio della vita di M. Pietro Bembo, 1521–1531* (Turin: Loescher, 1885), pp. 229, 240; see also Francesca Bortoletti, 'Reviviscenze del Parnaso', in *L'attore del Parnaso: profili di attori-musici e drammaturgie d'occasione*, ed. by Francesca Bortoletti (Milan: Mimesis, 2012), pp. 13–95 (p. 73).
10. Michel de Montaigne, *Journal de voyage*, ed. by François Rigolot (Paris: Presses Universitaires de France, 1992), pp. 145–46.
11. Giorgio Vasari, *Le vite de' più eccellenti pittori, scultori e architettori nelle redazioni del 1550 e 1568*, ed. by Rosanna Bettarini and Paola Barocchi, 8 vols (Florence: SPES, 1966–87), *Testo*, IV, 16.
12. Nino Pirrotta, *Music and Culture in Italy from the Middle Ages to the Baroque: A Collection of Essays* (Cambridge, MA: Harvard University Press, 1984), p. 168. Studies of improvised song

in this period include James Haar, '*Improvvisatori* and their Relationship to Sixteenth-Century Music', in *Essays on Italian Poetry and Music in the Renaissance, 1350–1600* (Berkeley: University of California Press, 1986), pp. 76–99.
13. Antonfrancesco Grazzini, *Le cene*, ed. by Riccardo Bruscagli (Rome: Salerno Editrice, 1976), III. 10, p. 359. As Bruscagli points out, the nature of the 'villania' is unclear, but it might refer to Manente's joining in the session without being a member of Lorenzo's circle.
14. Ibid., p. 344. 'A desco molle' means during light meals.
15. See Mario Martelli, 'Gli strambotti di Lorenzo', in *Studi laurenziani* (Florence: Olschki, 1965), pp. 135–78 (pp. 144–47). Martelli discusses a letter to Lorenzo from Niccolò Michelozzi, dated 10 July 1473, that refers to the possible setting to music of 'quattro de' vostri strambotti'. Martelli suggests that some of Lorenzo's verse has been lost, including improvised poems, but also that some of these were transcribed and polished by him and inserted in other works: for example, the *Selve* in the case of his strambotti. Raffaella Castagnola rejects Martelli's thesis that the *Selve* were composed gradually: see her edition of the *Stanze*, as she terms the work (Florence: Olschki, 1986), pp. lxx–lxxxviii. Paolo Orvieto is inclined to accept that the work grew over the years and points out that some stanzas are transmitted as single strambotti or in small groups: see his 'Nota introduttiva' to the *Selve* in Lorenzo de' Medici, *Tutte le opere*, 2 vols (Rome: Salerno Editrice, 1992), I, 535–40 (pp. 537, 538).
16. *Aldo Manuzio editore: dediche, prefazioni, note ai testi*, intro. by Carlo Dionisotti, ed. and trans. by Giovanni Orlandi, 2 vols (Milan: Il Polifilo, 1976), I, 100–01 and II, 271, doc. LXVI. See also Giovanni Battista Vermiglioli, *Memorie di Jacopo Antiquari e degli studi di amena letteratura esercitati in Perugia nel secolo decimoquinto* (Perugia: Francesco Baduel, 1813), pp. 110–12. Translations not otherwise attributed are mine.
17. *La vita*, p. 108.
18. Giraldi, *Modern Poets*, I. 188, pp. 104–05, translation modified.
19. Giovio, *Gli Elogi*, LXXXII, p. 106; Gnoli, p. 122. The allusion may be to Virgil, *Georgics*, II. 93–94: 'tenuisque lageos | temptatura pedes'.
20. Giraldi, II. 116, pp. 174–75.
21. Lodovico Guicciardini, *L'ore di ricreazione*, ed. by Anne-Marie Van Passen (Leuven: Leuven University Press; Rome: Bulzoni, 1990), no. 347, pp. 175–76.
22. *Canzoniere*, no. XXIX, in *Tutte le opere*, ed. by Paolo Orvieto (Rome: Salerno Editrice, 1992), I, 77–78, with 'tanto' for 'tanta' in line 13. Charles Dempsey suggests that it was written in reply to Pulci's canzone 'Da poi che 'l Lauro più, lasso, non vidi', sent to Lorenzo in 1466: see his *Inventing the Renaissance Putto* (Chapel Hill: University of North Carolina Press, 2001), p. 152.
23. No. 467, p. 218. In no. 481 (p. 223), Boiardo declaims a stanza on avarice, in reaction to a real-life instance; but a near-identical stanza is found in his *Inamoramento de Orlando* (II. 17. 1).
24. Baldesar Castiglione, *Il libro del cortegiano con una scelta delle opere minori*, ed. by Bruno Maier, 2nd edn (Turin: UTET, 1964), I. 9, pp. 95–96.
25. In Venice, Biblioteca Marciana, MS It. IX 203 (6757), fols 50^v–51^r, the sonnet is attributed to Accolti and follows another more complex sonnet on a similar topic, beginning 'Se latina è la lettera che porti'. A sonnet in praise of a young Florentine by Cristoforo Fiorentino, known as l'Altissimo, 'Sopra uno F.', is based on words starting with 'f', and this tautogrammatic technique could have been favoured by improvisers. It begins: 'Fortunato figliuol, formosa fronte, | fa a mie forze fral fermo favore, | fa ch'io diffonda, faticando fore, | l'F. fatal che ti fu fatto al fonte'; see *Strambotti e sonetti dell'Altissimo*, ed. by Rodolfo Renier (Turin: Società Bibliofila, 1886), *Sonetti*, XXXII, p. 56. For some further cases of improvisation, see Brian Richardson, '"Recitato e cantato": The Oral Diffusion of Lyric Poetry in Sixteenth-Century Italy', in *Theatre, Opera, and Performance in Italy from the Fifteenth Century to the Present: Essays in Honour of Richard Andrews*, ed. by Brian Richardson, Simon Gilson and Catherine Keen (Leeds: Society for Italian Studies, 2004), pp. 67–82 (pp. 71–72), *Manuscript Culture in Renaissance Italy* (Cambridge: Cambridge University Press, 2009), pp. 251–54, and 'The Social Connotations of Singing Verse in Cinquecento Italy', *The Italianist*, 34 (2014), 362–78 (pp. 366–68).
26. Some Latin and vernacular works by Acciaiuoli are mentioned in Girolamo Tiraboschi, *Biblioteca modenese*, 6 vols (Modena: Società tipografica, 1781–86), I, 76–77.

27. The poems are in Biblioteca Marciana, MS Lat. XII 210 (4689), fols 2bis^r-7^v. See Paul Oskar Kristeller, *Iter italicum*, 6 vols (London: Warburg Institute, 1963–92), II, 260; Vittorio Cian, 'Per Bernardo Bembo: le sue relazioni letterarie, i codici e gli scritti', *Giornale storico della letteratura italiana*, 31 (1898), 49–81 (pp. 78–80); Nella Giannetto, *Bernardo Bembo umanista e politico veneziano* (Florence: Olschki, 1985), pp. 176–77.
28. On transcription in the eighteenth and nineteenth centuries, see Michael Caesar, 'Poetic Improvisation and the Challenge of Transcription', in *Theatre, Opera, and Performance*, ed. by Richardson, Gilson and Keen, pp. 173–84.
29. On lines such as this, consisting of two *senari*, see G. E. Sansone, 'Appunti sul tredecasillabo e sull'endecasillabo ipermetro', *Giornale storico della letteratura italiana*, 128 (1951), 176–83 (p. 181).
30. Riccardo Fubini and Anna Menci Gallorini, 'L'autobiografia di L. B. Alberti: studio e edizione', *Rinascimento*, 2nd ser., 12 (1972), 21–78 (p. 73), and see Martin McLaughlin, 'Alberti and the Classical Canon', in *Italy and the Classical Tradition: Language, Thought and Poetry 1300–1600*, ed. by Carlo Caruso and Andrew Laird (London: Duckworth, 2009), 73–100 (p. 89).
31. *La vita di Castruccio Castracani da Lucca*, in Niccolò Machiavelli, *Opere storiche*, ed. by Alessandro Montevecchi and Carlo Varotti, 2 vols (Rome: Salerno Editrice, 2010), I, 1–66 (p. 56).
32. Cristoforo Landino, *Comento sopra la Comedia*, ed. by Paolo Procaccioli, 4 vols (Rome: Salerno Editrice, 2001), I, 252.
33. Cristoforo Landino, *Proemio al commento virgiliano*, in *Scritti critici e teorici*, ed. by Roberto Cardini, 2 vols (Rome: Bulzoni, 1974), I, 203–25 (p. 224).
34. From a letter to Francesco Pucci of late 1489 or early 1490, in Angelo Poliziano, *Opera* (Basel: Nicolaus Episcopius iunior, 1553), *Epistolae*, VI. 5, p. 79. On Poliziano as an improviser, see Elisa Curti, '"Udii cantar improviso": alcune osservazioni su Poliziano e la musica', in *L'attore del Parnaso*, ed. by Bortoletti, pp. 211–23 (p. 213). James Hankins describes 'improvised monodic song to the lyre' as 'the humanists' favorite musical genre', in 'Humanism and Music in Italy', in *The Cambridge History of Fifteenth-Century Music*, ed. by Anna Maria Busse Berger and Jesse Rodin (Cambridge: Cambridge University Press, 2015), pp. 231–62 (pp. 252–57).
35. *Oratio in expositione Homeri*, in Poliziano, *Opera*, pp. 477–92 (p. 479).
36. *Oratio super Fabio Quintiliano et Statii Sylvis*, ibid., pp. 492–98 (p. 494).
37. Raffaele Brandolini, *On Music and Poetry (De musica et poesia, 1513)*, ed. and trans. by Ann E. Moyer (Tempe: Arizona Center for Medieval and Renaissance Studies, 2001), pp. 82–83.
38. *La redazione manoscritta del Libro de natura de amore di Mario Equicola*, ed. by Laura Ricci (Roma: Bulzoni, 1999), I. 11, p. 265. See also Celio Malespini's praise for Andrea Alberti delle Pomarancie, cited in Philippe Canguilhem, 'Singing Poetry *in compagnia* in Sixteenth-Century Italy', in *Voices and Texts in Early Modern Italian Society*, ed. by Stefano Dall'Aglio, Brian Richardson and Massimo Rospocher (London: Routledge, 2016), pp. 113–23 (p. 118).
39. *De cardinalatu* ([San Gimignano]: Simone Nardi, 1510), Book III, fols Q12^v-Q13^r. See also Carlo Dionisotti, *Gli umanisti e il volgare fra Quattro e Cinquecento* (Florence: Le Monnier, 1968), p. 73. According to a letter of Stefano Taverna to Lodovico Sforza of 18 February 1493, Corsi, 'quale stava col Reverendissimo cardinale [Federico] Sanseverino et diceva in proviso et in sonetti', had recently been assassinated, allegedly on the orders of Cardinale Giuliano della Rovere, for having 'contato [probably an error for 'cantato'] improviso alcune cose poco honorevole de luy' at a dinner. See Pio Paschini, 'Una famiglia di curiali nella Roma del Quattrocento: i Cortesi', *Rivista di storia della Chiesa in Italia*, 11 (1957), 1–48 (p. 33).
40. Giraldi, I. 88, pp. 56–57.
41. Ibid., I. 44, pp. 38–39.
42. Ibid., II. 101, pp. 164–65.
43. Ibid., II. 85, pp. 154–55; see also II. 68, pp. 146–47.
44. Bill Overton, 'Embedded Extempore Verse in the Intimate Letters of John, Lord Hervey (1696–1743)', *Modern Language Review*, 110.2 (2015), 379–98 (p. 379).
45. Niccolò Machiavelli, *Opere*, III, *Lettere*, ed. by Francesco Gaeta (Turin: UTET, 1984), no. 229, p. 442. 'In gote' may mean 'chubby-cheeked' or, according to the *Grande dizionario della lingua italiana*, s.v. *gota*^{7}, 'with a serious air'. On this letter, see John Najemy, *Between Friends: Discourses of Power and Desire in the Machiavelli–Vettori Letters of 1513–1515* (Princeton: Princeton University Press, 1993), pp. 264–70.

46. See the perceptive analysis of Najemy, pp. 313–34.
47. Ovid, *The Art of Love and Other Poems*, trans. by J. H. Mozley (London: Heinemann, 1969), pp. 178–79.
48. No. 247, pp. 488–89. The arms of Cupid are also a theme of Machiavelli's madrigal 'Chi non fa prova, Amore', on which see Brian Richardson, 'Gli intermedi del Machiavelli e i madrigali asolani', *Quaderni veneti*, n.s., 2 (2013), 251–58 (pp. 254–55).
49. Annibal Caro, *Lettere familiari*, ed. by Aulo Greco, 3 vols (Florence: Le Monnier, 1957–61), no. 3, I, 9.
50. Ibid., no. 200, I, 275. 'Giovaresco' may have the sense of 'pleasant'.
51. Girolamo Ruscelli, *Del modo di comporre in versi nella lingua italiana* (Venice: Giovanni Battista and Melchior Sessa, 1559), chapter 7, fol. k1^{r-v} (first state). On the significance of this passage, see Luca Degl'Innocenti, 'Machiavelli canterino?', *Nuova rivista di letteratura italiana*, 18.1 (2015), 11–67, especially pp. 13–26.
52. Benedetto Varchi, *L'Hercolano*, ed. by Antonio Sorella, 2 vols (Pescara: Libreria dell'Università, 1995), II, 878.
53. Quintilian, *The Orator's Education, Books 9–10*, ed. and trans. by Donald A. Russell (Cambridge, MA: Harvard University Press, 2001), pp. 372–89.
54. On memory and extemporaneity in medieval preaching and authorship, see Mary Carruthers, *The Book of Memory: A Study of Memory in Medieval Culture*, 2nd edn (Cambridge: Cambridge University Press, 2008), pp. 255–60. On improvisation in the *commedia*, see Richard Andrews, *Scripts and Scenarios: The Performance of Comedy in Renaissance Italy* (Cambridge: Cambridge University Press, 1993), especially pp. 169–203, and Robert Henke, *Performance and Literature in the Commedia dell'Arte* (Cambridge: Cambridge University Press, 2002), especially pp. 12–30, 32–38, 43–49, 52–54. Compare Philippe Canguilhem's observation that musical improvisation in the fifteenth century did not equate to an absence of planning, in 'Improvisation as Concept and Musical Practice in the Fifteenth Century', in *The Cambridge History of Fifteenth-Century Music*, ed. by Berger and Rodin, pp. 149–63 (esp. pp. 154–56).
55. Giraldi, I. 141–42, pp. 82–83. See David Bloch, *Aristotle on Memory and Recollection* (London: Brill, 2007), pp. 24–25.
56. Francesco Luisi, 'Minima fiorentina: sonetti a mente, canzoni a ballo e cantimpanca nel Quattrocento', in *Musica franca: Essays in Honor of Frank A. D'Accone*, ed. by Irene Alm, Alyson McLamore and Colleen Reardon (Stuyvesant, NY: Pendragon Press, 1996), pp. 79–95 (pp. 86–89).
57. See, too, the anecdote of Domenichi discussed by Degl'Innocenti, 'Machiavelli canterino?', pp. 21–25, in which Machiavelli improvises a strambotto based on Ovid, *Metamorphoses*, IV. 167–89. Machiavelli cites the concluding Latin line of this passage in a letter to Vettori of 25 February 1514 (*Lettere*, no. 231, p. 450).
58. Martin McLaughlin, *Literary Imitation in the Italian Renaissance: The Theory and Practice of Literary Imitation in Italy from Dante to Bembo* (Oxford: Clarendon Press, 1995), pp. 5–6.
59. See, for example, Peter Mack, *A History of Renaissance Rhetoric, 1380–1620* (Oxford: Oxford University Press, 2011), p. 315; Ann Moss, *Printed Commonplace-Books and the Structuring of Renaissance Thought* (Oxford: Clarendon Press, 1996), pp. 51–65, 92–100.
60. Luca Degl'Innocenti, *I 'Reali' dell'Altissimo: un ciclo di cantari fra oralità e scrittura* (Florence: Società editrice fiorentina, 2008), pp. 264–67, and 'Verba manent: precisazioni e supplementi d'indagine sulla trascrizione dell'oralità nei cantari dell'Altissimo', *Rassegna europea di letteratura italiana*, 39 (2012), 109–34 (p. 121). On recurrent words and phrases used by Bernardino Perfetti in the early eighteenth century, see Françoise Waquet, *Rhétorique et poétique chrétiennes: Bernardino Perfetti et la poésie improvisée dans l'Italie du XVIIIe siècle* (Florence: Olschki, 1992), pp. 107–24.
61. Plautus, *Casina*, ed. by W. T. MacCary and M. M. Willcock (Cambridge: Cambridge University Press, 1976), line 837, p. 83.
62. Machiavelli, *Lettere*, no. 247, p. 491.
63. Najemy, p. 320.
64. Machiavelli, *Lettere*, no. 301, p. 570. Further possible instances are found in letter no. 210, p. 371, where 'sfogare' replaces Petrarch's 'celare'; no. 230, p. 445, where 'atti' replaces Petrarch's 'cenni'; no. 247, p. 489, where 'Petreia' replaces Ovid's 'Penei'. On this last change, see Najemy, pp. 322–23.

65. Paola Ventrone, *Gli araldi della commedia: teatro a Firenze nel Rinascimento* (Pisa: Pacini, 1993), pp. 108–14; Degl'Innocenti, *I 'Reali' dell'Altissimo*, pp. 190–201; Blake Wilson, '*Canterino* and *improvvisatore*: Oral Poetry and Performance', in *The Cambridge History of Fifteenth-Century Music*, ed. by Berger and Rodin, pp. 292–310 (p. 292); id., 'The *Cantastorie/Canterino/Cantimbanco* as Musician', in *The Cantastorie in Renaissance Italy: Street Singers between Oral and Literate Cultures*, ed. by Luca Degl'Innocenti, Massimo Rospocher and Rosa Salzberg, *Italian Studies*, 71.2 (2016), 154–70. See, too, on 'semi-improvisation', Peter Burke, 'Oral and Manuscript Cultures in Early Modern Italy', in *Interactions between Orality and Writing in Early Modern Italian Culture*, ed. by Luca Degl'Innocenti, Brian Richardson and Chiara Sbordoni (Aldershot: Ashgate, 2016), pp. 21–30.
66. Luca Zuliani, *Poesia e versi per musica: l'evoluzione dei metri italiani* (Bologna: il Mulino, 2009), pp. 7–19 (p. 14).

CHAPTER 8

Piero Vettori and France

Richard Cooper

> Piero Vettori [...] may be regarded as possibly the greatest Greek scholar of Italy, as certainly the foremost representative of classical scholarship in that country during the sixteenth century, which, for Italy at least, may well be called the *saeculum Victorianum*.[1]

Vettori's distinction as a humanist scholar, witnessed in his many publications over a very long life (1499–1585), and in the orations on his death,[2] has been reaffirmed in biographical studies,[3] and most recently by the work of Raphaële Mouren.[4] Although an anti-Medicean republican, he finally came to terms with Cosimo I,[5] and taught for over forty years at the Florentine Studio. Much is known about his Florentine connections,[6] whether with Benedetto Varchi, with Giovanni Della Casa,[7] or with Donato Giannotti,[8] the last of whom did not make terms with Cosimo, and lived in exile.

But Vettori was at the centre of a pan-European network of correspondents:[9] work has been done on his links with German humanists and pupils,[10] drawing on collections of such letters,[11] many of which were preserved in his archive in the Bayerische Staatsbibliothek, Munich,[12] which contains his library and some of his papers.[13] Apart from some German correspondence printed in his lifetime, another 220 letters were published in 1586 just after his death.[14] But this leaves much to explore in what is one of the richest correspondences of the Renaissance, the bulk of which (4000 letters) was purchased in the nineteenth century by the British Library.[15]

Comparatively little work has been done on his French network, which proves much more extensive than might be expected from a man who never set foot in that country. The Republic of Letters was no respecter of national boundaries in this *saeculum Victorianum*, and we find Vettori closely engaged with French scholars and printers, ambassadors and poets, students and bankers, aristocrats and even a monarch, over a period of fifty years. The exchange with Germain and Nicolas Audebert (1574–78) has been studied,[16] as have Vettori's quarrels with Muret[17] and with Scaliger in the confrontation of Italian and French schools of philology.[18] The publication of the Pinelli-Dupuy correspondence has shed light on Claude Dupuy's links with Vettori.[19] A recent article has shown the importance of Sebastian Gryphius as a printer of some of Vettori's earliest works,[20] as well as the capital role of the Lyon *fuoruscito*, merchant and banker, Riniero Dei, as intermediary.[21]

In the crisis following the fall of the Florentine republic, Vettori and his friends were faced with difficult choices. Vettori withdrew from Florence, and was tempted by the possibility of a post in Rome. But he was also tempted, like many *fuorusciti*, by France. His cousin, Francesco Vettori, who had been ambassador in France (1515–18), encouraged him to dedicate his forthcoming edition of Cicero to François Ier, who would surely reward him generously: 'Siccome non fu mai altro Re, da cui più amati, e pregiati fossero i valentuomini'.[22] Although Vettori chose to dedicate it to Florentine friends like Nicolò Ardinghello (living in Rome) and Bartolomeo Cavalcanti (living in Ferrara), this does not mean he was not attracted by the prospect of financial security in France. An unpublished letter to him of 22 December 1537 from Riniero Dei shows Vettori not only already engaged with Gryphius, but also putting out feelers about a possible powerful patron in France.[23] Dei alludes to the political turmoil, which Florence was experiencing in 1537 following the assassination of Alessandro de' Medici,[24] and which was causing some to consider emigration. He has been in discussion with another Italian émigré, Girolamo Fondulo, now back in France under Cardinal de Tournon's protection, who in the course of long periods spent in France had acquired 'de' signori di questo Regno bona notitia': they can think of no suitable patron at the French court with the necessary wealth or character — 'quella satisfattione d'animo che richiede la natura vostra libera' — with one exception, the second son of the Duke of Lorraine, Nicolas, future Duke of Mercœur (1524–1577). This would have a double advantage, because the young teenager is being educated

> in quella vita et in quelli studii, dei quali vi delettate voi, la cui compagnia vi saria stata honorevole come à luy la vostra, et non gravosamente, perché quella è una corte stabile, et non vagabunda come questa di Francia.[25]

The idea may have been for Vettori to be his tutor, and to reside at court in Nancy. Fondulo has subsequently sought the advice at court of Robert II de Lenoncourt, Bishop of Châlons (1510–1561), 'che governa tutta quella casa' [= Lorraine], but who sees no likelihood of this for Vettori, who will finally opt to accept Cosimo's offer of a post in Florence. France had had its own turmoil at this time, with the Imperial army invading Provence in the summer of 1536, and the sudden death of the Dauphin François, about both of which Vettori's republican colleague Lorenzo Benivieni (1495/96–1547), sent him a report, expressing the wish that, for the sake of Christendom, 'questi due principi diventassino amici e posassino le armi.'[26]

The links Vettori had made with the Lyonnais *fuorusciti* and printers were, however, to prove very fruitful, both for Vettori as regards international distribution of his writings, and as a moneyspinner for Gryphius.[27] Robert Estienne had already in 1538 reprinted Vettori's *Explicationes suarum in Ciceronem castigationum*, followed by the *Opera* in 1539. But from 1540, Gryphius was to bring out a series of editions of Vettori's texts and commentaries, especially on Cicero, Varro and Cato, for the production of which we have a detailed diary in the form of Riniero Dei's numerous letters to Vettori for the years 1537–42, and for which Gryphius's distribution channels to Switzerland, Frankfurt, Italy, Spain and France made him an intelligent choice.

Vettori maintained close links with Lyon through the network of Florentine *fuorusciti* and other Italians passing through the city. For instance, in 1556, he received a letter from Bastiano Antinori (1524–1592), a future member of the Florentine Academy and corrector/expurgator of Boccaccio[28]: Vettori had entrusted him with a letter to his contacts in Lyon, and with seeing what was hot off the press in Lyon or Paris, but all Antinori could find was Nicolas de Grouchy's *De comitiis Romanorum*, published two years before.[29]

Among those more established in Lyon, we find his former collaborator Girolamo Mei (1519–1594),[30] one of his two pupils who had found the manuscript of Euripides, *Electra*, which had allowed Vettori to publish the *editio princeps* in Rome in 1545.[31] Uncertain about his future, and perhaps through Vettori's contact with the *fuorusciti*, Mei had, between 1549 and 1554, taken up a post in the wealthy household of Guillaume, son of Thomas II Guadagni. A cache of unpublished letters to his former tutor[32] reveals his unhappiness in the service of this rich young man, who expects constant attendance, whether in Lyon, or his country estate,[33] or in Avignon, or his properties in Languedoc, Toulouse and Marseille.[34] The social round leaves Mei no time for study: 'tornando da la caccia e da le dame e da banchetti e da le feste e da tutte l'altre simigliante tresche, nelle quali la mia fortuna doppo trentadue anni à mio dispecto per più non potere m'ha sepellito'.[35] Embarked on a new project on Ancient Greek music (on which he was later to become an authority),[36] he can find no one with whom to discuss it, and, once the hunting season starts, he will have no leisure till the following March: 'subito che rinfreschi, il padron' uscirà in campagnia, allora buona note à Plutarcho e à Boëthio e à Cleonide e à Franchino e al Glareano e à tanti quanti e' sono'.[37] His stay in Avignon raises his hopes, because Cardinal Farnese is in residence as legate, with whom Mei hears that Vettori is now *familiarissimo*:[38] he asks for a letter of introduction to the cardinal, or at least the name of a kindred spirit in the cardinal's retinue, who might be 'un quasi rifugio et sfogamento à le volte di tanta solitudine d'huomini secondo il gusto e disiderio nostro, quanto io n' ho, da poi che io mutai aria in quà, provato già quattro anni continui o poco meno'.[39] In the legate's circle he finds people interested in music and poetry, an evidently more courtly pastime than studying Ancient Greek:

> Io hò à questi dì havuto certe lezioni di canzone e di sonetti, e ragionatone tanto e tanto sentito disputar di rime e non rime da certi huomini da bene qui di corte in camera del cappello, che io son' tutto tutto *plenus rimarum*, ché tutte getton fuor rime.[40]

As time goes on, with no time for study, his discontent rises, 'che maledetta sia la corte', and overflows:

> Ma che diavol farebbe qui Aristotile stesso? Ben lo vorrei vedere, se già egli non pigliasse moglie per disperazione, e ritirassesi con essa in un villaggio di bassa Provenza o di bassa Brettagnia, dove è tanto da mangiare, ché à dimenarsi un poco solamente l'huom' si guadagnia à vivere, e se voi sentissi una volta che il tedio de lo star più à questa vita, m'havesse fatto far come disperato un fatto scappuccio, videteve ne la prima cosa, e poi habbiatemene compassione[41].

One of Mei's letters reports on the high esteem in which Cardinal Farnese held

Vettori, as reported to him by one of his circle, Bernardo Cappello, 'affezionatissimo Vostro,' and from the cardinal's own mouth,

> udì dire à Mons R^{mo} che M Pier' Vettori gli piaceva tanto, et che gli pareva tanto buono, et persona che non bisogniava con lui se non haver voglia d'imparare, che del resto bisognia lasciar fare à lui et à la sua diligenza più che ordinaria, et che gli haveva lecto senza mai perdere una sera ò una mattina, et che fra l'altre cose desiderrebbe grandemente udir la Rettorica da lui, et che n'haveva una gran' voglia.[42]

Vettori was keen to satisfy the cardinal's appetite for his writings, two of which he had recently dedicated to him in 1552 and 1553.[43] Among the many letters over some thirty years between Farnese and Vettori,[44] where the cardinal calls him 'amico carissimo,' and 'beneficio universale del nostro secolo',[45] there is a very familiar one of 1553 thanking Vettori for sending him books via Lorenzo Capponi in Lyon.[46] A member of his retinue, Pierantonio Anselmi,[47] had accompanied the legate to Avignon for his triumphal entry to the city,[48] and had reported the cardinal's keen interest in knowing whether printing had been completed in Florence of the *Variae lectiones*, which were being dedicated to him.[49]

In this same year of 1553, Cardinal Bernardino Maffei (1514–1553) arranged for Vettori to be visited in Florence by Henri Estienne, 'giovane dotto, et ben costumato, et degno della conoscenza et amicitia di V. S.'.[50] Vettori already had experience of the Estienne presses, which had reprinted his Cicero edition and commentary in 1538/39,[51] the Cicero letters in 1541,[52] and the Cato and Varro text and commentary in 1543.[53] Henri showed to Vettori the manuscript of Anacreon he had found in Louvain in 1551, and which he was to publish in 1554.[54] Perhaps on the strength of this, the Florentine entrusted to him for publication his own *editio princeps* of the seven tragedies of Aeschylus, based on manuscripts collated by Girolamo Mei.[55] Estienne published this, probably in Geneva, in 1557, to international acclaim,[56] but not before Vettori's German correspondent in Venice, Arnoldo Arlenio, had expressed doubts about Estienne's reliability as a printer, 'per esser persona pocho stabile e desiderosa d'abracchiare assai'.[57] The choice of Estienne to print his new book may have been dictated by the difficulty of finding reliable printers of Greek elsewhere: Vettori's collaborator on Aeschylus, Girolamo Mei, had written to him from Lyon in 1551, lamenting the lack of Greek presses in that city:

> Ma dovete sapere che qui, ancora che ci sia ben' quaranta stamperie, non ce n'è nessuna che stampi libri greci, e quelli pochi che si vendon qui vengono ò di Parigi ò de' Svizeri ò d'Alamagnia, e parte anco d'Italia.[58]

But this choice of a French Protestant printer will not be the only example of the Florentine's relations with Huguenots in the Republic of Letters following the outbreak of religious dissension.

In the preface to his 1557 Aeschylus, Vettori acknowledged his debt to Adrien Turnèbe's 1552 edition,[59] which his own edition, however, greatly surpassed. In a chapter on Varro, Turnèbe acknowledged Vettori's supremacy as a textual scholar,[60] although Vettori himself felt Turnèbe was too inclined to make conjectural readings.[61] In a letter to Turnèbe, the Paduan humanist Johannes Faseolus had attempted to compare him with Vettori, only to be roundly contradicted by his correspondent: 'ille in interiora Musarum sacraria penetraverit, ego vix primum limen calcaverim. [...] *Victorius* singularis, et unicus est [...] omnibus doctrinae ornamentis excultus, et perpolitus'[62] ('[Vettori] had passed into the innermost sanctuary of the Muses, while I had hardly trodden the outer threshold. [...] Vettori is extraordinary and unique [...], ennobled and polished with all the graces of learning'). Turnèbe died before the tensions grew worse, and Huguenot scholars fell victim to religious strife. A case in point is Ramus, who had had to leave France in 1568 after his house was sacked and his library burnt. In exile in Switzerland, he was involved in an approach to Vettori with the major Basel printer Pietro Perna (1519–1582),[63] one of Ramus's publishers. Perna wrote to Vettori on 2 March 1569,[64] reminding him that they had met before, and seeking his help on a project to publish a complete edition of Aristotle in Greek with Latin translation. He has consulted Ramus, 'qui nunc Gallicos declinans tumultus apud nos egit aliquot menses' ('who has spent some months with us avoiding the disorder in France'), who in turn has no doubt whom Perna should approach:

> neminem (dixit ille) tibi ea de re consilium dare, aut opem praestare salubrius potest, quam vir eruditissimus, et in eo auctore versatissimus, D. *Petrus Victorius* Florentinus, neque quisquam Reipublicae literariae magis et utilius, praesertim in hoc genere, unquam fuit, atque ille.[65]

> [No one, he said, can give you advice on that matter, or give you more useful support, than that most learned man, one well versed in that author, the Florentine Petrus Victorius, nor was there ever anyone greater in the Republic of Letters, or more valuable than he, especially in that subject.]

He writes therefore to ask for advice on the best Latin translation and on the choice of manuscripts, spicing up his request with a mock-rhetorical appeal to Vettori's patriotism from the Lucchese ex-Dominican he was before his exile in Basel: 'E voi, Sig. *Pietro Vittorio*, non farete questo servizio a un' Oltramontano barbaro? il quale però quando Oltramontano fusse, a domandar questo non sarebbe barbaro, ma quasi un vostro compatriotta.'[66] Even the tempting offer of 'un Indice il più bravo, che fusse mai fatto a libro da uomo dottissimo in lingua greca, e buon filosofo,' seems not to have moved Vettori, whose reply, though not traced (Nonas Aprilis 1569), evidently pleaded old age, and reluctance to undertake this new project. Perna showed the letter to Ramus, who himself enclosed a letter to Vettori with Perna's reply,[67] which asked for suggestions of younger scholars who could help. The project seems to have come to nothing, and three years later Ramus was killed in the St Bartholomew's Day massacre.

Another victim of that massacre was Denys Lambin, who died of grief at the news of Ramus's murder. Vettori had much in common with him as textual editor of Cicero, and translator of Aristotle's ethics and politics, and may have met him during Lambin's visits to Italy.[68] But while admiring him as 'magni ingenii virum, magnaeque doctrinae' ('a man of great talent and great learning'),[69] he feels Lambin makes excessive emendations to the text of both Cicero and especially Aristotle.[70] Vettori's relative and correspondent, Pierantonio Giacomini, sent him news from

Paris of Lambin's death: 'Harà di già inteso la morte di Mons di Labino, dicon era dietro alla traduttione de libri di Platone et sperava lasciarsi molto adietro il Ficino quando la morte gli ha interrotto si nobil desiderio.'[71]

A number of Huguenots (or latterday Erasmians) stayed on in France despite the growing intolerance and danger. One prominent figure is the royal printer, Jean II de Tournes, who, unlike his family, did not go into exile in Geneva till 1585. When Vettori launched a new project to print Dionysius Halicarnassus's lives of Isaeus and Dinarchus, based on new manuscripts, he again consulted Giacomini about the best available printers of Greek. Giacomini reported in the autumn of 1580 that the situation in Paris was grave, with all the Colleges closed by the plague and the presses stationary, so there was no prospect there for at least six months. He therefore turned to de Tournes in Lyon, 'dottissimo et accurato libraio et forse dopo lo Stephano il piu dotto di Francia. Ha belli caratteri greci piccoli et grandi',[72] as witness his recent edition, which Vettori had seen, of Alciati's emblems, where there are many Greek verses. He describes de Tournes as 'intelligente della lingua greca', and one who 'vi darà tale conto della sua diligenza che non vi dispiacerà havergli fatto tale favor'. The offer is therefore made: 'Hora egli mi ha conchiuso che, se vi piace mandare este due vite, le stamperà subito nel modo giustamente che le mandrete [...] in favore delle buone lettere';[73] and Vettori duly sent his text in December (dedicating it to Giacomini), which the printer proposed to bring out in quarto rather than octavo, using larger Greek type than in the Alciati.[74] De Tournes sent Vettori a proof page to show what the type was like, and promised to have it out for carnival, so it could be sold at the Frankfurt fair.[75] Publication was delayed when the printer found mistakes and meaningless passages in the Greek text submitted to him, and suspected copyist errors: unwilling to 'far cosa che vi dispiaccia o che gli possa diminuare la sua reputazione,' he has halted production, 'et è talmente sbigottito che non sa se debba abbrusciare 13 primi fogli'.[76]

De Tournes was not the only royal printer to seek Vettori's custom. Taking over the Royal Press in Paris following his father's death in 1583, Frédéric II Morel (1552–1630)[77] wrote to Vettori, again citing Giacomini as a common friend, and enquiring whether he was still using Lyon presses for his Greek books. He has informed Giacomini that he would not turn down anything Greek Vettori had ready, especially if it concerned either Aristotle's *Eudemian Ethics*, or his *Magna Moralia*.[78] To show he was serious about Greek, Morel lists his recent and future Greek editions: George Pisida's *Hexameron* (which was to appear in 1584, and on which he asks Vettori to see if the Medici library had an authoritative manuscript, accompanying his request with a Latin poem and some Greek lines);[79] Planudes' commentary on Theophrastus (which had appeared in 1583 and been sent to Vettori); and St Gregentius's dialogue with the Jews, based on a manuscript brought to him from Constantinople, and which was to appear in 1586; he was also hoping to prepare editions of Nicephorus Blemmyes' writings on logic and physics, and St Anathasius's life of St Anthony. It is interesting to note how much post-classical material Morel was editing. Vettori's reply again pleads old age, and commitment to a previous major project (the *Ethics*?), 'opus arduum, ac difficile admodum' ('a very hard and arduous work'), but wishes the printer well to 'Graecas litteras, monimentaque optimorum ingeniorum è tenebris eruere, ac pervulgare' ('bring to light and make public Greek texts and the records of the finest minds'); given, however, that 'non possum otiosus esse' ('I cannot be idle'), Morel offered to print a future work for him,[80] a hope which Vettori's death the following year left unrealised.

The profound effect on France of the Wars of Religion is reflected in Vettori's correspondence. During the first war of 1562–63, Vettori was in correspondence with the poet and author Bartolomeo (Baccio) Del Bene (1514–c.1588), a favourite of Catherine de' Medici (and of her sister-in-law Marguerite), who sent him on missions to Italy.[81] The situation was increasingly tense following the Protestant defeat at Dreux (December 1562), the assassination of the Duke of Guise (24 February 1563) and the armed truce imposed by the Edict of Amboise (March 1563), during which moderates like the Chancellor Michel de L'Hospital, Paul de Foix and Jean de Monluc were seeking to apply Catherine's policy of tolerance and reconciliation. Vettori had written to Del Bene in Blois about a manuscript of the Homeric scholia which he had found in the library of Cardinal Salviati, and which he hoped the Chancellor, whom Vettori had met in Italy,[82] would be keen to see published. He also addressed to the Chancellor and the Queen Mother printed copies of his oration on the death of Cosimo's wife, Eleonora de Toledo,[83] given on 29 December 1562, whilst also reporting that the French ambassador in Tuscany had taken exception to some inclusion or omission in Vettori's eulogy, and had exploded with rage. Del Bene duly presented 'l'oratione fatta nel mortorio della duchessa,' and read out Vettori's accompanying letter to L'Hospital, who was only too aware of the ambassador's irascibility: 'il quale si rise di questa così subita excandescentia, e mi disse che da sua parte io vi scrivessi che voi non vi turbassi per sì poco di cosa, et che s'ei ne sentiva parlare vi scuserebbe'.[84] The moment is judged inopportune to talk to the Queen Mother, 'perché ella ha bene altri pensieri che simil baie', locked as she is in negotiations for peace. But the Chancellor expresses interest in the Homeric scholia: 'desiderebbe infinitamente che venissino in luce, ma dubita che, fin che questo regno sia pacificato, non si truovi chi ci voglia attendere';[85] he also asks Vettori to let him know of any new projects. Nil desperandum, Del Bene promises to raise the prospect with the major Paris scholarly printer, Michel Vascosan, on his next visit to the capital, although nothing seems to have come of the initiative.

The correspondence with Bartolomeo Del Bene adds a further dimension, when we learn that he had soon after entered the service of Catherine's sister-in-law Marguerite de France, who in 1559, as part of the peace settlement, had married Emanuele Filiberto, Duke of Savoy. Marguerite's circle in Turin and Mondovì included a number of refugees from religious persecution. Del Bene wrote to Vettori from Nice in early 1564, on his way to the newly established Savoy court in Turin,[86] reporting his conversation with L'Hospital about Vettori's new project on the cultivation of olives, one of his rare works in Italian, which was not to be completed and published till 1569.[87] L'Hospital had promised, before leaving Nice, to complete a poem of some hundred lines in praise of Vettori's works, including the one on olives, which press of urgent business had not yet allowed him to polish: Del Bene promised to obtain and send the verses, 'perché veggiate in quanta buona opinione et veneratione ei vi habbia'. The future chancellor's admiration is evident in the published verse epistle, in which he envies Vettori his pastoral *otium*, far from the turmoil of court and city:

> [...] solus tu vivere nosti,
> Solus, Victori, magnos contemnere reges,
> Insanique fori strepitus, turpemque repulsam
> Plebis, et oblatos indignis semper honores.[88]

[you alone have learned how to live, you alone, Vettori, how to disdain great kings, and the din of the maddening court, and the rejected shame of the mob, and the honours always bestowed on the unworthy.]

The same letter of Del Bene from Nice refers to a friend of Vettori's who is entering service with Emanuele Filiberto. This seems to be the German Hellenist and editor Arnaldo Arlenio, who had been recommended by Vettori's friends Bartolomeo Del Bene and his son Giuliano (1533–1611),[89] and invited by the duke to open a printing press in Mondovì;[90] when the enterprise came to grief, Marguerite was to take him under her wing 'come litterato [...], et certo n'haveva bisogno perché credo più praticho nelle buone lettere che nel bel negotiare'.[91] Other contacts of Vettori were to join the Savoy court, not least Jacques Cujas, who was for a time a Huguenot, and was invited to Turin in 1566, before returning to Bourges, where among his students was Vettori's former pupil Lelio Ubaldini.[92] According to Arlenio, one of Cujas's pupils, Claude Dorsan, was also teaching in Turin in 1567.[93]

As the wars progressed, travel in France became more insecure. Two pupils of Vettori, Carlo and Annibale Rucellai,[94] went to Turin in 1573 on their way to Carcassonne, where Annibale was to take possession of the bishopric. Carlo di Filippo Rucellai (1530–1598) was a juriconsult and philosopher, a recent member of the Florentine Academy, whom Vettori had praised in the preface to his commentary on book III of Aristotle's *Ethics*.[95] Annibale (ob. 1601),[96] the supposed addressee of his uncle Giovanni Della Casa's *Galateo*, had spent time in France as almoner of Catherine de' Medici, and had been rewarded in 1569 with the see of Carcassonne, which the wars had so far prevented him from occupying. Carlo describes meeting in Turin two of Vettori's pupils, Bartolomeo Del Bene and the mathematician Francesco Ottonaio,[97] as well as the papal nuncio in Turin, Vincenzo Lauro (1523–1592),[98] who had been hunting heretics among Marguerite's household.[99] They had then crossed the Alps to Avignon, but, for fear of the Huguenots in Nîmes, had had to take a circuitous route via Montpellier, and to avoid another Huguenot stronghold, Albi, in order to reach Carcassonne.[100] Although Carlo is enthusiastic about the fortified city, the Protestant threat prevents him and the bishop from venturing far afield, leaving them to focus on reading Terence, Cicero's speeches and letters (which they translate together into Italian), before moving on to Greek rhetoricians like Isocrates and Demosthenes, whilst Carlo is studying French grammar with a *dittionario*.[101]

Annibale Rucellai did not stay long in Carcassonne, any more than another bishop in southern France, Antoine Hébrard de Saint-Sulpice, Bishop of Cahors since 1577. Giovanni Matteo Toscano dedicated to this young bishop in 1578 his survey of Italian dignitaries, *Peplus Italiae*, with a liminary poem by Dorat.[102] But the political situation in Quercy was dangerous (Antoine's brother Bertrand would be killed at Coutras), and Hébrard was given permission by the king in June 1579 to go to Italy to study, accompanied as tutor by a famous local jurist, François Roaldès (1519–1589).[103] Travelling via Lyon, Milan and Venice, he spent the winter in Padua studying Law, History and Italian.[104] On his way to Rome in March 1580, he fell ill in Florence,[105] and during his two-week convalescence visited Vettori, before leaving from Rome to meet the Pope and various cardinals. From Rome he wrote to Vettori to assert that his friendship had proved better than all 'gli sciroppi e le medicine de quei vostri medici, gli quali come poco intelligenti delle nature et complessioni de' Francesi, et in particolare della mia, giudicavano et pronosticavano della mia partita et continuazione del mio viaggio'.[106] But while Hébrard was in Rome, Henri de Navarre's army captured Cahors after a siege at the end of May, sacked the town and the cathedral, and left the bishop without income.[107]

Another Italian correspondent of Vettori, obliged by the wars to relinquish his see in France, was Luca Alamanni, doctor of law,[108] and a descendant of the poet Luigi, whose son, Giovanni Battista, had held the major see of Mâcon. On his relative's death, Luca was elected in July 1583 to succeed to the see. Vettori's correspondent, Giacomini, had announced two years before that Luca would be coming to France, 'il quale piacendo a Dio farà rivivere la gloria del S. Luigi Alamanni suo parente e vostro amico'.[109] Vettori charged the new bishop, as he passed through Lyon, with seeing the Lyonnais printers about an edition in France of his commentary on the *Nicomachaean Ethics*. Luca wrote apologizing that 'fui constretto partir di Lione con gran prestezza per venirmene a questa corte, non potetti trattare con alcuno stampatore'.[110] He has, however, spoken to Giacomini, and to the poet and historian of Florence, Paolo Mini (1526–1599),[111] who undertake to have the commentary published. This is the work which Frédéric Morel had been hoping to print, but Vettori finally chose to publish it in Florence.[112] On his way through Lyon in late 1583, Luca also spoke to Paolo Mini, who was working there as a doctor, about the symposium of Athenaeus Sophistes: 'Dell'Ateneo dissi al sig^r Mini quanto V. S. desiderava, et mi par' di vedere che quell'altro medico franzese si varrà volentieri della offerta amorevole, che V. S. gl'ha fatta.'[113] The Frenchman in question was the distinguished botanist Jacques Daléchamps (1513–1588), a doctor at the Hôtel-Dieu in Lyon since 1552, whose forthcoming Latin translation of the *Deipnosophists* clearly interested Vettori.[114] Scarcely was the book printed (23 February 1583/84 n.s.), than Daléchamps sent Vettori a copy on 1 March 1583/84, citing their mutual friend Mini, and expressing his esteem: 'eruditionem singularem tuam me religiose venerari, benignitatem, comitatemque tuam inpensissime laudare'[115] ('devotedly venerating your remarkable learning, and zealously praising your kindness and courtesy'), handsomely acknowledged in an elegant reply from Vettori.[116] A year later, Daléchamps was to compose a Latin epitaph for Vettori.[117]

Having performed his task, Alamanni wrote to Vettori from court, expressing the hope that, by the beginning of 1584, he would be in his see of Mâcon, where he entered on 15 January; from there he wrote about a conversation with the local *procureur du Roi*, a humanist and admirer of Vettori, seeking enlightenment on a passage in book II of Statius's *Achilleid*, describing a dance among the Amazons, and wondering if this is reported in any other authors.[118] Such scholarly curiosity is touching given the political situation in Mâcon, which had been captured and sacked by the Huguenots in 1567, and was the theatre of dispute between both sides, culminating in the pillaging by the Ligue of Alamanni's *seigneurie* of Romenay in Bresse.[119] Alamanni took advantage of the forthcoming marriage of Christina of Lorraine to Ferdinando I of Tuscany to accompany the bride to Florence, and to abandon his diocese for Rome.

Another member of the same family, Vincenzo Alamanni (1536–90), was Florentine ambassador in France in 1572–76, at the height of the troubles. On behalf of the Grand Duke, Francesco I, he attempted to help another correspondent of Vettori, Marco Antonio Dovizi,[120] a nephew of Cardinal Bibbiena, who had come to Paris to try to recover his French inheritance, which proved to be saddled with debts. Dovizi wrote to Vettori in 1575 reporting lack of progress, as well as a certain anti-Italianism in 'queste parti così turbulenti et seditiosi, et dove il nome nostro Italiano è così generalmente odioso, come ogn'uno sa'.[121] He has had some help from the Duke of Montpensier, Louis de Bourbon (1513–1582), and especially from another correspondent of Vettori, Bon de Broé (1523–1588), president of the Chambre des Enquêtes at the Parlement de Paris,[122] to whom Vettori had addressed a letter of introduction for Dovizi. Broé replied directly to Vettori, thanking him for 'mutuam inter nos benevolentiam' ('the shared goodwill between us'), and expressing his admiration for this 'literarum decus, et ornamentum' ('glory and ornament of letters'), together with his impatience, and that of 'plerique nostrates viri docti, tuique studiosi' ('many of our learned fellowcountrymen who are devoted to you'), to read Vettori's commentary on Aristotle's *Politics*, which he hopes Vettori will send as a gift.[123] Dovizi confirms Broé's desire for the commentaries, 'quali dice che sono ancora molto desiderati da più altri suoi colleghi, co' i quali n'ha ragionato, et i quali amano grandemente li suoi scritti',[124] clear evidence of Vettori's esteem among Paris lawyers. Vettori replied in February, sending him the book,[125] which he entrusted to a relative, Roberto Venturi, who has been fighting in the wars in France, and whom he hopes Broé will be able to help.[126]

Vettori's letter also speaks of a recent visit to him in Florence of Paul de Foix (1528–1584), an old friend, 'qui me plurimum amat' ('who loves me greatly'), and who shares his esteem for Broé. De Foix had been, with L'Hospital, an architect of Catherine's policy of tolerance, and was suspected of unorthodoxy by both Pius V and Gregory XIII, who prevented his appointment as Archbishop of Toulouse.[127] His recent visit to Vettori was probably on his return from his embassy to Rome in 1572–74; and he wrote to Vettori in 1582,[128] when back in Rome as ambassador to Gregory between 1581 and his death in 1584, being one of those to whom Vettori sent a copy of his edition of Athenaeus.[129]

De Foix had succeeded as ambassador another correspondent of Vettori's, Louis Chasteigner, sieur d'Abain et de La Roche-Posay (1535–1595),[130] the patron of Scaliger, with whom he had travelled widely in Europe, before serving as ambassador in Rome in 1579–81. Nicolas Audebert had advised him on how to reach the ambassador by letter,[131] and Vettori wrote to him twice during his embassy, the first time calling on his 'exquisitam honestam artium scientiam, magnumque usum rerum' ('particularly distinguished knowledge of the arts, and wide experience') to help him resolve a doubt about what is said in Cicero and Plutarch about Themistocles and memory.[132] A second longer letter, six months later, discusses close details of the emendations he is making to the text of the *Nicomachaean Ethics*, and reports on the Salviati manuscript he has found of the Homeric scholia.[133] It is striking how Vettori treats the ambassador La Roche-Posay as an equal, one whose advice as a humanist scholar he values.

Two other young French scholars visited Vettori in Florence shortly afterwards. A Hellenist and bible scholar, Jean Courtier,[134] wrote to Vettori in early 1580, recounting his trip to Rome 'cum Randanis nostris' ('with our friends of the Randan family'), and his meeting on the return journey with Vettori, 'quem aetati nostrae Graecarum, Latinarumque literarum fontem uberrimum, et parentem vere omnes agnoscunt'[135] [whom all truly acknowledge as the rich fountain and father of Greek and Latin letters]. Courtier has done a translation of Hierocles of Alexandria's commentary on the Pythagorean *Golden Verses*, but he believes the text to be corrupt, and asks Vettori to see if the Medicean Library has a better manuscript. Vettori replied promptly that the duke does not allow any manuscripts to be loaned, pleaded his own old age, but saluted Courtier's two companions.[136] The publication in 1583 of Courtier's translation[137] reveals the identity of these companions, namely the future cardinal François de La Rochefoucauld (1558–1645), an avid collector of books and manuscripts,[138] accompanied by one of his brothers, probably Jean-Louis.

Vettori's interest in promising young scholars like La Rochefoucauld visiting Italy extends to young Italians studying in France. A case in point is Lelio Ubaldini, a great-nephew of the future pope Leo XI, who may be identified with a future devotional writer and poet.[139] Vettori had written to him, 'senza havermi conosciuto o veduto', apparently after his brother Marcantonio had shown him some of Lelio's poems. Lelio reported from Paris in 1578 that he had just completed a course on philosophy and, having now moved on to languages, especially Greek, was attending lectures by Jean Dorat.[140] He passed on greetings from (the future cardinal) Ottavio Bandini, who was with him in Paris studying. In a second letter later in the summer,[141] he sent Vettori a copy of Giammatteo Toscano's *Peplus Italiae*, just printed by Morel, and containing two hundred epigrams and short biographies of distinguished Italians.[142] Published with the support of Jean Dorat,[143] it was dedicated to Vettori's correspondent, the young Bishop of Cahors, Antoine Hébrard. Although Vettori is included,[144] Ubaldini considers that many worthy writers have been excluded from the book, especially in the field of letters, but he claims to have suggest the title *Peplus* to Toscano. After the summer vacation, we find Ubaldini in Bourges doing something he had been reluctant to do in his letter of 1 April, namely studying law, 'il quale mercé del Sig. Cuiatio fiorisce hoggi più in questa città che in altra di Francia'.[145] He expects Scaliger's *Manilio* to be published shortly, and will send it to Vettori. 'Ma in vero che ne dite Sig. Piero di quell'huomo?' Ubaldini admires his 'ingegno raro per certo e divino, ma fa troppo a sicurtà di quei poveri huomini che essendo morti non posson dir le lor ragioni.' It is interesting to see others participating in the quarrel between Vettori and Scaliger.

The mention of Dorat raises the question of Vettori's contact with the French court and its poets. Pierantonio Giacomini had kept him abreast of events, such as the preparations for the baptism of Charles IX's daughter Marie-Élisabeth de France, due to take place on 2 February 1573. Giacomini was well informed of the fine diplomatic balancing in the choice of godmothers, one of whom was Elizabeth I, represented by her ambassador, William Somerset, Earl of Worcester, and the other the Empress Mary of Austria, also represented by her ambassador, whilst the godfather was Emanuele Filiberto of Savoy, represented by Jacques, Duke of Nemours.[146] Giacomini observes that this ceremony was taking place against the background both of the royal army under the Duke of Anjou laying siege to La Rochelle, and of the Duke's prospective election to the throne of Poland, to which end M. de Langeac had been dispatched, armed with Latin letters by Guy Du Faur de Pibrac, which had been circulating, and of which Giacomini sends Vettori copies. These may be manuscript copies of Pibrac's *De rebus Gallicis*, published in November 1573. In a later letter following Henri's election,[147] Giacomini sent Vettori the two Latin orations (Vettori's own speciality), which had convinced the Polish Diet, given by Jean de Monluc, Bishop of Valence,[148] whom Vettori knew of when ambassador to Venice, but who was about to be declared a heretic by Rome (1574). He also reports the publication in Lyon of Guillaume Paradin's *Memoires de l'histoire de Lyon*, which he will send him because of Vettori's interest in antiquities; and he reports the death on 12 July 1573 of a member of the Capponi family of bankers, Lorenzo, a correspondent of Vettori,[149] who had married into the Guadagni family,[150] and had been ennobled by Catherine de' Medici.[151] Capponi was sincerely lamented by the Lyonnais for his generosity to the poor of the city, 4000 of whom he had fed for three months during the severe famine of that year.

A later letter sends Vettori the latest piece of court festival, performed at the Louvre on 15 August 1573, to greet ambassadors from Poland, who had come to offer Henri the crown. This *Ballet des Polonais* comprised texts by Dorat and Ronsard, published in Latin for the benefit of the Poles,[152] describing the dance of sixteen nymphs from different parts of France. It is this illustrated volume which Giacomini sent to Vettori:

> oltre che è accompagnata da alcune compositioni latine et franzesi che potranno piacerle, se non per altro almeno per essere cosa nuova. L'Aurato (et Ronsardo in parte) ne sono li autori, che hanno introdotto le ninfe di tutte le provincie et governi generali de la Francia a fare un dono al nuovo re di Polonia delle cose che ciascuna Provincia suole produrre più stimati et migliori, per segno et memoria del loro amore verso il detto signore.[153]

A letter from Lyon of Pietrantonio Giacomini in April 1580 contains the sentence, 'Il poeta De Portes, l'uno de più eccelenti di questi tempi, la saluta'.[154] Behind this greeting from the fashionable court poet Philippe Desportes lies a network of relations at court, mainly through the Florentine Gondi family, one branch of which had become bankers in Lyon, and risen high under the last Valois. Vettori's correspondence includes four letters from Jean-Baptiste I Gondi (1501–1580),[155] *maître d'hôtel* and emissary for Catherine de' Medici.[156] Jean-Baptiste had apparently approached Vettori for documentation about the history of the Gondi family, and for proof of their nobility, for which his cousins, Albert and Pierre de Gondi, showed their appreciation. Albert (1522–1602),[157] who had fought with distinction for France, and had been created Maréchal de Retz, wrote three letters thanking Vettori for having dug out 'les aliances, et degrés, qui la concernoient, une partye des quelles nous estoient incogneues',[158] and offering him his patronage:

> J'ay esté de tout temps affectionné aux vertus qui reluisent en vous, et les quelles ne sont pas moins reconnues en ce royaume, que aux autres pays, qui m'ont incité à honorer et vous, et votre nom. [...] Vous asseurant, que vous avés en ces quartiers un amy, qui desire vous monstrer qu'i[l] vous est tresaffectionné amy.[159]

Vettori had already been in contact the previous year with Albert's brother Pierre (1533–1616), Bishop of Paris, and had sent him a new work of his, the commentary on Aristotle's *De arte dicendi*,[160] just off the press from Giunta, with praise of both the bishop and his brother Albert, 'nobilissimi viri' [most noble men]. He has also arranged for Giacomini to send a copy of it to Henri III, which Giacomini has had specially bound

> con oro et con le cifere del Re dal suo legatore di libri. Non vi dirò le lodi che e' vi dette e la buona stima che e' fa di voi per non offendere le v^{re} orecchie raccontandovi este vostre lodi.[161]

Vettori had accompanied the gift with a letter to the King,[162] praising him as a patron of letters and of scholarship, and promising to send him some future work if his advanced age allowed. This letter reveals that the King had written to him previously, expressing admiration for his scholarship. Henri's reply reveals the role of Alberto Gondi as intermediary, as well as the esteem in which Vettori was held in France:

> J'ay receu les livres, que m'avez faict presenter par mon Cousin le Marescial de Retz, les quelz m'ont esté fort agreables, tant par le rapport qui m'a esté faict de vous, la connoissance que j'ay de votre sçavoir, que pour la tres grande affection que portez à mon service. A ceste cause j'ay bien voulu vous en remercier, et vous faire entendre, que en consideration de votre bonne volonté, et de vos qualitez, je vous feray toujours plaisir, là où l'occasion se presentera.[163]

Ths letter had been forwarded to Vettori by Giacomini, who had had the volume bound,[164] and it is in this letter that the greetings are passed on of Desportes. We also learn that Giacomini has lent another book by Vettori to the Bishop of Paris, 'il quale con i suoi nipoti che sono di grande espettatione et studieranno esto libro'.

The following letters of Giacomini show that the link with the Gondi was maintained. When another of member of the family died in Lyon in the summer of 1580, Vettori was asked to compose the epitaph for his tomb,[165] which he did, whilst Giacomini also sent him news of the Maréchal de Retz's successful campaign in Saluzzo and Carmagnola in the winter of 1580.[166] Vettori fulfilled his earlier promises in 1584, sending both to Pierre Gondi[167] and, via him, to the King,[168] letters accompanying his newly published commentary on the *Nicomachean Ethics*.[169] The letter to the King praises both him and the Kings of France in general, whom he describes as surpassing all other princes in humanity and piety, this despite the work being dedicated to the Duke of Urbino.

Vettori's extensive correspondence covers much of Europe, including a surprising number of French nationals, or of Italians in France. These correspondents range from Vettori's own pupils visiting France, French visitors to Florence, *fuorusciti* in Lyon, right up to senior members of the Parlement and even court grandees and the King himself. French humanists keep up with Vettori's publications, which most admire, whilst others openly contest his methods. In pursuit of accurate printing and wide distribution, Vettori turns to presses in Lyon and Paris, who bring out some sixty editions of his works. It is hardly surprising that he should merit an entry in Toscano's *Peplus Italiae*, given that all those listed in it are Italian. It is more of an achievement to be recognized in a French catalogue of worthies, such as that by Guillaume Roville, which starts with Adam (and his improbable medallion portrait), and presents (and portrays) Vettori among a short and select number of living celebrities, reviewing the wide range of his writing, and concluding: 'Finalement cet homme disert a si bien fait, estant versé et entendu en toute sorte de lettres, que son nom ne mourra jamais.'[170] It is a final irony that he should be portrayed here adjacent to his critic and sparring partner, Marc-Antoine Muret.

Notes to Chapter 8

1. John Edwin Sandys, *History of Classical Scholarship*, 2nd edition, 3 vols (Cambridge: Cambridge University Press, 1906–08), II, 135; reiterated by Rudolf Pfeiffer, *History of Classical Scholarship from 1300–1850* (Oxford: Clarendon Press, 1976), p. 135.
2. Raphaële Mouren, *Biographie et éloges funèbres de Piero Vettori: entre rhétorique et histoire* (Paris: Classiques Garnier, 2006).
3. Angelo Maria Bandini, *Memorie per servire alla vita del senator Pier Vettori* (Livorno: A. Santini, 1756); id., *Victorius, seu de vita et scriptis Petri Victorii* (Florence: n. pub., 1759); Francesco Niccolai, *Pier Vettori (1499–1585)* (Florence: Succ. B. Seeber; Leipzig: Gustav Fock, [1912]).
4. Raphaële Mouren, 'L'Auteur, l'imprimeur et les autres: éditer les oeuvres complètes de Cicéron (1533–1540)', in *Écrivain et imprimeur*, ed. by by Alain Riffaud (Rennes: Presses Universitaires de Rennes, 2010), pp. 123–46; ead., 'La Lecture assidue des classiques: Marcello Cervini et Piero Vettori', in *Humanisme et Église entre France et Italie du début du XV*ᵉ *siècle au milieu du XVI*ᵉ *siècle*, ed. by Patrick Gilli (Rome: École française de Rome, 2004), pp. 433–63; ead., 'Un professeur de grec et ses élèves: Piero Vettori (1499–1585)', *Lettere italiane*, 59.4 (2007), 473–506; ead., 'Une longue polémique autour de Cicéron: Paolo Manuzio et Piero Vettori', in *Passeurs de textes: imprimeurs, éditeurs et lecteurs humanistes*, ed. by Yann Sordet (Turnhout: Brepols, 2009), pp. 80–91.
5. Salvatore Lo Re, *La crisi della libertà fiorentina: alle origini della formazione politica e intellettuale di Benedetto Varchi e Piero Vettori* (Rome: Istituto Nazionale di Studi sul Rinascimento, 2006).
6. Raphaële Mouren, 'The Role of Florentine Families in the Editions of Piero Vettori', paper

give to the panel *Family Affairs: Kinship and Society in Renaissance Italy*, Renaissance Society of America annual meeting, Chicago, 3 April 2008, <http://raphaele-mouren.enssib.fr/chicago2008> [accessed 28 April 2016]; see also Cecil Roth, 'I carteggi volgari di Piero Vettori', *Rivista storica degli archivi toscani*, I (July-September 1929), VII, fasc. iii.

7. Eliana Carrara, 'Il carteggio in volgare di Giovanni Della Casa con Piero Vettori', in *Giovanni Della Casa, ecclesiastico e scrittore*, ed. by Stefano Carrai (Rome: Edizioni di Storia e Letteratura, 2007), pp. 1–46.
8. Donato Giannotti, *Lettere a Piero Vettori* (Florence: Vallecchi, [1932]).
9. Raphaële Mouren, 'Écritures et réseaux: l'exemple de Piero Vettori', in *Lettere come simboli: aspetti ideologici e simbolici della scrittura tra passato e presente*, ed. by Paola Degni (Udine: Forum, 2012), pp. 197–210.
10. Lucia Cesarini Martinelli, 'Pier Vettori e gli umanisti tedeschi', in *Firenze e la Toscana dei Medici nell'Europa del '500* (Florence: Olschki, 1983), II, pp. 707–26.
11. Piero Vettori, *Epistolarum ad Germanos missarum libri tres*, ed. by J. Caselius (Rostock: Jakob I Lucius, 1577); Angelo Maria Bandini, *Clarorum Italorum et Germanorum Epistolæ ad P. Victorium* (Florence, n. pub., 1758–60), 2 vols.
12. Bayerische Staatsbibliothek, MS Clm 734 (1526–68); 735 (1569–85); 736 (undated).
13. Raphaële Mouren, 'Quatre siècles d'histoire de la bibliothèque de Vettori: entre vénération et valorisation', in *Early Modern Books as Material Objects*, ed. by Bettina Wagner and Marcia Reed (Munich: De Gruyter Saur, 2010), pp. 241–67.
14. Pier Vettori, *Epistolarum libri X* (Florence: Giunta, 1586).
15. BL, Add. MSS 10263–78.
16. BL, Add. MS 10263, fol. 162, Nicolas Audebert — Vettori, Paris, 17 March 1583; Vettori, *Epistolarum libri X*, pp. 185–86, 189–90; Bandini, *Clarorum Italorum*, 1760, II, 103–05, 121–22; Emile Picot, *Les Français italianisants au XVIe siècle*, 2 vols (Paris: Champion, 1906–07), II, 153–80; Lino Pertile, 'Un umanista francese in Italia', *Studi mediolatini e volgari*, 21 (1973), 89–214; Silvia d'Amico, 'Alterum amant oculi. Doctis placeat auribus alter', in *Le Poète et son œuvre, de la composition à la publication*, ed. by Jean-Eudes Girot (Geneva: Droz, 2004), pp. 83–119.
17. Niccolai, *Pier Vettori*, p. 169; Jill Kraye, 'Italy, France and the Classical Tradition: The Origins of the Philological Commentary on Aristotle's *Nicomachean Ethics*', in *Italy and the Classical Tradition: Language, Thought and Poetry 1300–1600*, ed. by Carlo Caruso and Andrew Laird (London: Duckworth, 2013), pp. 124–30. An unpublished letter to Vettori from the Vatican scriptor Gabriello Faerno, 30 November 1546, BL, Add. MS 10266, fol. 107^{r-v}, accuses Muret (and Antonio Gouvea) of having 'ruinato' or 'fracassato' the text of Terence in their editions.
18. Niccolai, *Pier Vettori*, pp. 324–25; Anthony Grafton, *Joseph Scaliger: a Study in the History of Classical Scholarship*, 2 vols (Oxford: Clarendon Press, 1993), I, 52–70, 85–95. An unpublished letter of Piero Del Bene to Vettori, Lyon, 20 September 1574, BL, Add. MS 10264, fol. 63, refers to the recent (1573) edition of Varro by Scaliger, 'giovane molto litterato', which he is sending to Vettori, who he is sure will approve of 'alcune scholie del detto Josepo Scaligero, il quale riverisce et honnora molto VS et è giovane di bellissimo ingegno'. At this date, at least, Scaliger seems to have thought well of Vettori.
19. Anna Maria Raugei, *Gian Vincenzo Pinelli et Claude Dupuy: une correspondence entre deux humanistes*, 2 vols (Florence: Olschki, 2001).
20. Raphaële Mouren, 'Sébastien Gryphe et Piero Vettori: de la querelle des *Lettres familières* aux agronomes latins', in *Quid novi? Sébastien Gryphe à l'occasion du 450e anniversaire de sa mort*, ed. by Raphaële Mouren (Villeurbanne: Presses de l'Enssib, 2008), pp. 287–339.
21. See his twenty letters to Vettori in BL, Add. MS 10266.
22. Bandini, *Memorie*, p. 12.
23. Riniero Dei — Vettori, Lyon 22 December, 1537, in BL, Add. MS 10266, fol. 55^r-55^v.
24. Olivier Rouchon, 'Les Troubles de 1537 dans le domaine florentin', *Histoire, économie et société*, 19 (2000), 25–48.
25. Dei — Vettori, 22 December 1537, in BL, Add. MS 10266, fol. 55^r.
26. BL, Add. MS 10264, fol. 110.
27. Mouren, 'Sébastien Gryphe et Piero Vettori'.

28. *Dizionario biografico degli Italiani (DBI)* (Rome: Istituto della Enciclopedia italiana, 1960–), 3, 460.
29. Bastiano Antinori — Venturi, Lyon, 29 July 1556, in BL, Add. MS 10276, fol. 67.
30. *DBI*, 73, 207–11.
31. Niccolai, *Pier Vettori*, pp. 225–27; Giannotti, *Lettere*, p. 115; Grafton, *Joseph Scaliger*, I, 57.
32. Ten unpublished letters to Vettori (1548–55), Harvard University, Houghton Library, MS Mus 136; there are also ninety-six letters from him over forty years in BL, Add. MS 10268.
33. MS Mus 136, n° 2, Château de Beauregard, Saint-Genis-Laval, 13 September 1549.
34. Ibid., n° 4, Avignon, 15 April 1552.
35. Ibid., n° 3, Lyon 3 July 1551.
36. Niccolai, *Pier Vettori*, pp. 115–16.
37. Houghton, MS Mus 136, n° 3, Lyon, 3 July 1551.
38. Ibid., n° 4, Avignon, 15 April 1552.
39. Ibid., n° 6, Avignon, 5 November 1552.
40. Ibid., n° 8, Avignon, 14 December 1552.
41. Ibid., n° 9, Lyon, 8 November 1553.
42. Ibid., n° 7, Avignon, 6 December 1552. The *Rettorica* may be Vettori's edition of Aristotle, *De arte dicendi libri tres*, printed in Basel in 1548, and in Paris in 1549.
43. Vettori dedicated to him in 1552 his edition of Demetrios Phalerios: see Niccolai, *Pier Vettori*, pp. 240–43.
44. Several in BL, Add. MS 10275; cf. Niccolai, *Pier Vettori*, pp. 181–82.
45. BL, Add. MS 10275, fol. 135.
46. Farnese — Vettori, St-Quentin, 3 October 1553, in BL, Add. MS 10275, fol. 107.
47. A law professor at Pisa: see Jacopo Rilli, *Notizie letterarie, ed istoriche intorno agli uomini illustri dell'Accademia fiorentina. Parte prima* (Florence: Piero Matini, 1700), pp. 236–37.
48. Richard Cooper, 'Legate's Luxury: The Entries of Cardinal Alessandro Farnese to Avignon and Carpentras, 1553', in *French Ceremonial Entries in the Sixteenth Century: Event, Image, Text*, ed. by Hélène Visentin and Nicolas Russell (Toronto: Centre for Renaissance and Reformation Studies, 2007), pp. 133–61.
49. Pierantonio Anselmi — Vettori, Avignon, 6 May 1553, in BL, Add. MS 10263, fol. 116; the dedicatory letter is dated August 1553; Niccolai, *Pier Vettori*, p. 261.
50. Maffei — Vettori, 6 May 1553, in BL, Add. MS 10275, fol. 178; Bandini, *Memorie*, pp. 33–34; Niccolai, *Pier Vettori*, pp. 170, 182–83.
51. Cicero, *Opera* (Paris: Robert Estienne, 1539), fol.; *Explicationes suarum in Ciceronem castigationum* (Paris: Robert Estienne, 1538), fol.
52. Cicero, *Epistolarum libri* (Paris: Robert Estienne, 1541), 8°.
53. *Libri de re rustica* (Paris: Robert Estienne, 1543), 8°; *Explicationes suarum in Catonem, Varronem, Columellam castigationum* (Paris: Robert Estienne, 1543), 8°; Niccolai, *Pier Vettori*, p. 224.
54. John O'Brien, *Anacreon redivivus* (Ann Arbor: University of Michigan Press, 1995), pp. 9–12, 14, 159–60.
55. Niccolai, *Pier Vettori*, pp. 245–48 ; Grafton, *Joseph Scaliger*, I, 58 ; Raphaële Mouren, 'Une édition de texte classique au XVIe siècle: Piero Vettori, Henri Estienne et Eschyle (1557)', in *Positions des thèses soutenues par les élèves de la promotion de 1994 pour obtenir le diplôme d'archiviste paléographe* (Paris: École des Chartes, 1994), pp. 145–51; Monique Mund-Dopchie, 'Un collaborateur de Pietro Vettori', *Bulletin de l'Institut historique belge à Rome*, 37 (1966), 109–14.
56. *Tragœdiæ VII eduntur Petri Victorii cura et diligentia* ([Geneva]: Henri II Estienne, 1557), 4°.
57. Arnoldo Arlenio — Vettori, Venice, 16 July 1558, in BL, Add. MS 10263, fol. 156.
58. Mei — Vettori, Lyon, 3 July 1551, in Houghton, MS Mus 136, n° 3.
59. Monique Mund-Dopchie, *La Survie d'Eschyle à la Renaissance* (Louvain: Peeters, 1984); John Lewis, *Adrien Turnèbe (1512–1565): A Humanist Observed* (Geneva: Droz, 1998), p. 124.
60. Adrianus Turnebus *Adversariorum libri triginta* (Paris: Martin Le Jeune, 1580), II, lib. XIX, ch. 28, p. 162.
61. Piero Vettori, *Variarum lectionum XIII novi libri* (Florence: L. Torrentini and C. Pettinari, 1568), bk XXXVI, ch. 11, p. 192; Niccolai, *Pier Vettori*, p. 170 ; Lewis, *Turnèbe*, p. 114.

62. Turnèbe — Giovanni Fagioli, Paris, 7 July n.d., in Bandini, *Clarorum Italorum*, III, n° xxxiv, pp. 253–55.
63. *DBI*, 82, 401–06.
64. Bandini, *Clarorum italorum*, II, 33–36.
65. Ibid., II, 34.
66. Ibid., p. 35.
67. Ibid., p. 46.
68. Kraye, 'Italy, France and the Classical Tradition', pp. 122–30.
69. Vettori, *Variarum lectionum XIII*, bk. XXXVIII, ch. 15, p. 239; Niccolai, *Pier Vettori*, p. 157.
70. Vettori, *Variarum lectionum XIII*, bk XXXV, ch. 1, p. 167; bk. XXXVIII, ch. 15, pp. 239–40.
71. Pierantonio Giacomini — Vettori, Paris, 27 January 1573, in BL, Add. MS 10267, fol. 42^v.
72. Giacomini — Vettori, Lyon, 19 October 1580, in BL, Add. MS 10267, fol. 52.
73. Giacomini — Vettori, 19 October 1580, in BL, Add. MS 10267, fol. 52.
74. Giacomini — Vettori, Lyon, 12 December 1580, in BL, Add. MS 10267, fol. 54; Niccolai, *Pier Vettori*, p. 260.
75. Giacomini — Vettori, Lyon, 30 December 1580, in BL, Add. MS 10267, fol. 55.
76. Giacomini — Vettori, Lyon, 21 March 1581, in BL, Add. MS 10267, fol. 59; Giacomini sent the finished product in May, with apologies for delay, ibid., fol. 57, 18 May 1581.
77. J. Kecskeméti, *Frédéric Morel II, éditeur, traducteur et imprimeur* (Turnhout: Brepols, 2014).
78. Morel — Vettori, Paris, 15 May 1584, in Bandini, *Clarorum Italorum*, II, 163–65; Niccolai, *Pier Vettori*, pp. 169, 266.
79. Bandini, *Victorius*, pp. cx–cxi.
80. Morel — Vettori, Paris, 21 June 1584, in Vettori, *Epistolarum libri X*, p. 217.
81. *DBI*, 36, 330–33.
82. Loris Petris, *La Plume et la Tribune* (Geneva: Droz, 2002), pp. 9, 255.
83. *Laudatio Eleanorae Cosmi I Medicis uxoris* (Florence: Torrentino, 1562).
84. Del Bene — Vettori, Blois, 7 March 1562 (= 1563 n.s.), in BL, Add. MS 10264, fol. 16.
85. Ibid.
86. Del Bene — Vettori, Nice, 15 February 1563 [= 1564 n.s.], in BL, Add. MS 10264, fol. 17.
87. *Trattato delle lodi et della coltivatione de gli ulivi* (Florence: Filippo II Giunta, 1569).
88. Michel de L'Hospital, *Epistolarum seu sermonum libri sex* (Paris: Robert II Estienne, 1585), pp. 336–38 (p. 337).
89. Arnaldo Arlenio — Vettori, Turin, 10 July 1567, in BL, Add. MS. 10276, fol. 84.
90. *DBI*, 4, 213–14.
91. Giulio Del Bene — Vettori, Turin, 20 Oct. 1571, in BL, Add. MS 10264, fol. 20.
92. Lelio Ubaldini — Vettori, Bourges, Oct 1578, in BL, Add. MS 10273, fol. 322.
93. Arlenio — Vettori, Turin, 10 July 1567, in BL, Add. MS 10276, fol. 84.
94. Niccolai, *Pier Vettori*, pp. 126–27, thought they were brothers; but Luigi Passerini, *Genealogia e storia della famiglia Rucellai* (Florence: M. Cellini, 1861), pp. 71, 109–11, shows they were from different branches of the family.
95. Rilli, *Notizie letterarie*, I, 247.
96. Vettori — Annibale Rucellai, Florence, 10 June 1564, in Vettori, *Epistolarum libri X*, pp. 118–19.
97. Tommaso Vallauri, *Storia delle Università degli Studi del Piemonte*, 3 vols (Turin: Stamperia Reale, 1845–46), I, 191–92; Niccolai, *Pier Vettori*, p. 117.
98. Carlo Rucellai — Vettori, Carcassonne, 18 March 1573, in BL, Add. MS 10272, fols 51–54.
99. *DBI*, 64, 125–28.
100. Carlo Rucellai — Vettori, Carcassonne, 18 March 1573, in BL, Add. MS 10272, fols 51–54; Carlo Rucellai — Vettori, Carcassonne, 2 April 1573, in Penn University Library, MS Coll. 196.
101. Ibid., Carlo Rucellai — Vettori, Carcassonne, 2 April and 22 May 1573.
102. Niccolai, *Pier Vettori*, p. 165.
103. Edmond Cabié, *Guerres de Religion dans le Sud-ouest de la France* (Paris: Champion, 1906, and repr. Slatkine, 1975), pp. ix–xi, 492; see Cujas's letter to Vettori, 5 April 1580, in BL, Add. MS 10271, fols 123–24.

104. Cabié, *Guerres de Religion*, col. 496, 534–37.
105. Ibid., col. 553–54
106. Antoine Hébrard — Vettori, Rome, 8 April 1580, in BL, Add. MS 10265, fol. 21. See other news from Rome in April and May, in Cabié, *Guerres de Religion*, col. 561, 571; he was back in Lyon in August 1580, ibid., col. 610.
107. Ibid., col. 577, 591.
108. Rilli, *Notizie letterarie*, I, 163.
109. Giacomini — Vettori, Lyon, 18 May 1581, in BL, Add. MS 10267, fol. 57.
110. [Luca] Alamanni — Vettori, Paris, 7 December 1583, in BL, Add. MS 10263, fol. 15.
111. *DBI*, 74, 638–40; his letters are missing from BL, Add. MS 10268.
112. *Commentarii in X libros de moribus ad Nicomachum* (Florence: Giunta, 1584); Niccolai, *Pier Vettori*, pp. 264–67.
113. Alamanni — Vettori, 7 December 1583, in BL, Add. MS 10263, fol. 15^v.
114. *Deipnosophistarum libri quindecim in Latinum sermonem versi* (Lyon: Antoine de Harsy, 1583), fol.
115. Daléchamps — Vettori, Lyon, 1 March 1583, in Bandini, *Clarorum Italorum*, II, 155–56; Niccolai, *Pier Vettori*, pp. 159, 168 ; see Charles B Schmitt, 'The Correspondence of Jacques Daléchamps (1513–1588)', *Viator*, 8 (1977), 399–434 (p. 432).
116. Vettori — Daléchamps, 11 June 1584, in Vettori, *Epistolarum libri X*, p. 217; Mini's name is Latinized by Dalechamps as Minutius, and by Vettori as Minius.
117. Bandini, *Victorius*, p. cxliii.
118. Luca Alamanni — Vettori, Mâcon, 23 February 1585, in Penn UL, MS Coll. 196.
119. Comte de La Rochette, *Histoire des Evêques de Mâcon*, 2 vols (Mâcon: E. Protat, 1866–67), II, 489–99; Ami Bost, *Histoire de l'Eglise protestante de Mâcon* (Maçon: André Ruel, 1977).
120. G. Goretti Miniati, 'Alcune notizie inedite sulla famiglia Dovizi di Bibbiena', *Atti e Memorie della R. Accademia Petrarca*, n.s., 20 (1936), 131–37.
121. Marco Antonio Dovizi — Vettori, Paris, 15 October 1575, in Penn UL, MS Coll. 196.
122. Albin Mazon, *Bon Broé de Tournon: Président de la Chambre des Enquêtes au Parlement de Paris: 1523–1588* (Privas: Constant Laurent, 1904); *Dictionnaire de biographie française (DBF)* (Paris: Letouzey et Ané, 1933-), 7, col. 395–96.
123. Broé — Vettori, Paris, 14 October 1575, in Bandini, *Clarorum Italorum*, II, 92; Niccolai, *Pier Vettori*, p. 168.
124. Dovizi — Vettori, Paris, 15 October 1575, in Penn UL, MS Coll. 196.
125. *Politikōn biblia oktō. De optimo statu reipublicae libri octo* (Paris: Guillaume Morel apud Jean Bienné, 1574), 4°.
126. Vettori — Broé, Florence, 4 February 1575/76 n.s., in Vettori, *Epistolarum libri X*, p. 174.
127. *DBF*, 14, col. 220–21; Noel Didier, *Paul de Foix et Gregoire XIII, 1572–1584* (Grenoble: Allier, 1941); Malcolm Smith, 'Paul de Foix and Freedom of Conscience', *Bibliothèque d'Humanisme et Renaissance*, 55 (1993), 301–15.
128. Paul de Foix — Vettori, Rome, 29 January 1582, in BL, Add. MS 10266, fol. 188.
129. Schmitt, 'The Correspondence of Jacques Daléchamps', p. 420, De Foix — Daléchamps, Rome, 14 March 1583.
130. *DBF*, 1, col. 19; Raugei, *Gian Vincenzo Pinelli*, II, 470–71.
131. Audebert — Vettori, Rome, 23 February 1577/78 n.s., in Bandini, *Clarorum Italorum*, II, 103–05.
132. Vettori, *Epistolarum libri X*, p. 200, 27 December 1578.
133. Ibid., pp. 203–04, 20 June 1579.
134. Raugei, *Gian Vincenzo Pinelli*, I, 482; II, 312; he died in late 1584.
135. Jean Courtier — Vettori, 1 February 1580, in Bandini, *Clarorum Italorum*, II, 135.
136. Vettori — Courtier, Florence, 10 February 1580, in Vettori, *Epistolarum libri X*, p. 210.
137. *Hypomnēma eis ta tōn Pythagoreiōn epi ta chrysa. Commentarius in aurea Pythagoreorum carmina*, ed. by Curterius (Paris: Etienne Prévosteau, Nicolas Nivelle, 1583).
138. Joseph Bergin, *Cardinal de La Rochefoucauld: Leadership and Reform in the French Church* (New Haven and London: Yale University Press, 1987); *DBF*, 19, col. 1028–29.
139. Giovanni Battista Ubaldini, *Istoria della casa degli Ubaldini* (Florence: B. Sermartelli, 1588), pp. 65, 127–30.

140. Lelio Ubaldini — Vettori, Paris, 1 April 1578, in Penn UL, MS Coll. 196.
141. Ubaldini — Vettori, Paris, 22 June 1578, in BL, Add. MS 10273, fol. 320.
142. *Peplus Italiae: opus in quo illustres viri grammatici, oratores, historici, poetae, mathematici, philosophi, medici, jurisconsulti eorumque patriae, professiones et litterarum monumenta tum carmine tum soluta oratione recensentur* (Paris: Frédéric Morel, 1578).
143. Hugo Tucker, 'Jean Dorat et Giovanni Matteo Toscano, lecteurs des Pytiques de Pindare en 1566', in *Jean Dorat: poète et humaniste limousin de la Renaissance*, ed. by Christine de Buzon and Jean-Eudes Girot (Geneva: Droz, 2007), p. 205; Hugo Tucker, *Homo viator* (Geneva: Droz, 2003), p. 56.
144. Toscano, *Peplus Italiae*, bk. IV, pp. 108–09.
145. Lelio Ubaldini — Vettori, Bourges, October 1578, in BL, Add. MS 10273, fol. 322.
146. Giacomini — Vettori, Paris, 27 January 1573, in BL, Add. MS 10267, fol. 42.
147. Giacomini — Vettori, Lyon, 29 July 1573, in BL, Add. MS 10267, fol. 44.
148. Hector Reynaud, *Jean de Monluc* (Paris: Thorin, 1893, repr. Slatkine 1971), pp. 125–51.
149. Lorenzo Capponi — Vettori, Lyon, 20 November 1556, in BL, Add. MS 10265, fol. 95.
150. Hélène, sister of Guillaume (Mei's employer) and Thomas III Guadagni.
151. Giuseppe Allegrini, *Elogj degli uomini illustri toscani*, 4 vols (Lucca, n. pub., 1772), III, cc-ccv.
152. *Magnificentissimi spectaculi a regina regum matre in horte suburbanis editi* (Paris: F. Morel, 1573).
153. Giacomini — Vettori, Lyon, 1 November 1573, in BL, Add. MS 10267, fol. 46.
154. Giacomini — Vettori, Lyon, 1 April 1580, in BL, Add. MS 10267, fol. 48.
155. In Bandini, *Clarorum italorum*, I, pp. lxxii-lxxiii.
156. DBI, 57, 652–54; Joanna Milstein, *The Gondi: Family Strategy and Survival in Early Modern France* (Farnham: Ashgate, 2014), pp. 60–65; Vettori's research may have been included in Jean Corbinelli's *Histoire et preuves généalogiques de la maison de Gondi* (Paris: J. B. Coignard, 1705).
157. DBI, 57, 639–47.
158. Alberto Gondi — Vettori, Paris, 23 March 1580, in Bandini, *Victorius*, p. lxxii.
159. Alberto Gondi — Vettori, Paris, 25 March 1579/80 n.s., ibid., p. lxxiii.
160. Vettori — Pierre de Gondi, Florence, 9 October 1579, in Vettori, *Epistolarum libri X*, p. 208.
161. Giacomini — Vettori, Lyon, 1 April 1580, in BL, Add. Mss 10267, fol. 48.
162. Vettori — Henri III, Florence, 21 April 1580, in Vettori, *Epistolarum libri X*, p. 209; Niccolai, *Pier Vettori*, p. 191.
163. Henri III — Vettori, Paris, 20 March 1580, in Bandini, *Victorius*, p. lxxvi.
164. Giacomini — Vettori, Lyon, 1 April 1580, in BL, Add. MS 10267, fol. 48: 'Mando a V. S. la lettera che il Re mi ha dato fu l'occasione della Ret^{ca} d'Aristotele arrichita da vostri comenti.'
165. Giacomini — Vettori, Lyon, 26 June 1580, in BL, Add. MS 10267, fol. 50.
166. Giacomini — Vettori, Lyon 30 December 1580, in BL, Add. MS 10267, fol. 55; *Lettres de Henri III*, vol. V, ed. by Jacqueline Boucher (Paris: H. Champion, 2000), p. 134, n° 4092; p. 142, n° 4114; p. 151, n° 4142.
167. Vettori — Pierre de Gondi, Florence, 25 October 1584, in Vettori, *Epistolarum libri X*, p. 222; Giacomini acknowledged receipt in a letter of 19 October 1580, promising a *ricompensa* from Retz, BL, Add. MS 10267, fol. 52.
168. Vettori — Henri III, Florence, 25 October 1584, in Vettori, *Epistolarum libri X*, p. 223.
169. *Commentarii in X libros Aristotelis De moribus ad Nicomachum* (Florence: Filippo II and Iacopo II Giunta, 1584); Niccolai, *Pier Vettori*, pp. 187–88.
170. *Seconde partie du Promptuaire des medalles* (Lyon: G. Roville, 1577), p. 275.

CHAPTER 9

From Shadows towards Light: Transformations of Allegorical Journeys in Dialogue II of Giordano Bruno's *Cena de le ceneri*

Hilary Gatti

At the fifth session of the Venetian part of his trial at the hands of the Roman Catholic Inquisition, Giordano Bruno described his *Cena de le ceneri,* the first of his six philosophical dialogues written in Italian and published in London between 1584 and 1585, as divided into five dialogues which discuss the motion of the earth: 'ho composto un libro intitolato *La cena de le ceneri*, il quale è diviso in cinque dialoghi, quali trattano del moto della terra'.[1] The first, third, fourth and fifth dialogues into which he divided his *Cena* correspond to this description, discussing and endorsing the new post-Copernican cosmology, while extending the universe to infinite dimensions. Dialogue II, on the other hand, makes only a fleeting reference to the subject matter of the whole work, offering instead a remarkably colourful and dramatic account of the night-time journey that took Bruno (the Nolan) and his party from Salisbury Court in London, the French Ambassador's residence in which Bruno was housed, to the rooms of Fulke Greville in Whitehall where the *Cena* is set.[2] Bruno dedicated this work to his host, the French Ambassador, Michel de Castelnau, seigneur de Mauvissière. Bruno clearly considered Castelnau, and the French Embassy, as providing him with a safe haven in an often hostile city.[3]

Dialogue II offers much more than a historical account of Bruno's night-time London journey. He himself, in his introductory remarks on the subjects treated in each dialogue of his work, defines it as: 'una descrizione di passi et di passaggi, che piu poetica, et tropologica forse, che historiale sarà da tutti giudicata'.[4] It is generally recognized that the whole of Dialogue II is packed with literary and philosophical echoes, many of which have been identified by editors and critics. It has also been recognised as important in establishing Bruno's problematical relationship with the Elizabethan social and political world of which he was a guest. Yet little attention has been paid to the role of this dialogue within the text as a whole. What is its purpose within a work dedicated primarily to astronomical and cosmological issues? Can it be dismissed, as it often is, with a few words, as simply a literary and sociological *divertissement,* unrelated to the cosmological discussion which is the subject of the work as a whole? My essay will attempt to address these issues, offering an analysis of the night-time journey in its literary and allegorical dimensions that places it more securely within the overall textual structure of which it is a part.

La cena de le ceneri, Dialogo II

(1). The cause (occasion) of the supper constitutes the *incipit* of this dialogue. Theophilus, an imaginary figure who acts as narrator and Bruno's mouthpiece, claims that Bruno (referred to here as 'the Nolan', from the name of his home town in Italy, Nola) was one day asked personally by Fulke Greville (courtier to Elizabeth I and friend of Sir Philip Sidney) to explain his reasons for believing that the earth moves. The Nolan answered that first Greville should explain to him why it does not, and then he would argue against the traditional thesis. At that point, Greville proposes a meeting a week later, on Ash Wednesday, during which the Nolan would be able to discuss his new post-Copernican cosmology with some gentlemen invited especially for that purpose. The invitation is accepted, but on the arranged day no-one appears to escort the Nolan to Fulke Greville's rooms, so he goes to visit some Italian friends instead. On his return to the French Ambassador's residence, he finds the Anglo-Italian man of letters John Florio and the dramatist Matthew Gwynne, sent by Greville to urge him to come to supper, as many knights and gentlemen had been waiting for him all day.[5] Although it is already dark (Ash Wednesday that year, 1584, fell on 15 February) the Nolan decides to set off with Florio and Gwynne on the journey through London to reach Fulke Greville's rooms in Whitehall. In the written text, the party includes the imaginary Theophilus, who becomes the narrator of the journey.[6]

(2). Salisbury Court, which appears at that time to have been the name of the French Ambassador's residence (no longer extant), bordered on the much larger Buckhurst House, which would be renamed Dorset House in 1604 when Lord Buckhurst became Earl of Dorset. A short passage to the north called Water Lane led from Salisbury Court into Fleet Street. Water Lane also ran to the south of Salisbury Court, adjacent to the large garden of Buckhurst House, leading down to the Thames.[7] Instead of going north directly into Fleet Street, and walking along the Strand to Whitehall, the Nolan and his party decide to go down to the river and call a boat to take them to the Whitehall landing stage. This decision figures clearly as a mistake, for their journey turns at once into a hellish night-time ride in a creaking and leaking boat, whose meaning is suggested through the use of multiple classical echoes.

First and foremost, it is specified that they leave from *il ponte de palazzo del Milord Beuckhurst*: a specification which, at most, has drawn from editors of this text a footnote reminding readers that Lord Buckhurst, better known to literary scholars as Thomas Sackville, had co-authored with Thomas Norton in 1561 the tragedy *Gorboduc*, the first poetic drama in English to employ blank verse. It seems not to have been noticed by Bruno scholars that Buckhurst was also the author of the *Induction* to the second part of the popular *Mirror for Magistrates*, published in 1563.

The poem introduces this text — which tells of the misfortunes of great historical figures come to grief — with an account of a nightmare journey in which Sorrow accompanies the poet to Hades, or hell. A protagonist of the poem is predictably Charon, the mythical helmsman who, from the times of classical antiquity, was considered to have ferried the dead to Hades over the dark waters of Lake Acheron, meaning in Greek the lake or river of pain. In Buckhurst's account of the journey to hell:

> We passed on so far forth till we saw
> Rude Acheron, a loathsome lake to tell,
> That boils and bubs up swelth as black as hell;
> Where grisly Charon, at their fixed tide,
> Still ferries ghosts unto the farther side.[8]

Surely it is no coincidence if the Nolan's party are met with at Lord Buckhurst's landing-stage by an ancient and surly boatman who seemed the helmsman of the region of hell, causing the Nolan to exclaim to his friends: *piaccia a Dio, disse, che questo non sii Caronte*. And if it should be objected that Bruno himself specifies later on in his work that he spoke practically no English, it should also be remembered that his party on this journey included the bilingual John Florio, who would have had no difficulty in furnishing Bruno with an off-the-cuff translation of Buckhurst's poem during their evenings together at the French Ambassador's residence, where Florio also resided, as tutor to the Ambassador's daughter, throughout Bruno's stay in London.

The intertextuality of this part of the dialogue is rich with further literary, mythical and historical echoes. After a frustratingly long wait, the party ends up in a boat that is clearly unsafe, and ironically recalls to the Nolan's mind a boat known locally as the 'lux perpetua', thus reminding the reader of the Catholic prayer of requiem for the souls of the dead:

> Requiem Aeternam dona eis, Domine
> *et lux perpetua luceat eis*

or in the English Catholic version:

> Eternal rest grant unto them, O Lord,
> *and let perpetual light shine upon them.*

This is immediately followed by a quotation from Virgil's sixth book of *The Aeneid*, the importance of which for Bruno's discourse here is underlined with an explicit reminder of two of Virgil's verses:

> Gemuit sub pondere cimba
> Sutilis, et multam accepit limosa paludem.[9]

Virgil's groaning and leaking boat, which carries Aeneas to the muddy shores of Hades, is a clear indication of the meanings of the story told by Theophilus of the Nolan's own journey along the Thames. Furthermore, the Nolan and his party travel in a boat whose ominous groans and whistling remind the party of the music of the walls of Thebes, built, according to Greek mythology, by the twin brothers Zethus and Amphion after they had taken their revenge on Lycus, the previous ruler of Thebes who had held their mother in slavery. The music of Amphion's lyre, a gift from the god Hermes, accompanied the building of the walls and led to the conviction that the walls themselves were what Bruno calls 'vocal', just like the boat in which he is travelling with forced and apprehensive laughter. His 'sardonic' and slightly hysterical laughter is a further reminder of a classical example referred to explicitly by Bruno here, as when the Carthaginian military general, Hannibal, after having led his army and some elephants successfully over the Alps and invaded parts of Italy, tried to laugh off the danger of the counter-attack by the Roman army, which would eventually lead to his defeat. Bruno is clearly expressing apprehension here of the counter-attack by the defendants of the traditional cosmology that he can expect once he reaches his journey's end, and participates in the supper organized, with that precise intention, by Fulke Greville. It should also be remembered, however, that Nola, the home town of 'the Nolan', counted among its past glories the distinction of having resisted more than one siege by Hannibal and his powerful army.[10] As the whole work demonstrates, Bruno has no intention of letting himself be overcome by the hostile forces put together to oppose his cosmological arguments.

In conclusion of this dense passage of classical references, the party's slow progress in the rotting boat is defined as '*festina lente*', the Latin for 'more haste less speed'. Although of Greek origin, this motto was adopted by the Roman Emperor Augustus as his own, and from Roman times it had been depicted by an emblem of a dolphin wound around an anchor. There could also be a tacit reminder here of the adoption of this emblem in the modern world by the famous printer Aldo Manuzio of Venice, who, at the beginning of the sixteenth century, was the first to publish a series of small books in octavo format, handy for carrying about, which reached a wide public, somewhat like our paperback editions. Bruno's printer in London, John Charlewood, published *La cena de le ceneri* in octavo, and it seems to have been fairly widely read, given that around 40 copies of the original printings of 1584 survive in libraries around the world today.[11]

The quote from *Aeneid* VI, right at the centre of this dense passage, would have reminded Bruno's renaissance reader that Aeneas, with the help of the Cumaean Sibyl, entered Hades carrying a golden bough, and that after visiting the dark underworld of lost souls he arrived at the happy Elysian Fields where the souls of heroes, including his dead father, were thought to reside. No golden bough for the Nolan and his party in this hellish phase of their journey; but they do find comfort in the thought of love, misfortune, the passing of time and of the seasons in this world (*amor, gli sdegni, i tempi, et le staggioni*) as sung by the poet Ariosto in his epic of folly, love and chivalry, the *Orlando furioso*. The extraordinary success of this poem in sixteenth-century Italy (it was originally published in a complete form in 1532) had led to it being memorized and frequently sung in public as a favourite entertainment, and it is John Florio who starts singing it in the creaking boat on the Thames with the opening line of Canto 8, stanza 76: '*Dove senza me dolce mia vita*' (Where, far from me, my sweet life, [have you remained so young and lovely]?).

Orlando's words of lament for the beautiful Angelica he has lost stimulate the Nolan to reply with the verses '*Il saracin dolente, ó femenil ingegno*', from Canto XVII, stanza 117, that introduce a long sequence of anti-Petrarchan critique of the female sex as far from angelic, but rather capricious, inconstant and lascivious. It is a passage that will underlie Bruno's own critique of the female sex that opens his anti-Petrarchan sonnet sequence, the *Heroici furori*, the last of his Italian dialogues written and published in London. But this is not his subject in the *Cena*, and he quickly lets it go by adding a dismissive 'and so on'. However, this is only one of the multiple references in this work to Ariosto's poem, which has been persuasively shown by Lina Bolzoni to contribute significantly to its development.[12]

The memory of Ariosto's *Furioso* has brought the party back from the shades of a mythical Hades to the reality of a far from perfect world, symbolized now by the surly boatmen who insist that their working day is over and brusquely deposit their passengers at a landing-stage only a short way from where they had started off. Their uncouth behaviour earns them an ironic comment from the superior servant, Frulla, who applies to them some verses of the satirical Latin poet, Juvenal, commenting on the behaviour of the worst of the plebs observed by him during a night-time walk through the streets of ancient Rome:

> Rogatus tumet,
> Pulsatus rogat,
> Pugnis concisus adorat.

[Pleaded with, he swells, when struck he struts, when soundly punched, he adores you.][13]

The boat ride down the river, with its multiple memories of classical antiquity, has not got the party far.

(3). Abandoned by the far from courteous boatmen, the party steps off onto a landing stage that Bruno locates as at about a third of the total distance of their journey, and just beyond the church known as The Temple (so presumably at the Temple Stairs themselves) and finally they attempt to head north into the Strand. Neither the precise specification that they are now at about a third of their journey's length, nor the specification that they have arrived at the church known as The Temple, are to be considered as incidental annotations with respect to the 'tropological' or allegorical sense of this journey. It is a journey that Bruno divides nicely into three parts, of which the first stage of travel down the river constitutes the first part only. Readers of his earlier works published in Paris in 1582 will remember that he initiates his philosophical enquiry in the first of those Parisian works, *De umbris idearum*, with a poem celebrating the waters of a river (with all its memories of the melancholy Heraclitus and his reality in constant flux) whose waters are life-saving only if they are consumed soberly and without excess. Instead, if too fully indulged in they lead to madness and an inglorious fall:

> Si nimium t'ingurgitas, te turbabunt,
> Inqu'insaniam t'adigent,
> Precipitemve gloriam.[14]

In this first third of the journey that has taken the Nolan and his party down the river, among a cluster of memories of the Hades of classical antiquity, there have clearly been some notes of excess somewhere. During this process the Temple has turned into a Church (as, of course, happened with the decline of the Roman Empire and, in its final phase, the rise of Christianity) and the question raised by Bruno is whether the landing at the Temple stairs will facilitate the second stage of their journey, or bring with it yet more problems and difficulties of a different sort. In fact, in Bruno's account of it, the next stage of their journey is even less illuminating than the first.

The first thing that happens is that the party falls into a ditch into which they sink, which makes it sound as if it was low tide. Bruno is explicit about the muse he calls on to describe this part of their journey. She is Mafelina, one of the muses of Merlin Cocai. This was the pseudonym under which Theophilo Folengo, a Benedictine monk (although for some years a lapsed one), had become famous as one of the principal sixteenth-century poets who wrote mock-epic poems in a macaronic Latin. In his major poem *Baldus* — a hero who succumbs to the abundant temptations of the material world — Mafelina, who cooks succulent dishes of *gnocchi* and *polenta* for her poet, is invoked as one of the poet's '*Muse pancifiche*'. These 'Muses with fat stomachs' thus precipitate the Nolan and his party into a realm of thick matter, the flesh and the temptations thereof.[15] The allegorical sense of which would seem to be that the Barbarian invasions have begun, bringing with them the end of the classical era.

The Nolan, however, thinks that he has spied a way out through what Bruno calls a '*porco passaggio*', and he urges the others to follow him through this swinish passage. Its significance is specified by what at first sight seems, in such a context, a curious explanation: the Nolan will be able to find a way out of the ditch of sensual indulgence because he has studied in the schools more than the other members of the party: *há studiato ne le scuole piú che noi*.[16] Little attention has been paid to this rather surprising comment, where Bruno is clearly referring to medieval scholasticism, based on the philosophy of Aristotle and culminating in the Christian theology of St Thomas Aquinas, which, in Bruno's youth, had constituted the foundation of his education at the Dominican monastery in Naples.[17] And if this is now considered by Bruno to constitute a '*porco passaggio*', it seems fair to ask if there is not a covert reference here to Richard Swineshead, one of the most famous scholastic philosophers of medieval Oxford. Swineshead, sometimes referred to by hostile critics as *Subtilis Swynshed*, was also called The Calculator, as his major work, known as the *Liber calculationem* (c. 1340–1355), amounted to an attempt to reduce all natural phenomena to logical mathematical definitions. Bruno himself was not hostile to mathematics as such, but excessive calculation abstracted from a natural philosophy seemed to him pernicious, and he had just criticized his intellectual hero Copernicus himself, in Dialogue 1 of the *Cena,* as being too much a mathematician and not enough of a natural philosopher.[18]

Scholasticism in general, then, and perhaps in particular the calculatory version of it, appear at first sight to the Nolan as the way out of the deep ditch of sensual barbarity. But this too turns out to have been a bad mistake, which only involves the whole party in even greater difficulties when, instead of emerging from the ditch, they fall into a deeper quagmire than the previous one, closed in by high walls, and are forced to wade through thicker and thicker layers of clinging mud that now reaches right up to their waists. Their situation appears to the party a desperate one, with their desperation expressed in the text through the quotation of a virtually suicidal sonnet by Luigi Tansillo, a poet of a previous generation, of Nolan origin, much quoted by Bruno throughout his Italian dialogues. The sonnet begins 'Qual uom che giace e piange lungamente', and is followed in Bruno's text by some equally suicidal lines spoken by one of the blind poets in Marc'Antonio Epicuro's pastoral drama, the *Cecaria*.[19] Marc'Antonio Epicuro, sometimes known as Antonio dei Marsi from his origins in Abruzzo, had achieved considerable public success with his deeply sentimental poetic dramas. He spent much of his artistic life in Naples, where he died in 1555. So both Tansillo's sonnet and the despairing lines from the *Cecaria* bring Bruno's text decidedly close to the Nolan's own youthful experience, and would appear to suggest that the scholastic education he had received at the Dominican monastery in Naples had dramatically failed to satisfy his intellectual appetite, although it was anything but superficial.[20]

Dante is not mentioned here by name (Bruno only ever mentions him in passing once, in his *Spaccio de la bestia trionfante*, also written and published in London in the same year, 1584), but Bruno must surely have remembered that in his *Inferno* Dante follows Virgil down through the Fourth Circle of Hell until they reach the banks of the dark and muddy river Styx.

> L'acqua era buia assai piú che persa;
> E noi, in compagnia dell'onde bige,
> Entrammo in giú per una via diversa.
> In la palude va c'ha nome Stige.[21]

Virgil and Dante see souls crouched on the bank, covered in mud, and striking and biting at each other. They are the Wrathful, those who were consumed with anger during their lives. Virgil alerts Dante to the presence of additional souls here, which remain invisible to him as they lie completely submerged in the Styx — these are the Sullen, those who muttered and sulked under the light of the sun. They now gurgle and choke on the black mud of the swampy river. They are people like Bruno's 'Malcontent', to whom he dedicates the introductory poem of the *Cena*: 'barbarous curs' with cynical teeth, always ready to argue, attacking and humiliating their opponents. As in Dante, so in Bruno's text they live in the deepest levels of swamp, which are dark and obscure, so that it is even more arduous now for the Nolan and his party to make any progress at all. Bruno calls this part of their journey a 'purgatory', and likens the quagmire to Lake Avernus in southern Italy whose waters produced fumes so lethal that birds were said to drop dead into its shadowy depths. Buckhurst's *Induction*, mentioned above, also dwells at length on the horrors of Lake Avernus, which was often considered the entrance to Hades itself. So the struggle through the mud, surrounded by multiple memories of medieval scholasticism, seems to represent Bruno's version of the dark ages — both of his own Neapolitan youth and of the historical Middle Ages — which also get the party almost nowhere at all.

(4). They do nevertheless reach dry ground at last — which symbolizes the end of the second stage of their journey — and they come out on to 'the wide main road', which must have been the Strand. At this point they stop to debate whether to continue this frustrating journey, or go back to their not very distant lodgings. The decision-making process is complex and lengthy, and leads to a number of digressions that are not unrelated to the journey itself. For example, the decision to continue leads to a reflection on the question of free will (one of the most hotly debated subjects throughout Europe at this time) in which an overriding 'fate' urges their will to choose to continue the journey. Here echoes of Erasmus, which were far from dormant in the London of that time, merge with echoes of Machiavelli's preference for a classical fate rather than Erasmus's Divine Providence. Bruno's principal point, however, is to emphasize how the reason and intellect now combine to accept or 'elect' the commands of fate, rather than being passively dominated by them: again a reminiscence of Machiavelli, who had famously argued in *The Prince* that fate dominates half our lives or thereabouts, but free will and our own *virtù* do the rest.[22] The Middle Ages, Bruno seems to be suggesting here, have finally modulated into the beginnings of modernity.

At the same time as specifying his position on the freedom of the will, Bruno at this point has characterised his journey to Fulke Greville's rooms as no everyday affair but rather a moment of his destiny. This gives a solemnity to the decision to continue — which seems exaggerated only to the fatuous neo-Aristotelian pedant Prudentius — on the basis of which Bruno can introduce various further reflections connected to the destiny fate has carved out for him as well as to the actual journey itself. For example, quoting some verses from Virgil's *Georgics* inciting those who wish to cultivate their fields with success to ever more strenuous efforts, he then reflects on the greater merits of poets who praise noble ideals rather than those who stoop to praising rustic and humble objects of everyday use.[23] This is followed by a reference to the biblical story of Saul, ordered by his father to go in search of their lost asses. Saul's search was rudely interrupted when he was unexpectedly crowned King of Israel by Samuel, who — in spite of Saul's humble birth as a member of the smallest of the tribes of Israel — urges him to forget the asses and concentrate on reigning over the kingdom of Israel instead.[24] The story seems introduced to suggest that sometimes fate holds great things in store even for those whose origins may not seem propitious (*Gran cosa adunque ne promette il cielo*), thereby justifying the fulsome praise that follows of Elizabeth I and her court, which Bruno claims to have visited in the company of the French Ambassador, Michel de Castelnau, to whom this work is dedicated. The world that Bruno now begins to celebrate is clearly one composed above all of the powerful renaissance courts, whose Princes (among whom Bruno sees the English queen, Elizabeth I, as one of the most politically and culturally gifted of them all) dominate, at least for the moment, the European scene.

Bruno cleverly uses an effective rhetorical strategy here to disclaim in advance any criticism of presumption he might have met with by using a negative mode of praise: 'it is not my place to say', for example, or 'far be it from me to presume to praise', and so on. But although he disclaims any personal acquaintance with the major figures of the English court — such as Elizabeth's treasurer, William Cecil, Lord Burghley, Robert Dudley, Earl of Leicester, or her principal secretary, Sir Francis Walsingham — he makes clear that he knows who they are, and their specific roles in the government of the realm, whose queen is given important recognition for her success in maintaining peace and stability in a time of ferocious religious wars elsewhere in Europe. The most fulsome praise, however, is reserved for Sir Philip Sidney, whose refined manners and remarkable culture had already been drawn to Bruno's attention in Milan, during his journey north. It is with a clear note of pride that Bruno mentions explicitly that, in England, he had been in the company of Sidney, who may indeed have been the unnamed knight who sits at the head of the table during the supper itself. In any case, later on Bruno would dedicate to Sidney, as if to a patron, two of his philosophical dialogues written and published in London, the *Spaccio de la bestia trionfante* and the *Heroici furori*.[25]

Bruno is not so tender with the common people of London, who are subjected to pages and pages of bitter invective for the rudeness of their manners, their violent modes of treating foreigners, and their distrust of all things Italian. It is a part of his work which can hardly have endeared him to the English reader, either now or then, and one cannot help wondering who it was that, in an apparently contemporary hand, wrote a decidedly negative '*Male*' in the margin of this part of the text in the very copy thought to have been presented by Bruno himself to the English queen.[26] In the midst of this passage of at times almost hysterical criticism of the English common people — historically known not to have welcomed Italian visitors, considered indiscriminately as Catholic infiltrators — we find a cameo portrait of the English servants: their hierarchical status according to the importance of their masters, their varying social origins, and even the different kinds of uniforms and badges that distinguished them. Bruno may not have liked everything he found in England, but he had clearly been observing the society around him with a precise and penetrating eye. It was pages like these in Dialogue II of the *Cena de le ceneri* that made Giovanni Aquilecchia remark in the *Introduzione* to his 1955 edition that Bruno's 'realistic narrative technique' occupies a unique place in sixteenth-century Italian literature:

> Non sarebbe ardito affermare che con queste pagine [...] Bruno occupa un posto a sé nella letteratura cinquecentesca, non facilmente classificabile nell'ambito degli schemi tradizionali di quella.[27]

(5). In spite of Aquilecchia's insistence on the historical and realistic level of discourse that Bruno never entirely abandons from beginning to end of Dialogue II of the *Cena*, the 'tropological' or allegorical level of his discourse is never completely abandoned either. After this lengthy series of parentheses, Bruno at last picks up the theme of the journey once more, with the party now following the direct route along the Strand, into Charing Cross and on to Whitehall. Here he continues the invective against the common people thronging the crowded street. The now well-lit road provides the Nolan and his party with little respite or relaxation thanks to the frequent collisions with the crowd of plebeian Londoners who swarm along it. The idea expressed here seems to be that the collisions, rather than happening in a random sequence, come about on purpose, with the specific intent of distressing a party of foreign visitors. The 'double' collision which throws the Nolan twice against a stone wall might be a further covert reference to The Calculator, or the medieval Richard Swineshead, who was particularly concerned with double measures of quality in terms of intensity and remissness.

In any case, the general implication is clearly that, owing to aggressive hostility to their venture, the party is still having great difficulty in getting anywhere at all. In this sense the whole journey to Fulke Greville's rooms is already a prediction of the frustratingly negative dialogue that will take place over the new cosmology in the central parts of this text — that is, Dialogues III and IV — with Bruno's two academic adversaries still strenuously arguing in conventionally scholastic terms for an Aristotelian-Ptolemaic closed and earth-centred universe, or, at most, for a Copernicanism reduced to a purely mathematical theory for facilitating astronomical calculations. So we can say today that Bruno's Protestant antagonists in the cosmological discussion that follows argue in entirely conventional terms according to the strictly mathematical interpretation of the Copernican astronomy originating with Luther's principal disciple Melanchthon, which Robert Westman has called the 'Wittenberg Interpretation of the Copernican Theory'.[28] The Nolan/Theophilus (who together represent Bruno himself) will argue against them in realist terms, proposing a heliocentric post-Copernican universe extended now to infinite dimensions. Bruno was one of only a very few sixteenth-century natural philosophers who put forward a realist reading of the Copernican theory, or, as Robert Westman again puts it: '[Bruno] made clear that his own epistemic fulcrum lay above all in the discovery of physical explanations'.[29]

(6). In spite of all the hurdles, then, the party does finally arrive at the Palace of Whitehall, the principal residence in London of Elizabeth I and her court, which Bruno calls simply '*Il Palazzo*'. They knock on a door that is opened by ill-mannered servants who unwillingly indicate the staircase the guests must take to reach Fulke Greville's rooms. The arrival takes place among unpleasant reflections on the communal drinking cup, still much used in England at that time: yet another sign, in Bruno's opinion, of the uncivil habits of the people in what he considered a still uncouth island. Fortunately, such habits are not to be seen at this refined table. Some commentators have seen in this passage an underlying critical reference to the passing of the cup at the Eucharist — particularly in its Protestant versions — which Bruno repudiated in all its forms and ceremonies in favour of a divinity that manifests itself as a universal intellect.[30] But if so, he is careful here, in the context of the royal palace, not to explicate his 'tropological' meaning too openly. Rather, he links this episode of the final moments of his narration to a little fuss about who should sit at the head of the table — it turns out to be an unnamed knight — and who at the foot of the table, a place finally taken by John Florio. The implication is clearly that such social hierarchies may be about to be challenged by a new, infinite cosmology with no fixed centre, where all values, including those of an aristocratic social order, become relative.

In this sense, the dialogue ends with the first lights of a new dawn, or a more civilized era, at last visible on the horizon. The ensuing dialogues with the two neo-Aristotelian doctors invited as opponents by Fulke Greville will be hostile and problematical and, at the supper itself, will leave the question of the new post-Copernican cosmology unresolved. But in the final Dialogue V, between Theophilus, who is Bruno's mouthpiece in the secondary discussion, and his English friend and counterpart Smitho, the full implications of Bruno's new cosmology will be carefully and closely argued. There Bruno lays down the foundations for his new cosmic vision which, as he had anticipated in Dialogue I, allow him — and any reader disposed to join him in his newly immense universe — the chance at last to free themselves from the shackles of a closed and static universal space, such as Aristotle's or Ptolemy's. The reader is invited to fly into the unknown vistas of an infinite world that, as Bruno will argue in his following two works, the *Causa, principio et uno* and the *De l'infinito, universo e mondi*, contains within it the divine order of a world soul or universal intellect, reflected in the individual intellect of the new natural philosopher. That is to say, it is an ordered universe knowable by the human mind, which means that travel into space suddenly becomes a possible reality. And so, in Dialogue I of the *Cena,* we have the famous passages of prophetic space travel, which are far from being merely metaphorical or even purely spiritual or magical flights of the imagination:

> [Il Nolano] ha disciolto l'animo humano, et la cognitione che era rinchiusa ne l'artissimo carcere de l'aria turbulento, onde a pena come per certi buchi havea facultá de remirar le lontanissime stelle, et gl'erano mozze l'ali, á fin che non volasse ad aprir il velame di queste nuvole, et veder quello che veramente lá su si ritrovasse.[31]

(7). In the *Cena* itself, Bruno's new cosmic vision, which he presents with what are clearly paradisiac implications (again recalling Dante), is defined rather than celebrated. That celebration is postponed until the final pages of the last of his six Italian dialogues written and published in London, the *Heroici furori,* where the Dantean echoes of a vision of the Divine One or Unity are far more explicit, albeit transposed into this world, this universe, rather than a transcendent one: or, as Bruno himself puts it, a vision of 'il sommo bene in terra'. Such is the final culmination of his English journey, which takes Bruno through the hell of oppressive classical and medieval mental shackles, the purgatory of debate with the pedants and academics who are unable to throw off the chains of their neo-Aristotelian mind-set, towards the 'new world' of his new vision of a universe infinitely infinite, or infinite both intensively (that is, filled with an infinite number of ordered worlds or solar systems) and extensively (that is, as an unlimited universal space).[32]

The *Heroici furori* culminates in a *canzone,* a poetic celebration of Bruno's final philosophical vision, which, in Ingrid Rowland's impressive verse translation, includes the following lines, sung by one of the previously blind philosophers, who are the heroes of the final parts of this work:

> The Third, with the lyre, played and sang:
> After such labours and such miseries
> Is this the port our tempests shall ordain?
> Then let no other task to us remain
> Than raising to the skies,
> Our thanks for veiled eyes:
> The light has made its presence known through these.[33]

It is important to emphasise that this *canzone* too is part of Bruno's English experience, and is sung in the final pages of the *Furori* under the benevolent gaze of English nymphs. The special reference here to a 'chief nymph', who gives the blind philosophers back their sight, is generally considered as an indication that Bruno is placing his cosmological vision under the protection of the English queen. It has been argued that these apparently miraculous powers attributed to Elizabeth I are a recognition of her role as the temporal head of the Anglican Church founded by her father, Henry VIII, but that Bruno's interest in the Anglican settlement was of a political rather than a religious nature: a recognition of the English Church's novel solution to the troubled question of the relations between church and state.[34] The documents at present available give no indication of any attempt on his part to join the Anglican Church.[35] However that may be, in the final pages of the *Furori* it is English nymphs who guard the now sparkling and refreshing waters of the river Thames. The journey in its entirety has taken Bruno from the obscure and hellish depths of the river gurgling under the creaking boat that set off in the dark from Lord Buckhurst's landing stage, to the Elysian Fields of the sun-lit meadows through which the Thames now runs as a river of redemption, not in a life beyond but in the here and now of a newly infinite universe.

Notes to Chapter 9

1. See Luigi Firpo, *Il processo di Giordano Bruno*, ed. by Diego Quaglione (Rome: Salerno Editrice, 1993), p. 188. All English translations of foreign language texts here are mine, unless otherwise specified.
2. The text of reference for the *Cena* here is the copy of the first edition of 1584 held by the British Library, call number C.37.c.14.(2.), available on EEBO. Dialogue II of the *Cena* presents a complex textual problem as it has survived in two different versions. Giovanni Aquilecchia, the foremost Bruno scholar of his time, proposed a version in print held only by the Trivulziana Library in Milan as representing Bruno's final intentions — see Giovanni Aquilecchia, 'La lezione definitiva della *Cena de le ceneri* di Giordano Bruno (1950)', in *Schede bruniane* (Manziana: Vecchiarelli, 1993), pp. 1–39 — but more recently this thesis has been challenged and the so-called 'vulgate' version, extant in multiple copies, is here considered to be Bruno's final version. See on this subject, Elisabetta Tarantino, 'Le due versioni del foglio D della *Cena de le ceneri*', *Bruniana e Campanelliana*, 10.2 (2004), 413–24, and Neil Harris, 'Il cancellans da Bruno a Manzoni: fisionomia e fisiologia di una cosmesi libraria', in *Favole, metafore, storie: Seminario su Giordano Bruno*, ed. by Olivia Catanorchi and Diego Pirillo (Pisa: Edizioni della Normale, 2006), pp. 567–602.
3. Castelnau was a figure of considerable intellectual and political stature. His autobiography covers only his earlier life, but throughout the period of Bruno's years in London, he was in constant contact with the major figures of Elizabeth I's government, although his credibility was somewhat diminished by his Embassy's rumoured connection with the Throckmorton Plot to assassinate Elizabeth I. Castelnau himself, however, was a moderate Catholic who wished to see

a reconciliation between Elizabeth and her cousin, the Catholic and imprisoned Mary, Queen of Scots. On Castelnau's years in London, see Gustave Hubault, *Michel de Castelnau, ambassadeur en Angleterre, 1575–1585* (Paris: Imprimerie Belin, 1856, repr. Geneva, 1970).
4. [Giordano Bruno], *La cena de le Ceneri* ([London: John Charlewood], 1584), fol. A3.
5. On Florio's essential role in Elizabethan London as its foremost Italian language teacher, see Michael Wyatt, *The Italian Encounter with Tudor England* (Cambridge: Cambridge University Press, 2005). Matthew Gwynne wrote university dramas in Latin. His *Tres sibyllae* may have influenced Shakespeare's *Macbeth*.
6. See Bruno (1584), pp. 23–25.
7. For the geographical topography of Bruno's London journey, see the useful indications in John Bossy, *Giordano Bruno and the Embassy Affair* (New Haven and London: Yale University Press, 1991), in particular pp. 10–12, and 'A Note on Castelnau's House', pp. 248–52.
8. See vv. 479–83 of Sackville/Buckhurst's *Induction* to the second part of the *Mirror for Magistrates*, 1563.
9. See *Aeneid* VI, 413–14. In his Spanish translation of the *Cena*, Miguel A. Granada noted how the multiple quotations from book VI of the *Aeneid* in this part of the text associate Bruno's London journey with the descent of Aeneas to the underworld. See Giordano Bruno, *La cena de las cenizas* (Madrid: Editora Nacional, 1984), p. 85, n. 6.
10. In the second Punic war (218–201 BC), Hannibal made three attempts to take Nola, which occupied a strategic position for supplies to his army, but each time he failed.
11. For details of the surviving copies of the *Cena*, see Rita Sturlese, *Bibliografia censimento e storia delle antiche stampe di Giordano Bruno* (Florence: Olschki, 1987), pp. 44–49.
12. See Lina Bolzoni, 'Images of Literary Memory in the Italian Dialogues: Some Notes on Giordano Bruno and Ludovico Ariosto', in *Giordano Bruno: Philosopher of the Renaissance*, ed. by Hilary Gatti (Aldershot: Ashgate, 2002), pp. 121–41. Bruno's explicit reference to Rodomonte's infernal journey has been further discussed by Stefano Jossa in 'Il viaggio infernale di Rodomonte: una fonte della *Cena de le ceneri* tra Doni e Aretino', *Giornale storico della letteratura italiana*, 185 (2008), 577–89.
13. The verses, which had become proverbial, derive from Juvenal's *Satires*, III, 293 and 300.
14. See Giordano Bruno, *Opere mnemoniche: Tomo I*, ed. by Marco Mattioli, Rita Sturlese, and Nicoletta Tirinnanzi (Milan: Adelphi, 2004), p. 10.
15. For the invocation of the Muses in the *Baldus*, see Merlin Cocai, *Le maccheronee*, vol. I, ed. by Alessandro Luzio (Bari: Laterza, 1927), p. 47. Folengo's macaronic mock-epic is founded on numerous classical epic sources, among which the reference to Lucian's anti-Virgilian *Pharsalia* has recently been underlined. See Alessandra Paola Macinante, 'Tra le "auctoritates" folenghiane: "plus quam" Lucano', *Filologia e critica*, 38 (2013), 99–121.
16. See Bruno (1584), p. 28.
17. In his 1925 edition of the *Cena* in his *Dialoghi metafisici*, Giovanni Gentile remarked in a footnote that this quagmire of mud should be interpreted allegorically as the education given in the schools of the time, and the note was maintained in the revised format edited by Giovanni Aquilecchia: see Giordano Bruno, *Dialoghi italiani*, I, *Dialoghi metafisici*, ed. by Giovanni Gentile and Giovanni Aquilecchia (Florence: Sansoni, 1958), p. 58, n. 2. More recent editions have often ignored this comment altogether.
18. See Bruno (1584), p. 5.
19. Tansillo's sonnet is in Luigi Tansillo, *Rime*, ed. by Tobia R. Toscano, 2 vols (Rome: Bulzoni, 2011), I, 327. For the recent revival of interest in Tansillo's poetry, see Erika Milburn, *Luigi Tansillo and Lyric Poetry in Sixteenth Century Naples* (Leeds: MHRA-Maney Publishing, 2003). In the last of Bruno's philosophical dialogues written and published in London, the *Eroici furori*, Tansillo (1510–1568) is introduced as one of the speakers in the dialogue, and in Dialogue II of Part I of this work is even claimed as a neighbour and friend of Bruno's father. The quotation from Marc'Antonio Epicuro's *Cecaria* refers to the terzine I and III of the opening speech of the drama by an Old Man. This author's highly conceptual and deeply sentimental pastoral dramas were very popular in sixteenth-century Italy. Printed for the first time in 1525, the *Cecaria* went through twenty-five editions before the end of the century. Modern editions are rare. It can

be found in Marc'Antonio Epicuro, *I drammi e le poesie*, ed. by Alfredo Parente (Bari: Laterza, 1942).
20. For a detailed reconstruction of the rigorous academic programme Bruno must have followed to obtain his degree and ordination as a preaching friar — which we know he did — see Michele Miele, 'La formazione di Giordano Bruno a S. Domenico Maggiore', in *Giordano Bruno: oltre il mito e le opposte passioni*, ed. by Pasquale Giustiniani and others (Naples: Facoltà Teologica dell'Italia meridionale, 2002), pp. 63–79.
21. See Dante Alighieri, *La divina commedia*, vol. I, *Inferno*, ed. by Natalino Sapegno (Florence: La Nuova Italia, 1978), Canto VII, 103–06.
22. See chap. XXV of *Il principe* entitled 'Quantum fortuna in rebus humanis possit et quomodo illi sit occurrendum', in Niccolò Machiavelli, *Il principe*, ed. by Gabriele Pedullà (Rome: Salerno Editrice, 2013), pp. 288–303.
23. See Virgil's *Georgics*, I, 197–203. The praise of humble and even rather unpleasant everyday objects had become a fashionable literary game with anti-Petrarchan poets such as the Florentine Francesco Berni and Niccolò Franco.
24. The story of Saul and his asses is in I Samuel 9. This episode was not included in the alternative version of Dialogue II, which is here considered a preliminary version. For Bruno's frequent references to biblical texts see Hilary Gatti, 'Bruno's Use of the Bible in His Italian Philosophical Dialogues', in *Essays on Bruno* (Princeton and Oxford: Princeton University Press, 2011), pp. 264–79.
25. For the importance Bruno attributed to the figures of the English queen Elizabeth I, and her most cultured and intellectual courtier, Sir Philip Sidney, see 'L'apoteosi di Sir Philip Sidney e della ninfa del Tamigi', in the entry *Inghilterra*, in *Enciclopedia bruniana e campanelliana*, vol. II, ed. by Eugenio Canone and Germana Ernst (Pisa and Rome: Fabrizio Serra, 2010), pp. 81–85. Bruno was not, however, always so positive about Sidney as he is in the *Cena*. For an analysis of his more critical attitudes to some aspects of Sidney, see 'L'Eccellente Cavalliero Signor Filippo Sidneo', in Diego Pirillo, *Filosofia ed eresia nell'Inghilterra del tardo cinquecento: Bruno, Sidney e i dissidenti religiosi italiani* (Rome: Edizioni di storia e letteratura, 2010), pp. 20–26.
26. See p. 37 (fol. D3) of the copy of the original edition, call mark BE.2.T.6*, held by the Österreichische Nationalbibliothek in Vienna. The copy can be consulted via their online database. The volume in which this copy of the *Cena* was originally bound, also containing other dialogues by Bruno, and thought to have been presented by him personally to Elizabeth I, later passed through the hands of John Toland. For details of its bibliographical history, see Sturlese, pp. xxiv–xxv and 49.
27. See Giordano Bruno, *La cena de le ceneri*, ed. by Giovanni Aquilecchia (Turin: Einaudi, 1955), p. 21.
28. See Robert Westman, 'The Wittenberg Interpretation of Copernicus's Theory', in *The Copernican Question* (Berkeley: University of California Press, 2011), pp. 141–70.
29. Ibid., p. 301.
30. Also this episode of the communal drinking cup is not included in the alternative version of Dialogue II, here considered a preliminary version.
31. See Bruno (1584), p. 9.
32. On Bruno's infinite worlds, see the entry by Miguel Granada entitled 'Synodus ex mundis' in *Enciclopedia bruniana e campanelliana*, II, 142–54; on Bruno's concept of an infinite space, and its influence up to and including Isaac Newton, see Hilary Gatti, 'Cosmological Space between Copernicus and Newton', *Memoirs of the American Academy in Rome*, 58 (2013), 3–16.
33. For the text and translation of these verses, see Giordano Bruno, *On the Heroic Furies*, ed. and trans. by Ingrid Rowland (Toronto: Toronto University Press, 2013), pp. 350–51.
34. For this argument, see Gilberto Sacerdoti, *Sacrificio e sovranità: teologia e politica nell'Europa di Shakespeare e Bruno* (Turin: Einaudi, 2002).
35. The known documents referring to Bruno's years in England are presented and discussed in Giovanni Aquilecchia, 'Giordano Bruno in Inghilterra (1583–1585): documenti e testimonianze', *Bruniana e campanelliana*, 1 (1995), 21–42.

CHAPTER 10

Sebastiano Serlio:
giudizio, mescolanza, invenzione

Francesco Paolo Fiore

Non siamo certi della data di nascita di Sebastiano Serlio a Bologna, che potrebbe essere posticipata di circa dieci anni rispetto al 1475, anno tradizionalmente indicato,[1] né abbiamo elementi per stabilire con certezza quanto a lungo si sia trattenuto a Roma accanto a Baldassarre Peruzzi, che Serlio cita come suo maestro. Formatosi come pittore in patria, potrebbe aver conosciuto Peruzzi a Roma tramite gli artisti bolognesi attivi accanto a Jacopo Ripanda fra il 1515 e il 1522 o quando nel 1522 Peruzzi fu a Bologna, per seguirlo a Roma nell'autunno del 1523. In quest'ultimo caso Serlio si sarebbe trattenuto a Roma con Peruzzi poco più di un anno, perché nella primavera del 1525 è documentato di nuovo a Bologna come pittore.[2] Un periodo troppo breve per maturare le conoscenze di Roma e delle antichità romane se non lo considerassimo in aggiunta ad una permanenza precedente. Nel 1528, da poco a Venezia, Serlio pubblicherà infatti la nota serie di incisioni di basi e capitelli di quattro dei cinque ordini annunciati nel privilegio di stampa[3] e che appariranno in forme nuovamente articolate nel suo trattato, a partire dal libro IV pubblicato per la prima volta nel 1537 a Venezia con il titolo: *Regole generali di architettura sopra le cinque maniere degli edifici, cioè, thoscano, dorico, ionico, corinthio et composito, con gli essempi dell'antiquità, che, per la magior parte concordano con la dottrina di Vitruvio*. Sempre a Venezia avrebbe pubblicato nel 1540, come è noto, *Il terzo libro di Sabastiano Serlio bolognese, nel qual si figurano, e descrivono le antiquità di Roma, e le altre che sono in Italia, e fuori d'Italia* che, come il precedente, riflette ricerche e teorie maturate a Roma dall'inizio del secolo al Sacco (1527) della città.[4]

È stato giustamente notato che la concezione del libro III, nel quale sono illustrate anche alcune delle più importanti architetture moderne della Roma del primo Cinquecento, trova la sua origine nell'incompiuto progetto di rilevare la città e i suoi monumenti illustrato da Raffaello nella cosiddetta *Lettera a Leone X*, sia per quanto riguarda il materiale trattato che lo scopo teorico-didattico dell'opera. E che l'affermazione contenuta nella *Lettera* che gli 'ornamenti [...] tutti derivano dalli cinque ordini che usavano gli antiqui' esprimerebbe già l'idea fondamentale posta alla base del IV e III libro di Serlio.[5] L'impostazione dei libri III e IV tornerà anche nei libri da lui completati e editati in Francia dal 1545 in poi, pur attraverso esperienze personali e artistiche profondamente mutate, sia nel caso dei libri dedicati alla geometria e alla prospettiva (I-II, Parigi, 1545) e agli edifici sacri (V, Parigi, 1547), che di quelli più fortemente legati alla vita quotidiana come i libri sulle abitazioni (VI, giunto solo alle prove di stampa e che possiamo meglio conoscere attraverso due importanti manoscritti)[6] o gli *accidenti* (VII, edito postumo, Francoforte, 1575).

La novità del trattato, costituito da libri a stampa nei quali le immagini sono parte decisiva di fronte a un testo talora ridotto a mera didascalia, ha indubbiamente determinato il successo, insieme agli argomenti trattati e al tono didascalico, dei libri di Serlio. Ha reso tuttavia più difficile inquadrare compiutamente le *Regole generali* serliane fra le teorie artistiche del Cinquecento, dovendosi rapportare il testo alle immagini e le immagini fra loro per interpretare il significato trasmesso dall'autore tramite la combinazione delle parti. È quanto si può constatare a partire dalla tavola dal titolo *De le cinque maniere de gli edifici* (c. VI^r) che inaugura il libro IV e che rappresenta per la prima volta fianco a fianco e in progressione proporzionale (1:6, 1:7, 1:8, 1:9, 1:10) cinque ordini architettonici, caratterizzati da rapporti interni e forme specifiche per piedestalli e trabeazioni, oltre che per basi e capitelli. Inserita al fine di rispondere subito alle aspettative dei lettori e di comunicare loro un chiaro messaggio, ha assunto al di là del volere dell'autore un valore riduttivamente normativo che, considerato il successo del libro, delle ristampe e delle traduzioni in Europa, si legherà alla diffusione dei *cinque ordini* così come a lungo intesi nell'architettura occidentale. Ne è evidente indizio il fatto che la *Regola delli cinque ordini d'architettura* di Vignola, priva di una simile tavola riassuntiva nella prima edizione del 1562, sarebbe stata dotata di una tavola sui cinque ordini direttamente ispirata a quella di Serlio in un'edizione pirata di poco successiva al 1572.[7] Per non parlare della condanna espressa da Lomazzo a proposito delle semplificazioni e della troppo facile applicazione delle regole in architettura a carico del bolognese. Eppure Serlio, cosciente della forza dell'immagine e della semplificazione trasmessa, avvertiva trattarsi solo di un prologo: 'Ho voluto nel principio di questo libro imitare i Comici antiqui, alcun de quali volendo rappresentar una Comedia, mandava uno suo nuntio innanzi, che in succinte parole dava noticia a i spettatori, di tutto quello che ne la Comedia si haveva da trattare' (IV, c. V^v).[8] Intendiamo perciò tornare a esaminare la teoria sottesa alle *Regole generali* di Sebastiano Serlio per coglierne le componenti che, derivando dall'esperienza romana di primo Cinquecento e dal tentativo di stabilire una nuova e matura lingua architettonica rapportata all'antichità, portarono Serlio a definire qualità e limiti dell'invenzione in architettura con una libertà e un'articolazione molto superiore alla tavola del IV libro che annunciava i cinque ordini.

Abbiamo citato il passo della *Lettera* nel quale Raffaello afferma che gli '*ornamenti* [...] tutti derivano dalli cinque *ordini*'. Dopo avere descritto i primi tre (dorico, ionico, corinzio) trattati da Vitruvio, Raffaello aggiunge: 'Sono anchora due altre *opere* oltra le tre dicte: cioè attica et toscana, le quali non fuoron, però, molte ussate dalli antichi.'[9] Potremmo dunque considerare almeno complementari, nella *Lettera*, i termini *ornamento*, *ordine* e *opera*. Serlio, che nel titolo del libro IV parla di '*maniere* de gli edifici' e di '*maniera* Corinthia' nella dedica dello stesso libro (IV, c. V^{r-v}), utilizza a sua volta i termini *ordine* ('De l'ordine Dorico', IV, c. XIX^r; 'Et perché Vitruvio ha distribuito quest'ordine Dorico in moduli', IV, c. XX^r) e *opera* ('opera Dorica [...] Ionica [...] Chorintia [...] Thoscana [...] rustica', IV, c. V^{r-v})

come apparenti sinonimi. Ma se da un lato rende più esplicita la coincidenza di significato fra *ordine*, *opera* e *maniera*, parla dall'altro di 'opera rustica' che non è propriamente un ordine architettonico. Il termine *opera* sembra anzi acquistare nel suo trattato, insieme a quello di *maniera*, un significato più ampio di quello albertiano di *ornamento*. In un passo del libro IV i due termini sono infatti accostati come complementari e non coincidenti: 'Ho promesso in questo presente volume di trattar solamente de gli *ornamenti*, et de le differenti *maniere* de gli edificii' (c. VIII^v). Pur valutando che esiste una certa approssimazione concettuale nell'esposizione di Serlio, potremmo vedere qui l'annuncio del tentativo di delineare regole più articolate di quelle vitruviane, tali da permettere agli architetti del suo tempo di realizzare edifici moderni attraverso la composizione di forme e proporzioni entro una *maniera* applicata non solo a colonne e capitelli, ma ai diversi piani o all'intero volume dell'edificio, comprendendo anche gli altri ornamenti, quali porte, finestre e camini. Come nel caso delle finestre ioniche di villa Lante o del camino ionico di villa Madama di Giulio Romano,[10] richiamato implicitamente dal camino ionico del libro IV (cc. XLVI^v-XLVII^r).

Per giungere alla formulazione della sua teoria, Serlio parte dalla discussione del *decor* trattato da Vitruvio.[11] Gli antichi dedicavano gli edifici, scrive Serlio nell'introduzione ai lettori, 'a i Dei accomodandosi a quelli secondo la lor natura robusta, o dilicata', e se l'opera dorica era per Giove, Marte e Ercole, la ionica, che 'partecipa del robusto, et del delicato', andava sia per Diana che per Apollo e Bacco, combinando così figura, complessione fisica e psicologia degli dei in questione ed estendendo quanto Vitruvio scrive a riguardo dei templi antichi. Il passaggio del *decor* alle chiese dedicate a Dio e ai santi cristiani ne deriva di conseguenza e così è per le abitazioni degli 'huomini, secondo lo stato, et la profession loro'. Per Serlio, gli ordini sono dunque espressivi del dedicatario e della committenza, mentre la mescolanza fra *robusto* e *delicato* si rende necessaria per declinare l'espressione più appropriata. Ecco perché, quanto all'*opera* rustica, che Serlio dichiara più conveniente all'opera toscana, la più 'rozza' e meno ornata, 'si potrà ben ancho, non ci discostando da quello, che han fatto gli antichi, mischiare, et communitare quell'opera rustica con la Dorica, et con la Ionica anchora, et talhor con la Corinthia, a voglia di chi volesse contentar un suo capriccio' (IV, c. V^v).

Tuttavia Serlio non vuole portare sino alle ultime conseguenze il metodo proposto e accostare qualità troppo lontane di robusto e delicato. Ancora molti anni più tardi definirà 'per capriccio' la mescolanza fra rustico e corinzio nel XVI esempio di porta corinzia nel libro *Extraordinario* (Lione, 1551), anche se proporrà assai seriamente simile mescolanza fra rustico e corinzio per la porta dedicata a Traiano nella sua ricostruzione dell'accampamento dei romani secondo Polibio rappresentata nel cosiddetto VIII libro manoscritto.[12] Serlio non vorrà dunque discostarsi eccessivamente nemmeno negli ultimi anni in Francia da quanto aveva appreso a Roma da Peruzzi e dalle sue prime mescolanze fra colonne tuscanico-doriche e bozze rustiche[13] e soprattutto da Giulio Romano, in palazzo Maccarani e nella casa romana di Giulio a Macel de' Corvi, dove grandi bugne dal profilo regolare erano state ammorsate alle semicolonne ioniche al piano nobile, sopra al portale tuscanico bugnato del piano terreno. A salvare il decoro sarà chiamato in causa da Serlio il *giudizio* del prudente architetto, lo stesso che presiederà alla formazione dell'ordine composto, il più ornato, slanciato e vicino all'ordine degli archi trionfali dei romani antichi, frutto di una opportuna mescolanza: 'la prudentia de l'artefice dee essere tale, che secondo 'l bisogno, dee spesse volte anchora de le predette semplicità far una mescolanza, riguardando alla natura del soggietto' (IV, c. LXI^v). Il richiamo a Vitruvio, commentato ed emendato sulla base dei migliori esempi di ordini antichi e delle loro parti rinvenute a Roma e fuori Roma, come ripetuto con più insistenza nel III libro, sarà a sua volta utile affinché i lettori, 'volendosi servire delle cose antiche, sappiano fare elettione del perfetto, e bene inteso, e abbandonar le cose troppo licenziose' (III, c. CLV).

Persino le soluzioni da adottare per l'ordine dorico erano state frutto della scelta e mescolanza fra le migliori parti e soluzioni delle architetture antiche che Serlio include nel libro IV e che raccoglierà ulteriormente nel libro III sulle antichità. Il testo e le tavole dedicate all'ordine dorico nel libro IV offrono a questo proposito un esempio più che esplicito. È qui che Serlio riconosce che a parere di alcuni le colonne doriche non avevano basi ma, considerati alcuni esempi antichi, ritiene che la base 'atticurga' descritta da Vitruvio nel terzo libro del *De architectura* sia quella dorica, così come realizzato da Bramante nelle sue opere romane. Passa poi a descrivere e ricostruire il capitello dorico secondo Vitruvio e gli giustappone un'alternativa più vicina 'a gli antiqui che si veggono' e di maggior sporgenza, per poi illustrare numerosi esempi di capitelli e trabeazioni tratte dall'antico 'acciò che lo Architetto possi fare elettion di quel che più gli agrada in qu[e]sto ordine dorico' (IV, c. XXI^v). A ben vedere, il metodo di Serlio è dunque ispirato allo stesso metodo di Bramante, che trae da diverse architetture antiche, mescolandole, le diverse soluzioni messe in opera per il dorico del cortile inferiore del Belvedere, del tempietto di San Pietro in Montorio, del coro e del tegurio di San Pietro così come, dopo di lui, da Raffaello e da Peruzzi. Del rapporto con quest'ultimo Benvenuto Cellini avrebbe detto, rendendo infine chiara l'origine del metodo illustrato e del valore del *giudizio* dell'architetto al quale Serlio tanto spesso si appellerà nel trattato:

> Et avendo il detto Baldassarre assai ragionamenti con il detto Bastiano, mostrandogli per chiarissime ragioni che Vitruvio non aveva dato la regola a quel più bello delle cose degli antichi; di modo che in su quelle fatiche copiate dagli antichi il detto Baldassarre aveva fatto una scelta, secondo il suo buon *giudizio*. [...][14]

Che la proposta di Serlio rispecchi i decenni delle elaborazioni romane precedenti il Sacco del 1527 è reso evidente dal fatto che, mutati i tempi, nell'*Introduzione* alle *Vite* del 1550 Giorgio Vasari riprenderà assai da vicino il IV libro di Serlio nel descrivere i cinque ordini, ma proporrà l'identificazione del tuscanico con il rustico[15] chiamando rustico l'ordine che Serlio chiamava tuscanico, come annunciato nel titolo del capitolo III: *De' cinque ordini d'architettura: rustico, dorico, ionico, corinto, composto, e del lavoro tedesco*. Al composto, di cui adotta nome e proporzioni serliane, Vasari attribuisce però un solo capitello, ispirato all'arco di Tito, e si appella a Vitruvio nel definire 'troppo licenziosi coloro che, pigliando di tutt'e quattro quegli ordini [rustico compreso, dunque], ne facessero corpi che gli rappresentassero più tosto mostri che uomini'.[16] In tal modo Vasari esalterà l'origine toscana e fiorentina del rustico e allo stesso tempo rifiuterà la proposta serliana di mescolare il rustico con gli altri ordini così come rifiuterà le mescolanze che sono alla base dell'ordine composto e le mescolanze in genere, ammirando piuttosto le diverse vie percorse da Michelangelo per raggiungere l'*invenzione*. Trattare le differenze fra le elaborazioni del linguaggio all'antica da parte di Michelangelo, seguito da Vasari, e di Serlio travalica gli scopi di questo saggio, tuttavia non solo la proposta dei cinque ordini, ma anche il *giudizio* che per Serlio presiede alle scelte dell'architetto,[17] può considerarsi un precedente del significato di *disegno* come scelta attribuitogli dallo stesso Vasari. E se l'ipotesi che al termine *maniera* Serlio attribuisca un significato più ampio del termine *ordine* comportando l'accordo di più parti di un edificio fosse accettabile, saremmo anche vicini al significato di raggiunta composizione delle parti più belle che Vasari avrebbe dato al termine *maniera* nelle *Vite*.

Come non solo l'ordine composto, ma l'*invenzione* intesa come idea progettuale di un intero edificio possa nascere per Serlio dalla *mescolanza* di ordini e soluzioni all'antica, viene resa con maggiore complessità nelle facciate di case 'al costume di Venezia', inserite fra gli esempi dorici del IV libro (cc. XXXIV^v–XXXVI^r). L'impostazione si rifà indubbiamente alla sovrapposizione degli ordini al bugnato basamentale del palazzo Caprini di Bramante ripresa anche dal coevo palazzo Corner di Jacopo Sansovino,[18] ma la disposizione delle aperture è chiaramente ispirata alle facciate della tradizione veneziana. Simmetria e ordini all'antica ne assicurano al tempo stesso il decoro, quello che Serlio perseguirà anche nel libro VI nell'illustrare esempi di casi alla francese o meglio alla francese 'in parte', perché, come a Venezia, frutto della disposizione tradizionale corretta e, per così dire, incrementata dall'aggiornamento all'antica proposto da Serlio. Il libro VI diviene a questo proposito più esplicito e decisivo sin dall'impostazione della trattazione delle abitazioni, divise per i diversi gradi degli uomini, dal povero al re, in campagna e in città. L'*incipit* del manoscritto di Monaco ne offre un chiaro annuncio (c. 1^r):

> Le abitazioni degli uomini furono primieramente trovate per il commodo loro senza decoro alcuno, come nara Vitru[vio] nel segondo libro al primo capitolo. [...] Di poi con meglior giudicio et ordine, di grossi legnami le fecero, et così di tempo in tempo con più esperiencia et meglior arte andarono aumentando le abitazioni loro, dandogli non scio che di ornamento; et segondo li paesi, di quella materia che trovavano al suo proposito si servivano, di maniera che gli uomini di meglior giudicio a longo andare de gli anni cominciarono accompagnare la commodità al decoro, et massimamente ne' luoghi più civili. Del qual decoro et commodità uniti insieme io intendo di trattare in questo mio sesto libro, incominciando dalla minima casipppola del povero contadino et seguitando di grado in grado fin alla casa del principe.[19]

La *commodità*, riferita agli usi abitativi e costruttivi dei singoli luoghi, va dunque combinata con il *decoro*, che nel significato più comune attribuitogli da Serlio deriva dall'applicazione dei princìpi della composizione all'antica, in primo luogo la simmetria e gli ordini da lui stesso codificati. Ciò non significa che l'applicazione di questi ultimi sia rigida e assistiamo non solo a mescolanze degli ordini con il rustico, ma anche a una variazione delle proporzioni degli ordini dettate dallo stesso Serlio nel libro IV, per adattamenti visivi e soprattutto per quelli espressivi in risposta al *decor* vitruviano propriamente inteso. Ivi compresa, si intende, l'assenza degli ordini laddove il grado del proprietario della casa o la sua funzione e collocazione lo sconsiglino, pur mantenendo un'impostazione d'insieme all'antica. Considerata la permanenza di Serlio in Francia durante la stesura del VI libro, entrano in gioco le finestre allungate, gli abbaini e i tetti acuti accanto al *decoro* all'antica applicato a case che seguono le *commodità* francesi e divengono perciò alla francese 'in parte', né mancano tentativi di una vera e propria sintesi: 'Il coperto di questa casa non è in tutto a la italiana, neanche alla francese, ma ho tenuto quella via che ciascuno deve tenere, cioè la strada di mezzo' (VI Monaco, c. 58^v).

Commodità e *decoro* si uniscono quindi nel generare l'*invenzione*, e il libro VI di Serlio offre numerosissimi esempi di architetture che, a partire dai modelli tratti dalla realtà italiana o francese, sviluppano mescolanze di piante e alzati dove gli ordini divengono solo una componente, variamente declinata in rapporto alle diverse funzioni e ai diversi destinatari. Ne possono variare le proporzioni in rapporto alla suddivisione delle facciate, dai piani non sempre diminuiti progressivamente di 1/4 — come Vitruvio indica per le scene dei teatri — utilizzando con libertà l'introduzione o meno della balconata che comprende i piedistalli di colonne, semicolonne o paraste, o in rapporto all'introduzione di mescolanze di queste con bugne rustiche. Né mancano i casi nei quali gli ordini scompaiono o sono sostituiti da targhe o rappresentati solo dalle trabeazioni marcapiano, per riapparire piuttosto nei cortili o concentrarsi in portali e edicole delle finestre. Il metodo progettuale raggiunto da Serlio diviene ancora più evidente nel cosiddetto libro VIII, anch'esso rimasto manoscritto, dove la ricostruzione dell'impianto dell'accampamento dei romani secondo Polibio gli offre il pretesto per passare dal disegno urbano con la definizione di diverse tipologie abitative, alle architetture principali e alle porte dell'accampamento dove gli ordini giocano un importante ruolo espressivo delle qualità dei diversi edifici, alle facciate semplificate e quasi piane degli alloggi dei soldati.

La ripresa di molti di questi temi, che appare nel libro VII edito postumo a Francoforte dopo essere rimasto a lungo anch'esso manoscritto,[20] arricchirà di ulteriori considerazioni il tema dell'architettura *soda* o *delicata*, da ottenere con un opportuno trattamento delle forme e della scelta degli ordini, ivi compreso il colore delle colonne e dei fondi, il che fa tornare alla formazione di Serlio come pittore oltre che ai suoi scambi con i letterati e in particolare con l'amico Aretino.[21] Esemplare e molto spesso citato è il brano di commento alla *Duodecima proposizione e disputa diffinitiva d'alcuni termini d'architettura: cap. LIII*, dove Serlio paragona due diversi trattamenti di una medesima facciata:

> La figura qui davanti segnata E. è d'opera Composita: la quale si potrà dimandare gracile, delicata et anche cruda e secca. Sarà gracile per la sottilità e sveltezza delle colonne: che così comporta però con tale ordine. Sarà delicata per la pulitezza de l'opera, e per gl'intagli, che vi sono. Si potrà dir cruda per la oscurità delle colonne, e per le pietre miste incassate ne' piedistalli. E secca si dirà per esser contraria alla morbidezza. E questo si vede nella parte dove sono le colonne di pietra mista. Ma la parte schietta senza intagli, e che non vi son

pietre miste, quantunque ella sia gracile, come l'altra, non vi è però crudezza, né anche ha del secco: ma si darà morbida, dolce e semplice.[22]

Rispetto alla discussione di un così ampio e complesso insieme di motivi, il libro *Extraordinario*, edito a Lione nel 1551 è un più diretto ritorno all'ordine architettonico, e le invenzioni che nascono dalle mescolanze vi si moltiplicarono al punto da apparire in alcuni casi eterodosse allo stesso Serlio.[23] Ma il commento sulle mescolanze che generano le trenta porte 'rustiche' e venti 'dilicate' rende in realtà esplicito il metodo già annunciato nel libro IV. Malgrado il libro *Extraordinario* abbia avuto numerosissime ristampe negli anni successivi e le invenzioni di Serlio siano state da più parti prese a modello per portali di palazzi, giardini e fortezze, non si può tuttavia dire che la sua proposta di moltiplicare e articolare le mescolanze alla ricerca di un'espressività delle architetture abbia avuto pieno successo. Sempre più lontane nel tempo dalle elaborazioni dei primi trent'anni del Cinquecento romano, le mescolanze contenute nel suo trattato devono essere apparse, alla metà del secolo, incerte nel riferirsi alle regole da lui stesso enunciate e alle possibili deroghe, troppo lontane dal contesto e dalle tradizioni locali e allo stesso tempo incapaci di superarle, troppo ardite e allo stesso tempo manchevoli di unità di fronte alle nuove sintesi proposte da Michelangelo e Palladio in Italia e Philibert de l'Orme in Francia.

Notes to Chapter 10

1. Richard J. Tuttle, 'Sebastiano Serlio bolognese', in *Sebastiano Serlio*, a cura di Christof Thoenes (Milano: Electa, 1989), pp. 22–29; Sabine Frommel, *Sebastiano Serlio architetto* (Milano: Electa, 1998), p. 39, n. 2.
2. Howard Burns, 'Baldassarre Peruzzi and Sixteenth-Century Architectural Theory', in *Les Traités d'architecture de la Renaissance*, a cura di Jean Guillaume (Parigi: Picard, 1988), pp. 207–26; Deanna Lenzi, 'Palazzo Fantuzzi: un problema aperto e nuovi dati sulla residenza del Serlio a Bologna', in *Sebastiano Serlio*, a cura di Thoenes, pp. 30–38 (p. 30); Maurizio Ricci, 'Peruzzi e Serlio a Bologna', in *Jacopo Barozzi da Vignola*, a cura di Richard J. Tuttle, Bruno Adorni, Christoph L. Frommel e Christof Thoenes (Milano: Electa, 2002), pp. 119–25.
3. Deborah Howard, 'Sebastiano Serlio's Venetian Copyrights', *Burlington Magazine*, 115 (1973), 512–16; Hubertus Günther, 'Studien zum venezianischen Aufenthalt des Sebastiano Serlio', *Münchner Jahrbuch der bildenden Kunst*, 3ª ser., 32 (1981), 42–94.
4. Sylvie Deswarte-Rosa, 'Introduction générale: le traité d'architecture de Sebastiano Serlio, l'œuvre d'une vie', in *Le Traité d'architecture de Sebastiano Serlio: une grande entreprise éditoriale au XVI siècle*, a cura di Sylvie Deswarte-Rosa (Lyon: Mémoire Active, 2004), pp. 31–66, con numerose schede e bibliografia sui singoli libri del trattato serliano e la loro diffusione. Cfr. Magali Vène, *Bibliographia serliana: catalogue des éditions imprimées des livres du traité d'architecture de Sebastiano Serlio (1537–1681)* (Parigi: Picard, 2007); Sabine Frommel, 'Le Traité de Sebastiano Serlio: oeuvre d'une vie et chantier éditorial magistral du XVIe siècle', *Histoire et civilisation du livre*, 9 (2014), 101–27.
5. Christof Thoenes, 'Prolusione: Serlio e la trattatistica', in *Sebastiano Serlio*, a cura di Thoenes, pp. 9–18 (p. 10).
6. Sebastiano Serlio, *Architettura civile: libri sesto, settimo e ottavo nei manoscritti di Monaco e Vienna*, a cura di Francesco Paolo Fiore (Milano: Il Polifilo, 1994).
7. Christof Thoenes, 'La pubblicazione della "Regola"', in *Jacopo Barozzi*, pp. 333–40.
8. La citazione è tratta da Sebastiano Serlio, *L'architettura: i libri I-VII e Extraordinario nelle prime edizioni*, a cura di Francesco Paolo Fiore, 2 voll. (Milano: Il Polifilo, 2001), così come le citazioni seguenti dai trattati di Serlio. I corsivi, anche successivi, sono di chi scrive. Per la traduzione

in inglese dei trattati, *Sebastiano Serlio on Architecture*, a cura di e trad. da Vaughan Hart, 2 voll. (New Haven: Yale University Press, 1996–2001).
9. Francesco P. Di Teodoro, *Raffaello, Baldassar Castiglione e la 'Lettera a Leone X'* (Bologna: Nuova Alfa, 1994), p. 127.
10. Christoph L. Frommel, 'Le opere romane di Giulio', in *Giulio Romano* (Milano: Electa, 1989), pp. 96–133.
11. Silvio Ferri, *Vitruvio (dai libri I-VII)* (Roma: Palombi, 1960), p. 59, con particolare riferimento a *statio*, intesa come concordanza della struttura architettonica con il significato della divinità (Vitruvio, *De architectura*, I. II. 5). L'interpretazione del *decor* vitruviano in Serlio è discussa da Alina A. Payne, *The Architectural Treatise in the Italian Renaissance* (Cambridge: Cambridge University Press, 1999), pp. 113–43.
12. Francesco Paolo Fiore, 'Sebastiano Serlio and the Roman Encampment', in *Andrea Palladio and the Architecture of Battle*, a cura di Guido Beltramini (Venezia: Marsilio, 2009), pp. 272–97.
13. Oltre agli ordini su una facciata di palazzo nell'affresco della *Presentazione di Maria al tempio* in Santa Maria della Pace a Roma, un interessante esempio di mescolanza fra dorico e rustico è realizzata da Peruzzi nel portale del palazzo Orsini di Bomarzo che precede simili portali di Serlio e Vignola secondo Christoph L. Frommel e Fabiano Tiziano Fagliari Zeni Buchicchio, 'Il Palazzo Orsini a Bomarzo: opera di Baldassarre Peruzzi', *Römisches Jahrbuch der Bibliotheca Hertziana*, 32 (1997–98), 9–133 (pp. 25–26).
14. Benvenuto Cellini, *I Trattati dell'orificeria e della scultura*, a cura di Carlo Milanesi (Firenze: Le Monnier, 1857), p. 225. Cfr. Yves Pauwels, 'La Méthode de Serlio dans le Quarto Libro', *Revue de l'art*, 119 (1998), 33–42; Hubertus Günther, 'Sebastiano Serlios Lehrprogramm: Spuren von architektonischen Leitlinien im dritten und vierten Buch', *Zurich Studies in the History of Art*, 17–18 (2010–11), 495–517.
15. James S. Ackerman, 'Tuscan/Rustic Order: A Study in the Metaphorical Language of Architecture', *Journal of the Society of Architectural Historians*, 42 (1983), 15–34.
16. Giorgio Vasari, *Le vite de' più eccellenti architetti, pittori, et scultori italiani, da Cimabue insino a' tempi nostri nell'edizione per i tipi di Lorenzo Torrentino, Firenze 1550*, a cura di Luciano Bellosi e Aldo Rossi (Torino: Einaudi, 1986), pp. 31–36 (p. 34).
17. Francesco Paolo Fiore, 'Il "giudizio" in Sebastiano Serlio', in *Studi in onore di Renato Cevese*, a cura di Guido Beltramini, Adriano Ghisetti Giavarina e Paola Marini (Vicenza: Centro Internazionale di Studi di Architettura Andrea Palladio, 2000), pp. 237–49. Sul significato di disegno in Vasari, vedi i passi vasariani e il commento in *Scritti d'arte del Cinquecento*, a cura di Paola Barocchi, 2 voll. (Milano e Napoli: Ricciardi, 1973), pp. 1912–20; sulla revisione e trasformazione nella lingua toscana dei termini serliani, vedi Francesco Paolo Fiore, 'L'edizione dei libri di Sebastiano Serlio rivista da Cosimo Bartoli', in *Cosimo Bartoli (1503–1572)*, a cura di Francesco Paolo Fiore e Daniela Lamberini (Firenze: Olschki, 2011), pp. 41–57.
18. Manuela Morresi, *Jacopo Sansovino* (Milano: Electa, 2000), pp. 118–29.
19. Serlio, *Architettura civile*, pp. 43–44. Il manoscritto preparatorio del VI libro conservato presso la Columbia University e pubblicato da Myra N. Rosenfeld, *Sebastiano Serlio on Domestic Architecture* (Cambridge, MA e Londra: Architectural History Foundation, MIT, 1978), non contiene questa premessa.
20. Tancredi Carunchio, 'Libro settimo: premessa', in Serlio, *Architettura civile*, pp. 249–77.
21. John Onians, *Bearers of Meaning: The Classical Orders in Antiquity, the Middle Age and the Renaissance* (Princeton: Princeton University Press, 1988), sottolinea l'uso di termini, da parte di Serlio, simili a quelli della critica letteraria (pp. 299–301) e propone che abbia anche potuto influenzare Vasari (pp. 277, 303). Vedi anche John Onians, 'Serlio and the History of Architecture', in *Art, Culture and Nature* (London: Pindar Press, 2006), pp. 358–76.
22. Serlio, *L'architettura: i libri I-VII e Extraordinario*, vol. II, VII, 124.
23. Mario Carpo, *La maschera e il modello: teoria architettonica e evangelismo nell' 'Extraordinario Libro' di Sebastiano Serlio (1551)* (Milano: Jaca Book, 1993).

CHAPTER 11

Giacomo Leoni: Unsung Intermediary between Alberti and Palladio

John Woodhouse

As I type these lines, some eighty firemen and a dozen fire engines are attempting to check the flames devouring the mansion at Clandon Park in Surrey, ancestral home of the Onslow family. The present Clandon had stood there since the 1730s, on the site of the Onslows' former Jacobean house, and in 1956 Clandon Park was handed over by the family to the National Trust, whose former director, Simon Jenkins, praised it as a masterpiece of its kind by the Venetian architect Giacomo Leoni (1685–1746).[1] Leoni had few enduring friends or patrons during his life and many critics, hostile or indifferent to him thereafter. Deprived of patronage, regarded with jealousy by competitors, who could not share his expertise in Italian or his familiarity with all of Palladio's works, he nonetheless persevered. His work schedule was formidable, and perhaps indicates that he had taken to heart Leon Battista Alberti's oft-repeated profession of faith on the avoidance of idleness: 'Sia adunque persuaso che l'uomo nacque, non per atristirsi in ozio, ma per adoperarsi in cose magnifiche e ample, colle quali e' possa piacere e onorare Iddio in prima, e per avere in sé stessi come uso di perfetta virtù, cosí frutto di felicità.'[2]

While Clandon was under construction during the 1720s, Leoni's work on the regeneration of another great house, Lyme Park in Cheshire, commissioned by Sir Peter Legh, was, by 1730, also well under way. Leoni was further occupied during most of that decade with the production of the first English translation, using Cosimo Bartoli's Italian version, of Leon Battista Alberti's architectural masterpiece *De re aedificatoria*. One of the subscribers to what became a very expensive edition of Alberti's great work was the second Baron Onslow, ambitious to replace his Jacobean family home with a new and fashionable house at Clandon. Another subscriber was Lord Onslow's neighbour, Sir William Scawen, Governor of the Bank of England, who was, coincidentally, planning to construct a new house at Carshalton. The *Alberti* edition also included eleven beautiful copper-plate designs commissioned from Leoni for Sir William. The volume was Leoni's second pioneering publication, following his production of a trilingual version (in Italian, French and English) of Andrea Palladio's *Quattro libri dell'architettura*, which he had first edited in five large fascicules between 1716 and 1720, publishing a second, English only, edition in 1721.

The two great mansions and the two great editions reflect in practical and theoretical ways the combinations of architectural development in Britain which helped create a style and fashion for a multitude of eighteenth-century Anglo-Palladian buildings, and a taste for that ordered architecture against which modern architectural performance is still so often measured. It was a glorious period for many other brilliant British architects, including the greatest of them all, Sir Christopher Wren, but most of them were not lacking in great fortunes or generous patrons, and their praises have long been sung. Rudolf Wittkower observed in 1954 that 'Although [Leoni was] a figure of considerable importance in English architecture of the first half of the 18th century, no attempt has yet been made to clarify the many problems concerning his life and work'.[3] The present essay, for its lack of technical architectural terminology, is evidently not meant to challenge professional architects or architectural historians. Its aim, rather, following on Rudolf Wittkower's statement of six decades ago, is to present a more human and humane account of the problems, and perhaps the triumphs, of this apparently lonely immigrant in a Georgian Britain more than a little troubled by political, social, and religious controversy.[4]

To the objective observer, the destruction of one of Leoni's prized buildings seems to add a particular sort of insult to injury. Forty years of honest work in architectural design and construction brought Leoni little kudos and less profit during his lifetime, and, a century after his death, his pauper's grave was swept aside to make way for the new railway station at St Pancras (following 1863), and for *The Adam and Eve Pleasure Gardens, Genteel and Rural* (now superseded by the present Local Authority's amenity park). Yet Leoni was responsible, not only for some fine architectural creations of his own, but also for helping to publicise, and indeed to immortalise for an English readership, the artistic reputations of Leon Battista Alberti (1404–1472) and Andrea Palladio (1505–1580). His was the first ever publication of complete English translations of the architectural treatises of each of those men, and this ensured that his volumes graced the libraries of the Georgian cultural and fashionable élite in Britain, prompting them to foster similar architectural techniques.

The preface 'To the Reader' of Leoni's *Palladio*[5] states, with some justification, 'As for what concerns the printing, there has been no book hitherto more beautifully printed in England'. Leoni was its entrepreneur, contacting subscribers, raising the funds for the considerable publishing enterprise, and acting as manager and general factotum. He engaged a translator (Nicholas Dubois, soon superseded, probably by the professional translator John Ozell), and commissioned the fashionable artist Sebastiano Ricci, who had learned his trade in Venice and was resident in London 1712–16, to create a faux Veronese portrait of Palladio (*Paulus Caliari Veronensis Effigium Pinxit*). This was reproduced in the frontispiece of the edition by the Flemish engraver, Bernard Picart (more truthfully *B.Picart delineavit et sculpsit*). The same elegant, fake-Veronese print has since figured as a 'genuine' portrait of Palladio in several respected studies. Leoni later employed Picart, and his school, as well as other engravers, to produce copperplates of many of his own beautifully enlarged and in part redesigned illustrations of the original Palladio woodcuts. Leoni's English edition of Palladio's *Quattro libri dell'architettura* is in most respects still unsurpassed three hundred years after that first appearance, yet a brief mention in this tribute to Martin McLaughlin will probably be the only public acknowledgement of that triple centenary. Let sympathisers, regretting such silence, comfort themselves by regarding Clandon's gigantic pyre as a variation on a noble Viking funeral. Leoni's equally luxurious English version of the other great Italian architectural work, Albert's *De re aedificatoria*, translated from Cosimo Bartoli's 1565 Florentine edition, remained for 250 years its only English source.[6] Not until 1968 was a successor forthcoming, a clear and workmanlike translation into English of Alberti's volume, published by an international trio of architect-scholars.[7]

Leoni's Clandon Park marked a fresh beginning in the early Georgian period for the kind of fashion which Leoni believed had been launched by Inigo Jones and Christopher Wren, thanks to their ability, that is, to unite the brilliance of Palladio with their own inventive ideas. 'The English nation need no foreign examples of perfection in the way of architecture', he observed.[8] Those two British architects were, for Leoni, complete masters, outstanding talents both in magnificence and fine taste. The even earlier appearance of Leoni's *The Architecture of Andrea Palladio* had helped to fix a new ideal in the hearts and minds of its noble British readership. Concerned with the practicalities of constructing his new buildings, Leoni was also preoccupied with the Renaissance notion of dynamic idealism, to target and if possible to surpass an ideal model, an ambition which had characterized Italian artists and scholars since the opening of the fifteenth century, and which he evidently saw inherent in the methods of Inigo Jones and Christopher Wren. His preface to the reader in the 1721 edition of his *Palladio* makes it clear that he has added elements to the original text:

> I have not only made all the draughts myself, and on a much larger scale than my Author; but also made so many necessary corrections with regard to shading, dimensions, ornaments, etc., that this work may in some sort be rather considered as an original, than an improvement.[9]

Towards the conclusion of his *Alberti*, Leoni could find authoritative support for such an 'improvement'.

Leoni was an architect, not a philologist, not a textual critic, and unfortunately his liberal views later led to his becoming *persona non grata* to the influential Lord Burlington, whose initial attitude to Leoni had seemed more benevolent. A decade after the first appearance of the *Palladio*, Lord Burlington, irritated by what he condemned as Leoni's alteration of Palladio's original work, commissioned a rival translation by Colen Campbell (continued, on the latter's early death in 1729, by Isaac Ware). His Lordship also subsidised a second volume of Campbell's fine study, *Vitruvius Britannicus*, as a possible spoiler in the market for Leoni's second and subsequent editions of the *Palladio*. However, the Ware/Campbell edition was delayed for almost twenty years and its publication, in 1738, meant that it was already late to catch the fashionable aura, and the nobility were quite happy to keep their Leoni versions. Leoni was not concerned with textual criticism; nor was Burlington, at least not until Leoni's statement deliberately declaring his innovations became clear to him. It is, however, surprising that Burlington and his acolytes did not have their suspicions aroused a decade earlier by the so-called Veronese 'portrait' of Palladio (of whom no known portraits exist) placed by Leoni in his eye-catching frontispiece. But Burlington had money and influence and his views prevailed, and survive in the Introduction to the latest (1968) translation of Alberti's *On the Art of Building in Ten Books*. But passing beyond that Introduction to the text, it is possible to find a greater mentor than Burlington, no less an authority than Alberti himself, implicitly supporting Leoni's improvements:

> Yet [the Architect] should not mistake the mere bulk of the work for a true achievement [...] and he should make it his practice not to approve of anything that is not wholly elegant or worthy of admiration for its ingenuity; and should he find anything anywhere of which he approves, he should adopt and copy it; yet anything that he considers can be greatly refined, he should use his artistry and imagination to correct and put right; and anything that is otherwise not too bad, he should strive, to the best of his ability, to improve.[10]

The most comprehensive and insightful studies into Leoni's development so far are the splendid articles published by Lionello Puppi in 1984, and Richard Hewlings in 1985.[11] Some further details of his youth in Italy may here help to highlight his passion for architecture, counter some adverse criticism, and create a more reasonable and less prejudiced assessment of his qualities.[12] Artistic and architectural beauty surrounded Leoni from his birth in the Venetian parish of San Cassiano, where he was baptised at the homonymous church of the small local Campo. The plain exterior of the church, consecrated in 1376, is entered through what seems to be a side door, but it conceals unexpected treasures, not least three works by Tintoretto, and a delightful Palladian/baroque interior reworked in 1663. Beneath a fine ceiling, slim columns once guided worshippers towards a unique Antonello da Messina, his 1475 altar-piece of the *Madonna and Child with Four Saints*. For local citizens such paintings represent even today a great source of pride, and, in the context of the time, pride bordering on idolatry.[13] Those details are worth mentioning because Leoni became typically imbued with pride in the beauty and artistic tradition of his native city.

Leoni must have been a talented boy, rapidly developing skills as a draughtsman, and at about the age of fifteen he was given his freedom by a liberal if humble family who recognized those youthful gifts. He was given moral, artistic and, Lionello Puppi convincingly implies, some financial support by his paternal uncle, Antonio Leoni, an engraver and jeweller, then working with other artistic migrants on the reconstruction of Bensberg Castle, near Düsseldorf. The youthful Leoni travelled widely both in the Veneto (as far north as Pola), and south, as far as Rome. In Rome he used Palladio's guide book on *L'antichità di Roma*. This concise volume was sufficient to show Leoni how far Palladio had made himself 'Master of the noblest ideas of the antients, for walking through the rubbish and other remains of these, he discover'd the true rules of an art which, till his time, were unknown even to Michel Angelo and Brunelleschi, his contemporaries. The exactness of his designs can't be too much commended'.[14]

That habit, even pastime, of exploring Roman ruins had, in the fourteenth century, generated an interest in the classical past, stimulated still further by the recovery of ancient texts, such as Petrarch's discovery of Cicero's oration *Pro Archia* at Liège (1333), or the letters *Ad Atticum* at Verona (1345), providing inspiration for early Renaissance literary scholars. Similarly, in 1414, at the Swiss monastery of St Gallen, Poggio Bracciolini's discovery of Vitruvius's ten books on architecture was to formalise a similar interest in mathematics and architecture, which attracted, among others, Leon Battista Alberti, a keen student of Vitruvian ideas, expressed, he regretted, in overcomplicated technical language. Alberti's own tours of the Roman ruins, his *Descriptio urbis Romae*, dated from 1446–47.[15] Palladio's small guidebook was to inspire Leoni in his personal exploration of the hidden archaeological remains of Rome's imperial past (even discovering, he says, a new type of column). Leon Battista's appreciation of the consoling effect of being free to wander and enjoy the pleasure of nature's beauty and of man's creativity would no doubt have found an echo in the heart and mind of both his successors:

> Indeed, one of the most immediate pleasures worthy of the free man is to wander through cities and provinces looking at the many temples and theatres, at walled defences and all other types of building, and walk around places which are by nature pleasant and gracious, and things made beautiful thanks to the hand and ingenuity of man, and rendered stronger to withstand the inroads of an enemy.[16]

Leoni had already spent years in a close study of the architectural masterpieces which Palladio had constructed in the Veneto. He appreciated the imaginative leap between Palladio's adaptation and dynamic imitation of past Roman glories in order to create a contemporary architectural beauty, which would satisfy the new tastes for the Palladian/baroque. He also declares that he had seen all the buildings he describes, a statement in part corroborated by Nicholas Dubois (a bilingual military engineer with Marlborough's forces), who later was to help Leoni with his translations.[17]

After his youthful experiences, Leoni left his native city, determined, like many of his fellow citizens, to seek his fortune abroad. Initially he worked with the group of Venetian specialists who were constructing Schloss Bensberg, the new castle for the Elector Palatine, Johann Wilhelm, Count of Megen. Count Matteo D'Alberti, the accomplished Venetian architect, who had received the commission from the Elector Palatine, was in charge of directing the operation, and Matteo's friendship and successful pursuit of rich patronage was later to provide a good model for his ambitious young fellow-countryman.[18] D'Alberti had learned his trade in Paris and there is evidence that Leoni, until at least 1708, was interested in taking his own talents to France. In that year he began to copy and, with Dubois's help, part-translate into French and English, the text of Palladio's *Architecture*. France, renowned as recently as 1661 for Louis XIV's commission of the Palace of Versailles, was a tempting attraction for itinerant architects and builders, but Leoni's incomplete handwritten copy of Palladio, including some very accomplished illustrations, was abandoned in 1708. The title page of the manuscript carries Leoni's name, the date 1708 and the place Düsseldorf.[19]

Following Marlborough's victory in the War of the Spanish Succession, Britain may well have seemed a more promising target for the young Venetian. Victory had finally imposed peace of a kind in Europe, bringing profits to successful generals. The magnificent public buildings and great mansions which military leaders had observed when campaigning in Europe, and particularly in Italy, were now imitable and financially viable. In 1705 Marlborough was being rewarded with the prize of Blenheim Palace, begun the year after the allies' final victory. Even earlier, in 1685, Marlborough's second-in-command, George Hamilton, later Earl of Orkney, had acquired the Cliveden estate, and Leoni was among the architects encouraged to submit plans for Lord Orkney's reworked mansion. His ambitious application failed, but much later the estate provided him with two less grandiose commissions.[20] In 1727 he was engaged to build the Blenheim Seat, draped in terracotta militaria, at the north-west garden of the Cliveden park, and in 1735 he built the pretty Octagonal Pavilion overlooking the Thames, which now, more solemnly, survives as the Astor Mausoleum, converted thus two centuries later by Waldorf Astor, then owner of Cliveden.

The new generation of rich and noble tourists and their admiration for the neo-classical buildings they discovered in the Italian peninsula made Palladio's work particularly popular in Britain during the late seventeenth and early eighteenth century. Thanks to the British ritual of the Grand Tour, less complex examples of Palladian architecture offered a much sought-after style for the rich and noble. For some practitioners of the art, that simplicity and regularity gave it added advantages. Indeed it may seem incongruous to modern eyes that many so-called Palladian buildings in Britain have such a relatively limited range of style as to seem stereotyped, when Palladio's buildings in the Veneto varied so greatly. Palladio's plan of the 'original' Villa Capra, for example, the splendid residence built uniquely for Canon Paolo Almerica Capra Valmarana, could be applied to sweet if uninhabitable British replicas. Thus, Colen Campbell's first imitation of the Capra 'Rotonda' was Mereworth Castle, built for the 7th Earl of Westmorland in 1722, and, ironically, since neither patron nor architect had seen the original, based on Leoni's copperplate of Palladio's drawing. Subsequently Burlington's Chiswick House of 1725 was an imitation of Mereworth Castle.[21] Lord Burlington might have been happy with the design, though his contemporaries were understandably sceptical about whether the house would be habitable in the British climate. At the same time Leoni would indisputably have been aware of the aesthetic folly of building fashionable imitations of structures such as the Villa Capra transposed to the south of England.[22]

In Leoni's pursuit of a British patron, Henry, Earl Grey, one of the most ambitious social climbers of the period, was a prime target. By 1715, Lord Henry's son Antony (the young Earl Harrold) was enjoying his first Grand Tour. From his correspondence with Antony and his tutor John Gerard, it is clear that Lord Grey's ambitious plans for a fashionable new house and gardens formed a major topic of interest.[23] Leoni's name was to percolate through to Lord Antony's father, who was anxious to see Leoni's plans for a reconstructed Wrest Park, the family home in Bedfordshire. Leoni had cleverly followed up any initial approaches with a brief personal account of building techniques, his *Compendious Directions for Builders*, which was accessioned in the Ducal library with the date 1713.[24] The small handwritten codex is signed, undoubtedly optimistically, 'James Leoni E[lectoris] Pa[alatinae] Arc[hitectus]'. At the time Thomas Archer (1668–1743), by then already an architect of renown, had been commissioned by Lord Grey (who would in 1710 acquire the coveted ducal coronet), to build his celebratory new pavilion on the long water, at Wrest.[25]

In August 1715 Earl Antony commented approvingly to his father on reading that Mr Archer was engaged on a redesign for the gardens at Wrest, that might restore old features which he remembered with pleasure and affection.[26] By July 1715 Antony's letters seem to take it for granted that Leoni's plans were being seriously considered for the Duke's proposed rebuilding. These had been seen by the Ducal Secretary at Wrest, who mentions slight amendments to an earlier design. In another letter, the Secretary writes to John Gerard, referring to a letter from the Duke dated 28 July 1715, which indicated that a plan would quickly be sent to the travellers, by then in Geneva. Leoni's draft of the new Wrest was to be vetted by Filippo Juvarra, the Royal Architect of Victor Amadeus. Juvarra's verdict, transmitted to Wrest, quibbled over Leoni's plans and generously declared himself ready to take over the task personally if required. His views seem to have been ignored.

Leoni had made a good choice in Duke Henry as his potential patron, but fortune turned against him at the last moment. The noble lord had unfortunately invested in shares of the South Sea Islands Company (1711), which by 1719 collapsed to little above flotation price (an investment shortly to burst as the South Sea Bubble). Tragically, too, both of the Duke's sons died prematurely, in 1717 and 1723, and without offspring. Next, a serious fire in 1725 burnt down the Greys' London family house at 4, St James Square, and it would have been natural to call upon Leoni to help in its restoration.[27] Leoni's draft plans for Wrest were held up and then frustrated permanently, and ever since have remained in the Luton and Bedford Archives along with other Grey documents. By an ironic coincidence, the South Sea Bubble was to bring a further commission for Leoni, thanks to a spectacular piece of insider dealing by the banker Benjamin Styles, whose brother-in-law warned him beforehand of the impending crash. Styles sold his South Sea shares at an enormous profit and spent £150,000 on rebuilding his new house, Moor Park, where Leoni was commissioned, after Styles's dismissal of Sir James Thornhill, to create a Palladian mansion, now the splendidly imposing headquarters of Moor Park golf club.[28] By 1715 Leoni had begun his edition of Palladio, which began to appear in instalments in English, Italian and French between 1716 and 1720, and in English alone in 1721.

Leoni's hope for advancement at Wrest was dashed. However, coinciding with George I's succession to the English throne, and with Leoni's new enterprises, the first of Lord Burlington's three Grand Tours of Italy began in 1714. In Italy Burlington was at once captivated by the neoclassical architecture of Palladio. By the time of his final tour in 1719, he was thoroughly convinced of the superiority of Palladio's architectural achievements. His passion for Palladio and an interest in any newly arrived Italian with artistic pretensions, would inevitably cause him to take note of Leoni. Initially Burlington seemed inclined to help, and allowed Leoni to design a new town house in the garden of the ancestral Burlington House. Leoni's Queensbury House (7 Burlington Gardens), the first such Palladian town house in London, was built originally for John Bligh, Lord Clifton.[29] Another similar, though smaller Leoni house was in King's Road Chelsea, the present Argyll House, and, at 21 Arlington Street, stands Lord Shannon's house, another example of an elegant Leoni 'small house in town', as he termed them. Burlington might have been a useful contact for the young Venetian. Lord Treasurer of Ireland (his was an Irish title), Lord Lieutenant for East and West Ridings of Yorkshire (Burlington was a synonym for Bridlington), Director of the Royal College of Music, Privy Councillor and sundry other titles added weight to his influence and advice. In particular, architecturally speaking, his influence over the appointment of the Deputy to the Surveyor General of the Royal Office of Works turned out to be disappointing for any hopes which Leoni might have had for his later career. At his great house along The Strand, Burlington hosted such luminaries as James Gibbs (1682–1754), who, in the face of occasionally stern Puritan disapproval, had the misfortune to be a Catholic during a particularly anti-Catholic phase of the Whig political establishment. Gibbs soon gave way in Burlington's favours to the more fashionable Colen Campbell, keen to publicise his fine edition of *Vitruvius Britannicus, The British Architect*, published in 1715. Favoured for a while by Burlington, who undoubtedly used his influence in 1718 to secure his protégé's appointment as Deputy in the Office of Public Works, Campbell's status was a guarantee of official public commissions. In turn, however, when Burlington learned that Campbell had never been to Italy, he was replaced as his favourite by William Kent. Like Burlington, Kent also hailed from Bridlington, used his five years' experience of Italy to add credence to his reputation, and cultivated his Lordship's acquaintance during the latter's second Grand Tour in 1719.

Burlington's influence as patron and entrepreneur for the new vogue of Palladianism became ever more formidable. He was undoubtedly a great promoter of Palladianism as he rather narrowly understood it. His own surviving work seems largely the result of the drafts and plans of other experts (parts of Burlington House, Westminster School, Chiswick House (ultimately dependent, as noted, on Leoni's plan of the original Villa Capra), Northwick Park, and the Assembly Rooms in York (lifted from Leoni's copy of Palladio's Vitruvian plan for an Egyptian Hall). This last, very fashionable, design, published in Leoni's 1729 edition of Alberti's *De re aedificatoria*, was in fact Leoni's only piece dedicated to Burlington. The finished Hall stands in Blake Street, York, and a small plaque indicating 'Burlington's' achievement is affixed to the left of the entrance to what was originally the main reception room.[30] For a while, during Leoni's first appearance in Britain, he seems to have been congenial to his Lordship. but that relationship was to disintegrate after the publication of the second edition of his *Palladio*. As Rudolf Wittkower remarked, *vis-à-vis* Burlington at least, 'that edition was also the ultimate source of

Leoni's professional failure', because of the manner in which Leoni had altered the original text. His Lordship, from Grand Tourist-cum-Aesthete, had been suddenly transformed into Philologist and Textual Critic. Quick to assert his newly acquired science, he commissioned Colen Campbell, and, following Campbell's death, another interesting protégé, Isaac Ware, charging them to produce an edition of Palladio's work, correcting the changes which Leoni had introduced.[31] It must have been very discouraging for Leoni to be accused of misleading his readers, when he thought he had done his utmost to appeal to proud Palladianists by pointing the way to greater architectural triumphs through tasteful dynamic imitations, citing Alberti's views on justifiable improvements.

In the 1721 edition of Palladio the carnet of designs which conclude the volume had been aimed to attract more custom for Leoni himself: 'In the mean time I offer my Service, either in Person or otherwise, to such of my Subscribers and others, as may have occasion for me in the way of my Profession'. Leoni undeniably achieved great success with his publication of the translation of his *Palladio*, despite the hostile attitude of Lord Burlington, and despite assertions from less friendly critics that Isaac Ware's edition had replaced Leoni's version definitively. From his flattering dedication to the Duke of Kent of his *Compendious Direction* in 1713–14, to the letters he would later write to Sir Peter Legh at Lyme Park, Leoni seemed to have expended a great deal of effort (and flattery) for little reward. His most recent employer, Sir William Scawen, ex-Governor of the Bank of England, had died just as Leoni had begun the preliminaries to building Carshalton Park. Sir William's nephew and heir, Thomas Scawen, immediately began to squander the £10,000 destined for Leoni's building, and the site for the projected new Carshalton House now remains a blend of municipal garden and redbrick offices, Carshalton's beautifully incorporated pools and their small footbridge being the only survivors of Leoni's efforts.

His next move was to attempt another publishing coup: he began work on the edition of Leon Battista Alberti's *De re aedificatoria.* as translated into Florentine by Cosimo Bartoli in 1565.[32] Preparing for this new initiative must have occupied Leoni during much of the period of construction of Clandon. His edition has an *imprimatur* date of 1726, but Leoni writes to Sir Peter Legh at Lyme Park regretting that he was unable to deliver the requisite volumes until 1730.[33] Leoni excuses himself on the grounds that he had been away supervising workmen on the newly designed (though shortly to be abandoned) great house at Carshalton Park. Yet with three such commisions on his hands, Leoni no doubt felt more reassured concerning the immediate future, and less anxious to use a carnet of his own designs in his new edition to advertise his skill as an architect as he had done with his *Palladio*.

He must have experienced great pleasure in what was to be his new publishing coup, sponsored by some three hundred subscribers, headed by the Prince of Wales who was about to ascend the throne as George II. By contrast to his earlier subservience to patrons, Leoni's preface to this next book, his edition of Alberti's *De re aedificatoria*, has a more confident approach, a much more assertive tone. The dedication itself, addressed to George, Prince of Wales, begins with a eulogy of great nations which, reaching the peak of their glory, empire, and arms, foster a flowering of the arts. 'Questo felice stato gode ora la Gran Britannia':

> L'architettura, una delle belle arti e prima esecutrice della magnificenza fiorisce ora più che mai in questa avventurosa nazione, ond'io che vi diedi già splendidamente in luce le opere del Palladio, celebre architetto, ho per nuovo incoraggiamento intrapreso di dar simile splendore alle tanto rinomate opere di Leone Battista Alberti, altro primo lume di così nobil arte.[34]

By now Leoni's mood had changed; with the authority of Alberti's great edition to support him, Leoni felt free to criticise adversely, in an address *To the Reader*, the clumsy design of certain modern buildings 'great heaps of stone piled up one upon the other, as it were by accident [...] alcoves and close corners that may be very convenient receptacles for rats and mice, but are very narrow habitations for the family'. Rooms so crammed with windows that they look like lanterns. The polemical tone continues throughout the so-called supplement: 'I have always observed that those who know the least of our art, nay that can scarce distinguish the Five Orders, are always the most fruitful inventors of whims and extravagancies, and they are generally talkative in proportion to their want of skill'. He warns his Reader to beware of 'any that pretend mighty things in the theory but are not able to draw, from which they excuse themselves by saying that they have others that draw for them'. Thinly veiled allusions to Burlington make several appearances.[35] And though Burlington is complimented on his patronage of the arts and promotion of elegant designs, and on his masterfully designed back gate to Burlington House, his position in the architectural hierarchy is subtly, but firmly shown to be as, at most, an imitator, well below Inigo Jones and Wren, who in turn stand on the shoulders of Alberti and Palladio.

To conclude this brief survey it might be useful to consider certain particular features of two of Leoni's most splendid buildings, Lyme Park and Clandon. Both of these houses have elements which point to Leoni's originality in an otherwise not unexpected conformist world of Palladianism. In his survey of early Georgian country houses, Christopher Hussey's discussion of the many aspirant Palladians in early eighteenth-century England has an interesting observation concerning the effect upon his work of Leoni's necessarily poor English: 'The classical front of Lyme, Cheshire, *c.* 1720, and the building of Clandon Park, his outstanding existing works, show him to have been the most faithful Palladian of the group — partly, perhaps, because he seems to have little command of English. (Hence Leoni's turning, for translation of Palladio's text, to Captain Nicholas Dubois).[36] Hussey's perceptive remark about Leoni's command of English is confirmed by some of the letters written to Sir Peter Legh, and by Leoni's unfailing omission of any claim to have personally translated the work of Alberti or Palladio. An inability to read quickly in English could well hamper his perusal of architectural treatises then current, constraining him to depend for his own designs upon his knowledge of the Palladian buildings he had studied *in situ* during his early years in Italy. 'By this means, as well as access to Inigo Jones's annotated copy of Palladio at Worcester College, Oxford, he was able to add much not shown in the sixteenth-century woodcuts'. Yet there was no profit to be made from building houses which would not please a client. Fashion dictated the shape of buildings and Leoni was shrewd enough to sacrifice variety when necessary. In the two cases which Hussey particularly mentions, Clandon was built for a family of distinguished lawyers, three of whom held the office of Speaker of the House of Commons. A sober practical building seemed to be called for, and to outward appearances, in the words of Simon Jenkins: 'Clandon is indeed a lawyer of a house, formal to the world behind a Victorian porch, but with a certain pompous jollity in private.'[37]

The southern façade of Clandon was carried by four enormous pilasters, not unlike the scheme of the pilasters of Alberti's Palazzo Rucellai, the capitals are not dissimilar to the capitals on the Loggia dei Rucellai, in part described in the *De re aedificatoria*, VII. 6. Clandon's main entrance to the west was, before the 'Victorian porch', a classical type of triumphal arch in stone, very typical of Leoni's work, ten or more metres in height, framed by two wings constructed with contrasting red brick In front is a double staircase with eight shallow steps leading into the marble hall described by John Cornforth as 'unquestionably among the grandest of all eighteenth-century interiors, its decoration by the best Italian stuccadores, and its chimneypieces by Rysbrack'.[38] The contrast between the marble interior and the rose-red brickwork on the otherwise unpretentious western façade is, in Simon Jenkins's words, 'sensational': 'White and dazzling, the walls rise through two storeys of orders past balconies to a spectacular ceiling. This might be an Italian *cortile* with the mythical gods romping across the *trompe-l'œil* sky above.'[39] There are other less startling Palladian features leading off the marble entrance hall, which evidently once led on into the Saloon. The so-called Palladio room continues the stucco work of Artari and Bagutti, and the marble fireplace, though less ornate than the two Rybrack fireplaces in the Marble Hall, is of similar origin.

The second of Christopher Hussey's choice of houses is placed by Simon Jenkins in the first hundred of England's thousand best houses, and awarded four stars. Jenkins's essay is easily accessible, and he is justly eloquent in his praise of the wonderful mansion, its southern façade, and the house's furnishings. The work done at Lyme Park to create a mansion more in tune with the fashion of the times began in 1725, when Leoni sent Sir Peter Legh his design for the southern facade, surely one of the most beautiful of all his works. He had to create a design which barely touched the Elizabethan entrance on the mansion's north front, no doubt shuddering the while at the positioning of a small Ionic pillar, placed by an earlier more rustic predecesssor, in a most unpalladian manner, precisely over the centre of the entrance pediment. The steepish walk up, through the northern forecourt, to Lyme's main entrance may initially give the impression that the great house is built on a sloping site, and perhaps imply the need to negotiate uncomfortable staircases within. Visitors need have no fear. That may have been the case for the servants' stairs (one for men and one for women!), but in fact the narrow entrance archway leads, stepless, directly and imperceptibly into Leoni's redesigned classical courtyard, of the type which might have graced a Roman villa. Alberti noted that whenever possible our predecessors avoided stairs (regarding them as obstacles to free transit in a dwelling), thus allowing occupants to move from a central courtyard to the rooms off with comfort and convenience (another of the great merits of designing a villa rather than a town house).[40] Alberti's concept of a courtyard was that of a traditional family meeting point in the villa, akin to the main piazza in a city, the heart of a house, or more comfortably, the bosom of house and family. In the case of Lyme, bereft of Mediterranean sunshine, the courtyard serves to shelter the great Doric portal, which admits visitors to the entrance hall, a comfortably welcoming ambience, 'a sort of overblown drawing room' writes Simon Jenkins. Its soft comfort is indeed a complete contrast to Clandon's Marble Hall coolness, but it lacks none of the elegance to be expected in such an environment. Leoni had strong views on the English climate, particularly in the north of the country, where he expressed amazement that there were no public ordinances obliging householders to construct porticoes to protect passers-by from rain and tempest. He was more than a little preoccupied with comfort. Lyme's courtyard is enclosed on three sides by an arcade which provides further protection against the elements and supports a corridor with doors off, leading through the *piano nobile*, and allowing occupants to circulate without passing through private rooms or state appartments on the north or south sides, and permitting access to the west range, also previously unreachable without traversing other rooms. No dark tunnel this, the corridor has been known from its inception as 'The Bright Gallery', lit by a score of elegant windows installed in 1735. Space evidently prevented Simon Jenkins from analysing Leoni's brilliant creation of this spacious arcaded renaissance *cortile*. Simultaneously Leoni has here created a much easier access to previously difficult corners, a blend of practicality and beauty which Alberti would have appreciated, and which was typical of Leoni's best designs. The colonnaded south front, is introduced as an extension of the inner court, a masterpiece which again appears spontaneously to the observer passing through the arcades to the south. Leoni was concerned with the elegance and beauty of the façade to the garden, but not at the expense of comfort and practicality.

By contrast with the censorious views and warnings which enliven Leoni's 'To the Reader', in his reading of Leon Battista Alberti's *De re aedificatoria* Leoni must have been impressed by Alberti's many allusions to the merits of the good architect: 'A great matter is architecture, nor can everyone undertake it. He must be of the greatest ability, the keenest enthusiasm, the highest learning, the widest experience, and, above all, serious, of sound judgment and counsel, who would presume to call himself an architect.'[41] He would have enjoyed the satirical reference in Alberti's *Momus* when Jove regrets handing the governance of the world to philosophers when he should, more sensibly, have chosen the architects.[42]

Leoni died intestate, leaving his widow Mary and their two sons, John Philip and Joseph, with few visible means of support. During his final illness his last employer, Lord Fitzwalter, gave him eight guineas, 'pour charité'. He was buried in the Churchyard of Old St Pancras (a place of great importance for the history of Catholicism in the locality) near to the resting place of other renowned figures. In 1854 the burials were removed to create space for the Midland Railway's clearances, thus allowing access for the main line of the new St Pancras station. The desecration by the Midland Railway was variously approved by political and legal means, along with the destruction of hundreds of poor working-class houses nearby. The names of the more illustrious dead, and notably the names of Roman Catholics, were saved and commemorated on the Memorial Stele set up in 1877 by Angela Burdett Coutts.[43] The names of notables once buried there include Johann Christian Bach, Mary Wolstonecraft, John Flaxman, Sir John Soane, and James Leoni, perhaps the most public appreciation of his brilliant, if difficult, life and career.

Notes to Chapter 11

1. See Simon Jenkins's articles lamenting the tragic fire the morning after the conflagration, *The Times*, 30 April 2015; his views on Leoni had been expressed a decade earlier when he ranked Clandon among the more distinguished of England's great houses; see Simon Jenkins, *England's Thousand Best Houses* (London: Penguin Books, 2003), pp. 731–33.
2. Leon Battista Alberti, *I libri della famiglia*, in *Opere volgari*, ed. by Cecil Grayson, 3 vols (Bari: Laterza, 1960–73), I, 134.
3. Rudolf Wittkower, 'Giacomo Leoni's Edition of Palladio's *Quattro libri dell'Architettura*', *Arte veneta*, 8 (1954), 310–16 (p. 310).
4. Leoni was, for instance, a Roman Catholic, and barred from executing public works, not least those which Lord Burlington controlled, directly or indirectly, through the Office of Public Works. His sole income seems to have been as a private consultant architect.
5. Andrea Palladio, *The Architecture of Andrea Palladio [...] Design'd and Publish'd by Giacomo Leoni*, in five instalments (London: Watts, dated 1715–20, though the first volume was published only in 1716). Another, English only, edition was published in 1721, a third (1742 and reprinted 1755) contains the annotations of Inigo Jones to Palladio's original text; Leoni's 'To the Reader' is in book IV, part II of the 1721 edition; it lacks page numbers.
6. This version, in its 1755 reprint, was reproduced in Joseph Rykwert's reprint (London: Tiranti, 1955).
7. Following the publication of Alberti's original Latin text, *De re aedificatoria*, and the Italian translation of Giovanni Orlandi and Paolo Portoghesi (Milan: Il Polifilo, 1966), Joseph Rykwert, Neil Leach and Robert Tavernor translated this last version, with some slight modifications, as *On the Art of Building in Ten Books* (Cambridge, MA: MIT Press, 1968).
8. Andrea Palladio, *The Architecture of Andrea Palladio*, 'To the Reader'; there are no page numbers.
9. Ibid.
10. Quoted from Rykwert, Leach and Tavenor's translation, *On the Art of Building in Ten Books*, p. 316 (Alberti's *De re aedificatoria*, X. 5).
11. Lionello Puppi, 'L'avventura europea di Giacomo Leoni', in *Studi di storia dell'arte in memoria di Mario Rotili* (Benevento: Banca Sannitica, 1984), pp. 463–80; Richard Hewlings, 'James Leoni, an Anglicised Venetian', in *Architectural Outsiders*, ed. by Roderick Brown (London: Waterstone, 1985), pp. 21–44. Other brief but important studies include Tim Hudson's articles extracted from his doctoral thesis 'The Origins of English Palladianism' (University of Cambridge, 1974), which now enriches many a page of *Country Life*. Howard Colvin's *Biographical Dictionary of British Artists* (New Haven and London: Yale University Press, 1995) pp. 608–11, is expectedly full, objective and informative. T. P. Connor's more recent biographical notes in the *Oxford Dictionary of National Biography* (Oxford: Oxford University Press, 2004, online edition 2007) carry the baton further. See also John Woodhouse, 'Venice's European Diaspora: The Case of James Leoni (1685–1746)', *Modern Language Review*, 103 (2008), xxxiii-liv.
12. Though even benevolent architectural historians seem to devote much space to showing how their confrères, including Leoni, imitated or copied from predecessors. Leoni was much more original in his designs, though he was often forced by commissions to conform to norms of

Georgian Palladianism, as for example when Lady Newton prevented him from putting a cupola on the new Lyme Park. Its place was later taken by Lewis Wyatt's awful box-like structure.
13. The painting was 'liberated' by Archduke Leopold Wilhelm, the Austrian military commander and Governor of the Spanish Netherlands, who added it to his great art collection in Brussels. Cut down, it is now on display at the Kunsthistorisches Museum in Vienna.
14. See Andrea Palladio, *L'antichità di Roma*, ed. by Francesco Paolo Fiore (Bologna: Polifilo, 2006), p. 58; Leoni's appreciative comments are from the 1721 edition of his *Palladio*, in his preface 'To the Reader'.
15. Alberti's work on the *Descriptio urbis romae* had given him experiences not dissimilar to those which were to inspire Palladio and Leoni, though it is unlikely that they needed his mathematical approach to the eternal city. The *Descriptio* was Alberti's ingenious geometrical design for tracing distances between the great ruins and physical features of ancient Rome; see the useful critical edition by J. E. Bouriaud and Francesco Furlan (Florence: Olschki, 2005).
16. Alberti, *De commodis litterarum atque incommodis*, ed. by Laura Goggi Carotti (Florence: Olschki, 1976), p. 50 (author's translation).
17. See Peter Collins, 'New Light on Leoni', *Architectural Review*, 127 (April 1960), 225–26.
18. Puppi, 'L'avventura europea', suggests that Matteo D'Alberti's appointment at Bensberg may have been eased through the offices of Fr. Antonio Alberti, confessor of Maria Luisa de' Medici (who happened to be Johann Wilhelm's Electress). Rudolf Wittkower suggests that it was Matteo who might have offered Leoni his opportunity to work at Bensberg; see Wittkower, p. 310.
19. Peter Collins has shown, from the McGill manuscript of this incomplete copy of Palladio's *Five Orders*, that Leoni was in Düsseldorf in 1708. He also shows that Nicholas Dubois was responsible for the French translation (cribbed from Fréart de Chambray's version of 1650), which Dubois later retranslated into English; see Collins, 'New Light on Leoni'.
20. His designs are still preserved in the *Cliveden Album*. See Gervais Jackson Stopps, 'The Cliveden Album, drawings by Archer, Leoni, and Gibbs, for the 1st Earl Orkney', *Architectural History*, 19 (1976), 5–16 and 77–88.
21. See Christopher Hussey, *English Country Houses: Early Georgian (1715–1760)* (London: Country Life, 1955), p. 58. Hussey goes as far as to attribute Burlington's dismissal of Colen Campbell from Burlington House to the latter's having no first-hand acquaintance with Italian originals (p. 24).
22. The locals of Bergamo and surrounding parts, even nowadays, add their practical view, that the 'circular' Villa Capra enabled its owners to observe from all compass points the state of their farmland and the industriousness or otherwise of their workers, a perfect example of Palladio's blend of elegance and practicality.
23. The young heir mentions his meeting there with Edward Wortley-Montagu, who, twenty-five years later, was to commission from Leoni the design for a reworked Wortley Hall, the family's country mansion overlooking Tankersley Moor, nine miles north of Sheffield, today an interesting hotel.
24. Its fulsome dedication mentions the Duke's elevation to the Order of the Garter, which was awarded by George I only after his succession to the throne, hence implying a date for the codex of 1714.
25. Archer was amongst the leading British architects, responsible for a series of other splendid buildings. His style was shortly to give way to the new vogue for Baroque/Palladianism. See Giles Worsley, *Classical Architecture in Britain: The Heroic Age* (Yale: University Press, 1995).
26. Letter catalogued 30/8/33/1.8 (1715), Grey Documents, Luton and Bedford Archives.
27. 4 St James Square (now occupied by the Naval and Military Club) is sometimes counted as a Leoni reconstruction. Ironically, the 'new' Wrest was designed in 1833 by Thomas, second Earl de Grey, later elected first President of RIBA (1834–59).
28. See Martin Pedrick, *The Grosvenor Legacy* (Rickmansworth: Riverside Books, 1989) pp. 21–24.
29. The house still stands, having done duty in its time as the Royal Bank of Scotland, the Bank of England, and latterly as an exclusive fashion house, most recently Jil Sander, and Abercrombie and Fitch. Leoni's plans for the house were published in his 1726–29 edition of Albert's *Ten Books on Architecture* (Plates 20–22).

30. Anyone interested in what Leoni's design was intended to be in the round may enter and admire the columns of this superb interior, their number slightly diminished at present to accommodate a reasonably priced Italian restaurant!
31. Burlington had saved the eight-year-old Ware from destitution as a street urchin and chimney-sweep, educating and grooming him as an architect and draughtsman worthy now of *The Dictionary of National Biography*.
32. *L'architettura di Leon Battista Alberti tradotta in lingua fiorentina da Cosimo Bartoli* (Florence: Lorenzo Torrentino, 1550). That edition was reprinted in 1565 (Venice: Francesco Franceschi). Translations from Latin into *Florentine* (and denying the existence of a *lingua italiana*) were deliberately aimed at boosting the cultural standing of Cosimo de' Medici and the city of Florence.
33. Legh of Lyme papers at the John Rylands Library, letter from Leoni to Sir Peter Legh, dated 30 May 1730.
34. *Dell'architettura di Leon Battista Alberti libri X, Della pittura libri III, e Della statua libro I*, tradotti in lingua italiana da Cosimo Bartoli, nova edizione divisa in tre tomi da Giacomo Leoni Veneziano, Architetto, con aggiunta di vari suoi disegni di edifici pubblici e privati (London: Edlin, 1726).
35. English quotations from the appendice 'To the Reader' towards the end of the third volume (no page numbers given). Burlington habitually gave the task of doing his drawing to William Kent, Henry Flitcroft and other acolytes. See John Harris, *The Palladians* (London: Trefoil, 1969), p. 18.
36. Christopher Hussey, *English Country Houses: Early Georgian 1715–1760*, rev. edn (London: Country Life, 1965), p. 24.
37. Jenkins, *England's Thousand Best Houses*, p. 731. The Victorian porch, which ruins Leoni's classical façade, is a Victorian *porte-cochère* built by the fourth Earl Onslow about 1875.
38. John Cornforth, *Clandon House* (London: National Trust, 1982), and compare *Country Life*, 4 and 11 December 1969.
39. Jenkins, *England's Thousand Best Houses*, p. 731.
40. Alberti, *De re aedificatoria*, IX. 2.
41. Alberti, *De re aedificatoria*, V. 14 (p. 141).
42. Leon Battista Alberti, *Momus*, ed. by Rino Consolo (Genoa: Costa & Nolan, 1986), p. 235.
43. Edward Walford, 'St Pancras', in *Old and New London*, V (1878), ch. XXV, at <http://www.british-history.ac.uk/old-new-london/vol5/pp324-340>, accessed 27 July 2015, notes: 'It is to be feared that in the process of improvement the weakest have been thrust rather rudely to the wall' (p. 340), with particular reference to the hundreds of houses also destroyed in the poorer local neighbourhoods.

CHAPTER 12

Repurposing Renaissance Literature for Language Learning: Giuseppe Baretti's *An Introduction to the Italian Language* (1755)

Vilma De Gasperin

1. Italian literature and language learning

The relationship between literature and language learning is indisputably close throughout the history of Italian as a foreign language in Britain, from its dawn in the mid sixteenth century to today. Historically, both from a literary and a language learning perspective, the two strands could hardly be disentangled, and yet the focus on one or the other may shift: literature can oscillate from being primarily the goal, or the substance, or means of language learning. Naturally, these 'roles' of literature overlap but they call for a different consideration of literature, which may subvert a covert hierarchical slant.

First, if reading, understanding and enjoying Italian literature is viewed as the goal, then language learning is no more than the necessary instrument to reap higher cultural rewards. This notion is implied in lexicographical and grammar works from the very beginning. The first dictionary and grammar of Italian for the English, William Thomas's *Principal rules of the Italian Grammer* (1550), explicitly claims to be 'for the better understandyng of *Boccace*, *Petrarcha*, and *Dante*'.[1] When Giacomo Castelvetro appealed to King James VI of Scotland in the hope of 'apprender a lei, od alla Ser^{ma} Reina sua consorte [Anne of Denmark], la mia natia lingua', he used literary grounds as leverage, and strengthened his appeal by alluding to the appreciation of the Italian language by Queen Elizabeth I, claiming she was

> solita di dire, che l'italica favella, non solamente per la sua rara belta, ma anchora per la quantita di rari libri, che in essa & non in altra si leggono, merita d'esser d'ogni nobile spirito saputa; e se non fosse mai per altro, sol per potere intendere i nobili poemi, da pochi anni in qua venuti a luce, del gran poeta Torquato Tasso.[2]

The fascination with Italian literary masterpieces encouraged the study of the language in which they were written. As Pizzoli notes, 'il grande prestigio culturale della tradizione letteraria italiana spingeva infatti molti stranieri a imparare la lingua per avere la possibilità di leggere in originale le opere di autori la cui fama aveva valicato i confini nazionali'.[3] By the time Italian language learning had broadened its appeal to a larger social spectrum, Evangelista Palermo still wrote in the preface to his 1755 grammar that the knowledge of Italian was useful to 'all Travellers, lovers of Music, Merchants, and to those who are desirous of reading the Classics in Italian'.[4] Literature may be said to have been the principal motivation for learning Italian before travelling to the continent, which reached its peak with the Grand Tour in the eighteenth century, brought to the forefront the more practical need to understand and communicate with foreigners.

Secondly, as substance, literature provides much of what made up the Italian written language. On the one hand, literary texts provided orthographical, morphological and syntactical structures, which were codified in grammars. Subsequently, several compilers of grammars claimed that the rules they set out were based on 'the best authors'. On the other hand, literature provided a source of words, which Giuseppe Baretti called 'le pietre e i mattoni, [...] i primi grossi materiali d'una lingua'.[5] Accordingly, Thomas's dictionary translates 8,000 words based on those 'that *Acharisius* and *Pietro Alunno* had collected oute of certeigne the best auctores in the tongue'.[6] Thomas's sources were in turn based on the language of the Three Crowns: Alberto Acarisio da Cento's *Vocabolario, grammatica et orthographia de la lingua volgare* (1543) is enriched by 'ispositioni di molti luoghi di Dante, del Petrarca et del Boccaccio',[7] and lists 650 words from Boccaccio with the aim of helping the user to 'seguire le pedate de gli scrittori da noi approvati';[8] Francesco Alunno's *Le ricchezze della lingua volgare sopra il Boccaccio* (1543) contains, as the title page claims, 'le cadenze o uero le Desinenze di tutte le uoci del detto Boccaccio, e del Petrarcha'.[9] Half a century after Thomas's first bilingual dictionary, John Florio's *Worlde of Wordes* (1598), collecting 40,000 words, had expanded its sources to 72 books, and while admitting non-literary works — on horsemanship, cookery, falconry, botany, zoology and history — it was nonetheless very much a 'Vocabulary of Italian Authors'.[10] In the eighteenth century, Ferdinando Altieri declared on the title page of his bilingual dictionary that it contained 'all the words of the Vocabulary della Crusca and several hundred more taken from the most approved authors', which he listed in a 4-page 'Tavola degli autori citati in quest'Opera'.[11] The overt emphasis on literary sources for Italian–English lexicography seems to have come to an end with Giuseppe Baretti, who omitted such a declaration (and the corresponding table) when he revised Altieri's dictionary in 1760.[12]

Thirdly, literature can be seen to abdicate temporarily its role as principal goal, and be rather at the service of language learning and teaching, as an instrument to achieve linguistic competence through reading and translating literary texts. In this light literature is, in fact, not too dissimilar from a mine of words and phrases for dictionaries and grammars, except that words are learnt within elegant strings of phrases, clauses and sentences. Giovan Battista Castiglioni set his pupil Princess Elizabeth, the future queen, passages from Petrarch's *Trionfi* to translate and she committed to memory stanzas of Tasso's *Gerusalemme liberata* while learning Italian.[13] Some language-teaching manuals include substantial literary passages, moving away from texts that were written especially with the aim of teaching Italian — such as collections of dialogues, phrases, proverbs and stories.[14] For instance, in 1723 the teacher of modern languages Angelo Maria Cori declared he had adapted phrases from the 'best ancient Authors' for teaching purposes consciously omitting the source in order to avoid the potential criticism of textual manipulation.[15] David Francesco Lates, who in 1755 established himself in Oxford where he taught French, Italian, Spanish, Portuguese and Hebrew,[16] includes in his grammar a section on 'the most beautiful Passages of the best *Italian* Poets' and exhorts the learner to make good use of them: 'If you will give yourself the Trouble of learning these by heart, or, at least, of reading the last Collection, and those which precede it, several times over, you will both speak and write *Italian* with the greater Ease'.[17] Such bibliographical lists or collections of excerpts ultimately anticipate the formation of a literary canon whose primary aim is to facilitate or refine a knowledge of the Italian language.[18] Other manuals provide the learner with more or less general recommendations as to which authors to read, recommendations which are interspersed in prefaces or dialogues. For instance, the eighteenth-century anonymous grammar *A short specimen of what is most necessary to be known to attain the Italian tongue* illustrates this situation in the dialogue 'Per parlar italiano', identifying in sixteenth-century Italian literature the preferred linguistic model:

> [L]a lingua italiana è facilissima, ed ella deve parlarla con spirito.
> Avrei gran piacere di poterla parlar con franchezza.
> Perchè non legge qualche libro d'istoria, o di lettere familiari?
> Adesso non ne ho alcuno; ma per l'avvenire voglio comprarne.
> [...] Quali autori ha intenzione di leggere?
> Penso leggere i migliori, e principalmente quei del cinque cento, che oltre all'essere in gran numero, sono i più stimati, e più famosi.[19]

Whether by merely giving brief reading recommendations, or by including a collection of excerpts from Italian literary works, these texts begin to repurpose Italian literature and shift its main focus on language learning. In the mid-eighteenth century Giuseppe Baretti began his long-lasting and multifarious contribution to the field of Italian language pedagogy with a work that established the idea of anthologizing original Italian texts as the best means for a student to attain advanced knowledge of the Italian language.[20] In 1755 he published *An Introduction to the Italian Language*, an anthology of literary texts collected specifically as a tool for learning Italian.[21] What textual genres did Baretti privilege, what authors and texts did he include, to what degree of textual manipulation did Baretti indulge in for his use of literary texts for language learning purposes? By exploring these questions we may understand his early practice of repurposing literature for language learning and the extent to which the pedagogical focus affects the texts, in terms of selection, omission, adaptation and textual apparatus.

2. Choice of texts in Baretti's chrestomathy

Giuseppe Baretti wrote his first short text on issues relating to language learning when he initially arrived in London in 1751. The 24-page pamphlet called *Remarks on the Italian Language* (1753) offers a linguistic and stylistic review of Italian authors for the benefit of an advanced foreign learner wishing to 'attain the purity of the Italian tongue'.[22] So, before publishing his chrestomathy in 1755, Baretti provided a kind of annotated reading list, where authors are presented in the light of their linguistic virtues and vices as well as literary value. Regarding the Three Crowns, Baretti advises that Dante's language is 'lofty, sublime, and haughty',[23] although he is 'sometimes very clownish, and even unintelligible';[24] Petrarch's Cantatas are 'very beautiful', his *Triumphs* 'extremely bad' and his language is 'very pure and good'.[25] Boccaccio 'abounds with beautiful, lively and natural expressions; and the disposition of his periods is admirable' in the *Decameron*, but 'His other pieces are not written with the same propriety of language'.[26] Among Renaissance writers Baretti praises Giovanni Della Casa's *Galateo*, written with 'wonderful perspicuity and elegance',[27] Firenzuola's 'much sweetness and grace' as well as his 'agreeable and beautiful manner', and Cellini's 'inimitable grace'.[28] Others, on the contrary, he decries, like Pulci, whose phrases are 'often coarse and obscure'[29], and Aretino who is 'as ignorant of his own tongue, as of good manners'.[30] Pietro Bembo and Sperone Speroni 'wrote well in prose, and want not their beauties', but, like *Castiglione* in the *Courtier* 'they are heavy, and disgust the reader by a certain air of pedantry'.[31] Boiardo's *Orlando innamorato* 'is travestied in pure style'.[32] If Ariosto 'has many admirable and original beauties, he has also several considerable blemishes'.[33] Tasso's style 'is not polite, nor harmonious' and 'his thoughts and phrases are too studied and far-fetched; so whoever would attain the purity of the *Italian* tongue will not find it in his works'.[34] In 1755, two years after publishing the *Remarks*, Baretti wrote the first anthology of texts aimed specifically for language learning, ushering in a succession of Italian literature anthologies that were to establish a 'canon of the classics' in Britain.[35] As Baretti stated in his preface, *An Introduction to the Italian Language* focuses on improving linguistic competence rather than teaching Italian literature, even though the latter may indeed be a worthy collateral gain: 'Io non intendo dare altro in questa Raccolta che un Volume iniziativo, una facile Introduzione alla Lingua Italiana'.[36] The collection is a corpus of texts aimed at developing the understanding of literary language (comprising epistolary, narrative, poetic, historiographical texts) so that 'chiunque leggerà con diligenza, dopo d'aver imparati gli Elementi del Parlar nostro, non avrà d'uopo di maggiore ajuto per acquistare un più che mediocre conoscimento de' nostri buoni scrittori'.[37] The selection of texts, many of which belong to the Renaissance period, is based on both quantitative and qualitative criteria:

> Io ho ragunata in questi Fogli la maggior quantità di nostra Lingua che ho potuto; e gli Autori, da' quali ho scelti i miei saggi, sono annoverati per universale consenso de' miei Paesani fra i più eccellenti che l'Italia ha prodotti. Redi, Galileo, Caro, Navagero, Fracastoro, Poliziano, Ariosto, Tasso, Petrarca &c. non sono ignoti Nomi a chiunque ha contezza di libri.[38]

Baretti claims that he has included texts whose quality and hence canonical status is proven by the fact that they have stood the test of time with readers: 'L'Opere loro durano da un pezzo; dunque sono buone; perché gli uomini mai non s'accordano a lodare un libro cattivo, e a sottrarlo dall'obblio'.[39] It might therefore be surprising to find that Dante does not feature in the anthology, whereas the diplomat Andrea Navagero and the historian Caterino Davila are both included. We must bear in mind, however, that Baretti's anthology is not meant as a collection of Italian literary masterpieces in specimen form, but rather, as the title suggests, an introduction to and thus a collection of specimens of *language*, offering a varied range of topics and genres.[40] The most notable features of this collection are the selection and arrangement of texts, the omission of contextual information on authors, the abridgement and adaptation of the original texts, the footnotes and the literal translation.

Baretti's anthology consists of 40 texts — either full or sections of longer works — from 27 authors with a total of 467 pages. The texts are not arranged in chronological order, which would serve to illustrate the development of the Italian language, as Baretti later outlined in 'A History of the Italian Tongue' that prefaced *The Italian Library* in 1757.[41] Baretti omitted any biographical information on the authors or introduction to the works, which means that a reader who was not already acquainted with the texts would be in the dark as to the identity or life of the authors and even the century in which the texts had been written. As Baretti explains in the Preface, this is part of his conscious repurposing of texts not for literary erudition but 'per altri fini', namely language learning:

> Nè dirò io quì chi costoro si sieno; che la mia Raccolta io non l'ho fatta per compiacere a' Curiosi, ma per assistere ed agevolar la via a chi vuole studiare: Basta che i Dotti li conoscono; e i non Dotti che cercano sapere la nostra Lingua per altri fini, non cureranno di una tale informazione, che pure riuscirebbe imperfetta quando io non m'allargassi più che non posso in questa Prefazione.[42]

Thus, in Baretti's view, learned men and women did not require contextual information because they would possess it already, and the less learned students of Italian would not require it because, presumably, they would not be interested in knowing it and, in any case, space constraints prevented it. This is not to say that Baretti deemed this information unnecessary. On the contrary, he must have felt there was a market niche for such a publication, because two years later he published *The Italian Library, Containing an Account of the Lives and Works of the Most Valuable Authors of Italy*, whereby those who might nonetheless wish to have such knowledge at their disposal were soon able to quench their bio-bibliographical thirst.[43]

The anthology is evenly divided between prose and verse, and texts are broadly arranged according to genre. Prose texts include family letters, histories, Castiglione's *Courtier* and Trissino's *Epistola*, verse by *melodrammi*, *canzoni*, an *inno* and sonnets. Family letters were an acknowledged model for mastering style and language, as well as a fruitful and efficient mode of exchanging ideas and work in progress.[44] As the author of the preface to a 1765 collection of Annibal Caro's *Lettere* writes:

> Non è cosa da mettersi in dubbio la utilità che si trae dalle Raccolte di Lettere di eccellenti Scrittori, o si voglia considerare lo stile in cui elleno furono dettate, o la materia, cioè le cose in esse contenute. E per ciò che riguarda lo stile, osservano dottissimi uomini, che a ben intendere qualunque idioma,

> e a perfezionarsi nel possesso di quello, giova mirabilmente l'assidua lettura dell'Epistole; conciossiachè per la infinita varietà delle voci, delle frasi, e de' modi di favellare chiamar si possano a buona equità una gran conserva de' tesori delle lingue in cui sono scritte. Nè fa mestieri qui di provare quanto convenga alle studiose persone di ben sapere la propria lingua.[45]

Although these lines advised Italians on how to refine their Italian, which could not be considered their *native* tongue, the same benefit could be gained by the perusal of family letters when learning Italian as a foreign language, as Baretti well knew. Baretti himself published two collections of letters, one of which, his *Scelta di lettere familiari fatta per uso degli studiosi della Lingua italiana da G. B.* (1779), was especially aimed at providing a stylistic model of exemplary Italian.[46] The letters are the only texts in the *Introduction* to give information as to the time of their composition since most of them bear a date, with the exception of four, which could be due to careless omissions, or to Baretti's not being privy to this information at the time. As with the entire collection, letters are not presented in chronological order, but rather move back and forth between the early eighteenth and early sixteenth century, as follows: Francesco Redi (1626–1698), Galileo Galilei (1564–1642), Eustachio Manfredi (1674–1739), Giampiero Zanotti (1674–1765), Annibal Caro (1507–1566), Antonmaria Salvini (1653–1729), and Raffaello da Urbino (1483–1520). Interestingly, of these writers, two were primarily men of letters (Caro, Salvini), three were scientists (Redi, Galilei, Manfredi), and two artists (Zanotti, Raffaello). Baretti thought very highly of Caro's prose. In his *Remarks* he wrote: 'The Letters of *Annibal Caro*, and some of his prose satires against *Castelvetro*, are easy and perspicuous; and whoever would write familiarly will not find a better model among the *Tuscans*'.[47] Unlike with other authors, Baretti's high opinion of Caro was consistent and in 1757 he wrote:

> Caro was a most elegant and easy writer, and his letters are, in my opinion, the best in our language; [...] A foreigner cannot read a better book, if he will learn the language of conversation that is spoken by the learned and polite Italians.[48]

The letters illustrate a variety of topics, ranging from Redi's letters on wine and spices, to Raphael's discussion of his commission to build San Pietro, to Salvini's insistence on the need to read all authors, not merely the geniuses. Thus Baretti seems to have aimed at variety in content and register across two centuries.

The four histories selected in the anthology are: 'Descrizione di Granata' from *Il viaggio fatto in Spagna, et in Francia* by Andrea Navagero (1507–1565);[49] 'Dal sedicesimo libro della istoria' by Francesco Guicciardini (1483–1540);[50] 'Dal primo libro della Istoria' by Caterino Davila (1576–1631);[51] 'Dal Settimo Libro delle Storie Fiorentine' and 'La vita di Castruccio Castracani' by Niccolò Machiavelli (1469–1527). This latter text presents an anomaly within the anthology, consisting of a 31-line comment by Baretti, passing moral judgment on the conduct of Castruccio:

> Such was the life of Castruccio Castracani, who Machiavel seems to recommend as an imitable character, not only in open defiance of the laws of God, but in my opinion, with contemptible ignorance of the state of man. [...] we shall

> find the conduct of Castruccio, foolish and detestable. He that commits ill, teaches others to commit it, and must suffer by the consequences of his own example. [...] What a Prince did to gain a city, a private man will be equally tempted to do that he may gain a house, and a man of lower condition that he may gain a piece of money; and what life could be safe when every man should think himself at liberty to supply his want whatever it might be, by rapine and murder.[52]

One marvels that Baretti should choose this passage if he found the content so deplorable. And yet, since the focus of the anthology was on language, and Baretti admired Machiavelli's style, the choice is consistent with his aims which are linguistic rather than moral. In his 'Prefazione a tutte l'opere di Niccolò Machiavelli' (1772) Baretti described the *Istorie fiorentine* quite favourably:

> La lingua in cui Niccolò le scrisse, è tratto tratto un po' sgrammaticale, quasi in tutte le cose sue: pure è nitida molto, e toscanissima. Lo stile nondimeno l'approverei più, se tenesse dietro più che non fa, all'ordine naturale delle idee. O sia, Niccolò si desse ad intendere che il fraseggiare trasposto de' Latini accresca dignità alle Istorie, o che l'ammirazione in cui aveva il Boccaccio gli facesse gabbo, egli ha, come il Boccaccio, formato soverchi de' suoi periodi al modo latino, cacciando loro il verbo in punta con troppa frequenza.[53]

In Baretti's view, although the *Vita di Castruccio* may not be reliable and even less commendable in terms of content, stylistically it is better than the *Istorie*, especially as it does not imitate Boccaccio's syntactical order with the verb at the end of the sentence:[54]

> Veridica o non veridica, il leggerla riesce molto piacevole, eccettuandone l'introduzione che è intralciata, e anzi puerile che no. Tutto il resto è steso in uno stile così corrente che io lo giudico assai migliore che non quello delle sue *Istorie fiorentine*, perché meno trasposto.[55]

The prose passages from Castiglione, Trissino and Boccaccio do not fit into the categories of family letters or history. In *The Italian Library*, *Il Cortegiano* is listed under the heading 'Filosofia Civile e Politica', with the comment that 'few books made so much noise as this when it was first published; now it is much praised, and little read',[56] a further intimation of what he had previously identified as a 'certain air of pedantry' in Castiglione. Baretti selected a long passage from Book III, sections II–XXXIII, but he does not mark the divisions, and he omits sections without signaling it every time.[57] Giovangiorgio Trissino's *Epistola della Vita che dee tenere una Donna Vedova* is listed under 'Filosofia Morale',[58] and Baretti unsurprisingly adapts Trissino's peculiar orthography, replacing the Greek characters 'ε', 'ω' and 'ς' (indicating open vowels and voiceless sibilant) with 'e', 'o' and 's'. Giovanni Boccaccio is listed under the 'Novellisti', and Baretti selected the description of the Plague in the Introduction of the *Decameron* rather than a novella, which aligns the text with the more descriptive histories that precede it.[59] However, it is somewhat surprising that Baretti selected this particular passage, considering what he wrote two years later when he compared Boccaccio's style in the two kinds of prose:

> In his introduction to his novels, for instance, which contains a description of

the plague that raged in Tuscany in the year 1348, he strives too much to be eloquent and pompous, and his style is here and there perplexed and embarassed [sic] by circumlocutions and parenthesis; but when he comes to describe and characterize ser Ciappelletto, frate Cipolla, Guccio Imbratta, or Calandrino, his expressions flow with precision and rapidity.[60]

Verse is represented in the *Introduction* by a variety of genres. For epic poems, Baretti selects Ariosto's *Orlando Furioso*, roughly from XIV. 30 to XVIII. 26.[61] Roughly, because, even more so than with Castiglione, Baretti leaves out stanzas with no indication of doing so, not even with a line break or other typographical signs, nor does he mention from which *canto* the passage comes, but merely states, 'Dall'Orlando Furioso dell'Ariosto'.[62] Instead, for Tasso's *Gerusalemme Liberata*, as for the histories and Castiglione, Baretti provides fuller information in the heading: 'Dal decimoterzo Libro della Gerusalemme Liberata del Tasso'. More specifically, the passage from Tasso reproduces XIII. 52–80, and no stanzas are omitted. It seems Baretti was eager to offer as much of Ariosto's narrative as possible, making it the second longest represented author (32 pages) after Navagero (37 pages), and this required substantial cuts. Ariosto has a privileged place in Baretti's estimation of the Italian language: 'Nations owe the chief powers and beauties of their languages to their poets; but few nations, either ancient or modern, owe so much to a single genius as the Italian to Lodovico Ariosto'.[63] And yet, previously, in *Remarks* he had commented that 'if this Poet's genius could have submitted to rules, and he had possessed a more perfect knowledge of the *Italian*, or at least if he had been better acquainted with the purity of the language, he would have been truly an original'.[64]

Lastly, of the fourteen poems included, five are longer poetical compositions: 'Inno di Lorenzo Giustiniano', who became the first Patriarch of Venice in 1451; a poem entitled 'Frammento sulla vita rusticale' by Buonarroti, with a rare note on the text, advising that 'These stanzas were found thus imperfect among the manuscripts of Michelangelo after his death';[65] a *canzone* by Poliziano ('Monti, Valli, Antri, Colli'); 'Canzona di Bacco' by Lorenzo de' Medici;[66] Petrarch's *canzone* 'Vergine bella e di sol vestita'. Nine are sonnets by: Michelangelo Buonarroti ('Carico d'anni e di peccati pieno', 'Carco d'un'importuna e grave salma', 'Giunto è il corso della vita mia', 'Per la via degli affanni e delle pene'); Girolamo Fracastoro ('Greco Cantor, qualora io fisso aperte' and 'Gli Angeli, il Sol, la Luna erano intorno'); Margherita di Valois ('Già disiai di fare al mondo conte'), Giovanni della Casa ('Cura, che di timori ti nutri e cresci'), Lorenzo Bellini ('Aimè, ch'io vedo il Carro e la catena') and the collection concludes with the sonnet 'Donna leggiadra, il cui bel nome onora' by John Milton, which was added on the advice of Samuel Johnson.[67]

This selection of texts produces a variety of genres, of topics, and of literary periods, and by being presented devoid of bio-biographical information, they loosen their ties with the context as well as the co-text while the linguistic function acquires priority.

3. Textual adaptations

Baretti adapts the selected texts to a certain extent. Adaptation can range from undeclared omissions of large chunks of texts, as seen above with Castiglione and Ariosto, to orthographic changes, omissions or substitutions of words or even lines. I am unable to determine exactly which editions Baretti was using, but it appears that he did not feel a philological obligation towards the originals; rather, he adapted the text as he saw fit for his purposes. In the Preface Baretti warns the reader that there are several spelling variants in Italian, due to the history of the language and the diverse geographical provenance of the authors.[68] Nonetheless, he makes some changes in the spelling, though not consistently. For example in Davila's *Historia*, the changes primarily concern the orthography, largely mirroring phonetic evolution: 'assuefatti' > 'asuefatti'; 'anco' > 'anche'; 'proportionate' > 'proporzionate'; 'conditione' > 'condizione'; 'commune' > 'comune'; 'hereditario' > 'ereditario'; 'havessero' > 'avessero'; 'haverebbono' > 'averebbono'; 'senz'alcun' > 'senza alcun'.[69] In *Il Cortegiano*, he occasionally changes or leaves out words altogether, e.g. 'Rise il Magnifico Iuliano e disse' > 'Il Magnifico Giuliano disse'.[70] With Ariosto, Baretti makes more substantial changes. In *Italian Library* he notes that the 'most valued edition is that of Francesco Franceschi, 1584, in quarto, because of the cuts by Porro'. The 'cuts' in question are engravings by the Paduan engraver Girolamo Porro who had produced the copperplates for this edition. Baretti lists seven 'principal' commentators and illustrators of Ariosto, including the very popular Ruscelli.[71] At times Baretti modernizes the spelling: 'Correno' > 'Corrono' (XIV. 46, l. 1), 'Truova' > 'Trova' (XIV. 76, l. 1), 'ramaricare' > 'rammaricare' (XIV. 101, l. 1). In other cases he substitutes words or phrases: 'Non fe' lungo camin' > 'Non fe' molto cammin' (XIV. 36, l. 1), or adapts the word order: 'Discorreva il Silenzio' > 'Il Silenzio scorreva' (XIV. 97, l. 1). Other lines present more substantial and puzzling changes: 'Poco era men di trenta piedi, o tanto' (XIV. 130, l. 1) > 'Quel era largo venti braccia o tanto'. By changing 'trenta piedi' > 'venti braccia' Baretti maintains roughly the same measure, between 9 and 12 metres.[72] Yet Baretti translates it as 'That was twenty enlits wide or near it',[73] unlike another translation of the time, which is closer to the original: 'Full thirty foot, or little less, the ground'.[74] I cannot find 'enlit' in Johnson's or Baretti's Dictionary, nor in the *OED*. A possible explanation is that the printer confused the first three letters of what should have been the English word for *braccia*, namely *cubit*, which means both 'forearm' and 'an ancient measure of length derived from the forearm', corresponding roughly to 50 cm (*OED*). Similarly, 'Ritruovar poche tempre e pochi ferri / può la tagliente spada, ove s'incappi' (XVI. 50, l. 1) becomes 'Cedon tutte le tempre e tutti i ferri / All'orribil Fusberta ovunque incappi'. Baretti here not only changes the first line to make it more translatable; he also replaces 'tagliente spada' with 'Fusberta', which appears in the previous *ottava*: 'Mena Fusberta sanguinosa in volta' (XVI. 49, l. 5). The meaning of *Fusberta* is clarified by Baretti's translation: 'He wheels around *his* bloody *sword* Fusberta'.[75] The words highlighted in Baretti's English translation make explicit the meaning that is only implicit in the Italian, in this case the possessive adjective *his* (already implied in Italian) and the apposition *sword* that clarifies what 'Fusberta' is. The most striking feature of Baretti's textual adaptation occurs when he rewrites two entire lines by Ariosto to make the abridged text run smoothly and coherently in spite of the omission. Baretti's version runs from XVI. 89 to XVII. 7, skipping the proem XVII. 1–6.

Ariosto	Baretti
Ode il rumor, vede gli orribil segni	Ode il *romor*, <u>vede</u> gli orribil segni
di crudeltà, l'umane membra sparte.	Di crudeltà, l'umane membra sparte.
Ora non più: ritorni un'altra volta	*Oh spettacolo pien di troppo orrore*
chi voluntier la bella istoria ascolta. [...]	*Agli <u>occhi</u> del pietoso Imperadore!*
Vede tra via la gente sua troncata,	<u>Vede</u> tra via *la sua gente* troncata,
arsi i palazzi, e ruïnati i templi,	Arsi i *palagi*, e ruinati i templi
gran parte de la terra desolata.	Gran parte *della* terra *rovinata*.[76]
(XVI. 89, l. 7–XVII. 7, l. 3)	

Some minor changes pertain to spelling and syntax (*rumor* > *romor, la gente sua* > *la sua gente, palazzi* > *palagi, de la* > *della*). Interestingly, in Castiglione Baretti leaves 'Donna di Palazzo', noting that '*Palazzo* is a word of the Roman dialect, for which the Tuscans say *Palagio*',[77] but with Ariosto he tuscanizes the spelling. The lexical substitution *desolata* > *rovinata* repeats *ruinati* of the previous line and yet in his translation he uses a synonym: 'the temples *ruined*; a great part of the town *destroyed*'. With the omission of the proem, Ariosto's allusion to the pause or digression in the narration ('Ora non più: ritorni un'altra volta / chi voluntier la bella istoria ascolta') would no longer make sense and is replaced by 'Oh spettacolo pien di troppo orrore / Agli occhi del pietoso Imperadore!', creating a link between the image of 'occhi' and the verb 'vede' in the preceding and following stanzas.

In adapting literature for language learning purposes, Baretti thus implements a varying degree of transformation, abridgment, and manipulation of the texts, which can, however, be detected only by textual comparison with the original, unlike the footnotes and translation, which openly serve to repurpose these literary texts.

4. Notes and translation

Baretti's *Introduction* is equipped with a linguistic apparatus to aid foreign readers: 'With a literal Translation and Grammatical Notes for the Use of those who being already acquainted with Grammar, attempt to learn it without a Master'. Notes give lexical or grammatical explanation, often achieved by providing a direct translation of the phrase, or by breaking the phrase into separate grammatical parts. For example, 'erami in tutto risoluto di partirmene' is explained as: '*erami*, compounded of *era* and *mi*. *Partirmene*, compounded of *partir me ne, partire*, to withdraw, *me* me, *ne* from him'.[78] Sometimes Baretti comments at greater length on variation of usage in different writers:

> *Desideravi*, the second person singular of the preter imperfect tense, for *desideravate*. This is a deviation from grammar, as the nominative either expressed or understood is the plural pronoun *voi*. This breach of syntax is

supported by the authority of Boccaccio, Lorenzo de Medici, Poliziano, Pulci, Berni, and many more, and is never used by Petrarch, Dante, and many more. The Florentine writers in general think it a great elegance.[79]

Some notes simply explain the verb forms, as in '*Rivolse*, the third person of the preter-tense definite of the verb *rivolgere*', or spelling variations: '*A dir del Cortegiano*. It is necessary to observe, once and for all, that the Italian infinitives are written with or without the *e* final, according to the caprice of the convenience of the author [...]', and later: '*Operazion*, for *operazione*. I will observe once more, that Castiglione delighted in rejecting the final vowel; but such elisions in substantives ending in *ione*, are harsh and unharmonious, especially in prose'.[80] As for lexical explanations, Baretti alerts the reader to double and even contrasting meanings of a word. For example, '*Che avvanza*, which remains. The verb *avvanzare* has two significations which seem opposite. One is *to go forward*, the other is *to remain*, or *to be laid up before hand*';[81] or '*Tristo* in Italian sometimes mean [sic] bad or wicked, sometimes sad or sorrowful'.[82] Or variations, as '*Giovinezza*, young age; we say also *gioventù*'.[83]

Some notes clarify the meaning of a phrase through a translation not only into English, but also into Latin, French and even Spanish, which shows that Baretti had a cultivated, multilingual reader in mind: '*Dalle quali essa deve in tutto esser aliena*. Literally, *from which she ought to be in every thing estranged*. In Latin, *a quibus in omnibus* (or *omnino*) *ipsa debet esse aliena*', which in the translation of the text is given as 'which she must be quite a stranger to'.[84] And from French: '*Benchè di molti di quelli ella debbe potersi servire*. Literally, in French, *parceque de plusieurs d'eux elle doit pouvoir se servir*'.[85]

For all texts Baretti provides a 'literal' translation on the right-hand page, a translation whose flaws he accounts for in the light of his own aims and of the differences between the two languages:

> Io non vo poi estendermi in apologie della mia Traduzione, che, considerata la differente indole delle due Lingue, ho fatta ad verbum quanto m'è stato possibile. Una Traduzione libera non fu mia intenzione di fare, perché non avrebbe quadrato col mio Disegno ch'è d'insegnare l'Italiano e non l'Inglese.[86]

Indeed, this passage highlights the everlasting translator's dilemma between being faithful to the source text and recreating it in elegant prose or verse in the target language. Any flaw in Baretti's translation into English could have reasonably been accounted for by the fact that he was translating into a foreign language in which he had seriously been immersed for only four years, since his arrival in Britain in 1751, even taking into account the talented linguist he was. But this is not the point, since Baretti's translation is rooted in his view that when translating literary texts in order to teach Italian it is best to adhere as faithfully as possible to the original text, and consequently he highlights words that are not directly discernible in the Italian, but required in English to make sense, either grammatically, or semantically: 'tolta la loro terra da' Cristiani' > 'their town *having been* taken by the Christians';[87] 'Nostro Signore' > 'Our Lord (*the Pope*)', and 'nè so se il volo sarà di Icaro' > 'nor do I know if *my* flight shall be *that* of Icarus'.[88] The translation should provide little more, Baretti suggests, than a convenient dictionary: 'Consideri dunque il mio libro come un semplice vocabolario, che davvero non è altro; e allora la mia traduzione non riuscirà inutile, quantunque non elegante'.[89] And it must have been an excellent exercise for Baretti's improvement of the English language. And yet this comes at a cost, and Baretti's warning may serve as an encouragement to the learner to read the original and not just content him/herself with a handy translation. For what happens, in Baretti's view, when we translate literally? Stylistically, it amounts to disaster:

> il semplice e il facile debbe in simil caso diventar rozzo e plebeo; il forte e il sublime cangiarsi in fantastico ed ampolloso; il chiaro e metodico in intricato ed oscuro; e l'ingegnoso e piacevole in freddo e puerile: Vedrà che i sali svaporeranno; che svaniranno le grazie; e che la proprietà delle parole, la sceltezza delle frasi, la giustezza delle allusioni, il concatenamento de' pensieri, la soavità de' numeri, e la musica delle rime, tutto trasformerassi in fiacchezza, in durezza, in dissonanza, in confusione.[90]

Such an apocalyptic warning should suffice to dissuade any budding translator from contenting her/himself with translation of a literal kind. And it should make readers of all ages feel grateful to truly brilliant translators, who enable us to read foreign texts in all their splendour.

Notes to Chapter 12

1. William Thomas, *Principal Rules of the Italian Grammer, with a Dictionarie for the Better Understandyng of Boccace, Petrarcha, and Dante* (London: Thomas Berthelet, 1550).
2. Letter by Giacomo Castelvetro to King James VI of Scotland dated 20 August 1592, cit. in John Purves, 'Fowler and Scoto-Italian Cultural Relations in the Sixteenth Century', in *The Works of William Fowler, Secretary to Queen Anne, Wife of James VI*, 3 vols (John Blackwood and Sons: Edinburgh, 1940), III, lxxx–cli (p. cxxix).
3. Lucilla Pizzoli, *Le grammatiche di italiano per inglesi (1550–1776)* (Florence: Accademia della Crusca, 2004), p. 85.
4. Evangelista Palermo, 'The Preface', in *A Grammar of the Italian Language [...]* (London: A. Millar in the Strand, 1755), p. viii.
5. Giuseppe Baretti, *La Frusta Letteraria*, ed. by Luigi Piccioni, 2 vols (Bari: Laterza, 1932), I, 270.
6. Thomas, 'The Occasion', preface to *Principal Rules*.
7. Added to the title of the second edition, Venice, 1550.
8. Ornella Olivieri, 'I primi vocabolari italiani fino alla prima edizione della Crusca', *Studi di Filologia Italiana*, 6 (1942), 64–192 (pp. 112–13).
9. See T. Gwynfor Griffiths, 'La prima grammatica e il primo dizionario italiano ad uso degli inglesi', in *Avventure linguistiche del Cinquecento* (Florence: Le Monnier, 1961), pp. 53–80.
10. Desmond O'Connor, 'John Florio's contribution to Italian–English lexicography', *Italica*, 49.1 (1972), 49–67 (pp. 51–52).
11. Ferdinando Altieri, *Dizionario italiano ed inglese. A Dictionary Italian and English Containing all the Words of the Vocabulary della Crusca And several Hundred more taken from the most Approved Authors; with Proverbs and Familiar Phrases. To which is Prefix'd A Table of the Authors Quoted in this Work [...]* (London: William and John Innys, 1726).
12. Giuseppe Baretti, *A Dictionary of the English and Italian languages. Improved and augmented with above Ten Thousand Words omitted in the last edition of Altieri. To which is added, An Italian and English Grammar*; and *Dizionario delle lingue italiana ed inglese [...]*, 2 vols (London: C. Hitch and L. Hawes, 1760).
13. Jason Lawrence, *'Who the devil taught thee so much Italian?' Italian Language Learning and Literary Imitation in Early Modern England*, 2nd edn (Manchester: Manchester University Press, 2011), p. 13.

14. On dialogues for Italian language learning, see Spartaco Gamberini, *Lo studio dell'italiano in Inghilterra nel '500 e nel '600* (Messina and Florence: G. D'Anna, 1970), pp. 76–94; Pizzoli, pp. 65–77; Brian Richardson, '"Varie maniere di parlare": Aspects of Learning Italian in Renaissance Italy and Britain', in *Ciò che potea la lingua nostra: Lectures and Essays in Memory of Clara Florio Cooper*. ed. by Vilma De Gasperin, *The Italianist*, Special Supplement, 30 (2010), 78–94 (pp. 85–89).
15. 'The Phrases are taken from the best ancient Authors, whose Names I do not mention, that by being concealed they may be secure from the Satyr of those that pretend to be nice, who may turn against me for having added some Words, in those Cases that required it, to give a true Sense to my Period, and for not having observed the affected Niceties of the Language: But my Intention is only, that those that apply to this Idiom, may improve without much Difficulty'; in Angelo Maria Cori, 'Preface. To all such as are Lovers of the Italian Tongue', in *A new method for the Italian tongue; or, a short way to learn it [...]* (London: Geo. James in Little Britain, 1723), p. 88.
16. Cecil Roth, 'An Italian family in Oxford in the eighteenth century', *English Miscellany. A Symposium of History Literature and the Arts*, 9 (1958), 163–71.
17. David Francesco Lates, *A new method of easily attaining the Italian tongue, according to the instructions of Signor Veneroni [...]* (London: printed for the Author, 1762), p. vi.
18. On authors included in language learning manuals, see Pizzoli, 'Il canone dei classici', pp. 85–88.
19. *A short specimen of what is most necessary to be known to attain the Italian language* (London: [n. pub.], [1750(?)]), p. 39. The copy, held at the British Library, has no title page and the author and publication details are therefore uncertain.
20. For an overview of Baretti's language learning works and pedagogy, see Vilma De Gasperin, 'Giuseppe Baretti's multifarious approach for learning Italian in 18th-century Britain', in *The History of Language Learning and Teaching: Part 1: 16th–18th Century Europe*, ed. by Nicola McLelland and Richard Smith (Cambridge: Legenda, forthcoming).
21. Giuseppe Baretti, *An Introduction to the Italian language. Containing Specimens both of Prose and Verse [...]. With a literal Translation and Grammatical Notes, for the Use of those who, being already acquainted with Grammar, attempt to learn it without a Master* (London: A. Millar, 1755).
22. Joseph Baretti, *Remarks on the Italian Language and Writers from Mr Joseph Baretti to an English Gentleman at Turin, written in the year 1751* (London: [n.pub.], 1753), p. 9.
23. *Remarks*, p. 6.
24. *Remarks*, p. 7.
25. *Remarks*, p. 14.
26. *Remarks*, p. 4.
27. *Remarks*, p. 5.
28. *Remarks*, p. 5.
29. *Remarks*, p. 7.
30. *Remarks*, p. 6.
31. *Remarks*, p. 5.
32. *Remarks*, p. 6.
33. *Remarks*, p. 8.
34. *Remarks*, p. 9.
35. On Baretti as precursor of literary anthologies of Italian in Britain, see William Spaggiari, 'The Canon of the Classics: Italian Writers and Romantic-Period Anthologies of Italian Literature in Britain', in *British Romanticism and Italian Literature. Translating, Reviewing, Rewriting*, ed. by Laura Bandiera and Diego Saglia (Amsterdam: Rodopi, 2005), pp. 27–39. Spaggiari refers primarily to the 'History of the Italian Tongue' (1757), which includes non-translated literary excerpts, but in my view the importance of Baretti's anthologizing endeavour applies even more to the earlier *Introduction to the Italian Language*.
36. 'Preface', in *Introduction*, pp. v–xi (p. vi). According to the *Dictionary of National Biography*, the English translation of the Preface was written by Samuel Johnson.
37. *Introduction*, pp. v–vi.
38. *Introduction*, p. vi.

39. *Introduction*, p. vi.
40. Dante's exclusion may also be 'in keeping with Dante's not altogether unanimous popularity in eighteenth-century Italy' (Spaggiari, p. 28).
41. Giuseppe Baretti, 'A History of the Italian Tongue', in *The Italian Library. Containing An Account of the Lives and Works of the Most valuable Authors of Italy. With a preface, exhibiting The Changes of the Tuscan Language, from the barbarous Ages to the present Time* (London: A. Millar, 1757), pp. i–xciv. Now in G. Baretti, *Prefazioni e polemiche*, ed. by Luigi Piccioni, 2nd edn (Bari: Laterza, 1933), pp. 117–44, from which I quote.
42. *Introduction*, p. viii.
43. For example, the entry for Michelangelo appears under 'Poeti Lirici, e di vario Genere' as follows: 'Rime di Michelagnolo suo Nipote. In Firenze, presso i Giunti, 1623, in quarto. This was the famous painter, architect, and statuary. Some of his verses are as good as Petrarch's, but his compositions are not all of equal perfection' (*Italian Library*, pp. 76–77). However, not all authors whose texts are included in *An Introduction* appear in *Italian Library*: Raffaello Sanzio, Andrea Navagero, Marguerite de Valois, Lorenzo Bellini and John Milton are not listed.
44. 'La lettera si prestava bene alla divulgazione e alla discussione di un lavoro che si andava definendo per tappe successive, per piccole conquiste progressive. Consentiva di coinvolgere direttamente il destinatario anche non in presenza, di lavorare in collaborazione, accumulando conoscenze e confrontando ipotesi e deduzioni. La lettera era forma di comunicazione rapida, poiché a fine Cinquecento il sistema postale conosceva già un perfezionamento che la rendeva mezzo di scambio efficace': Erminia Ardissino, 'Postfazione', in Galileo Galilei, *Lettere*, ed. by E. Ardissino (Rome: Carocci, 2008), p. 242–54 (p. 243).
45. 'Prefazione', *Delle Lettere del Commendatore Annibal Caro scritte a nome del Cardinale Farnese [...]* , 3 vols (Padua: Appresso Giuseppe Comino, 1765), I, pp. ix–xxiii (p. ix). The author is probably the printer Giuseppe Comino.
46. Giuseppe Baretti, *Scelta di lettere familiari fatta per uso Degli Studiosi di Lingua Italiana*, 2 vols (London: Giovanni Nourse Librajo di Sua Maestà, 1779). Reprinted in G. Baretti, *La scelta delle lettere familiari*, ed. by Luigi Piccioni (Bari: Laterza, 1912). The letters in this collection purport to be exchanged between fictional characters, but in fact they are all written by Baretti himself, with the exception of the first one by Annibal Caro.
47. *Remarks*, p. 5.
48. *Italian Library*, p. 284.
49. Passage selected from Andrea Navagero, *Il viaggio fatto in Spagna, et in Francia, dal Magnifico M. Andrea Navagiero [...]* (Venice: Domenico Farri, 1563), pp. 18–27.
50. Passage selected from XVI. 1 to the beginning of XVI. 2; in Francesco Guicciardini, *Storia d'Italia*, ed. by Seidel Menchi, 3 vols (Turin: Einaudi, 1971), III, 1601–09.
51. Baretti selects the opening of *Historia delle Gverre Ciuili di Francia di Henrico Caterino Davila [...]* (Venice: Paolo Baglioni, 1650), pp. 1–9.
52. *Introduction*, p. 198.
53. *Prefazioni*, pp. 175–76. Originally 'Prefazione alle opere del Machiavelli di Giuseppe Baretti Segretario per la corrispondenza straniera della Reale Britannica Accademia di Pittura, Scultura, e Architettura', in *Tutte le opere di Niccolò Machiavelli*, 3 vols (London: Tommaso Davies, 1772), I, pp. i–xlx.
54. Baretti was frequently critical of Boccaccio's syntactical style and especially of his imitators: 'I cannot help thinking that [Boccaccio's] style is a little embarrassed by his frequent transpositions and parenthesis within parenthesis' (*Italian Library*, p. 248). Baretti believed that syntax must reflect 'l'ordine naturale delle idee, le quali non ne presentano mai il verbo prima del nominativo, e non ce lo collocano mai in punta a' periodi e a una gran distanza da quello', in *Frusta letteraria*, I, 88.
55. *Prefazioni*, p. 177.
56. *Italian Library*, p. 40.
57. For example, section V and VI run on in the same paragraph (*Introduction*, p. 50). Baretti's text signals with two lines of asterisks the omission of sections XVI–XVIII (p. 64), but does not do so when leaving out the second half of section XX resuming after the first sentence on XXI

(*Introduction*, p. 66). In *Il Cortegiano* (Milan: Garzanti, 2000) the omitted passages appear on pp. 279–82 and 284–85.
58. *Italian Library*, p. 31.
59. Selected passage in Giovanni Boccaccio, *Decameron*, ed. by Vittore Branca, 2 vols (Turin: Einaudi, 2005), I, 14–28.
60. *Prefazioni*, p. 129.
61. *Introduction*, pp. 358–421.
62. Based on the final 1532 edition of the *Furioso*, starting in XIV. 30 and finishing with XVIII. 26, Baretti leaves out the following stanzas: XIV. 63–64; XV entirely; XVI. 1–20; XVI. 53–55; XVI. 59–84; XVII. 1–6; XVII. 17–135 and XVIII. 1–9.
63. *Prefazioni*, p. 133.
64. *Remarks*, p. 8.
65. *Introduction*, p. 442.
66. Lorenzo de' Medici, *Opere*, ed. by Tiziano Zanato (Turin: Einaudi, 1992), pp. 391–94.
67. Spaggiari, p. 29.
68. 'Gl'Italiani scrivono e pronunziano in più maniere una stessa parola [...]. La ragione di questo è che la Lingua nostra fu primamente scritta da molte persone da più parti d'Italia', *Introduction*, pp. ix–x.
69. Davila, p. 4; *Introduction*, pp. 130–32.
70. Castiglione, p. 288; *Introduction*, p. 70.
71. Baretti mentions also: 'Lodovico Dolce, Giovanni Orlandi, Giuseppe Malatesta, Girolamo Ruscelli, Orazio Toscanella, Francesco Gaburacci, Gregorio Caloprese, and Laura Terracina'; *Italian Library*, p. 60. Quotes from the original are from *Orlando furioso*, ed. by Carlo Muscetta and Luca Lamberti, 2 vols (Turin: Einaudi, 1962), I, which is based on the edition by Lanfranco Caretti (Milan: Ricciardi, 1954).
72. *Braccio* = *c*. 60 cm, was used in some areas of Central and Southern Italy in antiquity; *piede* = *c*. 30 cm (T. De Mauro, *Grande Dizionario Italiano Dell'Uso*).
73. *Introduction*, p. 395.
74. *Orlando furioso*, trans. by William Huggins, 2 vols (London: Rivington and Fletcher, 1757), I, 212.
75. *Introduction*, p. 407.
76. *Introduction*, p. 410. My emphasis.
77. *Introduction*, p. 52n.
78. On Caro, *Introduction*, p. 22n.
79. On Caro, *Introduction*, pp. 24–25n.
80. On Castiglione, *Introduction*, pp. 56–57n.
81. On Castiglione, *Introduction*, pp. 40–41n.
82. On Trissino, *Introduction*, p. 208.
83. On Lorenzo de' Medici, *Introduction*, p. 451n.
84. On Castiglione, *Introduction*, pp. 46n and 47.
85. On Castiglione, *Introduction*, p. 47n.
86. *Introduction*, p. vii.
87. On Navagero, *Introduction*, pp. 88, 89.
88. On Raphael, *Introduction*, pp. 38, 39.
89. *Introduction*, pp. viii–ix.
90. *Introduction*, p. viii.

CHAPTER 13

Goldoni and Gozzi: Disquisition on a Statue that Walks

Joseph Farrell

One of Carlo Goldoni's early plays, premiered in 1736, was *Don Giovanni Tenorio, o sia Il Dissoluto*, a fresh but sceptical treatment of a work which had already attained privileged status in the recognised European tradition. The original work by Tirso de Molina had been produced in Spanish in 1630 and had, as Goldoni himself writes in his introduction, not only been translated twice into Italian but also been produced in more than one popular version, adapted to give parts to the masked characters of the *commedia dell'arte*. The play had met with enormous success in every part of the country, but this success baffled Goldoni, and in his account astonished even the companies who staged it. In his introductory *Autore a chi legge*, Goldoni could not have been more explicit in giving expression to a derisive, disdainful assessment, based on his rationalist outlook, of previous adaptations of the play:

> Non si è veduto mai sulle scene una continuazione d'applauso popolare per tanti anni ad una scenica rappresentazione, come a questa, lo che faceva gli stessi comici maravigliare, a segno che alcuni di essi, o per semplicità, o per impostura, solevano dire, che un patto tacito col Demonio manteneva il concorso a codesta sciocca Commedia.[1]

A contemporary French writer had used the popularity of this work in Italy to ridicule Italian drama as such, and Goldoni implies that the need to uphold the honour of the nation was one of the principal reasons for his decision to produce a new version. The only redeeming quality which Goldoni would allow the previous adaptations was their strenuous defence of sound moral principles, but even these had to struggle to make themselves felt amidst the 'mille inezie e improprietà' with which the work was burdened. Goldoni had little regard even for the variations on the theme written by Molière and Thomas Corneille, since both, especially the Molière version, were marred by two factors which offended Goldoni: the 'empietà eccedente di Don Giovanni' and the excessive respect Molière had shown towards the original, specifically 'facendo e parlare e caminare la statua del Commendatore.'[2] Goldoni's revisions of this work can be seen as his first, albeit inchoate and tentative, attempts at reform of the tradition of *commedia all'italiana*. His objections to the standard versions of the Don Juan/Don Giovanni story go to the heart of his aesthetic and philosophical principles and help clarify his wider relationship with tradition. His reform programme, when more fully developed, would bring him into conflict with Carlo Gozzi, who claimed to be the upholder of the tradition he believed Goldoni was undermining.

The final scene with the Commendatore, who had been killed earlier by Don Juan in a duel, and whose memorial statue in the graveyard accepted the Don's casual invitation to dinner, is central to the plot as devised by Tirso. The statue makes his ponderous way to Don Juan's residence, and is there to witness the arrival of the devil to carry off to hell the soul of the sinful Don. It is an enigmatic, mysterious scene, pregnant with multi-layered implications, and was retained both by Molière and by Lorenzo da Ponte (who knew Goldoni's work)[3] in his libretto for Mozart's opera, premiered in Prague in 1787. Goldoni, however, suppressed it entirely, and indeed this scene appears to be the main reason why he derided the whole play so robustly. He spends a paragraph giving a caricature summary of the original plot, reaching a climax of satirical condescension in his analysis of the incidents involving the statue which walks and talks. In his eyes, nothing is more grotesque or absurd, more lacking in rationality, plausibility and measure:

> per non perdermi inutilmente a far l'analisi d'una commedia, che in ogni scena ha la sua porzione di spropositi e d'improprietà, basta per tutte le altre la Statua di marmo eretta in pochi momenti, che parla, che camina, che va a cena, che a cena invita, che minaccia, che si vendica, che fa prodigi, e per corona dell'opera, tutti gli ascoltatori passano vivi e sani in compagnia del protagonista a casa del diavolo, e mescolando con le risa il terrore, si attristano i piú devoti, e se ne beffano i miscredenti.[4]

The excision of the statue scene leaves Goldoni with a problem, since he believes, or affects to believe, that crimes and sins such as those committed by the protagonist inevitably draw punishment. In a similar spirit, the full title of the Da Ponte-Mozart opera inverts Goldoni's to become *Il dissoluto punito, ossia Il Don Giovanni*, giving, at least superficially, primacy to the moral element. Goldoni's Don Giovanni too is struck down for his wicked ways, not by the intervention of some supernatural force or action by the wronged Commendatore but by a stroke of lightning. Goldoni plainly felt the need to justify even the intervention of this force, so he informs his readers that such events are recorded in Holy Scripture, and adds, significantly, 'i fulmini a ciel sereno cadono purtroppo naturalmente.' The word *naturalmente* is key, since it establishes the standards of reasonableness, naturalness or *vraisemblance* from which Goldoni never deviated during his long career as playwright. In nature, statues do not walk or talk, therefore there is no justification for depicting them as so doing on the stage. Lightning, however, is an empirically observed, natural phenomenon. Theatre should restrict itself to what can be witnessed as happening *naturalmente*. Fantasy has no place in Goldoni's theatre, unlike in Gozzi's.

Differing attitudes to a statue that defies or transcends its natural condition offer a convenient symbol for any discussion of the contrasting poetics of Goldoni and Gozzi. The question over what is acceptable on stage, the liberties creative inventiveness can afford itself, the choice to reflect society and imitate nature as against the licence to transcend reality in imagination can, by serendipity, be discussed with reference to walking statues in the oeuvre of the two men. Carlo Gozzi never viewed his creativity in theatre as limited by the parameters of observable reality and so his mind was unencumbered by any need to respect canons of *verosimiglianza*. The presence of a living statue on stage represented no *a priori* problem to him, quite the reverse, as is apparent from *L'augellin belverde* (1765), in many ways a sequel to the first *fiaba*, *L'amore delle tre melarance* (1761). It was premiered at the Sant'Angelo theatre by the company of Antonio Sacchi, the very venue where the same troupe had performed Goldoni's later masterpieces. The play features among the cast list two living statues, one a stern moralist and the other a chastened but seductive female. The first, Calmon, makes an unexpected appearance on a deserted beach to address the two quarrelling twins, Renzo and Barbarina, whose journey through enchanted lands, representing a voyage from the cult of the Enlightenment notion of *amor proprio* to a more exalted view of human motivations, is the spine of the play and of the imaginatively devised, allegorical, ideological polemics inherent in the plot. The twins had been engaged on a recondite philosophical discussion on the nature of self-love, with Renzo holding that it represented the peak of human spiritual potential, and Barbarina sustaining the opposite view. To their surprise, they are interrupted by the arrival of a statue, named Calmon. The statue takes sides with Barbarina:

> Calmon: Barbarina ha ragione: Renzo apri gli occhi
> Barbarina: O Dio, Renzo: una statua che cammina!
> Una statua, che parla!
> Renzo: È questo un caso
> Che un filosofo mai nol crederebbe,
> E pur è vero. Statua, mi dì, chi sei. (Act 1, scene 10)[5]

Renzo's Voltairean notions are inadequate, Calmon states, but Renzo is also forced to concede that some events, like the arrival of a philosophising statue, can be true even if its existence represents a mystery beyond the reach of sensist philosophy. In addition to the statue's verbal rebuttal of notions advanced by Enlightenment thinkers, the very presence of a statue onstage and his encounter with the human twins has wider implications for the theatrical debates of the age. Gozzi accepted, as Goldoni did not, that fantasy is a justifiable and valuable element in theatre, which need not be restricted to the representation of reality. The playwright's imagination can take wings and operate in a never-never land of its own devising.

Calmon is not the only statue encountered by the twins on their travels. Renzo later falls in love with the statue of Pompea, who had been turned to stone because of her vanity, or self-love, but who lacks the mobility of Calmon. Renzo soliloquises on his love for the statue:

> Renzo: No, che donna non v'è, che di bellezza
> Avanzi quella statua, ch'ebbe forza
> Di tener fin' ad or questi occhi fisi
> Sempre conversi in lei, nel mio giardino. (Act III, scene 4)

Renzo's ardour brings Pompea back to life. Her punishment had served to demonstrate that self-love has dire consequences and that the human heart is more unpredictable than the barren thought of the *philosophes* would allow. Like Goldoni's *Don Giovanni,* the play has didactic purposes, but Gozzi, unlike his rival, did not agonise over issues of plausibility. Nothing else so markedly sets the one apart from the other. The subtitle of *L'augellin belverde,* 'una fiaba filosofica' indicates that while this work, his masterpiece in the eyes of many, did not eschew the exotic, the fantastic, the romantic, the fairy-like, the bizarre, the magical or even the madcap, it was anything but an act of whimsy. Gozzi intended his play, even if he gave it what he described as 'un titolo fanciullesco,'[6] to be an assault on the intellectual climate of his time. Although he had lived some four hundred years before the Enlightenment, Calmon's transformation from human to stone was a consequence of his being an adherent *ante litteram* of the central tenets of sensist philosophy, which held that reason was the slave of the senses, and that human beings were incapable of genuine altruism. In consequence, his heart was turned to stone and in due course his body too became a statue, but one which retained the power to walk and talk, and so goad others to reconsider their beliefs and conduct. He was not an agent of vengeance like Tirso's Commendatore, but he had a mission to fulfil.

In few other works did Gozzi so successfully marry fantasy with polemics. Marina Warner, in her study of fairy tales, is intrigued by the nature of Gozzi's plots:

> The case of Gozzi, the last self-declared, and valiant champion of *commedia dell'arte* conventions, discloses the connections that bind modern fairy tales to theatre. In a spirit of enlightened, light-footed scepticism, Gozzi concocted joyful fantasies from his wanderings through *Arabian Nights,* Basile's *Pentamerone* and other collections of fairy tales.

There is, however, a paradox of which she does not seem to be fully aware:

> ... the example of Gozzi also illuminates a crucial dimension of the modern fairy tale: its emergence in symbiosis with the Enlightenment.[7]

The symbiosis is a purely chance event since Gozzi was opposed to every tenet of the Enlightenment. In *L'augellin belverde* the author glories in flights of fancy, luxuriant wonders, marvels, transformations, capricious theatricality and adventurous creativity. There are echoes of familiar works of other times, fairy tale or not. While still in the cradle, the twins had been exchanged by the wicked Queen Mother, Tartagliona, for a pair of puppies, and the children themselves thrown into a river, but instead of drowning they were found by two peasants, Truffaldino, a humble *salsicciaio,* and his wife, Smeraldina. It is unnecessary to labour the comparisons with the biblical story of Moses. In spite of their modest upbringing by the good-hearted couple, the twins were exposed to, and corrupted by, current philosophy. When grown to adulthood they callously desert their adoptive parents and set off on a journey of discovery which takes them through wonderlands and exotic realms where magic is routine, before ending up in a garden with the 'acqua che balla e i pomi che cantano.' The garden may be Eden, but it is here that Renzo and Barbarina are finally convinced by the statue of Calmon of the error of their ways. There is no reason to suggest any connection between the statues they encounter and the statue of the Commendatore in the Don Juan plays, although it is not inconceivable that Gozzi took the idea from that source. The mysterious statue that reasons and pleads for good sense is a wholly acceptable element of theatre for Gozzi, not an object of incredulous scorn. His imagination, or his search for appropriate allegories for his didactic purposes, is not bounded by *vraisemblance* or some acceptance of an idea of nature. As Beniscelli puts it, "per Gozzi, contrariamente a Voltaire (e a Goldoni, beninteso!) la *verité* non doveva avere nulla di *vraisembable*."[8]

The question of the opposing draw of reason and fantasy in literary creativity has wide implications, not only for the Enlightenment. Melchiorre Cesarotti was in residence in Venice between 1760 and 1768, the period of the staging of Gozzi's *Fiabe*, and was the author of treatises on translation, linguistics and aesthetics.[9] His debt to Diderot is beyond debate, but he may also (although this is speculation) have been influenced in his own aesthetic thinking by the contrast between the theatrical output of Goldoni and Gozzi. In his writing, Cesarotti identified the core elements of inventiveness as being *la ragione, la fantasia e il sentimento*. The issue of the emotional appeal of *il sentimento* requires separate treatment, but the most basic of all divisions is that which, in different guises and under names which vary from generation to generation, separates observation from imagination, realism from fantasy, *la ragione* from *la fantasia*. For the latter Cesarotti also proposes the near-synonym, *l'imitazione fantastica*, which serves as a reminder that no fantasy is ever an act of pure and total invention *ex nihilo*, but has roots in life.[10]

When Gozzi makes reference to the inspiration driving his own work, it is customarily in terms of dubious self-deprecation, as for example in his preface to *L'amore delle tre melarance*. After drawing attention to the 'caricata parodia buffonesca' of his two rival playwrights, Goldoni and Pietro Chiari, in the plot itself, he writes:

> Altro che cercai con questa, sennonché di scoprire, se il genio del pubblico potesse essere suscettibile d'un tal genere favoloso puerilmente in teatro.[11]

Goldoni was equally given to thinking in the abstract about his own writing, most famously in the much debated passage in the introduction to the Bettinelli edition of his works, where he identified the twin sources of his inspiration:

> Trattati di poetica, Tragedie, drammi, commedie d'ogni sorta ne ho letti anch'io in quantità, ma dopo avermi già formato il mio particolare sistema, e mentre me lo andavo formando dietro ai lumi che mi sommistravano i miei due sovrallodati gran libri, Mondo e Teatro...[12]

It is a more subtle, balanced, yet less transparent statement than has been recognised, and the antithetical balance of the two terms, *mondo* and *teatro*, is crucial. There is no precise explanation of either concept offered, but it is reasonable to interpret *mondo* as indicating for Goldoni the reality which surrounded him, including society, life as it is lived on a day-to-day basis, human relations in their entirety and people he knew whether remarkable or ordinary, with their defects, qualities and idiosyncrasies. The *mondo* was a well from which he drew inspiration which was then transformed into theatre. *Teatro* involved the grasp of convention and tradition, an acquired command of technique, an acceptance of the requirement to model ideas and emotions according to accepted dramatic canons, but also a willingness to stretch and challenge those canons. In modern terms, Goldoni's twin books would be mimesis and stagecraft, making Goldoni a playwright in whom mimesis is tempered by the craft and the métier of theatrical writing and performance. He was profoundly aware that the *mondo* could be transposed onto the stage only via the accepted conventions, the learned artistry and acquired mastery which make up stagecraft, not to mention the collaboration with actors and the recognition of the demands of the audience. The book that is *teatro* conditions and embellishes that of the *mondo*. It is not the case that in Goldoni the distance between observation and performance was minimal, as it would be for later realists. Francesco De Sanctis defined Goldoni as a *poeta* unlike the contemporary Pietro Chiari who was a mere *mestierante*, but Goldoni too was a *mestierante*-craftsman of the theatre.[13] He claimed not to follow masters, but to look outwards.

> Non ho cercato di imitare né i Greci, né i Latini, né i Francesi, né gli Spagnuoli, né gl'Italiani nostri medesimi, ma fissando la meta nella verità e nella ragione, mi sono condotto poi per quella via, per dove la natura mi ha trasportato.[14]

The core concepts, *verità* and *ragione,* employed in that statement are the common currency of the Enlightenment, even if Goldoni was, in spite of Gozzi's accusations, hardly a total proponent of Enlightenment culture. What he observed in the *mondo* could inform his theatre in the most varied ways. *Gl'innamorati*,[15] a dark work which predates the insights of Freud and Strindberg in its depiction of the forces of *eros* and *thanatos* in the psyches of a young engaged couple, illustrates his willingness to borrow from life. It was, he wrote, based on his observations of a quarrelsome couple in a Roman house where he had been guest. In a wider sense, it would be possible to construct aspects of the world of eighteenth-century Venice from his theatre. He depicts mockingly in such works as *La locandiera* or *La bottega del caffè* the plight of the *barnaboti*, the impoverished nobility of the city, and portrays admiringly the new wealth-creating, bourgeois, industrious class in the same two plays, as well as in others such as *L'uomo prudente*. He offers varying visions of the condition of women in many dramas, such as the twin works, *La putta onorata* and *La buona moglie*. The world of *Il campiello* was a real place, not part of a fantasy city, for Goldoni had no wish to create some parallel universe of magic and hyper-reality. At times, he seemingly comes close to fantasy, for instance in his musical theatre, but always shies away. *Il mondo della luna,* written as a *melodramma giocoso* and later set to music by Haydn, has episodes supposedly set on the far side of the moon, but this belief is an illusion, or more precisely an elaborate prank devised to give a wayward, stubborn individual the impression that he has been spirited away to an unearthly place. In the denouement the truth that he had never left his own garden on earth is unequivocally revealed.

In Gozzi's works, on the other hand, the magic kingdom is reality. The after-life of *L'augellin belverde* could be compared to that of another eighteenth-century work, *Gulliver's Travels*, also intended by its author as a trenchant satire on contemporary life but written in the style of fantasy and read by later generations as a children's fairy-tale. Fantasy is the reverse side of realism, and there were many such fantasy lands in the shadows of eighteenth-century rationalism. The division between Gozzi and Goldoni cannot be relegated to a dispute over the standards acceptable in drama in eighteenth-century Venice, but is the first edition of an irresolvable dispute between the claims of unfettered creativity as against meticulous observation.

The poetics, as well as the politics and the philosophy, of Goldoni and Gozzi were at the antipodes one from the other, as was fully recognised at the time, making it paradoxical that the first task for today's critic or theatre historian is to affirm, or re-affirm, the objective fact of a genuine division between the two playwrights and of a gulf founded on contrasting aesthetic visions of theatre and life. There has been a trend in recent critical writing to minimise the divide, and to suggest that, whatever the personal rancours and resentments that set Gozzi and Goldoni against each other, the two playwrights were, because they operated within a shared tradition, more united than they believed.[16] It is pointed out that they had a shared distaste for the degeneracy of the theatre of their own time, that Gozzi after an initial attempt in the early *Fiabe* to restore *commedia dell'arte* came to accept the main tenets of Goldoni's *riforma,* while Goldoni retained more elements of *commedia dell'arte* than he admitted. Gozzi believed he was restoring the centrality of the improvising performer, but after *L'amore delle tre melarance* the *fiabe* are in fact not *canovacci* but fully written scripts. He *de facto* accepted that part of Goldoni's reforming programme which changed Italian theatre from being actor-centred to author-centred. Even the figure of *Pantalone,* whose character switch from roué to respectable businessman can be taken as emblematic of Goldoni's reform, acquires basically identical traits in Gozzi. On the other hand, Ludovico Zorzi advances the theory that Goldoni's supposed reform of *commedia dell'arte* was not as radical as he himself imagined, so that Gozzi's counter-attack was in many ways redundant.[17] In other words, the conventional notion of a reform-minded Goldoni facing a reactionary Gozzi will not, it is now suggested, stand up to scrutiny. How strong was the tradition both men inherited, and how radical their attitude to it?

Any doubts over disagreement between the two would have astonished contemporary writers, gazetteers and exponents of the emerging trade of literary criticism, for whom the existence of an embittered split was an article of faith. In 1768, Giuseppe Baretti published in London his celebrated and controversial *Account of the Manner and Customs of Italy,* which contained a eulogy of the work of Carlo Gozzi and an attack on the theatre of Carlo Goldoni.[18] Baretti was an acute observer of cultural trends and a man of strong, individualistic judgement, but his idiosyncrasies do not mean that his acuteness of analysis should be underestimated. His book was enormously successful and influential not only in Britain but also in translated versions in France and Italy. Baretti made the assertion that Gozzi had by himself utterly changed 'the taste of the Venetian public.'[19] In the chapter on theatre, he was fulsome in his praise of Gozzi, whom he defined the 'greatest dramatic writer Italy had ever produced,' even going so far as to refer to 'Gozzi's genius, the most wonderful, in my opinion, next to Shakespeare, that any age or country every produced.'[20] Perhaps these extravagant assessments were intended more as polemical jibes than as reasoned criticism, as is the view of Alberto Beniscelli, who dismisses them as 'una provocazione.'[21]

In the debates following the publication in Venice of Baretti's *Account*, critics and writers divided even more firmly into Goldoniani and Gozziani. The lively theatrical creativity in the *Serenissina* thrived on disharmony. The first dispute had seen Carlo Goldoni, who worked for the Sant'Angelo and San Luca theatres, pitted against Pietro Chiari in San Samuele and later in the San Giovanni Crisostomo, a rivalry which culminated in the decision in 1749 of the authorities in Venice to order the closure of both Goldoni's *La vedova scaltra* and of Chiari's *La scuola delle vedove*, a play in which Chiari satirised and ridiculed the work of his rival. Goldoni himself had requested the government to intervene to defend the honour of the Republic, although whether he expected their actual response is not clear. At that point, Gozzi himself was still in the sidelines, sniping as a critic against the degradation of theatre, of public morals and political order, a decay for which he held Goldoni principally responsible. He lampooned Goldoni mercilessly in the period between 1757 and 1762, the first date, following the chronology established by Paolo Bosisio, being the year of the publication of *La tartana degl'influssi invisibili per l'anno bisestile 1756* and the latter being the year when an exhausted Goldoni left Venice for Paris.[22] The years from the premiere in 1761 of *L'amore delle tre melarance* until 1768 saw Gozzi at the peak of his creativity.

The support each received was not constant, as the allegiances of even the most seemingly partisan enthusiasts wavered and varied. If we leave aside certain constant admirers of Goldoni, like Pietro Verri,[23] or Domenico Caminer and his daughter Elisabetta, journalist and translator, alignments were faltering and uncertain. Francesco Capacelli Albergati, always desperate to have his abilities as playwright recognised, dedicated his play *Il sofa* (1770) to Carlo Gozzi. He followed Gozzi in employing magical effects and transformations from the human to the animal in the work, only to medise later with words whose scathing scorn equalled in force the earlier flattery, and to declare himself in favour of the Goldonian tradition.[24] Even Baretti, a few years after the publication of the *Account*, was writing of his dismay that Gozzi had had the gall actually to publish his *fiabe*, meaning the old *maschere* in his work were now taken out of their traditional life on the stage and endowed with the inappropriate dignity of print. His later words on the Gozzi are acid:

> L'animale ha guasti tutti i suoi drammi ficcando in essi quei suoi maledetti Pantaloni, e Arlecchini, e Tartagli, e Brighelli, che non doveva mostrare se non sulla scena per dar gusto alla nostra canaglia.

The entire *opus*, concluded Baretti in 1784, could be viewed as a 'mucchio d'oro e di sterco.'[25]

Anna Scannapieco may be right in suggesting that for Gozzi enmities, real or invented, were the psychological mechanism which unleashed his creativity, and that it is no coincidence the ending of his most fertile period of creativity coincides with the departure of Goldoni from Venice.[26] Gozzi attacked Goldoni with bitter animosity in a variety of pamphlets, squibs, satirical poems, proceedings of the Accademia dei Granelleschi and finally plays, all recorded and meticulously and insightfully analysed by Paolo Bosisio.[27] Even in the midst of the lightness and tomfoolery of *L'amore delle tre melarance* (1761), the figures of Goldoni as Celio Mago and of Pietro Chiari as Fata Morgana are introduced as figures of ridicule. The various headings under which Gozzi expressed his abomination for Goldoni are given definitive form in the resentful closing chapter of *Parte Prima* of his *Memorie inutili,* or to give it its full, Pecksniffian title: *Memorie inutili di Carlo Gozzi scritte da lui medesimo e pubblicate per umiltà.*[28] In this chapter, in a series of aggressive paragraphs each opening with the uncompromising, dogmatic formula, *Sostenni e provai,* Gozzi denounces Goldoni for a series of flaws, vices, crimes, and misdemeanours: for lack of originality, for having suppressed the traditional *commedia all'italiana,* for having suppressed the *maschere,* for having given the best parts in his plays to the proletarian characters, for having ridiculed the aristocracy, for having preached immorality among women, for having demeaned the craft of dramaturgy by writing for money, for having undermined social order and for having decreased the respect in which the church was heard. Malignity sharpens the critical faculties, and many of Gozzi's points were acute observations, but in all his writings on Goldoni, his main aim was to create a Goldoni who was an uncritical, indeed rabid, proponent of Enlightenment thought, and thereby responsible for the spread of atheism and of notions inimical to the stability of the Republic. He himself preferred light-fingered fantasy which left the social order untainted and unthreatened. His only contact with contemporary reality lay in his savaging of Goldoni.

The fundamental distinction is between those who, in the Shakespearean phrase, hold a mirror up to nature and those who use theatre as a magic lantern. If Goldoni held up the reflecting mirror to his own times, the magic lantern was picked up by Carlo Gozzi. His description of his plays as *Fiabe* smacks of false modesty, although he also referred to them in his autobiography as his 'poetiche fantasie,' or as his 'generi favolosi, poetici, allegorici.'[29] The *fiaba* of Gozzi, while having allegorical and satirical intentions,[30] is an excursion into the realm of fantasy and into wonderland, a journey towards a purity of invention and towards a theatricality of marvel, an area Goldoni never explored. Goldoni ventured at a certain point in his career into the territory of the exotic, but this is not synonymous with the fantastic, as was underlined, acutely but paradoxically, by Gozzi in his introductory discussion of *Turandot.* Gozzi was riled by critics who had asserted that the use of enchantment, the revival of the *maschere* and the appeal to the unlettered sections of the Venetian population were the only reasons for their success. Polemicist he may have been, but Gozzi nourished also the pride of authorship. In the introduction to the published version of *Turandot,* he set out he techniques adopted in his earlier plays and the reasoning behind the transformations of characters from one condition to the next, saying that they were not only a means of ensuring condign retribution on the guilty, but also that they had been prepared by the deft mechanism of the plot. *Turandot* eschews magic, he writes, and was designed to show that the success of his plays did not depend solely on the use of enchantment:

> Codesti ingrati furon cagione, ch'io scelsi dalle fole persiane la ridicola fola di Turandot per formarne una rappresentazione, bensí colle maschere, ma appena fatte vedere, e col solo fine di sosternerle, e spoglia affatto del magico mirabile.[31]

Turandot was an act of homage to the current audience demand for exoticism.

Goldoni too had deferred to that demand with works such as his Persian trilogy *La sposa persiana* (1753), *Ircana in Julfa* (1755), and *Ircana in Ispaan* (1756)[32] or *La bella selvaggia* (1758), the first three reflecting contemporary taste for *chinoiserie,* and the second the cult of the noble savage, but none of these can be termed works of fantasy, or works featuring the *magico mirabile*. As Goldoni himself states in his introductory passage to the first of the trilogy, he worried over the suitability of having the lower orders in tragedy, but decided that the characters he had invented were appropriate for comedy. 'Questa è una commedia fondata sulla passione,' he writes, adding 'altre ne ho fatte di un simile stile,'[33] as though to reassure readers that he would not be trespassing into unfamiliar territory. Eighteenth-century travellers had spread knowledge of the Orient, and this setting allowed Goldoni to indulge prurient curiosity over the harems of the East, but mainly to examine the jealous quarrels of Fatima and Ircana, a common theme in Venetian drama.

Even in the long decline which fascinated outside observers, Venice was a theatrical centre of primary importance, with more theatres than Paris or London, and as such became a European arena for the discussion of ideas, poetics, ideals, value and genres, in theatre above all. The imaginative cosmos of Carlo Goldoni is not that of Carlo Gozzi, but the importance of the disagreements between them transcends their city and their century. The former is representative of that company of writers who view, judge and represent the society in which they have their being. The latter is the champion of those who create realms of gold, who inhabit a dreamscape of marvellous, haunting lands inhabited by unicorns, mermaids, dragons, goblins and, above all, walking statues, a cosmos willed into being by imagination or by subconscious aspirations and fears. The aesthetics behind the two creative processes are incompatible. The reader must make a choice.

Notes to Chapter 13

1. All quotations from Carlo Goldoni, *Opere,* ed. by Giuseppe Ortolani, 14 vols (Milan: Mondadori, 1935–56). Present quote from *Opere,* I, 215.
2. Ibid, p. 216.
3. Tim Carter, 'Lorenzo da Ponte', in *Mozart and his Operas,* ed. by Stanley Sadie (London: Macmillan Reference, 2000), pp. 124-25.
4. Goldoni, *Opere,* IX, 215–16.
5. Carlo Gozzi, *Fiabe teatrali,* introduction and notes by Alberto Beniscelli (Milan: Garzanti, 1994). All references to this edition.
6. Gozzi, p. 295.
7. Marina Warner, *Once Upon a Time* (Oxford: Oxford University Press, 2014), p. 160.
8. Alberto Beniscelli, *La finzione del fiabesco* (Casale Monferrato: Marietti, 1986), p. 127.
9. I would like to express my indebtedness to Moreno Stracci's unpublished thesis, *L'Ossian di Cesarotti.*
10. Melchiorre Cesarotti, *Sopra l'origine e i progressi dell'arte poetica,* 1762. Republished by Reink, Delhi, 2015, p. 45.
11. Gozzi, p. 6.
12. *Opere,* I, 772.
13. Francesco de Sanctis, *Storia della letteratura italiana,* 2 vols (Milan: Feltrinelli, 1964), II, 794.
14. *Opere,* V, 513.
15. *Opere,* VII.

16. See, for example, Ginette Herry, *Goldoni à Venise* (Paris: Champion, 2002), pp. 96–103, or the same author's chapter '1756–1758: Venezia a teatro ossia Carlo Gozzi prima di Carlo Gozzi,' in *Carlo Gozzi, scrittore di teatro,* ed. by Carmelo Alberti (Rome: Bulzoni, 1996), pp. 33–82.
17. Ludovico Zorzi, 'Goldoni e la Commedia dell'arte,' in Marza Pieri, *Il teatro di Goldoni* (Bologna: Il Mulino, 1993), pp. 217–29.
18. Giuseppe Baretti, *An Account of the Manners and Customs of Italy* (London: T. Davies, L. Davis and C. Reymers, 1768), I, 175–77. I am grateful to Prof. Francesca Savoia for letting me see her paper, *Baretti e la commedia dell'arte,* unpublished when this piece was in preparation.
19. Baretti, *An Account,* p. 176
20. Anna Scannapieco, *Carlo Gozzi: la scena del libro* (Venice: Marsilio, 2006), pp. 26–27: Alberto Beniscelli, 'Gozzi e il mercato del teatro', in *Il teatro di Goldoni,* ed. by Marzia Pieri (Bologna, Il Mulino, 1993), pp. 146–47.
21. Alberto Beniscelli, 'Introduzione' to *Il ragionamento ingenuo* (Genoa: Costa & Nolan, 1983), pp. 18–19.
22. Paolo Bosisio, *Carlo Gozzi e Goldoni: una polemica letteraria con versi inediti e rari* (Florence, Olschki, 1979), p. 21. See also Goldoni's dedication to Verri of *Il festino,* in *Opere,* V, 431–36.
23. See Pietro Verri, article republished in *Il caffè,* ed. by Sergio Romagnoli (Milan: Feltrinelli, 1960), p. 45.
24. Piermario Vescovo, *Per una lettura non evasiva delle'Fiabe':* preliminari, in Alberti, pp. 172–74: see also Scannapieco, p. 105.
25. Letter of 12 March 1784 to Francesco Carcano, now in Giuseppe Baretti, *Scritti scelti,* ed. by Pietro Custodi (Milan: G. B. Bianchi, 1822–1823), II, 319.
26. Scannapieco, especially the chapter *Creare un nemico a cui difendersi,* pp. 29–42.
27. Bosisio.
28. Carlo Gozzi, *Memorie inutili,* edizione critica a cura di Paolo Bosisio con la collaborazione di Valentina Garavaglia, 2 vols (Milan: LED, 2006), pp. 374–407.
29. Ibid., II, 437.
30. Ibid., II, 436.
31. Gozzi, *Fiabe teatrali,* pp. 117–19.
32. See Herry, *Goldoni à Venise,* pp. 199–225.
33. *Opere,* IX, 522.

CHAPTER 14

Romantic, romantico, romanzesco: An Aspect of Walter Scott's Reception in Italy

David Robey

> But oh! that deep romantic chasm which slanted
> Down the green hill athwart a cedarn cover!
> A savage place! as holy and enchanted
> As e'er beneath a waning moon was haunted
> By woman wailing for her demon-lover![1]

Coleridge's use of the word *romantic* in 'Kubla Khan' (written in 1797 but only published in 1816) has a long history in English. Of the many meanings listed in the *Oxford English Dictionary* (*OED*), it comes closest to the fourth: 'Characterized or marked by, or invested with, a sense of romance...; arising from, suggestive of, or appealing to, an idealized, fantastic, or sentimental view of life or reality; atmospheric, evocative, glamorous.' The related meaning of *romance* (5a in the *OED*) is 'The character or quality that makes something appeal strongly to the imagination, and sets it apart from the mundane; an air, feeling, or sense of wonder, mystery, and remoteness from everyday life; redolence or suggestion of, or association with, adventure, heroism, chivalry, etc.; mystique, glamour'. These meanings derive, of course, from the features associated with medieval and Renaissance romances and their successors, and the term is used in this way either of landscapes and other physical settings or of human properties and actions. In 'Kubla Khan' the association of *romantic* with imagination and mystery is particularly strong and significant: the chasm is 'savage', 'holy', 'enchanted', with gothic overtones added by the reference to the demon-lover. Whatever one takes the poem's meaning to be, it is intimately connected with Coleridge's view of the imagination and its central importance in poetry.

Romantic in this sense does not necessarily have such gothic associations with the magical or supernatural, but it does have a consistent association with the imagination, and, in varying degrees, with difference, strangeness, often wildness: we can think of the meaning as a kind of sliding scale, with the gothic at one end, and a mild kind of difference at the other. The first occurrence given in the *OED* of this sense of the word is in Pepys's diary for 1666, in this case at the milder end of the scale, since the reference is to Windsor Castle. Later in the next century it recurs extensively, among other places, in Ann Radcliffe's *The Mysteries of Udolpho* (1794), the novel which gets Catherine Morland into such trouble in *Northanger Abbey*, and even more in the novels of Walter Scott, the subject of the present chapter; these occurrences are sometimes at the wilder end, verging, in Ann Radcliffe's case and occasionally in Scott's, on the gothic.

Other senses of *romantic* that exist alongside this one, again from the mid seventeenth century, relate to literature (having the characteristics of literary romances), more negatively to writing or statements in general (fictitious, fanciful), and also more negatively to human beings (impractical, quixotic, etc.). The literary-historical use of the word, to refer to late eighteenth- and early nineteenth-century writers, does not appear in English until the middle of the nineteenth century. The so-called English Romantics did not think of themselves as such: Byron, according to Vincenzo Monti, 'fremea di sdegno' if anyone praised the Romantic School.[2] The opposition between romantic and classical writing, so important for German and Italian literature and criticism in the first decades of the nineteenth century, had very limited impact in Britain. The narrower association of *romantic* and *romance* with love and passion, now so common, seems to have established itself somewhat later: definition 5b of *romance* in the OED, 'Ardour or warmth of feeling in a love affair; love, esp. of an idealized or sentimental kind', is not attested until 1858, while the modern sense of *romance* as 'a story of romantic love' is not attested until 1901. The coexistence of so many different meanings of both *romantic* and *romance* points to an essential degree of fluidity and ambiguity in the terms, from the eighteenth century onwards. Any definition is heavily context-dependent, and it is sometimes difficult in an individual case to determine which one applies. This is compounded by the possibility of both positive and negative connotations, at least when the referent belongs to the human rather than the natural world: views obviously vary as to the personal merits of privileging imagination over realism and practicality. Used of the natural world, the connotations of *romantic* tend to be positive.

For convenience, I shall call the meaning of *romantic* in 'Kubla Khan', and the associated meaning of *romance* (OED 5a), the extended English meanings of the words, because there is no exact equivalent of *romance* in this sense in Italian, and because the Italian Romantics used the term *romantico* quite differently, as is well known, and as some of them explicitly recognized. As I indicated, both words in the extended English sense feature quite prominently in Scott's novels, alongside other senses as well. My purpose is to look in detail at this aspect of Scott's work in the context of the enormous impact of his novels in Italy, the very different history of the term *romantico* and its cognate *romanzesco* in Italian, and the very different characters of English and Italian Romanticism. I shall focus, though not exclusively, on Italian versions of *Waverley*, the first of Scott's novels and, with four translations in at least 15 editions, one of the most widely read in Italy.[3] The reason is that romance in the extended English sense is a central theme in the novel, more so than in any of the others, and correspondingly the terms *romantic* and *romance* occur far more frequently, respectively 30 and 21 times by my count; the next most frequent occurrences are 20 of *romantic* in *Quentin Durward*, and 12 of *romance* in *Ivanhoe*, though *romance* is used not just in the extended sense, but also to denote the literary genre. In most of the novels *romantic* occurs fewer than 10 times, and *romance* even less. As I shall try to show, the ways in which these terms are translated in *Waverley* have a considerable effect on the overall meaning of the text, and therefore, necessarily, on its Italian reception.

In the Middle Ages and Renaissance *romance* and its cognates in other Western European languages stood for any kind of long fictional narrative in the vernacular. The absence of an exact equivalent in Italian of *romance* in the extended English sense results from the distinctive later history of the word in English where, by the middle of the eighteenth century, it came to be used for a particular kind of fictional narrative, usually in prose, characteristic of the Middle Ages and Renaissance, but also continued into modern times: in the *OED*'s definition (3a) 'A fictitious narrative, usually in prose, in which the settings or the events depicted are remote from everyday life, or in which sensational or exciting events or adventures form the central theme'. By the late eighteenth century the distinction between the romance in this sense and the more realistic novel of manners was becoming common, though not consistently observed. Scott subsequently defined the romance as 'a fictitious narrative in prose or verse; the interest of which turns upon marvellous and uncommon incidents', and the novel as 'a fictitious narrative, differing from the Romance, because the events are accommodated to the ordinary train of human events, and the modern state of society'.[4] Thus *Ivanhoe* (1819) is the first of the Waverley novels that Scott subtitles *A Romance*, and it marks his departure from the setting of Scottish history of the preceding two centuries to the more distant chivalric world of medieval England.[5] *Waverley* has a borderline status in this regard, for reasons we shall consider shortly: it is introduced as 'neither a romance of chivalry, nor a tale of modern manners' (p. 4),[6] though Scott also refers to the 'Novel or Romance of *Waverley*' in the introduction to his second novel, *Guy Mannering*.[7] In Italian, on the other hand, as in most other Western European languages, *romanzo* and its cognates stand for any kind of long fictional prose narrative; even today, if Italian writers need to distinguish romance as a sub-genre of the novel, they have to use a qualifier, as in *romanzo cavalleresco* or *romanzo rosa*, or resort to the English word. It is the absence of any exact equivalent for *romance* in this literary sense in Italian or other Western European languages that accounts for the absence of any exact equivalent of what I have called the extended English sense of the word; this too can only be rendered by approximations or circumlocutions.

In Italian *romantico* does not appear before the debates between Classicism and Romanticism in the early nineteenth century. Then it is used in the sense derived from A.W. Schlegel, whose lectures *Ueber dramatische Kunst und Literature* were first published in 1809, translated into Italian by Giovanni Gherardini in 1817, and popularized by Mme de Staël's *De l'Allemagne*, itself first published in 1810 and translated into Italian by the novelist Davide Bertolotti in 1814.[8] The term *romantisch* is linked by Schlegel to the concept of the Romance languages, but also to the narrative romances of the Middle Ages. It stands for a literature that is distinctively modern because it is based on Christian as opposed to classical culture, and deploys a more spontaneous and natural way of writing than the classicism that dominated the previous century. This is the sense in which the word *romantico* is widely diffused by the so-called manifestos from 1816 onwards, which gave Italian Romanticism its distinctive programme and character, calling for a literature that was modern, natural, 'popular' (in practice appealing to the relatively small literate classes), and grounded in reality. The word appears in Italian at least two years earlier in 1814, in a translation, edited by Bertolotti (p. 67), of an issue of Conrad Malte-Brun's journal *Le Spectateur ou Variétés historiques, littéraires et critiques*, which included a favourable review of Mme de Staël's *De l'Allemagne*.[9] On the other hand in Bertolotti's own translation of *De l'Allemagne*, which appeared in the same year, Mme de Staël's *romantique* is rendered by the established term *romanzesco* (I, pp. 218–24), a fact which indicates, as Olga Ragusa has put it, 'a certain degree of uneasiness in making use of a word that is not part of the Italian lexicon'.[10] The quality of Bertolotti's translation was derided by at least two of the manifesto writers, Ludovico Di Breme and Pietro Borsieri.[11]

If *romantico* in this sense rapidly becomes part of Italian literary debates, there is much more uncertainty about the equivalent of *romantic* in the English sense. The first occurrence of *romantico* cited by the *Grande Dizionario della lingua italiana* with this meaning is from 1817, the year after the first manifestos, in one of Gherardini's notes to his translation of Schlegel (III, pp. 351–55). This concerns the expression 'in questa romantica selva', for the German 'in diesem romantischen Walde' (III, p. 120), to describe the arcadian atmosphere of dream-like freedom that characterizes the forest of Arden in *As You Like It*, a usage by then well established in German — and of course rather different from the main meaning of *romantisch* in the rest of Schlegel's lectures.[12] The note is interesting both because it shows how novel such a use of *romantico* was in Italian, and because it underlines the difference between this and the related *romanzesco*. Gherardini observes that such a sense of *romantico* was long established in English, quoting the definition of *romantic* in Baretti's Italian/English dictionary: 'scenico, solitario, romitico, selvaggio, capriccioso; e dicesi per lo piú d'un luogo vagamente campestre.' The sense fills a gap in the related paradigm of Italian terms, as he argues by quoting in Italian from a preface (published in 1776) by the French translator of Shakespeare, Le Tourneur. French has two terms to describe scenes that 'rivolgano a sé gli sguardi altrui, e signoreggino l'immaginazione', *romanzesco* and *pittoresco* (*romanesque* and *pittoresque* in French);[13] neither conveys fully the 'dolce e tenera commozione', the imaginative stimulus that a scene can inspire, the former because of its connotations of fictitiousness and fantasy, a synonym of *chimerico* or *favoloso*; the latter because it is limited to physical appearances.[14] The same applies, evidently, to Italian. The contrast between the negative connotations of *romanzesco*, and the more positive connection with the imagination in *romantic*, will be central to my analysis of the Scott translations.

Some of the manifestos show a clear awareness that Romanticism has a distinct meaning in the Italian context. Giovanni Berchet's *Lettera semiseria a Grisostomo* (1816) commends two folkloric narrative poems by Gottfried August Bürger (also admired by Coleridge and translated by Scott) for their spontaneous, 'popular', and therefore non-classical nature, but doubts that they are likely to be well received in Italy because of the elements of the marvellous, the terrible, the magical; such elements he believes are best avoided by Italian poets, since they are not particularly congenial to an Italian 'popular' readership.[15] Much the same point is made in Berchet's later *Della Romanticomachia*.[16] Similarly in Ermes Visconti's 1818 synopsis of the Italian Romantics' arguments, *Idee elementari sulla poesia romantica*, magic and phantoms are seen as an interest of the peoples of the North, naturally inclined to reflection and melancholy, whereas modern Italian poets should deal with modern subjects, and the only element of the marvellous should be that of the Christian religion. The superstitions of the Ossian poems, so attractive to Northern writers (including Scott), have an interest, he argues, that is purely local to the region from which they come; the romantic as the Italians understand it has nothing to do with the English *romantick*, which should be translated by *romanzesco*.[17] In his 1823 letter to Cesare D'Azeglio, Manzoni takes much the same line. The famous argument that Romanticism should be concerned with 'il vero, l'utile, il bono, il ragionevole' leads him to reject, similarly to Berchet and Visconti, the association of the term with 'non so qual guazzabuglio di streghe, di spettri, un disordine sistematico, una ricerca stravagante, una abiura in termini dei senso comune'.[18] The rejection of the gothic side of Northern Romanticism would include Coleridge's 'deep romantic chasm'. It does not explicitly extend to the more measured interest in difference, strangeness, or wildness that we can see in Scott, but the general tendency of Italian Romanticism is against this — a tendency given its strongest theoretical form in the firm subordination of imagination to the service of truth by Manzoni, Scott's great admirer.[19]

Ermes Visconti claimed, wrongly, that *romantick* should be translated by *romanzesco*. A few years later another leading Romantic, Pietro Borsieri, also explicitly addressed the issue of translation, in his version (1823–24) of Scott's third novel, *The Antiquary*, in which *romantic* occurs frequently, if not nearly as much as in *Waverley*. Borsieri's version is based on a French translation, as were, we shall see, the earlier Italian versions of Scott's novels; in this case as in others it was that of Scott's semi-official French translator Defauconpret. On the first occasion where Defauconpret uses *romantique* for Scott's *romantic* (I, p. 41), Borsieri follows him with 'questa scena romantica', and observes, in a footnote, 'Prima che questa voce denotasse un genere della letteratura diversa dall'antica, e che ebbe origine colle lingue romanze, essa adoperavasi e tuttora si adopera in Inghilterra per indicare i bei punti di vista e le scene pittoresche [sic] della natura' (I, p. 132). To use *romantica* in this sense was clearly a novelty, as evidenced also by the fact that, out of the four occasions in the rest of the book where Defauconpret uses *romantique* for *romantic* in the same landscape-related sense (I, p. 141; II, pp. 113, 115, 140), Borsieri uses *romantica* twice (II, pp. 103 and 127), *pittoresche* once (II, 189), and once, for 'ce paysage si romantique', 'la bellezza del punto di vista' (II, p. 105). The use of *romantico* in the English sense was clearly slow to establish itself in Italian.

The first Italian translation of *Waverley* appeared in 1822, by Virginio Soncini, later a member of Manzoni's circle, though suspected by Niccolò Tommaseo of being an Austrian spy.[20] The first Scott novel to appear in Italian was *Kenilworth*, the thirteenth of the Waverley novels, published in English in 1821 and in Italian the same year, the first of many translations of Scott by the mathematician Gaetano Barbieri.[21] This is followed by four translations published in 1822, in addition to Soncini's *Waverley*: *The Black Dwarf, Old Mortality,* and *Ivanhoe* by Barbieri, and *A Legend of the Wars of Montrose* by Vincenzo Lancetti. All of these translations were made not from the originals but from French versions, by Defauconpret in the case of Barbieri's and Lancetti's, by Joseph Martin in the case of *Waverley*.[22] Tracing the rendering of *romance* and *romantic* in this early group of translations is therefore largely to trace their rendering in French sources that are themselves frequently quite free versions of the English. Before turning to *Waverley*, let us see how *romantic* fares in the other translations in the group; they do not contain any instances of *romance* in the extended English sense.

In the four novels that Barbieri translated from Defauconpret's versions, where Scott uses the word *romantic* either of places or of people (25 instances in all), Barbieri mostly either replaces the French *romanesque* with *romanzesco* (in one case with *da romanzo*), or, about as often, follows Defauconpret in omitting the term altogether. In *Kenilworth* Defauconpret once translates *romantic* (p. 291) with *chevaleresque* (IV, p. 2), and Barbieri follows him with *cavalleresca* (II, p. 6: 'una rispettosa e cavalleresca galanteria'). In *Ivanhoe* (p. 235), Barbieri once replaces Defauconpret's *romanesque* (III, p. 68) with *magico* (III, pp. 69–70: 'quel magico effetto che l'immaginazione attribuisce agl'incanti di fata benefica'). In *Old Mortality* for 'romantic ruins' (p. 288) the French has 'ruines encore majestueuses' (III, p. 80), and Barbieri follows it with 'rovine tuttavia maestose' (III, p. 110); for 'strange and romantic scene' (p. 336) Defauconpret has 'scènes sublimes et imposantes' (III, p. 190), and Barbieri follows it with 'sublime e portentosa' (III, p. 257). In only two passages in these novels, both of them relating to places, is Scott's *romantic* translated by Defauconpret's *romantique* and Barbieri's *romantico*: 'quel romantico asilo' (IV, p. 65; compare Defauconpret IV, p. 59) in *Kenilworth* (p. 315); and 'Romantico veramente era tal luogo' (I, p. 136; compare Defauconpret I, p. 117) in *Ivanhoe* (p. 66). In neither case does there seem to be a particular textual motivation for this departure from the translators' usual practice. In *A Legend of the Wars of Montrose* (*L'officier de fortune* is the subtitle in French, *L'officiale di fortuna* the main title in Italian) there are two occasions (pp. 13, 140) where Defauconpret's French has *romantique* referring to scenery ('ce paysage romantique' (I, p. 39) and 'la vallée romantique' (II, p. 141)); in Lancetti's Italian version of the French the first *romantique* is omitted altogether (I, p. 32: 'quel colpo d'occhio'), and in the second translated as *romantica* (II, pp. 124–25). Both French and Italian translators thus seem willing to use *romantique* / *romantico* from time to time about scenery, but not about human beings or their attributes.

In these novels the term *romantic* is often significant, but by no means thematically central; in contrast *Waverley; or 'Tis Sixty Years Since,* to give it its full title, is largely about romance and the romantic. Published anonymously in 1814, it was not only the first but arguably the most personal of the series that took its name. The designated heir of a large Southern English estate, its eponymous hero Edward grows up on a diet of chivalric romances, as Scott tells us he did himself.[23] Waverley devours the English and Italian poets 'who have exercised themselves on romantic fiction, of all themes the most fascinating to a youthful imagination, before the passions have roused themselves, and demand poetry of a more sentimental description' (p. 15). Ariosto and the imaginary world of the *Orlando furioso* are recurrent points of reference in the rest of the narrative. The distinction between 'romantic' and 'sentimental' is a point we shall come back to at the end.

Scott's borderline designation of *Waverley* as 'neither a romance of chivalry, nor a tale of modern manners' (p. 4) is picked up again a little further into the novel, when, at the end of his account of Waverley's English upbringing and of the national politics of the time, he makes a playful apology to his female readers for the prosaic but essential nature of this part of the narrative, and promises to take them, if they persevere with the book, into a 'more picturesque and romantic country' (p. 26).[24] This happens when, brought by a series of events to the Scottish highlands, Waverley finds himself irresistibly attracted, partly under the influence of his reading and partly as a result of his innate imaginative sensibility, to the landscape, to the beauty of Flora, the sister of his chieftain host Fergus Mac-Ivor, and then to the ill-fated cause of the Jacobite Young Pretender, Charles Edward Stuart, that Mac-Ivor has embraced. The rest of the book is the story of Waverley's involvement in the Jacobite insurrection of 1745 (*'Tis Sixty Years Since* refers to a fictional composition date of 1805) and its eventual failure, then of his rescue and return to a more ordinary life. The terms *romance* and *romantic*, both referring to chivalric romances and in their extended English senses, recur particularly frequently in the account of Waverley's first encounter with the Highland landscape and Fergus and Flora, especially in the pivotal Chapter 22 ('Highland Minstrelsy'). He feels like a 'knight of romance' entering into the 'land of romance', where he sees a 'romantic waterfall' and a 'romantic reservoir'; he is overcome by the 'romantic wildness of the scene' and, when he hears Flora sing, by a 'wild feeling of romantic delight' (pp. 112–15). Flora is just the woman to appeal to a 'youth of romantic imagination' (p. 122); Waverley is overcome by 'Love, with all its romantic train of hopes, fears, and wishes' (p. 141); and in rejecting his suit, as she does, Flora refers to his 'romantic tenderness of disposition' (p. 143). Here and elsewhere in the novel, both in the landscape and in the description of Waverley's state of mind, wildness and romance seem closely associated: he is 'wild and romantic in his ideas and in his taste of reading' (p. 61), and the 'wild romance of his spirit' (p. 70) is particularly captivating to Rosa, the woman he eventually marries. Later, Charles Edward is like a 'hero of romance' (pp. 206 and 220), and towards the end of the novel, after the failure of the insurrection, Waverley concludes with a sigh that 'the romance of his life was ended, and that its real history had now commenced' (p. 301).

Waverley is certainly not an unqualified celebration of romance and the romantic. Near the beginning of the novel, Scott states his aim as showing 'that more common aberration from sound judgment, which apprehends indeed occurrences in their reality, but communicates to them a tincture of its own romantic tone and colouring' (p. 20), contrasting this with the madness of Don Quixote, which is wholly delusional. Waverley's Highland adventure is indeed a sort of aberration, underlined by its failure and his return to a conventional mode of life at the end. There are other occasions too, though not many, when the terms *romance* and *romantic* are applied to Waverley negatively, notably by Charles Edward: 'He is really, though perhaps somewhat romantic, one of the most fascinating young men whom I have ever seen' (p. 224). Nevertheless the novel is not a simplistic argument for sound judgment or practical sense, and for the most part *romance* and *romantic* are used with more positive meanings, or at least with a suggestive degree of ambiguity. Events are seen mostly from Waverley's point of view, with a highly sympathetic portrayal of youthful imagination, and the enthralling strangeness of the romantic attractions to which he succumbs is richly and powerfully represented. Here as in later novels, a most engaging aspect of Scott's writing is his ability, and inclination, to represent opposed viewpoints with a substantial degree of even-handedness. This applies particularly to his treatment of Scottish religious and dynastic politics in the preceding century, an issue I shall return to at the end, and a leading theme of Lukács's classic discussion of Scott as the seminal historical novelist.[25]

Following his French source, Soncini's translation of *Waverley* frequently uses *romanzesco* (*romanesque* in the French) for Scott's *romantic*. For a 'youth of romantic imagination' (p. 122), we have 'un giovane dato al romanzesco' (II, p. 82); for 'romantic tenderness of disposition' (p. 143), 'il vostro pensare romanzesco' (II, p. 130). Similarly, when Waverley is struck by the 'romance of his situation' in the Highlands (p. 84), the Italian version has 'pensò quanto romanzesca fosse la propria situazione' (I, p. 207), and for the 'wild romance of his spirit' (p. 70), 'pieno il capo delle romanzesche sue idee' (I, p. 175). Also following the French, *romance* and *romantic* can be replaced by a more conventional term or omitted: the 'land of romance' (p. 112) becomes 'un paesetto maravigliosamente delizioso' (II, p. 62); the 'romantic waterfall' and 'romantic reservoir' (p. 113) become 'una cascata bellissima a vedersi (II, p. 63) and simply 'quel bacino' (II, p. 64). For Waverley's 'wild feeling of romantic delight' (p. 115), Soncini has 'Odoardo rimase assorto ed immobile come una pietra' (II, p. 66). 'Love, with all its romantic train of hopes, fears, and wishes' (p. 141) becomes 'combattuto da mille pensieri differenti' (II, p. 126); 'his romantic spirit' (p. 193), 'il suo immaginare caldo' (III, p. 31). On the other hand there are six occasions where *romantico* is used for *romantic*, precisely the six occasions where *romantique* is used in the French version (I, pp. 65, 68; II, pp. 67, 102, 141; III, p. 53), and in all cases in relation to landscapes: 'È romantico il sito' (I, p. 63); 'certe situazioni pittoresche, romantiche' (I, p. 68); 'quel sito solitario e romantico' (II, p. 64); 'questo romantico deserto' (II, p. 94); 'in un sito romantico' (II, p. 132); 'quel sito romantico' (III, p. 49). As one would expect, *romanzo* is only used to refer to the literary genre; it never has the extended English meaning that Scott frequently gives *romance*.

Plainly Soncini and/or his French source felt more comfortable using *romantico* and *romantique* of landscapes, though it is hard to tell what real force the words had for them, given the reservations we have seen Borsieri express in his translation of the *Antiquary* the following year. Conversely, there are contexts in which *romanzo* and *romanzesco* are the right translation for *romance* and *romantic*, when the reference to the literary genre is clear or when the connotations are more negative, as in Charles Edward's reservations about Waverley: 'egli ha un tantino del romanzesco' (III, p. 96). Yet the frequent use of *romanzesco*, with its connotations of fiction and falseness, for *romantic*, or the omission of *romantic* and *romance* altogether, tend to collapse Scott's sympathetic and complex portrayal of youthful imagination into a more simplistic kind of morality tale. However qualified, the original *Waverley* is a celebration of romantic imagination in a way that Soncini's translation is not.

For all its limitations, the many editions of Soncini's version, at least twelve up to 1847, are a strong index of its popularity, which seems to have been much greater than that of the subsequent, for the most part much better, translations based directly on the English.[26] The first of these, by Giambattista Bazzoni, appeared in 1830 and seems not to have been republished at all after that; Bazzoni was himself a liberally-inclined lawyer and the author of a historical novel, *Il castello di Trezza* (1826), on the basis of which he has been claimed as the first true disciple of Scott in Italian.[27] Despite working from Scott's original English, Bazzoni does not use the word *romantico* at all. Scott's *romantic* is mostly translated by *romanzesco*, on occasion by other terms, and on occasion is omitted. For 'a more picturesque and romantic country' (p. 26), Bazzoni has 'In un paese pittoresco e singolare' (I, p. 73); for 'the exercise of a romantic imagination' (p. 84), 'un'immaginazione naturalmente esaltata' (I, p. 208); for 'the land of romance' (p. 112), the 'regno delle fate' (II, p. 12); for 'a romantic waterfall' (p. 113), 'una pittoresca caduta d'acqua' (II, p. 13); for 'the romantic wildness of the scene' (p. 114), its 'naturale silvestre attrattiva' (II, p. 14); for 'the romance of the scene' (p. 114), the 'poetico aspetto del luogo (II, p. 15); for 'the wild feeling of romantic delight' (p. 115), 'un'estasi quasi affannosa' (II, p. 16); for 'romantic effect' (p. 125), 'effetto pittoresco' (II, p. 40); for 'the country around was at once fertile and romantic' (p. 197), 'la contrada era fertile e d'aspetto pittoresco' (II, p. 197). As the page references here should show, many of the alternatives to *romanzesco* occur in the passages where *romantic* and *romance* are repeated with particular frequency in the original, mainly in the pivotal 'Highland Minstrelsy' chapter (pp. 110–17), and no doubt to avoid excessive repetition of the Italian term. For all the greater overall fidelity of his version, Bazzoni is open to the same observation as has been made of Soncini, that he fails to render anything like the full complexity of Scott's use of *romantic* and *romance*.

The third translator of *Waverley* was Carlo Rusconi, also a historical novelist in his own right, a translator of Shakespeare, and later a liberal politician. In fact he produced two quite different versions of the novel. The first appeared in 1837, purportedly based on the 'edizione di Berlino fatta da Adolfo Martin nel 1822', an edition I have not been able to find, nor have I been able to find a possible German publisher named Martin. The music publisher Adolph Martin Schlesinger brought out other novels by Scott in Berlin in the original English, but I cannot trace any version of *Waverley*: the nearest German edition of the original English that I have found was published, also in 1822, in Zwickau by Schumann. The question of the source text is relevant, because Rusconi's first translation is drastically and quite freely abridged. If it was based on the Zwickau edition, a complete version, then the abridgment must have been carried out by Rusconi; otherwise it is possible, but perhaps not very likely, that there was an abridged version published by Schlesinger which Rusconi simply translated. For what it is worth, Schlesinger's 1823 edition of *A Legend of the Wars of Montrose* does not appear to be abridged.[28]

Many of the key passages on romance and the romantic are omitted altogether in this abridged version of *Waverley*, along with a great deal else. On the other hand a number of instances of *romantic* in Scott are now translated by *romantico*, referring both to places and to people: 'romantiche grazie' (I, pp. 15–16); 'un uomo caldo, entusiasta, romantico' (I, p. 25); 'pregi più romantici e fantastici' (I, pp. 59–60); 'militari e romantiche avventure' (I, p. 64); 'idee romantiche' (I, p. 68); 'Una romantica caduta d'acqua' (I, p. 100); 'romantica immaginazione' (I, p. 110); 'linguaggio romantico' (I, p. 114); 'L'amore, con tutto il suo romantico séguito di desiderii e di paure' (I, p. 128); 'effusione romantica' (I, p. 130); 'romantiche bellezze' (I, p. 186); 'un romantico giovine' (I, p. 187). All of this may indicate that by the later 1830s the English sense of *romantic* was more widely established in Italian usage. Interestingly, *romanzesco* is not used at all in the translation, though there are a number of other occasions where, for no very evident reason, the adjective *romantic* is simply omitted, or replaced by more conventional terms: 'a romantic imagination' (p. 84) becomes 'alla sua vivace fantasia' (I, p. 69); 'without diminishing the romantic wildness of the scene' (p. 114), 'Aggiungevano soltanto grazia alla scena' (I, p. 100); 'the wild feeling of romantic delight' (p. 115), 'Il celeste diletto' (I, p. 102). In the last two instances, notably, Scott's strong association of *romantic* and wildness is wholly elided by the traditional neoclassical terminology.

Rusconi's second translation of *Waverley* is a great deal more faithful, produced for the Florentine publisher Passigli in 1844 as the first of a projected collection of all Scott's novels and poetry. Though probably the best of Scott's nineteenth-century Italian translations, Rusconi's collection was not much republished,[29] no doubt because the enthusiasm for Scott's work was by then on the wane. Interestingly for our purposes *romanzesco*, nowhere present in Rusconi's previous translation, is now brought back for *romantic* alongside *romantico*. This occurs on a number of occasions, all referring to humans, mainly Waverley, and their attributes, including some where Rusconi's earlier translation had *romantico*: for instance, 'romantic imagination' (p. 122) is now 'immaginazione romanzesca' (II, p. 86) instead of the previous 'romantica immaginazione' (I, p. 110). On the other hand *romantico* is frequently used of places and settings ('una cascata, veramente romantica' (p. 80)), and in a number of instances of humans as well: 'romantic imagination' is also, twice, 'un'immaginazione romantica' (pp. 52 and 60). More revealing are the instances where *romantic* and *romance* are reduced to more conventional terms. On another occasion 'romantic imagination' (p. 202) becomes 'un'immaginazione poetica' (p. 137); the 'romance of the scene' (p. 114), the 'sublimità della scena' (p. 81); 'the wild feeling of romantic delight' (p. 115), 'le sensazioni deliziose' (p. 81); 'the land of romance' (p. 112), 'una terra incantata' (p. 80); 'The country around was at once fertile and romantic.' (p. 197), 'Il paese circostante era fertile e pittoresco' (p. 134); 'a romantic idea' (p. 319), 'un rispetto immaginario' (p. 212). The difficulty of finding a consistent rationale behind most of these variations reflects a continuing uncertainty, even at a time when the English sense of *romantico* seems to have been more widely established, about its exact application.

All of this is evidence, therefore, not so much of the transmission as of the lack of transmission of a literary theme, and a significant lack given the considerable freight that the terms *romantic* and *romance* carry with them. Their English meaning was not part of a literary programme, in the way that *romantico* and *romanticismo* were in Italy, but, through the connection between the imagination and ideas of difference, strangeness, or wildness, they encapsulated a significant element of late eighteenth- and early nineteenth-century English literature. Given the central importance of this connection in *Waverley*, the Italian translators' struggles with these two key terms, and the tendency to reduce them to the conventional categories of the established literary language, produced versions of the novel in which, for Italian readers, a large aspect of the its force was lost, and which conformed much more closely than the original to the characteristic interests of Italian Romanticism.

There is a parallel to this finding in a study published a few years ago, to which reference has already been made, on Defauconpret's French translations of Scott.[30] Here Paul Barnaby traces the ways in which, in Restoration France, the translator 'tailors the Waverley novels to a Legitimist, Catholic, post-Napoleonic readership' (p. 32). In *Old Mortality*, for instance, which Defauconpret translated in 1817, the sympathetic presentation of moderate Presbyterian opposition to English rule is effectively elided, so that Scott becomes for his French readers an implicit supporter of their newly re-established royal dynasty. A corresponding point could obviously be made of Barbieri's translation of the same novel, published in 1822 in Restoration Milan, since it is based on Defauconpret's. We can also see something comparable in the way the balance and complexity of *Waverley*'s treatment of the romantic imagination is elided by the Italian translators, or by Soncini's French source. Here too one could even find political consequences: if Waverley's attraction to the Jacobite insurrection is *romanzesco* in the Italian version, there is a stronger implication that it is delusional, and a consequent reduction of the sympathy with which Scott represents the cause. But given the liberal associations of the translators (unless Soncini really was an Austrian spy), it would be stretching the point to see this as covert support for the restored Austrian regime. The greater simplification and one-sidedness of the Italian versions seems to be the product not of political motives, but of fundamental cultural differences and lexical constraints.

Outside the world of translations, it may come as something of a surprise that the *Grande Dizionario*'s second citation of *romantico* in the English sense is by the polemically anti-Romantic Leopardi. In a letter dated 12 November 1827 to his sister Paolina, written shortly after his revivifying move to Pisa, he describes the city's mixture 'di città grande e di città piccola' as 'un misto cosí romantico, che non ho mai veduto altrettanto'.[31] This was no slip of the pen: the word *romantico* is repeated to make the same point about the Pisan cityscape in two further letters written on the same day.³² On the sliding scale of the English meaning of *romantico*, Leopardi's use is certainly at the mild end, but there is still the essential dimension of difference in the word: the mixture of opposites that he sees in Pisa transcends conventional categories, and, by implication, appeals to the imagination as a result. In fact there is some affinity between this response and Leopardi's vigorously classicist, though somewhat idiosyncratic, position in the classic/romantic debate. His *Discorso di un italiano intorno alla poesia romantica*, the wordy anti-Romantic diatribe written in 1818 though not published until the following century,³³ opposed both the Italian Romantics' arguments for modernity in content and expression, and the gothic interests of the English and Germans. Yet it rests on an idea of the poetic imagination that has a certain amount in common with that of Coleridge, though with a significantly different view of the way in which the imagination operates. It also introduces a distinction between the imaginative and the sentimental that overlaps to a degree with Scott's contrast, cited above from *Waverley* though in a very different kind of context, between romantic fiction and 'poetry of a more sentimental description' (p. 15). One can see how the extended English sense of *romantico* may have been congenial to Leopardi in a way in which the Italian sense was not. There may even be some connection between the appearance of the term in the letters of 1827, and Leopardi's narrative of the revival of his imaginative powers in the poem 'Il risorgimento', written in Pisa a few months later.

There is thus some shared ground between Leopardi's evocation of the illusions of youthful imagination in the *Canti*, for all his neo-classicist and Petrarchan idiom, and Scott's celebration of youthful romanticism in *Waverley*. This is not to argue for any influence or contact between them: there seems to be only one, purely passing reference to Scott in all of Leopardi's writings,³⁴ and it is very possible that neither had read the other. The point of highlighting the affinities is simply to illustrate the complexity of Scott's relationship to his Italian contemporaries. It is symptomatic, indeed paradoxical, that his romantic side, in the English sense, has its most eminent parallel in Leopardi's idiosyncratic classicism, whereas the aspects of his work that inspired the flood of Italian historical novels from the 1820s onwards were of a quite different order. What the great majority of Scott's Italian followers — including, in his own unique way, Manzoni — took from the Waverley novels were the techniques of historical representation, the plots of action and adventure, and, to use the distinction just cited, the 'poetry of a more sentimental description': the emphasis on passion and pathos, that is, as opposed to imagination and romance. Partly because of the deficiencies of the translations, but also, if not more so, because of the general thrust of Italian Romanticism, *Waverley*'s central interest in these last two themes seems to have provided little material for the historical novelists, however much the book may have been enjoyed by its Italian public.

List of Italian and French Translations

This study has been made possible, or at least feasible, through the use of Google Books. The translations of Scott's novels are dispersed across a large number of European and American libraries, and the effort of viewing them in person would no doubt not have been justified. I have therefore listed below, under the titles of the original texts, the editions of the translations I have used in this chapter together with their Google IDs, wherever available; only in the case of the second and third translations of *Waverley* was I unable to find an on-line version (copies are in the National Library of Scotland), although I was not always able to find first editions of other translations on line and therefore made use of later ones (I have noted wherever this was the case). For the original versions of Scott's novels I have cited a modern scholarly edition. There is some uncertainty as to the identity of some of the French translators, but for present purposes that makes no significant difference. To save repetition, I have not given a full URL for each text but only the Google ID(s) required to retrieve it, within brackets and separated by commas where there is more than one: usually there is one ID for each volume of a text but sometimes two or more volumes are combined in a single Google version. Each text or volume can be retrieved with the URL

  https://books.google.com/books?id=XXXXXXXXXXXX

replacing XXXXXXXXXXXX with the 12-character ID code. Such items are not always easy to find because of the vagaries of Google's metadata system, but I hope that these additional details provide some indication of the potential of Google Books for research projects far larger in scope than the present one.

MALTE-BRUN, CONRAD (ed.), *Le Spectateur ou Variétés historiques, littéraires, critiques, politiques et morales*, XII (Paris: Poulet, 1814) (ID: SchTAAAAcAAJ).
 ——*Lo Spettatore ossia Varietà istoriche, letterarie, critiche, politiche e morali del Signor Malte-Brun*, trans. by Davide Bertolotti, XII (Milan: Fortunato Stella, 1814) (ID: kXgEAAAAQAAJ).
SCHLEGEL, AUGUST WILHELM, *Ueber dramatische Kunst und Literatur*, 3 vols (Heidelberg: Mohr und Zimmer, 1809–11) (IDs: alwOAAAAYAAJ, s3VKAAAAcAAJ, SxoCAAAAYAAJ).
 ——*Corso di letteratura drammatica*, trans. by Giovanni Gherardini, 3 vols (Milan: Giusti, 1817) (IDs: qNZYAAAAcAAJ, wNZYAAAAcAAJ, 3dZYAAAAcAAJ).
SCOTT, WALTER, *The Antiquary*, ed. by David Hewitt (Edinburgh: Edinburgh University Press, 1995).
 ——*L'antiquaire*, trans. by A.-J.-P. Defauconpret, 4 vols (Paris: Gosselin, 1823) (IDs: hkHfnI9b5zEC, ld-fOQTGKbQC).
 ——*L'antiquario*, trans. by Pietro Borsieri, 4 vols (Naples: Borel, 1827) (IDs: HCQ-nMweozYC, TFMEdsZmBFAC, -oLsRlLyyGYC, nMlZaTyW7t8C) (first edition Milan: Ferrario, 1823–1824).
SCOTT, WALTER, *The Black Dwarf*, ed. by Peter Garside (Edinburgh: Edinburgh University Press, 1993) and *The Tale of Old Mortality*, ed. by Douglas Mack (Edinburgh: Edinburgh University Press, 1993) (first published together as *Tales of My Landlord* in 1816).
 ——*Les puritains d'Écosse et le nain mystérieux*, trans. by A.-J.-P. Defauconpret, 4 vols (Paris: Nicolle, 1821) (IDs: izaigcqWYhsC, 2pfwUqGjE_oC, S_xarmxhIIwC).

——*Racconti del mio ostiere o sia I puritani di Scozia e Il nano misterioso*, trans.by Gaetano Barbieri, 4 vols (Milan: Tipografia di Commercio, 1822) (IDs: jAdYAAAAcAAJ, HgdYAAAAcAAJ, NAdYAAAAcAAJ, egdYAAAAcAAJ).

SCOTT, WALTER, *Ivanhoe*, ed. by Graham Tulloch (Edinburgh: Edinburgh University Press, 1998).

——*Ivanhoe, ou le retour du croisé*, trans. by A.-J.-P. Defauconpret, 2 vols (Paris: Gosselin, 1822) (IDs: CaocSZ3yp6MC) (first edition Paris: Nicolle, 1820).

——*Ivanhoe ossia Il ritorno del crociato*, trans. by Gaetano Barbieri, 4 vols (Naples: Marotta e Vanspandoch, 1826) (IDs: _4-pHa6o-mAC, Cn806p7tSiQC, XspFk7cv8L4C, SlYahAxL_ugC) (first edition Paris: Nicolle, 1820).

SCOTT, WALTER, *Kenilworth: A Romance*, ed. by J. H. Alexander (Edinburgh: Edinburgh University Press, 1993).

——*Kenilworth*, trans. by A.-J.-P. Defauconpret, 4 vols (Paris: Nicolle, 1821) (IDs: 5hVMAAAAcAAJ, dhZMAAAAcAAJ, ixZMAAAAcAAJ, 6RVMAAAAcAAJ).

——*Kenilworth*, trans. by Gaetano Barbieri, 4 vols (Naples: Marotta e Vanspandoch, 1825) (IDs: RtmsaoEfKB4C, aK3KkLDubu4C, nSszCCBEfcwC, 9MOunAKwWPAC) (first edition Milan: Ferraio, 1821).

SCOTT, WALTER, *A Legend of the Wars Of Montrose*, ed. by J. H. Alexander (Edinburgh: Edinburgh University Press, 1995).

——*Épisode des guerres de Montrose, ou l'officier de fortune*, trans. by A.-J.-P. Defauconpret, 2 vols (Paris: Gosselin, 1823) (ID: H_j__LYzcUMC) (first edition Paris: Nicolle, 1819).

——*L'officiale di Fortuna, episodio delle guerre di Montrose*, tr. Vincenzo Lancetti, 2 vols (Naples: Marotta e Vanspandoch, 1825) (IDs: wR8ewxUzLaUC, LYdUA3tp-5QC) (first edition Milan: Ferraio, 1822).

SCOTT, WALTER, *The Tale of Old Mortality*: see *The Black Dwarf*.

SCOTT, WALTER, *Waverley*, ed. by Peter Garside (Edinburgh: Edinburgh University Press, 2007).

——*Waverley ou L'Écosse il y a soixante ans*, trans. by Joseph Martin, 2 vols (Paris: Gosselin, 1822) (ID: gcMUJHLIe5MC) (first edition Paris: Perronneau, 1818).

——*Waverly o sia la Scozia sessant'anni addietro*, trans. by Virginio Soncini, 4 vols (Naples: Marotta e Vanspandoch, 1825–26) (IDs: R9TnfivY8EwC, AnPvFUT6TzIC, d19ROyzWN4oC, WrZCoXUnK8UC) (first edition Milan: Ferraio, 1822).

——*Waverley, o, Sessant'anni sono*, trans. by G.B. Bazzoni, 3 vols (Milan: Crespi, 1830).

——*Waverley, ovvero sessant'anni fa*, trans. by Carlo Rusconi, 2 vols (Padua: Minerva, 1837).

——*Waverley o Son già sessant'anni*, trans. by Carlo Rusconi (Florence: Passigli, 1844) (*Collezione dei romanzi storici e poetici di Walter Scott, Volume 1 Parte prima*) (ID: pyqDTZl3jI4C).

STAËL-HOLSTEIN, ANNE LOUISE GERMAINE DE, *De l'Allemagne*, 3 vols (London: John Murray, 1813) (IDs: 04ANAAAAQAAJ, 90ANAAAAQAAJ, AYENAAAAQAAJ) (first edition Paris: Nicolle, 1810).

——*L'Alemagna opera della signora baronessa di Staël Holstein*, trans. by Davide Bertolotti, 3 vols (Milan: Silvestri, 1814) (IDs: sdDh4QP7p-4C, tYl_ph-yfTsC, 886jOKodeTIC) (this is based on the 1813 edition above).

Notes to Chapter 14

1. *The Complete Poetical Works of Samuel Taylor* Coleridge, ed. by E.H. Coleridge, 2 vols (Oxford: Clarendon Press, 1912), I, p. 297. I am very grateful to Jeanne Clegg, Pamela Clemit, and Peter Hainsworth for comments and advice on this chapter.
2. *Grande dizionario della lingua italiana*, ed. by Salvatore Battaglia and Giorgio Bàrberi Squarotti (Turin: UTET, 1961–2009), s.v. *romantico*; *Prose e poesie di Vincenzo Monti* (Florence: Le Monnier, 1847), p. 451. See also Marilyn Butler, *Romantics, Rebels and Reactionaries* (Oxford: Oxford University Press, 1981), p. 1ff.
3. Anna Benedetti, *Le traduzioni italiane di Walter Scott e i loro anglicismi* (Florence: Olschki, 1974), p. 44, lists 11 editions, and there are a further 5 in the on-line *OPAC SBN* <http://www.iccu.sbn.it/>: see note 26. The novel with the largest number of editions in Italian seems to be *Ivanhoe*, with 16 listed by Benedetti (pp. 30–31), and no doubt more that have come to light since then.
4. Walter Scott, *Essays on Chivalry, Romance, the Drama* (Edinburgh: Cadell, 1834), p. 129.
5. *Ivanhoe; A Romance*, 3 vols (Edinburgh: Constable, 1820).
6. Where page numbers are given in the main text of this chapter, they refer to the editions listed at the end.
7. *Guy Mannering, Waverley Novels,* III (Edinburgh: Robert Cadell, 1829), p. i.
8. Details of the translations referred to in this chapter to are listed at the end, under the titles of their originals.
9. See *Dizionario Biografico degli Italiani*, s.v. Bertolotti, Davide <http://www.treccani.it/enciclopedia/davide-bertolotti_(Dizionario-Biografico)/>.
10. See Olga Ragusa, 'Italy / Romantico — Romanticismo', in Hans Eichner (ed.), *'Romantic' and its cognates: the European history of a word* (Manchester: Manchester University Press, 1972), p. 303. Ragusa's general discussion of the word *romantico* in the early 19th century is fundamental to the present discussion, though I have added further details. The analysis and discussion of the Scott translations are mine.
11. See *I manifesti romantici del 1816*, ed. by Carlo Calcaterra (Turin: UTET, 1970), pp. 114, 142.
12. The text is also in *Discussioni e polemiche sul romanticismo*, ed. by E. Bellorini, 2 vols (Bari: Laterza, 1943), I, pp. 205–07. See also Eichner (ed.), *'Romantic' and its cognates*, p. 99.
13. Ibid., p. 86.
14. Ibid., p. 265, where it is pointed out that by the end of the 18th century *romantique* had begun to establish itself in this sense in French.
15. Calcaterra, *I manifesti romantici*, pp. 297–321.
16. Ibid., pp. 414–18.
17. Ibid., pp. 364–81.
18. Alessandro Manzoni, *Opere*, ed. Lanfranco Caretti (Milan: Mursia, 1973), pp. 1156, 1158.
19. Ibid., p. 1156; also *passim* in *Lettre a M. C*** sur l'unité de temps et de lieu dans la tragédie* (1820) and in the later *Del romanzo storico e, in genere, de' componimenti misti di storia e d'invenzione, Opere*, pp. 855–910, 1163–1211. In the latter (p. 1168) Scott is famously described as 'l'Omero del romanzo storico'; but Manzoni also criticized him for not being sufficiently true to history in the depiction of Richard Lionheart in *Ivanhoe* (letter of 1822 to Claude Fauriel in Alessandro Manzoni, *Tutte le opere*, ed. by A. Chiari and F. Ghisalberti, 7 vols (Milan: Mondadori, 1970), vol. 7, ed. by Cesare Arieti, part 1, p. 245).
20. In a letter of 1827: N. Tommaseo and G.P. Vieusseux, *Carteggio inedito*, ed. by R. Ciampini and P. Cureanu (Rome: Edizioni di Storia e Letteratura, 1956), I, pp. 97–98.
21. Franca Ruggieri Punzo, *Walter Scott in Italia, 1821–1971* (Bari: Adriatica, 1975), particularly pp. 20–21.
22. See Benedetti, *Le traduzioni italiane*, pp. 47–72. Benedetti does not identify Defauconpret as the anonymous translator of *Old Mortality* used by Barbieri, but more recent work takes the opposite view: see Paul Barnaby, 'Another Tale of Old Mortality: The Translations of Auguste-Jean-Baptiste Defauconpret in the French Reception of Scott', in *The Reception of Sir Walter Scott in Europe*, ed. by Murray Pittock (London: Bloomsbury, 2006), pp. 31–44 and 328 (for reasons that

are not explained, this very useful volume does not, unfortunately, include a chapter on Italy). See also the on-line *Bibliography of Scottish Literature in Translation* <http://boslit.nls.uk/vwebv/holdingsInfo?searchId=13&recCount=25&recPointer=2&bibId=24774>.

23. General Preface to Walter Scott, *Waverley Novels*, 48 vols (Edinburgh: Cadell, 1829–33), I, p. ii ff.
24. See also the interesting discussion, leading to rather different conclusions, of *Waverley* as romance in Edgar A. Dryden, '*Waverley* and American Romance: The Thematics of Form', *Genre*, 18 (1985), 335–61.
25. Georg Lukács, *The Historical Novel* (London: Penguin, 1969), pp. 29–69. We need not attach much weight to Scott's description of Waverley in a letter of 1814 as a 'sneaking piece of imbecility' (*Letters*, ed. by Sir Herbert Grierson, 12 vols (London: Constable, 1932–37), III, 478). Scott the letter-writer and Scott the novelist are not necessarily the same.
26. Benedetti, *Le traduzioni italiane*, p. 44, lists eight editions of Soncini's translation, and there are a further four in the on-line *Catalogo SBN* <http://www.iccu.sbn.it/>: Naples: Marotta e Vanspandoch, 1826; Naples: Giovanni Rusconi, 1829; Naples: Marotta e Vanspandoch, 1830; Naples: Gaetano Nobile, 1847. In the same catalogue there are no further editions of Rusconi's 1837 translation, and one further edition of his 1844 translation (Rome: Natali, 1847).
27. See Benedetti, *Le traduzioni italiane*, p. 57ff.; Luigi Fassò, *Giambattista Bazzoni (1803–1850): Contributo alla storia del romanzo storico italiano* (Città di Castello: S. Lapi, 1906).
28. *A Legend of Montrose of the Author of Waverley In Two Volumes* (Berlin: Adolph Martin Schlesinger, 1823). Volume I is at <https://books.google.co.uk/books?id=c8JMAAAAcAAJ>; I have not seen volume II.
29. See note 26.
30. Barnaby, 'Another Tale', pp. 31–44. In addition to Lukács's discussion in *The Historical Novel*, see the brief account of Scott's political attitudes in Butler, *Romantics, Rebels and Reactionaries*, pp. 109–12.
31. Giacomo Leopardi, *Opere*, ed. by Giovanni Getto (Milan: Mursia, 1967), p. 903.
32. Ibid., p. 1088; see *Tutte le opere di Giacomo Leopardi. Le lettere*, ed. by Francesco Flora (Milan: Mondadori, 1949), pp. 796–97.
33. Leopardi, *Opere*, pp. 445–507.
34. In a letter to Giampietro Vieusseux, Recanati 1828: *Tutte le opere di Giacomo Leopardi. Le lettere*, p. 658.

CHAPTER 15

Hypatia of Alexandria, Pagan or Christian? Propaganda Wars between John Toland's *Hypatia* of 1720 and Diodata Saluzzo's *Ipazia* of 1827

Letizia Panizza

Diodata Saluzzo (1775–1840) worked on *Ipazia, ovvero delle filosofie: poema* ('Hypatia; or, concerning philosophical schools: in verse') for many years. Her heroine, the eminent philosopher Hypatia of Alexandria, born *c.* 370, was put to death cruelly in 415. Saluzzo, of a cultured aristocratic Piedmontese family, was famed mainly for her poetry, *novelle*, tragedies and comedies. *Ipazia*, published in 1827, was at the time her crowning glory, though it is only recently that it has begun to receive attention. Her father had been one of the founders of the Reale Accademia delle Scienze di Torino, and she was the very first woman to be admitted. (Membership of an Academy was limited to a chosen few, distinguished for their contributions to the arts and sciences.) She acknowledged the honour in a short Dedicatory Letter to the Academicians at the beginning of *Ipazia*. Saluzzo astounded the literary world by publishing her first poetry collection, *Versi* (Turin, 1796) when she was only twenty; Ludovico Di Breme thought her poem *Le rovine*, a melancholy meditation on the ruins of the family castle at Saluzzo, to be the perfect Romantic poem; and the chief literary celebrity of the age, Alessandro Manzoni, aided her personally in the publication of her *novelle*. She was brought up among Catholic intellectuals, and enjoyed a correspondence with other cultured women poets like Luisa Bergalli and Faustina Maratti Zappi.[1]

A premonition of the kind of philosophy her poem is concerned with is furnished by a quotation from Dante on the verso of the title page:

> 'Filosofia [...] a chi l'attende
> nota, non pare in una sola parte,
> come Natura; lo suo corso prende
> dal divino intelletto e sua arte.'[2] (*Inferno*, XI. 97–100)

The context tells all: Dante and Virgil have been in the circle of heretics, just inside the walls of the City of Dis, appropriate region for hardened sinners. The heretics are buried in open flaming tombs on sterile, rocky ground. The last heretic, identified only by an inscription on a tombstone, is Pope Anastasius II who, according to legend, sympathized with a cleric belonging to a Greek heretical sect that denied the divinity of Christ. Pope Anastasius died in 498, the same century as Hypatia and Cyril, one full of theological and philosophical disputes and violent confrontations. The message is ominous: fomenting or supporting religious 'error' leads not only to eternal punishment in hell, but also to personal annhilation. A large part of Canto XI is devoted to Virgil's lecture on the organization of Hell, including the ways God is offended by the abuse of His gifts, especially the gift of reason. Just as a child resembles his father, so Nature resembles God, its creator. Likewise human industry, *arte*, imitates Nature and can be called God's grandchild. Virgil then links philosophy with the philosophy of nature, the content of Aristotle's *Physics*, carefully studied by Dante, as Virgil reminds him:

> e se tu ben la tua *Fisica* note,
> tu troverai, non dopo molte carte,
>   che l'arte vostra, quella, quanto puote,
> segue, come 'l maestro fa il discente;
> sì che vostr'arte a Dio quasi è nepote.
>   Da queste due, se tu ti rechi a mente
> lo Genesí dal principio, convene
> prender sua vita ed avanzar la gente. (XI. 101–08)

Anastasius should have learned about nature from Aristotle and Genesis that Christ's nature came from God as well as from a human being. Saluzzo's entire twenty cantos are in *terza rima* — Dante's own choice — interspersed with lyrical rhymes in varying metres. Dante is Saluzzo's guide, showing her how to deal with the *filosofie* of her title. The various sects have denied or misconstrued the supreme source of truth, the Christian God, and are consequently heretical, except for Aristotelianism, never condemned by Dante or Saluzzo, and some aspects of Neoplatonism. Furthermore, they erred precisely in not following Aristotle's *Physics*, in not understanding that, as told in Genesis, Nature is God's child, the divine *arte*. As *Ipazia* unfolds, Saluzzo illustrates how divine revelation, found in the Catholic faith, trumps imperfect human knowledge. Saluzzo binds Hypatia to the Dante quotation by emphasizing (see Preface, below) that Hypatia's speciality was natural philosophy. Its inadequacy then led her to higher truths and Christianity. This is a strange decision to take, and contrary to historical evidence: Hypatia was never a Christian. So why did Saluzzo insist? A clue lies in the same Preface, where she points to those who blacken the Catholic Church by affirming that it connived in the murder of the pagan philosopher Hypatia: Saluzzo names one person, 'il troppo celebre inglese, Tolando' (p. xviii). Condemned by Catholics and High Anglicans, adulated by a whole cabal — as Saluzzo puts it — of eighteenth-century French *philosophes*, she is referring to the English free-thinker and, by reputation, atheist, John Toland, author of a pamphlet on Hypatia. The words 'troppo celebre' are a sarcastic, scornful epithet implying that his fame for writing *Hypatia* is worthless, achieved by mendacity. She, Saluzzo will write the correct version of events.

My aim here is to show that Saluzzo's *Ipazia* makes sense in order to absolve Christians, especially the Bishop of Alexandria at the time, St Cyril, from all guilt.

Hers is a polemical response to Toland and others like him, just as his is polemical. So in examining each work, I shall focus on the kind of sources each author makes use of in portraying Hypatia and Cyril, and on the two issues at the heart of their works: was Hypatia pagan, as Toland argues, or Christian, as Saluzzo asserts?

John Toland's *Hypatia* (London, 1720)

Born a Catholic in Northern Ireland in 1670, Toland renounced Roman Catholicism as a teenager, studied at Protestant English and European universities, learned Latin, Greek, Hebrew and other Biblical languages, and became a renowned Orientalist, follower of the Biblical criticism of Richard Simon on the Old and New Testaments,[3] and a historian of early Christianity.[4] Toland pored over Greek Christian theologians and historians of the Church, recording mainly in English the many clashes, disagreements and assimilations between Greek pagan culture and the new religion. His scholarship, however, served to disillusion him about the validity of institutional religion, which included for him Judaism, Christianity and Islam, because none of these religions could be verified by reason. Instead, they appealed to the authority of written texts whose interpretation lay in the hands of self-appointed clerics.

Toland was not an atheist, but a Deist and a Pantheist; that is, he based his notion of God on philosophy and rational argument.[5] He upheld public toleration of religions, however, even writing a pamphlet defending citizenship for Jews in England. He also upheld republicanism, which made him a political outcast as well as a religious one: he was not averse to criticizing monarchies for using religion to justify oppressive laws. Nevertheless, by the year of his death, 1722, his writings were eagerly read by Enlightenment thinkers in England, where he had absorbed Hobbes and Locke, and in turn was taken up by Hume. In France, *philosophes* such as Voltaire, Bayle and Spinoza admired him, all of which further added to his notoriety among Catholics and Protestants. Toland, they said, was 'godless', an amoral persecutor of pious, upright believers.[6] Italians could have read some of his writings in French, and perhaps through the Socinian Protestants, founded by Lelio and Fausto Sozzini in the sixteenth century. Toland found support for his anti-Trinitarian opinions in their writings.[7]

Toland's *Hypatia*, the third in a group of four essays called *Tetradymus*, was the first serious study of the life and death of Hypatia based entirely on Greek material. He wrote it in English with marginal notes giving precise details about the sources. Toland is erudite, but he is also angry, as the very title indicates:

> *HYPATIA. OR THE HISTORY* of the most virtuous, most learned, and every way most accomplished LADY; WHO was torn to pieces by the CLERGY of Alexandria, to gratify the pride, emulation, and cruelty of their ARCHBISHOP, commonly but undeservedly stil'd St. CYRIL.

Nothing could be more black and white: Hypatia is the glory of her sex, Cyril the disgrace of his, 'for women have no less reason to value themselves that there existed a Lady of such accomplishments without the least blemish, than men could be ashamed that any could be found [...] of so brutal and savage a disposition' (I, 104).

Most of the sources, he tells us, agree on her supreme position as head of the Academy in Alexandria, and the manner of her death. Furthermore, Toland is impressed by the number of women philosophers active in these early centuries, of whom he has chosen only one, Hypatia, who had a large number of historians and philosophers write about her. The two most important for Hypatia are the ecclesiastical historian, and lawyer, Socrates Scholasticus (c. 380–450), and Synesius of Cyrene (c. 370–413), her most brilliant student and lifelong correspondent, both contemporaries.[8] Another contemporary historian, Philostorgius, also knew her, and wrote that he considered her superior in astronomical matters to her father Theon.[9] The other sources Toland cites are Damascius (462–540), who wrote the *Life of Isidore*, a philosopher who was his teacher; Nicephorus (two of them, Gregoras and Callistus, both of the fourteenth century, and paraphrasers of Socrates); Hesychius of Milesius (sixth-century compiler of an encyclopedia, *Onomatologus*, and the *Suda* (an invaluable tenth-century compilation of excerpts from works of literature, history and philosophy).[10] Modern scholarship has not improved on Toland's list; it has merely refined some details. Toland's animosity towards Cyril was not just due to his hatred of Hypatia; Toland loathed Cyril's theology: the Patriarch was a fervent follower of an earlier Patriarch of Alexandria, Athanasius, who fought Arians at the Council of Nicaea in 325, had the Council declare them heretics, burn their books, and banish Arians to a remote part of the Empire. For Toland, these bitter disputes made toleration impossible.

Putting together all his sources as in a mosaic, and careful to cite in the margin which one he uses, Toland concentrates on Hypatia's character and achievements first, and then the conflicts between Cyril and civic authorities under the Roman prefect or governor, Orestes, a Christian. Toland is moved by the deep admiration shown by Synesius in his letters to Hypatia: 'the grateful testimony he everywhere bears to the Learning and Virtue of Hypatia, whom he never mentions without the profoundest, and sometimes in terms of affection coming little short of adoration' (VII, p. 111). Synesius discussed with her abstruse matters such as the astrolabe and the hydroscope, turned to her for advice about his treatise *On Dreams* (used for divination, dreams needed 'correct' interpretation), and addressed her as 'The Philosopher'. Deakin, a mathematician himself, gives us more detailed descriptions of her achievements than any other writer. The two great masters of mathematics in Alexandria were Euclid, known even today for his *Elements* of geometry; and Ptolemy, famous for his description of the solar system and the motion of the planets, the *Almagest*. Euclid also wrote on *Conics,* which received fuller treatment from Apollonius; and other parts of geometry were developed into algebra or number theory by Diophantus. Theon, Hypatia's father, wrote commentaries on the *Almagest*, and credited his daughter with adding to and improving an earlier version. Hypatia herself commented on Apollonius in her *Conics*, and also contributed to number theory with her own commentary on Diophantus, thus attaining renown as a mathematician and astronomer.[11] Toland is aware of her production, and also of the fact that she received public acclaim. Deakin concludes that, in an age of few great mathematicians and astronomers, she was the best, and enjoyed the highest reputation. Toland knew that she attracted pupils to Alexandria from far and wide, and within the city had bent the ears of magistrates and the Roman Prefect, Orestes. Toland reports that, according to the *Suda*,

> she explained all the Philosophers, that is, all the several sects with the particular tenets of their founders, which shows an inexpressible elevation and capacity, each of these separately being thought a sufficient province to exercise the diligence of any one man. (IV, p.108)

Cyril was apparently incandescent with anger and envy, and so were his followers. The sources conflict on an issue essential for Saluzzo's later depiction of Hypatia: did she marry? Her contemporaries, Synesius and Socrates Scholasticus, never mention marriage, but Damascius's *Life of Isidore* says that a Hypatia married the philosopher Isidore. Since Damascius was writing about his own teacher flourishing at the end of the 400s, several decades after Hypatia's death, Toland is rightly sceptical: 'I frankly confess that I more than suspect many of the things he reports, as knowing that Damascius was a great visionary [...] but this ought not to affect his credit in matters of an ordinary nature' (XIII, p. 120). Nevertheless, Toland is still puzzled that Damascius does not waste many words on such a prominent woman in the *Life of Isidore*. He even insults Hypatia, saying that she was inferior to Isidore as a philosopher to a geometer, or as a man to a woman! Toland is shocked; this problem cannot be solved without more and better manuscripts (XIV, p. 122). Modern critics confirm that the Hypatia in Damascius could not be our Hypatia.

One author comes in for criticism: Cesare Baronio, an Italian priest, member of St Philip Neri's Oratorians, and Vatican Librarian. He put together the first truly scholarly history of the early Church up to 1198, making use of manuscripts in the Vatican and ones sent to him from all over Europe. His *Annales ecclesiastici* were published in twelve volumes from 1586 to 1607.[12] Baronius's account of Hypatia's death, however, may have added to Toland's dislike of him. On the one hand, his praise of Hypatia is unreserved: a pagan, 'she made progress in so many branches of letters that she surpassed all the philosophers of her age by far; at home and elsewhere; and people called her the most famous philosopher'.[13] On the other hand, he absolves Cyril of all culpability for Hypatia's torture and murder. Toland is also critical that Synesius, the Neoplatonic pupil of Hypatia, was made a bishop, 'not withstanding his protestation that he disbeliev'd some of the most essential articles of the Christian religion'. Toland shows that he had read letters of Synesius where he expresses his reluctance at being made bishop, and also other works where after his profession of faith, Toland remarks, Synesius appears as heathen as before. Why did not anyone seem to care about such a serious matter? Instead, they covered up the deficiency by 'pitiful excuses, or rather prevarications, invented by some learned men to defend him [...] the principal is Baronius' (VI, pp. 110–11). Toland was quick to sniff out a forgery when he read one: a letter purported to be written by Hypatia to Cyril discussing the Nestorian heresy and the calculation of the dates for Easter. The Nestorian heresy flourished at the end of the fifth century, long after Hypatia's death. Saluzzo would later accept the letter as genuine, proof of Hypatia's conversion.[14]

About Cyril and the circumstances leading up to Hypatia's murder, there is no such hesitation. Cyril's fierce reputation manifested itself shortly after he succeeded his uncle Theophilus as Bishop of Alexandria in 412. At the time — Toland follows Socrates — Hypatia was an advisor to Orestes, a pagan advising a Christian. Why wasn't Orestes turning to him, Cyril, for spiritual advice? Cyril resented her dominance. His first target were the Novatians, a Christian splinter group; Cyril closed down their churches and plundered their sacred vessels. Their doctrines were the same as Cyril's, Toland asserts, but they differed in discipline; that is, they owed obedience to a different authority. Toland's judgment is sour: 'if [a Christian] be ever so right, or at least ever so agreeable to that prescrib'd in the society whereof he's a member; yet if he boggles at any part of the public ritual and discipline, he ... rends the Unity of the Church, that is, he weakens the Government of the Clergy' (XVI, p. 125). Cyril's next target was the Jews; he objected to their Sabbath outdoor celebrations, and sent a spy to cause mischief. He was reported to Orestes, who had him tortured. When the spy died, Cyril unleashed a whirlwind, leading a pogrom that resulted in the expulsion of all the Jews from Alexandria, where, Toland specifies, 'they had liv'd in great opulence from the time of Alexander the Great, to the no small benefit of the place' (XVII, p. 126). Cyril in these forays had at his disposal a private militia of five hundred monks from Nitria. The Roman governor Orestes did not.[15] Perhaps realizing his excesses, especially his usurpation of the laws and authority of the state, Cyril tried to ingratiate himself with Orestes, who spurned this offer of a supposed reconciliation.

After the Jews came Orestes. Cyril ordered his shock-troops to taunt Orestes' bodyguard. Orestes was then hit on the head with a rock and nearly died, despite calling out to the military monks that he was a Christian. On his recovery, he had the leader of the Nitrian monks tortured and put to death. Cyril lost no time in making him a martyr and a saint. Now it was the turn of Hypatia, blamed for preventing the reconciliation of Orestes with Cyril: this time, Peter the Lector was the ringleader: 'and watching their opportunity, when she was returning home from some place, they dragg'd her out of her chair, dragg'd her to the church call'd Cesar's, and stripping her stark naked, they kill'd her with tiles. Then they tore her to pieces, and carrying her limbs to a place call'd Cinaron, they burnt them to ashes' (XIX, p. 130). Toland does not depart from Socrates about the gruesome facts of her death.[16]

Given Cyril's record of brutality against his opponents in the name of religious zeal, it is hard not to believe that he played a part in this murder, or at least did nothing to prevent it. These monks owed obedience to him alone, and could be rounded up in a few days. Toland is at a loss for enough suitable words to condemn this crime: nothing can be found to parallel the savagery against Hypatia, a woman of such distinction. Toland spends the last chapters evaluating Cyril's character and actions. Cyril, he believes, could not acknowledge any authority superior to his own, certainly not the state, in the hands of laymen, and even less the authority of a woman like Hypatia. Toland denies that Cyril should be considered a Christian, let alone a saint: 'I would think it no difficult task to show that neither the doctrines nor the distinctions in vogue were ever taught by Christ or his Apostles.' Prophetically, he condemns writers who distort the truth: that is, 'those that resemble [the murderers] by substituting precarious Traditions, Scholastic fictions, and an usurp'd Dominion, to the salutiferous institution of the holy Jesus' (XXI, p. 134). How could orthodox Catholics be pleased by this reversal of roles?

Diodata Saluzzo's Preface to *Ipazia*

Saluzzo's Preface instructs readers about her literary construction of Hypatia's story. Immediately, she defines her genre as the *romanzo*, that is, the novel; not just any kind of novel, she qualifies, but the 'romanzo istorico e filosofico', a demanding type of novel requiring erudition as well as imagination. Most of the preface is given to justifying or at least defending her poetic licence, her right, as it were, to stretch the boundaries of verisimilitude. Her choice of subject-matter, the philosopher Hypatia and her horrifying death, has been made, as mentioned above, with polemic intent: to crush the perversity of Toland. As we might expect, her narrative turns the tables on him: Cyril is restored to sanctity, a kind and humble priest. Hypatia is converted to Christianity by his words and deeds. She is put to death by mad, fanatical pagans. Her observation of various philosophical sects dissatisfies her. Only religion, the Christian religion, bestows the truth.

Her settings are clear enough. Time: 'sul principio del Quinto secolo dopo Gesù Cristo, nello scemare e finire dell'immenso potere romano' (Preface, p. xi). Where does this bold assertion of the decline and fall of the Roman Empire at the beginning of the fourth century come from? Her sources are few, as we shall see, but revealing. But in any case hers is not a lament that Rome had fallen, but a triumphal hymn: Christianity had vanquished paganism. As in Dante, there is a *selva oscura*, where stands a temple dedicated to the pagan Egyptian gods, Isis and Osiris. Near the temple are a marshy lake and a cemetery, where unspeakable pagan rites take place. On the other side, a pleasant open space: 'la valle abitata dai Cristiani,' appropriate for lowly self-effacing Christians. And, yes, there is a plain, simple 'chiesetta' under Cyril's ministry.

Most objections arise with the chronology of her historical characters. The 'personaggio principalissimo' is of course 'la celebre Ipazia', daughter of Theon (who is banished from her poem without any mention of his intellectual standing). For Saluzzo, Hypatia is a resolute virgin for whom marriage and being a Christian are incompatible. She refuses marriage to a noble pagan Isidore, not the philosopher of Damascius's *Life of Isidore*, but the last of the Ptolemy dynasty, one of Saluzzo's fictions:

> Ho lasciato a lei [Ipazia] quel certo, soave, e direi divino candore, che adorna la bellezza e l'anima d'una vergine in qualunque culto ella viva. L'Ipazia di questo Poema è Cristiana; misteri del suo cuore agitato sono ugualmente il nobile amor suo [per Isidoro], e la religione santa che lo combatte. L'amante suo, invitto liberatore della patria, non è Cristiano; ed ella, nel rifiutarne le nozze, trova una morte terribile fra il tumulto e la Guerra civile. (Preface, p. xvii)

Famous Neoplatonists like Plotinus and Iamblichus suffer strange fates, even though she grants that 'non veri gli eventi che riguardano costoro nel Poema' (p. xx). This is a gross understatement. Plotinus (205–69/70) was the illustrious head of the Academy in Alexandria before he left in 250 for Rome. He died in Italy. Saluzzo has reduced him to the status of guardian and mentor to both Hypatia (born, remember, over a century and a half later in 370), and her royal lover Isidore. He has no position in the Academy. Iamblichus, who died in 325, a good half-century before Hypatia's birth, is presented as a recently dead spirit in Hell. A mathematician and follower of Pythagoras, he also practised Chaldean magic. He is mourned by a fictitious besotted pagan lover, Aristea, who tries to converse with his spirit. Saluzzo's other historical character is Anfilia, described as 'donna di gran fama e d'ingegno [...] professava la filosofia'. In Saluzzo's *romanzo*, she is the sister of Aristea. I suggest she is Amphiclea, married to Iamblichus's son Ariston. The philosopher would thus not be her father, but her father-in-law.

Saluzzo's fiction would have us believe that the Academy is in the hands of a villainous usurper: 'Finsi nel Poema [...] un lascivo ambizioso ministro e sacerdote, che professando tutte le religioni, né ad alcuna credendo, serve a tutti i tiranni ed a tutte le sette' (p. xiv). This pretender, furthermore, is the ringleader of a plot to overthrow, with the aid of the dark arts, 'tutti gli altari della religione cristiana'. Within the structure of the poem, he is undoubtedly the dramatic opposite of Cyril. Is this arch-doubter meant to bring to mind the heretics of Dante, or perhaps more modern heretics like Toland, who did indeed examine many religions, and preached Deism and Pantheism, which for Catholics was the same as atheism? No wonder that Hypatia wants nothing to do with devil-worshippers.

In the course of her Preface, Saluzzo draws in Lodovico Muratori to determine that the year of Hypatia's death, 415, was also the year of 'fieri tumulti succeduti nella città d'Alessandria' (p. xvi). This, too, is twisted into a struggle of Egyptians against their occupiers, the Romans, and pagans against Christians. Muratori, instead, is referring to the expulsion of the Jews from Alexandria by Cyril![17] Saluzzo never alludes to Cyril's persecution of the Jews, or to conflicts among Christians. She weaves a tapestry of her own. The conflict is part of a revolution in which the Egyptians are fighting 'ora per la possanza delle loro passioni, ora per quella non minore delle loro opinioni' (Preface, pp. xiii-xiv). Departing even further from history, the conflict takes on the colours of a crusade of good versus evil, in which strong patriotic hues merge with expected moral and religious ones:

> Scopo morale del mio scritto è, prima di ogni altra cosa, mostrare che porre lo stato in civili contese, onde mutarne le leggi proprie ed antiche, è colpevole mezzo di menzognera felicità. [...] [I]l saldo operoso amore della venerata terra non cresce, se non in petti generosi ed amatori così delle rigide virtù come del culto religioso avito; e finalmente, che ammirabili sono l'ingegno ed il valore solamente quando sono con fede sincera adoperati per la vera gloria della patria. (pp. xxi-xxii)

In the above passage, it is hard to believe that Saluzzo is writing about ancient Alexandria, but rather about contemporary Europe and especially northern Italy.

The wars she is referring to reflect the French Revolution, which threw over old laws and religious rites with little respect for the *ancien régime* and Catholic religion, the 'culto religioso avito'. Perhaps she also had in mind Napoleon's invasion of northern Italy and the subjection of most of the peninsula to French rule.[18]

Despite the high praise, there is nothing in these pages about Hypatia's specific accomplishments, merely a general allusion to her learning. Hypatia's fictional refusal to marry the last of the pagan Ptolemies is the reason for her downfall and death. Suspecting some doubts about her version of events, Saluzzo faces her ancient sources and modern enemies, singling out Toland as the one who dared to attribute her death to the Christians:

> Dalla maggior parte degli antichi istorici vien detta Ipazia acerba nemica dei Cristiani; ed anzi non mancò chi loro apponesse la morte di lei. [...] Il troppo celebre Inglese Tolando niega essere d'Ipazia una lettera, che sua credevasi da molti, scritta a S. Cirillo intorno al ciclo pasquale, lettera in cui Nestorio vien chiamato empio.[19] (p. xviii)

This alleged letter of Hypatia to Cyril is the only shred of evidence Saluzzo relies on for Hypatia's conversion. As for Hypatia being an 'acerba nemica' of Christians according to the majority of ancient historians, this is another false claim: either she knows nothing of Hypatia's long friendship with Synesius, a Christian bishop, or she chose to ignore it. Saluzzo ties herself up in further knots by stating that since there is no certainty about Hypatia's conversion, she can say what she wants; and then asserting that, since Hypatia was exceedingly virtuous and a virgin, she must be a Christian: 'siccome sarebbe, nella oscurità di quei secoli, difficile l'indagare qual fosse la credenza d'Ipazia, ci basterà di ricordare, siccome tutti concordemente dicono che altissimo avea l'animo, la virtù severa e non dubbia giammai, e nobilissimo il costume' (pp. xviii-xix). At this point, Saluzzo concedes that her Hypatia is a literary hermaphrodite, half-historical, half-fictional, and appeals to the French historical-didactic novel about the son of Ulysses, Telemachus, and the ancient Greek poet Sappho. Why shouldn't she be allowed to do the same with Hypatia? And why does it matter if she chooses to keep the name and invent a fictional character?[20]

> E, se pure si vuole ch'ella cristiana non fosse, allora l'Ipazia di questo Poema, assomigliantesi alla vera Ipazia, sarà personaggio non istorico, con nome vero e celebre, qual'è Telemaco tra' i Francesi. [...] Mi sarebbe stato facil cosa sostituire altro nome di donna allora vivente al caro nome d' Ipazia se mai l'incredula filosofia richiamasse per proprio quel fantasma poetico, sotto il cui velo ho adombrata la dotta e casta vergine cristiana. (p. xix)

At the core of statements like this is a deep confusion about the historical novel, the *romanzo*, in a period when this genre was at its zenith in Western Europe.[21] Saluzzo was a member of an Academy which had contacts with literary figures in France; she corresponded with Alessandro Manzoni, who took care to see that two of her *novelle* were published.[22] Cesare d'Azeglio, father of Massimo who married Manzoni's daughter, wrote a kind review of *Ipazia*, mentioning he knew Diodata and her poetry.[23]

Saluzzo is defiant: Hypatia is a Christian, no matter what the historians say. Moreover, competing philosophies (by which we are meant to understand ideologies, especially religions) subvert a nation because there can be no coherent ethical system to underpin law and order. Therefore, she concludes, how much better, how much more powerful is the perfect, universal Christian philosophy (p. xxii).

It is highly unlikely that Saluzzo read Toland's *Hypatia* first-hand, or that she read the Greek sources even in translation. Her information was second-hand: if we glance at the last page of her Preface, headed 'Annotazioni' (p. xxiv), there are four notes. The first is about geography. The second refers to an Egyptologist, 'Signor Letronne', who published his *Recherches* on the history of Egypt in 1823.[24] The third is a much older Italian contemporary, Agatopisto Cromaziano (1717–1793), also known as Appiano Buonafede, a polymath priest, satirist and historian ceaselessly debunking all critics of Catholicism and its clergy. He is almost certainly the authority for her knowledge of the philosopher Isidore and his marriage to Hypatia. Saluzzo lets slip in this note that Cromaziano discusses 'frammenti dell'opera di Damascio raccolti da Suida'. Damascius was the author of the *Life* of the philosopher Isidore who lived after Hypatia's death and mentions briefly a wife called Hypatia (see above, p. 219). Cromaziano's work, *Della istoria e della indole di ogni filosofia* (7 vols, Lucca: Riccomini, 1766–81), is cited a few times throughout the poem. Beginning with John the Baptist, Cromaziano takes his readers through the Egyptians, Greeks, Romans and moderns (including Ralph Cudworth, John Locke and Toland), to prove that Christian philosophy — philosophy, theology, religion are all the same — brings truth to full bloom as in Saluzzo's interpretation of her Dante epigraph. Written in Italian and meant for the well-educated, lay Catholic reader, it constitutes his *vademecum*. Most importantly, Cromaziano has a section on Hypatia and Cyril, and frequently quotes Greek and Latin sources for the philosophies he discusses. Saluzzo uses the same names in her own few notes.[25] What he has to say about Hypatia is fairly brief; what he has to say about Cyril includes a long polemic against those who blame him.

Oddly, Cromaziano does not fit Hypatia into a chapter on Neoplatonism, but into Eclectic philosophy, which includes Cynics, Stoics, Plutarch and Proclus.[26] He follows Socrates on Hypatia's beauty and learning:

> Ipazia, bella e dotta Vergine ad Alessandria, la quale da Teone suo padre matematico di buon nome [...] avendo già apprese le Lettere e la Geometria e l'Astronomia [...] amplificò il saper suo oltre l' angustie paterne. [...] [L]a sua casa parve il Tempio della Sapienza [...] e insieme il Santuario della Castità.
> (Vol. V, p. 226)

There is no mention of Theon's position within a philosophical community, nor of Hypatia's. When he comes to her death, Cromaziano departs from Socrates, falsifying the ancient Greek sources. Hypatia was murdered by a gang of thugs, 'una masnada di uomini' opposed to Roman Orestes, the Prefect. They killed her, tore her limb from limb and burned her remains. It was a 'terribil tragedia'. What about Cyril? Some have accused Cyril and his monks, he says, but this is 'falsa e immaginaria', spread by enemies of Christianity. A more moderate opinion is given by Socrates, continues wily Cromaziano, who wrote that Orestes' opponents thought Hypatia was influencing him. That is as far as Cromaziano will go regarding Hypatia's death. His real concern is exonerating Cyril of all blame. He expresses false surprise that the noted Protestant historian Jacob Brucker, on whom Cromaziano depends for his own history of philosophy, aired the view that Cyril was not without blame, and that Hypatia's murder did not displease him. Worse than Brucker is the author of the French *Encyclopédie* (Pierre Bayle?) who dared to attack Cyril. Cromaziano translates from the French, yet the words are suspiciously like Toland's. Cyril was 'imperioso, violento, strascinato da zelo malinteso, geloso [...] irritator della plebe contro la Vergine innocente' (Vol. V, p. 228). This is just what Saluzzo thinks.

One other name occurs in note four; the earlier and more historically rigorous Sebastian Le Nain de Tillemont (1637–1698), an aristocratic Jansenist historian, also a priest. From him, she maintains, comes knowledge of Hypatia's alleged letter to Cyril — recognized by Toland as a forgery — 'dov'ella mostra la volontà di farsi Cristiana'. These two historians, especially the latter, endow some superficial respectability to her *romanzo*; nevertheless, Cromaziano is her major source as far as philosophy goes. As he treats each philosophy separately, there is no history of philosophy as such, no sense of what philosophy was at a given time or a given place. Saluzzo does the same; the result is a failure for historical verisimilitude: she imagines all of them in Alexandria in 415, the year of Hypatia's death.

The Poem

Saluzzo's poetry, in an archaizing Italian, while using *terza rima* for the narrative, bursts into several metrical forms for hymns, prayers, incantations and philosophical rhapsodies. I shall give a few examples that also show how she puts Cromaziano to use in combating her arch-enemy Toland. From the beginning, Saluzzo depicts the happy family of Plotinus and his two wards Hypatia and Isidore last of the Ptolemies, whom he brings up together: 'Nessun severo studio ad essa increbbe; | Plotin, tra' muri del Liceo, la diva | fanciulla ed Isidoro uniti crebbe' (p. 7). In her note on Canto I, Saluzzo again cites Cromaziano on the religion and rites of the Egyptian Magi (p. 22); she has had Hypatia observe the Magus Artapane in the dark forest with Aristea surrounded by torches calling up the spirit of her lost lover, Iamblichus:

> Minacciose le fiaccole ardenti
> son degli astri ne' cieli roventi,
> su la nube la nube ricade,
> ed i venti — con lunghi lamenti
> van dicendo: ritorna chi fu.
>
> I portenti — de' nuovi momenti
> rivolventi — la polve de' spenti
> agli spirti nudriti di fuoco
> schiudon loco — fra carmi possenti;
> nuovi carmi d'immensa virtù. (p. 13)

Catching sight of Hypatia, the Magus turns prophet:

> Trema, infeconda vergine,
> trema, ché il vero mancati
> primo d'Iddio tesoro,
> santa fecondità. (p. 14)

Hypatia listens to the incantations that bring up the dreadful sight of the dead and the damned, still the onlooker:

> Già le pare di veder gl'immondi spirti
> sorgere pel nefando altrui potere,
> ed in mostri cangiarsi e palme e mirti. (p. 18)

There is no doubt that these are 'spiriti perduti', like Dante's damned in *Inferno*; Artapane's sinister rites are broken only by the sudden arrival of Isidore, 'il magnanimo guerrier,' to sweep Hypatia away, and the welcome break of dawn.

    The message that these ancient Egyptian rites deal with demonic forces far from the 'truth' is reinforced in Canto II, where Hypatia experiences a worse priest, Altifone. Isidore has her spy on him to gather intelligence about a plot he is hatching to overthrow Roman rule. Isidore wants to prevent the rebellion. Altifone has many roles: high priest of Osiris, arch-conspirator, and, most unbelievable of all, head of the Platonic Academy (which should be Hypatia's position). Recognizing Hypatia, he delivers another doom-laden prophecy: 'esce dal cuore | la tua favella, e pure il dì veloce | s' appressa, in cui prevedo il tuo dolore' (II, p. 30). At the end of the canto, Saluzzo mentions Cromaziano again, plus an essay on the rites of Isis and Osiris by Plutarch (from his *Moralia*); and also a hymn in Apuleius, *The Golden Ass*, in praise of Isis. The last two are listed by Cromaziano.[27] After a hymn in praise of the sun, bringer of life, Altifone intones a more philosophical hymn, Neoplatonic in tone — after all, he is head of the Academy — praising an unknown, unspeakable One, creator and sustainer of all:

> Ignoto, alto, terribile
> del ciel, dell'orbe Dio,
> Tu lo calpesti il Tartaro,
> né te nomar poss'io
> né ragionar di te.
>
> Il divin nome incognito
> labbro mortal non mormori;
> Te col gran nome adorano
> l'etere, il sol che illumina,
> i mondi ch'alto ruotano,
> gli astri che ti rispondono,
> l'estate, il verno, l'aere,
> il mar, che a te favellano,
> e le potenze eteree,
> O d'ogni cosa Re! (pp. 38–39)

A prophet as well as all his other roles, Altifone tells her that she is already a Christian, does not want to marry her worthy suitor Isidore, and does not want worldly honours the secular authorities wish to bestow on her. He will use this foreknowledge to bring about her downfall. While Artapane and Altifone represent darkness and terror, in the next canto Cyril appears in contrast, a messenger of light, hope, harmony, decency and peace. Altifone is the villain Saluzzo had excoriated in the Preface (see above, p. 222): 'in volto | aveva la pace, in cuor desio di frode'; most shockingly, 'Amava Ipazia d'amor vano e stolto' (II, p. 41). He is convinced that Rome will not permit the marriage between a Christian Hypatia and a pagan Isidore. Saluzzo sums up the two priests:

> Pure Artapan men vile, fraudolento
> è d'Altifone; egli sé stesso inganna
> pria che altrui con fanatico ardimento. (II, p. 43)

Canto III is set in the modest Christian church, where Cyril preaches to a rapt congregation. Hypatia is no longer fearful, she listens to Cyril's sermon explaining the Old Testament; that is, how all the events from Adam and Eve were ordained by divine providence to prefigure the coming of a Redeemer, also foretold by the prophets. At the very end, as if in an opera, Christians break out in a chorus: 'Ah del tuo servo popolo, | che in le tue leggi adorati, | abbi pietà, Signor!' (p. 61). Saluzzo depicts these Christians as if they had never heard of Emperor Constantine the Great, whose Edict of 325 made Christianity the official religion of the Empire. Cyril, we remember, was anything but meek and mild.

Canto IV plays a key part in the poem, entirely preoccupied with Cyril's conversion of Hypatia from mere human geometry and the natural sciences to divine mathematics and astronomy. Cyril is able to read her mind, and while he sees her desire to become Christian, he also feels obliged to reprove her of un-Christian sentiments; namely, vanity and longing for human glory. Hypatia is mute, entranced by Cyril's omniscience and dazzling foreknowledge of developments in astronomy and mathematics. As he devastates her intellectual pride, her own achievements are made to seem puny in comparison:

> Pur, vedi Sapienza! Il regno suo
> cresce coll'età nuove, e sarà fiume
> con onde immense, se un ruscel già fuo;
> ché a poco a poco ha da crescer costume
> quel saver, se coltivalo l'ingegno.
> Una meta hai sol certa: è questa il Nume.
> Tu che con Dïofante il primo segno
> dell'umana scïenza oggi hai toccato,
> che universal delle grandezze è regno,
> che su se stessa intorno hai raggirato
> retta triangolar forma, e traesti
> da quella il cono, ed il cono hai tagliato,
> fama nell'avvenire aver credesti?
> Mal credi. (Canto IV, pp. 66–67)

Saluzzo understates Hypatia's philosophical and scholarly excellence to create her own Hypatia, one who is the opposite of what history and Toland had brought to light. Hypatia's Christian virtue lies mainly in her virginity. Saluzzo usually refers to her as 'la vergine', 'la verginella', 'la casta vergine', 'la vergine immortale' and so on. Hypatia's brilliance is a flickering candle, her fame a delusion. In fact, the model Saluzzo holds up as the finest feminine ideal is that of a nun, or a virgin-martyr, as we find in Jacopo da Voragine's medieval *Legenda aurea*. Did she realize that she was undermining herself, a cultured, famous, learned and highly articulate woman who was in no way meek and silent like her heroine?

Saluzzo, however, had yet to consider the *filosofie* of her title. This review begins in Canto v with a change of scenery. Hypatia wends her way from the site of religion to that of reason — the Neoplatonic Academy — to be accosted by Epicureans, Eleatics, Cyrenaics and Cynics. The speakers are unidentified members of their sects rather than named individuals. They are like tempters rather than exponents of doctrines. Some try to seduce her. Hypatia, apparently the only Neoplatonist on hand, rebuts them all with doctrines of lofty Platonic love. The first speaker, a ridiculous Epicurean, is a middle-aged man with a lyre who sings, dances and laughs, accompanied by a chorus of cherub-like little boys, 'fanciulletti.' Their song 'induce gioia e maraviglia' (v, p. 88), is a praise of mere undiluted sensual pleasures — the *carpe diem* motif. All of Nature's gifts, the cherubs sing,

> piacciono all'animo inebriato,
> che, mentre chiuso nel seno palpita,
> Natura gridagli per ogni lato,
> il soavissimo piacer t'invita;
> dentro al creato voluttà celasi;
> voluttà provida del mondo è vita. (v, p. 89)

> Di gioie abbellasi voluttà vera;
> fra mille gioie convienti scegliere
> pria che del vivere giunga la sera. (v, p. 90)

Hypatia, distressed by the amorous advances of the mature Epicurean, reminds him of his responsibilities and duties to the gods; but, becoming more serious, he reminds her that the gods do not govern the cosmos, that only atoms exist, 'volti al loro ballo eterno!' There follows a poem that could be called 'The Dance of the Atoms,' inspired by Cromaziano:

> È fuoco leggiero,
> è un aura il pensiero
> che d'atomi brevi
> il caso formò.
>
> Ma tutta gentile,
> al corpo simìle,
> è l'anima ristretta
> nel seno soletta;
> immagine bella,
> lievissima ancella,
> anch'essa pur muore,
> qual aura, qual fiore,
> se un atomo, un ente,
> volvente mutò. (v, p. 94)[28]

Hypatia is next assaulted by an Eleatic philosopher, about whom a note refers us to Cromaziano. A pre-Socratic fifth-century BC sect, they were already ancient in Plato's day, and would not have existed in Hypatia's. Saluzzo has him preach that nothing comes from nothing, and that Nature is a continual cycle with no beginning and no end. God is Nature, indifferent to human concerns, and inaccessible.[29] She then encounters the Cyrenaic sect, founded by Aristippus of Cyrene in Northern Africa in the early fourth century BC. Again, it is unlikely that Hypatia would have met him or his followers. Saluzzo picks out their doctrine of egoistic hedonism; nothing else is above the immediate experience of sense pleasure — there lies one's supreme happiness. Their spokesman tries to seduce Hypatia: 'Tu cerchi le cagioni, e 'l cor non odi. | Ti grida il cuor: lascia virtude astratta, | fugge 'l duolo; e gioisce in tutti i modi' (v, p. 100).[30] Hypatia flees. Her next suitor is another Cyrenaic. He, too, is a lecher, whose words once more defy plausibility by echoing the medieval motif of 'plucking the rose' of virginity as well as Torquato Tasso's *Aminta*:

> vezzosa fresca verginella,
> schiude la rosa un'aura beatrice,
> e co' baci le dà vita novella:
> a te, rosa d'amore, si disdice
> severa fronte nell'etade acerba:
> giova cosa che piace, e sempre lice. (v, p. 99)

The canto ends with the Cynics (meaning 'dogs'), another pre-Socratic group equally materialistic, anti-social and misanthropic to boot, typified in antiquity by sour Diogenes. The adept in the Academy growls: 'Il maggior bene è 'l sonno e poi la morte; | e poco basta a cui nulla desira' (v, p. 103). Saluzzo's sombre representations of these three sects are meant to contrast sharply with Hypatia's innocence and spirituality.[31]

It comes as a relief in Canto VI as we proceed from the inside to the gardens of the Academy. There, a brief encounter with the Gnostics ensues, and for the first time the great Plotinus holds forth with Hypatia and Isidore at his side. He has been marginalized by the wicked Altifone, who has made himself the head, but still has disciples. He dwells in a *magionella* in the Academy's grounds. Plotinus delivers a theological speech in a high register, expounding the doctrine of emanations from God, the One, down the great chain of being to the ever-changing world of nature. For Christians, Plotinus was interpreted as referring to the Trinity:

> Escon da Dio le essenze in l'intelletto
> divino nate; per sé stesse han vita;
> sono pur Dei; ché da quel luogo eletto
> nulla cosa mortal si vede uscita;
> variano il nome; in Dio ragione, in noi
> intelligenza son de' mondi suoi.
>
> Emanando emanata una discende
> serie di cose sol da Dio verace;
> le prime a lui simili il fonte rende;
> lontano il fonte, è la cosa fallace. (VI, p. 115)

The tone alters when he is alone with the two, imagining they are in love as Isidore sings a love-song to Hypatia. Like an affectionate but emotionally blind father, he expresses his longing to see the two of them covered in worldly glory, and also married. Hypatia, under pressure from both Plotinus and Isidore, bursts out: 'Ricuso il lauro e l'imeneo; il cammino | di vita è breve. Deh! Tu lo ricorda, | che Gloria è sogno, ed ha morte vicino' (VI, p. 123). The truth of Hypatia's conversion begins to dawn on Plotinus, who despises Christianity. Canto VI ends with an angry Plotinus banishing Hypatia from his sight: 'Ma piangi? tremi? ... In cor ti veggio ... e cedo. | Va, fatti ancella di vil setta atroce. | [...] Statti donzella di Cirillo appresso' (pp. 123–24). In the following two cantos, Hypatia listens first to a lecture about the Stoics from the philosopher Anfilia (Amphiclea), and then the Eclectics, whom she allies with the Neoplatonists, following Cromaziano. The last two cantos of volume I focus on Isidore and preparations for battle. There is time, however, for a meeting with a Pythagorean in Isidore's camp. The Pythagoreans were fascinated by numbers, believing that some had symbolic meanings. Saluzzo ingeniously composes a hymn in which each stanza is devoted to a number. Two, for example, was unlucky:

> Ma l'Uno seguita
> un fatal numero,
> di colpe immagine,
> il Due terribile;
> invan, ché vincerlo
> Iddio saprà. (IX, pp. 175–76)

Plots, counter-plots and romantic intrigues fill the rest of the volume, and do not concern Hypatia.

Hypatia's death and Cyril's role

Most of Volume II is taken up with what Saluzzo sees as the conflict between 'good' Egyptians led by the warrior Isidore, and the 'bad' Egyptians led by Altifone. Then there is the struggle between the alien conquering power, Rome, with its Roman prefect Orestes, and the mixed populace, mainly Egyptian. Saluzzo describes the situation as a fight for freedom from oppression, whether against Romans, against pagans or against tyrannical Egyptians. Hypatia and Cyril are caught up in the conflicts as victims whose only desire is for peace. Here Saluzzo follows the 'party line', which is the nineteenth-century Catholic view that the Church is a force for good, an instrument of divine providence. The Patriarch of Alexandria and Archbishop must be a holy man. No one embodied this view more than Saluzzo's contemporary, Alessandro Manzoni. His writings circulated in the Turin Academy Saluzzo and her father and brother belonged to. Manzoni's *Osservazioni sulla morale cattolica*, which was published in 1819, would have helped to shape Saluzzo's own attitudes.[32] Most of Volume II focuses on Cyril, whose conduct regarding Hypatia's death had been vilified by Toland and French *philosophes*. His reputation will now be saved, by hook or by crook.

The last attempt to unite Hypatia with Isidore takes place in Cantos XI and XI. Altifone swears to make Ipazia his or, if unsuccessful, kill her. He also swears to end Roman domination of Egypt and make himself king. To that purpose he wins over Orestes and Plotinus with honeyed words. Isidore also wants to drive the Romans out, because he fears they are spreading Christianity. Crisis point is reached in Canto XIII, where both of them are to be crowned with the laurel wreath: Isidore for winning in all the games, and Hypatia for her excellence in scientific research. As high priest, Altifone makes sure that the programme includes their public marriage before the (pagan) altar of Hymen. When the moment comes, Hypatia tears off her veil, and rushes through the crowds, shrieking:

> io son cristiana,
> (gridò), cristiana, né celarlo curo.
>
> Nulla! Nulla può sul mio cuor possanza umana!
> Nulla! Saria delitto or l'occultarlo,
> e delitto appressar l'ara profana. (XIII, p. 56)

She faints. Isidore is left in a state of shock; Plotinus continues to grumble:

> ingrata donna; più padre non sono.
> [...]
> Va! perdesti il mio amor; va, ti abbandono ...
> Va, crescesti al mio duolo ... e, se pur vile
> perdono vuoi, ti sprezzo, e ti perdono.

He hopes she will suffer like him, 'a cui desti la morte' (XIII, p. 59). Fortunately, Cyril has received a divine message telling him about Hypatia's plight. On finding her, he commands her: 'Seguimi! Vieni, vergine felice.' From now on, God replaces Plotinus and Isidore as her spiritual father, groom and guide:

> Tuo Dio t'aspetta; il Dio che luogo tenne
> a te di padre, ti fia sposo, e duce;
> ei che al giusto rifiuto il cuor sostenne. (XIII, p. 64)

Saluzzo keeps us in suspense, holding back Hypatia's death until Canto XIX, and concentrating on military matters. In Cantos XIV and XV, Isidore and Orestes recognize Altifone's perversity and build up their own troops. Saluzzo inserts a final philosophical sect among Altifone's men, a Pyrrhonian sceptic, expert at sowing despair. Each stanza of his mournful chant begins with 'Incerto, dubbioso'; and after a series of images of an evanescent wave, cloud, breeze, sound and divinity, ends with a question: 'Ma 'l vero, dov'è?' (XVI, pp. 120–22).[33] Among the troops, the sceptic undermines confidence: is their side right or wrong?

During the prolonged and bloody battle, Cyril becomes a model of brotherly love, comforting the wounded and dying; Hypatia and other Christian women become in turn angelic nurses, helping all, no matter what religion or political side. No taint of fanaticism or arrogance stains Cyril's behaviour: 'Egli forte, egli santo, in età prava | molti solve, niun sprezza, amor sol vanta' (XVIII, p. 164). Isidore wins the battle but Altifone escapes into the Christian church to spy on Hypatia.

Saluzzo packs Canto XIX with high melodrama, as poetic licence takes control of events. Calamity after calamity interspersed with miraculous interventions befall the characters. First, there is a fire in the valley started by Altifone and his thugs. He promised them that if they razed the village to the ground, they would find gold the Christians had hidden. Second, the fire reaches the church, where Cyril, Hypatia, Altifone and Isidore seek shelter for good and bad reasons. Third, inside the burning temple, Hypatia, moved by an inner premonition, makes her way to the altar with Cyril, only to find escape impossible. Fourth, consumed by his obsession with Hypatia, Altifone loses his mind. Then, a miracle in the midst of this desolation: Cyril is enveloped in a heavenly light that spreads peace: 'L' aura celeste che il Profeta invade, | pace intorno all'afflitta verginella | sparge, fra i nembi dell'iniqua etade' (xix, p. 180). The scene is set for Hypatia's death. She collapses at the disintegrating altar, and utters her dying prayer, followed by Cyril's blessing:

> fuggì lieve com'ombra il viver mio,
> che qual arida cade erba novella:
> io dal profondo suolo esclamo a Dio:
> 'Prendi mia vita; dammi eterna pace;
> ch' io provo un dolce di morir desio.'
> Il ministro del Ciel ascolta e tace;
> alza sul capo a lei la man pietosa,
> benedicendo la sua fede verace. (xix, p. 181)

Cyril orders her to rise as the flames grow more menacing, but as she staggers to her feet, there is a fifth, more serious, calamity. Having seen and heard Hypatia's prayer and Cyril's blessing, Altifone's lust turns to hate. He swoops, thrusting his dagger into Hypatia's heart three times. She falls, and dies clasping a still upright cross. Saluzzo has spared her heroine the historical indignity of being torn limb from limb, and having the bodily remains burned to ashes. Hypatia dies the perfect Christian death, ministered to by a perfect Christian saint who Saluzzo makes sure condemns violence and hatred. At this point, Isidore rushes in to find his beloved Hypatia dead, and Cyril prostrate, murmuring a final prayer for her soul: 'Ti chiama a lui dinanzi un Dio pietoso; | Dio t'ha redenta, o misera, o felice.' God welcomes her to a heaven where 'la vera scienza è vincitrice' (xix, p. 183). The phrase 'la vera scienza' brings us back to the Dante epigraph, and the limitations of human knowledge versus the infinite sea of divine illumination available only after death. Isidore immediately seeks out Altifone, chasing the murderer who meets his death by stumbling — appropriately — into a pit of flames. A further miracle: Isidore returns to the church to seek conversion. His change of heart, Cyril tells him, is due to Hypatia's prayers. Isidore finds that the flames have receded from the church thanks to Cyril's prayers and divine intervention, then returning to Hypatia's body. Like Beatrice in Dante's *Vita nuova*, 'Parea bella la morte in sul bel volto.' Isidore gazes at her with longing: 'In cuor bramoso di morir con seco | stava l'amante, il guardo in lei rivolto' (xix, p. 187). With more heavenly light on his face, Cyril experiences a prophetic ecstasy: his hymn rejoices in the defeat of the Romans and the future collapse of their Empire:

> Non più l'impero e l'imperante or sono.
> Unico avanzo di battaglie orrende
> restan le tombe poste in abbandono;
> mira le tombe il Romano, e comprende,
> com'è d'incerto evento
> un popolo invilir che non è spento. (XIX, p. 189)

Isidore, plainly moved, begs for baptism, and to be buried next to Hypatia in the valley of the Christians. Kept apart in life, they will be united in death. Once that is settled, he returns to lead his troops.

With Hypatia dead, Orestes and the Romans on their way back home, and Cyril's reputation for holiness at its zenith, the last canto could seem an anticlimax. Instead, Saluzzo keeps Cyril in the foreground, adding patriotism to his virtues in order to celebrate the triumph of Christian civilization over a dead pagan one. Saluzzo signifies this by linking Isidore's death with Cyril, so giving it a similar dignity to Hypatia's. The great warrior must die a hero battling a treacherous enemy with all his might. The struggle is gruelling, and the death-scene full of pathos. Isidore has seen the Romans routed, their standard, the eagle, captured. As the last of the Ptolemies, he has fulfilled his duty; he wishes death would hasten:

> parmi
> colpa l'indugio ... il mio destin vel mostra ....
> Fuggon sul mare vele romane ... è nostra
> preda l'Aquila avversa. ... aperto è 'l reo
> speco ... ed io moro! ... al Re dei Re ti prostra. (XX, p. 210)

Turning to his men, he wishes them peace, and to the Romans, war. He dies with the words 'patria' and 'Ipazia' on his lips.

No sooner have the Egyptian priests sung their hymns and performed their rites, and are about to bear the body to the Necropolis, when they are stopped dead in their tracks by Cyril, divinely forewarned. Isidore cannot be buried among pagans; he is a Christian, and furthermore Cyril has promised to bury him next to Hypatia: 'il battesimo ebbe Isidoro, espresso | ha 'l desir alto di diversa tomba | nel divo tempio, a casta sposa appresso' (XX, p. 214). Cyril is now supreme, the last Egyptian ruler has turned to the true God, his mission to advance Christianity has been fulfilled. Saluzzo gives Cyril the very last words of the poem:

> Lo [Isidoro] trasse or ora la guerriera tromba
> dal loco u' quel battesmo a lui diè pace;
> e dove l'inno santo ancor rimbomba.
> Nunzio al Signor d'ogni poter verace,
> popoli dell'Egitto, oggi son io;
> incerto è l'avvenir, l'età fugace;
> ma 'l patrio amor nasce e ritorna in Dio. (XX, pp. 214–15)

Concluding remarks

In her Preface, Saluzzo had emphasized that she was writing a 'romanzo istorico e filosofico'. She was presenting historical characters — Hypatia, Cyril, Plotinus, Iamblichus, the Roman Prefect — and various philosophical sects, and creating fictional events that could have taken place around the year 415. Saluzzo also wanted verisimilitude: that is, characters and events that were probable and therefore credible to the reader. As is apparent from the above analysis of Ipazia, Saluzzo is no historian and no philosopher. She abuses her sources (Muratori and even Cromaziano) and also her historical characters, especially Plotinus, Iamblichus, the Roman Prefect (who was a Christian), and above all her two main characters Hypatia and Cyril. By qualifying that she is writing a *romanzo*, can she be excused? If she were writing about fictional characters, there would be no problem; but if she is writing about historical people about whom there is a consensus as to the basic facts of their existence, then even Saluzzo cannot rewrite history. Verisimilitude goes out of the window, and so does the author's reputation. In addition, there is Saluzzo's conspicuous lack of historical sense. The most glaring fault is her anachronisms. There was no need to transfer Plotinus to a much later era and make him Hypatia's mentor. Why could Theon, her real father, mentor and collaborator, not serve in that role? Plotinus was the greatest Neoplatonist philosopher of all time, whose metaphysical doctrines became widespread among Christians, leading to the language used by Christian mystics like John of the Cross and Teresa of Avila. Furthermore, he was not even living in Alexandria for most of his adult life, but in southern Italy. Saluzzo has no grasp of Neoplatonism, let alone Plotinus's difficult *Enneads*; she makes him an absurd figure as he storms off stage when Hypatia confesses she is a Christian. Iamblichus, too, is a travesty of himself, and so is Anfilia, her translation of Amphiclea. Iamblichus was born around 245, and Amphiclea was his daughter-in-law, not his lover, and certainly not a contemporary of Hypatia. Most surprising is Saluzzo's exclusion of Synesius of Cyrene, the most important witness for Hypatia's character, and for what she taught. We can only surmise that he was left out because he was too strong a proof of Hypatia's life and death as a pagan. As for Hypatia herself and Cyril, they are the stuff of dreams.

Saluzzo's fictional characters have difficulty passing the verisimilitude test. Take the arch-villain Altifone, a treacherous head-priest of the Egyptian rites, head philosopher of the Neoplatonic Academy, and commander-in-chief of the rebel army. His two-dimensional character comes out of an adventure book for boys. Saluzzo's intent was to defame all philosophy, another historical mistake, as Christianity absorbed many teachings of the Stoics and Platonists, as well as the Aristotelians. Christians themselves were in disarray in the fourth century, their disagreements leading to schisms and doctrinal conflicts. Persecutions were not infrequent, as we see in the life of Cyril.[34]

In the propaganda war between Toland and Saluzzo over Hypatia, it must be said that Toland sticks closer to his historical sources than Saluzzo. What if Saluzzo had left out her ambition to write a 'romanzo istorico e filosofico' and limited herself to a *romanzo*? Could her story in verse pass muster? Saluzzo's gift for various metrical forms is exceptional; some of her verse, I have tried to show, touches the sublime; some is ingenious, some is entertaining. Unfortunately, her polemical desire to beat 'il troppo celebre Tolando' overcame her search for truth.

Notes to Chapter 15

1. *Ipazia*, 2 vols (Turin: Tipografia Chirio e Mina, 1827). An earlier version, published in 1824, was heavily revised for the 1827 definitive edition followed here. In English, on Hypatia herself, two studies stand out: Maria Dzielska, *Hypatia of Alexandria* (Cambridge, MA: Harvard University Press, 1996), excellent for the history of the controversies surrounding Hypatia's beliefs; and Michael A. B. Deakin, *Hypatia of Alexandria: Mathematician and Martyr* (Amherst: Prometheus, 2007), excellent for analysing the Greek sources, for translating into English all relevant passages, and giving the best presentation of her mathematics and astronomy. On Saluzzo, see the chapter by Adriana Chemello in *A History of Women's Writing in Italy*, ed. by Letizia Panizza and Sharon Wood (Cambridge: Cambridge University Press, 2000), pp. 144–47. On Saluzzo's reputation among contemporaries, see *Saffo tra le Alpi*, ed. by Laura Ney (Rome: Bulzoni, 1990), with sections on *Ipazia*; and *Il Romanticismo in Piemonte: Diodata Saluzzo*, ed. by Marziano Guglieminetti and Paola Trivero (Florence: Olschki, 1993), a collection of twelve essays on Saluzzo's life, literary circle and works, including *Ipazia*.
2. I have transcribed Saluzzo's spelling and punctuation; modern critical editions differ slightly. For the Preface, see pp. xi-xxii. The further quotation is taken from *La Divina Commedia: Inferno*, ed. by Natalino Sapegno (Florence: La Nuova Italia, 1959), pp. 132–33.
3. A French priest, Richard Simon (1638–1712) was one of the foremost Biblical scholars of his age, studying the manuscripts of the Old and New Testaments in their original languages and documenting faulty translations, omissions and additions. As this method raised doubts about doctrine, Catholics tried to suppress his published *Histoire critique du Vieux Testament* as well as his later *Histoire critique du texte du Nouveau Testament,* but his work was taken up by Protestant printers and patrons.
4. The literature on Toland is vast. See *The Oxford Dictionary of National Biography* entry by Stephen H. Daniel, vol. 54, pp. 894–98, and the entry by Justin Champion, 'John Toland', in *The Routledge Encyclopedia of Philosophy* (London and New York: Routledge, 1998). For a complete bibliography on Toland up to 1978, see Giancarlo Carabelli, *Tolandiana: materiali bibliografici per lo studio dell' opera di John Toland (1670–1722)* (Florence: La Nuova Italia, 1975), followed by *Tolandiana: errata addenda ed indice* (Ferrara: Università degi Studi, 1978). See also Justin Champion's study, *Republican Learning: John Toland and the Crisis of Christian Culture, 1696–1722* (Manchester: Manchester University Press, 2003).
5. Toland was the first to write a substantial treatise, *Pantheisticon*, which he worked on for two years and published in Latin in 1720, the same year as *Hypatia*. It was then issued posthumously in 1751 in English. See *Pantheisticon: A Modern English Translation*, trans. by Jason Cooper (Milton Keynes: Open Archive Books, 2014). See also Gavina Cherchi, *Satira ed Enigma: due saggi sul 'Pantheisticon' di John Toland* (Lucca: Maria Pacini Fazzi, 1985). Two years earlier, Toland published *Nazarenus, or Jewish, Gentile, Mahometan Christianity*, ed. by Justin Champion (Oxford: Voltaire Foundation, 1998), in which he arrives at the conclusion that all religions are equal and should coexist in mutual respect and toleration. These two works provide an appropriate backdrop for *Hypatia*.
6. *Hypatia*, the third of four essays in a pamphlet collection called *Tetradymus*, runs from pp. 103 to 136, and is divided into twenty-two chapters. I shall give chapter and page in my text.
7. See Robert E. Sullivan, *John Toland and the Deist Controversy* (Cambridge, MA: Harvard University Press, 1982), chapter 3, 'The Varieties of Socianism,' pp. 82–108.
8. Socrates Scolasticus continued the *Historia Ecclesiastica* of his predecessor Eusebius (*c.* 263-*c.* 340) up to the year 439. For passages in English relevant to Hypatia, see Deakin, pp. 143–48. Synesius is a fascinating example of a Neoplatonist baptized a Christian and made a bishop, although

not believing in some basic Church doctrines like the Resurrection and the Trinity. He kept a wife and children, loved hunting, and acted more as a civic administrator than as a priest. Several writings by him are extant, including a large body of letters, some to Hypatia. See J. C. Nichol, *Synesius of Cyrene: His Life and Writings* (Cambridge: E. Johnson, 1887) for a complete account; and, for his letters to Hypatia, Deakin, pp. 150–58. The most thorough analysis of Synesius's intellectual development, see Henri Marrou, 'Synesius of Cyrene and Alexandrian Neoplatonism,' in *The Conflict between Paganism and Christianity in the Fourth Century*, ed. by Arnaldo Momigliano (Oxford: Clarendon Press, 1963), pp. 126–50.

9. Philostorgius (368–c.439) wrote an *Ecclesiastical History*, including an account of the Arian heresy. His history has been preserved in an *Epitome* by a tenth-century scribe, Photius of Constantinople.

10. Information from *The Oxford Classical Dictionary* (London: Oxford University Press, 1970), and Deakin, passim.

11. Deakin, pp. 88–89; on Hypatia's contribution to the *Almagest*, pp. 91–94; on *Conics*, pp. 95–96; on her commentary on the *Arithmetic* of Diophantus, pp. 98–101. In his evaluation, Deakin corroborates what Toland states, but without the mathematical expertise of Deakin. In the 390s she and her father were the leading mathematicians of Alexandria. Once he died, she would be 'the Empire's most accomplished mathematician' (pp. 110–11). He continues: 'It was not a good time for mathematics in either China or India. [...] It may come as a disappointment to some to learn that, although Hypatia was in her time the world's best mathematician, she cannot realistically be classed as one of the world's great mathematicians' (p. 111).

12. See the perceptive evaluation by Carlo Ginzburg in the *Dizionario biografico degli Italiani*, vol. 6, pp. 470–78. Coming to maturity just after the Council of Trent, Baronio set himself the task of answering Protestant historians, headed by Mattia Flacio in the *Centurie* of Magdeburg. They are credited with starting research into primary sources on Christian origins. Baronio's *Annales* represent a great feat of scholarship, they aim to prove an unbroken line of papal authority and supremacy over all Christendom. Ginzburg concludes: 'Il Baronio è un cospicuo rappresentante dell'intransigenza controriformistica' (p. 470). A tireless searcher for the truth, Ginzburg admits, Baronio never allows himself to find fault with what has happened. As for Hypatia, see the next note.

13. '[Hypatia] tantos in litteris fecit progressus, ut omnes philosophos sui temporis longe superaret'(p. 320; 'She excelled in every discipline; that she surpassed all the philosophers of her age by far'); but 'invidiae flamma contra eam incensa est' (ibid., 'the flame of envy was ignited against her'), *Annales ecclesiastici*, vol. V, 395–440. Baronius excuses Cyril by placing the entire blame on Peter the Lector and the infamous Nitrian monks: 'Hoc facinus cum Cyrilli tum Ecclesia [...] non exiguam labem aspersit' (ibid.; 'The deed brought about no little shame to Cyril and the Church').

14. Toland objects to historians abusing this document to declare Hypatia Christian: 'As for a ridiculous Letter, pretended to be written by her to Cyril about the Paschal Cycle, tis a manifest forgery.' Nestorius (380–450) would not have risen to prominence until after Hypatia's death in 415. He was made Archbishop of Constantinople in 428. His fiercest opponent was Cyril, put in charge of convoking the Council of Ephesus in 431, where he had Nestorius declared a heretic. Yet the letter imagines him already a heretic, for Hypatia calls him *impious* (XXI, p. 134)! Nestorius denied that Mary was *Theotokos*, 'bearer of God', because God, being eternal, could not be born.

15. Toland does not give much detail about Cyril's violence against the Jews, but he had just written *Nazarenus*, a plea for toleration among the three great religions (see note 5 above).

16. Toland has followed Socrates accurately, and so has Deakin, who thinks Hypatia was dragged to a church to obtain divine sanction for the atrocity (pp. 73–75); perhaps also, as she was a heathen, to de-Satanize her.

17. Saluzzo mentions Muratori and the *Annali d'Italia* earlier (p. xii), where she gives the names of Emperors and other dignitaries for the year 408. Her short quotation is correct but misleading: Muratori is recording the history of Italy, year by year. There are only a few lines about Alexandria at the very end of the chapter. The tumult has to do with the expulsion of the Jews

by Cyril. Hypatia is not even named: 'Succedettero ancora in quest' Anno [415] de I fieri tumulti nella Città d' Alessandria per gli quali di colà furono scacciati i Giudei. Socrate Storico incolpa forte di tali scandali Cirillo Vescovo di quella Città, e i Monaci di Nitria, ma sopra ciò è da vedere Cardinale Baronio': *Annali d'Italia, dal principio dell'era volgare al 1749*, 12 vols (Modena: Giovambattista Pasquali, 1744–49), III (1744), *Dall'anno 401 ... all'anno 600*, year 415, p. 56. For Muratori, see the entry by Girolamo Imbruglia in the *Dizionario biografico degli Italiani*, 77, pp. 443–52.

18. For the history of the effects on Italy of the French Revolution, see Martin Clark, *The Italian Risorgimento*, Seminar Studies in History (Harlow: Longman, 1998); and Harry Hearder, *Italy in the Age of the Risorgimento 1790–1870* (London: Longman, 1983).
19. This letter, found in an account by Pope Damascius in the tenth century, was declared apocryphal by Toland, both because it is so late with respect to the events, and because it is protecting Cyril from blame. If Hypatia were Christian, obviously Cyril would not want to murder her.
20. Telemachus, the son of Ulysses in Homer's *Odyssey*, is the hero of a moralistic novel, *Les Aventures de Télémaque*, by Fénelon, tutor to the grandson of Louis XIV. In the novel, Telemachus is instructed on his travels by Mentor, who turns out to be the goddess Minerva in disguise. The novel was first published in 1699 anonymously, and went through many editions and translations in the next century with the author's name. Sappho is the Romantic heroine in Alessandro Verri's *Le avventure di Saffo, poetessa di Mitilene*, published in 1780. Her 'adventures' of the title are purely fictional.
21. For the historical novel, see Sandra Bermann's Introduction to her translation of Alessandro Manzoni, *On the Historical Novel* (Lincoln: University of Nebraska Press, 1984), pp. 1–59, and Olga Ragusa's essay on Manzoni in *The Cambridge Companion to The Italian Novel*, ed. by Peter Bondanella and Andrea Ciccarelli (Cambridge: Cambridge University Press, 2003), pp. 42–60. With a wider range, see also Jerome de Groot. *The Historical Novel* (London: Routledge, 2010), which discusses Manzoni but not Saluzzo.
22. Manzoni's letter to Saluzzo is in *Saffo tra le Alpi*, ed. by Ney, pp. 92–94.
23. See item 25 in *Saffo tra le Alpi*, ed. by Ney, pp. 112–14.
24. Jean Antoine Letronne, 1787–1848, a distinguished archaeologist, was a member of the Académie des Inscriptions et Belles-Lettres from 1827, and then professor of archaeology at the Collège de France from 1837 to his death. He published numerous books and articles on ancient Egypt.
25. Livio Berardo, a classicist, in 'Ipazia o delle ideologie', in *Il Romanticismo in Piemonte*, ed. by Guglieminetti and Trivero, pp. 143–54, is scathing about Saluzzo's abuse of her Greek sources and Muratori, accusing her of 'mistificazione ideologica.' He agrees she relies mainly on Cromaziano's *Istoria*, which he declares unsound historically. Cromaziano does, however, give plenty of sources in his own notes, ranging from Greeks — Diogenes Laertius, *The Lives of the Philosophers* and the *Suda* are favorites — to Latin — Cicero *De natura deorum* and *De finibus* are relied on — to moderns. Cromaziano freely uses Protestant and Catholic historians and philosophers: Jacob Brucker, Francis Bacon, Ralph Cudworth, Henri Bayle (his *Dictionnaire*), Jean-Jacques Rousseau and John Toland (not *Hypatia*) on the Protestant and Deist side; Baronius, Tillemont and a host of theologians on the Catholic side. Saluzzo, on the other hand, is haphazard about her references, perhaps not wanting her readers to trace them. In addition to Dante, there are echoes of Petrarch, Poliziano and Tasso (*Gerusalemme liberata*, *Aminta* and perhaps *Il mondo creato*) in her poem. History and philosophy are subordinate to her fictions.
26. Vol. V (Naples, 1787), chapter 68, 'Dell' Ecletticismo', pp. 217–26; on Hypatia, pp. 225–26. The term was first used by Brucker, and then the *Encyclopédie*. It may be that Cromaziano's revelation of Cyril's enemies motivated Saluzzo to write a rebuttal.
27. After enduring life as an ass in punishment for curiosity about black magic, Lucius is transformed back into a human being thanks to the goddess Isis.
28. Epicurus, he says, bought a pleasant orchard where he taught doctrines that were 'facili e dilettevoli'; he purged philosophy from 'austerità e tristezza'. As for the atoms, they are the material elements of everything, ruled by chance, their seeming busy movement determined by the swerve, *declinazione*. The gods are blessed, with no interest in caring for humans. Vol. III,

chapter 33, pp. 140–48. Christians denounced them mainly for their denial of an afterlife, and of divine providence.

29. Saluzzo for once is precise, giving volume and chapter for this little-known sect: Vol. II, chapter 28: 'niuna cosa potere esistere dal niente, e quindi quello che ora esiste essere sempre stato, non avendo principio dove comincia né fine dove finisce'. The senses deceive us; all movement and changes in the natural world are mere appearances. Nature, the universe and God are One. He gives Plato, Cicero, and the Englishman Ralph Cudworth (1617–1688) as his sources; see pp. 342–64.

30. Cromaziano, Vol. III, chapter 38, pp. 232–58. He presents Aristippus (the Elder) of Cyrene in Northern Africa as another pleasure-seeking materialist.

31. For the Cyrenaics in Cromaziano, see Vol. III, chapter 38, pp. 232–58; for the Cynics, chapter 41, pp. 354–89.

32. The first and most influential part of *Osservazioni* was completed in Milan, 1818, the result of correspondence with and reading of French and Italian Catholic intellectuals. It was intended to be an answer to the Swiss Protestant historian J. C. L. Sismondi, critical of the corruption of the clergy in the Italian Middle Ages. Manzoni wished to square the New Testament ethics with Church doctrine, and with moral philosophy to produce a seamless garment of immutable and eternal truth. The good Christian lived in hope despite suffering because eternal life awaited. See S. B. Chandler, *Alessandro Manzoni: The Story of a Spiritual Quest* (Edinburgh: Edinburgh University Press, 1974), pp. 37–45.

33. Saluzzo gives no indication of sources. She only identifies the sect: 'Filosofia Pirroniana' (p. 131). The main source for these extreme sceptics is Sextus Empiricus, *Adversus mathematicos* ('Against the Philosophers'), translated into Latin in the sixteenth century. See Cromaziano, Vol. III, chapter 41, entitled 'La Seconda Accademia', which deals with Pyrrho, pp. 321–53.

34. For the fourth-century religious context in which Hypatia lived, see Robin Lane Fox, *Pagans and Christians* (New York: Alfred Knopf, 1980). See also Arnaldo Momigliano's introductory essay in *The Conflict between Paganism and Christianity*, ed. by Momigliano, pp. 1–16. And for this essay see also chapter VI by H. I. Marrou, 'Synesius of Cyrene and Alexandrian Neoplatonism', pp. 126–50.

CHAPTER 16

John Dickson Batten's Illustrations to the *Inferno*

Peter Hainsworth

I

This chapter aims to chime with Martin McLaughlin's interest in the history of Dante's reception in England, and particularly in Oxford.¹ In it I discuss an artist, also with Oxford connections, who stands out among nineteenth-century English illustrators of the *Inferno*, but whose Dante work is little known even to specialists. This neglect or ignorance derives in part from changes in taste, but historical and contingent factors have also played a major part, as will, I hope, become evident.

We tend to think of nineteenth-century artists, especially the Pre-Raphaelites, as being eager and prolific illustrators of Dante. In fact most picked on episodes from Dante's life, particularly ones deriving more or less fancifully from the *Vita nuova*. Illustrations of the *Divine Comedy* are much less numerous and concerted sequences rare. Of the three best known illustrators (Flaxman, Blake, and Doré), it is Doré who for generations of English Dante readers becomes almost canonical, from the first publication of his work alongside Cary's translation in 1866.² This translation, once Samuel Taylor Coleridge had given it his stamp of approval in 1815, became the most reprinted and widely read version of Dante in nineteenth-century England and has continued to be reprinted, with the Doré illustrations, up until today.³

Together Cary and Doré offered a viable solution to the notorious problem of Dante's difficulty. Cary kept fairly close to Dante's literal sense, but his blank verse was both readable and poetic, with some of Milton's sonorities without Milton's complexity and with a consistently maintained heightening of tone and idiom in accordance with contemporary expectations of what poetry should be. Doré, perhaps more excitingly, gave Dante's afterlife a detailed, dramatic texture, which was full of movement and in the case of Hell (where he was probably most successful) dark horror. In some ways the gap between his Hell and his realist images of Victorian London was not great, and not that remote from Dickensian portrayals either.⁴ At the same time Doré and Cary plainly situate themselves in a subordinate position with respect to Dante. They of course interpret and intervene, but it is evident that primarily they want to convey in a different language (Cary) and in a different medium (Doré) what they take Dante to be doing, not to assert a personal poetic or artistic vision which uses Dante primarily as a starting point. In this respect, no doubt in part because they are not great figures in their own right, the approach of both of them seems modest and traditional, and quite unlike that of many of their more recent successors, as it is unlike that of Blake, whose visual interpretations of the *Comedy* are likely to be read much more for what they say about Blake than for what they say about Dante.

At the same time it was evident to any nineteenth-century reader of Dante with an acquaintance with the original that Cary's was anything but the last word. Too much of the poetry, however defined, had been lost; most obviously blank verse was not *terza rima*. From the mid-century onwards there was a succession of further translations, some of the *Inferno* alone, but many of the whole *Comedy*.[5] The translators were clergymen, lawyers, scholars, essayists, critics and novelists, both men and women, the publishers reputable. Though most received little more than grudging critical approval, the struggle to capture what is doomed to remain elusive became an established one and translations of the *Comedy* into English verse have continued to appear in large numbers up to and including the present day, contemporary translators now being mostly poets and academics.

One of the late nineteenth-century translators was George Musgrave (1855–1932), a graduate of St John's College Oxford and a well-off lawyer who published a version of the *Inferno* in 1893, with the intention, never realised, of following it up with *Purgatorio* and *Paradiso*.[6] The distinctive and determining feature of his translation is the choice of the nine-line stanza that Spenser had used in the *Faery Queen*, in iambic pentameters rhyming ABABBCBCC, with a twelve-syllable final line. Here is the meeting with Brunetto Latini (*Inf.* 15.25–33).

> Then reacht he up his arms to me, whilst I
>   With fixèd stare scanned his baked lineament,
> Which, albeit scorcht with fire so terribly,
>   Was all too well remembered. So I bent
>   My face to his, and back this answer sent:
> 'Oh! SER BRUNETTO, art *thou* here?' And he:
> 'Nay but, my Son — ah! be not ill content
>   'If thy LATINI turn aback with thee
> 'But for a little space, and quit this varletry.'

The sense is quite carefully maintained, as is the length of the passage, and the rhymes do give a certain musicality, but the form imposes syntactic distortions which the archaic idiom barely justifies. And of course the final line introduces a weightiness and a pause which are not there in the original, though in some places there is enjambement between one stanza and another. Musgrave was not satisfied with his translation as it was first published and quickly set about revising it for a second edition that he seems initially to have hoped would appear within a few years. He also decided that the second edition should be illustrated.

In this he departed from the general rule. Apart from Cary, almost all nineteenth-century translations that I have seen were unillustrated except perhaps for a frontispiece portrait of Dante and (more rarely) diagrams or maps of the three regions of the afterlife. The exceptions are few and unexciting. One is Frederick Pollock's version of 1854,[7] which has fifty drawings by George Scharf, Junior, all appearing at the beginning of the cantos to which they relate. They are small, unambitious and very much in the manner of Flaxman. In 1890 Phoebe Traquair (who had illustrated Elizabeth Barratt Browning's *Sonnets* and the *Vita nuova*) produced a set of twenty Dante illustrations with notes by John Sutherland Black[8]: these are line-drawings of an almost topographical nature, intended presumably to help the readers of Dante with orientation, but unaccompanied by the text of the poem in the limited edition in which they appear. Musgrave was thus looking back to Thomas Hope, who had commissioned Flaxman, and John Linnell, who had commissioned Blake, when he selected an established artist and illustrator, John Dickson Batten (1860–1932), to produce a set of illustrations for his revised *Inferno*.

Like Musgrave himself, Batten had a degree in law. But after graduating from Trinity College, Cambridge, he had trained as an artist at the Slade under Alphonse Legros. He had then had considerable success as a book-illustrator, working principally with Joseph Jacobs (1854–1916), who published various collections of folk-stories and children's stories in the 1880s and 90s,[9] some of which continue to be available today, still with Batten's illustrations. He was particularly interested in techniques of printing and was one of the prime movers in the introduction of Japanese wood-block processes into England.[10] He also became a successful painter, working in an aestheticising neo-classical idiom not far from that of Lord Leighton and with some Pre-Raphaelite resonances. An interest in early Italian art and poetry showed itself particularly in a series of illustrations to Maurice Hewlett's *A Masque of Dead Florentines*,[11] a set of rhyming verses on great Florentine writers and painters of the Middle Ages and Renaissance, the flavour of which can be gauged from the addendum to the title: 'wherein some of Death's Choicest Pieces, and the Great Game that he played therewith, are fruitfully set forth.' One of the first illustrations shows Dante's Beatrice, Petrarch's Laura and Boccaccio's Fiammetta dancing together with Death in the foreground playing a lute, another Dante, Petrarch and Boccaccio together. Then follow portraits, mostly death-haunted, mostly of artists, from Giotto to Michelangelo.

Over a period of three years, between 1897 and 1900, Batten completed forty-five pen-and-ink drawings of scenes from the *Inferno* for Musgrave. Forty-three were exhibited at Leighton House in January 1900[12] and then passed to the printer Richard Taylor for plates to be prepared. At this stage it was envisaged that a second edition with the illustrations would be published by David Nutt during the same year.[13] But for reasons that we do not know publication was to be long delayed, though a number of folio collotype prints of the illustrations were made over the next few years, perhaps for a projected book edition. At some point Musgrave decided to commission another series of illustrations from another artist, Edmund Hort New (1871–1931), whose speciality was rural and urban scenes. New accompanied Musgrave and his wife to Italy in the autumn of 1913 and over the next few months produced a substantial set of drawings of places connected with Dante and the *Divine Comedy*, plus others of coats of arms of noble families of Dante's time and an overall map of the globe showing Hell, Purgatory and the Heavens.[14] Musgrave appears to have thought of incorporating at least some of New's work in the second edition alongside or instead of Batten's illustrations. He also intended to include as a frontispiece Lord Leighton's portrait drawing of Dante. In the event, when the edition did eventually appear, it included forty-four of Batten's drawings but none of New's drawings nor the Lord Leighton portrait.

Apparently because of ill-health and eventual blindness, Musgrave was never able to carry out the revisions to his full satisfaction. Publication did not come about until 1933, a year after both he and Batten had died, and the final editing of the text was completed by Musgrave's friend and executor, Edward Adams Parker.[15] For all the tinkering the text was not significantly improved. Here is the stanza quoted above in its second version:

> Then stretched he out his arm to me, whilst I
>   So fixedly scanned his baked lineament,
> That, albeit scorched with fire so terribly,
>   It baffled not remembrance. So I bent
>   My face to his, and back this answer sent:
> 'Oh, Ser Brunetto, art *thou* here?' And he:
>   'Nay but, my son — ah! be not ill content
>   If Brunetto Latini back with thee
> Turn for a little space, and quit this varletry.

Some of the archaic patina has been removed, but the style and idiom remain much as it was. In 1933 Musgrave must have seemed distinctly old-fashioned, even alongside Melville Best Anderson, Geoffrey Bickersteth, Laurence Binyon, and other none too modernising translators of the time.[16] So far as any general readership was concerned, his version quickly vanished from sight.[17]

The Batten drawings were also eclipsed. Unlike his illustrations to fairy-tales and folk-stories, they had no literary context in which they might re-appear. One (Beatrice looking down on Dante struggling to climb the mountain) is reproduced in Eugene Paul Nassar's 1994 anthology of Dante illustrations[18] but so far as I know that is all. Unlike many other drawings by Batten, they are not reproduced or available on the web. But they had not vanished. For reasons that are not clear Musgrave left in his will all the Dante material he owned to Lady Margaret Hall, Oxford: it included the original New drawings, copies of the Leighton portrait, Batten's original pen-and-ink drawings and multiple copies of full-size collotype reproductions of all of them. The original drawings give the impression of not being particularly valued, in spite of being mounted, presumably for the 1900 Leighton House exhibition. The mounts are discoloured and ragged and details in the original drawings have been touched up in white in various places, presumably by Batten himself before he passed them over to be engraved. But the collotype versions are generally in good condition.[19] Most of these are on stiff white paper, with further copies, in some cases more than one, of each of the images on finer off-white paper, dated to 1912–13. In the year following Batten's death the drawings were loaned at the request of his widow for an exhibition at the Art Workers Guild.[20] It was the last time they were made available for viewing by a wider public. Thereafter the only display was in Lady Margaret Hall itself, where a selection of the collotypes hung for years along the walls of one of the corridors in the main building, which continues to be known as Hell Passage long after the pictures were taken down and replaced by notice-boards.

II

The drawings were of course intended from the start for publication in book form, and the edition in which they appear includes all but one of them (Virgil and Dante struggling against the wind blowing over the ice at the bottom of Hell), with an additional drawing not among the pen-and-ink originals nor the collotype reproductions. This shows the stars as they were at the beginning of Dante's journey and is placed before the start of Canto 1. So far as the rest are concerned, though the clarity of the images is remarkable, the inevitable reduction in size tends to blur lines together a little in some instances and to lose some of the subtler variations in line texture of others.[21] Inevitably the overall impact is diminished, even though each illustration has a page to itself and often occupies the whole of it. It is the larger collotype images which display the clarity and force of Batten's line drawing and which, given the intrusiveness of the corrections to the pen-and-ink originals, are probably the best realizations of his artistic intentions.

There is normally one illustration per canto, though a good proportion contain visual references to events or aspects of Hell that appear later or in some cases earlier in the narrative.[22] Some of the earlier cantos and again some of the concluding ones have two illustrations (1, 3, 7, 8, 32) and in a few cases three (cantos 5, 12 and 34), though the illustration of Charon in the 1933 edition is placed before the start of canto 4, not towards the end of canto 3 where it belongs narratively. Further on there is an illustration set on the bridge between the two relevant *bolge* showing both Bertrand de Born (canto 28) and Geri del Bello (canto 29), which in the 1933 edition appears within canto 28. The image of Beatrice looking down on Dante struggling to climb the mountain appears as a frontispiece. Otherwise the second canto where it belongs is unillustrated, as are a few others (11, 27, 30 and 33). Of these the most striking omission is canto 33, given that since the time of Chaucer Ugolino has been the Dante character who has most captured the imagination of English readers and translators. Conversely Batten follows nineteenth-century taste in devoting two images to Paolo and Francesca (one showing Dante first catching sight of them among the rest of the lustful and the second the two figures swirling through the air in close-up), the third image for the canto in which they appear being of Minos seated above a crowd of sinners waiting to be assigned their places of punishment. Most unusual in terms of the distribution of images is that three are given to canto 12, the first showing a melancholy-looking Minotaur, the second the meeting with the centaurs Chiron and Nessus and the third Dante riding on the back of Nessus.

These three moments, so close to each other in the poem, were perhaps chosen because the subjects offered Batten particular scope for his aestheticising and classicising inclinations. The third (Fig. 16.1), for instance, has the posed, almost decorative air of a pottery design. Virgil and Dante are depicted as they are in all

Fig. 16.1. The Centaur Nessus Carries Dante across the River of Blood

Fig. 16.2. The Meeting with Homer, Horace, Ovid and Lucan

the images. Virgil is a bearded, older figure, in a long robe, with something of an Old Testament prophet about him rather than a Roman poet. Dante is wearing the familiar scholar's cap and gown, but his features are those of the youthful portrait attributed to Giotto rather than having the curved Roman nose and the fierce, lined face we are more familiar with. Both faces are delineated with the simplest of lines, though neither figure is as expressionless as they might seem at first glance. Dante's position on Nessus's back as he carries him through the shallows of the river of boiling blood shows a certain nervous tension (as is understandable), while Virgil seems to be exchanging benevolent glances with the centaur, who indeed is designated in the text as a 'scorta fida' (12.100) and is generous with the information he provides about the river of blood and the souls submerged in it. Horror is largely relegated to the background figures and the dark cliffs behind. The bush marking the wood of the suicides which Virgil and Dante are about to enter is a controlled rather than fearful tangle and the fumes rising from the river wind around in attractively stylised coils. Leaving aside the attention to landscape and to texture, there is much here that suggests a calculatedly less muscular version of the idiom of Flaxman.

A similar sort of classicism is evident in the images representing the opening scenes of the poem. When Dante is still in the world above, light and brightness are suggested by keeping largely to firm line-drawing with only delicate suggestions of texture. Even more striking is the use of line and untextured space to evoke brightness in the image of Dante walking forwards conversing with Homer and the other ancient poets, two of whom (Horace and Lucan, assuming Batten is following Dante's order) look like handsome youths from Renaissance paintings, while Homer and Ovid are bearded sages similar to Virgil (Fig. 16.2).

Batten's stylised romantic classicism achieves its most lyrical effects in the representations of Beatrice and of Paolo and Francesca. Interestingly and justifiably, given the parallels between Francesca and Beatrice suggested in canto 5 with all the distress they cause Dante, Batten's Francesca is physically very similar to his Beatrice, only somewhat more girlish. But the chaste love of the one is suggested by her modest robe, her controlled hair and her hands clasped in a concern that is almost prayer, as she looks down at a distant earth-bound Dante struggling to climb the mountain. (Fig. 16.3). Francesca on the other hand, her hair loose and naked apart from a wispy veil that winds around both herself and the youthfully handsome Paolo to whom she has surrendered her hand, is almost dancing with him through the darkness, the two seeming as light on the wind as Dante says they are (Fig. 16.4) In contrast with the famous 1835 Paolo and Francesca of Ary Scheffer (now in the Wallace Collection), the iconography of which may well have been at the back of Batten's mind, the physical sensuality of the lovers' passion is gently transformed into the sort of rhapsodic poetry that many nineteenth-century readers found in the episode and that more recent critics have often wanted to qualify.

At the opposite extreme are the representations of devils and monsters. Here Batten seems to draw on his experience as an illustrator of folk- and fairy-stories. His grotesque Cerberus and Pluto and even more the cavorting bands of devils

Fig. 16.3. Beatrice Watches from Paradise

Fig. 16.4. Paolo and Francesca

further down have the sort of fearful, comic energy to be found in medieval pictures of the Last Judgement as well as in early illustrated manuscripts of the *Comedy*. It is an aspect of Dante that Doré's realist idiom finds particularly difficult to deal with, since its underlying assumption is that everything in *Inferno* is to be presented in a key of gloom and horror. Batten's version of the devils having to be rescued from the pitch into which they have tumbled is much closer to the black, none-too-tasteful comedy of the episode in Dante's actual text. (Fig. 16.5).

His triumphs in the monstrous are the much more serious images of Minos and Geryon, both of which have a quite remarkable pictorial and psychological complexity to them that is grounded in a careful and imaginative reading of Dante's text, if again not always one that modern scholarship would agree with. Minos (Fig. 16.6), who can easily be imagined as little more than a howling dog with a monstrous tail, becomes a grandly implacable and thoughtful figure, his royal character (which Dante largely deletes) indicated by his crown. He sits towering over the terrified crowds of sinners pushing forwards and at the same time trying to press back who are waiting to be assigned their places. His tail is already wound about him the appropriate number of times to indicate to the sinner on the right where he is to go. Beyond and below can be seen in miniature the souls of the first circle of Hell proper, with the lustful (whom Dante will meet immediately he and Virgil leave Minos behind) being whirled through the darkness by the infernal storm,.

Batten's Geryon (Fig. 16.7) is more mysterious and less foul than Dante declares him to be, but has all the features Dante picks out (17.10–27) — the deceitfully righteous face, the hairy arms and the reptilian forefeet suggested by the word 'branche', the serpent's body with its surface patterned with knots and circles, and the forked tail of a scorpion. On his back Dante hunches himself against an upright and supportive Virgil, looking fearfully down while Geryon directs his gaze directly to the front as if concentrating on calibrating the circling descent that Dante describes and which is suggested visually by the snaking of his body. Dante says that he could see nothing beyond the body of the beast during the descent itself, only hear the sound of rushing water (which turns out to be the River Phlegethon) and then of wailing, and that it is only when they dismount that he makes out, and rapidly describes for his readers' benefit, the tenfold divisions of Malebolge with its connecting bridges and the bottommost pit of Hell at its centre (18.1–18). Partly prompted no doubt by this description that is about to be offered after the descent itself, Batten has chosen to show the whole of lower Hell, including features that Dante does not mention at this point. There are three small figures in the bottom right-hand corner, who are three of the giants positioned in a well around the rim of the lowest circle, the frozen waste of Cocytus, their figures made tiny by distance but with enough definition for us to make out their reflections in the ice. And there are fissures in the rocky surface of Malebolge and indications that the bridges across the sixth bolgia are broken. The cause is the earthquake that occurred at Christ's death on the Cross, which Virgil talks about in an earlier speech (12.31–45) and which one of the devils, Malacoda, says more about later (21. 105–17). The broken bridge will cause Dante and Virgil some trouble in canto 24, their climb out being

FIG. 16.5. The Devils Fallen in the Pitch

the subject of another illustration (Fig. 16.8).

In making so much visible Batten may be departing from the letter of Dante's text in Canto 17, but everything he introduces into the Geryon illustration is grounded in what Dante says about the geography and history of Hell, and with the remarkable attention to getting the details right that he shows in his illustrations generally. He was almost pedantically interested in Hell's topography. The catalogue of the exhibition of the drawings of 1900 has at its end a diagrammatic representation of Malebolge in profile which brings out what Batten saw as its almost vertical steepness. He also remarks that from what Dante says in various places the divisions between the trenches of Malebolge are quite narrow, but that the 9th and 10th bolge are separated by a a considerable gap, as is indeed suggested by the opening section of canto 29. Batten proposes in the catalogue that the gap is something like one-and-a-quarter miles (though if anything ll. 37–39 suggest that it could be much larger). In the Geryon drawing the precise distance does not matter of course, but it is made plain that the gap is larger than any of the preceding ones.

It is not just details of the text that concern Batten but also questions of scale and texture. Only a small number of drawings foreground the sinners and their punishments, most notably, as well as Paolo and Francesca, the Avaricious and the Prodigal, and Caiaphas. In the majority groups of sinners appear in a broader setting, as do representations of Virgil and Dante. Unlike Flaxman, but like Doré, Batten follows Dante in wanting to bring out the material reality of Hell as a place, taking especial pains with Malebolge. He uses his formidable command of line to accentuate its sheer hardness, picking out the details of great boulders, broken cliffs, and roughly smoothed causeways, the darkness and hardness of which is contrasted visually with the much lighter figures of Virgil and Dante and also of

Fig. 16.6. Minos, the Judge of Hell

Fig. 16.7. Geryon Carries Virgil and Dante down to Malebolge

FIG. 16.8. Virgil and Dante Climb out of the Sixth Pit of Malebolge

the sinners, who are repeatedly reduced to small figures that our eyes have to seek out. In the drawing of Dante and Virgil climbing out of the Sixth Bolgia (Fig. 16.8) our attention goes first to the massive wall looming towards us on the right and occupying almost half the picture, then to Virgil standing above Dante and urging him on. It is only when we follow the line down from them towards the bottom left-hand corner that we see the backs of the hypocrites trudging on their endless way. A somewhat similar effect is achieved with the illustration to the Ulysses canto, which picks up on what Dante says about stopping himself from falling into the bolgia by holding onto a rock and shows a quite unemphatic version of the double flame of Ulysses and Diomedes below, the taller of the two tips waving as it speaks, as Dante says it does.

The vastness of Hell is impressively conveyed in drawings such as that of Geryon, more so of course in the larger collotype reproduction than in the book-illustration. And the giants, which appear there, appear in two other drawings in similarly reduced size to bring out the fearful vastness of lower hell. In one remarkable drawing (Fig. 16.9), however, it is their immensity which is emphasised, even more so than in the comparable Doré drawing which it echoes in some ways. Both artists bring out the giants' size partly by reducing Dante and Virgil to almost doll-like figures. Batten reinforces the effect by depicting the traitors plunged in ice in the Ninth Circle on a similar scale and also by foregrounding the crouching figure of Antaeus, making him occupy more than a quarter of the picture space and suggesting through the perspective of the wall and the other two giants (Nembrot — or Nimrod — with the horn and Ephialtes in chains) that, were he to stand

Fig. 16.9. Antaeus

up, he would be a truly enormous figure. Following Dante, Batten gives his face an expression that suggests grudging acceptance of his role and at the same time makes the hands indicate the care with which he carries it out. He has taken some minor liberties with the text, not least in having Antaeus crouch, whereas Dante suggests a more rigid movement from the vertical, comparing the giant first to the tower of the Garisenda in Bologna seeming to lean over a person looking up and then, when he has put the two figures down, rising up like the mast being hoisted in a ship (31.136–45). More interestingly we might well feel Batten has given the moment of descent a somewhat different tone from that which it has in Dante, whose focus is first on Virgil's resoluteness and then (almost comically) on Dante's fear. Those features are rendered schematically in the positioning of the two figures. But Batten's three giants are not at all grotesque or frightening, nor for that matter inhuman apart from their size. In fact they seem rather Michelangiolesque and more languorous than threatening. Again Batten's aestheticising classicism seems evident. As such, it is arguably not out of place. Dante's account of the encounter with the giants is not simply a record or an evocation of fear and trembling before massive brute power (as Doré makes it). It is also studded with references to classical myth and history and to a lesser extent to the Old Testament. Not all of these have an obvious narrative or expressive function and may well be seen as rhetorical ornamentation deliberately made to clash with the subject-matter of the episode. Batten's classicism does something similar and in that regard is quite Dantesque.

III

In the letter to Lady Margaret Hall mentioned above, Mary Batten writes that 'it was great trial to my husband that these drawings, the work of three years, were hidden from the world for over thirty years' and that they were 'the culmination of my husband's work in book illustration'. She was right. His illustrations to fairy- and folk-tales have a quirky imaginative freedom and vigour, but only those for the *Arabian Nights* stories have some of the complexity of the Dante drawings.[23] Those he did for Hewlett's *Masque of Dead Florentines* have some analogies with the Dante work (particularly the drawings of female figures), but are imaginatively simpler and more schematically realised. The Dante drawings are a major project, without parallel in late nineteenth-century Britain, and are more elaborately and thoughtfully worked and much more disciplined in their combinations of fantastical and classicising imagery than his earlier work. In a variety of different and quite individual realisations of late nineteenth-century English artistic idiom, Batten engages closely with Dante's text, attempting to find as exact pictorial equivalents as possible for the events, characters and topography that Dante describes verbally. That inevitably means interpreting the original text, and Batten is a subtle and careful interpreter. He does not aim to impose a strong personal vision in the manner of Blake and many more modern illustrators (Dalì, Phillips, etc.) but nonetheless offers a particular way (or ways) of looking at Dante's Hell. If illustration is expected to help flagging readers (of which in the case of Dante there are always many) and to give them pleasures that have a bearing on the text but also have value in their own right, then Batten is outstanding. David Nutt was barely exaggerating when he wrote in the endnote to the 1900 catalogue, that 'Mr Batten's designs speak for themselves, but the publisher may be allowed to emphasise the fact that they essay to interpret as well as to illustrate, and that they thus form a valuable addition to the exegesis of the *Inferno*, as well as an artistic achievement of the first rank.'[24]

Batten seems to have abandoned book-illustration after 1900 and turned his energies to recuperating Renaissance techniques of fresco and tempera painting, becoming secretary of the Society of Tempera painters. He was also active in the Art Workers Guild. He carried out painting commissions for English churches,[25] well as continuing a successful career as a painter in oils. He also published a book of poems, almost all centred on his paintings of the 1880s and 90s,[26] and more curiously a treatise on the possibility of human beings achieving winged flight.[27] Overall he was a highly talented and individual figure, whose work deserves serious re-evaluation, his Dante illustrations above all.[28]

Notes to Chapter 16

1. See in particular *Italy's Three Crowns: Reading Dante, Petrarch and Boccaccio*, ed. by Zygmunt G. Barański and Martin McLaughlin (Oxford: Bodleian Library, 2007), and *Dante in Oxford: The Paget Toynbee Lectures*, ed. by Tristan Kay, Martin McLaughlin and Michelangelo Zaccarello (London: Legenda, 2011).
2. Cary's translation was first published in its entirety in 1814. The first illustrated edition seems to have been an American one of 1845, which included twelve of the Flaxman drawings. The 1866 two-volume folio (London: Cassell, Petter and Galpin and New York: P. F. Collier) was the first to include the Doré illustrations and was followed by most later ones. (See R. W. King, *The Translator of Dante: The Life, Work and Friendships of Henry Francis Cary (1772–1844)* (London: Martin Secker, 1925), p. 284.)
3. For discussions of Cary's work and its reception see King, *passim*, especially Chs. 4 and 6: William J. De Sua, *Dante into English. A Study of the Translation of the 'Divine Comedy' in Britain and America* (Chapel Hill: University of North Carolina Press, 1964), pp. 26–39; Valeria Tinkler-Villani, *Visions of Dante in English Poetry: Translations of the* Commedia *from Jonathan Richardson to William Blake* (Amsterdam: Rodopi, 1989), pp. 173–234; Alison Millbank, *Dante and the Victorians* (Manchester: Manchester University Press, 1998), pp. 17–25; Antonella Braida, *H. F. Cary's 'The Vision of Dante': Its Literary Context and its Influence* (Unpublished D.Phil thesis, Oxford, 1997); Edoardo Crisafulli, *The Vision of Dante: Cary's Translation of the 'Divine Comedy'* (Market Harborough: Troubador, 2003), especially pp. 97–166. For the overall history of Dante's reception by English readers, translators and adapters see above all Nick Havely, *Dante's British Public* (Oxford: Oxford University Press, 2014).
4. See Millbank, pp. 196–200.
5. First comprehensively surveyed by Paget Toynbee, *Chronological List of English Translations of Dante from Chaucer to the Present Day*, Twenty-Fourth Annual Report of the Dante Society (Boston: Ginn and Company, 1906). Toynbee counted 22 complete translations of the *Divine Comedy* as having appeared by 1904, all but 3 since 1850. Gilbert Cunningham (*The Divine Comedy in English: A Critical Bibliography*, 2 vols (Edinburgh: Oliver and Boyd, 1965–66), I, 1) counts forty translations of one or more *cantiche* before 1900 and forty-two between then and 1965.
6. *Dante's Divine Comedy, Consisting of the Inferno-Purgatorio and Paradiso. A Version in the Nine-line Metre of Spenser*, by George Musgrave. *The Inferno or Hell* (London: Swan, Sonnenschein and Co, 1893).
7. London: Chapman and Hall, 1854.

8. Edinburgh: T. & A. Constable, 1890.
9. Notably *Celtic Fairy Tales* (1890): *English Fairy Tales* (1890); *Indian Fairy Tales* (1892); *More Celtic Fairy Tales* (1894); *More English Fairy Tales* (1895); *The Book of Wonder Voyages* (1896). All these were published by David Nutt, London. Batten also illustrated E. Dixon's *Fairy Tales from the Arabian Nights* (1893) and *More Fairy Tales from the Arabian Nights* (1895), both published in rather luxurious editions by J. M. Dent, London.
10. See his 'Woodcut Printing in Colour after the Japanese Manner', *The Studio*, 3–4 (1894–95), 110–15 and 144–48.
11. Maurice Hewlett, *A Masque of Dead Florentines*, Pictured by J. D. Batten (London: J. M. Dent, 1895).
12. Those exhibited were reproduced in *Catalogue of an Exhibition of Forty-three Drawings by John D. Batten Held at Leighton House, Whitsuntide, 1900. A.D.* (Long Acre: David Nutt, 1900), and then, again in 1900, in *Dante's Inferno: Forty-three Illustrations by John D. Batten,* Engraved by Richard Taylor and Co.
13. The announcement is contained in an endnote by Nutt to the 1900 Catalogue.
14. E. H. New, letter to S. C. Cockerell, 23 October 1913 (British Library, Additional MS 52742).
15. *Dante's Inferno: A Version in the Spenserian Stanza, by George Musgrave, with Forty-four Illustrations by John D. Batten* (London: Humphrey Milford [for Oxford University Press] 1933).
16. The decade 1928–38 saw five translations of the *Inferno* published and two of the entire *Comedy*. See Cunningham, Vol. 1, 9.
17. A review in the *New Statesman and Nation* (23 July 1933) by W. J. Turner quotes the opening lines of the translation and comments: 'The effect, as a whole, is even more ridiculously remote from Dante than those three lines taken above; but again, much literary skill has gone into the making of this version; poetry, however, does not derive from literary skill.' Later judgements are only slightly less damning. See De Sua, pp. 75–77, and, for a summary of initial reviews, Cunningham, Vol. 1, 186–91.
18. Eugene Paul Nassar, *Illustrations to Dante's Inferno* (Rutherford: Farleigh Dickinson University Press, 1994).
19. A letter from Parker to the Principal of Lady Margaret Hall, dated 16 January 1933, says that the drawings are valued at £80 4s. 6d, but that the collotypes 'can be regarded as valueless' (LMH, Domestic Papers Box 3, Musgrave Bequest).
20. Mary Batten, Letter to the Principal, Lady Margaret Hall, 20 January 1933 (Also in DP3 — see preceding Note).
21. The size of the pages is approximately 7.5 × 5.5 inches (19 × 14 cm).
22. The full list, with the titles (which may well be Parker's) given in the 1933 edition, is as follows: 1. Beatrice watches from Paradise; 2. The Stars at the Beginning of the Journey; 3. Dante essays to climb the Mountain; 4. He meets the Lion and the She-wolf; 5. The Gate of Hell; 6. Ante Hell. The Sluggards; 7. Charon; 8. Limbo. The Hemisphere of Light; 9. The Meeting with Homer, Horace, Ovid, and Lucan; 10. Minos, the Judge of Hell; 11. The Carnal Sinners; 12. Paolo and Francesca; 13. Cerberus, the Dog-Fiend; 14. Plutus, the God of Riches; 15. The Avaricious and the Prodigal; 16. The Ferry of Phlegyas; 17. The Devils at the Entrance to the City of Dis; 18. A Messenger descends from Heaven; 19. Farinata; 20. The Minotaur; 21. The Meeting with Chiron; 22. The Centaur Nessus carries Dante across the River of Blood; 23. The Wood of the Suicides; 24. The Edge of the Third Belt of the Seventh Circle; 25. Brunetto Latini; 26. Virgil throws Dante's Girdle over the Precipice; 27. Geryon carries Virgil and Dante down to Malebolge; 28. Panders and Seducers; 29. Simoniacs; 30. Soothsayers; 31. Virgil parleys with the Devils; 32. The Devils fallen in the Pitch; 33. Caiaphas; 34. Virgil and Dante climb out of the Sixth Pit of Malebolge; 35. Thieves; 36. Evil Counsellors. The Flame of Diomede and Ulysses; 37. Bertran de Born and Geri del Bello; 38. Approaching the Last Pit of Malebolge; 39. The Giants; 40. Antaeus; 41. The Lowest Depth of Hell; 42. Satan; 43. Virgil and Dante pass the Centre of the Universe; 44. The Stars at the End of the Journey.
23. See Note 9 above.
24. See Note 11 above. Such later judgements as I have seen are, to say the least, restrained. So Cunningham, p. 191: 'The drawings are wood-engravings, of varying relevance and interest,

more likely to be admired for some degree of technical skill than for any light they shed on the poem, though R.A.[Anning] Bell says that Batten's studious mind revelled in the preliminary labour of working out a thorough understanding of the complex geographical plan of the *Inferno*.' Nassar (p. 23) is dismissive of Batten's drawings and those of others he sees as influenced by William Morris and Art nouveau. 'Essentially decorative they rarely capture a complex Dantean tonality. The scenes of the *Inferno* are paraded, often with delightful line, but with little of Dante's inner life...'

25. Notably St Martin's Church, Kensal Rise, and Christ Church, Lichfield.
26. John D. Batten, *Poems* (London: Chiswick Press, 1916). This had been preceded by an earlier collection, *Verses* (Cambridge: Devana Press, 1893).
27. John D. Batten, *An Approach to Winged Flight* (Brighton: Dolphin Press, 1928).
28. Acknowledgements: I should like to thank the Principal and Fellows of Lady Margaret Hall for permission to reproduce nine of Batten's illustrations. My thanks also go to Roberta Staples and Oliver Mahony for invaluable help with library and archival material, and to Allan Doig and Nicholas Shrimpton for much-needed advice and encouragement.

CHAPTER 17

Turns of Chance:
Modern Luck and Italian Modernism
(Marinetti, Montale, Pirandello)

Robert S. C. Gordon

The problems of chance and indeterminacy, of the 'slings and arrows of outrageous fortune' that beset human lives, loom large in our philosophical conceptions of being and in our everyday experiences. We all feel acutely our inability to control the course of events in our lives and we are all tempted to give the force that deprives us of that control a name, a label, an existence as an entity we can imagine, if not quite contain. Some idea of fortune and misfortune, of the unpredictable outcome of events and how we might mitigate them — in other words, some idea of luck — is a 'human universal', to use a phrase adopted by anthropologist Donald Brown,[1] a constituent element of all human cultures and, we might speculate, perhaps also an element of consciousness or mind itself, as if an emanation of some underlying animal instinct for coming to terms with risk and danger.[2]

But human universals always and necessarily express themselves in culturally specific and historically delimited ways. We find them coded into specific historical-cultural re-elaborations, into forms that enact a dialectical transformation, reprising extant patterns whilst also overlaying them, in a process of more or less apparent and destabilising adaptation, with new tropes and new topoi. Where we see such universals take an especially disconcerting or radical turn, we might deduce that a profound shift in values and / or aesthetics has taken place and we might identify the symptoms of a new cultural paradigm with the re-invention of shared categories such as luck and chance. One instance of such an epochal shift that has been posited and traced in innumerable categories of knowledge and value is the nineteenth- and early twentieth-century entry into 'modernity' in European culture. This transition to modernity over the course of the long nineteenth century has been variously described and labelled with epithets such as industrial, democratic, scientific, secular, mass-cultural, urban, colonial, secularizing; moving on, in the early twentieth century, into an implosion of war, imperial collapse and radical cultural 'modernism'. We might therefore well expect, and hope to explore, a shift in this period in the imagining of the 'human universal' of fortune, chance and luck, as one amongst many other categories in a phase of radical transformation. If, previous to the convulsive era of modernity, talk of fortune had been dominated by millennial traditions of belief in a divine force of fate — whether that be the blind goddess Fortuna or the hand of Christian Providence, guiding destinies through forces beyond our control[3] — modernity instead prepared the ground for, on the one hand, a radically new set of assumptions around the individual and his (more rarely, her) capacity to shape their destiny (the self-made-man of bourgeois Europe);[4] and, on the other hand, a broad assumption of scientific social knowledge, often implying a new statistical knowledge, that contained and tamed the wilds of chance.[5] In short, as this bird's-eye purview suggests, modernity brought with it new forms, ideas, images and stories of luck, undermining although never quite abandoning older shared myths of Fortune and Providence.

Such a broad-brush sketch of an hypothesis leaves open to analysis and discovery a more textured sense of precisely how and what emerged in this transition to new conceptions of chance. Closer attention is needed to discern the working patterns in the emergence of a new myth, to trace its transitional, founding symptoms and the minutiae with which the new replaced or built a new synthesis with the old. This chapter proposes one way to test out the larger hypothesis, to tease out its manifestation at the level of textual form and aesthetics, to put flesh on the bones of an assumption that modernity transformed our image and idea of luck.

It does so by revisiting three well-known early twentieth-century works of modernist literature in Italian, looking in each them for markers of a specific literary and cultural modernist turn in the history of luck. It searches for a series of localized motifs of chance in these texts that might provide the framework for a genealogy of modern luck. The selection of these particular works might be said in itself to have something of the random about it, given their markedly diverse forms, tones and styles and their chronological range from across the first quarter of the twentieth century: in a sense, they share little more than their much-anthologized status as canonical works of the period. As is often the case with apparently random (or pseudo-random) selections, however, there are biases at work. The texts are useful precisely because they stand for some of the fundamentals of European modernism and also, as we shall see, embrace key dynamics of chance, resonating with an array of contemporary literary and cultural production so that they seem like the tip of an iceberg of modernist luck.

The texts in question are, in the order they will be treated here: Filippo Tommaso Marinetti's first Futurist manifesto (1909), Eugenio Montale's first major poetry collection, *Ossi di seppia* (1925), and Luigi Pirandello's most important novel, and perhaps the first of any modernist work of fiction in Italian, *Il fu Mattia Pascal* (1904).[6] The brief analysis of each offered here will be loosely governed by a single motif of modern luck, which is thrown into particular new light by the work in question and around which other related motifs, and so a general picture of modernist luck, seems to cluster and revolve. These are, respectively, the figures of accident, contingency and curiosity.

1. Futurism. Accident

As in so many other aspects, Italian modernism finds one of its focal and foundational points in relation to genealogies of chance in the avant-garde explosion of Futurism, and in particular in Marinetti's 'Fondazione e manifesto del futurismo' of 1909.[7] This much analysed hybrid piece of late-symbolist, sub-Nietzschean, early modernist rhetoric combines, in its full version, two strikingly distinct sections or performed movements: first, a florid narrative preamble in a form and style approaching that of a prose poem; and secondly, a programmatic list of revolutionary statements of intent, the manifesto proper, signed off with a declamatory coda. What interests here is less the enumeration of Futurist principles found in the manifesto section, for all its pioneering force as the inaugural statement of avant-garde, collective cultural activism, than its strange underpinning in the preceding narrative section.

Marjorie Perloff, in her influential work *The Futurist Moment*, identified elements of the narrative preamble as key to Marinetti's transformation of the manifesto form from its more pompous and directive nineteenth-century predecessors into something more performative and compelling.[8] Perloff placed particular emphasis on the non-psychological and collective aspect of the adventure narrative in the preamble, as it evokes an exalted night vigil spent in some fantastical hybrid realm, which combines echoes of Marinetti's exotic Egyptian childhood and the mechanized spaces, bodies and machines, real and imagined, of contemporary industrial Milan.

Marinetti and his friends head off at dawn in their three beast-like automobiles ('gli automobili famelici [...] le tre belve sbuffanti', 'Fondazione', pp. 3–4), heedless, headlong, self-forgetting, thrusting towards danger and death: 'La furente scopa della pazzia ci strappò a noi stessi e ci cacciò attraverso le vie, scoscese e profonde come letti di torrenti' 'Fondazione', p. 4). The climactic moment of violence and revelation — and, for the reader or audience of the manifesto, the moment that sets the scene for and the seal on the proclaimed truth of the manifesto to follow, the proclamation of the birth of Futurism — is a half-heroic, half-comic car crash:

> ... Diamoci in pasto all'Ignoto, non già per disperazione, ma soltanto per colmare i profondi pozzi dell'Assurdo!
> Avevo appena pronunziate queste parole, quando girai bruscamente su me stesso, con la stessa ebrietà folle dei cani che voglion mordersi la coda, ed ecco ad un tratto venirmi incontro due ciclisti, che mi diedero torto, titubando davanti a me come due ragionamenti, entrambi persuasivi e nondimeno contradittorii. Il loro stupido dilemma discuteva sul mio terreno.... Che noia! Auff!... Tagliai corto, e, pel disgusto, mi scaraventai colle ruote all'aria in un fossato....
> Oh! materno fossato, quasi pieno di un'acqua fangosa! Bel fossato d'officina! Io gustai avidamente la tua melma fortificante, che mi ricordò la santa mammella nera della mia nutrice sudanese.... Quando mi sollevai — cencio sozzo e puzzolente — di sotto la macchina capovolta, io mi sentii attraversare il cuore, deliziosamente, dal ferro arroventato della gioia!
> Una folla di pescatori armati di lenza e di naturalisti podagrosi tumultuava già intorno al prodigio. Con cura paziente e meticolosa, quella gente dispose

> alte armature ed enormi reti di ferro per pescare il mio automobile, simile ad un gran pescecane arenato. La macchina emerse lentamente dal fosso, abbandonando nel fondo, come squame, la sua pesante carrozzeria di buon senso e le sue morbide imbottiture di comodità.
>
> Credevano che fosse morto, il mio bel pescecane, ma una mia carezza bastò a rianimarlo, ed eccolo risuscitato, eccolo in corsa, di nuovo, sulle sue pinne possenti!
>
> Allora, col volto coperto della buona melma delle officine — impasto di scorie metalliche, di sudori inutili, di fuliggini celesti — noi, contusi e fasciate le braccia ma impavidi, dettammo le nostre prime volontà a tutti gli uomini *vivi* della terra: [...] ('Fondazione', pp. 5–6)

The scene is quite a remarkable one of injury, miracle and resurrection, of machine, nature and man tangled and emerging from a watery ditch ('melma delle officine — impasto di scorie metalliche, di sudori inutili, di fuliggini celesti'). It is worth asking precisely what auratic qualities Marinetti was intent on invoking in this incoherent vision of this careening vehicle, as the specific source and inspiration of his 'dictation' of the principles of the new futurist life, which follows on immediately from this extract.

Jeffrey Schnapp, in an important 1999 essay, argued that this foundational car crash places Marinetti at a cultural-historical cusp between two versions of modern subjectivity, in relation to the motion technology of transport, looking back to Rousseau's *Rêveries du promeneur solitaire* (1782) and forward to J. G. Ballard's 1973 novel *Crash*:

> [I] place Futurism's founding myth at the culminating point of an anthropology of speed and thrill that evolved over the course of two prior centuries: an 'anthropology' inasmuch as it envisages accelerated motion not as a neutral physical event that leaves the traveler and the context traveled through unchanged. On the contrary, the transportation revolution of the eighteenth and nineteenth centuries precipitated fundamental perceptual and psychic changes in human subjects and in the fantasies that governed their modes of interconnection with landscapes traversed and viewed: changes that suggest a tight linkage between the history of transportation technologies and that of optical devices, from phantasmagoria to moving pictures, such that the story of moving vehicles is, from the start, the story of moving cameras; changes that so blur the distinction between the categories of realism and the hallucinatory or the fantastic that they demand a rethinking of the commonplace notion that modernism marks a revolt against naturalism.[9]

Schnapp sees in Marinetti's crash a combination of Futurism's aesthetic of speed and its fascination with the perception and materials of technology (metal, surface, contact), which looks forward to the erotics of techno-modernity that Ballard will later make explicit in his novel *Crash*. The figure of the accident, the flashpoint of the crash, is what ties all these features together.

Karen Beckman has recently extended Schnapp's insight into the modernist topos of the crash by linking Futurism to the slapstick crashes and collisions of silent film comedy, for example in her analysis of early car-crash shorts such as Cecil Hepworth's *How It Feels to Be Run Over* (1900) and *Explosion of a Motor Car*

(1900).[10] Beckman notes how, in these experiments in motion, the accident is not necessarily or exclusively marked by speed but rather by a more subversive 'series of possible alternatives to a notion of bourgeois progress that is repeatedly aligned with capitalism, adulthood, heterosexuality, the couple, and the car's forward motion' (p.64). Beckman is in fact writing here not of Hepworth, but of Laurel and Hardy. Marinetti's own disastrous, muddy, tumbling crash, its sudden disruption of the direction of travel, has something of the same subversive (and comic) quality.

Part and parcel of this somewhat dizzying brew of intersecting modernist topoi, and closely related to those touched on by Schnapp and Beckman, is an underlying abstracted dimension to Marinetti's thickly materialized crash: that is, the category of the 'accident' or 'accidental', the event as a figure of pure chance, of the indeterminate and uncontrolled break in the flow of movement, without apparent purpose or function, uncaused and uncausing although by no means without consequence:[11] on the contrary, since the grandiose consequence of the absurd crash in Milan, is nothing less than the hallucinatory birth of Futurism. This dimension of accidental chance has not only a mechanical aspect — the sudden collision of two bodies or of bodies, objects, machines and natural surfaces — but also aesthetic, ethical or philosophical aspects that are at least as pertinent to the Futurist revolution as its erotic or techno-subjective implications.

The aesthetics and ethics of Futurism that the 1909 manifesto goes on to declare is subtended by values and energies that derive in part from this open embrace of the accidental. Marinetti's state of mind and art in his crazed car dash prior to the crash is one of, among other things, an openness to risk, danger, death, and an indifference to consequences: in other words, an openness to chance. It has the quality of blind, uncontrolled abandon, much as the classical goddess of Fortune was pictured as blindfolded — and we might usefully compare in passing this ancient-modern analogy with Marinetti's own much-quoted analogy later in the manifesto between classical beauty and modernist techno-aesthetics ('un automobile ruggente, che sembra correre sulla mitraglia, è più bello della Vittoria di Samotracia', 'Fondazione', p. 6). And the manifesto section repeatedly taps into this same conjunction of elements:

> 1. Noi vogliamo cantare l'amor del pericolo, l'abitudine all'energia e alla temerità. [...]
> 3 Noi vogliamo esaltare il movimento aggressivo, l'insonnia febbrile, il passo di corsa, il salto mortale, lo schiaffo ed il pugno. [...]
> 5. Noi vogliamo inneggiare all'uomo che tiene il volante, la cui asta ideale attraversa la Terra, lanciata a corsa, essa pure, sul circuito della sua orbita.
> ('Fondazione', p. 6)

Having recovered the abstracted quality of the accidental that frames and subtends the manifesto, we can usefully return to Marinetti's material embodiment of chance and the accidental. In both the narrative and the manifesto sections of the founding document — and indeed in many later Futurist manifestoes and creations in different media — the material, multi-sensory presences in the crash scene begin to look like material markers of chance, in the shape of chaos, collision, noise and mess. The car crash is, literally, mired in confusion, filth, mud, burning, tangled wreckage and tumult. David Trotter has written compellingly about late nineteenth-century English and French fiction and painting — from Turner to Melville to Flaubert — as recurrently stained by dirt and mess, by clutter, litter and mud.[12] This material, cultural and mimetic debris is to be distinguished, Trotter notes, from 'waste', which is the systemic, planned, constitutive and necessary by-product of (industrial, capitalist) labour and production. 'Mess', on the other hand, tends to be unproductive, deviant and thus deeply disruptive: as a marker of disorder, it creates a space for chance and contingency: 'mess is what contingency's signature would look like, if contingency had a signature' (Trotter, p. 15). Marinetti's 'melma', the debris of the car and the blackened faces that emerge from the wreckage, are, we might suggest, no less than the materialized image of the pure chance of the accident, envisioned as mess. The sheer mess of stinking mud, metal and sweat, together with the abstracted randomness of the accidental, and indeed together with the timbre of death and the erotics of speed, add up in Marinetti's florid invocation to a revelation; a staged, chance epiphany, an epiphany of modern chance. And, in Marinetti's tale of origin, Futurism flows directly from it.

2. Montale. Contingency

Marinetti's epiphany reaches its peak of imagined intensity at a double turn. The beast-automobile veers and turns from its path of heroic progress; coming face-to-face with the querulous cyclists, it turns again, vertically this time, overturning, before crashing into the watery, maternal ditch. This double turn as a figure of accident — and more broadly of chance — as a prelude to an epiphany (of the revealed 'Word' of Futurism), recalls other moments of modernist epiphany, other moments of chance vision through turning movement, which work as a sort of counterpoint to the images of blind chance, loss and abandon that accompany it. These other moments could not, however, be further in tonality and in the negative valency of their epiphanies from the bombast of the Futurist moment.

Secular epiphanies in modernism are a well-worn object of study, perhaps first explicated by James Joyce in *Stephen Hero* ('a sudden spiritual manifestation, whether in the vulgarity of speech or of gesture or in a memorable phase of the mind itself [...] the most delicate and evanescent of moments') and further elaborated in *Dubliners*, but with roots in Romantic visionaries and analogues in other modernists from Woolf to Mansfield to Faulkner.[13] But where Marinetti's Futurist revelation, much like the transcendent epiphanies of monotheistic religion, is linked to a truth and a call to proselytise, Joyce's and other modernists' tend to be fleeting and fragile, unpredictable, the opposite of providential, rooted in and an enactment of contingency.

A key analogous case in Italian modernism is that of the muted, impossible miracles of Montale's *Ossi di seppia*.[14] *Ossi*'s tone of dark entrapment and sunlit absorption precludes any facile form of enlightenment, but the fragile possibility of a moment of illumination is staged with almost as much drama as Marinetti's crash, also around an accident and also around a turn. Montale's epiphanies come not from heroic abandon to danger, but instead from a chance stumble or an incidental glance that opens onto a glimpse of miraculous change or return, a new light. The prefatory 'In limine' and the opening poem 'I limoni' give us each of these accidents, the stumble and the glimpse, in turn:

> Un rovello è di qua dall'erto muro.
> Se procedi t'imbatti
> tu forse nel fantasma che ti salva: [...] ('In limine', *Ossi*, p. 5)

> Quando un giorno da un malchiuso portone
> tra gli alberi di una corte
> ci si mostrano i gialli dei limoni;
> e il gelo del cuore si sfa,
> e in petto ci scrosciano
> le loro canzoni
> le trombe d'oro della solarità. ('I limoni', *Ossi*, p. 12)

The scene or moment of the Montalean miracle is perhaps most purely, almost abstractly evoked in one of the brief, ostensibly simple lyrics of the 'Ossi di seppia' section, 'Forse un mattino andando' (*Ossi*, p. 42). Here, the dynamic figure of the turn returns, in the form of a sudden turn and snatched look that cheats grim reality, catches it unawares, thereby performing the impossible (and also terrifying) miracle of knowledge or self-knowledge:

> Forse un mattino andando in un'aria di vetro
> arida, rivolgendomi, vedrò compirsi il miracolo:
> il nulla alle mie spalle, il vuoto dietro
> di me, con un terrore di ubriaco

The terror of the vision is another kind of abandon ('di ubriaco'), not to the exhilarating danger of death and risk of the Futurists, but rather an abandonment to nothingness, the vacuum that lies beneath and behind our 'screen' realities.[15]

Throughout *Ossi*, Montale holds out half a hope for his beachcomber's noonday miracle, sketching out a negative metaphysics caught sight of on the turn. And there is a particular structural and lexical pattern to its evocation, to its dependence on a banal look, turn, or stumble, and thus to its origin and end in contingency: all the stagings of Montale's fragile miracle — in 'In limine', 'I limoni' and 'Forse un mattino', and indeed in many other poems besides in *Ossi* — are conditional or hypothetical in mood, and thus always suspended, no more than possible, fundamentally contingent, dependent on an 'if', a 'when', or a 'maybe'. The poet imagines repeatedly what escape, an opening, revitalized euphoria or awesome self-knowledge would feel like, when and where it would burst in; but he repeatedly also couches the possibility in doubt, as an event that may happen but may well not, and as all the more elusive, miraculous, all the more uncontrolled and saturated with the negative capability of chance for that. And the characteristic, simple marker of that contingency in *Ossi* is the banal adverb 'forse'.

A search of *Ossi di seppia* shows that Montale uses the word 'forse' a remarkable 19 times in the collection as a whole, often at moments and in poems of structuring importance for his vision and poetics. To name a few, these include, 'Arremba su la strinata prode', 'Mediterraneo', 'Arsenio', 'Crisalide' and 'Incontro',[16] as well as two poems already cited, 'In limine' ('t'imbatti / tu forse') and 'Forse un mattino'.

Like the violent veerings of Marinetti's accident, Montale's 'forse' imagines a momentary bifurcation or a deviation, a swerve in space and time.[17] 'Forse un mattino' gives us at the start the blandly generic 'mattino' and 'andando' to set as a non-place and a non-time for the swerve ('rivolgendomi') — this could be anywhere, any morning — and it closes in its second stanza with an equally simple binary between those who have seen, who know the secret, who have turned, and those who have not ('gli uomini che non si voltano'). But the moment is merely an iterative ghost of a possibility: it and all the terrifying consequences of revelation it brings could happen on any and every day, but might never happen at all. The split, the gap between revelation and nothingness, is infinitesimal and arbitrary, stripped of efficient cause and hence by definition contingent, led by empty chance. All this is cast as a result of its simple incipit, the insidiously destabilizing adverb 'Forse [...]'. The resulting vision is most likely a chimera, a future that is all but stolen away in its moment of imagining. In this, 'Forse un mattino' sets the paradigm, with its hanging, muted opening, a seeping marker of the contingent, lingering over and bleaching all that follows, dissolving the spectrum of metaphysical and physical possibility into a possible nothing, just as they seem to herald truths, certainties and a sense of a future.

There is a contrast of scale (time and space) and also of noise, here. The muted 'Forse' contrasts with the trumpet blasts of 'I limoni', with grander revelations. Waiting on the random swerve of chance, Montale's moment of contingent epiphany is also — unlike Marinetti's loud and loudly proclaimed crash — a near noiseless, imperceptible moment, as is evident also in poems such as 'Arremba su la strinata prode', where the moment of rupture is all but silent (again, perhaps): 'Viene lo spacco; forse senza strepito' (*Ossi*, p. 48). In the sequence 'Mediterraneo', 'forse' clusters in no fewer than six occurrences and the term accompanies the infinitesimal voice of the poet as he contemplates the vast roar of the sea, oscillating between the contingency of the self and the contingency and certainty of the vast world of nature around him. This latter is an important point in the usage of uncertainty and chance in *Ossi*, since the poet's doubt goes so far as to doubt the very idea that uncertainty is so rooted in the world. Perhaps, in other words, it is just a symptom of his own subjective pathology, his flaw; perhaps chance is an illusion and the world is in reality strong, stable, determined, the opposite of chance:

> e forse
> m'occorreva il coltello che recide,
> la mente che decide e si determina ('Mediterraneo', *Ossi*, p. 59)

> e forse tutto è fisso, tutto è scritto,
> e non vedremo sorgere per via
> la libertà, il miracolo,
> il fatto che non era necessario! ('Crisalide', *Ossi*, p. 89)

The paradox is at its bluntest in 'Crisalide' — perhaps there is no perhaps — and the fundamental affinity of the miracle to chance and contingency is at its deepest: chance or a lucky turn is not only the condition and cause of the miracle here, but it is its very substance. The 'miracolo' *is* 'il fatto che non era necessario', a definition of contingency worthy of a dictionary entry;[18] and it is as pervasive and present an absence as one could possibly imagine.

Other familiar Montalean images resonate in the light of the contingent presence-absence of the 'forse'. The Montalean object is a case in point: *Ossi* is peppered with the fragments, the debris and the bric-à-brac that litters the Ligurian beaches, and this litter evokes once again the clutter and mess of modernity that Marinetti's mud and noise played on in another key. David Trotter analyses the litter on Turner's Brighton beaches as a visual field-marker of chance.[19] And something similar also holds for those other half-presences, the other evanescent figures that haunt *Ossi di seppia*'s fragile moments of rupture and escape and their permanent suspension in contingency: figures of ghosts, half-lives and shadows:

> Se procedi t'imbatti
> tu forse nel fantasma che ti salva ('In limine')
>
> Se un'ombra scorgete, non è
> un'ombra — ma quella io sono. ('Ciò che di me sapeste', *Ossi*, p. 36)

The negative-positive voice in 'Ciò che di me sapeste' (the affirmative 'quella io sono', where 'quella' is, however, a shade or shadow, insubstantial) is a far more compelling and characteristic Montalean subject than the more often quoted, blunt Montalean negative, 'ciò che non siamo'; it is the voice of suspended contingency, rendered posthumous by chance.

3. Pirandello. Curious incidents

The ghostly presence of possible worlds and selves in Montale, opened (perhaps) by a chance turn or trip or (more likely) never opened at all, calls to mind the first living shade and figure of ghostly chance in Italian modernism, Pirandello's 'late' Mattia Pascal. Mattia speaks from the outset of *Il fu Mattia Pascal* as a phantasm: he is narrating his life from the 'afterlife' of the dusty Boccamazza library at Miragno, where he has taken refuge following a series of devastating epiphanies that fate or chance has dealt him. His writing of his story is prompted by the realization that he cannot ressurect his first life as Mattia, having returned from his second life — in reality, another ghostly and insubstantial first afterlife, as it turns out — as Adriano Meis.

The library itself is already a site of a kind of serendipitous chance — and indeed another site of mess and clutter — in its accumulation of dusty tomes and of eclectic knowledge.[20] Its books have been piled up without order or reason and left to rot, oddly coupled, some even stuck to each other. Mattia's reading is fed by the librarian don Eligio, who hurls books as he stumbles upon them, down onto the table at the centre of the disused church for Mattia to debug and dip into:

> Molti libri curiosi e piacevolissimi don Eligio Pellegrinotto, arrampicato tutto il giorno su una scala da lampionajo, ha pescato negli scaffali della biblioteca. Ogni qual volta ne trova uno, lo lancia dall'alto, con garbo, sul tavolone che sta

> in mezzo; la chiesetta ne rintrona; un nugolo di polvere si leva, da cui due o tre ragni scappano via spaventati: io accorro dall'abside, scavalcando la cancellata; dò prima col libro stesso la caccia ai ragni su pe 'l tavolone polveroso; poi apro il libro e mi metto a leggiucchiarlo. (*Il fu Mattia Pascal*, p. 49)

Mattia's own strange story ('strano e diverso', p. 47), seems to echo don Eligio's 'libri curiosi e piacevolissimi', not least as it is, like them, told from the half light of the library. Don Eligio recommends to Pascal that he ape the tone of Boccaccio and Bandello for his own tale; but Mattia's self-conscious autobiographical musings rather stage a sort of self-conscious invention of the modernist novel, as the family melodrama of inheritance, jealousy and betrayal of the novel's opening chapters morphs into the philosophical contrivances and paradoxes of Adriano's story and its problematic of identity and self-(re)invention. What is striking for our purposes is the extent to which, just as the library and its oddball librarians exist under the sign of serendipity and phantasms, so markers of different iterations of chance and luck cast their shadow over the entire narrative of *Il fu Mattia Pascal*, and especially over its pivotal moments of turn and transformation.

As so often in the nineteenth-century novel of which Mattia's early life story is an epigone, the source of all his family's troubles lies in a family fortune, won and lost. Mattia's father had acquired his wealth and property — and then suddenly died of fever following a boat trip to Corsica — all, according to local gossip, in mysterious circumstances of trade, investment and games of chance:

> Qualche vecchio del paese si compiace ancora di dare a credere che la ricchezza di mio padre (la quale pure non gli dovrebbe più dar ombra, passata com'è da un pezzo in altre mani) avesse origini — diciamo così — misteriose.
> Vogliono che se la fosse procacciata giocando a carte, a Marsiglia, col capitano d'un vapore mercantile inglese, il quale, dopo aver perduto tutto il denaro che aveva seco, e non doveva esser poco, si era anche giocato un grosso carico di zolfo imbarcato nella lontana Sicilia per conto d'un negoziante di Liverpool (sanno anche questo! e il nome?), che aveva noleggiato il vapore; quindi, per disperazione, salpando, s'era annegato in alto mare. Così il vapore era approdato a Liverpool, alleggerito anche del peso del capitano. Fortuna che aveva per zavorra la malignità de' miei compaesani.
> Possedevamo terre e case. Sagace e avventuroso, mio padre non ebbe mai pe' suoi commerci stabile sede: sempre in giro con quel suo trabaccolo, dove trovava meglio e più opportunamente comprava e subito rivendeva mercanzie d'ogni genere; e perchè non fosse tentato a imprese troppo grandi e rischiose, investiva a mano a mano i guadagni in terre e case, qui, nel proprio paesello, dove presto forse contava di riposarsi negli agi faticosamente acquistati, contento e in pace tra la moglie e i figliuoli. (*Il fu Mattia Pascal*, p. 52)

By the time of Mattia's early years, his father's property and investments have all but disappeared, and Mattia's impossible character and family circumstances combine to propel him into an acute (Pirandellian) awareness of the catastrophic absurdity of his life. He flees, and at this point, the novel returns to the scene of a game of chance, marking a point of closure of the first cycle of this parody of a life-story. In place of Mattia's father's picaresque card-game, evoking the spirit of trade and adventure, however, the son seems rather to stumble upon the tawdry, *faux-*

glamorous surroundings of the roulette tables at Monte Carlo. It is as if the arch-capitalist model of risk and return staged in the former have been superseded in the latter by a degraded version of the same, by the purely random spin of the wheel, desperate, productless and valueless. But it turns out that Mattia's very subjecthood, his life and death indeed, are at stake in this absurd turn of chance.

The game at Monte Carlo occupies the entirety of Chapter Six of the novel, 'Tac tac tac...' (*Il fu Mattia Pascal*, pp. 88–102), and it acts as a sort of set-piece interlude between Mattia's old and new lives, a prelude to the surprise revelation of the novel's central conceit in Chapter Seven, 'Cambio treno', when Mattia will happen upon news of his own suicide. 'Tac tac tac...' opens with dozens of players hanging on the spinning, tapping, ivory roulette ball, praying to it as to the age-old goddess of fortune, or the reduced version of it, that it embodies. Mattia looks on, his own presence for now a more mundane and empty, ironically detached, product of chance: 'Ero capitato là, a Montecarlo, per caso' (p. 88). Tellingly, he happens upon Monte Carlo as an alternative to a failed project to embark on the great modern adventure of emigration, a sea-borne lighting out (like that of his father) to new worlds. His first fantasy had been to escape from Miragno to Marseille and from there to America: 'mi sarei imbarcato, magari con un biglietto di terza classe, per l'America, così alla ventura' (p. 88). Feeling too tired and old for such a risky venture, however, he has second thoughts and a chance sighting of a shop display on roulette (including the book — another serendipitous encounter with an arcane book — *Méthode pour gagner à la roulette*) tempts him instead to the Casino. There, he finds a microcosm, an isolated community of obsessives devoted to either hyper-rational or hyper-emotional theorems to tame chance and wrench control over their own destinies, even if the theorems and their destinies are both reduced to money, numbers and the spinning wheel. Thus, one player has fallen head over heels in love with 'his' number ('Era innamorato del numero 12', p. 91), whilst others work furiously on formulae and systems to break the bank, as Mattia looks wryly on:

> Vi seggono, di solito, certi disgraziati, cui la passione del giuoco ha sconvolto il cervello nel modo più singolare: stanno lì a studiare il così detto equilibrio delle probabilità, e meditano seriamente i colpi da tentare, tutta un'architettura di giuoco, consultando appunti su le vicende de' numeri: vogliono insomma estrarre la logica dal caso, come dire il sangue dalle pietre; [...] (p. 90)

Initially cynical and immune to the allure of risk, Mattia's sudden and quite random success at the tables leads him to return for 12 days running, astonishing his fellows by winning for nine of these, before his luck turns. This creates an remarkable aura of tawdry charisma around him, as others cling to his magical, almost materialized luck (he is touched, pursued, as the target of deals and desperate offers). The deluded air of excitement is shattered only by the grim suicide of one of the fauna of the locale, whose bloody, shattered face fascinates both Mattia and his fellows gamblers as they watch themselves and their own future in him.

That the Monte Carlo suicide — random, meaningless, directly 'caused' by and encapsulating an uncausing and absurd realm of luck — permeates the whole novel and Pirandello's radical philosophical turn in *Il fu Mattia Pascal* is only confirmed by the symmetries between this and three other suicides that together form the matrix of the book's structure: first, there was the sea-captain, from whom Mattia's father had won his fortune; then, this nameless dandy at Monte Carlo; shortly afterwards, the man at the mill in Miragno, whose corpse is misrecognised as Mattia; and finally, the staged, fake suicide of Adriano Meis in the Tevere in Rome, setting the seal on the impossibilty of Mattia's (and indeed any of our) living and constructing a new life for him/ourselves.

Two of these suicides follow closely on from each other — the anonymous man at the Casino and at the mill at Miragno — making up a powerful diptych that unveils the novel's central trick and paradox, and through which Pirandello embraces the absurd extremes of impossible chance, and the useless systems designed to tame it, and through which he declares both of these as somehow more revealing of our human reality than the banalities of steady, regular lives. Chapters Six and Seven of *Il fu Mattia Pascal* mark a philosophically and psychologically revelatory moment in his work, and they turn on a dual aspect of chance: first the spinning, random tables and ivory balls of the Casino resort; and then the contrivance of the newspaper report of a mangled suicide, and the curious incident of a case of mistaken identity, of a man who reads of his own death.

Famously, Pirandello added as an appendix to the 1921 edition of *Il fu Mattia Pascal* a defence against accusations of anti-naturalism, of 'inverosimiglianza', that had been levelled at the absurd contrivance of events in the novel, under the heading 'Avvertenza sugli scrupoli della fantasia' (*Il fu Mattia Pascal*, pp. 249–55). To clinch his defence, he quoted at length from a newspaper report of 27 March 1920 in *Corriere della sera* that seems lifted directly from his novel: a story of a suicide, a body found in a canal, misrecognised by his wife and her future husband, and finally also the return of the 'dead' man, in this case from prison.[21] The chain of unlikely and (un)lucky circumstances both in the novel and in the reported case, and indeed the lucky strike of Pirandello's happening upon the *Corriere* article twenty years after writing the novel, saturate the novel in coincidence, error and chance, as well as in acutely post-*verista* Pirandellian paradoxes of the real and the realistic, 'il vero' and 'il verosimile'. But the *Corriere* report recalls vividly also the newspaper aspect of Mattia's discovery of his own death, the announcement in a local newspaper under the heading 'Suicidio' that he glimpses on the train and the excessively flowery obituary he manages to obtain by telegraphed copy published in the local Miragno paper, *Il Foglietto* (*Il fu Mattia Pascal*, pp. 106–12).

The newspaper dimension to both the false suicide story and the 'Avvertenza' is of great interest, linked to, but somehow also superseding the origin of the novel in the nineteenth-century melodramatic plot. Both newspaper stories are rooted in the genre of journalistic 'cronaca', the minor, gossipy, 'stranger-than-fiction' reportage of life's odd happenings, typically fished out from the invisible mass of ordinary lives. This form emerges in a distinctively modern form in nineteenth-century France, and as a result is often labelled in Italian also with the French term 'fait divers'.[22] An analogous English term might be 'human interest story', but perhaps a more resonant parallel here is suggested by the phrase used above to describe the story of Mattia's discovery of his own death, a 'curious incident'. This phrase has its origin in Conan Doyle's Sherlock Holmes stories (reminding us that many 'fait divers' stories are also crime stories), and points to the almost incidental element in these stories, the low-level, microscopic scale of detail, akin to the clue, that triggers human curiosity, surprise but also a form of recognition.[23]

Both the 'fait divers' and the 'curious incident' connote disturbances, exceptions and coincidences, often also errors and misprisions,[24] that ripple almost invisibly on the surface of normality; both thereby also connote dynamics of chance, fortune and misfortune. In fact, Italian usage gives us a better indicator than either French or English of the bonds that tie all these threads together into a single and singularly modernist understanding of luck and chance. The homonym 'caso' gives us all three meanings: 'caso' as chance; 'caso' as singular event or happening; and 'caso' as criminal case or mystery to be solved. *Il fu Mattia Pascal* hints in its flashes of newspaper reportage that the novel itself, Mattia's story, is little more than a self-consciously hyper-elaborated reflection on the comic 'fait divers', the curious incident, the 'caso'. The 'Premessa' to the whole convoluted tale tells us as much directly, in the simple phrase already quoted above: 'il mio caso è assai più strano e diverso' (p. 47).

The modernist turn and chance's disproportionate role in it are neatly encapsulated here, in the elevation of the throwaway fragment of the 'fait divers', the unlikely curious incident that life throws up and is then forgotten, into the structuring principle of, or rather the clue to a new interrogation of our deepest sense of self and being; to Pirandello's own version of the 'human universal', the 'senso *universalmente umano*' (p. 255; emphasis in the original).

The motifs thrown up by an exploration of chance and luck in Italian modernism are varied and hardly make for a coherent whole: accident, contingency and curious incidents, but also mess, uncertainty, collision, risk, turn and inversion, swerves and spins, incidents and 'fait divers'. Taken together, they nevertheless begin to suggest a certain constellation of effects, a possible genealogy of modern(ist) luck, rooted in the provisional, the improbable and the unstable, concentrated on moments, sudden turns, and oblique angles, which turn out (perhaps) to change everything. Modern(ist) luck is a refocalizing instrument, in a sense, an often ironic double-take effecting a fragmentation and a rescaling of reality, form and vision to focus on the perception of the infinitesimal, ongoing moment.[25] Many of the motifs share further a mood of abandon, including self-abandon — to a collective, to an other, to danger and death, to the isolated moment — that suggest modern luck is driven by a willing loosening of (self-)control. Jackson Lears, in a compelling study of the evolution of ideas of luck in the popular culture of America — from Puritan pioneers to two-bit gamblers of nineteenth-century dens to high capitalists of the twentieth century — sees its entire long history as a struggle between cultures of control and cultures of what he calls 'grace' in American life.[26] For Lears, the culture of luck, chance, gambling and risk-taking, of abandon — the 'persistent allure of accident', as he calls it (pp. 273–317) — amounts to a search for something like secularized grace, a recovered magic or even freedom in a disenchanted world of increasing rationalization and control; or at the very least an expression of anxiety at the loss of that freedom. Marinetti, Montale and Pirandello, and the high culture of Italian and European modernism in general — although not yet confronted with American-style Fordist management controls, nor even yet with fully-fledged modern totalitarian control — nevertheless seem to feel something of the same allure; and to respond to modernity by embracing the freedom and anxiety of the moment, the turn, the possible apotheoses and catastrophes of chance.

Notes to Chapter 17

1. Donald E. Brown, *Human Universals* (New York: McGraw-Hill, 1991).
2. There is a vast field of scholarship on traditions of cultural and philosophical conceptions of fortune, chance and luck: see, for example, José M. Gonzalez García, *La diosa Fortuna: metamorfosis de una metafora politica* (Madrid: Antonio Machado, 2006); Erich Köhler, *Le Hasard en littérature: le possible et la nécessité* (Paris: Klincksieck, 1986).
3. See Gonzalez García, passim.
4. Franco Moretti has some interesting reflections on the bourgeois hero, typified in Robinson Crusoe, shaping his world against the vagaries of fortune and adventure, in *The Bourgeois. Between History and Literature* (London: Verso, 2013), pp. 25–29. This bourgeois figure develops and adapts a Renaissance trope, in turn an adaptation from classical traditions, of the individual grasping at the chance opportunity (*occasio*) thrown in his way, often figured in a goddess's tuft of hair. Aby Warburg traced this image of Renaissance 'Fortune' in one of the panels of his Mnemosyne Atlas (1924–29): see Gonzalez García, pp. 33–41, 93–102.
5. On the transformation of social knowledge and its concurrent revolution in conceptions of chance in this period, see Ian Hacking, *The Taming of Chance* (Cambridge: Cambridge University Press, 1990).
6. The editions quoted from here are as follows: Filippo Tommaso Marinetti, 'Fondazione e manifesto del futurismo' (1909) in *I manifesti del futurismo* (Project Gutenberg, 2009), available at <http:www.gutenberg.org/ebooks/28144>; Eugenio Montale, *Ossi di seppia* (1925) in *Tutte le poesie*, ed. by Giorgio Zampa (Milan: Mondadori, 1990), pp. 3–105; Luigi Pirandello, *Il fu Mattia Pascal* (1904) (Milan: Mondadori, 1983).
7. Marinetti drafted his manifesto in French and in Italian with this title in 1908, circulated it under the imprint of his journal *Poesia* in January 1909, and then published it in various Italian newspapers in early February 1909, but without its preamble or coda. The full manifesto appeared in Paris as 'Le Futurisme', *Le Figaro* (20 February 1909), with a wider dissemination and reaction following. See Paolo Tonini, *I manifesti del futurismo italiano* (Gussago: Edizioni dell'Arengario, 2011).
8. See Marjorie Perloff, *The Futurist Moment: Avant-Garde, Avant-Guerre, and the Language of Rupture* (Chicago: University of Chicago Press, 2004), pp. 85–90.
9. Jeffrey Schanpp, 'Crash (Speed as Engine of Individuation)', *Modernism/Modernity*, 6.1 (1999), 1–49 (p. 3).
10. Karen Beckman, *Crash: Cinema and the Politics of Speed and Stasis* (Durham, NC: Duke University Press, 2010), pp. 14–19 (on Schnapp); pp. 29–36, 44–47 (on Hepworth).
11. On the *longue durée* history of this concept of the accidental, from Aristotle to the Surrealists, see Ross Hamilton, *Accident: A Philosophical and Literary History* (Chicago: Chicago University Press, 2007).
12. David Trotter, *Cooking with Mud: The Idea of Mess in Nineteenth-Century Art and Fiction* (Oxford: Oxford University Press, 2000).
13. James Joyce, *Stephen Hero* (1905) (London: Jonathan Cape, 1956), p. 216. On epiphany in modernism, see for example Hugo Azérad, *L'Univers constellé de Proust, Joyce et Faulkner. Le Concept d'épiphanie dans l'esthétique du modernisme* (Oxford: Lang, 2002); Morris Beja, *Epiphany in the Modern Novel* (London: Peter Owen, 1971).

14. For the influence of and affinities between Joyce and Montale, see Romano Luperini, *L'incontro e il caso: narrazioni moderne e destino dell'uomo occidentale* (Bari: Laterza, 2007), pp. 27–28, who comments especially on the poem 'Incontro'; and Antonella Amato, 'Montale, Joyce e l'incontro con la modernità', *Moderna*, 1 (2013), 61–87.
15. Calvino commented in a reading of 'Forse un mattino' on the paradox of reverse vision, on the split in our visual field ('spazio bipartito') between a visible front and an always unknowable, invisible reverse field, as a figure for knowledge, perception and their limits. Only half in jest, Calvino went on to suggest this zoological-anthropological fact (front vision), and Montale's poetic insight, had been shattered by the 'uomo motorizzato' and his invention of the rear-view mirror: perhaps the link drawn here to Marinetti's futurist crash is not so implausible after all (Italo Calvino, '"Forse un mattino andando"', in *Letture montaliane in occasione dell'80° compleanno del poeta* (Genoa: Bozzi, 1977), pp. 38–45). I'm grateful to Martin McLaughlin for pointing out this essay by Calvino to me, some time in the early 1990s.
16. *Ossi*, pp. 48, 51–61, 83–84, 87–88, 98–99.
17. The term 'swerve' evokes the *clinamen* of Lucretius, a key figure and influence on all materialist and anti-determinist conceptions of the rule of chance in the world, and a significant influence on modern refigurations of chance: see Warren Motte, 'Clinamen Redux', *Comparative Literature Studies*, 23.4 (Winter, 1986), 263–81; Pierpaolo Antonello, *Il ménage a quattro: scienza, filosofia, tecnica nella letteratura italiana del novecento* (Florence: Le Monnier, 2005), pp. 170–94.
18. E.g. 'contingency, n. [...] II. 3. C. The condition of being free from predetermining necessity in regard to existence or action; hence, the being open to the play of chance [...]' (*Oxford English Dictionary*, s. v. 'contingency').
19. Trotter, *Cooking with Mud*, pp. 33–59.
20. On don Eligio's library, see Ilaria de Seta, 'From Cage to Nest: the Library of *Il fu Mattia Pascal*', *Pirandello Studies*, 30 (2010), 55–74; Matteo Pedroni, 'La biblioteca di Mattia Pascal. Fonti, funzioni e figure', *Studi novecenteschi*, 2 (2008), 377–99. Another space of 'bricolage' that the library recalls is the early-modern *Kunstkammer* or 'cabinet of curiosities', whose accumulated collections of objects of art, science and natural history were disordered precursors of modern libraries and museums as rationalised spaces of knowledge. This link foreshadows further dimensions of 'curiosity' in *Il fu Mattia Pascal* discussed below. (Thanks to Guido Bonsaver for suggesting the connection.)
21. On the importance of newspaper 'casi' as sources for Pirandello's short stories, novels and plays, see Marco Manotta, 'Il caso', in *Luigi Pirandello* (Milan: Mondadori, 1998), pp. 41–43.
22. On the 'fait divers' and its links to a mode of narrative driven by luck (*le hasard*), see the essay by Roland Barthes, 'Structure du fait divers' (1962) in *Essais critiques* (Paris: Seuil, 1964), pp. 188–97.
23. 'The curious incident of the dog in the night-time' appears as a phrase in Arthur Conan Doyle, 'Silver Blaze' in *The Memoirs of Sherlock Holmes* (1894) (Harmondsworth: Penguin, 1976), pp. 7–34 [p. 28]. It is especially noteworthy for Holmes's ingenious use of a sort of non-clue: the case is solved because of a dog that did *not* bark. On the significance of Holmesian clues for modern paradigm of knowledge (and indeed chance), see the influential essay by Carlo Ginzburg, 'Spie: radici di un paradigma indiziario' (1979), in *Miti, emblemi, spie: morfologia e storia* (Turin: Einaudi, 1986), pp. 158–209.
24. A case in point of error as a driver of unexpected consequences is the misrecognition (or presumed misrecognition) of the dead man at the mill as Mattia. On links between recognition, chance and plot contrivance, see Terence Cave, *Recognitions* (Oxford: Oxford University Press, 1990), p. 2; discussed further in Alison James, *Constraining Chance: Georges Perec and the Oulipo* (Evanston, IL: Northwestern University Press, 2009), p. 70–74.
25. The phrase 'the ongoing moment' is an echo of Geoff Dyer's study of the photograph, another figure for modernity's attention to the encapsulated, chance moment: see Geoff Dyer, *The Ongoing Moment* (London: Abacus, 2006) and cf. Roland Barthes's formula of the 'punctum' as a term for the photographic moment (*La Chambre claire* (Paris: Seuil, 1980)).
26. Jackson Lears, *Something for Nothing: Luck in America* (London: Penguin, 2004).

CHAPTER 18

Johnny's Epic Resistance: Classical Echoes in Fenoglio's *Il partigiano Johnny*

Rosalba Biasini

In the aftermath of World War II many Italian writers felt the urge to write about the common experience of the Resistance and to contribute to the creation of a national, shared memory. The time seemed ripe for a national *epos*, a tale to remember the founding moment of a new Italy, which would establish a much needed system of ethical values, based on tradition and communal beliefs.[1] Yet proposing an epic account of the Resistance seemed difficult: becoming like Homer, as Calvino wrote in 1948, proved impossible.[2] But why, asked the young writer? Why, in a crucial moment for the whole country, was it not possible to reach the realistic and historical totality admired by our ancestors in literature? Why could Italian writers not create an *epos* to celebrate the birth of a nation and the reunion of a people, after the horrors of Fascism and the war? With the Resistance and the creation of the Republic, times were ready for a national renaissance which would need a celebratory 'holy book'.[3] Unfortunately, though, the distance from the war and its tragic events was not enough, the linguistic and stylistic choice constituted a problem, and finally the risk of falling into empty rhetoric discouraged any attempt at a national epic tale.

The holy book took slightly longer to appear. Partisan Beppe Fenoglio started as early as WWII to take notes and write accounts of what he described immediately as a civil war.[4] Throughout his remaining short life — born in 1922, Fenoglio died prematurely in 1963 — while employed in a clerical job, he dedicated his free time to writing, and especially to the memories of the Resistance. His partisan masterpieces, *Il partigiano Johnny* (1968) and *Una questione privata* (1963), were both composed in different versions in the 1950s and published posthumously, showing that most of Fenoglio's writing was carried out privately, and that behind the relatively few publications which appeared during his life lay a hidden world of attempts and rewritings.[5] *Una questione privata*, the first to appear after Fenoglio's death, was immediately hailed as the book of a generation.[6] Yet a few years later *Il partigiano Johnny*, with its total, all-consuming war, larger-scale vision and broader perspective, its epic connotation, as it will be argued, was destined to become the holy writing of the Resistance.

In the following pages, I will reflect on how Beppe Fenoglio succeeded in creating an epic yet not rhetorical representation of the Resistance with *Il partigiano Johnny*.[7] After having established what is meant by 'epic', I will trace its presence in PJ, investigating also textual links between this text and Classical epic. Finally, I will propose an interpretation of Fenoglio's intentions, linking its literary choice with the wish to show the universality of man's experience, and that in this light tragedy, albeit deeply connected to history, is a timeless human condition.

It is now certain that the text now read as PJ was not written immediately after the war, as some critics suggested, but in the 1950s.[8] In those years, Fenoglio had started work on a longer story, 'un libro grosso', with Johnny — a student, then a soldier, eventually a partisan — as the main character.[9] The first part of Johnny's story had been adapted by the author into the published *Primavera di bellezza*, while in the months following its appearance Fenoglio and his publisher Livio Garzanti continued to discuss its sequel, presented by Fenoglio as the second, 'superior' part of the book, a narrative entirely centred on the Resistance — what we read today as PJ.[10]

When it appeared in 1968, this 'duplice tentativo di romanzo'[11] received significant attention from the critics, especially for the presence of stylistic and content features that seemed to go beyond the expressive and formal structures of the novel. Some of these early reviewers recognised an 'epic' inspiration, and a connection with Classical epic — Paolo Milano focused on the centrality of the death as a theme, with Johnny's co-fighters falling one after the other 'like in the *Iliad*', leaving the eponymous character to a solitary resistance.[12] And if Fenoglio's partisans fearlessly fight, their chiefs look similar to heroes or deities, as Comandante Nord, who, in Walter Pedullà's words, is an incarnation or a descendant of Achilles.[13] Indeed the cover of the book itself, although presenting the story as an 'antiheroic saga', encouraged the reading of the story as an Odyssey inside the partisan war ('l'Odissea della guerriglia').[14]

Beyond these initial comments, PJ's epic connotation has been recognised by several critics, and variedly discussed. Many talked in favour of it and focussed on several elements including: the language and especially its 'grand style', an attempt at heroic writing (Beccaria),[15] the existential importance of the fight and the futility of solitary death (Galaverni, Casadei),[16] connections with various epic texts (Bessi, Bàrberi Squarotti, Muñiz Muñiz, Gabriele Pedullà).[17] However, others denied the overall epic nature of the text, despite their acknowledgement of the presence of single elements that can be identified as epic.[18]

Much of the debate originates from different perceptions of what is intended by epic. Following Bakhtin, Beccaria considered PJ's epic character as a sign of the author's will to put Johnny's story at an epic distance, meant as an out-of-time dimension which is typical of the epic genre.[19] In such dimension, human actions are not seen as individual gestures, but as part of an absolute, collective experience. Not many agreed with this conclusion.[20] On the basis that PJ is instead a text deeply grounded in its time, the idea of 'epic text' was refused. However, as we will discuss, disagreeing with the application of Beccaria's bakhtinian interpretation of epic to PJ and denying its epic traits are two different matters.

On this basis, one must conclude that the debate on epic is merely the umpteenth on Fenoglio's works, following the fierce discussions on philological and chronological issues. However, it seems unproductive to list how many and which epic elements are present in PJ, in an attempt to ascribe the text to the epic tradition; instead, the effectiveness of the epic component in the text must be analysed, along with Fenoglio's reasons behind his writing. The creation, both in terms of language and content, of an atmosphere that recalls Classical epic is sought by the very author, who, in order to reproduce a specific tone to its writing, makes frequent references to other epic texts, generating in the reader a quest for recognition that renders PJ, and Fenoglio's writing style and habits, particularly interesting.

Yet before we do so, we should ask: what is meant here by epic? Why do many describe PJ — an unfinished long narrative — not as a novel, but as a 'modern epic'? To answer, it is worth making a distinction between 'epic genre' and 'epic connotation' — in Italian, 'epicità'. With the former, a codified yet diverse literary genre is intended, with the latter a broader character, typical of some texts, obtained by the explicit reference to the epic genre via stylistic and linguistic features as well as contents. By the definitions of epic genre, an epic text is an extended writing, generally poetic, characterised by high linguistic style. It recounts an event, often a war, or a journey, and is generated in a community — in its most ancient form, epic does not have a single author.[21] In its original form, epic is moreover a primal artistic expression, celebratory of the founding myth of a society.[22] Its hero acts in momentous circumstances and is the repository of ethical and civil values.[23]

Starting from Hegel's reflection, epic as a genre has often been analysed in contrast with the novel and its genre. In this perspective, epic is an original form, voice of a universal condition reflected in human actions, while the novel is a secondary form, condemned to a fragmentary expression and damned by the continuous and unsuccessful aspiration toward a lost totality.[24] Bakhtin reinterpreted this opposition, seeing in epic a static, sterile form, and in the novel the expression of a multifaceted, deeper view of the world, representing a plurilinguistic, polyphonic reality.

The modern world recognised the end of epic as a literary genre, but continued to use the term to describe several artistic forms — novels, but also theatre, cinema, music — that share with the epic genre grandiosity of expression and representation.[25] Beyond the genre, the epic content of a work — the aspiration to fixed ethical values and to celebrate a people, the heroic vision of the world, the use of a grand style — is hence retraceable in texts that are not part of the genre itself. Such texts can be described as universal, 'encyclopaedic', 'hybrid' in some cases. Franco Moretti used the definition 'opere mondo'.[26] For Moretti, *epos* has not completely disappeared with the growth of the novel, but has continued to exist and renew itself, stressing its uniqueness and its wish to produce holy books for different communities. In this light, the term 'epic' is associated with contents and actions that express grandiosity, and has been used for several works across the nineteenth and twentieth centuries. These works, although deeply grounded in the absolute present of a modern, often technological era, offer an attempt to grasp the totality of the human condition.[27]

More interesting then, in modern literature, is the initial distinction we made in terms of 'genre' and 'connotation'. This last can be identified with the concept, theorised by Northrop Frye in the 1950s, of literary mode: a wider 'mood' inspired by literary genres — the epic genre, for instance — and traceable in modern literary and artistic works through the explicit references to features pertaining to the genre.[28] Important here is the fact that in a single text more modes can cohabit, so for instance the presence of epic elements, that can be grouped under the definition of epic mode, can appear along with elements pertaining to different modes.

The epic connotation clearly visible in PJ, but difficult to categorise on account of the presence, in the same text, of elements not ascribable to epic — for instance, irony and the grotesque — can then be described as an instance of the epic mode.[29] Some examples will help us. According to the definition of epic mode,[30] the story must take place in a distant time; Johnny's adventure is indeed set in the Resistance, in a time clearly identifiable and close to the act of writing. However, one can argue that, while representing a modern war, Fenoglio provides a representation of such war that unequivocally establishes a connection with all human conflicts, especially since his character Johnny seems to experience war as a timeless condition, that pairs his struggle to that of ancient heroes.[31] The war described in the following excerpts is unmistakably identifiable, yet the language and the style employed — notably the inversion adjective-noun, the use of metaphors, the repetitions — contribute to the creation of what has been perceived as epic:

> Scorrevano con gli occhi e le punte dei fucili l'immoto, dorato, quasi irridente rettilineo, ma il cannoneggiamento sulle alte colline era troppo assorbente, soggiogante. Così, pensava Johnny, la mia vita e quella di costoro è di nuovo in ballo, dadi in fondo al bossolo. Bene, egli era nuovamente pronto. (PJ² XI 11; see also PJ¹ XV 6)[32]

> Nell'immensa ondata del primo tocco di mezzanotte Michele aprì il fuoco e tutti gli uomini gli tennero dietro. E un attimo dopo dietro le alte mura le rauche trombe fasciste squillarono al parossismo dell'intolleranza.
> I partigiani raddoppiarono, le trombe impazzirono, e come in parossistica esaltazione i ragazzi di Johnny si scoprivano da dietro le cataste e s'avvicinavano ai ciechi muri della caserma, ma follemente, ma ciecamente, come se volessero darvi del capo. (PJ¹ XIX 25–26)

Moreover, a second component of the epic mode is a heroic protagonist, a semi-divine fighter able to perform superhuman actions. In his perception of himself at least, Johnny embodies such a character:

> Scavalcò la ripa sul ventre, si rizzò e corse nel prato, nudo, sconfinato. Tumulto esplose alle sue spalle, ma era solo tumulto di urli, Johnny correva e si chiedeva quando, quando sarebbe arrivata la prima pallottola. Arrivò, ed altre ancora, infinite altre, ora di lato anche, dai suoi primitivi ricercatori, tutto il mondo si rimpinzò dei loro spari e urli, urli di indicazione, di incoraggiamento, di revisione e di maledizione. Johnny correva, correva, le lontane creste balenanti ai suoi occhi sgranati e quasi ciechi, correva ed il fuoco diminuiva al suo udito, anche il clamore, spari e grida annegavano in una gora fra lui e loro.
> Correva, correva, o meglio volava, corpo fatica e movimenti vanificati. [...] I pensieri vi entravano da fuori, colpivano la sua fronte come ciottoli da

> una fionda. — Pierre ed Ettore sono morti. Ettore aveva il mal di ventre, non poteva correre come doveva. Li hanno uccisi. Io sono vivo. Ma sono vivo? Sono solo, solo, solo, e tutto è finito. (PJ¹ XXX 18–20)

Johnny feels as invincible as an ancient warrior, does not run but flies, believes himself to be the sole one to escape bullets and death — we will later learn that his comrades Pierre and Ettore have both survived. So if Johnny is not an ancient hero, his perception of the war is certainly influenced by his readings. When he made his partisan choice, Johnny walked to the hills convinced that the whole destiny of Italy depended upon him:

> Partì verso le somme colline, la terra ancestrale che l'avrebbe aiutato nel suo immoto possibile, nel vortice del vento nero, sentendo com'è grande un uomo quando è nella sua normale dimensione umana. E nel momento in cui partì si sentì investito — nor death itself would have been divestiture — in nome dell'autentico popolo d'Italia, ad opporsi in ogni modo al fascismo, a giudicare ed eseguire, a decidere militarmente e civilmente. Era inebriante tanta somma di potere, ma infinitamente più inebriante la coscienza dell'uso legittimo che ne avrebbe fatto.
> Ed anche fisicamente non era mai stato così uomo, piegava erculeo il vento e la terra. (PJ¹ IV 39–40)

His engagement, felt as a mission, requires a higher style. Language adapts to the content, while Johnny becomes the Hegelian hero, destined to originate the founding myth of his people. However, it must be noted that behind this there is also the hint of a smile by the author, who observes the young partisan following his same destiny, with the same strength and determination. The whole passage can then be read as an expression of ironic intentions, with Johnny as a mock-heroic character unaware of his real role in the world.

And if Johnny acquires the traits of a hero, everything around him is described in epic terms, habits, gestures, objects,[33] while Comandante Nord's sudden and numinous arrival in a car, as with epiphanies in Classical epic, is heroic as much as grotesque:

> Springò in piedi, alto sul fuoco della miseria, dell'impossibilità, serrò il libro con uno schiaffo secco come se volesse schiacciarci tra i fogli tutti i pidocchi di quella sua miseria. Salì al piano superiore, socchiuse appena la finestra aperta alla tarda sera piemontese, all'aquatile vibrazione del fogliame sotto vento. (PJ¹ I 25)

> Venne il ventoso, massivo fruscio dell'autovettura di Nord. Essa e gli occupanti erano pronti per l'ingresso di gala. Due autisti, rigidi fin d'ora, e sul sedile posteriore, solo, Nord, inguainato nella sua tuta di gomma nera con le cerniere cromate: dominante, monolitico e arcano come un duce assiro. (PJ¹ XX 3, see also PJ² VI 3)

A whole village can be described with the tools of Classical epic, but the spell is easily broken:

> Il brusio del paese veniva viaggiando sui raggi dorati, ma Ettore scoccò all'indietro un'occhiata insimpatetica e si domandò perché diavolo mai Nord li avesse destinati di guarnigione a quel paesaccio [...]. (PJ¹ XXIV 4; PJ² X 8)

The same happens when, after the long winter of 1944–1945, the partisans again gather together to resume the fight, and Nord gives his famous speech (second example):

> Il vicino di Johnny scoppiò a ridere: — Sai? Sembra che abbiamo tutti passato il più gran raffreddore della nostra vita -. Ed era vero, tutti apparivano spenti, gocciant e rabbrividenti, i cento uomini che risposero all'appuntamento del 31 gennaio sul poggio di Torretta. (PJ² XXIV 1)
>
> — Lasciatemi dirvi un altro paio di cose, necessarie, perché io stesso sto diventando mortalmente stufo di questo discorso — . E quando il nuovo ripple di riso dileguò sulla glabra, ventosa cresta, spiegò le armi e l'equipaggiamento per cinquemila. (PJ¹ XXXIX 11; see also PJ² XXIV 10)

Following the style and the images of epic stories, Fenoglio retells Johnny's partisan adventure, choosing epic modalities because they best suit Johnny, a character that lives his life as an epic, an existential and moral condition.[34] Epic, then, is the measure that seems to satisfy the urge to retell Johnny's war, the story of all partisans. On the basis of these considerations, we can partially conclude that with the use of appropriate distinctions and tools, it is possible to use the term 'epic' when analysing PJ in both versions.[35]

The creation of the epic mode resides in a dialogue with the genre and its texts, and its presence in PJ is indeed linked to the use of Classical epic, at various levels, ranging from a broad inspiration to textual references. Several studies suggested interesting connections, and the high number of references would require a more detailed discussion. In this limited context, and in order to illustrate the reflections so far highlighted, it will be worth analysing at least a few of these aspects, focussing on the effectiveness of the Classical epic in representing some thematic fields, such as the description of fighters, first of all Nord:

> L'uomo era così bello quale mai misura di bellezza aveva gratificato la virilità, ed era così maschio come mai la bellezza aveva tollerato d'esser così maschia. [...] L'aurea proporzione del suo fisico si manifestava fin sotto la splendida uniforme, nella perfezione strutturale rivestita di giusta carne e muscolo. [...]
> I prigionieri fascisti usavano riconoscerlo di primo acchito, al solo apparire lontano, anche prescindendo dall'individuale splendore della sua divisa. [..]
> Johnny si riprendeva lentamente dallo shock di Nord, e braced himself per non soccombere all'immediata, integrale, colpo-di-fulmine devozione indiscriminata. (PJ¹ XIII 8–10)

Not many details are offered, yet the picture is clear: Nord's beauty and charm are so powerful as to captivate both his enemies and his own men, including Johnny. His beauty is perfectly harmonious, to fulfil Classical ideals. To evaluate the importance of physical appearance, we must recall how the Greeks tried to disfigure Hector's body after his death (IL XXII 369–71), while the gods tried to preserve it from decomposition (IL XXIII 185–91; IL XXIV 18–21).[36] And beauty and physical power certainly play a big role during the *teichoscopia*, the observation from the walls (IL III), when from the walls of Troy King Priam asks Helen to point out to him the Greek warriors.[37]

Other descriptions are present in PJ, for instance Pierre's (PJ¹ XIII 16) and Kyra's (PJ¹ XIV 3), and they all seem to follow the same pattern, which is: at their first appearance, the partisans are described with fixed characteristics, namely their physical appearance — not always positive — their competence in the use of weapons, their clothes. It must be noted that in classical epic the 'vestition' is treated as a ceremonial, especially before the fight.[38]

When discussing Nord's description, we focused on its power to charm. However, the fascination with Johnny and his comrades seems to fade as the partisan war progresses, and PJ clearly shows a growing sense of disillusion and loss of faith towards commanders, Nord in particular.[39] Yet Nord's 'epiphanies' always renew his power over his men, as can be seen in PJ¹ XVIII 29 and PJ¹ XXXI 15, and especially in PJ's final pages, when Nord harangues the fighters:

> [F]urono riscossi dal boato d'evviva che salutò l'arrivo di Nord da oriente.
> Il suo ascendente fisico trionfò ancora una volta e definitivamente sugli uomini raccolti, reimbandatisi. Per quel che ne lasciava vedere lo stretto cerchio delle guardie del corpo, vestiva il prestigioso cappotto da ufficiale inglese impellicciato di astrakan: ma quanto frusto e guasto, dicendo a prima le marce e i nascondimenti e le salite e discese a stalle e fienili. Sul capo portava, con una certa coquetry, il suo berretto da ufficiale di marina [...]. (PJ¹ XL 5–6, see also PJ² XXIV 4)

The commander's aura includes his clothes and his famous astrakhan coat, witness of the long winter.[40] However, a subtle irony must be read here towards Nord's 'coquetry', despite the seminal moment. Nord's power resonates the typical suggestion that Greek commanders had on their warriors, for instance Achilles' speech in XVI, to prepare the Myrmidons to fight under Patroclus' leadership and his savage cry that scares the Trojans fighting around Patroclus' body (IL XVIII 222–29).

In wartime, death is part of everyday life, as Fenoglio experienced, and its description can reach the sublime in Homeric poems — for example, those of Patroclus (XVI 791–867) or Hector (IL XXII 322–63), which inspired that of Turnus in AEN XII. In PJ death is quick and its description essential, especially when it concerns Johnny's closer friends: 'Tito cadde fulminato, col fucile imbracciato, fu forse quel ferro-ligneo supporto a farlo cadere giù così interito, come un palo' (PJ¹ IX 6).[41] Indeed it is not the actual death that interests Fenoglio, but its effects on the survivors, especially Johnny, as well as the ceremony that accompanies the burials. In these traits, the epic re-agent is traceable, for instance in the description of the recovery of Tito's body and of his funeral. His comrades need to come to terms with the loss:

> E allora Johnny si ricordò di Tito, e lo pensò, ma *come un morto morto secoli fa*. Fred intanto aveva ripreso la articolata favella, dopo la reazione, e lamentava Tito, in modo sconnesso, babbling e lancinante.
> Puntavano, ma inconsapevoli, a un casale [...].
> Fred cominciò — Hanno ammazzato il nostro compagno, e preso un altro. Il nostro compagno Tito è morto. Tito è morto [...]. Johnny si sorprese a dire le stesse parole di Fred, col medesimo tono: — Hanno ammazzato un nostro compagno, e preso un altro. Il nostro compagno Tito è morto. Tito è morto –.
> (PJ¹ IX 16–18)

In this excerpt, for Johnny Tito is dead 'secoli fa', he does not belong to their fight any more, but to the number of valorous fighters who died for a common cause — the defence of his homeland. War is then a universal experience, and even the lamentation following death refers to memories of the Classical world.[42] In IL's last book, when Hector body's is finally returned to Priam (IL XXIV, 723–75), Andromache, Hecuba and Helen cry over the dead, stating the significance of his death for his community and for the war.[43] In PJ, when Tito's body arrives, Johnny sees in it 'un sigillo di eternità, come fosse un greco ucciso dai Persiani due millenni avanti' (PJ¹ IX 22), and, like the women in IL, he is saddened at the thought of a future life without his friend. As has been noted, Cassandra's cry in the Homeric verses recalls the 'apostrofe' given by Tenente Biondo, who invites partisans and civilians to come closer to observe and honour the dead (PJ¹ IX 24–25).[44]

The uses of the 'grand style' and the reference to classical epic here are intended to celebrate the fighter, and especially the ethical engagement that led him to a premature death. In this view, a heroic death is highly desired, as in Classical epic. At several points in PJ, Johnny wishes to die in action, not in banal circumstances — and resorts to his usual irony to calm his fear of death:

> Rotolava, leggero ed anestetizzato come in sospensione stratosferica. [...] — Mi son salvato lassù, ma ora vado a sfracellarmi nel ritano? — pensò con un'angoscia pigra. Ma si fermò e si rizzò in tempo [...]. (PJ¹ XI 23)

> Meglio era morire come Tito, al suo tempo e nel suo luogo, col terrore così repentino e breve da annullare quasi la terribilità del piombo penetrante. Stava così invidiando Tito, quando dovette alzare gli occhi al ciglione, dov'era erettasi l'ombra dell'ombra dei fascisti. (PJ¹ IX 10)

It is a memory that comes from his studies and readings, linked also to the wish to receive the great honours we mentioned:

> Anch'io così, se ugual destino m'è preparato,
> giacerò, morto; ma adesso voglio aver nobile gloria. (IL XVIII 120–22)

> Oh tre fiate fortunati e quattro,
> Cui perir fu concesso innanzi a Troia,
> Per gli Atridi pugnando! E perché allora
> Non caddi anch'io, che al morto Achille intorno
> Tante i Troiani in me lance scagliâro?
> Sepolto i Greci co' funèbri onori
> M'avriano, e alzato ne' lor canti al cielo.
> Or per via così infausta ir deggio a Dite. (OD V 392–99)

> [...] O terque quaterque beati,
> quis ante ora patrum, Troiae sub moenibus altis,
> contigit oppetere! [...] (AEN I 94–96)

Death and near-death experiences are primary themes in PJ.[45] For this, funeral honours acquire a ritual meaning that acts also as an inspiration for the other fighters. In his moments of despair, Johnny tends to remember his dead comrades, knowing that he will have to count solely on himself. Like ancient warriors, he asks his heart, his *thumos*, to sustain him, as in PJ¹ VIII 16. But his heart does not always hear:

> Il cuore di Johnny decadde, si squagliava, ecco non era già più consistente della neve intorno corrotta dall'arsenicale precoce, ingannevole disgelo. (PJ¹ V 9)
>
> E Johnny sospirò e il cuore gli cadde, stremato dalla giornata, dal vagabondaggio, da quella vergognosa cattura e dalla pietà del prigioniero. (PJ² XIX 23)

In OD, reference to the *thumos*, our emotional inner part, identified by the moderns with the heart, are countless, but some seem to offer a precedent to PJ's pages (OD IX 530–32, OD V 382–83).

However, as a good soldier, Johnny fights fiercely. Despite the uncertainties, he knows that his war must be completed, since with his comrades he is deemed to protect and defend his land, just like Hector, 'il combattente popolare, l'uomo che difende la sua casa, la sua famiglia', 'il patriota, il partigiano'.[46] And that land, the Langhe, becomes the setting for Johnny's story. Natural elements, 'elementi primi della costituzione fisica del mondo (acqua, aria, terra)' and landscape participate in the action, reviving the epic connection between man and nature that is not always pacified:[47]

> Lasciò che il paesaggio lo assorbisse, immaginò cosa avrebbe voluto e potuto fare, e con chi, via via per quella lustra strada parallela alla bealera di visiva sorgentezza alpina, sotto quei filari di pioppi così argenteamente freddi e vivi, nelle piazzette dei paesini così ovviamente pacifici con un loro sentore di caffè-latte. (PJ² I 7)

Amongst the natural elements, the river has a special place, at times personified, as in IL XXI 211–71, when the river Scamandrus rebels against Achilles' deadly rage:

> Il fiume aveva annullato gli argini di ottobre, le sentinelle erano rinculate addirittura contro la scarpata del viale grande. Il fango brulicante appariva anche più tremendo e letale delle acque impazzite, gli altissimi flutti, veloci e come gettati in cemento, sfioravano le superstiti arcate del ponte. Nel tuonare del fiume potevi però cogliere i colpi di tosse delle invisibili sentinelle. Il caotico cielo, forgia di quel diluvio, era odioso, si tirava le bestemmie.
> Scivolò giù a quel cosmogonico caos d'acqua e fango e si accostò alla sentinella. (PJ² VIII 4–5)[48]

But in Johnny's sentimental geography, a special place is taken by the city of Alba, that can produce in him the same feelings that Aeneas has for his lost Troy as well as for his promised land in Italy, and Odysseus for Ithaca:

> Bevuto che ebbe, Johnny andò a una finestrella orizzontale intagliata nel muro nudo e attraverso essa vide le ombre delle mura della città nei vapori bassi danzanti, le torri e i campanili svanivano nel cielo cinerognolo. Mai come in quel momento capì quanto ci tenesse alla città, quanto pericolo essa corresse e quanto poco egli potesse fare per essa. (PJ² IX 10)

The city, in PJ, is often connected to the life that Johnny had before as well as to some 'sospension[i] di partigianesimo' (PJ¹ XII 1) that occur during the war. It has been observed that the weakest parts in PJ, which are deleted or reduced in PJ², are concerned with Johnny's private activities, such as his relation with his parents and his encounters with women — 'la ragazza della collina' (PJ¹ II 1–7) or Sonia (PJ¹ XXXVI 1–9), who disappears from PJ² — and these are mostly set in the city or in villages. It has been argued that this shows Fenoglio's wish to eliminate from the final version (PJ²) traces of bourgeois individualism.[49] Actually, this theme — Johnny's private dimension as opposed to his public and historic function — is not unconnected to epic: these intimate moments can be linked to the descriptions of love encounters in IL, for instance between Hera and Zeus in XIV, 159–86, or in III 379–450, when Paris, divinely saved from Menelaus, finds himself in Helen's arms. AEN IV, the story of Dido and Aeneas, is also an example of a private moment, which ends when Aeneas decides to continue his quest, upon which an entire people rely, rather than prolong his idyll with the queen.

In IL VI, Hector returns to the city for a last visit. In this book, every element connected to the city is a symbol of a world that no longer belongs to the warrior, but represents a distraction from his mission, from which he must flee, sacrificing his loved ones. Before joining the partisans, Johnny, hidden in a 'casa in collina', feels the urge to visit the city, and meets his parents. His distance from them is already clear, especially in his capacity to observe the Germans without being terrified:

> Tornò a casa, che gli apparve più nuova ed insolita [...]. I suoi stavano già cenando, sentì per le scale il chiocchiare delle posate, scorato. Suo padre si limitò a scrollare il capo per la sua imprudenza, ma sua madre insorse contro di lui per quel suo mettersi con volontaria leggerezza alla perdizione, e allora Johnny scoprì l'unico modo di placarla, invece di minimizzare il pericolo, disse pianamente: — Ho visto i tedeschi –. (PJ¹ III 6)

As the decision to join the partisans becomes steadier, the thought of his parents grows in Johnny, and marks his departure for the hills as well as his partisan beginnings (PJ¹ IV 27 and PJ¹ XIX 24). However, his parents constitute a tension that pulls him in the opposite direction, preventing his movement towards opening, travel, quest.[50] In this view, Johnny must distance himself from his family in order to fulfil his mission: like Hector, who must remember his role of fighter and defender of his wife Andromache during their poignant farewell (IL VI 441–45).

In Alba occupied by the partisans, Johnny, now a fighter amongst them, can meet his father. Yet his changed position and his role amongst the partisans and in the fight does not allow time for affection:

> Egli scoprì suo padre tra la folla che gremiva il mercato coperto: stava muto e ciondoloni, visibilmente tremante; e più tremò quando individuò suo figlio nella rear-profluvie dei partigiani tornati. Johnny gli accennò d'incontrarlo al primo crocicchio. Là suo padre non lo abbracciò, ma molto accuratamente lo palpò dappertutto. — Lascia andare, ho soltanto una terribile emicrania. — Vieni a casa con me, a riposarti. — Non posso, debbo pranzare con gli uomini. — Tua madre... — Verrò stasera e mi fermerò fino a mezzanotte, va bene? [...] A proposito, hai sempre un pensiero per tua madre, quando ci sei dentro? Per tua madre e per me? — Sicuro, ce l'ho sempre... ma subito dopo. (PJ¹ XXI 41–42)

In IL VI during his walks from the city walls to the palace, Hector makes several encounters, and recognises loved faces (237–529). The same happens to Johnny, when, fed up with the 'nostalgia della città che lo travagliava ferocemente' (PJ¹ XII 10), he decides to visit Alba. Like Hector, Johnny meets some people, including a terrorised young lady with a girl, who cries like Astyanax at the sight of Hector's helmet.[51] When finally Johnny meets 'Industriale enologico B.', who invites him to his house to listen to music and meet some girls, their power is again an opposition to Johnny's tension, and their presence creates disturbance as much as Odysseus' sirens. Johnny resists, as Hector resists Helen (vv. 344–68), and moves away from his old life's attractions, feeling stronger in his engagement: 'Johnny riguadagnò la collina, l'alte colline' (PJ¹ XII 44), and ready for a deeper and absolute commitment to his choice.

This analysis, which cannot exhaust the possible connections between PJ and Classical epic, wishes to propose a contribution towards further explorations. With this stylistic decision, Fenoglio looks back at the years immediately following WWII, when one could still hope in a national *epos* and in its redeeming power. However, writing in an epic-like style in the 1950s has a different flavour: knowing the outcome, the author was able to use an epic tone to describe the Resistance without sounding rhetorical or excessively celebratory.

It has been noted that amongst the reasons that would not allow us to consider PJ an epic is the author's awareness of the failure of the ideals of the Resistance: having lost faith in the triumph of such ideals, the writer would abandon the project of the 'libro grosso'.[52] Actually, another interpretation is possible: it is following such failure that Fenoglio felt the need to embark on a broader project, deciding to put it aside only to write in a different, lighter form — a short novel rather that an extended saga — but still about the Resistance.

As has been argued, assessing PJ's epic components still proves difficult to his critics; however, as we have seen, PJ, like all 'modern epic', should not be assigned to a genre, but put in relation with the modalities of storytelling and representation of such tradition, tracing in it the effectiveness of the epic mode, a connotation that finds its origin in the genre. Fenoglio knew clearly the perception that he wanted to create for his readers, and he successfully achieved it by looking at texts that are part of the epic genre, such as the Classical epic. What the author meant was clear: to create for Johnny an epic Resistance.

Johnny's adventure was important to Fenoglio, who needed to put in words his personal story in order to prevent the same oblivion that affected many of his contemporaries. Writing in the 1950s Fenoglio made a last attempt to revive, at least in his pages, the greatest period of Italian modern history: his epic choice is hence ethical, and the use of epic as a literary re-agent is connected to the will to represent human experience and the tragic nature of life in its totality. As Beccaria rightly states, Fenoglio is interested in the absolute and existential human condition. However, this intuition can be accepted only if we recognise that, although concerned with universal tragedy, men have been and always will be influenced by their personal experience, which is part of the history of their times.[53] This means that Johnny's war shares traits of classical era battles because fighting, and especially protecting one's own land, is a common, shared experience. Yet his very experience takes place in the middle of the Italian Resistance, in a time and space that, albeit sublimated by Johnny's perception and Fenoglio's writing, are clearly recognisable.

This is Fenoglio's approach to the Resistance in PJ. In order to represent *that* tragedy, *that* part of a totality, he created Johnny and his epic. The textual relations with other works constitute a literary resource to retell a human experience that becomes exemplary. Fenoglio chooses the epic of the Resistance to tell us about mankind, the sadness of human solitude and the power of belonging to a community, and to overcome history and grief with a shared perception of common history. As Pavese wrote in 1945, what will save us is the reaching out of man to other men ('l'apertura dell'uomo verso l'uomo').[54] Suffering and anguish marked a new beginning, made of shared memories and recovered joy. What PJ seem to tell us, then, is that embracing this common tragedy, despite our individual moments of abandonment, can help us find our natural dimension, which must be within our community and inside our times.

Notes to Chapter 18

1. Remo Ceserani, *Guida breve allo studio della letteratura* (Rome-Bari: Laterza, 2003), p. 233. See also Sergio Zatti, *Il modo epico* (Rome-Bari: Laterza, 2000).
2. Italo Calvino, 'Saremo come Omero', *Rinascita* (December 1948), p. 448, now in Calvino, *Saggi, 1945–1985* (Milan: Mondadori, 1995), pp. 1483–87.
3. According to Hegel, an epic reflects the founding moment for a community and as such it constitutes the 'holy book' of a people or a nation, being part of the foundation of a people's ethical beliefs (G. W. F. Hegel, *Estetica* (Turin: Einaudi, 1997 [1967[1]]), p. 1168 [*Vorlesungen über die Ästhetik*, ed. by Heinrich G. Hotho (Berlin: Duncker & Humblot, 1842–43)]).
4. In 1949 Fenoglio presented to Einaudi a collection of short stories entitled *Racconti della guerra civile*, while on 8 March 1960, in a letter to Livio Garzanti, he used the term 'civil war' to describe the Resistance (Beppe Fenoglio, *Lettere 1940–1962* (Turin: Einaudi, 2001), p. 133).
5. Fenoglio, *Il partigiano Johnny* (Turin: Einaudi, 1968) was 'created' by editor Lorenzo Mondo, who chose the title and put together parts of two different versions of Johnny's story (PJ[1] and PJ[2]) found amongst Fenoglio's writings. This edition made the text known to readers, but did not meet the expectations of philologists. A scientific edition of Fenoglio's published and unpublished works followed: Fenoglio, *Opere* (Turin: Einaudi, 1978). In this edition, the two versions of *Il partigiano* are offered one after the other. A further attempt to render the text accessible — the form in which it is currently read — was made by Dante Isella in 1992: Fenoglio, *Romanzi e racconti* (Turin: Einaudi; Paris:Gallimard, 1992; new edition: Turin: Einaudi, 2001). Isella clearly indicated his interventions and choices (he used PJ[1] for the first twenty chapters, and PJ[2] for the remaining twenty-one) in Isella, *Schede critiche — Il partigiano Johnny*, in Fenoglio, *Romanzi e racconti*, pp. 1583–98.
6. Calvino's 1964 preface to *Il sentiero dei nidi di ragno: Prefazione 1964* in Calvino, *Romanzi e racconti* (Turin: Einaudi, 1993), pp. 1185–1207, especially pp. 1201–02.
7. From here on, I will refer to *Il partigiano Johnny* with the abbreviation PJ.
8. Two different schools viewed PJ as an early, possibly the first, or a later work. Several facts, including the discovery of the *Appunti partigiani 44-'45* in 1994, proved that PJ should be dated in the 1950s. Informed accounts of the philological debate are in Philip Cooke, *Fenoglio's Binoculars, Johnny's Eyes; History, Language, and Narrative Technique in Fenoglio's 'Il Partigiano Johnny'* (New York: Lang, 2000) and in Giancarlo Alfano, 'Presente assoluto e campo della scrittura nel *Partigiano Johnny* di Beppe Fenoglio', in Giancarlo Alfano and others, *Omaggio a Beppe Fenoglio, nel quarantesimo della morte, Testo. Studi di teoria e di storia della letteratura e della critica*, 45 (January-June 2003), 9–38.

9. 'Sto effettivamente lavorando a nuovo libro. Un romanzo propriamente non è, ma certo è un libro grosso (alludo allo spessore). Non ne ho ancora terminato la prima stesura e mi ci vorrà certamente un sacco di tempo per averne la definitiva. Il libro abbraccia il quinquennio 1940–1945' (Fenoglio, *Lettere*, p. 82).
10. See letters to Garzanti on 8 and 12 September 1958 (Fenoglio, *Lettere*, pp. 91–93 and pp. 95–96). Gabriele Pedullà has recently edited Fenoglio, *Il libro di Johnny* (Turin: Einaudi, 2015), an attempt to reassemble Johnny's story. In Pedullà's words, '[l]a soluzione [...] adottata [...] si basa sulla scelta di valorizzare innanzitutto la redazione più antica di *Primavera di bellezza* [...], ancora sprovvista della conclusione [...]. [...] Quanto alla seconda parte, [si è optato per la] sola redazione più antica, [...] l'unica a esserci giunta completa' (Gabriele Pedullà, *Le armi e il ragazzo*, in Fenoglio, *Il libro di Johnny*, pp. v–lxxvi (p. xiv)).
11. Maria Antonietta Grignani, 'Virtualità del testo e ricerca della lingua da una stesura all'altra del 'Partigiano Johnny'', *Strumenti Critici*, 36–37 (October 1978), 275–331 (p. 275).
12. Paolo Milano, 'Il partigiano che pensava in inglese', *L'Espresso*, XIV, 32, 11 August 1968, p. 19.
13. Walter Pedullà, 'La Resistenza momento della verità» di Fenoglio', *Avanti!*, 15 August 1968.
14. Fenoglio, *Il partigiano Johnny*.
15. Gian Luigi Beccaria, *La guerra e gli asfodeli: romanzo e vocazione epica di Beppe Fenoglio* (Milan: Serra e Riva, 1984), recently republished (Turin: Aragno, 2013).
16. Roberto Galaverni, 'Una vita come resistenza. Le occasioni uniche di Beppe Fenoglio', *Intersezioni*, 13 (1993), 125–47. Alberto Casadei has written widely on Fenoglio and epic; see for example *Dagli Appunti partigiani al Partigiano Johnny*, in *Omaggio a Beppe Fenoglio*, pp. 39–54; *L'epica storia di Fenoglio*, in *Beppe Fenoglio. Scrittura e Resistenza*, ed. by Giulio Ferroni, Maria Ida Gaeta and Gabriele Pedullà (Rome: Edizioni Fahrenheit 451, 2006), pp. 107–17); *Epica inutile e morte dell'eroe: 'Il partigiano Johnny' di Beppe Fenoglio*, now in Casadei, *Romanzi di Finisterre. Narrazione della guerra e problemi del realism* (Rome: Carocci, 2000), pp. 61–88. Most of his reflections are now in the third chapter of *Stile e tradizione nel romanzo italiano contemporaneo* (Bologna: Il Mulino, 2007).
17. Rosella Bessi, 'Fenoglio e l'epica classica', *Inventario*, 5–6 (December 1982), 169–89, Giorgio Bàrberi Squarotti, *L'eroe, la città, il fiume*, in *Beppe Fenoglio oggi. Atti del convegno di S. Salvatore Monferrato, 1989*, ed. by Giovanna Ioli, intro. by Gian Luigi Beccaria (Milan: Mursia, 1991), pp. 33–62, Maria de las Nieves Muñiz Muñiz, 'Spazio e resistenza in Fenoglio', *Allegoria*, 54 (September-December 2006), 23–36, now in *Beppe Fenoglio. Scrittura e Resistenza*, pp. 29–43; Gabriele Pedullà, *Le armi e il ragazzo*. Recent contributions on epic include: Veronica Pesce, 'Il partigiano Johnny, un caso di epica moderna', *Maia*, I, LXII (January-April 2010), 91–114, Marialuisa Sipione, *Beppe Fenoglio e la Bibbia: il 'culto rigoroso della libertà'* (Florence: Cesati, 2011), Valter Boggione, *La sfortuna in favour; saggi su Fenoglio* (Venice: Marsilio, 2011), Stefano Jossa, *Un paese senza eroi: l'Italia da Jacopo Ortis a Montalbano* (Rome-Bari: Laterza, 2013), pp. 225–37.
18. Amongst others, Cooke, Alfano, Vittorio Spinazzola, *L'egemonia del romanzo* (Milan: Il saggiatore, 2007); Franco Petroni, 'Misura breve, misura lunga nella narrativa di Fenoglio', *Moderna*, 1 (August 1999), 125–42.
19. Mikhail Bakhtin, 'Epos e romanzo. Sulla metodologia dello studio del romanzo', in *Estetica e romanzo* (Turin: Einaudi, 2001 (1975¹)), pp. 454–82.
20. See Cooke, p. 41, and Gabriele Pedullà, 'Nota bibliografica', in Fenoglio, *Il libro di Johnny*, pp. lxxvii–lxxxi.
21. For a definition, see Maurice Bowra, *From Virgil to Milton* (London: Macmillan, 1945), p. 1, and Zatti, p. 15. On authorship see Hegel, pp. 1173–74.
22. Epic has been divided into 'original', linked to oral tradition (Homeric poems, for instance), and 'literary' (the *Aeneid*, to focus on Classical epic) — Bowra, pp. 1–32 and Zatti, p. 16. David Quint, *Epic and Empire: Politics and Generic Form from Virgil to Milton* (Princeton: Princeton University Press, 1993) sees literary epic as an expression of political power, used in some contexts to favour imperialism.
23. J. Brian Hainsworth, *The Idea of Epic* (Berkeley: University of California Press, 1991), especially p. 10.
24. Hegel, p. 1186, György Lukács, *Die Theorie des Romans* (Berlin: Cassirer, 1920). For a recent

exploration of the continuous contamination between epic and novel, see Massimo Fusillo, 'Fra epica e romanzo', in Franco Moretti (ed), *Il romanzo* (Turin: Einaudi, 2001), vol. II, *Le forme*, pp. 5–34.

25. 'In our modern vocabulary the proper secondary use of *epic* expresses admiration for more than scale [...]. We commend grandeur of subject, vision, and moral force — in a word, depth and breadth [...]' (Hainsworth, p. 149).
26. Moretti, *Opere Mondo. Saggio sulla forma epica dal 'Faust' a 'Cent'anni di solitudine'* (Turin: Einaudi 2003 [1994^1]).
27. A recent discussion on the state of Italian contemporary novel is Wu Ming's *New Italian Epic. Memorandum 1993–2008: narrativa, sguardo obliquo, ritorno al futuro*, first published online <http://www.carmillaonline.com/2008/04/23/new-italian-epic/> [accessed 3 July 2015]), now in Wu Ming, *New Italian Epic. Letteratura, sguardo obliquo, ritorno al futuro* (Turin: Einaudi, 2009).
28. Northrop Frye, *Anatomy of Criticism* (Princeton: Princeton University Press 1957).
29. Muñiz Muñiz, p. 30.
30. For a recent definition, see Ceserani, pp. 232–33.
31. Cooke.
32. Quotes from PJ are from Fenoglio, *Il partigiano Johnny*, in Fenoglio, *Opere*. The abbreviations PJ^1 and PJ^2 are used to refer to the version of PJ that have been variously used.
33. Beccaria, pp. 35–37.
34. Giovanni Falaschi, 'Fatti straordinari', *L'indice dei libri del mese*, 11, November 2007, p. 10.
35. It has been noted that in PJ^2 some epic traits disappear (Bessi, p. 186). However, this 'potatura di figure ed episodi accessori' (Grignani, p. 307) is not intended as a passage from epic to novel, but represents part of Fenoglio's constant work to make the text more readable, since '[q]uando la misura (e il lessico) di un grande stile, tra l'omerico ed il biblico, è raggiunta di primo acchito [...] il testo non è più mutato, o lo è di ben poco' (Beccaria, p. 96. For examples see pp. 96–97), providing actually 'la conferma che [PJ] tenta di conciliare epico e popolare, sublime e libresco, senso letterale e senso figurale' (Elisabetta Soletti, *Beppe Fenoglio* (Milan: Mursia, 1987), p. 127). Hence the epic quality is not meant to disappear.
36. I will use the abbreviations: IL, *Iliad*, OD, *Odyssey*, AEN, *Aeneid*. I used the following editions: IL: Omero, *Iliade*, trans. by Rosa Calzecchi Onesti (Turin: Einaudi, 1990 [1950^1]), as suggested by Bessi; OD: Omero, *Odissea*, trans. by Ippolito Pindemonte (Rome: Newton Compton, 2008 [1822^1]); AEN: Virgilio, *Eneide*, trans. by Rosa Calzecchi Onesti (Turin: Einaudi, 1989 [1967^1] — for the *Aeneid* the Latin text as been used for reference, following linguistic studies on PJ that revealed the effectiveness of Latin in Fenoglio's language (Pier Vincenzo Mengaldo, *Storia della lingua italiana: Il Novecento* (Bologna: Il Mulino, 2006); Isella, 'La lingua del *Partigiano Johnny*', in Fenoglio, *Romanzi e racconti*, pp. xv–xlvi).
37. An episode of 'observation from the walls' is in PJ when Johnny, from a hill, witnesses helplessly the killing of the partisans Ivan and Louis (PJ^1 XXXVIII 1–4; PJ^2 XXII 1–4).
38. On this topos see Jossa, *L'eroe nudo e l'eroe vestito*, p. 12). For examples, see for instance IL X.
39. Cooke, p. 113, and Spinazzola, p. 224.
40. This changed aspect for the always impeccable Nord can be read in line with AEN II 274–75, when Hector — whose body, we said, was preserved by the gods — appears to Aeneas in miserable conditions, surprising the hero.
41. See Cooke, p. 144.
42. Bessi, p. 177.
43. The women, and especially Helen, lament their own destiny. A similar element appears in PJ during Tito's funeral, when the mother of a soldier missing in Russia pities herself together with the young partisan.
44. On rituals in ancient Greece and Rome see Ernesto De Martino, *Morte e pianto rituale: dal lamento funebre antico al pianto di Maria* (Turin: Bollati Boringhieri, 2000 [1975^1]), especially pp. 275–82.
45. See Casadei, *Epica inutile e morte dell'eroe*.
46. Calvino, 'Omero antimilitarista', *L'Unità*, 15 September 1946, now in Calvino, *Saggi*, pp. 2118–19.
47. On the natural elements and their impact see Eugenio Corsini, 'Paesaggio e natura in Fenoglio',

in *Beppe Fenoglio oggi*, pp. 13–32, as well as Gian Luigi Beccaria, p. 72 and p. 69, and Elisabetta Soletti, *Beppe Fenoglio*, p. 121.
48. See Pesce, pp. 99–101.
49. Grignani, pp. 299–307, and Petroni, p. 130.
50. Ettore Canepa, 'Il partigiano Johnny di Beppe Fenoglio', in Canepa, *Per l'alto mare aperto: viaggio marino e avventura metafisica da Coleridge a Caryle,d a Melville a Fenoglio* (Milan: Jaca Book, 1991), pp. 121–60 (128).
51. Bessi also analyses an episode in PJ (PJ¹ XXVI 9) where Johnny and his comrade Ettore joke about Ettore's 'casco di cuoio, molto massiccio ed imponente', claiming that the helmet will have the power to scare away fascists and Germans, much like in classical times would have done weapons, and helmets in particular. Amongst IL hypotexts retraced by Bessi include XV 308 ff., XIX 12 ff., XVI 769–71, XV 608–10, and of course (IL VI, 466–74), when Astyanax is scared by the sight of Hector's helmet and rejects his embrace, making Hector and Andromache smile at the difficult moment of their final farewell.
52. See for instance Petroni.
53. Beccaria pp. 114–15.
54. Cesare Pavese, 'Ritorno all'uomo', in Pavese, *La letteratura americana e altri saggi* (Turin: Einaudi, 1951), pp. 217–19 (p. 218). The essay appeared in *L'Unità* in 1945.

CHAPTER 19

Una questioncella privata: su un racconto inedito di Italo Calvino

Mario Barenghi

Comincerò con una citazione.

> I sogni dei partigiani sono corti e poco fantasiosi. Sogni di uomini affamati, nati dalle notti di fame, legati alla storia del cibo sempre poco e da dividere in tanti: sogni di pezzi di pane morsicati e chiusi in un cassetto. I cani randagi devono fare sogni simili, di ossa rosicchiate e nascoste sottoterra.
>
> Solo se si dorme vicino al fuoco, la pancia è piena, e non si è camminato troppo durante il giorno, ci si può concedere di sognare una donna nuda e al mattino ci si sveglia sgombri e spumanti con una letizia come d'ancore salpate. Allora si prende a parlare di ragazze, con i compagni stesi nella paglia, e si racconta e ci si passa le fotografie.

Al lettore di Calvino questo brano suonerà familiare. Parole simili, se non proprio identiche, le ha già incontrate da qualche parte... Dove? Ma certo: nel *Sentiero dei nidi di ragno*. Più precisamente, all'inizio del cap. VII, quello che termina con l'incendio dell'accampamento del Dritto. Verifichiamo:

> I sogni dei partigiani sono rari e corti, sogni nati dalle notti di fame, legati alla storia del cibo sempre poco e da dividere in tanti: sogni di pezzi di pane morsicati e poi chiusi in un cassetto. I cani randagi devono fare sogni simili, di ossa rosicchiate e nascoste sottoterra. Solo quando lo stomaco è pieno, il fuoco è acceso, e non s'è camminato troppo durante il giorno, ci si può permettere di sognare una donna nuda e ci si sveglia al mattino sgombri e spumanti, con una letizia come d'ancore salpate.
>
> Allora gli uomini tra il fieno cominciano a parlare delle loro donne, di quelle passate e di quelle future, a fare progetti per quando la guerra sarà finita, e a passarsi fotografie ingiallite.[1]

Si tratta evidentemente di due versioni dello stesso passaggio; quella del *Sentiero* è la seconda. Le differenze principali s'incontrano all'inizio e alla fine; identica rimane l'allusione alle polluzioni notturne, perfetta nella sua levità ed esattezza espressiva. La riscrittura dell'attacco, puramente formale, serve a evitare un paio di ripetizioni (*I sogni/ Sogni*; *uomini affamati/ notti di fame*); più significativo l'intervento sulla conclusione, che amplia la durata temporale. Bastano due tocchi — il verbo all'infinito anziché all'indicativo, un aggettivo in più — perché la scena acquisti profondità: dietro l'ingiallirsi delle fotografie ci sono lo scorrere dei giorni e dei mesi, i disagi, le intemperie. Nel romanzo, poi, è uno dei brani in cui in cui è più evidente il distacco della narrazione dal punto di vista di Pin. Lo stesso fenomeno si verifica, ad esempio, poco dopo l'inizio del cap. II:

> La sorella di Pin è sempre stata sciatta nelle faccende di casa, fin da bambina: Pin faceva dei grandi pianti in braccio a lei, da piccolo, con la testa piena di croste, e allora lei lo lasciava sul muretto del lavatoio e andava a saltare con i monelli nei rettangoli tracciati col gesso sui marciapiedi. Ogni tanto tornava la nave del loro padre, di cui Pin ricorda solo le braccia, grandi, e nude, che sollevavano in aria, forti braccia segnate da vene nere. Ma da quando la loro madre è morta, le sue venute sono state sempre più rade, finché nessuno l'ha più visto; si diceva che avesse un'altra famiglia in una città di là dal mare.[2]

Pur rimanendo ben lontana dall'onniscienza, non prevista dalla strategia narrativa del *Sentiero*, la prospettiva è più ampia di quella del protagonista, che ovviamente non può aver memoria di quand'era così piccolo. In prima approssimazione, potremmo parlare di punto di vista del vicinato: le notizie riferite corrispondono a quanto sa chi abita in Carrugio Lungo. Qualcosa del genere accade anche nel cap. IX, quando il commissario Kim annuncia il tradimento di Pelle. Il commento che segue dà voce a sentimenti estranei a Pin, eppure molto personalizzati. A fungere da *focus* narrativo sarà la coscienza di combattenti adulti, di partigiani politicamente consapevoli (mentre su Pin ritornerà il capoverso seguente, con il motivo, davvero tutto suo, della preoccupazione per la pistola nascosta).

> Questa è una di quelle notizie che mettono nel sangue una disperazione cieca, e impediscono di pensare. Pelle appena qualche sera prima era lì con loro che diceva: facciamo un colpo come dico io, sentite! Par quasi strano di non sentire il suo respiro intasato dal raffreddore, dietro di loro, mentre si mette a oliare il mitragliatore per l'azione dell'indomani. Invece ora Pelle è laggiù nella città proibita, con una grande testa di morto sul berretto nero, con armi nuove e bellissime, senza più paura di rastrellamenti, e sempre quella sua furia che gli fa sbattere gli occhietti arrossati dal raffreddore, umettarsi le labbra sbavate dall'arsura, furia contro di loro, i suoi compagni di ieri, furia senz'odio o rancore, così come in un gioco tra compagni che ha per posta la morte.[3]

È il punto di vista degli uomini del Dritto? Almeno in parte, sì. Ma l'enfatica iterazione della parola «furia» sembra quasi un'anticipazione del discorso di Kim al comandante Ferriera, nel capitolo successivo: «Perché c'è qualcosa d'altro, comune a tutti, un furore [...] tu sai che c'è coraggio, che c'è furore anche in loro [...] E basta un nulla, un passo falso, un impennamento dell'anima e ci si trova dall'altra parte, come Pelle, dalla brigata nera, a sparare con lo stesso furore, con lo stesso odio».[4] Non sappiamo abbastanza dell'esperienza partigiana di Calvino per azzardare ipotesi; difficile è tuttavia sfuggire all'impressione che l'accorato fervore del tono (il sangue, la cieca disperazione) tradisca l'impronta di un episodio personalmente vissuto.

È probabile che i risvolti autobiografici del *Sentiero* siano più numerosi di quanto si possa sospettare. Ad esempio, secondo quanto riferisce Esther Calvino, corrisponde a un episodio preciso la cruda scena della fucilazione dei prigionieri ad opera dei cognati calabresi, che nella realtà facevano i macellai, e che si cibarono del cuore degli uccisi (o dell'ucciso). Italo ne fu così colpito che perse i sensi. Non a caso, la Prefazione 1964 al *Sentiero dei nidi di ragno* sottolinea l'impatto traumatico con la violenza in guerra:

> Ero stato, prima d'andare coi partigiani, un giovane borghese sempre vissuto in famiglia; il mio tranquillo antifascismo era prima di tutto opposizione al culto della forza guerresca, una questione di stile, di «sense of humour», e tutt'a un tratto la coerenza con le mie opinioni mi portava in mezzo alla violenza partigiana, a misurarmi su quel metro. Fu un trauma, il primo...[5]

Lo stesso sentiero dove i ragni — *Nemesia caementaria*? — fanno i nidi esisteva davvero (devo anche questa notizia a Esther Calvino) e probabilmente esiste ancora: era uno dei luoghi prediletti di Italo, lungo un corso d'acqua nei pressi di Baiardo.

Torniamo al brano sui sogni dei partigiani. La sua collocazione in quel punto del *Sentiero* non manca di ragioni. Al centro del cap. VII è infatti l'emergere dell'attrazione erotica fra la Giglia e il Dritto, che Pin prontamente intuisce («Ehi, speriamo che non vengano su i tedeschi, il comandante si sente sentimentale, stasera»).[6] Tuttavia la sua origine è diversa. E nella versione primitiva — la prima che abbiamo citato — il nesso con la trama era molto più stretto, perché il protagonista era un giovane, non un bambino. Era la storia di un amore acerbo e controverso, troncato dalla scelta di unirsi alla Resistenza: titolo, «*Flirt» prima di battersi*.

Il testo, emerso di recente tra le carte di Calvino, consiste in 24 fogli dattiloscritti numerati, con un numero abbastanza cospicuo di correzioni a penna; dell'ultimo foglio è stata tagliata la metà inferiore, giusto sotto sotto la firma (nome e cognome in caratteri maiuscoli). Mai pubblicato, il racconto sembra rimasto però a lungo sulla soglia di una possibile edizione. Il titolo *Flirt prima di battersi* (in questo caso, senza virgolette) compare in un elenco di 95 racconti, suddivisi per anno, dal 1945 al 1959, stilato sul *verso* di una bozza dell'*Orologio* di Carlo Levi (che era stato edito da Einaudi nel 1950). Si tratta del quinto titolo dei sedici registrati nel 1946, dopo *Il grasso resta a terra*, *Attesa della morte in un albergo*, *La banda internazionale*, *Il settimo si riposò*, e prima di *Paura sul sentiero*; quindi il nono in assoluto, visto che il 1945 ne comprende solo quattro (*Angoscia in caserma*, *Come un volo d'anitre*, *La stessa cosa del sangue*, *Andato al comando*). In sintesi, ecco la storia.

★ ★ ★ ★ ★

Riviera ligure, agosto 1944. La vita di Attilio, studente universitario, è divisa in due: da una parte un'apparenza di normalità sociale (le vacanze, i bagni, il giro di amici, le ragazze), dall'altra i contatti clandestini con gruppi antifascisti. Al centro della vicenda è il rapporto con Vanda, la più bella ragazza della spiaggia, tanto avvenente quanto superficiale e frivola («la sua vita, la sua bellezza erano come sullo sfondo di una cartolina patinata a colori, come l'ignoranza del male nel mondo»). Benché il suo primo fidanzato sia morto in Russia, abbattuto con il suo aeroplano, Vanda appare del tutto disinteressata alle vicende della guerra. Quando vede Attilio confabulare in disparte con l'amico Edmondo, che lo informa sugli ultimi eventi («— Ieri battaglia a Pian del Carpe [...] Due camion carichi di tedeschi messi fuori combattimento. Il terzo è arrivato dopo e li ha sorpresi. Un morto: Gordon. Kim è ferito»), la sua curiosità nasce solo dalla gelosia, come se non concepisse altra realtà oltre agli amori e ai *flirts*. Sempre più incline a lasciare la città per unirsi ai partigiani, Attilio non sa se parlarne a Vanda oppure no; dapprima medita di raccontarle una bugia, poi prova a entrare in argomento di sbieco, divagando sulla sua attrazione per la montagna.

— A me piace un po' Cortina, il Breuil; da questa parte non c'è nulla che valga la pena, paesetti senza vita, ci si annoia. — Non era un inizio confortante.
— Tutte le estati facevo un giro, sacco in ispalla. Peccato quest'anno con questi ribelli, questi tedeschi. Si rischia di prendersi una raffica in pancia. — Bel gusto! — fece Vanda. Attilio inghiottì saliva, riprese: — Eppure, di un po' di montagna ne ho proprio voglia; sarei quasi tentato d'andarmene coi partigiani; dev'essere una vita pittoresca; mi attira. — Era un modo d'arrivarci vergognoso, vigliacco: ma Attilio, ad andare con Vanda, s'era avvezzato a questo torpido mentire, a questa maschera grigia e avvilente; perché?
— Mamma mia! — fece Vanda. — I ribelli! Vorrei proprio vederti!
Attilio non si smontò. — Non ti piacerebbe che fossi un partigiano, uno barbuto che gira nei boschi vestito di telo da tenda, col *thompson*, la cartuccera...?
— Era un'immagine ridicola, creata apposta per Vanda, ma in fondo anche lui i partigiani li immaginava così.
— Ma perché poi fanno i partigiani? — Rispondere a queste domande di Vanda era difficilissimo; non bisognava tirare in ballo le idee, neppure sfiorare le idee, neppure far sospettare che si aveva delle idee: Vanda si sarebbe ritratta spaventata come una cavalla a un'ombra sconosciuta. Bisognava muoversi nel vuoto pneumatico, indicarle qualche immagine che fosse catalogata nei suoi schemi, come in una scrittura a geroglifici.

Pur consapevole che la sua idea di darsi alla lotta armata ha qualcosa di astratto, Attilio la coltiva come unica via d'uscita dalla sospensione vagamente irreale di un ambiente ostinato a vivere quell'estate come tutte le altre («Era una società che moriva in costume da bagno»). D'altro canto, non gli sfugge che Vanda, con tutta la sua fatuità, rappresenta quel vecchio, solido mondo borghese di cui egli stesso fa parte, ed entro il quale i lineamenti del suo futuro sarebbero già ben prefigurati: un avvenire comodo, sicuro, gratificante.

Doveva essere dolce e soffice la vita accanto a Vanda, come in un mondo di zucchero filato e di croccante, una vita senza problemi, lievemente animalesca, da sani animali soddisfatti: i borghesi! Perché non accettava Attilio questo suo posto di borghese assegnatogli dal destino, dalla natura? Perché pretendeva di risolvere le contraddizioni del mondo, e s'impelagava in contraddizioni ancora più stridenti?
In quel suo spirito di ribellione, in quel suo consumarsi in una passione letteraria o politica, quanto non era residuo dell'ombrosa solitudine dell' adolescenza, quando la donna è una terra misteriosa e irraggiungibile? Ora egli aveva la donna, così, senza ribellione, senza gloria: la sua vita sarebbe stata soddisfatta anche così, ereditando l'agiata professione paterna, considerando con moderato umorismo quel piccolo mondo provinciale, accanto ad una moglie elegante ed invidiata: Vanda.

Così la storia prosegue, tra infingimenti e incomprensioni, senza mai valicare i limiti di un'intimità fisica che entrambi temono. Naturalmente agli occhi degli estranei le cose possono assumere un aspetto diverso, più lusinghiero per la vanità maschile di Attilio. Così, mentre Edmondo continua ad aggiornarlo sugli sviluppi della guerra, sulle azioni partigiane, sulle questioni ideologiche («– Una carica di tritolo sotto il ponte... Saranno cento, centocinquanta uomini... Il capo è Anselmo: è stato in Spagna con Negrin... Il Cotentin è libero... Puntano su Bordeaux... Tra i socialisti e i comunisti c'è questa differenza... — ») Attilio si accorge che gli operai dell'organizzazione clandestina, vedendolo insieme a Vanda, assumono nei suoi confronti un atteggiamento diverso, insieme ammirato e complice: «non era come avere una bella casa, dei bei libri, cosa di cui quasi si sentiva umiliato, di fronte a loro, cosa che dichiarava solo uno squilibrio sociale, tra lui e loro; nell'avere una bella donna era in gioco qualcosa di comune tra lui e loro».

Altre presenze femminili agiscono però nella sua immaginazione. Non le amiche della spiaggia, oggetto della gelosia di Vanda, né la partigiana jugoslava coi calzoncini corti e il mitra, di cui ha sentito parlare Edmondo, e chissà se esiste davvero: bensì la ragazza «dalla bellezza raccolta e dignitosa», dallo sguardo fiero e triste, che gli trasmette un messaggio urgente del partito. Occorrono materiali, vestiti, armi, soldi: i partigiani hanno bisogno di tutto.

> Attilio voleva battersi: sentiva una volontà cupa e disperata in lui, avrebbe vendicato i morti, punito i traditori, ma capiva che ogni suo atto, ogni suo gesto sarebbe stato dettato da un segreto bisogno del rispetto, dell'ammirazione di quella ragazza bassa e nera.

La decisione è presa. Il giorno prima di andare in montagna Attilio organizza una specie di festa in un podere della famiglia. Ora deve proprio parlare con Vanda, verso la quale sente di nutrire uno strano rancore. Ma vedendolo accigliato e pensieroso, la ragazza lo previene: è inutile che parli, ha capito tutto. Luisa, eh? quella civetta: se n'era accorta subito. Preso in contropiede, Attilio sceglie la via più facile e le dà ragione. Anzi, si spinge oltre: dà una spiegazione della sua immaginaria infedeltà. «– È che lei non fa tante storie, come te. Con lei si può arrivare subito al sodo, si può arrivare. — Si stupì d'aver parlato così. Per vendetta? Per orgoglio d'uomo?» Una volta di più, la reazione di Vanda sorprende Attilio. Abbandonata contro un albero, si ravvìa i capelli e gli chiede: «Mi sposerai...?»

Qui la scena s'interrompe. Dopo un doppio interlinea (uno dei nove che scandiscono il racconto) la storia riprende con il brano sui sogni dei partigiani e la scena dei combattenti che esibiscono le fotografie delle ragazze.

> Toccò anche a Attilio mostrare la sua, portata sempre in fondo al portafoglio. I compagni pidocchiosi, malrasi, si sporgevano dietro le sue spalle, sbarrando gli occhi imbambolati davanti al viso, al corpo della più bella ragazza della spiaggia. Essa sarebbe rimasta così nei loro occhi di uomini assetati e così l'avrebbero sognata, nei loro sonni interrotti dai turni di guardia e dagli allarmi.
>
> E ad Attilio parve in quel momento che, ad abbandonarla alle fantasie di quei suoi compagni pidocchiosi e stracciati, avesse esaudito un suo ultimo desiderio di vendetta.

Così il racconto si conclude.

* * * * *

«*Flirt*» *prima di battersi* presenta corrispondenze assai notevoli con quanto Calvino dichiara nella già citata Prefazione 1964 al *Sentiero* riguardo ai primi abbozzi narrativi sulla Resistenza.

> Per mesi, dopo la fine della guerra, avevo provato a raccontare l'esperienza partigiana in prima persona, o con un protagonista simile a me. Scrissi qualche racconto che pubblicai, altri che buttai nel cestino; mi muovevo a disagio: non riuscivo mai a smorzare del tutto le vibrazioni sentimentali e moralistiche; veniva fuori sempre qualche stonatura; la mia storia personale mi pareva umile, meschina; ero pieno di complessi, d'inibizioni di fronte a tutto quel che più mi stava a cuore.
> Quando cominciai a scrivere storie in cui non entravo io, tutto prese a funzionare [...][7]

Come Attilio — nome che include, anagrammaticamente, «Italo» — Calvino ha trascorso un periodo di collaborazione clandestina con gruppi antifascisti attivi in città, prima di raggiungere in montagna un reparto combattente. Secondo l'accurata ricostruzione di Claudio Milanini, Calvino viene reclutato dall'esercito della Repubblica Sociale Italiana all'inizio del 1944; dopo una serie di controlli medici viene assegnato come scritturale al tribunale militare di Sanremo, dove presta servizio fino alla metà di giugno, quando si unisce al distaccamento garibaldino del comandante Erven.[8] A guerra conclusa, in una presentazione del 1960 che più tardi intitolerà *Autobiografia politica giovanile*, Calvino dichiara di essersi avvicinato al partito in febbraio, subito dopo aver appreso della morte del giovane medico comunista Felice Cascione, e di aver avuto il compito di organizzare gli studenti nel Fronte della Gioventù; «un mio scritto fu ciclostilato e pubblicato clandestinamente».[9] In *Flirt* la ragazza nera chiede ad Attilio se è lui «il compagno degli articoli». Il protagonista conferma, non senza un pizzico di orgoglio («Io sono quello di "Rinascere nel sangue", "Parole agli schiavi", "Italia senza italiani"»), ma la ragazza taglia corto: «– Non si tratta di questo, adesso: tu organizzi studenti, no?».

In realtà Attilio rappresenta il più impegnativo sforzo di sintesi dei due estremi fra i quali — come ha mostrato Bruno Falcetto — oscillano i protagonisti della narrativa calviniana degli anni Quaranta, i «buoni a nulla» e i «partigiani». Il protagonista di *Flirt* non è ancora un partigiano, anche se pensa che sia giunta l'ora di diventarlo; non è più un buono a nulla, perché qualcosa ha pur già cominciato a fare: e tuttavia appare ancora esposto alle insidie di una neghittosa indolenza, che frena la sua risoluzione. Impacciato e insicuro di sé, avverte con penosa noia la mancanza di senso della vita che conduce; ma di fronte alla decisione esita, tentenna, tergiversa (non a caso "decidere" viene da *caedo*, taglio). Come in uno dei più interessanti raccontini giovanili editi postumi, *Come non fui Noè*, a profilarsi è il tema della «chiamata per la quale non si è pronti».[10]

Particolarmente stretta appare poi la parentela con il «ragazzo rastrellato» di *Angoscia in caserma*, uno dei tre racconti di *Ultimo viene il corvo* dei quali Milanini ha riconosciuto la radice autobiografica. Esclusi sia dalla grande silloge del 1958 *I racconti*, sia dall'edizione 1969 del *Corvo*, ricompaiono nella versione definitiva, che però è corredata da una postilla che equivale a una presa di distanze (per tutta questa vicenda è d'obbligo il rinvio alle notizie fornite da Falcetto nell'apparato del «Meridiano»).[11]

> Questa edizione (1976) riproduce [...] i trenta racconti del 1949 nello stesso ordine, compresi i racconti «rifiutati» dall'autore nelle raccolte successive. Tra essi, come testimonianza d'epoca, sono i primi racconti che Italo Calvino scrisse nel 1945, nei mesi seguenti alla Liberazione (*La stessa cosa del sangue*, *Attesa della morte in un albergo*, *Angoscia in caserma*), e che l'autore non aveva più voluto ripubblicare perché l'esperienza della Resistenza vi viene resa ancora attraverso un'evocazione emotiva, che contrasta con lo stile da lui elaborato in seguito.

Come l'Attilio di *Flirt*, l'anonimo protagonista di *Angoscia* prova un senso di repulsione nei confronti dell'ambiente che lo circonda: che in questo caso non è il tranquillo mondo ipocrita della buona borghesia provinciale, bensì la caserma, dove si respira un clima di mediocrità squallida, di opportunismo meschino. Sintomatico è che l'argomento di discussione preferito sia l'«otto settembre», ovvero l'inattesa messe di occasioni di profitto personale che il caos seguito all'armistizio aveva offerto a lesti e scaltri. Pure, anche qui biasimo e disgusto si mescolano a un'inconfessabile attrazione, all'intuizione (o al timore) di una segreta sintonia: alla tentazione — infine — di adeguarsi, cedendo al contagio di un pragmatismo della più bassa lega.

> Il ragazzo rastrellato, a vivere in mezzo a loro, sentiva questo grosso fiato di viltà affoltirglisi intorno, congiungersi a una sua vena segreta, e il rampicante polveroso che cresceva a tappezzare le mura del cortile tappezzava lui pure, era un insinuarsi di solidarietà tra lui e loro, che l'inchiodava a quelle mura, a quelle brande.[12]

Di qui l'impulso del protagonista a reagire, troncando di netto con il contesto avvolgente da cui rischia di essere sopraffatto. In *Angoscia* è la fortunosa evasione durante un trasferimento; in *Flirt* una scelta politica sicuramente coraggiosa, che però sul piano umano e personale ha comunque qualcosa della fuga. Rivelatrice, al termine del dialogo fra Attilio e Vanda sulla possibilità che lui si unisca ai ribelli, è l'occorrenza della parola-chiave del ragionamento che il Kim del *Sentiero* fa al comandante Ferriera, «furore». Vanda non prende sul serio i discorsi di Attilio: come può pensare di andare a menar le mani uno come lui, che ha paura di tuffarsi dal trampolino alto?

> Attilio si sentì ferito, quasi si fosse messa in dubbio la sua virilità; era una velleità intellettuale, questo suo voler fare il partigiano, ora lo capiva, nient'altro che una velleità intellettuale, ma lui ci si accaniva con furore.

Tutti coloro che combattono, secondo il Kim del *Sentiero*, sono mossi da una «ferita segreta». La ferita segreta del protagonista di *Flirt* ha due cause: da un lato il disagio di appartenere a un ceto privilegiato (studente di giurisprudenza e figlio di un avvocato o di un notaio, Attilio vive la propria condizione con un imbarazzo simile al rimorso), dall'altro una sessualità ancora immatura e inibita, che conserva tratti adolescenziali. Utile, da questo punto di vista, è ricordare un'importante variante del cap. IX. Rileggiamo il passo del monologo di Kim:

> Tutti abbiamo una ferita segreta per riscattare la quale combattiamo. Anche Ferriera? Forse anche Ferriera: la rabbia a non poter fare andare il mondo come vuol lui.[13]

Il costrutto di «rabbia» con la preposizione «a» anziché «di», grammaticalmente anomalo, è la traccia di una sostituzione, e forse l'indizio di una correzione, se non affrettata, non del tutto convinta. La stesura del 1947 infatti non parlava di «rabbia» e «ferita», bensì di «impotenza» (che si costruisce appunto con il dativo).

> Tutti abbiamo un'impotenza segreta per riscattare la quale combattiamo. Anche Ferriera? Forse anche Ferriera: l'impotenza a non poter far andare il mondo come vuol lui.[14]

Come già accennato, nella loro storia Vanda e Attilio si trattengono da effusioni troppo spinte. I motivi coincidono solo in parte. In lei si direbbe prevalga un oculato ossequio alla morale borghese; in lui, una sostanziale insicurezza. Vanda, nello schermirsi, è del tutto padrona di sé; la prudenza di Attilio ha invece qualcosa di più indistinto: «Anche in Attilio era un guardingo senso di pericolo [...] Attilio non era un ragazzo scapestrato o cinico; si ritraeva con una segreta *furiosa paura*» (corsivo mio). L'insolito accoppiamento aggettivo-sostantivo suggerisce un confuso ripiegarsi dell'eccitazione, come se, per eccesso (o difetto) di ardore, l'impulso si aggrovigliasse prima ancora di esplicarsi. L'autocontrollo ha facilmente la meglio: alla larga dalla pazzia, siamo ben lontani dalla «furia» amorosa dell'Orlando ariostesco — più ancora che dal «furore» dei combattenti di cui parla Kim. Sia in *Flirt* sia nel *Sentiero* il lessema sta a designare una perturbazione dell'animo indeterminata, ma abbastanza forte da sopraffare l'intenzione volontaria e la razionalità. Questo è insieme vizio e pregio: gli esiti possono essere positivi o rovinosi, secondo la capacità del soggetto di arginarla, di incanalarla, cioè di avvalersene senza reprimerla, evitando però di esserne travolto. Dare un senso politico al furore dei partigiani è appunto il compito del commissario Kim. E non sarà un caso se il principale saggio ariostesco di Calvino si intitolerà *La struttura del «Furioso»*:[15] né che, come ha notato Guido Bonsaver, nel *Castello dei destini incrociati* Orlando pazzo per amore scopra l'impotenza della Durlindana negli umidi recessi del bosco femminile.[16] In una parola, il problema è sempre come trasformare un impeto in una risorsa.

E non è detto che l'impeto sia, in senso proprio, amore. Quello di Attilio è particolarmente spurio e controverso: qui non è in gioco una travolgente passione, bensì — giusta il titolo — di un *flirt*. Il senso esatto della parola (una relazione superficiale e poco impegnativa, non comprommettente, senza rapporti sessuali) è ben illustrato da una pagina del *Giardino dei Finzi-Contini*, il dialogo telefonico tra il protagonista e Micòl nel cap. I della parte II:

> — [...] E quest'autunno, di mettermi lì buona buona me la sento ancora meno. Lo sai cosa mi piacerebbe fare, caro te, invece che seppellirmi in biblioteca?
> — Sentiamo.
> — Giocare a tennis, ballare, e flirtare, figùrati!
> — Onesti svaghi, tennis e ballo compresi, a cui, volendo, potresti benissimo darti anche in Venezia.[17]

A questo punto potremmo interrogarci sulla trama di *«Flirt» prima di battersi*, e ragionare su quel che è successo o che non è successo alla fine della festa, il giorno prima che Attilio si unisca ai partigiani. Tra la battuta di Vanda e la ripresa del racconto intercorre infatti una vistosa ellissi, un «non detto» carico di significato: per usare i termini di Nicola Gardini, una «lacuna» da manuale.[18] Vanda, sciocchina finché si vuole, non manca di capacità di seduzione: il prezioso dettaglio dei puntini di sospensione («Mi sposerai...?») getta un'ombra ambigua su ciò che accade quella sera, e su quanto precede il brano sui sogni erotici dei giovani combattenti, a sua volta preambolo alla futile e ingenerosa «vendetta» di Attilio. Perché Attilio sente il bisogno di vendicarsi? Di che cosa si vendica? Rigorosamente parlando, la lacuna non esclude alcuna congettura possibile. Ad alimentare il rancore del protagonista potrebbe essere qualunque cosa: un amplesso appagante, perché l'appagamento fisico non sarebbe bastato comunque a compensare la scarsa intesa fra i due; un amplesso non appagante, a maggior ragione; un'improvvisa resistenza di lei, verosimilmente dettata meno dal pudore che dal calcolo; un'inopinata *défaillance* del protagonista, non impotente (come si evince dal seguito), ma senza dubbio goffo e insicuro.

Il valore di questa ellissi, tuttavia, sta proprio nel non rivelare un dettaglio per dare maggior risalto all'insieme. Il punto è che tra Attilio e Vanda non può funzionare, sono troppo diversi. Il giovane intellettuale cerebrale e introverso e la fanciulla spensierata e conformista sono fatti per deludersi reciprocamente. Attilio lo intuisce, sia pur con rammarico; e alla fine ne trae le inevitabili conseguenze, portandosi dietro uno strascico di astioso malumore.

A ben vedere, anche questa storia ce ne ricorda un'altra. Quale? Torniamo, un'ultima volta, alla Prefazione 1964. Come tutti ricordano, Calvino ripete a più riprese, con piccole varianti, il medesimo interrogativo: Questo romanzo è il primo che ho scritto, che impressione mi fa leggerlo adesso? Le risposte offrono un affascinante ventaglio di verità parziali: il *Sentiero dei nidi di ragno* è il risultato di un clima storico, è un'opera collettiva, è una risposta personale alle polemiche politiche di quegli anni, è l'esito della convergenza di una serie di modelli letterari, è il frutto di una particolare vicenda biografica... Non riuscendo a venire a capo del problema — e non occorrerà sottolineare che si tratta di un sovrano artificio retorico — Calvino coglie il destro di rivolgere un altissimo elogio al romanzo postumo di Beppe Fenoglio *Una questione privata*, il libro che tutta una generazione avrebbe voluto scrivere, miracolosamente apparso quando nessuno ci sperava più; e dopo aver elencato le motivazioni del suo giudizio — che ora non mette conto di citare per esteso — conclude: «è al libro di Fenoglio che volevo fare la prefazione: non al mio».[19]

Una questione privata è probabilmente il capolavoro di Fenoglio; *«Flirt» prima di battersi*, un racconto giovanile che Calvino non si è mai risolto a pubblicare. Ciò nondimeno, e a dispetto delle apparenze, le affinità tra i protagonisti delle due opere sono forti. Benché Milton sembri un uomo, e per moltissimi versi lo sia, ha più o meno l'età di Attilio, visto che sono entrambi studenti universitari. Certo, all'altezza di quei fatali quattro giorni del novembre '44 in cui si consuma il suo destino, Milton ha già alle spalle molti mesi (non è dato sapere quanti) di militanza partigiana, mentre Attilio si accinge a partire solo nell'agosto dello stesso anno:

rispetto alla guerra, si matura in fretta. Ma anche Milton è schivo, scontroso, incline a interrogarsi e arrovellarsi; e, soprattutto, è altrettanto impacciato e ingenuo di Attilio nei rapporti con l'altro sesso. Inoltre il suo amore per Fulvia, per quanto profondo, soffre fin dall'inizio di velleità letterarie (come ha ben illustrato Gabriele Pedullà),[20] che ne inficiano la schiettezza. Lo stesso vale per, non diremo l'amore, ma l'attrazione fisica che il protagonista di *Flirt* prova per la sua bella. Un indizio: ammirandone i seni, «piccoli come campanule sotto la veste azzurra», Attilio richeggia la famosa analogia del *Cantico dei cantici* mormorando una parola («cavriuoletti») di cui Vanda non capisce il senso, e che lui si guarda bene dallo spiegare.[21]

In sostanza, *Flirt* e *Una questione privata* mettono a tema una medesima congiuntura esistenziale: il divario tra una precoce maturazione politica (incipiente in Attilio, acquisita in Milton), frutto evidente della guerra, e una persistente immaturità psicologica ed emotiva, che trattiene gli eroi dei due racconti entro l'ambito di una sessualità inibita e insicura, da adolescenti, quali da poco hanno in realtà cessato ambedue di essere. Le differenze dipendono dalla chiave in cui l'autore sceglie di giocare tale disparità di sviluppo. Il romanzo di Fenoglio punta sull'interiorità della rappresentazione, effetto della distanza temporale (Fulvia esiste solo nei ricordi di Milton) e sul progressivo isolarsi del protagonista (la vicenda documenta un distacco sempre più forte dalla realtà), e nell'insieme presenta un carattere eminentemente tragico (l'infausta conclusione giunge come esito pressoché fatale di una sorte segnata). Calvino mette in scena invece una situazione aperta, interlocutoria: il destino di Attilio è ancora tutto da costruire, l'avvenire è impregiudicato, tutto quello che si può registrare per ora è che nel suo instabile legame con Vanda egli si dimostra insieme più consapevole di lei e al tempo stesso più sprovveduto. Rispetto alla tranquilla adesione della fidanzata al ruolo di ragazza borghese che non ha altro pensiero se non quello di assicurarsi il miglior partito possibile (non a caso, di lei si dice che ha prossime origini contadine), Attilio si mostra infatti più problematico e inquieto, più cosciente della complessità delle scelte, ma anche più incoerente e ondivago. Il risultato è che nella sua decisione storicamente e moralmente giusta di schierarsi con i partigiani entrano anche motivi personali poco nobili e un tantino puerili.

Il che, sia chiaro, è oltremodo verosimile, sul piano storico e psicologico. Né si può dire che *Flirt* sia un brutto racconto — tutt'altro. Ma impostata in quei termini, l'immagine della Resistenza non poteva assumere il carattere epico che premeva a Calvino. Un carattere non celebrativo, certo, non trionfalistico, ma epico tuttavia, come avverrà nel *Sentiero*: che giustamente sarà — secondo la definizione di Martin McLaughlin — un'epica su scala minore, *a small-scale epic*.[22] Per raggiungere questo obiettivo occorrerà rinunciare a un protagonista simile all'autore: al giovane borghese, al «ragazzo intellettuale dalle scapole sporgenti e dalle natiche magre», o, secondo Vanda, a «quell'orso che *dice* sempre stramberie», e che ella cerca senza successo di ricondurre al rispetto delle convenienze. Occorrerà inventarsi il personaggio di Pin, il bambino che vive tra la strada e l'osteria, il fratello della Nera di Carrugio Lungo, anche lui fuori fase rispetto alla realtà circostante, ma per ragioni diverse: anche lui un misto di inferiorità e superiorità, di inadeguatezze palesi e di nascoste risorse. E ci vorranno altri diciassette anni, fino al 1964, perché l'autore razionalizzi, e arrivi finalmente a proclamare, come il creatore di Madame Bovary: *Pin, c'est moi*.

In questa prospettiva appaiono ancora più chiare le ragioni dell'ammirazione di Calvino per *Una questione privata*. Fenoglio era stato capace di fare quello che a lui, tanti anni prima, non era riuscito: parlare insieme di amore e di guerra. Come in un poema cavalleresco, come nell'*Orlando Furioso*. Ma Calvino, cultore dei momenti aurorali, scrittore degli inizi (e *di* inizi), le vicende concluse non sarebbero state comunque congeniali. Il suo romanzo partigiano rimane appunto la storia di Pin, il *Sentiero*, dove i morti ammazzati sono ben sette, a fronte dei tre della *Questione privata*, ma dove la dimensione funebre è confinata tra parentesi, perché lo sguardo rimane puntato verso il futuro. Quanto alla «questione privata» di *Flirt*, be', non si trattava, come nel caso di Milton, di una domanda senza risposta, né di una *quête* cavalleresca o di un quesito da cui dipende la vita o la morte dell'eroe: era solo un piccolo groviglio di malintesi, un grumo di incomprensioni in una giovane coppia male assortita. Insomma: una questioncella.

Il testo di *Flirt* non appare del tutto pronto per la pubblicazione: ci sono alcune vistose ripetizioni non emendate. Una è proprio in apertura: «I giardini municipali erano d'un gusto convenzionale e chiassoso, *da cartolina patinata a colori*» (corsivo mio): la stessa similitudine usata poche righe sotto nella descrizione di Vanda. Tuttavia le correzioni manoscritte muovono con grande coerenza nella direzione di sfrondare il testo dai particolari superflui, di renderlo più asciutto ed essenziale, di ridimensionare il suo carattere introspettivo. Detto in altre parole, se Attilio con tutti i suoi limiti sta diventando un partigiano vero, Calvino, per parte sua, sta diventando Calvino. *Flirt* non è solo un'importante tessera del discontinuo mosaico autobiografico che sottostà ai racconti degli anni Quaranta (buona parte dei quali entrati in *Ultimo viene il corvo*): è anche un momento-chiave del suo apprendistato letterario. Tale, possiamo presumere, la ragione di un «rifiuto» d'autore che serba — carte alla mano, almeno fino al 1959 — qualche margine di incertezza.

Notes to Chapter 19

1. Italo Calvino, *Romanzi e racconti*, a cura di Claudio Milanini, Mario Barenghi e Bruno Falcetto, coll. «I Meridiani», 3 voll. (Milano: Mondadori, 1991–94), I (1991), 78.
2. *Romanzi e racconti*, I, 15.
3. *Romanzi e racconti*, I, 101.
4. *Romanzi e racconti*, I, 105–06.
5. *Romanzi e racconti*, I, 1197–98.
6. *Romanzi e racconti*, I, 82–83.
7. *Romanzi e racconti*, I, 1198.
8. Claudio Milanini, 'Calvino nella Resistenza' [2006], in *Da Porta a Calvino: saggi e ritratti critici*, a cura di Martino Marazzi (Milano: LED, 2014), pp. 327–46 (p. 329).
9. Italo Calvino, *Saggi 1945–1985*, a cura di Mario Barenghi (Milano: Mondadori 1995), p. 2754.
10. Bruno Falcetto, 'Buoni a nulla e partigiani: immagini di gioventù nella narrativa calviniana degli anni quaranta', in *Leggere l'adolescenza*, a cura di Barbara Peroni (Milano: Unicopli, 2008), pp. 157–77: 163. *Come non fui Noè (Buon a nulla)* si legge in *Romanzi e racconti*, III, 826–30 (nonché in *Prima che tu dica «Pronto»*, Milano: Mondadori, 1997).

11. *Romanzi e racconti*, I, 1261–1305.
12. *Romanzi e racconti*, I, 328.
13. *Romanzi e racconti*, I, 109.
14. *Romanzi e racconti*, I, 1252.
15. Devo questa osservazione a Domenico Scarpa. *La struttura del «Furioso»* (1975) è riprodotta, con un titolo leggermente alterato, in Calvino, *Saggi*, pp. 759–68.
16. Guido Bonsaver, *Il mondo scritto: forme e ideologia nella narrativa di Italo Calvino* (Torino: Tirrenia Stampatori, 1995), p. 229.
17. Giorgio Bassani, *Opere*, a cura di Roberto Cotroneo (Milano: Mondadori 1998), p. 377.
18. Nicola Gardini, *Lacune: saggio sul non detto* (Torino: Einaudi, 2015).
19. Calvino, *Romanzi e racconti*, I, 1202.
20. Gabriele Pedullà, *La strada più lunga: sulle tracce di Beppe Fenoglio* (Roma: Donzelli, 2001).
21. «I tuoi due seni Son come due cavrioletti gemelli che pasturano fra i gigli» (*CC*, 6, 5: versione di Giovanni Diodati). Per inciso, ad Attilio sfugge la regola cosiddetta del dittongo mobile, cui il teologo secentesco invece si attiene: «Io vi scongiuro, figliuole di Gerusalemme, Per le cavriuole, e per le cerve della campagna» (*CC*, 3, 5); «Riduciti prestamente, o amico mio, A guisa di cavriuolo, o di cerbiatto, Sopra i monti degli aromati» (*CC*, 8, 14).
22. Martin McLaughlin, *Italo Calvino* (Edinburgh: Edinburgh University Press, 1998), pp. 19–34.

CHAPTER 20

Calvino's *Il barone rampante* and Leopardi's *Elogio degli uccelli*

Emanuela Tandello Cooper

Leopardi è sempre presente in qualche modo in quello che scrivo.[1]
ITALO CALVINO

'Sono contento anche dei riferimenti leopardiani, perché le *Operette Morali* sono il libro da cui deriva tutto quello che scrivo.' Thus Calvino, in a letter sent to Antonio Prete, delighted that a major *leopardista* should have recognized, and praised, the distinctive Leopardian imprint of *Palomar*.[2] 'Quel libro senza eguali della nostra letteratura', as Calvino called the *Operette morali*, and indeed its author, loom large in Calvino's essays, interviews and letters. Numerically, references to Leopardi come second only to references to Vittorini and Pavese, and are infinitely more numerous than references to Dante and Petrarch, or even Ariosto.[3] As for his creative works, if we consider the *Cosmicomiche*, *Ti con Zero* and *Palomar* as owing the greatest debt to Leopardi, we should acknowledge that 'la "scelta leopardiana" so frequently declared and reaffirmed by Calvino points to 'implicazioni più vaste'.[4] As the eminent Leopardi scholar Lucio Felici stressed in 2006, 'Negli interventi critici che si susseguiranno negli anni, essa determinerà una catena di considerazioni imprescindibili per chi si accosti ai testi creativi di Calvino.'[5] Interestingly, critical interest seems to have come mainly from Leopardi scholars. Antonio Prete, as we shall see, adopts Calvino's category of *leggerezza*, from his *Lezioni americane* (Milan: Garzanti, 1988), in order to discuss Leopardi's notion of *infinito*, in one of the most inspiring and influential books on Leopardi of the second half of the twentieth century, his *Finitudine e infinito*;[6] Felici, and above all Novella Bellucci and Andrea Cortellessa, choose to spearhead their exploration of the presence of the *Operette morali* in the Novecento through Calvino's own homage to the book.[7] As for criticism on Calvino, the view expressed by Felici that the Leopardian influence is to be found predominantly in the *contes fantastiques*, and eventually in *Palomar*, is reflected in the — still too few — studies devoted to this major literary affiliation.[8]

The aim of this essay is to pursue the 'imprescindibile' trail in one of Calvino's relatively early works. It will endeavour to show how *Il barone rampante* can, and should, be considered a highly significant tribute to Leopardi, not only as the author of the *Operette*, but also as the poet of the *Canti*, the philosopher of the *Pensieri* and the *Zibaldone* — and, indeed, as the 'character' that inspires the figure of Cosimo itself. The absolutely pervasive presence of Leopardi in this book requires a far more extended treatment than the scope of this article will allow. The discussion will therefore limit itself to a single example, which will thus be treated as paradigmatic of the extraordinarily complex and detailed nature of Calvino's dialogue with the discourse and poetics of the *Operette morali*. It will argue that behind chapter XXIV — in which we witness Cosimo's ethical forays into ornithology, and the eighteenth-century roots of a discourse on multiplicity and biodiversity — lies Leopardi's masterpiece, the *Elogio degli uccelli*. The discussion will ultimately suggest the centrality of Leopardi's poetics for the ethos of *Il barone rampante* as a whole.

Cosimo and birds

As Biagio tells us at one point, Cosimo goes mad, thus living up to the expectations — and early diagnosis — of the good citizens of the 'vil borgo selvaggio' of Ombrosa: 'Che Cosimo fosse matto, a Ombrosa s'era detto sempre' (Ch. XXIV, RR 735).[9] This is not the destructive, Orlando-like madness induced by his love for Viola, but rather a 'real' madness, according to Biagio, which nearly turns him from *homme sauvage* into another species altogether:

> Se prima andava vestito di pelli da capo a piedi, ora cominciò ad adornarsi la testa di penne, come gli Aborigeni d'America, penne d'upupa o di verdone, dai colori vivaci, ed oltre che in testa ne portava sparse sui vestiti. Finì per farsi delle marsine tutte ricoperte di penne, e ad imitare le abitudini di vari uccelli. (BR, 735)

It could be argued that this is an example of a metaphor turning into literality. From the moment he climbs into the trees, Cosimo is shown to move 'come un uccelletto'. So far, in *Il barone rampante* the image of birds has been used to define Cosimo's lightness: not only does he live in trees, as birds do, but he is described by Biagio as moving with bird-like agility and joyous lightheartedness:. Cosimo is like 'un uccelletto', climbs 'il nodoso albero, muovendo braccia e gambe per i rami con la sicurezza e la rapidità che gli venivano dalla lunga pratica fatta insieme' (BR 559); he hops about with 'quell'aria indaffarata e rapidissima degli animali selvatici, che magari li si vedono anche fermi acquattati, ma sempre come se fossero sul punto di balzare via' (BR 594); he sports a 'leggero passo di codibugnolo', BR 777). The alien (i.e. non-human) gestures of hopping, leaping and flying find an elegant expression in Cosimo's free, joyous movement in his aerial realm — where books themselves are 'like birds', balancing on the precarious shelves built by their reader:

> Per tenere i libri, Cosimo costruì a più riprese delle specie di biblioteche pensili, riparate alla meglio dalla pioggia e dai roditori, ma cambiava loro continuamente di posto, secondo gli studi e i gusti del momento, perché egli considerava i libri un po' *come degli uccelli* e non voleva vederli fermi o ingabbiati, se no diceva che intristivano. (BR 653–54; my italics)

The aerial dimension — the epitome of the quality Calvino would define, many years later, as *leggerezza* — is necessary to books, they belong to it. Libraries are like a 'marmoreo cimitero', before which 'il mondo lussureggiante che nei suoi pensieri s'inaridiva' (BR 652). Equally, the books themselves, and consequently the ideas within them, become sad if forced into stillness. 'Airiness' equals the imagination, without which ideas become sad and die. It is, however, one thing to act like a bird, another to try and become one. The former neatly serves the metaphor that Biagio has been carefully constructing. It is now Cosimo who proclaims himself to be 'ora codibugnolo ora barbagianni ora pettirosso': 'Finì per farsi delle marsine tutte ricoperte di penne' (BR 735). Birds — which so far he has happily hunted with the help of Ottimo Massimo, and unceremoniously shot — take centre stage, threatening the anthropomorphism that informs Biagio's biographical project through what today we would call a case for biodiversity. Birds, claims Cosimo, are 'veri amici', so much so that they seem to understand his own change of heart ('s'erano accorti di questo suo mutamento d'idee, e gli venivano vicino, anche se sotto c'era gente ad ascoltarlo' (BR 736). He alone, he claims, understands the admirable qualities — physical, but above all cultural, even linguistic — of our avian friends, and fulminates against the stolidity of his fellow men, who cannot recognize them as such. Indeed, he turns to advocacy: he improvises 'discorsi d'accusa agli uomini [...] discorsi che erano poi d'accusa a tutta la società umana, sotto forma di parabole', and he takes to writing and publishing his own treatises:

> Cosimo si mise anche a comporre certi scritti, come *Il verso del Merlo*, *Il Picchio che bussa*, *I Dialoghi dei Gufi*, e a distribuirli pubblicamente. Anzi, fu proprio in questo periodo di demenza che apprese l'arte della stampa e cominciò a stampare delle specie di libelli o gazzette (tra cui *La Gazzetta delle Gazze*), poi tutte unificate sotto il titolo *Il Monitore dei Bipedi*. (BR 736)

This account by Biagio, in its mock-serious style of a bibliographical compilation, is a (not-so-gentle) satire of Cosimo's dialogue with eighteenth-century culture, with its passion for encyclopaedic knowledge, taxonomy and generally for scientific study and discovery. As the reader has discovered in chapter XIII, after the unfortunate incident of Gian dei Brughi, Cosimo turns, with the inevitable enthusiasm of the young, into a veritable *gentiluomo illuminato*. His hunger for knowledge ('Cosimo aveva preso una smisurata passione per la lettura e per lo studio', BR 650) leads him to devouring 'libri d'ogni specie': on 'Rousseau che passeggiava erborizzando per le foreste della Svizzera', on 'Beniamino Franklin che acchiappava i fulmini cogli aquiloni', and the 'Barone de la Hontan che viveva felice tra gli Indiani dell'America' (BR 650). Like Monaldo Leopardi, Cosimo also accumulates a cripplingly large bill with his personal bookseller, entrusted with acquiring volumes from Amsterdam and Paris, and gets poor Fauchelafleur, that affectionately vague and yet ambiguous figure who spends most of his time musing and digressing, arrested by the Inquisition for being the unlikely owner of the complete works of Pierre Bayle ('tutte le opere del Bayle') 'e di tutte le pubblicazioni più scomunicate d'Europa'. Furthermore, like many of his much-admired models, he engages in long epistolary exchanges 'coi maggiori filosofi e scienziati d'Europa, cui egli si rivolgeva perché gli risolvessero quesiti e obiezioni, o anche per il piacere di discutere cogli spiriti migliori e in pari tempo esercitarsi nelle lingue straniere'. His curiosity, however, goes well beyond philosophy, taking him not down to earth, but down to the next level, his forest and the lands and gardens that lie by it or underneath it. This knowledge therefore — if he is to yield to his 'bisogno di fare qualcosa di utile al suo prossimo' (BR 654) — needs to be of an essentially empirical nature. If entries from Diderot's and d'Alembert's *Encyclopédie*, such as '*Abeille, Arbre, Bois, Jardin*', fire his imagination, certain 'manuali d'arti e mestieri, per esempio d'arboricoltura' that begin to crowd his aerial bookshelves lead him to become a skilled gardener, almost the embodiment of that most British of notions, that 'woodland flourishes under good human management',[10] turning him almost into a prophet of biodiversity. Cosimo fancies himself a 'philosophe', his *spirito illuministico* stretching out to the treatises that can be considered as the result of this 'studio matto e disperatissimo': the all-encompassing utopian *Progetto di Costituzione per Città Repubblicana con Dichiarazione dei Diritti degli Uomini, delle Donne, dei Bambini, degli Animali Domestici e Selvatici, compresi Uccelli Pesci e Insetti, e delle Piante sia d'Alto Fusto sia Ortaggi ed Erbe* (which Biagio describes as 'un bellissimo lavoro, che poteva servire d'orientamento a tutti i governanti' (BR 764)) and the never-completed *Progetto di Costituzione d'uno Stato ideale fondato sopra gli alberi* (BR 695). Again, however, the difference between these and Cosimo's parables, dialogues and gazettes is that the latter are supposed to be the work of a madman. The whole fabric of Cosimo's life in the trees as a metaphor (and a very eighteenth-century one at that) risks collapse (literally!) when Cosimo introduces to his aerial world — no longer only his own — a printing press, which gets almost phagocitized by the flora and fauna of Ombrosa:

> Alle volte tra il telaio e la carta capitavano dei ragni, delle farfalle, e la loro impronta restava stampata sulla pagina; alle volte un ghiro saltava sul foglio fresco d'inchiostro e imbrattava tutto a colpi di coda; alle volte gli scoiattoli si prendevano una lettera dell'alfabeto e se la portavano nella loro tana credendo fosse da mangiare, come capitò con la lettera Q. (BR 737)

When Cosimo is not busy printing his broadsheets, he hangs 'come un nidiaceo' from a tree, only to be stirred out of this torpor — or regression into a state of nature — by the adventure with the wolves. Serving the community again eventually brings him back to less outlandish ways, shown in the far more 'reasonable' title of his new broadsheet, 'Il Vertebrato Ragionevole', which seems to assert a less alarming synthesis of avian and human nature under the normalizing term of 'vertebrate'. Biagio's satire and containment of Cosimo's behaviour to another instance of 'madness' ('Cosimo matto lo era stato sempre') does not entirely hide his scientific and literary pedigree. Not only do the dialogues, discourses and gazettes inevitably hark back to the intellectual practice of a century in which, as he admitted himself, Calvino would have felt at home,[11] their genre undeniably connects to the varying forms of writing articulated in the *Operette morali*, from the dialogue to the Lucianesque narrative, the philosophical *discours* and *conte philosophique*. The ethos they proclaim — the celebration of birds as man's best friends — is plainly resonant of Leopardi's own views in the *Elogio*, and so is the suggestion that they are capable of some kind of understanding, and thus of evolution. Indeed, Cosimo's madness itself can be read as a *reductio ad absurdum* of the Leopardian desire to turn into a bird ('convertito in un uccello', that is to say not to become 'like one', but being one) and, even more importantly, as a Menippean-style reversal of evolutionary transformation. Cosimo's desire to be a bird (not *like* one) which as we shall see, echoes Amelio's, in the *Elogio degli uccelli,* echoes the ideas that inform Leopardi's own writings on animals and birds — ideas that are acknowledged to reflect some of the most influential scientific theories of the Enlightenment, on the biological similarities between species, and ornithology in particular. Being (like) a bird, therefore, both in *Il barone* and Leopardi's *Elogio,* stands for a different kind of understanding of our being animals amongst many, and leads to an altogether different type of discourse over our inexorable separation from the world of nature, and the need for an 'ultrafilosofia', 'che conoscendo l'intiero e l'intimo delle cose, ci riavvicini alla natura' (Zib 115).[12]

Leopardi's birds

Always in Leopardi the idea of flight embodies a gesture of freedom, and a state of ecstatic joy: 'Forse s'avessi io l'ale | da volar su le nubi, | e noverar le stelle ad una ad una [...] più felice sarei' ('Canto notturno di un pastore errante dell'Asia'). But what could be interpreted (as it has been, and in many ways continues to be, for the reasons we shall see later on) as a poetic metaphor/simile raised to the status of a symbol, risks making us lose sight of the depth and extent of Leopardi's familiarity with eighteenth-century scientific theories, and the far from generic adoption of these creatures as embodying the kind of ideal creature that human beings would dearly like to be, but cannot because they have lost that 'natural' way of being a long time before. It is Calvino himself, in his Memo on *Esattezza,* who turns upside down the notion of Leopardi's *vago* as essentially abstract and symbolic. Starting from his own assumption that the celebration of *vago* should be diametrically opposed to his own praise of accuracy and precision, he embarks on a re-reading of renowned, pivotal entries in the *Zibaldone* from 20 to 28 September 1821, and comes to a very different conclusion:

> Ecco cosa richiede da noi Leopardi per farci gustare la bellezza dell'indeterminato e del vago! È una attenzione estremamente precisa e meticolosa che egli esige nella composizione d'ogni immagine, nella definizione dei dettagli, nella scelta degli oggetti. [...] Il poeta del vago può essere solo il poeta della precisione. (*Lezioni americane*, pp. 680–81)

We need to consider *vago* in relation to Leopardian and Calvinian lexis: nowhere in Leopardi, it can be argued, do we encounter the range and richness of Calvino, and *Il barone rampante* is a very good example of this. However, this does not mean that Leopardi's birds are just any generic bird. Several different birds populate his bestiary. This is particularly relevant to our discussion here, as the generic noun *uccelli* in Leopardi reveals a far from imprecise knowledge of the ground-breaking ornithological studies by Buffon, and many others, including Condillac and Voltaire. In order to see this, we need to pursue first of all the two most important birds mentioned by Leopardi: his 'Passero solitario' and his 'Gallo silvestre'.

Traditionally considered as the symbol of isolation and exclusion, and the poet's own veritable *alter ego*, the 'passero solitario' is far from being a generic domestic bird, as Fernando Bandini was to reveal as late as 1975:

> Il passero solitario è un uccello della famiglia dei turdidi (*Monticola solitarius*) di colore bruno azzurro. La nota ignoranza ornitologica dei letterati italiani ha fatto scorrere fiumi di inchiostro su una questione assai semplice: passero solitario è denominazione antichissima, almeno dai tempi di Alberto Magno, di questo uccello: presente come tale da secoli in molti dialetti italiani e in numerose lingue europee. Leopardi, così estraneo all'uso di un linguaggio tecnico [...], può qui riferire il nome preciso di una specie.[13]

Bandini, however, also goes as far as to suggest that the bird's behaviour, as described in the eponymous poem of the *Canti*, resembles more 'quella dell'*Histoire des oiseaux* del Buffon (cfr. *Le merle solitaire*) dove già il passero è umanizzato come simbolo patetico della solitudine'. This bird, then, is allowed to enter the bestiary of Italian poetry as a proper species, together with Pascoli's 'Puffini' and Montale's 'Upupa'. It has to be said, however, that a sparrow ain't no blackbird, and that it is not so much ornithological ignorance that critics ought to be charged with, but, more relevantly perhaps, with tardily (perhaps even reluctantly) acknowledging the importance of Leopardi's reading of the scientific treatises and manuals conserved in his father's library.

Buffon's *Histoire naturelle générale et particulière, avec la description du cabinet du roi* (1749–88), and in particular his *Discours naturel sur l'histoire des oiseaux* (of which a copy is still held in the Recanati library, in its Italian translation: *Storia naturale, generale e particolare*, Venice: Fratelli Bassaglia, 1782) ought, in my view, to be considered as another source for a bird that would appear to possess a pedigree entirely steeped in myth: the 'gallo silvestre'. For this *operetta*, Leopardi makes use of the narrative device of the discovered manuscript, of which the text is a translation from the sacred language of Hebrew ('una mescolanza babelica di parlate derivanti dall'ebraico, di cui esse rappresentano una dispersione'). Rigoni also mentions Buxtorf's *Lexicon* (another text held in Leopardi's library: Ioan Buxtorfius, *Lexicon Chaldaicum, Talmudicum et Rabbinicum*, Basel: König, 1639) which Leopardi himself quotes in *Zibaldone* 1282 in relation to rabbinical texts. However, if we were to apply both Calvino's elective sympathy with Leopardi's actual appreciation of detail, and if we were at the same time to consider the initial description of the creature itself, we would actually find this bird is none other than the ostrich (*autruche*) described in Buffon's *Discours*:

> Affermano alcuni maestri e scrittori ebrei, che tra il cielo e la terra, o vogliamo dire mezzo nell'uno e mezzo nell'altra, vive un certo gallo salvatico; il quale sta in sulla terra coi piedi e tocca con la cresta e col becco il cielo. (PP 161)

The original language of the *Cantico*, as Rigoni writes, whether belonging to the bird or to men, is indefinable. What we do know is that the *operetta* 'a sua volta una versione in prosa più possibilmente "fedele" a un "originale" poetico, dichiara nel suo preambolo l'offuscamento del Senso simbolico e tradizionale, evocandolo in forma essenzialmente musicale (sonora, ritmica e infine metrica)'.[14] In it, Leopardi again (as in 'Il passero solitario') isolates the image, of a creature excluded from the consolation and joys of his fellow-creatures; a sombre, lugubrious song, which summons humankind back from the illusions of sweetest sleep, to remind them that 'a tutti il risvegliarsi è danno', that 'il misero non è prima desto, che egli ritorna nelle mani dell'infelicità sua'. It is thus a death song, like that of Ruysch's mummies (*Dialogo di Federico Ruysch con le sue mummie*), where the bird, which is endowed with the gift of reason (either that, says Leopardi, or he has been instructed like a parrot) can be seen as embodying yet another alter ego of the poet. The melancholy is thus conveyed through the lyrical tone of the *Cantico*, but far more so by the philosophical dimension of the argument it gives voice to. This bird, then, would appear to be in a different league from the 'passero solitario'. And yet, there is a passage in Buffon — which I traced through a search of the excellent Gallica online edition by Pietro Corsi and Thierry Hoquet — that throws further light on what kind of bird this might well be. In the first instance, 'gallo silvestre' is not a scientific term, but 'gallo cedrone' (a species foreign to the British Isles, and referred to with approximation as a grouse) in Italian, is. This led to *Tetrao urogallus*, or *tetras*, the closest French equivalent, which in turn led to *autruche*:

> Elle la [sa voix] fait rarement entendre, car très-peu de personnes en ont parlé; les Écrivains sacrés comparent son cri à un gemissement, et on prétend même que son nom hébreu jacnah est formé d'ianah, qui signifie hurler. Le Docteur Browne dit que ce cris ressemble à la voix d'un enfant enroué, et qu'il est plus triste encore.[15]

It seems highly likely that this reference too, should be considered as one of the main sources for the *operetta*: because of the initial description — this bird is very tall — and because of the references to Hebrew sources, which Buffon himself quotes; and because of the descriptions of the bird's immensely sad, indeed lugubrious, song.

This is a long digression, but it is important to understand where Leopardi is coming from in the *Elogio*, and the potential importance of the 'Gallo silvestre' itself for the author of BR, as the image of a creature that occupies, utopically, both air and ground, and more importantly, 'ha uso di ragione'.

This brings us to the idea of these birds actually possessing a soul (*anima*) or a rational mind, an idea that undermines the philosophical and religious anthropocentrism in Leopardi's time. This hypothesis had been heralded in the *Dissertazione sull'anima delle bestie* (1811), which Leopardi had written at the early age of thirteen. Contradicting Descartes, Malebranche and Fontenelle, Leopardi had boldly advocated that 'l'anima delle bestie sia spirituale', and that they possess 'uno spirito dotato di senso, di libertà, e di un qualche barlume di ragione', thus aligning himself (not always confidently, or consistently, and often indulging in second-hand erudition) with Voltaire, d'Holbach, Condillac and, with some reservations, Buffon himself. This presumed 'reason' of birds (and indeed of all animals), however, must not be believed to be used in the same way as human beings do: 'se le bestie avessero la ragione [...] come noi e se ne usassero come gli uomini? Il disordine, la crudeltà, la devastazione sarebbono state enormi sopra la terra' (PP 516).

> '*Chi riunisce questo popolo di uccelli? Chi presiede al consiglio dove si determina il giorno e*

> *l'ora della partenza? Chi forma la falange? Chi gli mostra il cammino?*' Io rispondo che, se si vuole ammettere la natura come regolatrice ed autrice di queste azioni, ciò non sarà che in quelle che riguarda la conservazione dei bruti, onde nelle loro altre azioni è necessario un qualche raziocinio ed un barlume di ragione.

The central idea of the *Dissertazione*, that animals possess 'una imperfetta libertà' that allows them to exercise their physical gifts according to their own will ('chi mai potrà negare che un augello sia libero di alzare o no il suo volo e di seguire in ciò gl'impulsi della propria volontà?': PP 508) would further mature and develop throughout Leopardi's career. Its intimations are present in the ninety-odd entries in the *Zibaldone* concerning animals (but briefer references abound throughout the journal), and as we have seen, they become the direct object of poetry in the *Canti*, in the *Operette*, and eventually in the searing anti-anthropocentric satire of the *Prolegomeni della Batracomiomachia* (which, for its powerful *azzeramento* of any biological, let alone cultural, hierarchical difference between the species, was to be condemned and banned by the Church, and even by many moderate admirers of Leopardi).[16]

Amongst all animals, birds are thus privileged by Leopardi, because they are the closest to the human species, with whom they are seen to interact 'naturally' through a Darwinian ability to evolve and adapt, which extends to the ability to respond to human social behaviour: 'gli uccelli, anco essendo liberi, pigliano alcun poco della civiltà di quegli uomini alle cui stanze sono usati' (PP 155). Truly, then, in Cosimo's terms, they are 'i loro veri amici'.

Amelio's desire

The *operetta Elogio degli uccelli* (composed between 29 October and 1 November 1824)[17] takes the form of an *encomium* preceded by a brief narrative passage, in which we are introduced to its author. Amelio (whose very name means carefree, lighthearted), 'filosofo solitario', striking a melancholy pose ('stando una mattina di primavera, co' suoi libri, seduto all'ombra di una sua casa in villa, e leggendo'), upon hearing the birdsong around him, sets pen to paper and writes down the thoughts that that wonderful sound has inspired. The landscape setting, characteristically marking in Leopardi the lyrical–metaphysical stance of many of the *Canti*, stages the moment in which sound and sight lead to the suspension of the act of reading, to meditation and finally to the act of writing of the text that we are then given to read. Amelio's greatest desire is to 'per un poco di tempo, essere convertito in uccello', because birds 'sono le più liete creature del mondo', 'sono di natura meglio accomodati a godere e ad essere felici'.[18] Among other animals, birds are closest to human beings because, 'anco essendo liberi, pigliano alcun poco della civiltà di quegli uomini alle cui stanze sono usati' (p. 155), and, what is more important, they share with them the capacity to laugh, that is to say, to feel pleasure. They are not simply delightful to us, but rather they are delighted in themselves, as their movements clearly reveal. As Calvino himself writes in his Memo on *Rapidità*, 'nella sua giovinezza quanto mai sedentaria, Leopardi trovava uno dei rari momenti gioiosi' when writing about the energy and strength inspired by velocity (*Saggi*, I, 665).

The corporeal exuberance of birds, their ability to cover huge distances and see things that we, in our own mind, cannot even begin to imagine ('l'animo nostro a fatica se ne può fare una immagine proporzionata') is accurately observed:

> Cangiano luogo a ogni tratto; passano da paese a paese quanto tu vuoi lontano, e dall'infima alla somma parte dell'aria, in poco spazio di tempo, e con facilità mirabile; veggono e provano nella loro vita cose infinite e diversissime. (*Elogio*, p. 157)

> vanno e vengono di continuo senza necessità veruna; [...] tu non li vedi mai star fermi della persona; sempre si volgono qua e là, sempre si aggirano, si piegano, si protendono, si crollano, si dimenano; con quella vispezza, quell'agilità, quella prestezza di modi indicibile. (*Elogio*, p. 158)

Just as they display — and this is considered to be Leopardi's stroke of intuitive genius — the ability to laugh ('partecipano del privilegio che ha l'uomo di ridere: il quale non hanno gli altri animali'), and thus to express as well as experience pleasure, they are capable of exercising their gift of flight for sheer delight: 'usano il volare per sollazzo'. In brief, they enjoy a superabundance of energy, vitality and speed that Leopardi considers to be directly related to a spiritual, inner life:

> veggono e provano nella vita loro cose infinite e diversissime; esercitano continuamente il loro corpo; abbondano soprammodo della vita estrinseca. E siccome abbondano della vita estrinseca, parimenti sono ricchi della interiore.

This must mean that birds are capable not only of some kind of 'reason', but of great imaginative powers:

> Per la qual potenza [fisica] godono tutto giorno immensi spettacoli e variatissimi, e *dall'alto* scuoprono, a un tempo solo, tanto spazio di terra e distintamente scorgono tanti paesi coll'occhio, quanti, pur colla mente si possono comprendere dall'uomo in un tratto; s'inferisce che debbono avere una grandissima forza e vivacità, e un grandissimo uso d'immaginativa.

> [immaginativa] quella ricca, *varia, leggera, instabile e fanciullesca*; la quale si è *larghissima fonte di pensieri ameni e lieti, di errori dolci, di vari diletti e conforti.*

They share with us the beauty of nature, but with that nature that is man-made: 'come dire i campi lavorati, gli alberi e le piante educate e disposte in ordine'. They respond, in other words, to a certain extent to civilized human environments, as suggested by Buffon (the reference, in the author's hand, is 'Buffon Uccelli t. 1 p. 52'):

> Dicono alcuni, e farebbe a questo proposito, che la voce degli uccelli è più gentile e più dolce, e il canto più modulato, nelle parti nostre, che in quelle dove gli uomini sono selvaggi e rozzi; e conchiudono che gli uccelli, anco essendo liberi, pigliano alcun poco della civiltà di quesgli uomini alle cui stanze sono usati.[19]

Sedentary Amelio/Giacomo finally abstracts and sublimates the suggestions and intimations of his readings into the complex discourse of his philosophy. Birds rise to the same status as ancients and *fanciulli* — or rather, the young and the ancients possess the very same qualities as birds. Our desire to 'be like' them is a profoundly modern desire that has its roots in our sense of a catastrophic loss, and the disconsolate (but 'vera') realization of the illusion of an anthropomorphic ethos.

Calvino is too intelligent a reader of Leopardi not to see that Amelio's desire (which is lyrically expressed and articulates an enthusiasm rarely seen in this author) is undermined by the modernity of the (cleverly disguised) scientific premises that inform it. It is as impossible for birds to become like us as it is for us to become like them. They are the 'fanciulli del regno animale' (Rigoni), they belong to the same dimension as the ancients: a dimension that has been lost forever, and, as Rousseau argued, a dimension that we can only presume to have existed, a dimension that we can only fathom through the imagination. Cosimo, like Amelio, is a 'moderno'. He may embrace, with his ever-youthful enthusiasm, the diversity of the avian world and even advocate shared *anime*, mutually conversant with each other. But, as the experiment with printing shows, there is no going back — because modern man is going forward (albeit, as the poet says, this going forward is actually a going back of the worst sort). Printing is at odds with the kind of reverse evolution he might be attempting to put into place. The world of human culture has no place in the trees, indeed it proves even more alienating: 'la civiltà allontana dalla natura, dalla corporeità fantasticante della vita dell'immaginazione'.[20] 'Tutte belle cose', Biagio wrily comments, 'però io avevo l'impressione che in quel tempo mio fratello non solo fosse del tutto ammattito, ma andasse anche un poco imbecillendosi'. And this, he adds, is more serious, because 'la pazzia è una forza della natura, nel male o nel bene, mentre la minchioneria è una debolezza della natura, senza contropartita' (BR 737). How 'minchione' Cosimo should be considered, however, is another matter. His temporary reply to the failed experiment of the press in the trees is to revert completely to the state of a 'nidiaceo', hanging from a bough inside a quilted cocoon, 'leggiucchiando [...] a borbottare tra sé, o a canticchiare', hibernating. When eventually he does return to 'sanity' ('non fece più tante stranezze'), he does so by continuing to print 'un ebdomadario', a weekly magazine, *Il Vertebrato Ragionevole*. Cosimo's learning curve ends with a notion — not a compromise, but an acknowledgement — that re-establishes that belief in (some) species as sharing some degree of 'reason'. 'Illusioni', Calvino would write, which nonetheless allowed mankind to 'manage' the world that, as we know, is in Calvino's present, as well as in Leopardi's, quintessentially unmanageable.

As Antonio Prete has admirably observed in his *Finitudine e infinito*,

> la rappresentazione aerea [nell'*Elogio*] rinvia a quell'immaginare che sin dalla fanciullezza attraversa e interrompe e rafforza il ragionare del poeta, anzi diventa il segno di una tensione [...] verso l'unità di pensiero e poesia.[21]

This 'energia fantasticante'[22] that Amelio recognizes in birds is the same found in the early years of our life, 'quando in nessun luogo soli interrogavamo le immagini e le pareti e gli alberi e i fiori e le nuvole, e abbracciavamo sassi e legni' as well as in the imagination of the ancients, 'Leggiadro tempo quando il poeta nella natura, fresca vergine intatta, vedendo tutto cogli occhi propri' (Zib 644). We could safely say that birds share the same qualities with *fanciulli*, with poets, and, I would like to add, with readers, as it is their *immaginativa* that supplies that which cannot be seen if not *in flight*:

> Trovansi gli animi alcune volte, per una o per altra ragione, in istato di mobilità, senso, vigore e caldezza tale [...] che seguono ogni menomo impulso della lettura, sentono vivamente ogni leggero tocco, e coll'occasione di ciò che leggono, creano in sé mille moti e mille immaginazioni.

It is thus a nostalgia for flight, and therefore for *fanciullezza*, and its powerful imaginative energy, which Amelio movingly expresses at the end of the *operetta*, when he writes 'io vorrei, per un poco di tempo, esser convertito in uccello'.

This is a crucial point of contact with *Il barone rampante*, as we have already intimated. Both texts celebrate *fanciullezza*, *leggerezza* and *immaginativa* as coterminous, and as central to their meditation over nature, and the nature of our desire. What *fanciulli*, savages and primitive men (and birds!) possess is the imagination 'che toglie i confini del mondo' (AP 41), that literally breaks down boundaries, and allowes 'un'erranza oltre i confini'. This is a particular kind of wisdom that both texts pursue in the figures of their two protagonists, Amelio and Cosimo, projections of desire (is Cosimo not Biagio's instrument, his eye as well as his ears, and soul?) that are nonetheless perfectly aware of the gravitational pull of 'il *vero*'.

Calvino, like Leopardi with Amelio, thus privileges in Cosimo, in his flight into the trees, and in Biagio's dream of Ombrosa, the epitome of Leopardian *fanciullezza*. If Cosimo is entrusted with the task of investigating the folly and spiritual poverty of the human world, he still emerges unscathed, sustained by ingenuity, *vision*, imaginative energy, vitality and solidarity with other creatures (not only birds, but trees and plants too). Time passes, experience is said to mark him, imbue 'reason' into him — but Cosimo never grows out of his original enchanted view of the world. It is up to Biagio to drag him, so to speak, down to earth, through the narrative, temporal laws of *bios*. Cosimo remains essentially untameable, because he after all embodies Biagio's own resilient, fabulously imagining, all-seeing, wild *fanciullezza*. Cosimo, in other words, is Biagio's *desire* — this is why he simply cannot be allowed to set foot on the ground again, not even (especially) in death. This is one of the reasons — possibly the main reason — why we should consider *Il barone rampante* a veritable homage to Leopardi, himself 'Dolce, amaro *enfant sauvage*'.[23]

A (very provisional) conclusion

This brief discussion demonstrates the need to consider seriously how many fundamental aspects of *Il barone rampante* owe a significant debt to Leopardi. Leopardi's voice, and in particular the voice of the *Canti* ('L'Infinito', 'La sera del dì di festa', to mention just two), is unmistakably heard in Cosimo's own early idyll in chapter II:

> [la magnolia] avvolgeva il ragazzo in un profumo fresco di foglie, come il vento le muoveva. [...] Ma era tutto il giardino che odorava, e se Cosimo ancora non riusciva a percorrerlo con la vista, tanto era irregolarmente folto [...]. C'era un gran silenzio.

Cosimo's outlook, which Marco Belpoliti has described as 'un occhio sui rami',[24] owes a great deal to Leopardi, as a later essay by Calvino testifies:

> quel qualcosa che *ferma la mia vista* da una parte e dell'altra, dosso di collina, tronco d'olivo, superficie cilindrica di serbatoio di cemento, *siepe di ginestre* [...] dando le spalle a un altro fondale e fronteggiando la ribalta del luminoso orizzonte.[25]

It is unthinkable to conceive the nature of Cosimo's eye without considering both authors' 'poetiche dello sguardo', the role of sight, the imagination and vision in the construction of a poetic landscape, the notion of freedom, and the dimension of time in the act of writing. Calvino's 'Dall'opaco', but also his 'Ipotesi di descrizione di un paesaggio', not only have a major influence on his novel, they also encourage an exploration of the notion of construction of a landscape that stretches a long way back to Leopardi's own ideas on space and natural landscapes, and the treatises by Berkeley and Burke[26] that helped to shape them. In particular, it could be argued that Leopardi's pivotal notion of 'double' vision, or 'double' object, offers a fruitful element of comparison with Calvino's own 'hypothesis' over the nature of literary landscape. Let us consider, briefly, the famous passage in the *Zibaldone*:

> All'uomo sensibile e immaginoso, che viva, come io sono vissuto gran tempo, sentendo di continuo ed immaginando il mondo, gli oggetti sono in un certo senso doppi. Egli vedrà con gli occhi una torre, una campagna, udrà con gli orecchi il suono di una campana; e nel tempo stesso con l'immaginazione vedrà un'altra torre, un'altra campagna, udrà un altro suono. In questo secondo genere di obbietti sta tutto il bello e il piacevole delle cose. Trista quella vita (ed è pur tale la vita comunemente) che non vede, non ode, non sente senon che oggetti semplici, quelli soli di cui gli occhi, gli orecchi e gli altri sentimenti ricevono la sensazione. (Zib 4418)

Leopardi's extraordinary intuition, a testimony to his awareness of the most recent and challenging theories of vision of his time,[27] matches Calvino's dynamic reading of space in *Il barone* and in the later essays mentioned above. An investigation would surely lead to the consideration of a double object/double vision in the novel itself: in other words, we do not *see* what Cosimo sees, but what Biagio imagines him as seeing (i.e. we see through — or thanks to — Biagio's imagination). But whilst for Leopardi imagining (which is the poetic act in itself) is dependent on memory (*rimembranza*), in Calvino writing means to trace a line between isolated individual memories a connection, a continuity:

> Tracciare una linea tra punti discontinui che la memoria conserva isolati, strappati dalla vera esperienza dello spazio; [...] ricostruire una continuità che si è cancellata nella memoria con l'orma dei miei passi.[28]

Despite the differences (but it is in difference, too, that this dialogue with Leopardi is rooted) both share a 'poetics of the gaze' that raises questions about the statute of the subject in relation to the objects that surround it, and help to define it (or not, as the case may be).

As Francesca Southerden writes in her book on Sereni (a contemporary of Calvino, whose dialogue with Leopardi is also pervasive):

The subject perceives the image interposed between the 'I' and the object as 'real', as a sign that the object as 'real', as a sign that the object is out there for the taking and that it is essentially offering itself to the subject for possession.[29]

With both Leopardi and Calvino, landscape bolsters, or undermines, the image of the Subject, forcing it into an aesthetic construction: a study of the natural landscape (woods, *selve*, and gardens) as it features in *Il barone*, and in Leopardi's own early writings (his *Memorie della mia vita* in the first instance) as well as in the *Canti*, does, I believe, reveal an even deeper affinity between the two. Further studies along these lines will, I suspect, only confirm that Leopardi is present in almost everything Calvino writes in *Il barone rampante*.

I am tempted, however, to conclude this first stage of what I hope will become a fully developed study with a suggestion that, tongue-in-cheek as it is, may well contain some truth. Leopardi's *Il barone rampante* can, and should, be considered an early, yet highly significant tribute to Leopardi as the 'character' that inspires the figure of Cosimo itself. Indeed, the pervasive presence of Leopardi in this book can be seen to begin with the profound sense of fun with which Calvino 'ci strizza l'occhio' by harking back, through his portrayal of a dysfunctional family, to perhaps the most notorious one in our literary history. A politically reactionary, financially insolvent father, a virtually ubiquitous authoritarian mother, two major siblings, a rebellious son driven to taking flight from the family home because of its stifling environment and its intolerable rules. It could be argued that this is Calvino having a laugh. Poor Paolina Leopardi, for example, although herself considered in the end 'la suora di casa' because of her notorious failure to marry, certainly never indulged in repellent culinary practices, but rather was educated with her brothers, and was definitely better at maths and writing than at so much as boiling an egg. The 'generalessa' turns out to be a real softy at heart, petite, feminine, and skilled in embroidery (albeit of military maps rather than lace) — but the energy and authority she exudes are not so far from Adelaide Leopardi's: as Leopardi's biographer Rolando Damiani writes,[30] quoting Paolina, their mother the Countess, 'che pure amava delle cose terrene i fiori più delicati e fragranti, il mughetto, le mammole, le resede, le gaggie', would haunt the whole household with the clomping sound of her boots and her iron-fisted discipline. Unquestionably the real *pater familias*, she wore heavy country boots, dominated the household with ruthless parsimony as she tried to stem the incessant flow of debt caused by her husband's incontrollable passion for books (in *Il barone*, it is actually Cosimo who accumulates debts with 'il libraio Orbecche', and has to be granted an allowance by his brother, in return for renouncing primogeniture). If Calvino — I suspect sympathizing with the young Conte over the unvaryingly puzzling, and thus alarming, nature of women — mercilessly constructs the figure of Battista, his portrayal of Cosimo's other sibling is certainly strongly reminiscent of Giacomo's favourite brother and playmate, Carlo. Like Carlo, Biagio basks in reflected light, like Carlo he experiences (or is made to experience), in a mimetic way, Cosimo's own inner life. More importantly, I think, a symbiotic relationship exists between them, such as characterized the Leopardi boys in their childhood and early youth. Cosimo, like Giacomo, claims autonomy and independence at a very young age: 'Quella volontaria segregazione tra i libri [...] un isolamento dalle opinioni dei genitori, la misteriosità della vita interiore', are shared with Biagio (and Giacomo shares them with Carlo, to whom he is bound by 'un affetto di sogno').[31] Furthermore, Calvino's characters and Leopardi and his siblings share together a passion for jokes and pranks: 'la passione per la burla' writes Damiani, drawing on the correspondence between Carlo and Paolina, is one of the most strikingly recurrent memories of their childhood with Giacomo'.[32] More importantly, stories and storytelling feature prominently family recollections, and in Giacomo's own *Memorie*, and in the *Zibaldone*. Here is Damiani, again, on Giacomo and Carlo:

> Nei mattini festivi, disteso a letto nella stanza condivisa con Carlo [compare Biagio: 'Avevamo una camera in comune, con due lettini ancora da ragazzi' (BR 575)], amava improvvisare avventure di Filsero, l'eroe un po' gradasso e ciarlatano di una saga fiabesca. [...] Ammaliato da un racconto protratto per giorni e settimane, Carlo rimase convinto fino alla vecchiaia che quella favola sarebbe piaciuta anche a chi non ne cogliesse i sottintesi.[33]

And here is Giacomo himself, from his *Memorie della mia vita*, concerning childhood, imagination, and stories:

> Mi dicono che io da fanciullino di tre o quattro anni, stava sempre dietro a questa o quella persona perché mi raccontasse delle favole. E mi ricordo ancor io che in poco maggiore età era innamorato dei racconti, e del maraviglioso che si percepisce coll'udito, o colla lettura (giacché seppi leggere, ed amai di leggere, assai presto). Questi, secondo me, sono indizi notabili d'ingegno non ordinario e prematuro. [...] Il piacere dei racconti, sebbene questi vertano sopra cose sensibili e materiali, è però tutto intellettuale, o appartenente alla immaginazione [...] l'esser divenuto capace di questi piaceri assai di buon'ora, indica manifestamente una felicissima disposizione, pieghevolezza ec. degli organi intellettuali o mentali, una gran facoltà e vivezza d'immaginazione. (Zib 1401–02)

It is difficult to believe that Calvino (who truly had read everything by Leopardi), in creating the narratorial relationship between Cosimo and Biagio, should not have been aware of this other eminent example of symbiotic affection that almost verges on identification and sibling idolatry. Not only this: as we will see, often in *Il barone* we encounter Leopardi through both Cosimo and Biagio — both in different ways engaging in storytelling and meditation in equal measure.

Last but not least, Cosimo's rebellion and wilfulness resound loud and clear: 'le mie risoluzioni', writes Giacomo shortly before the doomed attempt to leave Recanati in 1819, 'non sono passeggere, come quelle degli altri, come mio padre stimo che si persuada'.[34]

It is, in short, by reading through Leopardi's letters, thoughts and journal that we are given access to his early life (and it is not surprising that this material should have been put to good use by Mario Martone in his biopic *Il giovane favoloso*).[35] The echoes of Cosimo's youthful *and* life-long rebelliousness are perhaps too many to be swept aside as mere coincidence.

Notes to Chapter 20

1. Interview with Fabrizia Ramondino, 'Il mondo incantato del Signor Palomar', *Il Mattino*, 8 January 1984, p. 3; published as 'Lo sguardo di Palomar', in *Sono nato in America: interviste 1951–1985* (Milan: Mondadori, 2012), p. 559.
2. Antonio Prete, '*Palomar* o la vertigine della misura', in *Italo Calvino / 2*, Special Issue devoted to Calvino, *Nuova Corrente*, XXXIV.100 (July-December 1987), 387–408.
3. Niccolò Pagani, *Calvino lettore di Leopardi: ricostruzione di un rapporto*, unpublished 'tesi di laurea', Università di Torino, Scuola di Scienze Umanistiche, Anno accademico 2014–15, p. 92; <https://www.academia.edu/14408874/Calvino_e_Leopardi._Tra_Operette_morali_e_Cosmicomiche> [accessed 12 October 2016]. This thesis contains the most up-to-date bibliography, and a list of references to Leopardi contained in Calvino's essays, articles, interviews and letters.
4. Lucio Felici, *La luna nel cortile: capitoli leopardiani* (Soveria Mannelli: Rubbettino, 2006), p.192. Felici here is referring to Calvino's 'Il fantastico nella letteratura italiana', Italian translation of a lecture given at the International University Menendez Pelayo in Seville in September 1984, in which Calvino devotes two important pages to the operetta *Federico Ruysch e le sue mummie*: Italo Calvino, *Saggi*, II (Milan: Mondadori, 1995), pp. 1672–82.
5. Felici, p. 192.
6. Antonio Prete, *Finitudine e Infinito: su Leopardi* (Milan: Feltrinelli, 1998).
7. '*Quel libro senza uguali*': *le 'Operette morali' e il Novecento italiano*, ed. by Novella Bellucci and Andrea Cortellessa (Rome: Bulzoni, 2000).
8. Franco Gallippi, 'Calvino, Leopardi e il non-sapere', *Rivista di studi italiani*, 28.2 (2010), 78–97; and id., 'Calvino's Reading of Leopardi', *Rivista di studi italiani*, 33.1 (2015), 226–45.
9. All references to *Il barone rampante* [BR] are from Italo Calvino, *Romanzi e racconti* [RR], ed. by Claudio Milanini, Mario Barenghi, and Bruno Falcetto, pref. by Jean Starobinski, I (Milan: Mondadori, 1991).
10. Sara Maitland, *Gossip from the Forest* (London: Granta, 2012), p. 5.
11. 'Ho sempre ammesso che la mia epoca era il Settecento, cioè un'epoca di preparazioni e di cambiamenti in cui si pensava ancora che il mondo e la società fossero qualcosa di padroneggiabile. Penso che in quel secolo mi troverei bene. Era un momento in cui la barbarie umana [...] e la capacità della civiltà di tenere sembravano aver raggiunto un certo equilibrio. Illusioni, naturalmente, però illusioni che permettevano di lavorare umilmente.' Calvino, *Sono nato in America*, p. 372.
12. All references to Leopardi's works, and specifically to *Operette morali* [OM]: *Poesie e prose* [PP], I: *Poesie*, ed. by Mario Andrea Rigoni, con un saggio di Cesare Galimberti; II: *Prose*, ed. by Rolando Damiani (Milan: Mondadori, 1988); *Zibaldone di pensieri* [Zib], ed. by Rolando Damiani (Milan: Mondadori, 1997); excluding: *Memorie della mia vita: edizione tematica dello 'Zibaldone di pensieri' stabilita sugli 'Indici' leopardiani* [MV], ed. by Fabiana Cacciapuoti, pref. by Antonio Prete (Rome: Donzelli, 2003).
13. Giacomo Leopardi, *I Canti*, ed. by Fernando Bandini (Milan: Garzanti, 1975).
14. Rigoni, in PP, II, 1340.
15. The encyclopaedia of Sir Thomas Browne (1605–1682), *Pseudodoxia Epidemica, or, Enquiries into Very many Received Tenets, and commonly Presumed Truths*, whose title refers to the prevalence of false beliefs and 'vulgar errors', is found in Leopardi's library in the Italian translation, but in a much later edition: Tommaso Brovvn [sic], *Saggio sopra gli errori popolareschi* (Venice: Lazzaroni, 1743).
16. By far the most influential discussion of the eighteenth-century texts consulted by, and/or referred to in the *Dissertazione* is to be found in the Introduction to Giacomo Leopardi, '*Dissertazione sopra l'anima delle bestie' e altri scritti selvaggi*, ed. by Gino Ditadi (Este: Isonomia, 1999). See also Liana Cellerino, *L'io del topo: pensieri e letture dell'ultimo Leopardi* (Rome: La Nuova Italia Scientifica, 1997).
17. For en extensive study of this *operetta*, see Franco D'Intino, *L'immagine della voce: Leopardi, Platone e il libro morale* (Venice: Marsilio, 2009)

18. Except perhaps hares: 'eccetto che delle lepri si dice che la notte, ai tempi della luna piena, saltano e giuocano insieme, compiacendosi di quel chiaro', p. 153; Calvino quotes the lines from 'La vita solitaria' in his Memo on *Leggerezza*: 'Cara luna, al cui tranquillo raggio | danzan le lepri nelle selve' (PP 58).
19. Rigoni, in PP, II, 1341, and note how that freedom to exercise their 'will' is seen here in the ability to adapt, to some extent, to human presence and behaviour.
20. Rigoni, in PP, II, 1341.
21. Prete, *Finitudine*, p. 34.
22. This is another felicitous expression coined by Antonio Prete, in his preface to MV, p. xiv.
23. Prete, *Finitudine*, p. 45.
24. Marco Belpoliti, 'Un occhio sui rami', in *L'occhio di Calvino* (Turin: Einaudi 1996), p. 65.
25. Italo Calvino, 'Dall'opaco', in *La strada di San Giovanni* (Milan: Mondadori, 2011), pp. 82–83.
26. George Berkeley, *An Essay towards a New Theory of Vision* (1709), and Edmund Burke, *A Philosophical Enquiry into the Origin of our Ideas of the Sublime and Beautiful* (1757), both present in Italian translation in the poet's library in Recanati.
27. See Alessandro Parronchi , *Le origini dell'Infinito, e altri studi leopardiani* (Montebelluna: Amadeus, 1989).
28. Calvino, 'Ipotesi di una descrizione di paesaggio', in *Saggi*, II, 2694.
29. Francesca Southerden, *Landscapes of Desire in the Poetry of Vittorio Sereni* (Oxford: Oxford University Press, 2012), p. 109.
30. Rolando Damiani, *All'apparir del vero: vita di Giacomo Leopardi* (Milan: Mondadori, 2002), pp. 37 and 39.
31. Damiani, *All'apparir*, p. 25.
32. Ibid., p. 27.
33. Ibid., p. 26.
34. Ibid., p. 34.
35. *Il giovane favoloso* is a film about Leopardi's life, directed by Mario Martone, and presented at the Venice Film Festival in 2014. Its truly impressive success with Italian audiences derives not only from the extraordinary acting of Elio Germano (who plays Giacomo) but also from the accuracy of the biographical details, drawn from the letters by Giacomo, Carlo and Paolina Leopardi. The film also won the heart of many young people thanks to Martone's sensitive use of Leopardi's poetry, through quotations in voiceover, and outstanding photography that captures the spirit of Leopardi's melancholy genius.

CHAPTER 21

Transformations in the *giallo*: Italo Calvino's Metafictional Anti-Detective Novel
Se una notte d'inverno un viaggiatore (1979)

Helen Anderson

Italo Calvino's postmodernist masterpiece *Se una notte d'inverno un viaggiatore*[1] is a metafictional anti-*giallo* that dramatizes the modern tendency to foreground the writing and reading of the text. Towards the end of the 1970s, writers were seriously considering the role of the reader and the function of literature, and research in narratology greatly influenced fiction. *SNIV* exemplifies these developments. The act of reading is the unconventional protagonist of the hypernovel, which, written after a prolonged creative crisis, fittingly describes the trials of a novelist suffering from writer's block. As Lazzaro-Weis outlines, the genre is a popular structuring principle for postmodernist writers:

> The detective story with its strong, well-known conventions, its own penchant to parody itself and its privileged status as a natural paradigm for the hermeneutic act of reading, serves well two main goals of much post-modern fiction, namely, the unmasking or flaunting of the linguistic or narrative structures of the text and the challenging of the reader to participate directly in creating or conferring meaning(s).[2]

SNIV is regarded as the best modern Italian exponent of these metafictional techniques, as the Lettore's pursuit of texts makes him a 'textual' detective.

With *SNIV*, the mature Calvino reworks the traditional detective novel in a metafictional vein to create a postmodernist hypernovel that both reflects and branches off from the experimental work of his French and Italian contemporaries. The detective novel has always been associated with scholarly inquiry since it foregrounds the similarities between reading and detection. Calvino develops this association by creating a literary mystery that a reader attempts to solve. *SNIV* is driven by the theme of communication, and underpinning motifs of *vuoto*, *vertigine* and *assenza* reveal that Calvino's interest in the fragility of humanity in the face of the cosmos, and by implication the difficulty of mimesis in literature, endures from his 1950s novels to his final works.

The hypernovel shares much with Calvino's other two main 1970s publications,

Le città invisibili (1972) and *Il castello dei destini incrociati* (1973). The semiotic trilogy is characterized by fervid experimentation, textual subversion and self-referentiality. Modular structures allow Calvino to interrogate the confines of the textual universe: *Città* is composed of descriptions of individual cities, *Castello* is told by means of tarot cards, and *SNIV* features an apparent series of interrupted novels. Their autonomous narrative universes seem suspended in the void, unrelated to external 'reality'. The trilogy utilizes techniques common in 1960s and 1970s literary experiments, such as self-reflexivity and geometric structures, which explore dimensions of existence and identity. These endeavours are epitomized in Calvino's semi-serious metatextual guide to *SNIV*, 'Comment j'ai écrit un de mes livres', which explains the hypernovel's Greimas-inspired architecture.[3]

This essay examines Calvino's parodic metafictional hypernovel, focusing on the *cornice*, or frame tale, the reader-detective's investigation, the criminal's anti-literary activities and the victims of textual sabotage. It will consider *incipits* 1, 5, 6, and 7 as manipulations of the *giallo* on the micro-novel level. It will demonstrate that, for Calvino, the former reassurance of the *giallo* needs to be problematized, for the world is not ordered and the adequacy of the human mind to things is impossible.

The novel contains twelve *cornice* chapters interwoven with ten novel *incipits*. The *cornice*'s heterodiegetic narrator addresses the reader directly (the characters Lettore and Lettrice, and the external, 'real' reader). The *cornice* narrator's authority is counterbalanced by the evanescence of the *incipits*' narrators and, whilst the *cornice* is narrated in the present tense, the *incipits* alternate between past and present tenses, confusing narrative levels. The *cornice* concerns the Lettore's pursuit of a complete novel and is indebted to genres as varied as the romance (the Lettore and Lettrice's relationship), the fairy tale (the quest), and the *giallo*; the *incipits* each represent a chapter of a different novel, together forming 'a summa of contemporary fiction'.[4] The whole point of *SNIV*, it appears, is to avoid categorization and to present the infinite potential of fiction. Each *incipit* ends abruptly, usually at the plot's climax, and the incomplete novel cycle leads the Lettore through a series of adventures in the *cornice*, including the unravelling of a book-counterfeiting conspiracy headed by Ermes Marana. The *cornice* concludes with a parody of the romance novel, as the Lettore and Lettrice marry and settle down to finish reading *SNIV*. Calvino insists throughout that life and literature are inextricably bound and that human logic is futile in the face of fiction and the universe.

Tani claims that the 'metafictional anti-detective novel' belongs in only a general way to detective fiction. I would argue that, even though conventional elements (the corpse, a murder) are not always present, *SNIV* belongs in a specific way to the genre, since Calvino develops a classical association, that of scholarly inquiry as a process of detection. Tani describes how 'the fiction becomes an excuse for a "literary detection", and if there is a killer in the fiction, he is a "literary killer", a killer of texts'.[5] *SNIV* promotes a new category of readership where the reader is the protagonist of the novel he is reading. There are two dialectical levels, the first where the 'real' or empirical reader is reading *SNIV* and the second, where fictional readers undertake to read the novel, whilst participating in it. The protagonist of each *incipit* addresses a hypothetical reader. The first *incipit*'s narrator declares: '[s]ono una persona che non dà affatto nell'occhio, una presenza anonima su uno sfondo ancora più anonimo, se tu lettore non hai potuto fare a meno di distinguermi tra la gente che scendeva dal treno.'[6] He is aware that he is both the narrator and the main character of the *incipits*. The repetition of 'anonima', following the tendency of the *nouveau roman*, however, signals a departure from stable identity. There are two parallel pronoun chains, one denoting 'io' as the narrator, 'tu' as the reader, 'lui' as the empirical author, 'esso' as the narrated novel, and a second involving 'io' as the writer, Calvino, 'tu' the Lettore, 'Lei' Ludmilla, and 'esso' the *incipit*. Calvino gives little access to the narrator's psychology, suggesting only that he is a projection of the author. The narrator of both the *cornice* and the *incipits* seems to know what the implied reader is anticipating: '[s]ei uno che per principio non s'aspetta più niente da niente' (4), but the narrator's confidence is undermined by metafictional discourse, which reveals that textual realms are unreliable.

When the first *incipit* ends, the readers both external and internal are expected to become textual detectives, (co-)producers of meaning and agents in the reconstruction of events. Modern theorists such as Roland Barthes and Umberto Eco claim that the meaning of a text is created through the reading process, implying the death of the author. Calvino multiplies the conventional reader, creating the Lettore, Lettrice, and a host of minor reader characters that exist one fictive level above or below the 'real' reader and convey varied perspectives on the infinite potential of reading.[7] Each reader has a different method: for example, one uses books as material for sculptures and another delights in the 'promise' of reading, going no further than the preface. Calvino showcases the places designed for the production or consumption of literature and illustrates how, from the moment it is written, a text is influenced by editor, publisher, and reader.

The Lettore assumes his role as detective at the end of the first *incipit* and is joined by sidekick Ludmilla. The Lettore is unnamed, illustrating a shift from the eponymous novel to the anonymous, favoured by *nouveaux romanciers*. Ludmilla, a more experienced reader, dominates the Lettore, reversing the usual power balance between detective and sidekick. Throughout *SNIV*, Ludmilla's readerly desires are met by the author(s) of the *incipits* she reads and the Lettore feels compelled to solve the mystery of the *incipits*. Desire, love and jealousy are the motors of his quest. When the Lettore meets Ludmilla, the narrator remarks that their 'romanzo da leggere' has become 'un romanzo da vivere' (36), highlighting the complex links between fiction and life. Like the traditional detective, the Lettore strives for order and explanations: '[l]a cosa che ti esaspera di più è trovarti alla mercé del fortuito, dell'aleatorio, del probabilistico, nelle cose e nelle azioni umane' (30). Calvino shows that the traditional *giallo*, designed to represent absolutes, must be challenged, since the world(s) of the text and the external world(s) are labyrinthine.

As the Lettore and Lettrice investigate the textual mystery, there begins a metafictional discussion on reader-response theory, in which the authorial voice questions the role of the reader, asking if the reader is born at the cost of the death of the author and if the reader dominates the text. Reader-response theorists generally agree that the reader (and in Calvino's case the reader as detective) is essential to the creation of textual meaning and admit that there is an intrinsic difficulty in analysing the role of the reader, since individual readers are shaped by different experiences. A text's meaning is not always explicit, as illustrated in a simile in the first *incipit*: '[s]ono le pagine del libro a essere appannate come i vetri d'un vecchio treno, è sulle frasi che si posa la nuvola di fumo' (11). *SNIV* fits Barthes's 'scriptible' description, denoting a modern text that invites readers to (co-)create meaning. The classic text, its opposite, is 'lisible', with passive, consumer readers. In his examination of Honoré de Balzac's *Sarrasine* (S/Z), Barthes argues that:

> Dans ce texte idéal, les réseaux sont multiples et jouent entre eux, sans qu'aucun puisse coiffer les autres; ce texte est une galaxie de signifiants, non une structure de signifiés; il n'a pas de commencement; il est reversible; on y accède par plusieurs entrées dont aucune ne peut être à coup sûr déclarée principale; les codes qu'il mobilise se profilent à perte de vue, ils sont indécidables, ayant pour mesure l'infini du langage.[8]

According to Barthes, the reader can become the prime source of power. Calvino acknowledges the modern focus on the involvement of the reader in the production of meaning, but his Lettore is no superhero. Often, other characters possess more imagination than him, particularly the open-minded Ludmilla. In *Le Plaisir du texte* (1973), Barthes proposes a typology of the pleasures of reading.[9] The sexual metaphor of the 'plaisir' of the text is extended and reversed by Calvino, as McLaughlin explains:

> If reading is a kind of intercourse, then this work moves backwards to celebrate both the literary foreplay that takes place before a text can be read as well as the central act of intercourse/reading itself (the sexual union of the male and female readers is described as a reading of each other's body by all five senses, not just by the eye as in the reading of a text). Throughout, of course, there is also a play on the ambiguity of climax in both its literary and sexual meanings, while the whole structure of the novel is a series of interrupted coitions.[10]

The author inquires into the place of pleasure within the reading process, by allowing the characters to pursue their desires. The author, reader and text are fragmented and multiplied and the different textual 'realities' presented in the *cornice* and *incipits* render the detective's task difficult by complicating the text's ontology.

Eco's *Opera aperta* (1962) and *Lector in fabula* (1979) discuss how the reader inserts 'possible worlds' into the text and how every literary work proposes a model reader. Calvino illustrates this in 'author' Silas Flannery's observation of Ludmilla: 'il romanzo resta bloccato alla pagina che hai sotto gli occhi, come se solo l'arrivo di Ludmilla potesse rimettere in moto la catena degli avvenimenti' (163), and '[d]irei che potrebbe essere la mia lettrice ideale' (217). The text depends on Ludmilla. As textual detective, the Lettore reflects Eco's concept of the reader of an 'open work': 'le lecteur est mis en état d'attente et d'anticipation'.[11] The 'open work' features postmodernist elements such as rhizome (the play of surface tropes, images and signifiers)[12] and intertextuality, both of which point to the overwhelming potential of fiction. Though he is not a professional detective, the Lettore is compelled to decipher the incomplete *incipits*. This requires him to navigate a labyrinth of intertextual and extratextual 'possible' worlds. Calvino implies that a good reader is always a detective, since he consciously or unconsciously strives for the unsaid. The parallels between sleuthing and scholarly investigation are thus highlighted. The Lettore's compulsion to detect is proportional to the fascination that texts provoke and his pursuit of the complete text aims at re-establishing order in reading and life. Ludmilla is a major catalyst; as the writer's muse, her desires dictate the styles of the *incipits*. She is the most important link in the competitive relationships of the *cornice* and drives the plot forward, since she is contended by the Lettore, Marana and Flannery. Reflecting the author's own reading habits, as McLaughlin observes, Ludmilla brings autobiographical elements to the text, further complicating its generic status.[13] Ludmilla has a paradoxical role, given that she is both the force driving the mystery and the 'sidekick' attempting to solve it.

In contrast to the epistemological *giallo*, in which a puzzle is solved according to a formula, the enigma presented by Calvino's ontological text is within such an intricate web of textual possibilities that the Lettore has no hope of solving it. The quest (a fairy tale topos) for a forbidden or stolen text is a theme found in several modern Italian novels (e.g. Luigi Malerba's *Il fuoco greco* and Eco's *Il nome della rosa*) that address the written expression of phenomenal reality and establish the fictive text as the bearer of the highest order of truth. Christopher Brooker defines the general quest as one of the world's 'basic plots': 'No type of story is more instantly recognisable to us than a Quest'.[14] The traditional quest (based on Propp's functions)[15] involves: a call; companions; a journey; helpers; a final ordeal; and a coming-together. In *SNIV*, the 'call' is the first *incipit* that the Lettore wishes to finish. He must find a design in both the 'viaggio testuale' and in life. He expects to find a beginning, middle and end contained within a physical book binding, but his textual experience is interrupted repeatedly as the novels he reads disappear or are lost or stolen. Authors and titles mean little, as the Lettore cannot work out where *incipits* begin and end. His expectations are constantly thwarted:

> Tu sai dove vuoi arrivare, è una sottilissima rete che stai tendendo. — Il più buffo sarebbe che come credevamo di leggere Italo Calvino ed era Bazakbal, adesso che vogliamo leggere Bazakbal apriamo il libro e troviamo Italo Calvino. (35)

The 'sottilissima rete' highlights the postmodern concern with rhizome and the suggestion that novels can be muddled up reinforces the impression established by *SNIV*'s intertexts: all texts belong to a collective network.

A constant play of references to infinite fictional networks complicates the quest. In the first *incipit*, we learn that 'tutti i luoghi comunicano con tutti i luoghi istantaneamente' (19). The narrator of the first *incipit* describes a mysterious 'limbo illuminato sospeso tra le due oscurità del fascio dei binari e della città nebbiosa' (15) and a powerful 'organizzazione'. The motif of a powerful network highlights the postmodern preoccupation with a loss of hierarchy. The only order present is represented by an omnipotent 'organization' that unnerves both 'real' and fictional reader. In two introductory notes written in 1973 for Balzac's *Ferragus* and Robert Louis Stevenson's *The Pavilion on the Links* respectively, Calvino references the notions of tentacles and occult omnipotence in literature.[16] The worldwide conspiracy is thus a staple of the novel in the West and is also a metaphor for the author, who teases in a play of absence and presence.

Throughout his investigation, the Lettore reads of fragmented selves and places.[17] Names, events and the topos of the love triangle between protagonist, lover and rival are repeated in several *incipits*, contributing to a sense of literary vertigo. The novel illustrates Julia Kristeva's concept of intertextuality, which she considers a replacement for intersubjectivity. Kristeva argues that meaning is not transferred from writer to reader, but is filtered through 'codes' imparted by other texts: 'every text is from the outset under the jurisdiction of other discourses which impose a universe on it'.[18] Kristeva implies that the meaning of an artistic work is formulated by its viewer. 'Guarda in basso dove l'ombra s'addensa', highlights the infinite potential of storytelling:

> Sto tirando fuori troppe storie alla volta perché quello che voglio è che intorno al racconto si senta una saturazione d'altre storie che potrei raccontare e forse racconterò o chissà non abbia già raccontato in altra occasione, uno spazio pieno di storie che forse non è altro che il tempo della mia vita [...]. (125)

The Lettore, Lettrice and external reader attempt to find a coherent discourse in the *incipits*, but the external reader also has to contend with the *cornice-incipit* structure. The presence of the *cornice* underscores the artifice of the micro-texts within it and reminds the reader of the act of reading. The *cornice* is common in classical fiction; Giovanni Boccaccio's *Decameron*, the *Thousand and One Nights*, and Miguel de Cervantes's *Don Quixote* show how storytelling can be debated self-reflexively in its own medium.

The non-linear *incipits* have numerous forward and backward links and the predicament of the eternal beginning establishes the dominance of text over reader, since the reader cannot see an ending. The Lettore is told: '[n]on chiedete dov'è il seguito di questo libro! [...] Tutti i libri continuano al di là' (81). The 'al di là' provokes ontological questions: where is the Lettore, and does this mean books end in Heaven, Hell or some Other realm? The absolutes of the epistemological *giallo* are denied in order to show the unknowability of the world. The reader's quest is interrupted by intertextual references (e.g. Hölderlin, Dostoevsky). The influence of Jorge Luis Borges is evident in the text's overall design but most densely in 'In una rete di linee che s'intersecano'. Borges's ideas that literature is a world governed by the intellect and that only the written world has a full ontological reality (the things of this world exist for Borges only in as much as they refer to things that have been written) influence Calvino, who adopts Borgesian motifs such as eternity, cycles and labyrinths, all mythical expressions of metaphysical concerns.[19] Borges writes: 'a book is not an isolated being: it is a relationship, an axis of innumerable relationships'.[20] Calvino mirrors this concept, suggesting that literature, a catalogue of texts and genres, is composed of systems in which various cultures place their texts.

'In una rete di linee che s'intersecano' is full of references to vision and mirrors, designed to disorient the reader:

> Di specchio in specchio [...] — la totalità delle cose, l'universo intero, la sapienza divina potrebbero concentrare i loro raggi luminosi in un unico specchio. O forse la conoscenza del tutto è seppellita nell'anima e un sistema di specchi che moltiplicasse la mia immagine all'infinito. (193)

The labyrinthine narrative emphasizes the impossibility of finding the essence of the world and highlights the inexplicable nature of reality. In *Cibernetica e fantasmi* (1967) Calvino states:

> Il labirinto è fatto perché chi vi entra si perda ed erri. Ma il labirinto costituisce pure una sfida al visitatore perché ne ricostruisca il piano e ne dissolva il potere. Se egli ci riesce, avrà distrutto il labirinto; non esiste labirinto per chi lo ha attraversato.[21]

The labyrinth motif disconcerts the Lettore, who is surrounded by possibilities but no conclusions. His quest becomes more complicated as the worlds of the *incipits* multiply or dissolve: 'il mondo si va disfacendo e tenta d'attrarmi nella sua dissoluzione' (73). The fictive universe is unstable, 'quell'universo tutto schianti e sbalzi [...] Sentii subito che nell'ordine perfetto dell'universo s'era aperta una breccia, uno squarcio irreparabile', and Calvino uses nouns such as 'nulla', 'vuoto' and 'ombra' to emphasize man's inability to comprehend the textual and extra-textual universe (76–77). 'Quale storia laggiù attende la fine?', the final, apocalyptic *incipit*, echoes the obliteration of the town of Macondo in Gabriel García Márquez's *Cien años de soledad* (1967). Its protagonist erases people and buildings until nothing remains: '[e]ccomi dunque a percorrere questa superficie vuota che è il mondo' (291–92). The Lettore is presented with confusing extremes: an empty textual world and a 'forest' of words: '[l]'aprirti un varco a fil di spada nella barriera dei fogli s'associa al pensiero di quanto la parola racchiude e nasconde: ti fai largo nella lettura come in un fitto bosco' (47). He struggles with the blank page: 'ti sembra d'esserti perduto nel libro dalle pagine bianche' (54) and is physically trapped within. 'Sporgendosi dalla costa scoscesa' best communicates the impossibility of transcribing reality in language: 'non può esistere alcun vocabolario che traduca in parole il peso di oscure allusioni che incombe nelle cose' (70). The Lettore's path is strewn with mysteries that cannot be unravelled:

> Ma tra questi normali argomenti di corrispondenza d'ufficio s'affacciano allusioni a intrighi, complotti, misteri, e per spiegare queste allusioni, o per spiegare perché non vuole dire di più, Marana finisce per lanciarsi in affabulazioni sempre più frenetiche e imbrogliate. (134)

The Lettore's quest is thwarted by infinite space and time, and both he and the external reader suspect that only the criminal knows the truth.

The textual criminal, translator and forger Marana, is described as 'uno con tutte le carte in regola' (114), but, when subjected to a kind of detective 'grilling', emerges as a deeply suspicious character:

> Chiamiamo il Marana, gli facciamo delle domande, lui si confonde, si

> contraddice... Lo mettiamo alle strette, gli apriamo il testo originale sotto gli occhi e gli chiediamo di tradurci un pezzo a voce...Confessa che di cimbro lui non sa neanche una parola! [...] il testo l'aveva tradotto da un altro romanzo... (114)

From this seemingly banal act, of pretending to be able to translate, we learn that Marana is a master forger and arch-enemy of literature who enjoys disrupting the reading experience. In Greek mythology, Hermes is an Olympian god of boundaries, a mediator who epitomizes the power of the spoken word. Calvino's Ermes is the opposite; he impedes communication. The Homeric hymn invokes Hermes as a contradiction: 'a bringer of dreams, a watcher by night, a thief at the gates'.[22] Calvino's Ermes forges texts, driven by a desire to destroy the relationships between text, author and reader. Rather than offer a detailed characterization, Calvino prefers to let Ermes lurk in the shadows of the text. Marana appears only when mentioned by others and represents the traditional author function: present, but rarely described.

Weiss suggests that Marana's lurking could be due to a wish, on Calvino's part, to comment on unseen translators, who are taken for granted. The critic explains that Calvino had an uneasy relationship with translators and compares Marana to Sherlock Holmes's arch-enemy Moriarty, considered the first literary criminal mastermind. Weiss posits that Calvino is parodying hermeneutics as a theory of interpretation, which reinforces my argument regarding Calvino's overturning of the *giallo*, since in the traditional *giallo* the enigma is solved, whereas in the anti-*giallo*, the disabled hermeneutic code means it remains an enigma.[23] Weiss describes Marana as a 'Calvino incarnation of deconstruction', because he challenges narrative conventions. Marana has a pessimistic view of the legacy of fiction and remarks that it may be forgotten or attributed to a collective or individual author:

> Che importa il nome dell'autore in copertina? Trasportiamoci col pensiero di qui a tremila anni. Chissà quali libri della nostra epoca si saranno salvati, e di chissà quali autori si ricorderà ancora il nome. Ci saranno libri che resteranno famosi ma che saranno considerati opere anonime [...]; o forse tutti i libri superstiti saranno attribuiti a un unico autore misterioso, come Omero. (116)

Marana is driven by jealousy: 'Pare facesse tutto per una donna' (280). Once Marana realizes Ludmilla prefers books to him, he sabotages her reading experience, forcing her to acknowledge his presence in her books: 'tra il libro e lei si sarebbe insinuata sempre l'ombra della mistificazione, e lui identificandosi con ogni mistificazione avrebbe affermato la sua presenza' (186). Marana and Ludmilla have opposing views of literature:

> — Per questa donna [...], — leggere vuol dire spogliarsi d'ogni intenzione e d'ogni partito preso, per essere pronta a cogliere una voce che si fa sentire quando meno ci s'aspetta, una voce che viene non si sa da dove, da qualche parte al di là del libro, al di là dell'autore, al di là delle convenzioni della scrittura: dal non detto, da quello che il mondo non ha ancora detto di sé e non ha ancora le parole per dire. Quanto a lui, invece, voleva dimostrarle che dietro la pagina scritta c'è il nulla; il mondo esiste solo come artificio, finzione, malinteso, menzogna. (281)

Ludmilla searches for new knowledge of the world, whilst Marana seeks to demonstrate that the world is artificial. In *SNIV*, Calvino presents both pessimistic and optimistic viewpoints of the meaning of literature and types of readers. Though troubled by writer's block and the unstable political climate of the 1970s, Calvino meditates on an ideal state of literature, in which we return to the blissful experience of reading and ignore critical debate (whilst, ironically, he is only too aware of it).

Marana also sabotages the writing process of the Irish novelist Silas Flannery, whose manuscripts disappear and return altered. Flannery comments on Marana's theory of the author as a character: '[h]a continuato a espormi le sue teorie, secondo le quali l'autore di ciascun libro è un personaggio fittizio che l'autore esistente inventa per farne l'autore delle sue finzioni' (210). This recalls 'I livelli della realtà in letteratura' (1978), in which Calvino discusses the 'sdoppiamento o moltiplicazione del soggetto dello scrivere'.[24] Calvino argues that 'la persona che scrive deve inventare quel primo personaggio che è l'autore dell'opera' and that the textual 'io' is not the 'real' author but a 'proiezione di se stesso che l'autore mette in gioco nella scrittura'.[25] The author concludes that literature knows only *levels* of reality, not reality, a concept that correlates to *SNIV* in many ways. Thus Marana reflects some of Calvino's own metafictional viewpoints.

However, critics disagree as to which character best reflects Calvino. Weiss asserts that Calvino is identifiable as both Marana (in metafictional discourse) and Flannery (experiences of writer's block) whilst Feinstein argues that there are three alter egos of Calvino in the novel: the earnest writer Silas Flannery, the devious translator Marana and the impossible-to-please female reader, Ludmilla.[26] I would agree, especially given that Ludmilla's readerly habits reflect Calvino's own. Feinstein notes that Marana is interested only in falsehood ('sognava una letteratura tutta d'apocrifi', 185), has abandoned illusions about a positive side to literature and therefore represents Calvino the critic's 'intellectual pessimism'.[27] Marana satirizes the supremacy of reading over writing by ensuring that the reader cannot decode the text. He belongs to the 'Organizzazione del Potere Apocrifo', which has fractured into two Wings (Light and Shadow), both of which want Flannery's latest manuscript. Feinstein interprets this allegorically, suggesting that the two factions represent traditional humanist critics on the one hand (interested in works of 'light', with moral value), and avant-garde anti-humanist structuralists or deconstructionists on the other (interested in works that show that 'individuals have no autonomy').[28] Their opposing truths cancel one another out, illustrating Calvino's desire to portray truth as elusive. Indeed, Calvino shows that even Marana, the textual terrorist, is impotent when confronted by reading: '[h]o capito i miei limiti — m'ha detto — Nella lettura avviene qualcosa su cui non ho potere' (282). Calvino demonstrates that man has limits that cannot be overcome in terms of knowledge of the world.

The main victim of Marana's literary sabotage is the author figure, whose works and relationship with his reader are targeted. The second victim is the (internal and external) reader, whose experience is disjointed and unfinished. The reading experience of the Lettore and Lettrice is a form of *coitus interruptus*, since their reading of each *incipit* is thwarted just as they become excited. Marana victimizes Flannery during his writer's block and causes him to lose all enjoyment: 'il piacere della lettura è finito per me' (197). Flannery's paranoia grows: '[a]nch'io vorrei cancellare me stesso e trovare per ogni libro un altro io, un'altra voce, un altro nome, rinascere; ma il mio scopo è di catturare nel libro il mondo illeggibile, senza centro, senza io' (211). This questioning of the authorial 'io' underlines the instability of fiction, as it highlights a plurality of authorial voices. Once Marana exposes the producers, consumers and artifice of fiction, it becomes an unnerving realm. Flannery has to accept his lack of authorial power and this serves to demonstrate the text's autonomy. In chapter eight, a *mise en abyme* of *SNIV* since it hints at the infinite regress of fiction by narrating the production of the book that is being read, Ludmilla rejects Flannery because, although she has read his work, she imagined a different author.[29] This reflects Marana's and Calvino's view of the fragmented author persona. Flannery has an idea for a story in which two authors (one of vacuous fiction, one of 'serious' fiction) observe each other's writing process. The tormented writer takes the productive writer as his model, for he writes efficiently and tailors his novels to his audience; whilst the productive writer is convinced the tormented writer's work must be richer. In their attempts to emulate each other, they write the same novel (this is one of many endings Flannery imagines). Here, Calvino suggests that authorial intention is redundant in the face of the autonomous text. The intermingling of the authors' identities underscores the complex intertextual realm of literature. Earlier, Flannery exclaims '[c]ome scriverei bene se non ci fossi!' (199), a statement that supports the notion of the autonomous text, and, in considering the verb 'to write', he wonders if the act of writing will ever be a consequential exertion of the writer's will to work: 'Potrò mai dire: "oggi scrive", così come "oggi piove" [...]?' (205), Flannery is a metafictional representation of the writer in crisis, who realizes that there is no certainty in literature other than falsification:

> scrivere è sempre nascondere qualcosa in modo che venga poi scoperto [...] non c'è certezza fuori dalla falsificazione. (226)

Flannery wants an abstract power to help him write, which confirms his feeling of inadequacy: '[s]e fossi solo una mano, una mano mozza che impugna una penna e scrive...Chi muoverebbe questa mano? La folla anonima? Lo spirito dei tempi? L'inconscio collettivo? Non so' (199–200). The idea of his hand being moved by an external force hints at the disappearance of the 'io', the first subject of writing. If a mysterious force guides the author then the reader cannot hope to decipher any textual 'reality'. Marana's machinations and Flannery's writerly crisis ensure that the Lettore's investigation is doomed.

In the novel's denouement, the Lettore is sent to South America by Flannery to find Marana, but Marana is in Japan. The *incipits* convey a sense of finality that reflects the hopeless nature of his mission: 'Intorno a una fossa vuota' talks of the final frontier of the inhabited world, of 'spaesamento' and 'vuoto', whilst 'Quale storia laggiù attende la fine?' describes a world that the protagonist erases until just a surface remains: '[I]nvece: niente: intorno il vuoto è sempre più vuoto' (293). Here the *vuoto* reflects the isolation of the individual. The final *incipit* ends on another note of emptiness:

> Il mondo è ridotto a un foglio di carta dove non si riescono a scrivere altro che parole astratte, [...]. Salto da una sponda all'altra, e in basso non vedo alcun fondo ma solo il nulla che continua giù all'infinito; corro su pezzi di mondo sparpagliati nel vuoto; il mondo si sta sgretolando... (295–96)

The world is reduced to a piece of paper, upon which no concrete words can be written. The Lettore's acceptance of the irrationality of this final *incipit* illustrates a progression from his initial need for order to the realization that literature is more powerful than him. Chapter eleven unfolds in a library, where the Lettore searches fruitlessly for the endings of the *incipits* and meets seven readers, who describe their different approaches to reading, allowing Calvino to reiterate the infinite potential of fiction in a final summary. The Lettore describes his approach to reading, which reveals he seeks order, like the traditional detective:

> a me nei libri piace leggere solo quello che c'è scritto; e collegare i particolari con tutto l'insieme; e certe letture considerarle come definitive. (301)

The sixth reader joins the *incipit* titles so that they form a single title. Although this suggests that the texts are bound together in a single purpose, it does not resolve the problem that the Lettore encountered: the lack of resolution. In a letter to Lucio Lombardo Radice, Calvino confirms that the *incipits* are actually complete: 'La tua osservazione che gli "inizi" sono, invece, delle narrazioni compiute mi pare giusta'.[30]

SNIV's array of genres represents a survey of attitudes towards the modern world and, as a philosophical meditation, it concludes that the world cannot be accepted as it is. The readers in the library lament the endings of stories of ancient times, with marriage or death providing simple closure. The Lettore marries Ludmilla in fairy-tale tradition, parodying the underpinning experimental characteristics of *SNIV* in a typically self-reflexive manner. The joined *incipit* titles and the marriage emphasize the artifice of the text, whose only reality exists in its own story. Whilst the Lettore did not find a fictional resolution in the *incipits*, he chooses his own conventional ending by marrying Ludmilla:

> Ora siete marito e moglie, Lettore e Lettrice. Un grande letto matrimoniale accoglie le vostre letture parallele.
> Ludmilla chiude il suo libro, spegne la sua luce, abbandona il capo sul guanciale, dice: — Spegni anche tu. Non sei stanco di leggere?
> E tu: — Ancora un momento. Sto per finire *Se una notte d'inverno un viaggiatore* di Italo Calvino. (305)

Calvino carries through the concept of the unbreakable link between fiction and life to the ending. Luisa Guj argues that their union is a metaphor of regeneration, with its promise of 'togetherness, fertility and offspring', and emphasizes the novel's final 'successes' (nuptial bliss and the Lettore's reading of the last few lines of *SNIV*).[31] However, the Lettore's conventional happy ending is destabilized by the text's metafictional commentary, which has prevented the dominance of a single discourse. Whereas the protagonist of the traditional *giallo* restores order following the chaos of the crime, the Lettore finds no answer to the textual mystery in the *cornice* or in the *incipits*.

The specific detective *incipits* must be considered when examining the role of the genre in the hypernovel. The first *incipit* sets the tone of mystery, while a central cluster of detective *incipits* (five, six and seven) precede a revelatory *cornice* chapter (eight), suggesting that the majority of the investigative work is completed before Flannery's thoughts are revealed. In the *incipits*, the logic of the traditional *giallo* is subverted, and Calvino depicts a world in which existential angst, criminal networks and disorder reign.

The first *incipit*, 'Se una notte d'inverno un viaggiatore', is indebted to the spy thriller, with its nameless narrator-protagonist, who waits at an unnamed station to exchange suitcases with a stranger, its *femme fatale* (in the tradition of the hard-boiled novel), and references to an all-powerful organisation. What makes this *incipit* subversive is its unrelenting metafictional commentary and ambiguity, chiefly conveyed through images of *nebbia*. Engine steam fogs up the book's pages, denoting the merging of extra- and inter-textual reality. The station is a *non-lieu*, to borrow Marc Augé's term, antithetical to the notion of anthropological place (a place of identity and history).[32] The narrator describes himself as 'quell'uomo che si chiama "io"' (12) and warns that the author may be luring the reader into a non-temporal trap, drawing attention to authorial control. The narrator attempts to define who he is but seems unaware of his role: 'è chiaro che dipendo da altri, non ho l'aria d'uno che viaggia per una sua faccenda privata o che conduce degli affari in proprio' (16). Characters in search of identity represent the shift from epistemology to ontology that has occurred in postmodernist fiction by drawing attention to the potential plurality of self.[33] Calvino questions time (an important element in detective fiction because it provides coordinates for the crime and the investigation) when the narrator reveals that he seeks 'il momento zero' (18) from which he departed. He would like clocks to run backwards and wonders how many different lives he could have, if he were to make different decisions at different junctures. His status as the 'ultimo viaggiatore in attesa' (19) suspends him in limbo, or a *non-lieu*. By emphasizing the power of time, the narrator highlights man's fragile status in the world. When describing the locals, the narrator notes that their conversational remarks form 'un brusio di voci indistinte' (20), giving a sense of a collective identity and numerous, simultaneous discourses. Having established the *femme fatale* Armida, the narrator comments that the other characters' memories blur her identity: 'c'è un velo d'altre immagini che si deposita sulla sua immagine e la rende sfocata' (21). The instability of Armida's image and identity contributes to the ontological questioning permeating *SNIV*. No resolution is reached, as the protagonist boards a train and gains no explanation as to the purpose of his aborted mission. Here, Calvino subverts the traditional *giallo*, which usually contains an explanation of narrative events and sees order restored.

Incipit five, 'Guarda in basso dove l'ombra s'addensa', is 'un romanzo cinico-brutale' that parodies the French hard-boiled novel.[34] The plot centres on the disposal of a corpse by Ruedi lo Svizzero and Bernadette. As this linear story is told, a series of flashbacks and digressions explain Ruedi's past and how the pair came to be lumbered with a corpse. The seriousness of the murder is undermined by a slapstick narrative and what makes the *incipit* subversive is its comedy and metafictional discourse, alongside the narrator's comments on how he is constructing a web of stories about his past lives (131). Ruedi's need to saturate the reader with stories, to show that even the most insignificant episode denotes numerous other events, contributes to *SNIV*'s thesis on the plurality of discourse in the textual world.

The sixth *incipit*, 'In una rete di linee che s'allacciano' (the 'romanzo dell'angoscia'), is an obsessive thriller set on an American university campus.[35] It opens with a commentary on nervous sensations produced by the sound of a telephone ring, which lacerates the continuity of space and time. The narrator-protagonist, a professor, often hears a telephone ring when he is out jogging. He answers a call through an open window, learns one of his students has been kidnapped and goes to the scene to find her tied up. The *incipit*, pervaded by a sense of the unknown, has no concrete resolution. The relentless ringing of the telephone, the professor's constant movement and his fear create a sense of narrative vertigo and disorder, while the web of telephone lines denotes plural discourse. The author expands upon the need for escape that was central to Ruedi's crime in the previous *incipit*, by turning an innocent object (the telephone) into a pursuer. Once again the plot of the traditional *giallo* (disruption then restoration of order) is subverted.

'In una rete di linee che s'intersecano', is a Borgesian geometric thriller. Calvino's description of Borges's *El jardín de senderos que se bifurcan* as a thriller containing a tale of logical-metaphysical suspense mirrors the plot of his own seventh *incipit*.[36] Thematically, it is a variation on the previous 'telephone' *incipit*, as the narrative concentrates on the power of another inanimate object, this time a mirror. This *incipit* contains intertextual references to 'occult' philosophical writers such as Athanasius Kircher and Plotinus, as well as to the inventor of the kaleidoscope, again stressing the relationships between text(s) and world(s). Like the narrators of the first, fifth and sixth *incipits*, the protagonist is pursued. He conceals himself amongst an army of doppelgängers and establishes a criminal organization. Counter-counterplans foil counterplans and he finds himself kidnapped and located at home in his catoptric room, where his mistress is tied up and his wife reveals herself as the engineer of the counter-counterplan. A hall of mirrors blurs the three characters, until the protagonist can see only one whole reflection. He has reached his goal of totality and yet the merging identities indicate the ontological nature of Calvino's text, which destabilizes absolutes. The metafictional commentaries that accompany each narrative highlight life's disorder on a small scale, by suggesting that textual reality is fragile.

In *SNIV*, Calvino subverts conventional features of the detective story genre by engaging in an extreme metafictional experiment. Readers both inside and outside of the text are forced to play detective, in order to unravel the mystery concocted by a master textual forger, a killer of fiction. Calvino's novel is an anti-detective story, in which textual realities are established only to be destroyed. The result is a novel that displays the infinite potential of literature, both from the author's and the reader's perspective. The author can create anything he desires and may interrupt the text at any point. The reader is free to impose his individual interpretation on the text, thereby forever altering its identity. The *romanzo da leggere* is given life and becomes a *romanzo da vivere*. Life and fiction are inextricably linked, each indecipherable from the other. Calvino is unafraid of showing the incompleteness of literature; in fact he rejoices in the massive presence of words, images and meanings in the fictive universe. Calvino takes the *giallo*'s traditional focus on scholarly inquiry to the extreme and explores the mysteries of the literary realm rather than a case of murder. Detective stories conceive reading and detection as identical activities, and Calvino uses this as a starting point for his parody. He questions the status of literature throughout and casts doubt on traditional expectations of plot, author and reader. Calvino's 'Per chi si scrive? (Lo scaffale ipotetico)' (1967) suggests that 'la letteratura vive oggi soprattutto della propria negazione' and just over a decade later *SNIV* cements this theory, as it questions and denies itself throughout.[37] In *SNIV*, Calvino continues to showcase the inevitable subjectivity of descriptions of reality, demonstrates that language cannot represent external referents and illustrates that literature is irremediably unfinished, but is, paradoxically, the only thing that remains. In *SNIV*, the narrative universe is autonomous and man is powerless in the face of the complex world(s) within and beyond the text. In the *cornice*, Calvino tells a traditional story, but ironically, whilst the *incipits* are entirely experimental and disorienting. He strikes a balance between experimentation and readability. Here, Kermode's assertion that 'since reality is incomplete, art must not be too afraid of incompleteness' is fitting.[38]

Calvino's textual experiments reached their peak in *Le città invisibili* (1972), but *SNIV* can be considered as a masterpiece for its intense exploration of reading and writing. In the hypernovel, geometric rationality continues to be used in the service of the *vuoto*: shapes and symbols are employed to expose man's vain attempts to order the universe. The hypernovel's precise ordering symbolizes the fragile nature of constructions produced by man's imagination. The traditional *giallo* relies on logic and therefore provides an excellent formulaic foundation that Calvino exploits to subvert order. Calvino's metafictional anti-*giallo* lays bare narrative constructs and expresses the irrationality of the universe, but his vision is not nihilistic. He does not aim to destroy literature like Marana; rather, he aims to show its potential, exemplified in ten *incipits*, which together form a dazzling survey of some of fiction's most exhilarating genres. Calvino takes the epistemological form of the traditional *giallo*, which works logically towards absolutes, and turns it into an ontological form, to illustrate the radically fragmentary world and man's inability to order it. Calvino's hypernovel draws on the metaphysical detective stories of Borges and joins the Italian ranks of Carlo Emilio Gadda's and Leonardo Sciascia's philosophical *gialli*, to demonstrate that the *giallo* no longer guarantees narrative purpose, a fixed format or a clear solution and is instead an open form delivering a resounding message that the world can be interpreted but never accurately represented.

Notes to Chapter 21

1. Italo Calvino, *Se una notte d'inverno un viaggiatore* (Milan: Mondadori, 1994 [1979]); henceforth *SNIV*.
2. Carol Lazzaro-Weis, 'The Metaphysical Detective Novel and Sciascia's *Il contesto*: Parody or Tyranny of a Borrowed Form?', *Quaderni d'italianistica*, 8.1 (Spring 1987), pp. 42–52 (42).
3. Calvino, 'Comment j'ai écrit un de mes livres', *Nuova corrente* 34, N.99 (1987), 9–28. Calvino explains the narrative organization of what would be *SNIV*. The author employs a personal slant on Greimas's semiotic square diagrammatics in the hypernovel's frame tale.
4. Martin McLaughlin, *Italo Calvino* (Edinburgh: Edinburgh University Press, 1998), p. 116.
5. Stefano Tani, *The Doomed Detective: The Contribution of the Detective Novel to Postmodern American and Italian Fiction* (Carbondale: Southern Illinois University Press, 1984), p. 113.
6. *SNIV*, p. 16.
7. Guido Bonsaver lists these perspectives in *Il mondo scritto: forme e ideologia nella narrativa di Italo Calvino* (Turin: Tirrenia, 1995), p. 71.
8. Roland Barthes, *S/Z* (Paris: Seuil, 1970), p. 12.
9. Roland Barthes, *Le Plaisir du texte* (Paris: Seuil, 1973)
10. McLaughlin *Italo Calvino*, p. 127.
11. Jules Gritti, *Umberto Eco* (Paris: Éditions Universitaires, 1991), p. 34.
12. According to Peter Brooker, rhizome is a term introduced by Gilles Deleuze (1925–1995) and Félix Guattari (1930–1992) in *A Thousand Plateaus* (1987), following *Anti-Oedipus: Capitalism and Schizophrenia* (1984). *A Glossary of Cultural Theory* (London: Arnold, 2003), p. 224. See also Umberto Eco, *Semiotica e filosofia del linguaggio* (Turin: Einaudi, 1984), p. 112.
13. 'In Chapter VII Ludmilla's evident taste for reading more than one book at a time and for having a different book to read in every room also derives from the author's own habits', McLaughlin, *Italo Calvino*, p. 121.
14. Christopher Brooker, *The Seven Basic Plots* (London: Continuum, 2004), p. 69.
15. Vladimir Propp, *Morphology of the Folktale* (1928)
16. *Nota introduttiva*, Honoré de Balzac, *Ferragus* (Turin: Einaudi, 1973), pp. v–ix. *Nota introduttiva* in Robert L. Stevenson, *Il padiglione sulle dune* (Turin: Einaudi, 1973), pp. v–ix.
17. Jonathan Usher, 'Interruptory Mechanisms in Calvino's *Se una notte d'inverno un viaggiatore*', *Italian Studies*, 45 (1990), 81–102.
18. Jonathan Culler, *The Pursuit of Signs: Semiotics, Literature, Deconstruction* (London: Routledge & Kegan Paul, 1981), p. 105.
19. Italo Calvino, *Saggi*, ed. by Mario Barenghi, 2 vols (Milan: Mondadori, 1995), I, 1293–94; henceforth *S*.
20. *Literary Philosophers: Borges, Calvino, Eco*, ed. by Jorge J. E. Gracia, Carolyn Korsmeyer, and Rodolphe Gasché (New York: Routledge, 2002), pp. 213–14. From Borges, *Labyrinths and other stories* (London: Penguin, 1964).
21. Calvino, 'Cibernetica e fantasmi', *S*, p. 224.
22. Diane J. Rayor, *The Homeric Hymns* (Berkeley: University of California Press, 2004), line 13.
23. Beno Weiss, *Understanding Italo Calvino* (Columbia: University of South Carolina Press, 1993), p. 175.
24. 'I livelli della realtà in letteratura', *S*, pp. 381–98 (p. 389).
25. *S*, pp. 389–90.
26. Wiley Feinstein, 'The Doctrinal Core of *If on a Winter's Night a Traveler*', in *Calvino Revisited*, ed. by Franco Ricci (Ottawa: Dovehouse Editions, 1989), p. 147.
27. Feinstein, p. 149.
28. Feinstein, p. 150.
29. Feinstein, 'Doctrinal Core' and McLaughlin, p. 121. McLaughlin describes how *SNIV*'s complex structure is reflected in this *mise en abyme*, which recalls the mythical 602nd night of *The Thousand and One Nights* mentioned by Borges. Calvino singles out Scheherazade's story in 'I livelli della realtà in letteratura' (1978), written in the same year as *SNIV*.

30. Letter to Lucio Lombardo Radice (13 November 1979), in Calvino, *Lettere 1940–1985*, ed. by Luca Baranelli (Milan: Mondadori, 2000), p. 1406.
31. Luisa Guj, '"Quale storia laggiù attende la fine?" The Lettore's Successful Quest in Calvino's *Se una notte d'inverno un viaggiatore*', *Italian Quarterly*, 30 (1989), 65–73 (p. 71).
32. Marc Augé, *Non-places: Introduction to an Anthropology of Supermodernity* (London: Verso, 1995).
33. E.g. Paola Capriolo, *Il doppio regno* (Milan: Bompiani, 1993 [1991]).
34. 'Presentazione', *SNIV*, p. xv.
35. 'Presentazione', *SNIV*, p. xv.
36. Calvino, 'Jorge Luis Borges' (1984), *S*, pp. 1292–1300 (p. 1298).
37. Calvino, 'Per chi si scrive?' (1967), *S*, pp. 199–204 (p. 201).
38. Frank Kermode, *The Sense of an Ending: Studies in the Theory of Fiction* (New York: Oxford University Press, 1967), p. 130.

CHAPTER 22

❖

'Senti 'n po', a Gregori Pècche...':
Shavelson's *It Started in Naples* and
Fellini's *La dolce vita* between
Italian and U.S. Culture

Guido Bonsaver

This essay addresses questions related to what is arguably the greatest influence on Italian culture during the twentieth century, that of the United States of America. The so-called 'Americanization' of Italian society has been at the centre of several works dedicated to various periods and to different areas of social and artistic endeavour.[1] This essay is devoted to the cinematic representation of this process. In this field, despite a number of films directly addressing the topic — with Steno's *Un americano a Roma* (1954) as its most popular example — not much attention has been paid to understanding their modes and *topoi*. From a historical and sociological viewpoint, the work of David Ellwood has been the most fruitful, particularly for his capacity to link developments in the film industry with the overall advancement of U.S. culture throughout Europe.[2] The 1950s, with the much publicised impact of the Marshall Plan on the one hand, and the return of the Italian film industry to a position of international prominence on the other, is a most stimulating decade on which to concentrate. These are years during which Italian cinema created its own images of the new, modern Italy emerging from the 'boom economico'. Ellwood suggests that these images were part of a defensive mechanism through which U.S. culture was demystified, thus participating in Italy's attempt to shape its own peculiar kind of modernity.[3] Whilst, in general terms, I agree to the presence of such tendency, in this essay I would like to offer a detailed analysis of two films which offer a different image of the meeting between U.S. and Italian culture.

The choice of Federico Fellini's *La dolce vita* and the less renowned *It Started in Naples* by Melville Shavelson, starring Clark Gable, Sophia Loren and Vittorio De Sica, derives from a number of reasons. Both films were produced in 1959 and distributed the following year, and thus, as a pair, they offer an interesting parallel between a Hollywood-based and an Italian overview of the new Italy emerging from economic recovery. At the same time, both films, in different ways, question our established understanding of a typical Hollywood production and an Italian one. *It Started in Naples*, as we will see, is not such a well-packaged cinematic product as one would expect, and *La dolce vita* invites a reconsideration of the notion of auteur film. Finally, two scripts which never saw the light of production, both written in 1948, will provide an intriguing insight into Fellini's early interest in the clash between U.S. and Italian culture and allow for some interesting parallels with Shavelson's film.

A note on methodology is also due at the end of this preamble. The essay will move between two distant poles: at one end the philological accuracy of archival reconstruction, and at the other the comparative analysis in search of similarities and echoes from one work to another. They are both vital to the content of this essay, and are indirectly a homage to the scholar celebrated in this Festschrift, who is master in both.

Writing a Film: Shavelson's 'Too Many Cooks'

Thanks to the extensive archival material related to Hollywood productions — Paramount, in this case — it is possible to reconstruct the genesis of *It Started in Naples* with a good degree of precision. The initial treatment was offered in 1957 by two British scriptwriters, Michael Pertwee and Jack Davies. It was meant to become a musical entitled *Song of Capri*, featuring two U.S. citizens, an army sergeant and a music-hall singer, both arriving on the isle of Capri, their lives variously intertwined with those of locals. Without entering into much detail, it will suffice to quote the short, cutting view of Paramount editor Allida Allen: 'This Italian musical has more to offer in scenery than in plot, which in addition to being slight is also rather old-fashioned. It stands in need of padding and polishing — otherwise, as musicals go, it is no better and no worse than most'.[4] Unsurprisingly, *Song of Capri* remained dormant for two years until another duo, this time made up of the experienced director Melville Shavelson and scriptwriter/producer Jack Rose, decided to take up the idea and develop it into a very different story. The result was roughly the script which went into production: Philadelphia lawyer Mike Hamilton arrives in Naples to sort out the estate of his brother who lived there in his last years. To his surprise, he discovers that the brother had re-married a local woman who had died with him in a boating accident, and that the two had left a child who is now looked after by his aunt, Lucia Curcio, on the isle of Capri. The meeting between Mike and Lucia leads to a romantic comedy in which the American's initial suspicion is won over by the Italian's vitality and beauty. The production took off with the signing of two of Paramount's biggest stars: the ageing Clark Gable — *It Started in Naples* was the last film released before his death — and the 25-year-old Sophia Loren. At the same time, it was decided that the script could benefit from some Italian polish. It was not the first time that Paramount had done this, famously so for one of its most successful runaway productions, William Wyler's *Roman Holiday* (1953). Indeed, one of the Italian authors who had helped then was hired again: it was Suso Cecchi d'Amico.[5] The existence of copies of the script before and after this round of revision gives us the unique opportunity of being able to examine the different authorial perspectives of this tale of clashing cultures.[6]

The most noticeable difference concerns the political overtones which characterise the first version of the script (I333). This happens mainly through the secondary character of Renzo, Lucia's work associate. In I333 Renzo is presented as a militant communist, constantly associating Mike's presence with the role of the USA as an oppressive colonialist power. For example, in a scene inside Lucia's kitchen he attacks Mike shouting: 'Why don't you get out of the Middle East? And you are building a missile base in Positano?', or when Mike offers to pay for Nando's education, Marco again intervenes and shouts: 'You cannot buy Italy with gold!' (I333, shot 22, p. 42). Or, more comically, when he realises there there is romance between Mike and Lucia, he says to Nando: 'You see? American imperialism! First, the Middle East, now Lucia! Tomorrow my grandmother — and then the world! (I333, shot 201, p. 92)

After Cecchi d'Amico's makeover, politics is replaced by a more nuanced representation of cultural difference. Renzo becomes a more neutral presence (one could argue that this is a net loss in terms of the comic potential of this character) whereas the metonymy of Mike standing for a general idea of U.S. attitudes remains dominant but is rarely made explicit. In the kitchen scene, for example, Cecchi d'Amico replaces the political innuendos with a dialogue in which Mike is asked to taste a tomato sauce which Lucia has prepared. Luigi, a paying guest in Lucia's house, complains about the sauce, at which point Mike, asked to give his opinion, suggests they should add a little bit of ketchup. The stage direction specifies: 'There is shocked silence. Luigi crosses himself', after which Luigi cuts the conversation short by saying: 'Is okay! I eat' (I334, shot 41, pp. 23–24). Another instance concerns the scene of one of the various fights between Mike and Lucia for the custody of the child. In I333, Nando steals Mike's wallet and when Lucia tries to defend him, Mike explodes with an angry outburst: 'I don't want that kid. I don't want you, I don't want your whole country. American go home! They ought to write that out in spaghetti on our Ambassador's forehead'. Lucia's reply is equally violent: she crushes her cigarette on the back of Mike's hand and says: 'You like American cigarettes?' (I333, shot 135 pp. 63–64). Suso Cecchi d'Amico entirely gets rid of both Nando's misbehaving and the following fight between Mike and Lucia. Instead, food comes back as a cultural symbol: this time, after befriending Nando, Mike asks the hotel kitchen to provide him with all the necessary ingredients in order to prepare a hamburger. This leads to a memorable scene in which Mike proudly teaches the child how to prepare and eat a proper American hamburger (I334, shots 113–24, pp. 55–63; see Fig. 22.1).

The initial script also contains a scene in which the USA vs Italy theme takes a meta-cinematic turn. Mike and Lucia, by now lovers, enjoy a picnic in the countryside. Reflecting on their relationship, Mike comments on how being happy is almost an obligation for an American, promoted everywhere, from the constitution to songs and films. To which Lucia replies:

LUCIA: Yes, all the time, I see the American movies.
[*Mike gets up and moves where some donkeys are*]
MIKE (*hitching up his belt in true Western style*) Ma'am, I just rode into town to tell you I love you... me and my trusty horse (he pats the donkey) Shorty.

FIG. 22.1. *It Started in Naples*. Set photo: Mike (Clark Gable) teaches Nando (Marietto Angeletti) how to prepare and eat a hamburger. (Courtesy of Margaret Herrick Library.)

>   LUCIA (*Western*): Aw, shucks now... Is that right? Shucks?
>   (I333, shots 204–07, pp. 94–96)

The explicit discussion of European versus American attitudes is entirely removed by Cecchi d'Amico, and so is the abrupt move into the Western genre which implied a very improbable knowledge of the expression 'Aw, shucks' on the part of Lucia. Instead, Cecchi d'Amico introduces a new sequence which returns to the development of the adult-child relationship and has Mike organise a firework display in memory of Nando's father.

These few notes make it apparent that Suso Cecchi d'Amico's contribution to the script had two aims: to avoid too explicit a discussion of the cultural clash experienced by Mike and to add psychological depth to Mike's growing fondness for young Nando. After her modifications, however, Shavelson and Rose returned twice to the script in the weeks immediately preceding shooting in Naples and Capri. The return of incorrect forms in the few Italian expressions which were added makes it almost certain that these last two rounds of modifications were added without Cecchi d'Amico's involvement.[7]

I335, dated 22 July 1959, is simply a re-typed version of I334 and hence it can be immediately discarded. More importantly, I336 (3 August 1959) and I337 (14 August

1959) show that Shavelson and Rose, literally just before flying to Italy — shooting started on 18 August -, returned to the script with a number of relevant cuts and additions. In the first instance there was a reduction of the number of shots which went from 268 in I334 to 253 in I336. This was mainly the result of the cutting of a couple of secondary scenes which added little to the narrative. More importantly, I336 reinstated the 'pre-Cecchi d'Amico' dénouement of the key scene in which Mike tests Lucia's moral stature. In all versions Mike anonymously sends his hotel room key to Lucia together with some banknotes cut in half in order to trick Lucia into behaving like a prostitute. However, whereas in I333 Lucia played the game despite finding out about Mike's plan, in order to humiliate him when he turned up in his room, Cecchi d'Amico tried to avoid the ambiguity of having Lucia sensually lying on Mike's bed and suggested that Lucia's revenge should involve her asking a friend to go into Mike's room in her place so that she could just spy on Mike's behaviour. This change, present in I334, was removed and the script returned to the original ending in I336. In this case, it is possible that the rejection of Cecchi d'Amico's modification was due to the desire to keep Sophia Loren in the spotlight during the most sensual scene of the entire film (indeed, the image of Sophia Loren lying in Mike's bed was later used for one of the film's publicity posters). It might even be that this was done to accommodate a demand by Sophia Loren or by her agent and partner, producer Carlo Ponti. It was a mistake which is in many ways symbolic of the main weakness of the plot: Mike and Lucia are not particularly credible in their triple move from cynical and cold-hearted antagonists to lovers-for-fun to truly-in-love companions. In this particular case, the final version keeps Lucia in an ambiguous light since it allows one to think that, had Mike decided to consummate the deal, she would have welcomed it. Cecchi d'Amico tried to avoid this but, perhaps owing to external pressure, Shavelson and Rose decided otherwise. The possible link to Sophia Loren's screen presence is also suggested by another modification. This is the main change related to the final version of the script, I337. It takes the form of an appendix to the film's ending. Whereas previous versions finished in Naples railway station, with Mike deciding to step out of his train, rejoin Nando and symbolically drink with him from a public fountain (he had refused to do so at his arrival, at the start of the film), the final version added a scene in which Mike and Nando, back in Capri, joyfully rejoin Lucia.

Beyond our examination of Suso Cecchi d'Amico's contribution, such detailed analysis allows us to show the degree to which even a most typical Hollywood production was subject to a constant evolution of the script, up until the week before shooting began. Indeed, changes continued to be introduced even at the editing stage. The most important was to be the change of the narrative voice over at the start of the film: from Lucia's voice in I333, to no voice over in I334/6/7 to the voice of Mike inserted in the final editing (I338 Release Dialogue Script, dated 1 June 1960). Later on in this essay we will return to an interesting development related to this change.[8]

Fellini's American Counter-Dreams

If we now move on to some considerations of Fellini's *modus operandi* with regard to scriptwriting, we can begin by addressing another type of generalization often raised in relation to Italian auteur film and to Fellini in particular. The image of the film director as a polyvalent artist, in control of the many skills and stages involved in the making of a film, often tends to overshadow the contribution of other collaborators. In the case of Fellini, this brought the recurrent complaints of his co-scriptwriters, in particular Tullio Pinelli and Ennio Flaiano, constantly sidelined in favour of the myth — cultivated by Fellini himself — of the all-encompassing artistic genius of the director. A recent study by Federico Pacchioni has rightly addressed this issue, examining both the quantity and quality of the contribution to Fellini's films by the group of authors who accompanied him at various stages in his career.[9] In the case of Fellini, one should also bear in mind that his early experiences as a scriptwriter were of a collaborative nature and many took place under the aegis of Lux Film, Italy's production company which, more than any other, had adopted a Hollywood-studio type of approach to film production. It is within this context that Fellini had his first experience in working on two scripts entirely devoted to the meeting of Italian and U.S. culture.[10]

The two texts, which have both recently come to light, are *Napoli-New York*, deriving from an idea of the film director Gianni Franciolini, and *Happy Country*, based on a concept by the journalist Luigi Barzini. Together with Tullio Pinelli, in 1948 Fellini was asked by Lux Film to produce a fully-fledged treatment.[11] Strictly speaking, these two are not the only examples of Fellini's early encounter with U.S. culture. One could list other instances, from the collaboration with Rossellini in what we could call the postwar 'Ur-film' on Italy and the USA, *Paisà* (1946), to the scriptwriting of Lattuada's American *noir Senza pietà* (1948), to the use of Hollywood genre conventions in films by Pietro Germi such as *In nome della legge* (1949) and *Il cammino della speranza* (1950) to which Fellini contributed as a co-scriptwriter.[12] At the same time, *Napoli-New York* and *Happy Country* are the two works in which the meeting of Italian and U.S. culture are at the very centre of the narrative and, at least potentially, they could have become a symbolic sequel to *Paisà* set in the early postwar years. They both failed and no critical revaluation can redeem that. In the context of our essay, however, they are useful examples of a thematic approach to the topic which led to a number of generalisations and narrative *faux pas* which, ultimately, they share with Shavelson's *It Started in Naples*.

Napoli-New York tells the story of two Neapolitan children, Celestina and Carmine, who cross the Atlantic hiding in the bowels of a merchant ship. Once in New York, Celestina looks for her older sister, Agnese, who migrated in search of the U.S. soldier who promised to marry her. At the very same time, Agnese is in court being tried for the murder of the soldier. The two storylines become entangled and the happy ending sees Agnese being acquitted in the wake of the news that her little sister had tried to commit suicide in desperation. By working in tandem, Pinelli and Fellini (and the latter, according to the documentation, was the bigger contributor) produced a detailed treatment.

The Achilles heel of the story lies in the self-conscious attempt to redress the negative perception of Italians and Italian-Americans in the USA. The treatment insists on the cultural difference which makes Anglo-Saxon Americans hostile towards 'il travaglio di un popolo lontanissimo e malnoto'. Their sense of superiority is matched by their ignorance: 'non afferrano i passaggi psicologici, nati da tradizioni, convenzioni, ambienti "esotici" e "inferiori"'.[13] The reference to 'ambienti "esotici"' is worth expanding. In fact, the weakness of this treatment lies in its 'exoticisation' — or, better, 'orientalisation' — of Neapolitans. The authors move the negative stereotype into a positive one based on the praise of a presumed candour and genuineness of Italians: in the end Celestina and Carmine become a sort of Rousseauesque *bons sauvages*, that is, their diversity is not negated, it is simply reinstated in a positive light.

There is, after all, a similar process at play in Shavelson's *It Started in Naples*. Lucia and her people represent a less civilised society, earthy, irrational, sentimental: there is no meeting between the two cultures, one of the two has to succumb to the other. If in *Napoli–New York* it was U.S. society which eventually accepted and praised the values of Italianness, in *It Started in Naples* it is Mike who eventually rejects his 'Americanness'. Very symbolically, in the final scene, when he decides to get off the train to rejoin Nando, Mike rejects the company of three compatriots in the compartment by refusing even to speak English with them. 'No spikka da English', he exclaims, his process of Italianisation now complete.

The same happens in the second script, *Happy Country*. Here the setting moves to a village in Tuscany, where an American oil company has decided to buy the rights to exploit the presence of crude oil in the area. Once again, the clash between the two cultures brings the defeat of one of the two. U.S. technology and pragmatism, impersonated by the engineer Robert Leonard, clash with the humanist values and humble customs of all locals, whether poor peasants or country gentry. If *Napoli–New York* attempted a revaluation of Neapolitans, *Happy Country* states the superiority of Tuscan humanism. Once again, America loses: Robert falls in love with the beautiful and cultured daughter of the local aristocrat and by the end his conversion to Italy's culture, similarly to Mike's, is total. A change of clothing is key to this: where, back in Capri, Mike asked Lucia to take his tie off, in Tuscany Robert appears in the final scene holding Fernanda's hand, happily dressed as a local farmer: 'in tenuta da agricoltore (stivaloni e giacca di velluto)' (p. 96).

In other words, in both 1948 scripts Fellini and Pinelli failed to convey a convincing narrative of the encounter of U.S. and Italian culture because in both cases they simply aimed at defending a pre-packaged, two-dimensional idea of Italian identity. The sophistication of Rossellini's episodes of *Paisà* — from the meeting of GIs with a Sicilian girl, to the meeting of different religions and mindsets in the monastery episode (entirely rewritten by Fellini), to the common deadly destiny in the final episode — are abandoned in lieu of a stylised, dualistic vision. In *Napoli-New York*, Fellini and Pinelli even tried to create a meta-cinematic bridge with Rossellini's film: whilst wondering alone through the streets of New York, Celestina enters a cinema attracted by the sight of a familiar expression dominating the posters,

Paisà. She then enters and watches the film unable to restrain her feelings, shouting 'Napule!... Chist'è Napule!...' (p. 137). Distraught and nostalgic, Celestina leaves the cinema and attempts to commit suicide by jumping into a canal (p. 140). It is difficult to imagine how such a scene could have been turned into a convincing and memorable piece of filmmaking.

Cars, Drinks, Babes and Rock'n'Roll

About a decade later, Fellini returned to the subject or, rather, with *La dolce vita* he attempted a more ambitious project: to represent Italian society in all the apparent glory of its new-found wealth. It is not a film about the encounter of Italian and U.S. culture. However, I would argue that *La dolce vita* convincingly represents the degree to which Italian society had absorbed U.S. culture by the late 1950s. The fact that this is not at the centre of the film's narrative is perhaps a blessing in disguise: Fellini and his team of co-scriptwriters (this time with Ennio Flaiano in the role of main collaborator) did not have to create an entire script around this phenomenon and hence there are no thematic simplifications such as those present in the two early scripts, nor defensive representations such as that of Steno's *Un americano a Roma* which only makes fun of the protagonist's infatuation with American culture. At the same time, in a more indirect way, the new Italy which noisily invades the screen in *La dolce vita* ends up revealing the extent to which Italy's modernity in the 1950s was deeply shaped by the USA as a cultural model. In this brief survey, Shavelson's *It Started in Naples* will provide a useful point of comparison.

Let us start with one of the status symbols of the 1950s: automobiles. When Suso Cecchi d'Amico was working on adding depth to *It Started in Naples*, she introduced a whole new scene concerning cars. When Mike meets his Italian lawyer, Mario Vitali (played by De Sica), the initial script had the two meet in the cemetery where Mike's brother is buried. Instead, Cecchi d'Amico decided to move the scene to Naples's crowded railway station: there, Mike's fears of being robbed are immediately tested plus the cultural clash is given an extra twist with the scene of Mike receiving a lift from Vitali in his miniscule Fiat 500 Topolino. It is a clever solution which adds a comic touch and at the same time provides a visual clue to Mike's culture shock (Fig. 22.2). Car enthusiasts could accuse Cecchi d'Amico of an anachronism: by 1959, the Fiat Topolino, built since 1936, had retired (production stopped in 1955). On the other hand, the car closely associated with the 'boom economico' is the more modern-looking Fiat 600 (produced in 1955–1969) which we briefly see in shot. It is an anachronism which serves the purpose of making the difference between Italy and the USA look even greater.[14]

In *La dolce vita*, from the very first shot, modernity is associated with U.S. technology. The iconic plexiglass bubble canopy of the helicopter carrying the statue of the Christ is that of a Bell 47G, a U.S. helicopter which had its baptism of fire during the Korean War (1950–53) and was later built under licence in Britain, Italy and Japan. Equally striking is the appearance of the first car outside the nightclub, owned by rich socialite Maddalena. It is a Cadillac Eldorado Brougham, whose size and shape immediately sets it apart from the rest. When Maddalena and

'SENTI 'N PO', A GREGORI PÈCCHE... 339

FIG. 22.2. *It Started in Naples*. Set photo: Mike (Clark Gable) tries to squeeze into the Fiat car of his lawyer (Vittorio De Sica) and his assistant (Giovanni Filidoro).
(Courtesy of Margaret Herrick Library.)

FIG. 22.3. *La dolce vita*. Film still: the prostitute and her pimp wait for Maddalena and Marcello to reappear whilst standing next to Maddalena's Cadillac.
(Courtesy of Cineteca di Bologna.)

Marcello use it to give a lift to a prostitute, the latter is excited and at the same time ironic: it is here that she addresses Marcello in Roman dialect, teasingly calling him 'a Gregori Pècche'. The luxurious car is alien and at the same time familiar to her. And similarly her pimp is unimpressed, only interested in squeezing as much money as possible from the couple (Fig. 22.3). The American car, in other words, is a symbol of wealth and privilege but it is not 'foreign': it simply represents the highest form of prosperity in a city — and by extension in a country– where poor and rich live side by side.[15]

When sitting in the Cadillac, Marcello is equally cool about such a show of foreign luxury. He too drives a foreign car. It's not American, though. It is the TR3 sports car of British car maker Triumph. I am certainly not intending to try and offer an overstretched interpretation of this detail as cryptically conveying Marcello's failed attempt to rival his rich, U.S.-equipped friends. At the same time, it is an intriguing detail if we consider a variant in earlier versions of the script: when Marcello meets his father in the Via Veneto, he begins to boast about the relative wealth afforded by his job as a journalist. This is how he tells his father about it:

> MARCELLO: Sai... il giornalismo... se uno è in gamba... può rendere molto... Io ho anche avuto una certa fortuna... Conosco tutti... se c'è qualche servizio importante, lo affidano a me... entro dappertutto, ai ministeri, in Vaticano... Mi sono già fatto la macchina... Americana..., l'appartamento... grande di lusso...[16]

Adding 'Americana' to the description of his new car was certainly a way to add glamour and a superior air to his new lifestyle. We do not know why Fellini eventually settled for a British spider (I am inclined to think that it was due to the atypically low cut of the car doors, which allowed an ample view of the overflowing beauty of Anita Ekberg). The result is that, in that scene, Mastroianni eventually resorts to a modified line, saying 'Mi sono già fatto la macchina... eccola là...'. Gone is the reference to American cars. But only in relation to Marcello. When Silvia lands at Rome airport, the chaotic car cavalcade which follows, taking her to the hotel where she meets the press, is spectacularly led by a U.S. Ford Fairlane monumentally leading a noisy convoy of Italian Fiats, Lancias and Vespas. More cryptically, in the sequence of the miraculous appearance of the Madonna (the only one which was entirely bolted on to the script by Fellini only a few days before shooting started), when Marcello arrives in his car at the squalid location, he is closely followed by a big U.S. car, this time a white Ford Thunderbird. When the two cars stop, the camera concentrates on Marcello, but in the background one can see a uniformed driver and his aide helping an old man and a woman out from the back seats of the luxurious Ford. It is a detail which is secondary but its effect is similar to that of Maddalena's Cadillac parked outside the prostitute's house. Rome is a city where extremes meet: everybody, rich and poor come to see the alleged miracle. Furthermore, the cryptic presence of the Ford Thunderbird acquires more sense if one pays attention to the last sequence of the film. Another car cavalcade, this time at night and at high speed, opens the first scene of the orgy sequence. Once again, a big U.S. car leads the lot and this time it is a Ford Thunderbird. More interestingly, it is the same white Thunderbird which we saw at the 'prato del miracolo'. This opens the field to possible interpretations. In my view, the car acts as the connecting point between two very different situations, pointing to a sense of moral confusion, if not hypocrisy, amongst Italy's establishment: devout during the day and dissolute at night.[17] One could argue that the ethical contradictions being described in *La dolce vita* are part and parcel of Italy's conversion to U.S. consumeristic materialism, hence the constant presence of American cars as a clear indicator of the source of all problems. This would be in tune with Pio Baldelli's interpretation of Fellini's vision as being ultimately nostalgic for his Catholic childhood.[18] At the same time, Baldelli is careful to point out that Fellini's vision contains little of the more direct and political denunciation of, say, the films of Francesco Rosi of those very years. Italy's newly-found wealth and moral conflicts are presented as a *fait accompli*, and the 'American' feel is their tale-telling trait.

Another indicator of Italy's changing habits is related to drinks. In Shavelson's *It Started in Naples*, this is given a heavy-handed treatment through an entire scene during which Mike and Lucia try to get the other one drunk by way of a cocktail of their own concoction. The duel turns into a sort of national competition whereby Mike orders a Kentucky Bourbon-based drink to which Lucia responds with a Cinzano-based one. The two bottles in clear display and a U.S.A. and an Italian flag in each of the glasses add evident signposting for the benefit of the more inattentive viewer. Throughout the film, wine is also presented as the typically Italian drink as opposed to Whiskey. Interestingly enough, this is something that happens in a similar way in the 1948 script of *Happy Country*: when Robert arrives in Tuscany he enters a local inn and orders some Whiskey, only to be served wine (p. 52). Fellini's approach in *La dolce vita*, whilst using the same paradigm, is subtler. This takes us back to the episode of the unannounced visit by Marcello's father. Whilst waiting for his son in an overcrowded bar on Via Veneto, we are made to understand that the father had ordered a beer for himself. Marcello's arrival immediately brings a breeze of American glamour in his wake. He asks his father if he wants another drink and suggests they have 'un Gin Fizz', a typical U.S. cocktail. The father's unfamiliarity is comically portrayed with his reply delivered in clear Romagnolo accent: 'Un Gin Fritz? Ma che Gin Fritz! La mia birra è ottima'. The 'Americanised' drinking habits of Marcello and his friends are subtly reiterated later on in the same sequence. Accompanied by Paparazzo, father and son end up in a night club which the father fondly remembers from his visits in the pre-war years. But times have changed. Marcello had already described it as 'un locale vecchio', and when they enter it, Paparazzo looks around in dismay and adds: 'Non ti pare una tomba?'. Here again, subtly, the same metonymy related to drinks is suggested: when they arrive, Marcello takes the initiative and proposes to order his father a glass of Whiskey. Excited by the sight of the half-naked ballerinas, the father this time cuts the conversation short and accepts the offer. However, with the second round of cabaret dancing, now with girls dressed in 1920s clothes, the American influence is replaced by the presence of the old icon of wealth and glamour in the Italian mind: Paris. First the father reminisces about his trips to Paris, and his visit to similar cabarets. Then Marcello recognizes one of the dancers, Fanny, who happens to be French.

When Fanny approaches the small group at the table, Marcello's father excitedly delivers some compliments in French, after which he decides to order a bottle of champagne. Paparazzo immediately disapproves but Marcello, who has decided to try and help his father relive his youth, silences Paparazzo. The father at that point mentions his intention to order one of the best, a Veuve Cliquot, to which Paparazzo replies with a sardonic smile and invites him to drink his Whiskey. 'Intanto beva questo', he says, the bottle of Black and White well in view on the table. And when eventually the French dancer turns up with a bottle of champagne and Paparazzo tries to open it, Marcello's father takes it off his hands saying: 'Cosa fa? No, no; può adoperare la sua abilità con la Coca Cola, ma lo champagne è roba mia'. In other words, within this sequence, so often praised by critics for its elegiac tones related to Marcello's ageing father, Fellini also manages to give visual form to Italy's former and present cultural models. The sophisticated Paris of the early twentieth century has been replaced by high-tech America, with its big cars and fancy drinks. Here we certainly see no intention to give a moral lesson: Italy has simply changed, and the lure of France of the interwar years has been replaced by that of the USA.

When it comes to female beauty, the representation acquires a meta-cinematic quality. Photographs and films are the modern means through which ideas and models of beauty are forged and disseminated. Hollywood and its star system immediately come to mind as the Western world's most influential factory of images of beauty. However, as suggested earlier, the 1950s are years during which the Italian film industry seemed to be competing with Hollywood, promoting its own images of female beauty. *It Started in Naples* is a good example of Hollywood buying into the Italian model.

Already by the early 1950s, Italian stars such as Rossana Podestà and Gina Lollobrigida were trying to establish themselves in the over-glamourized world of Hollywood. In February 1954, when the U.S. magazine *Cosmopolitan* decided to devote a long feature article on emerging Italian actresses, the chosen headline was: 'Italian Stars: Sex Without Glamour'. According to the author, the common characteristic of Italian actresses was their being sensual and yet unsophisticated beauties.[19] Some of them had crossed the Atlantic in order to foster their international career — Alida Valli blazing a trail — others were making use of the opportunities offered by U.S. runaway productions set in Italy. Indeed, together with the growth of the Italian film industry, the 1950s saw the arrival of the so-called 'Hollywood on the Tiber', a period during which U.S. studios began to invest in productions filmed abroad. Italy, or rather Rome, with its studios and picturesque locations, became their first choice (beating Britain into second place already in 1950).[20] Sophia Loren, thanks also to Carlo Ponti's managerial abilities, became the most successful star, managing to land a multi-film contract with Paramount of which *It Started in Naples* was to be the last one.[21]

One can certainly question *Cosmopolitan*'s definition of Italian female stars but there is no doubt that the type of the beautiful working-class woman, sensual and roughly-educated, was a recurrent one. Sophia Loren's 'American' debut took place in 1950, with a non-speaking part as a slave girl in the runaway blockbuster *Quo Vadis*, and she again played the part of the slave in her first film as a co-protagonist, in Clemente Fracassi's *Aida* (1953). But the film which launched her career and image is De Sica's *The Gold of Naples* (*L'oro di Napoli*, 1954; released in the USA in 1957) in which she played the part of an exuberant 'pizzaiola'. Paramount developed the image without moving too far from those confines: from the equally sexy Italian housemaid in *Houseboat* (1958), to the wild west singer of *Heller in Pink Tights* (1960), Loren's characters would often rotate around the uneducated, salt-of-the-earth persona, and it is in that part that she was to achieve her Academy and Cannes awards as Best Actress for *Two Women* (*La ciociara*, 1960).

The character of the beautiful but penniless nightclub singer Lucia Curcio in *It Started in Naples* complied with the model. However, within the boundaries of this essay, what makes this character particularly interesting is her central role in the film's narrative of Italian *joie de vivre* triumphing against American cold-heartedness. The scene already mentioned, in which Lucia faces Mike's bourbon-based cocktail with a bottle of Cinzano and an Italian flag, makes it clear that her character symbolically stands for the entire Italian people. From the very start of the film, Mike's fears of being swindled concentrate on her. The prejudiced vision of Italy as a country of fraudsters and petty criminals is introduced by Mike's voiceover comments during the establishing shots taking us from the credits to the first sequence of the film. He reminisces about his former visit to Naples as a soldier in the 5th Army and his memories of flirting with the local beauties is mixed with his other experiences: 'The Neapolitans cheered us all the way up from the beachhead. Half an hour later they were selling our gasoline on the black market. And those kids on the street: scrounging cigarettes, swiping k-rations'. Incidentally, and amusingly so, in the Italian dubbed version of the film, Mike's denigrating comments are replaced with the following words: 'I napoletani ci accolsero col più grande entusiasmo e con la gioviale vivacità che avevano conservato nonostante gli innumerevoli bombardamenti subiti e la fame sofferta'. The decision to avoid a translation of the original is an interesting example of what one could call 'script adjustment to a different national audience'.[22] After his comments on children, however, Mike's attention concentrates on two young women on the station platform and here he delivers another sneering memory about an older sister of theirs probably having stolen his good conduct medal.[23] Unsurprisingly, when Mike first meets Lucia, dressed up as a queen for a folk pageant (embodying a persona which she tries to convince him reflects her personal wealth), he is immediately suspicious of her. The ideological backbone of the rest of the film rests entirely on Lucia's mission to change Mike's mind. In the end, she is successful but, one should add, despite being Italian. What is meant by this is that the many prejudices about Italians — being a cunning, ragged people always ready to improvise and lie to serve their interests — are not questioned. Lucia manages to convince Mike that she is a good substitute-mother, a good lover and a good prospective companion, but all the prejudices with which Mike returned to Naples remain true to him. What we witness is simply an orientalising conversion by an educated white Anglo-Saxon man to a foreign country whose simplicity and Rousseauesque primitivism appears a radical alternative to a supposedly cold-hearted American life.[24]

With Fellini's *La dolce vita*, the first image which comes to mind is that of Sylvia who spectacularly enters the narrative with her arrival at Rome's airport. She is presented as the ultimate Hollywood diva, very much reflecting the status and biographical traits of the actress impersonating her: Sylvia is Swedish like the real Anita Ekberg, as much as the other Hollywood icon of the 1950s, Ingrid Bergman, and the script immediately makes it clear that she should be seen as part of a more general idea of American-made glamour. When, provocatively dressed as a nun, Sylvia reaches the top of St Peter's dome, she happily comments: 'This is the right way to lose weight. I must remember to tell Marilyn'. The reference to Marilyn Monroe confirms Sylvia as the impersonation of a Hollywood beauty.[25] Marcello's girlfriend, the Italian brunette played by (French) actress Yvonne Furneaux is no contest. Emma is beautiful and sensual but she has none of the positive qualities with which stars like Sophia Loren could win the day: she is maniacally jealous, over-caring and irrational. However, Fellini's representation of the triumphant Hollywood star is far from simplistic.

First of all her presence only lasts the length of one sequence. Her persona is not part of the film's narrative backbone as one could have expected or might later misremember. Moreover, Sylvia's goddess-like status is questioned throughout the sequence. When she exits the Douglas DC-4 airliner in all her glamorous self, the mask drops momentarily when the photographers ask her to take her glasses off. For a second, her smiling composure is replaced by the annoyed gesture of a spoiled child. Later on, despite Marcello's infatuation, her faultless image is eroded again and again: at the top of St Peter's she mistakes Rome for Florence; her husband is an alcoholic; her empathetic attraction to the animal world is shallow (she forgets about the cat as soon as she sees the Trevi fountain), and her only reaction when slapped in the face by her husband is to say: 'You shouldn't do things like that, particularly in front of people'. On a more comic note, the end of the Trevi fountain scene, with the water being turned off at the very moment Marcello and Sylvia are about to kiss, brings back to earth her beatification as the perfect dream woman. Within the overall structure of the film, Sylvia or, better, Marcello's fruitless encounter with Sylvia, becomes the second 'cerchio' of his descent into the hell of his personal crisis. Does this allow us to suggest that Marcello's existential predicament is linked to the 'Americanization' of Italian society? This would be too crude an interpretation; however, there is no doubt that images of modernity, beauty and wealth recurrently come to Marcello — and are owned by him, like his drinking habits, or are dreamt of, as with Sylvia — through U.S. cultural models.

Sound brings us to the last of our thematic wanderings. Those who remember only a few snippets of *It Started in Naples* are likely to have Sophia Loren's nightclub singing performance in the front of their minds. In the entire film she sings three times, and twice the same song: 'Tu vuo' fa' l'americano'. Once again, Shavelson did not tread lightly on symbolism. Whereas the other song, 'Carina', is a musical vehicle for Loren to engage in a sensual dance which is part of her seduction of

FIG. 22.4. *It Started in Naples*. Set photo: Lucia (Sophia Loren) sings *Tu vuo' fa' l'americano* accompanied by guitarist Renzo (Paolo Carlini). (Courtesy of Margaret Herrick Library.)

FIG. 22.5. *La dolce vita*. Film still: Adriano (Adriano Celentano) singing *Ready Teddy* the moment before he slips and falls to the ground. Sylvia (Anita Ekberg) and Frankie (Alain Dijon) are visible to the right. (Courtesy of Cineteca di Bologna.)

Mike, the popular Italian song on wannabe-Americans is part and parcel of the film's representation of the Italy vs USA battle. Composed in 1956 by Renato Carosone, 'Tu vuo' fa' l'americano' is a song which two years later was associated with a film featuring Neapolitan comedian Totò: *Totò, Peppino e le fanatiche*, directed by Mario Mattoli. In tune with the song, Mattoli's film develops an anti-consumeristic/anti-Americanization theme, with the male protagonists' complaints condensed in three by then unusual English expressions: camping, weekend, hobby. Despite the collaboration of two renowned authors — Steno and Age — the film's lack of originality and taste touches its lowest point when the two male protagonists fail to bed two German tourists because of the 'American' tranquillizers their wives had given to them.

In *It Started in Naples*, Carosone's song becomes the music score of Lucia's decision to reject the 'Americanization' offered by Mike. She sings it first in English at the nightclub (Fig. 22.4) and then, later on, she sings it in Italian, dancing with Nando, celebrating their winning the court case against Mike. The diegetic function of the song is clarified by Lucia's line before she starts singing: 'Can you imagine? He wanted you to go to America and become an American, like in the song'. Once again, it is a battle between two different lifestyles: you are either American or Italian.

In *La dolce vita* we have no such close, mechanical correlation between music score and narrative. However, Italy's new 'Americanized' culture is present through sound too. Despite appearances, and as shown by an in-depth study of the film's soundtrack, the music score works on the repetition of a limited number of motifs, mainly composed by Nino Rota.[26] In our case, there is a specific scene which deserves careful attention. This is Sylvia's bacchanal dance at the ruins of Caracalla. The scene begins with a medium shot of a black saxophonist playing the melody of *Arrivederci Roma*. Subtly, we are already placed in Italian/American cinematic territory: this is the song which gave the title in the Italian release to the 1957 U.S.-Italian co-production *Seven Hills of Rome* starring the Italian-American tenor Mario Lanza. It is a typically Italian melodious song (it was composed by Italian comedian, Renato Rascel) which Marcello seems at ease with, hence he continues his courtship of Sylvia. However, Marcello's plans are disrupted by the arrival of Frankie, a Hollywood actor in town for the shooting of another film. Under his instructions, the band begins to play a cha-cha (composed by Nino Rota) which contains a parody of the Italian military tune Marcia dei Bersaglieri. Here Marcello begins to lose control, unable to fight back Frankie's animalistic energy. But it is the following song, loudly requested by a group of people shouting 'vogliamo il Rock'n'roll!' which takes us to the core of Italy's 'Americanization'. A then unknown young singer, Adriano Celentano, steps on to the stage, grabs the microphone and sings the iconic 1956 rock'n'roll number *Ready Teddy*, originally sung by Little Richard and most famously by Elvis Presley. What English-speaking listeners to the song will immediately notice is the fact that Celentano does not reproduce the original lyrics nor seems able to add any sense to his mumbling sounds. He is pretending to speak English whilst simply babbling a meaningless phonetic near-equivalent of the original.[27] Adriano Celentano, in other words, seems to embody

Italy's aspiration to absorb the U.S. model. It is an aspiration which is shown to be as energetic and inspiring as at the same time ridiculous. The latter is suggested not just by Celentano's linguistic limitations but also by his incapacity to complete a flawless performance. Half way through the song he steps off stage, loses balance and falls flat on the floor. Sylvia kindly comes to his rescue and from then on she takes over and leads the second part of the song (Fig. 22.5).

The choice of Adriano Celentano took place following the suggestion of Fellini's friend and biographer, Tullio Kezich, who had seen Celentano perform in Milan. No doubt they were well aware of the singer's use of mock-English.[28] Once again, the connection with U.S. culture is presented as a recurrent feature of 1950s Italy, and at the same time Fellini seems to point indirectly at the flaws of this enthusiastic absorption of foreign mannerisms.

Conclusion

The comparison between the work of Shavelson and Fellini has provided the opportunity to observe opposite extremes in the representation of the encounter between two cultures during the very same period. As suggested earlier, in *It Started in Naples* the two worlds of Italian and U.S. society meet in Naples with the arrival of Mike, but the Italy that Mike meets seems free from any U.S. influence. If nothing else it is fighting to resist it, hence its only presence in the song *Tu vuo' fa' l'americano* which is used to ridicule the idea of an 'Americanised' Italian. This attitude is embodied first and foremost in the character of Nando. Given his family background — U.S. father, Italian mother — he could have been the ideal vehicle for an image of the fusion of the two cultures. Instead, his character is a familiar one to an Italian and foreign audience: he is presented as the typical 'sgugnizzo', the little boy grown up too early, acting like an adult in a world where school has been replaced by the law of the street. His only non-Italian trait is the fact that he speaks good English.[29] Nando has very good memories of his U.S. father, whom he has idealised, but his personality and manners reveals no trace of it. Overall, one could suggest that, apart from the scriptwriters' lack of interest in — and probably little knowledge of — of Italian culture in the 1950s, the cultural clash is so central to the status of *It Started in Naples* as a comedy that it has to be maintained as such. Mike's final conversion to 'Italianness' is a sudden change of heart, literally, which moves him from one side to the other of the invisible fence dividing the two cultures. Suso Cecchi d'Amico's attempts to add a more nuanced treatment of this theme ultimately failed. I would not go as far as to suggest that this is at the root of the film's relative lack of success. Good comedy does not necessarily need good social insight (although that is what might make it memorable). As already mentioned, the film ultimately fails in building a convincing love story between the two protagonists, despite flawless performances by Sophia Loren and Clark Gable.

As we have seen, Fellini's early scripts dealing with Italian and U.S. culture were equally unsuccessful. *La dolce vita*, however, is a film which has left memorable impressions on critics and audiences around the world for a whole series of good and bad reasons. The aim of this essay is not to comment upon this, apart from the caveat that, in any case, it is not my intention to present *La dolce vita* as an example of auteur cinema's superiority over Hollywood superficiality.[30] If *It Started in Naples* presents us with a story of the existential conversion of a U.S. American to an allegedly simpler but more genuine foreign culture, *La dolce vita* offers us a story of the existential crisis of an Italian in a society which has absorbed a lifestyle mimicking U.S. values. In the film there is no discussion regarding this, not even at the intellectuals' party in Steiner's house, which could have provided a platform for such meta-thematic conversation. Moreover, differently from the archival clarity behind the scripting of *It All Started in Naples*, with *La dolce vita* we have only a vague idea of the individual contribution of each of the three main authors of the script — Fellini, Flaiano and Pinelli.[31] I would argue, however, that the social critique present in the film derives mainly from the cynical eye of Ennio Flaiano. Other instances in his own writings of the period reveal his critique of consumerism as a U.S.-derived trait of 1950s Italy.[32] At the same time, Flaiano's sardonic view is tempered on the one hand by Pinelli's interest in the spiritual dimension of Italy's changing nature, and on the other by Fellini's joyful tolerance for all the contradictions and foibles of human nature. The key perhaps lies in the words of the prostitute when she mocks Marcello, calling him 'a Gregori Pècche'. Marcello is not the ridiculous Nando Moriconi of Steno's *Un americano a Roma*. But, still, the prostitute thinks he is somebody who 'wants to be an American': glamorous, cool and handsome like a Hollywood star. The difference is that whereas Moriconi was an isolated village idiot, *La dolce vita* presents us with an entire society which is living the dream, with Marcello as its foremost example. When mentioning U.S. culture, Fellini as much as other intellectuals of his generation such as Italo Calvino and Ferdinanda Pivano suggested the extent to which, during their youth under Fascism, the idea of 'America' loomed large in their mind and implied a world of freedom and fantasy enthusiastically derived from novels, comics and Hollywood films.[33] The 1950s are the years in which an entire generation seemed to be given the chance to create that world within the old walls of their own nation. The Italy following the 1948 general elections, the Italy of the Marshall Plan, of the first car, television, fridge and washing machine for every family, was an Italy inebriated by its 'American dream come true'. *La dolce vita* is a resonant, compelling acknowledgment of that.

Notes to Chapter 22

1. See for example *Mal d'America. Da mito a realtà*, ed. by Ugo Rubeo (Rome: Editori Riuniti, 1987); *Nemici per la pelle: sogno americano e mito sovietico nell'Italia contemporanea*, ed. by Pier Paolo D'Attorre (Milan: Angeli, 1991); Stephen Gundle, *I comunisti italiani tra Hollywood e Mosca: La sfida della cultura di massa: 1943–1992* (Florence: Giunti, 1995); Daniela Rossini, *Il mito americano nell'Italia della Grande Guerra* (Rome-Bari: Laterza, 2000); Massimo Teodori, *Maledetti americani. Destra, sinistra e cattolici: storia del pregiudizio antiamericano* (Milan: Mondadori, 2002); Pietro Craveri and Gaetano Quagliariello (eds), *L'antiamericanismo in Italia e in Europa nel secondo dopoguerra* (Soveria Manelli: Rubbettino, 2004); Victoria De Grazia, *Irresistible Empire: America's Advance Through 20th Century Europe* (Cambridge, MA: Harvard University Press, 2005).
2. See in particular David W. Ellwood, *Rebuilding Europe: The U.S. and the Reconstruction of Western Europe* (London: Longman, 1992); and *The Shock of America: Europe and the Challenge of the Century* (Oxford: Oxford University Press, 2012).

3. See Ellwood, *The Shock of America*, pp. 416–17, and his close analysis of Steno's film: '*Un americano a Roma*: A 1950s Satire of Americanization', *Modern Italy*, 1.2 (1996), pp. 93–102.
4. The report by Allida Allen is dated 7 August 1957; in Paramount Pictures Production Records: Scripts, file I-331: 'Song of Capri' (Margaret Herrick Library, Los Angeles; from now on abbreviated as MHL). In his biography of Clark Gable, David Bret suggests that this initial treatment meant to involve Gracie Fields, the famous British singer and actress who lived in Capri at the time. The choice of a musical makes this suggestion credible although Bret is mistaken in suggesting that it was still part of Jack Rose's and Melville Shavelson's later project. David Bret, *Clark Gable: Tormented Soul* (London: Aurum Press, 2014), p. 240.
5. According to Paramount's records, Suso Cecchi d'Amico was paid a flat fee of $6,400 (then 4 million Lira) for her contribution to the script. Interestingly, the contract specified that Cecchi d'Amico's role was not going to be acknowledged in the credits and publicity for the film in its Italian release. Indeed, all publicity related to *La baia di Napoli* made no mention of Suso Cecchi d'Amico (see: MHL, Paramount Picture Production Records: Costs, 66 'It Started in Naples', file 8). A comparison with *La dolce vita*, also provides an idea of the generosity of Hollywood productions. Ennio Flaiano, whose role as co-scriptwriter was enormously more intensive than that of Suso Cecchi D'Amico, received 2 million Lira for his treatment of the film and another 2.5 million Lira for his contribution to the script. Flaiano's contract, dated 30 July 1958, is held in the Archivio Prezzolini at the Biblioteca comunale di Lugano (from now abbreviated as APL), Fondo Flaiano, 2.3 Materiale cinematografico: Contratti 52.1 Una bella vita (1958).
6. Script no. 333, dated 1 May 1959, is attributed to Shavelson and Rose; Script 334, dated 11 July 1959, is attributed to Shavelson, Rose and Cecchi d'Amico. Both scripts are held at MHL, Paramount Pictures Production Records: The scripts are registered as respectively I333 and I334 under the then working title 'Bay of Naples'. The more sophisticated grammatical accuracy of the few Italian quotes in I334 confirms the fact that it was revised by an Italian native speaker.
7. Unfortunately Suso Cecchi d'Amico's personal papers and correspondence do not contain material which might help shed more light on the making of this script. In her published conversations with her granddaughter she makes only passing reference to the film, defining it as 'bruttissimo' and simply adding that her role was of 'soltanto un lavoro di revisione'; see Suso Cecchi d'Amico, *Storie di cinema (e d'altro) raccontate a Margherita d'Amico* (Milan: Garzanti, 1996), p. 208. I am grateful to Masolino d'Amico for looking into his mother's personal papers in search of references to the production of *It Started in Naples*.
8. The expression 'too many cooks' used in the title of this section refers to a review of the film which identified the lack of coherence in the protagonists' plotline and attributed it to a script which had been worked on by too many hands. Lowell E. Redelings, 'It Started in Naples', in *Hollywood Citizen-News*, 22 September 1960, p. 15.
9. Federico Pacchioni, *Inspiring Fellini: Literary Collaborations Behind the Scenes* (Toronto: University of Toronto Press, 2014).
10. Given what I just wrote about collaborative work, one should immediately add a caveat: in both cases, the film concept was penned by somebody else and Fellini was one of the two authors who developed them. We should therefore be careful before discussing these texts as a Fellini-only product. They are, however, very indicative of the cultural milieu in which Fellini was working.
11. Federico Fellini and Tullio Pinelli, 'Happy Country (Paese felice)', ed. and trans. by Federico Pacchioni and Peter Bondanella, in *Fellini Amarcord*, 1–2 (October 2006), pp. 49–148. Federico Fellini and Tullio Pinelli, *Napoli–New York*, ed. by Augusto Sainati (Venice: Marsilio, 2013). I am grateful to Peter Bondanella for pointing me in the direction of these two works.
12. See Peter Bondanella, 'Fellini e le sceneggiature "americane": Paisà, Senza pietà, Happy Country', in Massimiliano Filippini and Vittorio Ferorelli (eds), *Federico Fellini autore di testi* (Bologna: Istituto per i Beni Artistici, Culturali e Naturali della Regione Emilia-Romagna, 1999), pp. 153–67.
13. All quotes are in Fellini and Pinelli, *Napoli–New York*, p. 138.
14. A similar convention was used by Fellini and Pinelli in *Happy Country*: Robert, the American engineer, leaves his country in a big U.S. airliner, then, in Italy, moves to a train, then to a

crowded bus and eventually to an old van which is what he is left with in order to reach the Tuscan village (pp. 50–54).

15. With regard to this, it is interesting to note that in a letter by Flaiano to the producer Dino De Laurentis, of 8 May 1957, when discussing the plotline of a treatment he was going to offer — the story of two young women who arrive in Montecarlo in search of a rich foreign man and instead end up with two Italians — he recapped it as follows: 'Finiscono insomma, dalla Cadillac tutta d'oro alla [Fiat] 600 per famiglia, un po' rimpiangendo la loro decisione ma poi consolandosi.'; in Anna Longoni and Diana Ruesch (eds), *Soltanto le parole. Lettere di e a Ennio Flaiano* (Milan: Bompiani, 1996), p. 136. Incidentally, the extra-diegetic song accompanying Maddalena's and Marcello's meeting with the prostitute is a jazzy song composed by Nino Rota entitled *Cadillac*. See Thomas Van Order, *Listening to Fellini: Music and Meaning in Black and White* (Madison: Farleigh Dickinson Press, 2009), p. 104.
16. This dialogue appears in two earlier versions of the script. One is to be found amongst the papers of Ennio Flaiano (held at APL, Fondo Flaiano, 52.III Sceneggiatura di Ennio Flaiano, 'La dolce vita' (1959), seq. 4, scena 9). The other, different in other details from the previous one but not in this passage, is the script published in Federico Fellini, *Quattro film* (Turin: Einaudi, 1974), p. 237. The latter publication is regrettably entirely devoid of any form of editorial notes, not even to suggest the origin and timing of the script, despite its evident differences from the film's final cut.
17. We should not forget that the social milieu represented in *La dolce vita*, particularly in the final sequence, was inspired by a renowned murder case in morally dubious circumstances, involving the son of a Christian Democrat minister. I am referring to the death of Wilma Montesi, found dead on a beach near Rome on 9 April 1953. On this see Stephen Gundle, *Death and the Dolce Vita: The Dark Side of Rome in the 1950s* (Edinburgh: Canongate, 2011).
18. I am referring to Pio Baldelli's long essay 'Dilatazione visionaria del documento e nostalgia della Madre Chiesa in Fellini', in Pio Baldelli, *Cinema dell'ambiguità: Rossellini, De Sica-Zavattini, Fellini* (Rome: Samonà e Savelli, 1969), pp. 285–379.
19. Alan D'Alessandro, 'Italian Stars — Sex Without Glamour', *Cosmopolitan*, February 1954, pp. 44–60.
20. As reported by the film industry paper *Hollywood Reporter*: Anonymous, 'Italy Runner-Up to Hollywood in Film Production', *Hollywood Reporter*, 15 June 1950, p. 12.
21. On Sophia Loren's multi-film contract with Paramount see Pauline Small, *Sophia Loren: Moulding the Star* (Bristol: Intellect Book, 2009), pp. 44–47.
22. Other dubbed versions — French, German and Spanish — retain the original lines. The modification actually damages the cohesion of the film to the Italian audience since the denigrating comment justifies Mike's suspicions and fears of being robbed as soon as he gets off the train in Naples. The only archival material related to this modification can be found in the correspondence attached to the submission of the script to the Ministero per il turismo e lo spettacolo: in a memorandum to the Direttore Generale Spettacolo, an anonymous censor, amongst other things, drew the attention to the recurrent critique of Neapolitan life contained in the film. Next to that passage, a handwritten note — presumably by the director — says 'Vedere se si può evitare con cautela' (memo dated 8.8.1959, in ACS, Ministero Turismo Spettacolo — Divisione Cinema, f. CF2990). It is therefore possible that the changes were discreetly agreed as a way of adding a more positive view of Neapolitan life.
23. Again, the Italian version entirely turns the table, and from victim Mike turns into an admirer of the 'belle ragazze', reminiscing: 'Anch'io per la verità mi detti abbastanza da fare'.
24. In his essay on Sophia Loren's as an Italian icon, Stephen Gundle convincingly suggests that the development of Loren's image in the 1960s, influenced by De Sica rather than Ponti, settled on a rather backward-looking image of Italians which coincided with foreign stereotypes. Stephen Gundle, 'Sophia Loren, Italian Icon', *Journal of Film, Radio and Television*, 15.3 (1995), 367–85 (pp. 371–79).
25. As Bondanella rightly suggests, another connection to Marilyn Monroe is added during the meeting with the press when Sylvia says that she goes to bed wearing only two drops of perfume (thus recalling a similar statement by Monroe in an interview by magazine *Marie Claire*). See

Peter Bondanella, *The Films of Federico Fellini* (Cambridge: Cambridge University Press, 2002) p. 86. Finally, the title of this sequence as it appears in an early copy of the script available at APL (Fondo Flaiano, 52.III Sceneggiatura di Ennio Flaiano, 'La dolce vita'), is 'La diva Americana'.

26. I am referring to the chapter on *La dolce vita* in the already quoted study by Van Order, *Listening to Fellini*, pp. 100–23, See also the Appendix, pp. 213–28.
27. Even in later years, during his phenomenal career as singer and actor, Celentano almost capitalized on this limitation of his, to the point that he composed songs in which he invented English expressions, most famously the title of his 1976 hit song *Svalutation*.
28. See Tullio Kezich, *Noi che abbiamo fatto La dolce vita* (Palermo: Sellerio, 2009), pp. 54–55. An equally symbolic use of U.S. music is made in the already discussed nightclub sequence. Here the 'French' atmosphere is disturbed first by the fact that the 1920s music is actually a U.S. jazz piece ('Yes, Sir, That's my Baby', 1925). Secondly, when Marcello's father and the French ballerina are dancing to a romantic waltz, they are interrupted by another U.S. jazz song ('Stormy Weather', 1933) following the request repeatedly shouted by a group of U.S. sailors. Thirdly, 'Stormy Weather' is sung again by an African American ballerina inside Marcello's car when they leave the nightclub whilst his father leaves in the French ballerina's car. See Van Order, *Listening to Fellini*, pp. 233–34.
29. This is useful for the film since in the its U.S. version, Nando's English is immediately justified as his natural language. The Italian dubbing of the film is once again troublesome: Nando speaks Italian all the time and so does everybody apart from the odd English expression, with the result that the moves between the two languages which are present in the original are entirely lost. More importantly, they make no sense of the scenes in which secondary characters who do not speak English are bodily acting as if they do not follow the protagonists' conversation. This is obvious in the first sequence of the film when Mike meets his Italian lawyer and their dialogue in English is clearly not understood by the lawyer's assistant.
30. I will only add that, for example, I share Baldelli's critique of the sequence of Steiner in *La dolce vita*. See Baldelli, 'Dilatazione visionaria del documento', pp. 347–51. As for the 'bad reasons' for the success of the film, that is, its metamorphosis from a harsh critique of 1950s Italian society into a vehicle for the promotion of Italian goods, see Stephen Gundle, 'Hollywood Glamour and Mass Consumption in Postwar Italy', *Journal of Cold War Studies*, 4.3 (Summer 2002), pp. 95–118.
31. A good indication of each author's role, at least from a quantitative viewpoint, comes indirectly from a contract for the rights of a musical version of *La dolce vita* which was signed by New York producer Joel Spector on 29 October 1968. The musical eventually never took off but the royalties paid in the first year were divided as follows: Fellini 41%, Flaiano 24%, Pinelli 23%, Rondi 11%; in APL, Fondo Flaiano, 52.III Materiale cinematografico. Contratti. La dolce vita (musical).
32. See for example the journalistic pieces published in *Il Mondo* and *L'Espresso-mese* in 1960: or the short text 'Some of these days', published posthumously; all in Ennio Flaiano, *Opere,* vol.1 (Milan: Bompiani, 1988), pp. 252–53, 588, 607, 625.
33. For Fellini, see for example Peter Bondanella, *The Cinema of Federico Fellini* (Princeton: Princeton University Press, 1992), p. 18. For Calvino, I am referring to his memoirs as a film-goer during the interwar years, topically published as a preface to Fellini, *Quattro film*, pp. ix–xxiv; now in *Romanzi e racconti*, vol. III (Milan: Mondadori, 1994), 27–49. I am grateful to Martin McLaughlin for pointing me in the direction of this essay. For Pivano, see her interview with Ugo Rubeo in Rubeo (ed.), *Mal d'America*, pp. 101–13.

CHAPTER 23

Diffracting Dante's *Paradiso* with Pasolini and Morante: Transformation, Identity and the Form of Desire

Manuele Gragnolati

This essay, which pushes further some concepts explored in my book *Amor che move. Linguaggio del corpo e forma del desiderio in Dante, Pasolini e Morante* (Milan: il Saggiatore, 2013), proposes a reading of Dante's *Paradiso* through texts by two twentieth-century authors: Pier Paolo Pasolini and Elsa Morante.[1] Rather than only looking at how Pasolini's and Morante's texts relate to Dante's or have been influenced by them, the way in which I read this constellation of works is inspired by the practice that epistemologist and feminist Donna Haraway has called 'diffractive reading'. Referring to the optical phenomenon of diffraction, according to which light waves encountering an object do not produce a shadow that repeats the exact form of the object but produce a complex diffraction pattern that depends both on the waves and on the object itself, Haraway proposes a strategy of reading that, instead of reflecting, diffracts and has texts interact beyond any apparent genealogy, studying them not only together but also one through the other, with the aim of offering a different perspective and producing something new:

> Diffraction patterns record the history of interaction, interference, reinforcement, difference. Diffraction is about heterogeneous history, not about originals. Unlike reflections, diffractions do not displace the same elsewhere, in more or less distorted form, thereby giving rise to industries of metaphysics. Rather, diffraction can be a metaphor for another kind of critical consciousness at the end of this rather painful Christian millennium, one committed to making a difference and not to representing the Sacred Image of the Same.[2]

If, methodologically, my analysis is inspired by Haraway's concept of diffractive reading, its aim is to understand the state of the souls in Dante's representation of Heaven, and indeed, as I hope will become clear, the terms 'Transformation' and 'Identity' in my title refer not only to the method of diffracting Dante with authors from a different period but also to how Dante imagines the condition of being in Paradise. More generally, I also aim to show how this condition is conveyed by the aesthetics of the *Divine Comedy* and the *Paradiso* in particular — and this is what

I mean with the concept of 'Form of Desire', also mentioned in the title of this essay.

My story begins on the shores of Purgatory, where the pilgrim encounters a shade who has also just arrived: Casella, an old friend from Dante's youth, before his exile from Florence. It is one of the most complex and discussed episodes of the whole poem and rewrites the Virgilian motif of the failed embrace between the living and the dead. When Casella, who has recognized Dante, leaves his group of shades and moves forward to embrace him, words such as 'abbracciarmi' and 'affetto' charge the episode with the same intimacy and affection characterizing the Virgilian models: 'Io vidi una di lor trarresi avante / per abbracciarmi, con sì grande affetto, / che mosse me a far lo simigliante' [I saw one of them come forward / with such affection to embrace me / that I was moved to do the same] (*Purg.* II, 76–78).[3]

Dante-the-pilgrim tries to embrace the shade in front of him, but fails three times because, in the *Divine Comedy*'s otherworld, the souls can unfold a body of air that allows them to have a shape and express sensorial faculties, but they have no substantiality.[4] Indeed — as the poet laments — shades in the otherworld have an appearance — 'aspetto' — but are 'vane', empty: 'Ohi ombre vane, fuor che ne l'aspetto! / tre volte dietro a lei le mani avvinsi, / e tante mi tornai con esse al petto' [Oh empty shades, except in seeming! / Three times I clasped my hands behind him / only to find them clasped to my own chest] (*Purg.* II, 79–81). After the pilgrim recognizes his old friend, Casella tells him that although he is now a soul deprived of its mortal body, he continues to love Dante in the same way that he did when he was in his earthly body: 'Così com'io t'amai / nel *mortal corpo*, così t'amo sciolta' ['Even as I loved you in *my mortal flesh*,' he said, / 'so do I love you freed from it'] (*Purg.* II, 89–90). The same affection is shown by Dante, who relapses into nostalgia for earthly pursuits, asking his friend to sing in the same way he used to sing in their youth — and Casella performs Dante's canzone *Amor che ne la mente mi ragiona* so beautifully that all the souls, enchanted by the sweetness of the performance, forget that they are in Purgatory to embark on a journey of purification that will eventually lead them to Heaven.

As is well known, the rest of the episode shows that the mutual affection that the two friends still feel for each other is wrong and that attachment to the body, affection for friends and beloved, and nostalgia for the past are also wrong and must change in Purgatory.[5] Indeed, the moral structure of Dante's understanding of Purgatory prescribes that the souls in Purgatory learn to detach themselves from anything transient and re-direct all their desires towards God. According to what Teodolinda Barolini has called Dante's Augustinian paradigm of desire, attachments to one's mortal body and nostalgia for earthly affections symbolized by the earthly body are considered as distractions that the soul must abandon in Purgatory, if it wants to attain the complete love for God that is necessary to reach Heaven.[6]

If this Augustinian discourse of desire is introduced from the pilgrim's arrival at the shores of the mountain of Purgatory, it is reiterated by Beatrice's reproach to him at the summit of the mountain:

> Quando di carne a spirto era salita,
> e bellezza e virtù cresciuta m'era,
> fu' io a lui men cara e men gradita;
> e volse i passi suoi per via non vera,
> imagini di ben seguendo false,
> che nulla promession rendono intera. (*Purg.* XXX, 127–32)
>
> [When I had risen to spirit from my flesh,
> as beauty and virtue in me became more rich,
> to him I was less dear and less than pleasing.
> He set his steps upon an untrue way,
> pursuing those false images of good
> that bring no promise to fulfillment.]

In her argument that her death should not have induced the pilgrim to stop loving her and to direct his desire towards mortal goods that may seem good but actually lead the person away from the right path to God, Beatrice indicates that when her soul separated from her flesh, she became more beautiful and virtuous.

In the second part of her speech, Beatrice explains that it is precisely when she died physically that the pilgrim should have loved her most because this would have meant loving her soul, the immortal part of her that will never fail him:

> Mai non t'appresentò natura o arte
> piacere, quanto le bella membra in ch'io
> rinchiusa fui, e che so' 'n terra sparte,
> e se 'l sommo piacer sì ti fallio
> per la mia morte, qual cosa mortale
> dovea poi trarre te nel suo disio?
> Ben ti dovevi, per lo primo strale
> de le cose fallaci, levar suso
> di retro a me che non era più tale. (*Purg.* XXXI, 49–57)
>
> [Never did art or nature set before you beauty
> as great as in the lovely members that enclosed me,
> now scattered and reduced to dust.
> And if the highest beauty failed you
> in my death, what mortal thing
> should then have drawn you to desire it?
> Indeed, at the very first arrow
> of deceitful things, you should have risen up
> and followed me who was no longer of them.]

Beatrice confirms that the correct way for Dante to love her is one in which it should make no difference for him whether she is in the flesh or not. Actually, she explains, he should love her more now that she is a shade than when she was in her fleshly body on earth: albeit beautiful, the earthly body is mortal, and one should neither love it as though it were not doomed to die nor, as the pilgrim did after her death, replace it with some other mortal good that distracts from fully directing one's love to God.

Beatrice's words not only reiterate that one should not love earthly goods too much, but also indicate that there is something problematic in the earthly, fleshly body that is related to an intimate attachment to others and that must be overcome in the soul's purgatorial apprenticeship. Flesh would not seem to be required in the eschatological panorama of the *Divine Comedy*, where by releasing a body of air, the souls are able to have full experience of the afterlife, including the glory of Paradise. As *Inferno* and *Purgatorio* placed emphasis on the intensity of the souls' pain, so the *Paradiso* is full of passages indicating that in Heaven the fleshless souls have access to the beatific vision, which satisfies all their desires and grants them perfect bliss: 'Lume è là sù che visibile face / lo creatore a quella creatura / che solo in lui vedere ha la sua pace.' [There is a light above that makes the Creator / visible to every creature / that finds its only peace in seeing Him.] (*Par.* XXX, 100–02)[7]

Interestingly, the intensity of the soul's happiness in Heaven is represented by the fact that beginning with the Heaven of Mercury, the shades' individual features are hidden by a light that surrounds them and is a manifestation of the joy provided by their beatific vision:

> Luce divina sopra me s'appunta,
> penetrando per questa in ch'io m'inventro,
>   la cui virtù, col mio veder congiunta,
> mi leva sopra me tanto, ch'i' veggio
> la somma essenza de la quale è munta.
>   Quinci vien l'allegrezza onde fiammeggio;
> per ch'a la vista mia, quant' ella è chiara,
> la chiarità de la fiamma pareggio. (*Par.* XXI, 83–90)

> [Divine light focuses on me, piercing
> the radiance that holds me in its womb.
>   Its power, conjoined with my own sight,
> raises me so far above myself that I can see
> the Highest Essence, the source from which it flows.
>   And this inflames the joy with which I burn:
> for, in the clarity of my sight,
> I match the clearness of my flame.]

The disappearance of the blessed shades' individual features can be taken as a sign that, in line with the Augustinian paradigm of Purgatory, in Heaven souls have indeed learned to relinquish the past and to transform personal and individual attachments into an absolute and unconditional love for God that opens the self and also becomes gratuitous love for everyone else.[8]

Several interesting studies have shown that this condition achieved and manifested by the souls in heaven corresponds to a state of merging with God that radically changes the self — and this is one of the senses of the transformation mentioned in the title of the present essay. Thus, for instance, Lino Pertile and Steven Botterill have indicated that Beatrice, who in a way can be considered as the symbol of the pilgrim's personal and individual attachments, must also eventually leave and be replaced by Bernard of Clairvaux before the pilgrim can reach the ultimate union with God and the Universe;[9] and Robin Kirkpatrick has spoken of a 'spirit of dispossession' that characterizes the condition of being in Heaven, while Christian Moevs indicates that the redirection of desire from mortal to immortal goods can be understood as a 'spontaneous crucifixion of the self' and that 'love is selflessness, and self is lovelessness'.[10]

There is something fascinating about the loss of self and identity that uniting with God implies in Dante's concept of heaven and in the openness and porosity that this loss implies and what I want to propose now is to read this condition of openness and porosity with a passage from Pier Paolo Pasolini's *Petrolio*, the ambitious magnum opus on which Pasolini was working when he was killed in 1975 and which represents the culmination of his long-standing engagement with Dante. There is neither God nor heaven in Pasolini's bleak portrayal of post-war Italy, but I want to consider the dissolution of the ego in two episodes in which the protagonist Carlo, after being transformed into a woman (but ultimately remaining a man), has numerous sexual encounters with several young men from the Lumpenproletariat. These episodes are veritable rhetorical and sexual *tours de force* insisting on the details of Carlo's masochistic submission; this submission shatters and annihilates his subjectivity and is experienced as a liberation from his bourgeois position and consciousness.[11]

A short passage from the second episode, in which Carlo has sex with Carmelo, a Sicilian waiter, should suffice to give a sense of the dimension of sacred ritual with which the protagonist undertakes his masochistic submission, which allows him to have access to the reality of the 'other' and to forget his own bourgeois identity and personal history:

> Se la pressione sulla mano era stata sconvolgente, quasi paralizzante — come quella di un padrone sulla bestia ammansita — la pressione sulla nuca fece quasi perdere i sensi a Carlo. Cosa voleva quella mano, larga e massiccia, posata sulla sua delicata nuca di borghese che era sempre stato debole e reso ridicolo davanti a se stesso dai suoi complessi e dai suoi doveri? Tutta la sua storia non esisteva più: la forza di un corpo esercitata con tanta prepotente delicatezza su di lui attraverso quel palmo di una mano callosa, riduceva anche lui a un corpo: un corpo rivalutato dal fatto che poteva essere fonte, sia pur misera, di piacere. [...] Una specie di soddisfazione comica coesisteva in lui con la meravigliosa vertigine e la sconvolgente contrizione di schiavo ubbidiente a cui quella pressione di Carlo sulla sua nuca lo costringeva. [...] Tuttavia il pugno, stringendo per pura obbedienza, cioè convenzionalmente, il membro di Carmelo non potè fare a meno di sentirne la realtà. E fu un nuovo sprofondarsi nel meraviglioso martirio. Ora egli aveva in mano il sesso nudo: il miracolo si era dunque realizzato compiutamente. Non c'era più nulla che dividesse Carlo dal suo desiderio finora sempre considerato irrealizzabile. I calzoni sacri di Carmelo erano sbottonati, gli slip sia pur faticosamente tirati giù sotto i testicoli, e il suo cazzo era fuori, allo scoperto, all'aria fredda, ma insieme stranamente tiepida della sera, sotto la luce torva della luna: nudo più della stessa nudità. [...] Ecco, Carmelo accarezzava la testa di Carlo come si accarezza la testa di un cane; anzi, di una cagna. (*Appunto 62*, 1509–12)[12]

As explicitly maintained in another Note, the value of sexual experience consists in its passive form of obedience and degradation that also frees oneself from the feeling of possession and power. Indeed the text establishes a link between sexuality, economics, and ethics, distinguishing between the act of possessing, symbolised by the penis, and that of being possessed, and also identifying possession with Power and Evil and being possessed with the only possibility of Good:

> Chi è posseduto perde la coscienza della forma del pene, della sua compiutezza limitata, e lo sente come un mezzo infinito e informe, attraverso cui Qualcosa o Qualcuno si impadronisce di lui, lo riduce a possesso, a un nulla che non ha altra volontà che quella di perdersi in quella diversa Volontà che lo annulla.
> Da parte di chi è posseduto colui che possiede è dunque sentito come un Bene, anche se esso implica il sacrificio, il dolore, l'umiliazione, la morte. L'urto che viola la carne, si estende su tutto l'infinito fronte della carne, non in un punto solo. L'intero corpo, la cui coscienza dall'interno è illimitata perché coincide con quella dell'universo, è coinvolto dalla violenza con cui colui che possiede si manifesta, e che non conosce pietà, mezzi termini, rispetto, proroghe: la sua voglia di possedere non concede limiti a chi è posseduto, che deve essere ciecamente passivo, obbediente, e a cui tutt'al più, anche nella sofferenza e la degradazione, può essere solo concesso di manifestare la sua gratitudine.
> D'altra parte è fuori discussione che il Possesso è un Male, anzi, per definizione, è IL Male: quindi l'essere posseduti è ciò che è più lontano dal Male, o meglio, è l'unica esperienza possibile del Bene, come Grazia, vita allo stato puro, cosmico. (*Appunto 65*, 1552–53)

Thus *Petrolio* makes fascination with masochistic surrender quite explicit and gives such surrender an ethical value that resonates with the work of contemporary queer theorists who propose radical passivity as the only way not to be complicit with power and domination.[13]

But — and this is the next point that I want to make — *Petrolio* also connects surrender and dispossession with aesthetic and textual choices. *Petrolio* breaks up the traditional form of the novel and authorship and has an 'open' and shapeless structure which refutes development and teleology. As the novel itself indicates, the course of narration is chaotic and swirly rather than linear and progressive and aims at inducing a feeling of disorientation in the reader: 'Il mio non è un romanzo "a schidionata", ma "a brulichio" e quindi è comprensibile che il lettore resti un po' disorientato' (*Petrolio*, 22A, p. 1275), where the phrase 'a brulichio' refers to the chaotic and irregular movement of bees and 'a schidionata' refers instead to the progressive logics of cause and effect represented by the 'schidione' (the long metal skewer used for the shish kebab). Indeed *Petrolio* is a text that proceeds as a chaotic accumulation of fragments, and explicitly resists completion and linearity, deploying what has been recently theorized as a 'queer temporality', that is, a temporality that resists progression and linearity and instead endorses repetition, circularity, and endless dilation.[14]

My point here is that *Petrolio* does not simply describe scenes of masochism and surrender, but also replicates, through its aesthetic choices, that form of sexuality. In this sense, while I have interpreted the textual operation of Dante's *Vita Nuova* as a successful performance that re-writes the original poems and lets a new, modern author emerge in an effective way, I consider *Petrolio* instead to embody a queer performance that embraces textual failure and destroys the modern figure of the author.[15] In particular, drawing on the concept of aesthetics that Leo Bersani developed with respect to some important texts by Freud (especially *The Three Essays on Sexuality* and *Beyond the Pleasure Principle*), my hypothesis is that *Petrolio* does not simply describe scenes of masochism, but also replicates, through its aesthetic choices, a form of sexuality founded on a paradoxical kind of pleasure.[16] In this respect, I find particularly interesting Bersani's reformulation of the concept of 'artistic sublimation' as the possibility not of purifying or transcending desire but, on the contrary, of extending it to the movement of the text, thereby expressing, enacting, and making the reader experience sexuality, which for Bersani is masochistic in its ontological state, that is, before being domesticated and sanitised by norms.[17] In other words, *Petrolio*'s anarchic aesthetics and de-structured and endless textuality replicate a masochistic sexuality and mobilize non-linear and non-domesticated pleasures linked to the shattering and undoing of the self — and this is what I mean by *forma del desiderio*, the 'form of desire'.

So far, I have focussed on transformation and shattering of the self, arguing that they represent an important component of the heavenly state as imagined by Dante and that, if looked at through Pasolini, the paradisial state of dispossession also contains a paradoxical desire and pleasure that can be replicated by the movement of textuality. I shall now go back to Dante's *Paradiso* and complicate things a little by moving to another concept mentioned in the title of this essay: 'Identity', that is, in this case, the idea that there is something about their past that the souls in heaven continue to be attached to and that cannot be tamed, disciplined, or fully abandoned — an identity, that is, that goes in the opposite direction of transformation. Here I will mention three passages in canto XIV of *Paradiso* which celebrate the Christian dogma of the resurrection of the flesh, that is, the doctrine that at the end of time the flesh will resurrect and will reunite with the soul, reconstituting the human being in its entirety — what Dante calls 'la persona tutta quanta', 'the person all complete'. In other words, according to the eschatological assumptions laid out in the *Divine Comedy* and, in particular, in canto XIV of *Paradiso*, the aerial body that the soul has at its disposal when it gets to the Afterlife, will, at the end of time, be replaced by its real, material body, made of resurrected flesh.

I shall not go into the intellectual complexity of *Paradiso* XIV, on which I have written extensively on other occasions, but I want at least to point out the sublime intensity with which this canto conveys nostalgia for one's own mortal body and the intimate affections that it represents. In the first passage the soul of Solomon answers Dante-the-pilgrim's doubts about what will happen to the blessed when their body is resurrected, explaining that the resurrection of the flesh and the material reconstitution of the person will allow for the increase of the beatific vision and happiness:

> Come la carne glorïosa e santa
> fia rivestita, la nostra persona
> più grata fia per esser tutta quanta:
>   per che s'accrescerà ciò che ne dona
> di gratüito lume il sommo bene,
> lume ch'a lui veder ne condiziona;
>   onde la visïon crescer convene,
> crescer l'ardor che di quella s'accende,
> crescer lo raggio che da esso vene. (*Par.* XIV, 43–51)

> [When we put on again our flesh,
> glorified and holy, then our persons
> will be more pleasing for being all complete,
> so that the light, granted to us freely
> by the Highest Good, shall increase,
> the light that makes us fit to see Him.
> From that light, vision must increase
> and love increase what vision kindles,
> and radiance increase, which comes from love.]

Solomon also explains that, while before the end of time the features of the blessed souls are hidden by the luminosity that surrounds them, when the flesh resurrects at the end of time, their features will be visible again:

> Ma sì come carbon che fiamma rende,
> e per vivo candor quella soverchia,
> sì che la sua parvenza si difende;
> così questo folgór che già ne cerchia
> fia vinto in apparenza da la carne
> che tutto dì la terra ricoperchia. (*Par.* XIV, 52–57)
>
> [But like a coal that shoots out flame
> and in its glowing center still outshines it
> so that it does not lose its own appearance,
> just so this splendor that enfolds us now
> will be surpassed in brightness by the flesh
> that earth as yet still covers.]

And the third passage in the same canto expresses the souls' enthusiastic reaction at Solomon's celebration of the resurrection of the flesh:

> Tanto mi parver sùbiti e accorti
> e l'uno e l'altro coro a dicer 'Amme!',
> che ben mostrar disio d'i corpi morti:
> forse non pur per lor, ma per le mamme,
> per li padri e per li altri che fuor cari
> anzi che fosser sempiterne fiamme. (*Par.* XIV, 61–66)
>
> [So quick and eager seemed to me both choirs
> to say their Amen that they clearly showed
> their desire for their dead bodies,
> not perhaps for themselves alone, but for their mothers,
> for their fathers, and for others whom they loved
> before they all became eternal flames.]

The joy with which the souls react at the prospect of reuniting with their fleshly body — that mortal body which has remained on Earth and is now a corpse — reveals the intensity of their nostalgia for that body ('disio d'i corpi morti').[18] Unlike many other passages of *Paradiso* that stress the souls' current happiness, here Dante's poem emphasizes the intensity with which they desire to recuperate their bodies, when they will be happier. In particular, the rhyme words 'amme' / 'mamme' / 'fiamme' express that after the recovery of what are now dead bodies, the separated souls — which in heaven have become splendid lights, enflamed by their beatitude and love for God — will become again veritable individuals with their own singularity, made of relations and memory.

What is important to note is that the souls' desire for their dead body is connected not only with the increase of their vision of God, but also with their personal attachments; it is the passionate 'expression of their desire to love fully in heaven what they loved on earth'.[19] The souls' 'disio d'i corpi morti' thus seems to contradict the Augustinian paradigm of detachment that, as we have seen, characterizes the process of Purgatory as an education in selflessness and dispossession. First I would like to point out that, as far as I know, the relational sense expressed by the souls' desire for their resurrected body was something of a novelty for contemporary theologians, who focused mainly on the exclusive relation of the individual to God and were less interested in the idea that personal and individual attachments continue in heaven among the blessed.[20]

Secondly, I would like to explore further the connection that the XIV canto of *Paradiso* makes between the body's materiality and fleshliness, memory, and individuality as fundamental parts of the heavenly experience by turning to consider how the motif of the resurrection is presented in *Aracoeli*, the last novel by Elsa Morante. Published in 1982 and conceived of as a dialogue with Pasolini, who was Morante's close friend, *Aracoeli* is a fascinating, complex text that I have explored in detail in my book and in a couple of other articles co-authored with the philosopher of language Sara Fortuna.[21] Here I shall not dwell on the novel's complexity or the queer subjectivity that it conveys, but I want to consider at least the passage in which the protagonist and narrator explains that his journey to Spain in search for his dead mother has been initiated by the re-emergence, in the memory of the body, of physical sensations originally shared with her and then forgotten.

The narrator's journey towards the realm of the dead is both geographical, towards the maternal Spain, and archaeological, through his psyche, and the motif of the resurrection is inverted from the future to the past and morphs into the possibility to recuperate shared bodily sensations and re-experience them in their corporeal fullness that brings back the past and mixes it with the present:

> La tentazione del viaggio mi aveva invaso recentemente con la voce stessa di mia madre. Non è stata una trascrizione astratta della memoria a restituirmi le sue primissime canzoncine, già seppellite; ma proprio la voce fisica di lei, col suo sapore tenero di gola e di saliva. Ho riavuto sul palato la sensazione della sua pelle, che odorava di prugna fresca; e la notte in questo freddo milanese, ho avvertito il suo fiato ancora di bambina, come un velo di tepore ingenuo sulle mie palpebre invecchiate. Non so come gli scienziati spieghino l'esistenza, dentro la nostra materia corporale, di questi altri organi di senso occulti, senza corpo visibile, e segregati dagli oggetti; ma pur capaci di udire, di vedere e di ogni sensazione della natura, e anche di altre. Si direbbero forniti di antenne e scandagli. Agiscono in una zona esclusa dallo spazio, però di movimento illimitato. E là in quella zona si avvera (almeno finché noi viviamo) *la resurrezione carnale dei morti*. (1047–48, my emphasis)[22]

This passage interests me because it highlights the significance of the body in its physical materiality as the carrier of one's memory and history both in its singularity and in its inter-subjective character, here connected with the relationship with the mother. But this passage also interests me because the experience retrieved and re-lived — indeed resurrected — is that of the infant suckling at the mother's breast, which the novel deploys as its central image and also connects with the origin of language (and as we know from Gary Cestaro's analysis, the image of suckling is also central to Dante's meditation on language and to the distinction therein traced between Latin as paternal and *volgare* as maternal[23]). In particular Morante's novel, which is set in an explicitly post-Freudian context, articulates the possibility of recovering an originary maternal component of language — i.e., a corporeal, affective, and libidinal substratum that originates in the experience of suckling and is thereafter forgotten but continues to be carried in the adult's body and can at times re-emerge through the body's memory, re-configuring subjectivity in a new way, free from Oedipal and normative paradigms. But what also interests me about *Aracoeli* is that, as in Pasolini's *Petrolio*, so too in Morante's novel a kind of 'artistic sublimation' is discernible which replicates the movement of desire through its aesthetic choices, albeit in a different way that is less about shattering and annihilating oneself than about recovering in a reconfigured way a condition of relationality with fluid, permeable boundaries. Not only does Spanish as the maternal language constantly emerge at the surface, weakening the rational structure of Italian as paternal language and making it 'invertebrate',[24] but the novel's narrative structure is also distorted and destabilizing in its continual interruptions and inversions of genres, rhythms, and perspectives. In this way, boundaries are lost along with norms and directions, in an operation of fluidification and integration which replicates the movement of a polymorphous sexuality that, in the final pages of the novel, is endorsed in its non-oedipal, non-binary, non-teleological, non-normative character.

So to recapitulate, what interests me about Morante's novel in connection with Dante's concept of the resurrection of the body are three aspects: first, the idea that, in its materiality, the body carries one's own memory and relational history that can be occasionally retrieved; second, the connection between this form of resurrection and the experience of suckling as the originary moment of the formation of a relational, corporeal, and fluid linguistic subjectivity that is subsequently lost; and third, the possibility for textuality to replicate that form of resurrection. Returning to Dante's *Paradiso* and to the blessed souls' 'disio d'i corpi morti', I want to conclude by making two points. The first point is that there seems to be a paradoxical and un-resolved tension in the *Divine Comedy* between the state of heaven as dissolution of the self and the blessed souls' 'disio d'i corpi morti', which arguably includes not only the desire to embrace Casella at the end of time but also to recover Beatrice.[25]

And the second point, on which I will linger a little more and conclude, regards the 'form of desire' deployed in the final cantos of *Paradiso*, where something interesting takes place that has to do with the resurrection. First of all, on a thematic level, the resurrection of the body is anticipated and imagined before the end of time and indeed, when Dante-the-pilgrim enters the Empyrean (the last immaterial Heaven where God and the blessed reside), not only is he granted the privilege of seeing the blessed with the resurrected body that they will only have at the end of time, but his own 'living' body has acquired the characteristics of a resurrected body.[26]

Moreover, as Gary Cestaro has noticed, in the last ten cantos of *Paradiso* dedicated to the pilgrim's experience in the Empyrean, the image of the child suckling at the mother's breast, which is central to Dante's meditation on the acquisition of the vernacular in the *De vulgari eloquentia* but is generally suppressed in the *Divine Comedy*, comes back with great insistence.[27] For instance, it is present in the moment in which Dante-the-pilgrim enters the Empyrean and observes a river of light turning into a circle:

> Non è fantin che sì subito rua
> col volto verso il latte, se si svegli
> molto tardato da l'usanza sua,
>   come fec' io, per far migliori spegli
> ancora de li occhi, chinandomi a l'onda
> che si deriva perché vi s'immegli;
>   e sì come di lei bevve la gronda
> da le palpebre mie, così mi parve
> di sua lunghezza divenuta tonda. (*Par.* XXX, 82–90)

> [No infant, waking up too late
> for his accustomed feeding, will thrust his face
> up to his milk with greater urgency,
>   than I, to make still better mirrors of my eyes,
> inclined my head down toward the water
> that flows there for our betterment,
>   and no sooner had the eaves of my eyelids
> drunk deep of that water than to me it seemed
> it had made its length into a circle.]

The image of the child craving his mother's milk expresses here the intensity of the pilgrim's desire to see God and is deployed at the crucial moment in which the pilgrim, now close to attaining the ultimate vision, is about to abandon a linear dimension of temporality (as of that on Earth or in Purgatory) and enter, instead, the circular and extra-temporal dimension of Eternity, where everything is simultaneously co-present — what theologians called *totum simul*. This passage confirms that the connection between the image of suckling and that of the resurrection, which is foundational in *Aracoeli*, is also operative in Dante's text, for which, as we have seen, the motif of the resurrection of the body is so important that it is staged before the end of time — and indeed the new circle of light from which Dante's eyes drink voraciously will soon turn into a flower formed by the resurrected bodies of the blessed which he can finally see in the Empyrean.

Moreover — and this will be my last point — the poem not only stages the resurrection of the body before the end of time, but also reproduces this experience in its textuality. That is, my hypothesis, which draws on Cestaro's reading but pushes it further through the concept of 'artistic sublimation' which I have exemplified with Pasolini's *Petrolio* and Morante's *Aracoeli*, is that the kind of desire informing the eschatological imagination of the *Divine Comedy* is also replicated in the movement of its textuality and conveyed by the form of the text itself. I found it indeed quite intriguing that the image of suckling at the mother's breast appears in precisely the three cantos of the *Paradiso* (XXIII, XXX and XXXIII) where, as Teodolinda Barolini has shown, the *Divine Comedy* deploys a different kind of textuality — a textuality that is no longer rational, logical, or linear but 'jumping': that is, a kind of textuality that transgresses the common mode of textuality, which is discursive, logical, linear, 'chronologized', and intellective, and is, instead, 'lyric', that is, 'nondiscursive, nonlinear or circular, dechronologized and affective'.[28] In other words, the antinarrative mode of cantos XXIII, XXX, and XXXIII, is 'resistant to subdivision and hence to logical exposition, and is characterized by apostrophes, exclamations, heavily metaphoric language, and intensely affective similes', subverting linearity and conveying the fullness of the *totum simul*.[29]

Here I will focus on canto XXXIII, the final canto of the poem, which together with XXIII and XXX, is a prime example of the jumping mode of *Paradiso*'s textuality. In this canto the image of suckling is found in the second part, after the pilgrim enjoys the first vision of God and his mind is fully absorbed in enjoying it: 'Omai sarà più corta mia favella, / pur a quel ch'io ricordo, che d'un fante / che bagni ancor la lingua a la mammella' [Now my words will come far short / of what I still remember, like a babe's / who at his mother's breast still wets his tongue] (*Par.* XXXIII 106–08). Commentators note that these lines also echo a verse from the Psalms stressing that the true praise of God is made by the mouths of infants who are still suckling at the mother's breast. Cestaro stresses that after Bernard's prayer to Mary, canto XXXIII asserts again the metaphorical concept of Christian charity as female, corporeal, and nurturing (and here one cannot but think of the image of 'Jesus as Mother' explored by Caroline Bynum): at a loss to convey the power of the final vision, the poet can only return to the primal scene of suckling at the mother's breast.[30] Indeed. But I would also add that canto XXXIII represents Dante's supreme attempt to mobilize the fractured, circular, equalized mode of antinarrative textuality, which in this case seeks to approximate what Barolini has defined as the 'circling, surging, orgasmic approach' of the soul to the fulfilment of its desire: through three waves of discourse, the pilgrim's final ascent approaches and backs off, approaches and backs off again, and finally arrives.[31] And it can arrive only when Dantethepilgrim's mind is hit by a light (*fulgore*) that allows it to attain the ultimate vision beyond a rational way of understanding and beyond the linear realm of temporality, joining instead the circular, extra-temporal dimension that defeats linearity and binary oppositions and where everything is present at the same time: 'ma non eran da ciò le proprie penne: / se non che la mia mente fu percossa / da un fulgore in che sua voglia venne', [But my wings had not sufficed for that / had not my mind been struck by a bolt / of lightning that granted what I asked] (*Par.* XXXIII 139–41), where *venne* could be another sign of the orgasmic, orgiastic qualities of the canto's textuality.

Ultimately, my point is that the poem not only represents the resurrection of the body (for both the blessed and the pilgrim) before the end of time, but also performs it through its corporeal, fluid, anti-narrative mode of textuality. If therefore, as we have seen at the beginning of this essay, the heavenly state can be interpreted as the dissolution of too rigid an identity into the movement of God's cosmic order and his love ('l'amor che move il sole e l'altre stelle'), this same state also expresses an individuality which is accepted in its singularity and relationality and persists in the body and in desire for the body. One could say that the subject which is no longer a subject, re-found and replicated in the poem's textuality and rhythm, not only opens itself up to a state of cosmic dissolution, but also maintains a corporeal depth which is connected to the inter-subjective development of the individual and her history. One could therefore say that, together with the sense of progression typical of Dante's poem and its epic form, the pyrotechnic, ardent, 'resurrected' character of the textuality of *Paradiso*'s last cantos replicates the paradoxical pleasure not only of losing but also of continuing to find oneself again. This is their 'form of desire'.

Notes to Chapter 23

1. Some material in this article partially overlaps with the following articles: Manuele Gragnolati, 'Differently Queer: Sexuality and Aesthetics in Pier Paolo Pasolini's *Petrolio* and Elsa Morante's *Aracoeli*', in *Elsa Morante's Politics of Writing: Rethinking Subjectivity, History and the Power of Art*, ed. by Stefania Lucamante (Madison, NJ: Fairleigh Dickinson University Press, 2014), pp. 205–18; Manuele Gragnolati and Francesca Southerden, 'From Paradox to Exclusivity: Dante's and Petrarch's Lyrical Eschatologies', in *Petrarch and Boccaccio: The Unity of Knowledge in the Pre-modern World*, ed. by Igor Candido (Berlin: De Gruyter, forthcoming 2017).
2. Donna J. Haraway, *Modest_Witness@Second_Millennium.FemaleMan$^©$_Meets_OncoMouse^{TM}: Feminism and Technoscience* (New York: Routledge, 1997), p. 273. See also Donna J. Haraway, 'The Promises of Monsters: A Regenerative Politics for Inappropriate/d Others', in *Cultural Studies*, ed. by Lawrence Grossberg, Cary Nelson, and Paula A. Treichler (New York, Routledge, 1992), pp. 295–337; and Birgit Mara Kaiser and Kathrin Thiele, 'Diffraction: Onto-Epistemology, Quantum Physics and the Critical Humanities', *Parallax* 20.3 (2014), 165–67. On the difference between reflection and diffraction, see Astrid Deuber-Mankowsky, 'Diffraktion statt Reflexion. Zu Donna Haraways Konzept des Situierten Wissens', *Zeitschrift für Medienwissenschaft* 1 (2011), 83–92.
3. On the motif of the failed embrace and its Virgilian intertexts, see Manuele Gragnolati, 'Nostalgia in Heaven: Embraces, Affection and Identity in the *Commedia*', in *Dante and the Human Body: Eight Essays*, ed. by John C. Barnes and Jennifer Petrie (Dublin: Four Courts Press, 2007), pp. 117–37. Quotations from the *Commedia* are from Dante Alighieri, *'La Commedia' secondo l'antica vulgata*, ed. by Giorgio Petrocchi, Società Dantesca Italiana, Edizione Nazionale, 2nd rev. edn, 4 vols (Florence: Le Lettere, 1994). English translations come from: Dante Alighieri, *The Divine Comedy*, trans. by Robert Hollander and Jean Hollander, 3 vols (New York: Doubleday, 2000–2007).
4. See in particular Statius's description of the formation of the aerial body in *Purg.* XXV, 85–108, and Manuele Gragnolati's discussion of it in *Experiencing the Afterlife: Body and Soul in Dante and Medieval Culture* (Notre Dame, IN: University of Notre Dame Press, 2005), pp. 67–77.
5. For readings of this episode, see for example, John Freccero, 'Casella's Song: *Purgatorio* II, 112', in his *Dante: The Poetics of Conversion*, ed. by Rachel Jacoff (Cambridge, MA: Harvard University Press, 1986), pp. 186–94; and Robert Hollander, '*Purgatorio* II: Cato's Rebuke and Dante's *Scoglio*', *Italica* 52.3 (Autumn, 1975), 348–63.

6. Teodolinda Barolini, *The Undivine 'Comedy': Detheologizing Dante* (Princeton, NJ: Princeton University Press, 1992), pp. 99–121, especially pp. 103–08.
7. On the fullness of the separated souls' experience in Hell and Heaven, see Gragnolati, *Experiencing the Afterlife*, pp. 77–87, and his *Amor che move*, pp. 69–90.
8. On the notion of productive pain in the *Purgatorio*, see Manuele Gragnolati, 'Gluttony and the Anthropology of Pain in Dante's *Inferno* and *Purgatorio*', in *History in the Comic Mode: Medieval Communities and the Matter of Person*, ed. by Rachel Fulton and Bruce W. Holsinger (New York: Columbia University Press, 2007), pp. 238–50; and Gragnolati, *Experiencing the Afterlife*, pp. 89–137.
9. Lino Pertile, *La punta del disio: semantica del desiderio nella 'Commedia'* (Fiesole: Cadmo, 2005), especially pp. 235–46; Steven Botterill, *Dante and the Mystical Tradition: Bernard of Clairvaux in the 'Commedia'* (Cambridge: Cambridge University Press, 1994), pp. 64–86, where he speaks of Dante's 'process of [...] detachment from Beatrice' as realized through Bernard's replacement of her as guide (p. 85).
10. See Robin Kirkpatrick, 'Polemics of Praise: Theology as Text, Narrative and Rhetoric in Dante's *Commedia*', in *Dante's 'Commedia': Theology as Poetry*, ed. by Vittorio Montemaggi and Matthew Treherne (Notre Dame: University of Notre Dame Press, 2010), pp. 14–35 (p. 23); and Christian Moevs, *The Metaphysics of Dante's 'Comedy'* (New York: Oxford University Press, 2005), pp. 89–90.
11. On these episodes and the bibliography on them, see Gragnolati, *Amor che move*, pp. 55–58. See at least Massimo Fusillo, 'Il protagonista androgino: metamorfosi e ruoli sessuali in *Petrolio*', in *Progetto Petrolio. Una giornata di studi sul romanzo incompiuto di Pier Paolo Pasolini*, ed. by Paolo Salerno (Bologna: Clueb, 2006), pp. 89–102; Francesca Cadel, 'Politics and Sexuality in Pasolini's *Petrolio*', in *The Power of Disturbance: Elsa Morante's 'Aracoeli'*, ed. by Manuele Gragnolati and Sara Fortuna (Oxford: Legenda, 2009), pp. 107–17; and Raffaele Donnarumma, 'Metamorfosi e nascondimenti. Pasolini e l'omosessualità in *Petrolio*', in *Inquietudini queer: desiderio, performance, scrittura*, ed. by Saveria Chemotti and Davide Susanetti (Padua: Il Poligrafo, 2012), pp. 293–321.
12. I quote *Petrolio* from Pier Paolo Pasolini, *Romanzi e racconti*, ed. by Walter Siti and Silvia De Laude, vol. 2 (Milan: Mondadori, 1998), pp. 1159–1830. For an English translation of Pasolini's novel, see Pier Paolo Pasolini, *Petrolio*, trans. by Ann Goldstein (New York: Pantheon, 1997), which is based on the first edition of *Petrolio* by Maria Careri, Graziella Chiarcossi, and Aurelio Roncaglia (Turin: Einaudi, 1992). On the differences between this edition and that by Siti and De Laude see Siti and De Laude, 'Note e notizie sui testi', in Pasolini, *Romanzi e racconti*, vol. 2, pp. 1993–96.
13. See, for instance, Judith Halberstam, *The Queer Art of Failure* (Durham, NC: Duke University Press, 2011).
14. See Carolyn Dinshaw and others, 'Theorizing Queer Temporalities: A Roundtable Discussion', *GLQ: A Journal of Lesbian and Gay Studies* 13 (2007), 177–95.
15. Manuele Gragnolati, 'Pier Paolo Pasolini's Queer Performance: *La Divina Mimesis* between Dante and *Petrolio*', in *Corpus xxx: Pasolini, Petrolio, Salò*, ed. by Davide Messina (Bologna: CLUEB, 2012), pp. 134–64.
16. Leo Bersani, *The Freudian Body: Psychoanalysis and Art* (New York: Columbia University Press, 1986). On the connection between sexuality and writing in *Petrolio* cf. especially Fusillo, 'Il protagonista androgino', but also Rino Genovese, 'Manifesto per Petrolio', in *A partire da Petrolio. Pasolini interroga la letteratura*, ed. by Carla Benedetti and Maria Antonietta Grignani (Ravenna: Longo, 1995), pp. 79–92; and Deborah Amberson, 'Neo-Capitalism, Acedia and Non-style in Pier Paolo Pasolini's *Petrolio*', *Quaderni d'italianistica* 29.2 (2008), 53–72. On the relationship between homosexuality and deviation from the traditional form of the novel, see Sergio Parussa, *L'eros onnipotente. Erotismo, letteratura e impegno nell'opera di Pier Paolo Pasolini e Jean Genet* (Turin: Tirrenia, 2003).
17. Bersani, *The Freudian Body*, pp. 47–50.
18. On the motif of the resurrection of the body in the *Commedia*, see Gragnolati: *Experiencing the Afterlife*, pp. 139–78, and his *Amor che move*, pp. 104–10 and pp. 149–61, both with ample bibliography. See also Anna Maria Chiavacci Leonardi, '*Le bianche stole*: il tema della

resurrezione nel *Paradiso*', in *Dante e la Bibbia. Atti del Convegno Internazionale promosso da 'Biblia': Firenze, 26–27–28 settembre 1986*, ed. by Giovanni Barblan (Florence: Olschki, 1988), pp. 249–71; and Caroline Walker Bynum, 'Faith Imagining the Self: Somatomorphic Soul and Resurrection Body in Dante's *Divine Comedy*', in *Faithful Imagining: Essays in Honor of Richard R. Neibuhr*, ed. by Sang Huyn Lee and others (Atlanta: Scholars Press, 1995), pp. 81–104.
19. Barolini, *The Undivine 'Comedy'*, p. 138.
20. See Colleen McDannell and Bernhard Lang, *Heaven: A History* (New Haven: Yale University Press, 1998), pp. 90 ff.
21. Gragnolati, *Amor che move*, pp. 111–48; Sara Fortuna and Manuele Gragnolati, '*Attaccando al suo capezzolo le mie labbra ingorde*: corpo, linguaggio e soggettività da Dante ad *Aracoeli* di Elsa Morante', *Nuova Corrente*, 55 (2008), 85–123; 'Allattamento e origine del linguaggio tra la *Commedia* dantesca e *Aracoeli* di Elsa Morante', in *Parole di donne*, ed. by Francesca Maria Dovetto (Milan: Aracne, 2009), pp. 271–303.
22. I quote *Aracoeli* from Elsa Morante, *Aracoeli*, in *Opere*, ed. by Carlo Cecchi and Cesare Garboli (Milan: Mondadori, 1990), ii, 1039–454. For an English translation of the novel, see Elsa Morante, *Aracoeli*, trans. by William Weaver (New York: Random House, 1984).
23. Gary Cestaro, *Dante and the Grammar of the Nursing Body* (Notre Dame, IN: Notre Dame University Press, 2003).
24. As Vincenzo Mengaldo writes, Spanish 'quasi fiacca le strutture razionali dell'italiano stesso, e lo rende invertebrato': 'Spunti per un'analisi linguistica dei romanzi di Elsa Morante', in *Vent'anni dopo 'La Storia'. Omaggio a Elsa Morante*, ed. by Concetta D'Angeli and Giacomo Magrini, special number of *Studi novecenteschi*, 21 (1994), 11–36 (pp. 29–30). On the language of *Aracoeli*, see also Graziella Bernabò, *La fiaba estrema. Elsa Morante tra vita e scrittura* (Rome: Carocci, 2012), pp. 271–75.
25. See Manuele Gragnolati, '*Paradiso* XIV e il desiderio del corpo', *Studi Danteschi*, 78 (2013), 285–309.
26. See Gragnolati, *Experiencing the Afterlife*, pp. 161–78.
27. Cestaro, *Dante and the Grammar of the Nursing Body*, pp. 154–56.
28. See Barolini, *The Undivine 'Comedy'*, pp. 218–56 (p. 221). Her notion of a 'jumping' textuality as fundamentally lyric rather than narrative in nature derives from her analysis of the terzina from *Paradiso* XXIII, 61–63, in which Dante acknowledges that he must leap over the moment of ecstatic, lyrical, mystical vision he cannot describe and rejoin his path further up: 'e così, figurando il paradiso, / *convien saltar* lo sacrato poema / come chi trova suo cammin reciso' [And so, in representing Paradise, / the sacred poem must make its leap across, / as does a man who finds his path cut off]. On the poetic language of the high *Paradiso* as incorporating a Kristevan dimension of semiotic affect which recuperates the fluid and maternal component of the vernacular, see Cestaro, *Dante and the Grammar of the Nursing Body*, especially pp. 135–66; and Gragnolati, *Amor che move*, pp. 149–61.
29. Barolini, *The Undivine 'Comedy'*, p. 221.
30. Cestaro, *Dante and the Grammar of the Nursing Body*, pp. 165–66; Caroline Walker Bynum, *Jesus as Mother: Studies in the Spirituality of the High Middle Ages* (Berkeley: University of California Press, 1982).
31. Barolini, *The Undivine 'Comedy'*, p. 252.

CHAPTER 24

'Poetry is not eggs':
Luigi Meneghello on Italian and Foreign Poetry, Translation and 'Transplants'

Diego Zancani

Luigi Meneghello liked collecting aphorisms, and quite a few are scattered in the large quantity of manuscripts and other material which he donated to the *Centro di Ricerca sulla Tradizione Manoscritta di Autori moderni e contemporanei* at the University of Pavia, both during his lifetime and after his death.[1]

In a passage (published in Italian in *La materia di Reading e altri reperti* (1997), but delivered in English at Edinburgh University) entitled 'Italian Flowers' on the subject of art and poetry, Meneghello said:

> Take an aphorism like the dramatic, to me almost explosive: *Poetry is not eggs* to counterbalance, if not wholly to replace, the Crocean view that 'poetry is intuition' or 'poetry is expression' which had seemed eternal truths to me. [...][2]

As usual in Meneghello, irony disguises something deeper, and in this case, the mention of Benedetto Croce reveals a secret relationship between poetry and philosophy, a subject which always fascinated him. Judging from his writings, he seems to believe that there is a secret link between poetry and truth, in a way which remains somewhat mysterious, and yet fascinating, something that he feels has to do with the 'functioning of our mind'.

It is relatively easy to prove a very early, and then constant interest for poetry in the works of Luigi Meneghello, even if, as he repeatedly pointed out, his own attempts at writing verse remained very poor. In one of his talks concerning his writings, he concentrated on the notion of rhythm in prose, and he added:

> Naturalmente sono di questa specie [i.e. rhythmical] anche gli effetti che più mi interessano nelle cose che scrivo io stesso. Mi rendo ben conto che si tratta di effetti tipici della poesia piuttosto che della prosa, e forse per questo tendo ad appoggiarmi ai poeti, scrivendo, non agli altri: per parte mia, però, versi in proprio cerco di non scriverne, non mi ci trovo, e quei pochi che ogni tanto mi arrivano in casa, per lo più sono brutti come l'orco ('come-orco' nella fraseologia di mia moglie). Scrivendo in prosa, invece, mi viene del tutto naturale puntare sulla forza poetica delle parole. (*Discorso in controluce*, *OS*, pp.1377–78)

Judging from the manuscript material, and some of the published work, the statement that he tries not to write verse of his own is not literally true, of course. One can find some very bad verse in the early manuscripts, especially in a section labelled 'trash' by the author himself, and excellent poems published, sometimes at the end of his books, such as 'Congedo' in *Pomo pero*, which could also be written as prose:

> Il piano inferiore del mondo
> Ha un orlo di monti celesti
> Ed è colmo di paesi.
>
> Nei broli annerisce l'uva
> Che nessuno vuole raccogliere,
> Ne prendono qualche graspo
> gli operai dell'officina,
> uno ne piluccano uno ne gettano,
> giacciono i gioielli neri
> sotto le viti tra le erbacce.
> Smurata è la mura dell'orto,
> Dilaniato il *core*,
> Mucchi di strame ingombrano
> La corte, coppi caduti,
> Rotti rametti, pali fradici.
> Intorno si vede sorgere
> Un mondo di cose nuove
> Questa roba si spazza via,
> Trionfa un rigoglio
> Banale e potente.
>
> Non è più una parodia,
> È vero uso moderno,
> I geometri se ne intendono
> Delle cose e dei loro nomi,
> Mio piccolo popolo
> Forzato da un ramo villano
> Di storia italiana,
> È una foto ricordo — sorridi.
>
> Va libretto mio, va a roccolare.[3]

In this passage Meneghello's love for plurilingualism is found in the central English word *core*, which could of course also be taken as a poetic term for 'heart'.

Or another longish, more complex, poetical composition published in *Jura*, in the section *L'acqua di Malo*, from which I shall quote only the first two stanzas:

> La mia vita mentale è marasmatica
> È un rush di correnti nella testa
> Ciò che vi prende forma si disfa
> L'acqua dinamica travolge le forme
> Ne rigenera altre le disintegra
> È un'acqua brunita, turchina in strati possenti
> Non la scorgevano gli occhi venuti a spiare
> Agli spiragli degli alti battenti di ferro

> Sento allo scroscio che è acqua quasi metallica
> Il suono trasmette i riflessi profondi
> Non si sa quale forza la agiti [...]⁴

In the opening part of *Jura. Ricerche sulla natura delle forme scritte*, published in 1987 and reprinted in 2003, in which Meneghello makes very subtle analyses of the relationship between the language that one speaks and the writing forms, he published a translation of a poem by Don Marquis, in a section called 'What I would have liked to do in life'. The implicit answer seems to be that the author would have liked to be a poet,⁵ and, in a typically ironic vein, an author of Latin verse.⁶

He wrote:

> Naturalmente mi sarebbe piaciuto riuscire a fare dei bei versi, in latino, se possibile, altrimenti pazienza, in volgare; ma 'fare lo scrittore', andiamo... (OS, p. 1384)

This notion is reiterated much later in a filmed interview of 2006.⁷

And in fact, in the section of *Jura* entitled 'L'anno del giglio', the author describes the way in which his alter ego S., around the age of 8 or 9, conceived the idea of writing a formal Christmas letter (addressed to his parents, but also to baby Jesus) in verse. Although S. was still uncertain about poetic refinements and with a tendency to rhyme 'speme' (hope) with 'Gerusalemme' and 'stile' with 'mille' (after all there was no difference in the single or double consonants at the spoken level in his part of Italy), 'S. andò tuttavia dritto agli estremi della creazione letteraria, la poesia'. 'Unfortunately', as Meneghello tells us, the 'central nucleus of his poetical opus' written around the 1930s, has actually come down to us, in a black notebook (he does not mention Heidegger) of the type used to keep shopping accounts, and with the title *Giglio* because, he explains, 'poetry means flowers, perfume, purity'. Among the samples from this early poetical period, the author quotes a couple of lines written for their maid from Slovenia, Jovanka, known in the family as Giovanna:

> Oggi è il dì di San Giovanni,
> La Giovanna compie gli anni

This, he tells us, represents the festive side of literary activity, involving good wishes, writing hymns to new-born babies, relatives' weddings and other important family events, where one can already sense a well-defined conception of the relationship between the artist and society.

The other perceived aim of poetry was a comic-satirical one. The subject's (S.) younger brother is represented as an expert pilot of a Caproni aeroplane:

> Mio fratello ch'è un bravo aviatore
> Del capron mette in moto il motore.

Then the brother goes fighting 'Ora vola nel ciel nuvoloso...' 'E nel cielo nemico ora sono...' and he starts shooting and even bombing enemy cities, in what is an obvious crescendo:

> Bombardando nemiche città
> Meneghello ora grida alalà!

But quickly the protagonist returns home, the war is over,

> E poiché, dopo grande battaglia,
> La vittoria arrise all'Italia

our hero decides to take his father for a ride in the clouds. But the emotion of reaching an altitude of 200 metres is too much and the poor father has an accident in his pants. The whole poem seems to derive from some 'pensierini' written at school about aeroplanes. Meneghello concludes: 'La poesia coi suoi strumenti fecali sgombra un pezzo di cielo e vi disegna il vero. E la gente ride.'

The following section deals with the obscure sources of poetry, and provides further examples of verses penned by S. in which he mentions the fear that his younger brother experiences when hearing the fireworks in a local festival, and the panic that seems to grasp him when he sees 'feminine beauty', in the shape of two pretty little girls, and if he meets

> Adriana oppur Marcella
> scappa via come fosse una gazzella

what to do? What is suggested is a kind of homeopathic treatment, as Meneghello remarks:

> Oimè dovranno mettergli le gonne
> A quel pauroso paura-di-donne

Then further thoughts on the value of the jocular elements in poetry follow, and in general on poetic apprenticeship as a foundation of literary activity and therefore a specific function of the writer.

This leads Meneghello to conclude that the poetical output of S., around the age of eight, did not really come from school lessons. There is an element of personal inventiveness, and the influence of children's magazines, such as the *Corriere dei piccoli* or its rival *Il balilla*, with their facile rhymes. This is what lies behind these precocious experiments of poems to be recited. But generally the *Giglio* collection has obscure sources, therefore — adds Meneghello — contrasting with Montale's *Ossi di seppia*, in which sources and 'ascendenze letterarie' are transparent.

There are other numerous references to poetry and to the origin of rhythm in other works.[8] In particular in the section 'UR-MALO' at the end of *Pomo Pero*, Meneghello has added hundreds of mostly archaic dialect words, divided into 21 sections, according to their syllabic structure, provided in a *Registro* (*OS*, pp. 726–47). As an example, the first part of section 13, dedicated to bisyllable nouns ending in *–ón*, will suffice:

> fotón pirón moltón galón sitón
> paión cocón cavrón parón giarón
> marón traión marsón
> tacón

If I had to provide a translation I would find it rather difficult, but I believe *fotón*[9] means 'a fit of anger', *pirón* 'fork', *moltón* 'mutton', *galón* 'thigh', *sitón* 'dragonfly', *paión* 'straw mattress', *cocón* 'barrel stopper', *cavrón* 'big goat', *parón* 'master', *giarón* 'gravel', *marón* 'chestnut', *traión* 'snow-plough', *marsón* 'small fish', *tacón* 'mending patch', but it must be added that Meneghello himself in an annotation at the end of *Pomo pero*, while explaining the significance of this 'example, limited to phonic and lexical aspects, of the linguistic background' from which the writing concerning Malo originated, adds that he regrets not having been able to explain the meanings of those words, because 'it would have been necessary to write another book'. (*OS*, 754).

On these rhythmical experiences and on the importance of childish rhymes in general Fernando Bandini has written an original essay in which he proves, among other things, that some of the archaic terms used by Meneghello, especially the ones in the 8th sequence of bisyllables, all ending in –*o*, the vowel variations (as in *pómo zugo figo bèco baso / cuco biso vèro gnaro sòco* [...] */giasso lógo buto risso pèro*) form a kind of cabalistic 'magic square' in which the tonic vowels at the top and left margin (*o u i e a*) are the same, but the series is inverted on the bottom and right margin (*a o u i* e), and one diagonal is made up of the same vowels, five *as*.[10]

In a passage belonging to *La materia di Reading* (*OS*, 1377–78) Meneghello discusses the phonic effect of the final –*o* in the two lines from T. S. Eliot's *The Love Song of J. Alfred Prufrock*, in which the stressed final vowel is emphasised:

> In the room the women come and go
> Talking of Michelangelo

But then he moves to an even stronger example of rhythm in a childish rhyme (used to exclude children in a game), which he quoted in *Libera nos a malo* (*OS*, p. 49):

> *An Pan*
> *Fiol d'un Can*
> *Fiol d'un Béco*
> *Muri Séco*
> *Cole Gambe Disti-rà*

In which, he claims, the powerful binary rhythm, especially in the last word, represents the 'expressive strength of the text'.

Later, important notes by Meneghello on rhythmical aspects of his prose, emerge in his conversations, as in a passage originally appeared in *L'acqua di Malo* and then published in *Jura* (*OS*, p. 1162):

> I ricordi relativi a quelli che erano già vecchi quando i vecchi di adesso erano bambini ci riportano lontano nel secolo scorso, e un giretto per il paese ci mette davanti agli occhi i frammenti del mondo di allora.
> A specchio degli sterpi della Proa c'è la casa dove crebbe mia bisnonna Candida: quelle mattonelle a spina di pesce nel portico sono le stesse su cui giocava da piccola, e qui passava vestita da festa per andare a messa la domenica da ragazza: su questo scalino davanti alla porta settecentesca avrà chiacchierato col moroso...
> Il nostro legame con quel mondo erano queste case, e i tronconi del ponte vecchio sulla Proa, da cui il nonno certamente saltava giù con gli altri bambini del suo secolo....

The author singles out one phrase as particularly significant and implicitly he asks:

what is the magic of a phrase like *A specchio degli sterpi della Proa* which he found so satisfying that he would have liked to chime the bells of the village church to celebrate? First of all it is a hendecasyllable, secondly the reminiscences from Montale's *Ossi di seppia* are remarkable. *Specchio* suggests the 'azzurri specchianti' and the possibility of being in the same phono-semantic area of the rhyming *secchio* of 'Cigola la carrucola del pozzo' (rhyming with *vecchio*) where memories come up to the surface. There is also the *sterpi*, line 3 of 'Meriggiare', with words like *schiocchi*, and the *esiguo specchio* in the Montalian *Osso* (*Ripenso il tuo sorriso*), which may well be the key intertextual element in this evocative passage

Apart from concerns of rhythm, there are others expressed by the author about his writings: for example in the weekly magazine *Epoca* of 7 December 1974, in a section entitled 'L'autore si confessa', Meneghello declared:

> Fra i molti crucci che potrei confessare c'è quello di non saper scrivere con perfetta autorità... cioè riuscendo a comunicare la sostanza intima, 'il vero' delle cose su cui si scrive.

This seems to recall the dialect phrase on which the title of his third book is based: *pomo pero dime el vero, dime la santa verità: Quale zéla? Questa qua* (*OS*, p.755). The preoccupation with 'the truth', the 'essence' of lived experience is indeed a constant in Meneghello's writings, but it seems to be underlined in an almost obsessive manner which allows the reader to suspect that frequently, and in various ways, through the use of irony, of foreign words, of dialect, of archaisms, he is actually practising a subtle form of 'dissimulation'.[11] This could be substantiated by some of the manuscripts in Pavia.

Together with this remark, there is also the one that we find in the important *Discorso in controluce*, mentioned above, where the author concentrates on the work which is necessary to transform 'experience into writing' or at least an attempt to reflect on the two elements, and what he calls

> una certa propensione, istintiva, per la gnoseologia, l'epistemologia, lo studio dei meccanismi (o non-meccanismi) della 'conoscenza': quasi l'idea di capire il modo di capire. (*OS*, p. 1384).[12]

On top of the evidence mentioned above to prove the importance of rhythm, and the accompanying one of the 'true experiences' for Meneghello, I would add a short piece, of only two pages, published in a plaquette by Rosario Morra in Venice, in June 2002, and entitled *Murazzi*. This work is hardly known, since the edition consisted of only 99 copies, but it is an example of a whole text written in a strong rhythmical, suggestive, prose. The second 'paragraph' will suffice:

> [...] ma ora li ho visti i murazzi e nell'abbacinante
> luce che investe la mente quando (non più giovane)
> ti capita la fortuna di trovarti a rimirare
> i lastroni della pietra luminosa e ti metti a correre
> saltando di masso in masso per chilometri;
> in direzione di chioggia
> ora non più giovane li ho visti e li ho rimirati
> e ho corso e saltato per lunghissimi tratti

> e la luce e le forme di pietra e il rapporto col mare
> erano perfetti, cose sognate, splendide benché cosparse
> di profonda malinconia e splendidamente inutili [...]¹³

in which lexical elements deriving from Dante's poetry (*mente, luce, luminosa, rimirare*) stand out, among other prominent rhythmical and alliterative elements (*-tr-* and *-rt-* in *fortuna, trovarti, lastroni, pietra, chilometri* and endings in *-etti -atti, metti, tratti, perfetti*), producing a satisfying result for the ever (apparently) dissatisfied author. It is also a good example of a text which gains from being read aloud.

Meneghello's attitude to celebrated Italian and foreign poets has also been studied and I shall summarise some of the findings here, with the addition of a few remarks coming from the massive collection of unpublished manuscripts that was mentioned earlier.

Among contemporary Italian poets there is no doubt that Meneghello had a special regard for Montale, and there are numerous intertextual references to him in his works, especially in *Libera nos a malo*, *I piccoli maestri* and *Pomo pero*.¹⁴ Later on Meneghello's interest seems to diminish or become more critical, or simply more ironical.¹⁵ And yet, the author himself had acknowledged in a private communication that some of Montale's verse (e.g. *... precipita / il tempo, spare con risucchi rapidi / tra i sassi* in 'Crisalide') affected him 'con forza ossessiva'.¹⁶ In a manuscript note, undated, but probably from the late 1950s [Temporary shelf mark MEN 01 0267, f. 17], and revisited in June 1999, Meneghello writes some notes which begin with the phrase: 'Scrivo per i miei coetanei' then adds

> Imparate il ~~cinese~~ l'inglese, 'Give up Italy as a bad job'. Apprezzate incoraggiate quel poco di buono che c'è, e disprezzate e deridete il resto. Esempi del poco di buono (in letteratura) qualche verso di Montale, una parte del suo lessico.
> Esempi del resto: la montatura della sensibilità montaliana.

He then suggests that ten 'very rich' bursaries should be given to demolish Ungaretti and thirty for the 'dissection of serious Montale' from 'Montale da strapazzo'. The author is conscious of the almost delirious elements in what he jots down, which he himself defines, in English, as 'trash' and 'spaventosa pappardella' in a note added on 21 June 1999. On 26 August 1999 he adds a personal note, presumably when revising his manuscripts to send to Pavia: 'indecenze goffaggini auto-lesionismi. Buttare? Lasciare mss? [per preservare le miserie imbarazzanti?]'.

Moving on to Ungaretti, already in *Libera nos* we find that a few words recorded as an invective against the poor food that was available to one of the beggars in the village

> Sempre ròcoli
> Stechetoni
> Cago verde
> Come rughe.¹⁷

are completed by Meneghello, in a typically lapidary way, with 'Allegria di naufragi'. (*OS*, p. 280). A similar attitude is expressed in *I piccoli maestri*, when the narrator is talking about sentinel duty:

> In quelle ore di solitudine assoluta, ghiacciata, uno si sentiva soldato, frate, fibra dell'universo, e mona. Il freddo era schifoso.

And these are not the only instances of ironic use of words taken from Ungaretti's early poetry. In *Pomo pero* there is another reference to one of Ungaretti's poems:

> Quando trovo in questi miei studi una vergogna (a parte che *resta scavata nella mia* vita, come avrebbe detto un Autore non Veneto che di vergogna avrebbe dovuto intendersene, ma non ne dava segno) resto male.

In *Bau sète!*, Ungaretti is also labelled as 'un ballista di prima riga'.[18]

And yet, judging from Meneghello's unpublished manuscript notes, *Allegria di naufragi* was considered 'the best' of Ungaretti's production, but the overall judgment is definitely scathing. In the same folder mentioned above (MEN 01 0267) on the same page (f. 17), Meneghello adds, as another example of 'what is bad in Italian poetry':

> [...]' L'intera opera di Ungaretti, poeta farabutto se mai ce ne furono, con la sola eccezione delle poesiole del tempo di guerra.'

Another poet that Meneghello considered in a very negative vein was Quasimodo, the 'ballista tindarico'. Not only do we find in Meneghello's works, the reference, in *I piccoli maestri* (OS, p. 391), to the period spent in Padua 'a suonare l'oboe sommerso, che poi non si sa che suono possa fare. Farà glu glu' but I can testify to an afternoon seminar at the university of Reading, around 1972–73 wholly dedicated to the demolition of Quasimodo's poetry, to the so-called 'hermetic poets' and even more to the criticism belonging to the same school, when it was proven that Carlo Bo had nothing to say, and did not say much, apart from waffle.

Meneghello and foreign poetry

In a passage towards the end of *Bau-sète*,[19] we find the following sentence: 'Le donne maledette del mio venerato Baudelaire mi facevano pensare a una sfilata parigina [...]'. What is striking here is the adjective *venerato*. We thought it was almost impossible for Meneghello to venerate anything or anybody, especially a poet. In fact there are occasional intertextual references to Baudelaire, for example at the beginning of *Libera nos*, when he is describing a struggle among children, specifically that of Gigi Meneghello himself with his girl-cousins Flora and Este, both taller than himself in the courtyard of their house in Malo: at a certain point the 'wrestlers' are tangled but stay there '*dans d'immenses efforts* senza combinar nulla'. The phrase comes from Baudelaire's 'La cloche fêlée' from *Les Fleurs du mal*, and the presence of the French collection fits well in a narrative which takes into account the name of one of the girls (Flora) to suggest a kind of *Fleurs de Malo*.[20]

In an interview with Ernestina Pellegrini, Meneghello was asked which foreign literature he read before his contact with British culture. And he answered that he read above all French literature, as well as Latin and some Greek, but mainly nineteenth-century French classics and more poetry than narrative; which confirms the impression that one gets from reading Meneghello's texts.

The next question that Pellegrini asked related to a forthcoming book which was going to be called *Trapianti*.[21]

And this is the point our investigation on poetry wanted to reach.

There are a few fragments of poems in dialect, and some early attempts at translating particularly difficult English poems in manuscript notes which are dateable to the late 1950s. The beginning of a short fragment in Italian, for instance, [MEN 220, ff. 61–65] with the date 17 May 1958, is almost certainly derived from the beginning of Gerald Manley Hopkins's *The Fell of Dark*: 'I wake and feel the fell of dark, not day'. In Meneghello's autographs we find: *Mi sveglio e c'è un'alba, buio pelo* and then, on the following leaves, the same with variants: *Mi sveglio e c'è non luce buio pelo*; *Mi sveglio e c'è pelo buio non luce (alba)*, and on f. 65, under the title 'Un delitto', *Mi sveglio in bocca al buio non al dì*. This will eventually be published in *Trapianti* as *Me sveio e palpo pelo, pelo scuro /nò dì*. This again shows the painstaking and prolonged *labor limae* of the author.

The idea of 'transplanting' poems from English to his own Vicenza dialect for publication may have come to Meneghello after his retirement from the University of Reading in 1980. In his manuscripts, one finds some early attempts, dated October 1984, at 're-writing' e.e. cummings's 'Buffalo Bill' in dialect. [Temporary shelf mark MEN 02 0311, ff. 3–23], and in the same folder we find a 'Progetto per un pezzo di 5000 parole (c. 15 pp.) sulla TRADUZIONE o piuttosto di TRADUZIONI' and the first authors mentioned are: 'Cummings, Larkin, Qualche Yeats, Qualche Lawrence?' (f. 3), then follows on f. 6 some attempts at finding a title, in two columns: 'Pezzo da intitolare p. es.'

> *Omaggi*
> *Lacerba*
> *Florilegio*
> *Fior da fiore*
> *Il fiore*

In the second column, with double underlining *Le biade / La biava*, and even, in a second folder, '*Companadeghi* oppure *Le biave / La biava*'.

Eventually *Le biave* was chosen with specific reference to sustaining food, fodder, as explained by Meneghello in the interview with Ernestina Pellegrini and in the filmed interview with Marco Paolini, and appeared in a miscellany dedicated to Giulio Lepschy in 1997.[22] On 19 October 1996 [MEN 01 0311, f.6] he compiled a list of 'poeti per La biave'[*sic*], with notes added to some of the names: Th. Hardy, [A. E. Housman], W. B. Yeats, Edward Thomas, D. H. Lawrence (Siegfried Sassoon), T.S. ELIOT with the addition in capital letters '*VEDAREMO*', [Wilfred Owen] with addition 'mah!', Roy Campbell, Sir John Betjeman, William Empson [W.H. AUDEN] Dylan Thomas, addition 'No', Philip Larkin 1–2., then reduced on f. 6v to a SHORT LIST: Yeats, Larkin, Donne, Hardy, Lawrence, Hopkins, M. Arnold, E. Thomas, Cummings. Eventually *Le biave* contained G. M. Hopkins (4 poems), e.e. cummings (5), W. Empson (4), W. B. Yeats (17), Shakespeare (1).

It is obvious that the practice of translation has occupied Meneghello through most of his life, and particularly in the 1960s when he actually translated half a dozen

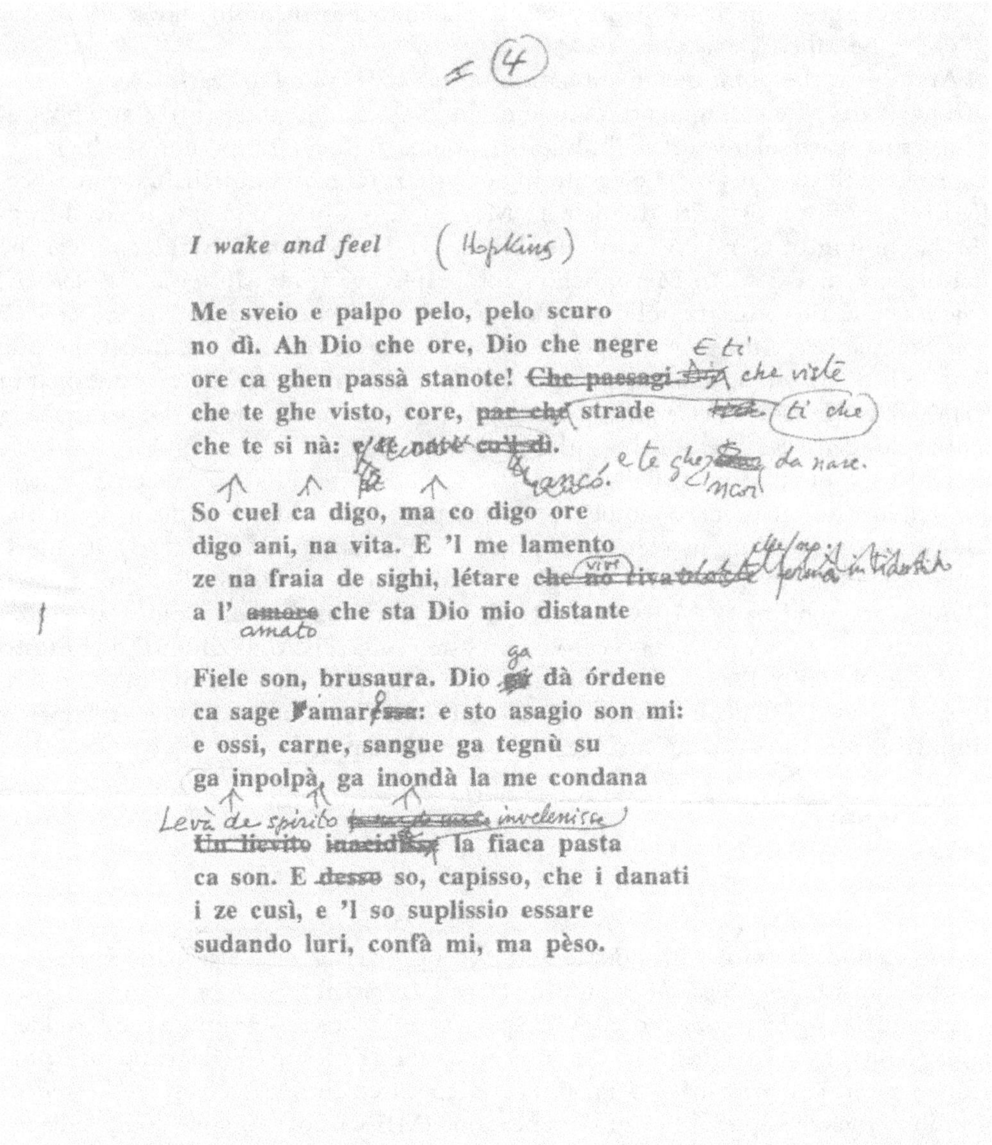

I wake and feel   (Hopkins)

Me sveio e palpo pelo, pelo scuro
no dì. Ah Dio che ore, Dio che negre
ore ca ghen passà stanote! Che passagi
che te ghe visto, core, par che strade
che te si nà:

So cuel ca digo, ma co digo ore
digo ani, na vita. E 'l me lamento
ze na fraia de sighi, létare
a l' amore che sta Dio mio distante

Fiele son, brusaura. Dio gà dà órdene
ca sage l'amarezza: e sto asagio son mi:
e ossi, carne, sangue ga tegnù su
ga inpolpà, ga inondà la me condana

Un lievito inacidiss la fiaca pasta
ca son. E desso so, capisso, che i danati
i ze cusì, e 'l so suplissio essare
sudando luri, confà mi, ma pèso.

FIG. 24.1. Gerard Manley Hopkins' sonnet 'I wake and feel the fell of dark, not day', translated by Luigi Meneghello into Vicentino dialect, with numerous autograph additions, to be compared with the published text in *Trapianti: dall'inglese al vicentino* (Milan: Rizzoli, 2002), p. 23. (Courtesy of the Centro di ricerca sulla tradizione manoscritta di autori moderni e contemporanei, University of Pavia.)

books from English,[23] a total of over one thousand five-hundred pages, as he tells us. And he claims that this activity helped him to write clearly and to understand the difference between Italian and English, where the latter seems able to express anything directly as if phrases and sentences to describe events or emotions already existed, while in Italian, one felt there was a large hiatus between the spoken and the written language.[24]

Apart from his published translations, there are numerous attempts at poetry translation in his manuscripts. When he was invited to give a lecture at the University of Ca' Foscari in Venice for the inauguration of a new postgraduate course in literary translation from English, he concentrated on the subject, and gave examples of his early poetical translations from English. The lecture was delivered on 15 April 1994, and published as *Il turbo e il chiaro* in 1995 (*OS*, pp. 1537–59). In this lecture his attitude to translation is clearly expressed:

> Per me tradurre significa spostare gli equilibri interni di un testo, che nel testo stanno lì, e nella vostra comprensione immediata e diretta del testo li vedete stabili, ma non appena tentate di tradurre vi può venir fuori dalla traduzione qualche cosa che non sapevate nemmeno che c'era nel testo: almeno questo è ciò che capita continuamente a me. Si va, traducendo, a colpire punti nevralgici del testo; si fanno emergere aspetti che non erano in rilievo, che forse nella lingua originale non potevamo nemmeno sapere se c'erano o no. Insomma la traduzione è quasi un nuovo testo [...]. (*OS*, p. 1539)

But what does it mean to translate difficult English poetry into one's native dialect? Is it the same as translating into a national language? And why does Meneghello prefer the notion of 'transplanting' rather than translating? It is well known that in his work there is a certain propensity to use terms which have to do with the 'cultivation' of the mind, with flowers, and in general with activities connected with a rural or rustic milieu. In this context he pointed out that the title *Trapianti* had nothing to do with hospital surgery, but was literally similar to the removal of a plant to put it into a different pot. In a way it is not dissimilar to what Montale had expressed in a famous poem of his *Ossi di seppia*, '*Portami il girasole*'.

From what we have seen above, at the beginning of the project for the miscellany *In amicizia*, the idea was still directly that of 'translation', presumably in the etymological sense, and in accordance with the principles investigated in *Il turbo e il chiaro*, according to which even the poet is not sometimes fully conscious of the 'sense' or the 'meaning' of what he/she is writing. Moreover, in the second part of the same conversation, Meneghello tries to give some practical advice to the would-be translators in the audience, where he insists on the possibilities of translation in 'refining the reading of a text, to look at it more deeply' (*OS*, p. 1551). He then moves on to give some examples, and the first one is perhaps one of the most famous in Meneghello's works. It is a rendering of the first lines from Coleridge's *Kubla Khan* (In Xanadu did Kubla Khan/ a stately pleasure dome decree [...]).

> A Sanadù chel can da l'os d'on Kubla Can
> El ghe dà ordene ch'i fesse on gran palasso,
> On capanón co la so cupola.

> Nobile capanón de Kubla Can.
> Orcocàn, Kubla Can, che capanón!
> Can da l'os d'on Kubla Can!

It is obvious that the 'ludic' element creates a much more comical effect in the dialect version, on the other hand, as Meneghello explains, the 'stately pleasure dome' of the original suggested to him a type of building that in the 1960s seemed to spring up everywhere in the Italian North East, 'il capannone, il mitico edificio-investimento che tanti miei conoscenti ed amici si erano messi a costruire' (*OS*, p. 1552). This, coupled with the play on the euphemistic 'Can da l'os' (*can da l'ostia*) and the phonic identity of Khan and Can, produces a comic effect, but also a dream-like atmosphere, with the repetition of syllables and the colloquial use of imprecations (*orcocàn*, for 'porco can'), and the language helps to make a refined text more homely, and much more suitable to be appreciated in a rural area of Northern Italy.

In *Il turbo e il chiaro* Meneghello also lists the poets that he would like to translate, the main ones being Donne, Hopkins, Yeats, e. e. cummings and Philip Larkin, the only one with whom he was personally acquainted, and whom he finds relatively straightforward to translate. The example he gives is the best known in Larkin's corpus:

> They fuck you up, your mum and dad —
> They may not mean to, but they do.

which seems to go very smoothly into another demotic language:

> I te ciava to mama e to popà
> No i fa mia posta, ma i te ciava.

Not all of the above have made it to the *Trapianti*, where we find Hopkins (6), e. e. cummings (6), W. Empson (3), W. B. Yeats (17), Roy Campbell (1) and Shakespeare (5), among other fragments from previously published works.

In April 2002 Meneghello must have been thinking of the publication of his adaptations from English, and on a piece of paper headed 'Palace Grand Hotel — Varese', we find: 'aut. Luigi Meneghello/ TRASPIANTI / dall'inglese al vicentino/ and below: '"S" balenata 26.4.02", then 'STRAPIANTI'.

In an interview by Luca Bernasconi (which was broadcast in Switzerland in 2005) one of the questions concerned 'The fascination of what's difficult' as found in a poem by Yeats, and Meneghello replies that Yeats has always fascinated him. The concept in the original English is something expressed 'perfectly'.[25] In view of this comment, it may be fruitful to focus on the rendering of the whole poem in Vicentine dialect.

> [From 'The Fascination of What's Difficult']
> *The fascination of what's difficult*
> *Has dried the sap out of my veins, and rent*
> *Spontaneous joy and natural content*
> *Out of my heart...*
>
> La me passion par cuel che zé difìssile [MS, MEN 320, f. 140: de cuel; *El fàssino de cuel*]

> La me ga sugà le vene
> La passión de 'l difìssile,
> La me ga tólto 'l contenuto naturale
> De le bale...

To achieve this striking result, in a typically irreverent, but totally justified, outcome in dialect, Meneghello has had to tinker with the original, not only in moving the imagery from above the belt to below, as Pietro De Marchi pointed out,[26] but in pretending to misunderstand the 'natural content' which in English must bear the stress on the second syllable and therefore could have become something like 'la sodisfasión naturale'. This would have underlined a further sexual meaning, and perhaps by using a standard Italian word like 'contenuto' he has tried to focus on the 'unnatural' element that poetry may convey. Can this be another instance of *dissimulatio*? In order to achieve concision, the phrase 'and rent spontaneous joy' seems to have been sacrificed. Moreover, the last term can be inserted in the semantic series of Vicentine *balòte* as indicated in *Maredè maredè* (p. 15), in which the term is immediately followed by *materia* ('pus'). Meneghello's choice, according to some, appears to justify the reference to the 'wrapping of the essence of life' which helps an effective 'transplant'.[27]

Before concluding I would like to mention the work which has gone in the achievement of *I Trapianti*. If we consider the English text as a 'fiore còlto' and the Vicentine dialect the 'fiore donato', in the context of the early poetry by Ungaretti, we would say that in between there is certainly not the 'inesprimibile nulla', on the contrary there is a flurry of correctional activity.

We shall illustrate it by looking at one important poem by Gerard Manley Hopkins, *I wake and feel* but in *Trapianti* it is given as [The Fell of Dark]:

> I wake and feel the fell of dark, not day.
> What hours, O what black hours we have spent
> This night! What sights you, heart, saw; ways you went!
> And more must, in yet longer light's delay.
>   With witness I speak this. But where I say
> Hours I mean years, mean life. And my lament
> Is cries countless, cries like dead letters sent
> To dearest him that lives alas! Away
>
>   I am gall, I am heartburn. God's most deep decree
> Bitter would have me taste: my taste was me;
> Bones built in me, flesh filled, blood brimmed the curse
>   Selfyeast of spirit a dull dough sours. I see
> The lost are like this, and their scourge to be
> As I am mine, their sweating selves; but worse.

The transition from the tormented language of Gerald Manley Hopkins to a satisfying and convincing Vicentine version starts a long time before publication.

In the Pavia manuscripts, after a note dated 4 December 1957: 'Maledizione! La letteratura costa parecchia fatica, e non dura', there are the early attempts mentioned above. The same folder (temporary 202) contains other fragments of dialect poetry, e.g. f. 68 *Inc*. 'A gato magnao / me ramenava par la camara'; f. 79, dated 'venerdì 14 nov. '58' 'I cigni che s'indormensa [...] / te piaseli i cigni?/ Vardeli: i pare barchete [...]'.

In turning the first line of Hopkins into Vicentine, the author goes for the current meaning of 'fell', a fur or hide, and disregards the other, older meaning of 'bitterness' possibly etymologically connected with Italian *fiele* 'gall': *Me sveio e palpo pelo, pelo scuro.* In order to visualise some of the continuous attention to the text and its variants, it may be worth looking at a reproduction of one typed version to see the way in which different stages are reached (Fig. 24.1).

ll.3–5: *ore ca ghen pasà stanote! Che paesagi e ti che viste/ che te ghe visto, core, par che ti che strade che te si nà: e te narè col dì ,e te ghe 'ncor da nare.*

l.8: 'létare che no riva' is first crossed out, and then *vive* written above the line, after the second version *che no fermà in trànsito* has been rejected.

l. 14 *Selfyeast of spirit a dull dough sours* becomes 'Un lievito inacidisse la fiaca pasta/ ca son', but then it is probably felt to be not sufficiently true to the dialect spirit, and *Levà de spirit invelenisse la fiaca pasta / ca son*, and in the margin, in a faint note, the word 'corompe' is suggested, presumably as a substitute for 'invelenisse' which in turn was written after an intermediate *fa n'da male*.

In this version which is already number 4 in a typescript, four different inks are visible, and the constant repeated attempts to achieve a satisfactory 'final' version are clear.

Alterations will continue until the text is printed. But in the case of a reprint, it is still possible to alter something (e.g. in some of the poems which are printed in OS, e.g. *La me cara ecetera* by e.e. cummings, imperceptible changes exist, for example *e se lu* vs *e che se lu*, and the more macroscopic *in meso metro de fango* vs. *in meso metro de paltàn* in *Trapianti*. The choice of lexical items, but also of prepositions and other grammatical elements, seems to go in the direction of a more 'authentic', even archaic, localised dialect. In some of the longer passages from Shakespeare Meneghello in his 'transplant' recreates a kind of popular form of Italian Shakespeare. But he still manages to keep a certain elevated tone in the spoken theatrical language. In the celebrated passage from *Hamlet* (Act II, sc. II, ll. 304 ff.)

> What a piece of work is a man! How noble in reason, how infinite in faculties, in form and moving how express and admirable, in action how like an angel, in apprehension how like a god! The beauty of the world, the paragon of animals! And yet, to me what is this quintessence of dust? Man delights not me: no, nor woman neither, though by your smiling you seem to say so.

Meneghello has given a dialect title to the piece in his *Trapianti* (p.93) 'Confidense a Rosencrantz e Guildenstern' and then, capturing the Hamletic irony perfectly:

> Casso, un omo! Che capo d'opera che l'zé, che nobile el so giudissio, che infinite le capacità! De figura e de ati, co che l'è s'ceto e amirevole! In assión, cuanto vissìn ai angeli! De comprendonio, cuanto someiante a un dio! La belessa del mondo! El pì togo de tuti i animai... Sì, ma par mi cossa zé sta cuintessensa de pólvare? A mi l'omo NO ME PIASE: nò, e la dona gnanca...Vedo ca fe un soriseto, ma ve sbaliè...

In general terms, the achievement of Meneghello's 'transplants' is similar to that mentioned by Leopardi in his *Zibaldone* according to which the forms, the words, the graces, the elegance that are found in any writing or speech in a foreign language can only be fully appreciated in one's own language:

> Tutto quello mai che può spettare alla lingua [...] non si sente mai né si gusta se non in relazione colla lingua familiare, e paragonando più o meno distintamente quella frase straniera a una frase nostrale, trasportando quell'ardimento, quella eleganza ec. in nostra lingua.[28]

It is a high achievement. And it almost reaches a diction which is reminiscent of some passages in Dante (e.g. *Par.* XXVIII, 84 *con le bellezze d'ogni sua parroffia*) , as in the opening of Hopkins' *Starlight Night:*

> Vara le stéle! Vàrdele, vara 'l celo!
> Vara, ma vara, i s'ciapi d'i omeniti
> Fiamanti sentà-zo parària!
> Le parochie che slùsega, là oltra, le sitadele [...]

Perhaps Meneghello's youthful, velleitarian desire to write good Latin verse could not be achieved nor realised, but, judging from most of his work, and in particular from the *Trapianti*, he has managed to achieve a high level of poetry in a Neo-Latin language from North-East Italy, which for him was definitely his *parlar materno*. And through his painstaking attempts to reach 'perfection' he proves to, be after all, an excellent craftsman, like the ones in his home town, including his father, a very able *fabbro*.

Notes to Chapter 24

1. A preliminary inventory of the manuscripts has been published by Chiara Lungo, 'Il fondo Luigi Meneghello di Pavia: Inventario (1984–2001)', in *Tra le parole della 'virtù senza nome': la ricerca di Luigi Meneghello,* ed. by Francesca Caputo (Novara: Interlinea, 2013), pp. 201–46.
2. The English text is in a manuscript at the Centro per gli studi sulla tradizione manoscritta di autori moderni e contemporanei at the University of Pavia, with the temporary shelfmark MEN 0110, ff. 34–35; the Italian is in the section *Fiori a Edimburgo* of *La materia di Reading e altri reperti* in Luigi Meneghello, *Opere scelte: progetto editoriale e introduzione di Giulio Lepschy,* ed. by Francesca Caputo (Milan: Mondadori, 2006), p. 1344. From now on this will be abbreviated to OS.
3. An explanation of the meaning of this verb, based on Vicentine dialect *rocolare*, in a form which Meneghello defines as 'trasporto', is given in *Leda e la schioppa* (OS, p. 1219) as, roughly, 'gather together, beg [something to survive]'.
4. OS, pp. 1168–69.
5. *Cosa avrei voluto fare nella vita,* was first published with the title *Com'era Shakespeare* in the daily *Giornale di Vicenza,* on 23 September 1984. Just before the actual translation Meneghello explains that the original title of Don Marquis is all in lower case 'pete the parrot and shakespeare' and is supposed to have been written by 'archy', a literary cockroach who typed the text by jumping on the keyboard. Meneghello also gives some information on the reasons why he decided to translate it.
6. '[...] già da adolescente avevo una mezza idea che sarebbe stato meglio morire a diciannove anni. [...] Però non prima di aver scritto un libro di poesie in latino. Naturalmente non ero in grado di scriverle, il mio latino non era certo all'altezza. Era un'ambizione campata in aria'. Luigi Meneghello, *Dialoghi,* Ritratti (Rome: Fandango libri, 2006), p. 56.
7. The passage has been cut in the DVD.

8. In *Leda e la schioppa* Meneghello devotes a few pages specifically to the rhythm of his prose, and exemplifies it by highlighting a passage from *Pomo pero*: 'Sul cantone di dESTRA, la mura smagliATA faceva una sELLA, da cui si osservAVA la grande campAGNA del Conte [...]' adding, at the end, 'Qui se non sentite il ritmo, non vi ho fatto sentire niente' (OS,1241). In the same 'conversation' he quotes various rhythmical series of terms from UR-MALO, including the ones mentioned above (*OS*, 1245).
9. *Fotone* is mentioned in *Libera nos a malo* (*OS*, pp. 40, 185, 310), and with further explanation (as *fotón*) in *Maredè, maredè... Sondaggi nel campo dell'eloquenza vicentina* (Vicenza: Moretti & Vidali, 1990), p. 170, and *sitón* is also mentioned on p. 223.
10. Fernando Bandini, 'Dialetto e filastrocca infantile in *Libera nos a malo* e *Pomo pero*', in *Su/Per Meneghello*, ed. by Giulio Lepschy (Milan: Edizioni di Comunità, 1983), pp. 73–83.
11. This is too complex an aspect of Meneghello's writings to discuss here, but it is worth looking at the following: Barry Jones, '*Pomo pero:* What's in a name?', in *Su/Per Meneghello*, pp. 85–95, and Franco Marcoaldi, in *La Repubblica* 27.6.2007.
12. In *Maredè, maredè* (p. 29), while talking about fragments and the organization of his thoughts he also mentions what he believed was his destiny: '[...] quando voglio fare ciò per cui m'immaginavo di essere nato: filosofare.'
13. No punctuation and no capitals in the original, of which we have respected the formatting.
14. See the illuminating article by Franco Marenco, 'Meneghello's Intertextual Strategies', in *Meneghello: Fiction, Scholarship, Passione civile*, ed. by Daniela La Penna, *The Italianist*, 32 (2012), Special Supplement, pp. 74–78, and Silvio Ramat, 'Luigi Meneghello e la memoria dei poeti italiani' in *Per 'Libera nos a malo'. A 40 anni dal libro di Luigi Meneghello*, ed. by G. Barbieri and F. Caputo (Vicenza: Terraferma, 2005), pp. 51–70.
15. See Diego Zancani, 'Montale in Meneghello', in *Su/Per Meneghello*, pp.109–18.
16. Private letter by Meneghello dated 2 July 1983.
17. *rughe* 'caterpillars'.
18. *Bau sète!* In Luigi Meneghello, *Opere*, ed. by Francesca Caputo, 2 vols (Milan: Rizzoli, 1997), II, 452.
19. In Meneghello, *Opere*, II, 555–56.
20. Diego Zancani, 'Le Flore di Malo ovvero Meneghello e la citazione di autori stranieri', in *Per 'Libera nos a malo'. A 40 anni dal libro di Luigi Meneghello*, pp. 73–83.
21. Ernestina Pellegrini, *Luigi Meneghello* (Florence: Cadmo, 2002) pp. 147–54.
22. *In amicizia. Essays in Honour of Giulio Lepschy*, ed. by Zygmunt G. Barański and Lino Pertile (*The Italianist*, 17, 1997), pp. 327–47. In MS 320 there is a copy of an autograph letter to Barański, accompanying the final typescript of *Le biave* in which the author concludes: 'Ho fatto più fatica del previsto, e non so se il risultato lo giustifichi. Ma ormai, come diceva il poeta, è tardi.'
23. 'La traduzione c'è dappertutto nella mia vita' Meneghello explains in *Il turbo e il chiaro*, and then mentions the large amount of translations 'pubblicate con altro nome' (*OS*, p. 1540–41); most of them are listed in the section *Bibliografia* by Francesca Caputo in *OS*, pp. 1759–69.
24. *Il turbo e il chiaro* (*OS*, p. 1541).
25. 'E allora, scrivendo, rimetti a posto le cose'. Intervista con Luigi Meneghello a cura di Luca Bernasconi, in *Volta la carta la ze finia. Luigi Meneghello. Biografia per immagini*, ed. by Giuliana Adamo and Pietro De Marchi (Milan: Effigie, 2008), pp. 203–11.
26. Pietro De Marchi, 'Traduzioni, trasporti, trapianti: Meneghello tra le lingue', in *Italia e Europa. Dalla cultura nazionale all'interculturalismo*, Atti del XVI Congresso AIPI Krakow, 26–29 August 2004, 2 vols (Florence: Cesati, 2006), II, 307–16.
27. See also Lucrezia Chinellato, '"Nel corso dei decenni cerco una versione viva". Meneghello e l'esperienza della traduzione in vicentino', in *Meneghello: Fiction, Scholarship, Passione civile*, pp. 139–53, 148–49.
28. Giacomo Leopardi, *Zibaldone* (963), mentioned by Lucrezia Chinellato, 'Nel corso dei decenni cerco una versione viva', p. 139.

CHAPTER 25

'Double trouble': Giampaolo Pansa's *Il sangue dei vinti* from Novel to Film

Philip Cooke

In his monograph on Calvino, published by Edinburgh University Press in its splendid series 'The Writers of Italy', Martin McLaughlin dedicates an entire chapter to the 1947 novel *Il sentiero dei nidi di ragno*.[1] McLaughlin's chapter, read by generations of scholars and students, describes the novel as 'a small-scale epic', as a 'canonical text of neorealism', but also as a work which 'occupies a problematic place in the history of post-war Italian literature'.[2] In 2015, in confirmation of the novel's canonicity, *Il sentiero* was placed on the syllabus for the *maturità* exam, with students asked to write a piece of textual analysis. In the run up to the exam one student posted a question on the web: 'Esiste un film tratto dal libro di italo calvino "il sentiero dei nidi di ragno"?'. The 'best response' was 'non c'è mi dispice (sic) se vuoi sapere la trama del libro eccola' — and indeed a helpful summary followed.

The inclusion of the novel in the *maturità* exam, coupled with the (rather surprising) absence of a film version,[3] perhaps in confirmation of the problematic status described by McLaughlin, raises a number of interesting questions about the interaction between Resistance literature and Resistance film in post-war Italy: which literary texts which offer an account of the Resistance have been transformed into films in the period from 1945 to the present day? Why do some texts not make it into a film version while others do? How are literary texts manipulated into film and what problems do they present to film makers? What kinds of changes occur in the page to screen process and what lies behind such changes?[4] In this chapter I will offer an overview of these issues, while making no claims to completeness. The chapter will discuss a number of well-known Resistance texts, such as Renata Viganò's *L'Agnese va a morire* and Elio Vittorini's *Uomini e no*, but will dedicate most attention to the film version of Giampaolo Pansa's novel *Il sangue dei vinti*, as it occupies an important and highly contested place in recent debates about the historical and cultural significance of the Resistance.[5] The chapter does not deal with films which are based on non-literary texts, of which there are many examples, particularly in the 1960s, with films like Nanni Loy's *Le quattro giornate di Napoli* (1962) and Gianni Puccini's *I sette fratelli Cervi* (1968) based on re-elaborations of historical texts or memoirs.[6] The *quattro giornate* is loosely based on Aldo De Jaco's 1952 book *La città insorge*, and the film about the Cervi brothers also has its basis in a text of the 1950s, Aldo Cervi's *I miei sette figli*.[7]

Calvino's *Il sentiero dei nidi di ragno* is one of a small group of literary texts published in the period from the immediate post-war to the late 1940s which went on to acquire the status of 'classic' Resistance novels — they have all been reprinted many times over the years, appear on school and university courses in Italy and abroad, and have been frequently anthologised.[8] These novels include Elio Vittorini's *Uomini e no*, Cesare Pavese's *La casa in collina* and Renata Vigano's *L'Agnese va a morire*.[9] *La casa in collina* has suffered the same fate as *Il sentiero dei nidi di ragno* and has never been made into a film. This may be because Pavese's literary executors have refused to give consent, or because the text's portrayal of an intellectual's separation from history does not sit well within the various Resistance narratives which have circulated since the Liberation. There are, however, film versions of *L'Agnese va a morire* and *Uomini e no*. In both cases many years elapsed between the publication of the literary text and the release of the film. In the case of the Viganò novel, the film version directed by Giuliano Montaldo was released in 1976, whereas Valentino Orsini's film of *Uomini e no* dates to 1980.[10]

For *L'Agnese va a morire* the delay can be attributed, in part, to Viganò's own reaction to the various scripts which were sent to her over the years, one of which turned Agnese into the lover of the partisan commander, but also to the vagaries of the market and the practical, as well as financial, problems encountered by film makers. Shortly after the novel won the Premio Viareggio in 1949 Viganò received the first approach from a film maker, which led to nothing. Subsequently, the first concrete idea for a film came from Gian Vittorio Baldi, who in the mid-1950s produced a number of documentaries including the ten-part documentary for RAI television, *Cinquant'anni 1898–1948. Episodi di vita italiana tra cronaca e storia*. Baldi never made the film of Viganò's novel but went on to direct the film *L'ultimo giorno di scuola prima delle vacanze di Natale* (1975), which depicts a massacre of civilians carried out by Fascists in Emilia 1944. Other subsequent proposals came from Glauco Pellegrini, a member of the cultural commission of the PCI, best known for his documentary of Palmiro Togliatti, and from Gianfranco De Bosio who in 1963 directed *Il terrorista*, a film about a Venetian *gappista* which starred Gian Maria Volonté and Anouk Aimée. The script was co-authored by De Bosio and the theatre director and playwright Luigi Squarzina.[11] Eventually Montaldo, who in 1961 had directed *Tiro al piccione*, a film about a young man who remained faithful to Mussolini's RSI and itself based on a literary text,[12] seems to have hit on a winning formula and to have persuaded Viganò that he was the right man for the job:

> Diverse volte mi avevano proposto di fare un film dal libro, c'era stata anche la proposta di ridurlo per la televisione. Però le sceneggiature non mi convincevano. Questa volta, dopo aver letto la sceneggiatura, ho detto di sí, perche rispecchiava veramente il senso del libro. Ho parlato a lungo con Montaldo e mi è piaciuto come lui vedeva il personaggio dell'Agnese.[13]

The first clear indication that a film based on the book was to be made can be found in a short article in *L'Unità*. At the time, so the article suggested, no decision had been taken as to who would play the key role of l'Agnese, but the cast would be 'di livello qualitativo', and include Franco Nero and Mariangela Melato, neither of whom actually appeared in the film.[14] A subsequent article suggested that none other than Simone Signoret would play l'Agnese, and that Ornella Muti would also make an appearance.[15] As it happened, Montaldo opted for the Swedish actress Ingrid Thulin, who is best known for her many roles in the films of Ingmar Bergman, such as *Winter Light* (1963) or *The Silence* (1963), both of which demonstrated her ability to play extremely demanding and, it goes without saying, bleak roles. In 1969 Thulin had played the part of Sophie Von Essenbech in Visconti's *The Damned*, the first of a series of attempts to give her a wider international status. It would be relatively easy to dismiss the choice of Thulin as one dictated by her undoubted star appeal and aesthetic qualities. However, Thulin uses her experience in Bergman's rather sombre films to create a version of l'Agnese which works effectively on screen, particularly during long takes and close ups of her stoic features.

In addition to Thulin, the cast of *L'Agnese va a morire* includes Stefano Satta Flores as the partisan commander, Michele Placido as Tom and Ninetto Davoli (famous for his many roles in the films of Pasolini) as 'La Disperata'. Satta Flores had previously had a role in the film *C'eravamo tanto amati* (1974) whose opening scene depicts a successful partisan action involving the three friends who then follow different — and mainly disappointing — paths in an Italy where the ideals of the Resistance are betrayed. Placido, on the other hand, was at the time an emerging actor who would go on to become one of Italy's best-known stars and, as we will see later, played the lead role in *Il sangue dei vinti*. In 1975 he had played Agramante in Luca Ronconi's film version of the *Orlando furioso*.[16]

As Viganò's own positive reaction to the script would suggest, the film version follows very closely the plot of the original novel, with only a few variations. Of these the most noteworthy is the addition of a scene at an early point in the film in which the partisans, led by Tom, efficiently execute a Fascist in what would appear to be Ravenna. The scene is immediately followed by the arrival of Rina, Tom's beloved, at the partisan HQ. The scene establishes Tom as a protagonist, and the film gives greater emphasis throughout to this character, possibly in an attempt to give him a more important role than was the case in the book, and so offer Placido more opportunities to display his many qualities. A similar process would appear to have taken place with the character of 'La Disperata'. In the book this character appears as if from nowhere, and is the subject of a separate micro-narrative (pp. 179–81) in which he kills a German patrol, an episode not included in the film. In the film, however, 'La Disperata' arrives on the scene when he brings the bad news of General Alexander's winter declaration to the partisan command. Played by Ninetto Davoli, he becomes in the film a very brash Roman who dies heroically in a hail of German bullets in the final battle scene. In the book La Disperata is a quiet local boy. It is likely that the changes to the character of 'La Disperata' were occasioned by the casting of Davoli, and the difficulty of fitting him into the script.

As with the novel, the opening scene shows l'Agnese giving assistance to a young Italian soldier journeying home after the armistice declaration of 8 September 1943. The soldier is spotted by la Minghina, her filofascist neighbour, who warns Agnese that this act of solidarity represents a risk. And indeed word gets through to the local German soldiers that l'Agnese's house is a safe haven for escaped soldiers, leading to the arrest of her husband Palita who is taken away to be sent to Germany. The involvement of the daughters in the betrayal of l'Agnese and her husband, and their acts of horizontal collaboration with the Germans are more explicitly stated (and displayed) in the film than in the book. Indeed, one characteristic of the book which is given particular emphasis in the film is that of the danger of spies and acts of betrayal, as if to emphasise the importance of working class solidarity in the Resistance period (as well as in the 1970s).

In many ways what the film of *L'Agnese va a morire* does is to restate, in terms which are readily comprehensible to viewers, the themes which were already present in the novel: the importance of women in the Resistance, the dominant role of the PCI in the organisation of the movement, the difficult relationship between the Allies and the Resistance, the brutality and inhumanity of the Germans, the solidarity of the partisans and the peasants, and the key role played by the elements. With the exception of nature, these themes were all at the centre of historical discussions in the 1970s. 1975, the year in which the decision to make the film was made, was International Women's year. During this period there were a number of conferences, major research projects and many publications on Italian women during the Resistance. In 1977 David Ellwood would publish his detailed study of the Allies and the Italian Resistance entitled 'l'alleato nemico'.[17] Likewise, the question of peasant solidarity during the Resistance was a much discussed topic during the period. The issue of the relationship between the peasants and their surroundings was not, however, a topic of interest to historians at the time, and it is this aspect of the film which makes it most interesting. In the novel Viganò tends to use nature in a fairly simplistic way, with bad weather reflecting the difficulties and pessimism of the partisans. The film, however, represents nature as more of a protagonist. The film was shot in the wetlands to the east of Ferrara, with a lot of the filming done in the Valli di Comacchio. From the very opening shot, in which l'Agnese pushes her barrow full of clothes against the backdrop of a huge grey sky, nature has an intimidating presence, emphasised by the number of panoramic shots taken from a low point of view. L'Agnese is frequently depicted as an isolated figure, fighting her way through driving rain or heavy snow, her face wrapped in a simple peasant scarf. As the Allies advance North the Germans blow up the dams, flooding the area and forcing the partisans to abandon their hide-out. In days long before the invention of CGI the flood is an impressive moment in the film. A further contribution to the film is made by the music of Ennio Morricone, particularly effective in the scenes when the partisans attempt to drive their rudimentary boats through the icy waters.

When *L'Agnese va morire* was released, the Resistance revival of the 1970s was at its height.[18] This might account, in part, for the film's subsequent and continued popularity — particularly among left-wing viewers. The film certainly touched a chord with wider developments of the 1970s, such as the women's movement, and the idea of a politicised Resistance movement engaged in a class war, summed up by the phrase 'la Resistenza è stata rossa e non tricolore'. By the time Orsini's version of *Uomini e no* came out in 1980 the Resistance spirit was beginning to decline, but the presence of the long-term antifascist Sandro Pertini as president of Italy meant that it remained on the agenda, above all in the fight against terrorism. It is within this context that the film version of *Uomini e no* needs to be analysed.

Vittorini's novel was first published in 1945, shortly after the liberation. It tells the story of the Milanese *gappista*, Enne 2, and focusses above all on his own anguish and isolation and his impossible love for Berta. Stylistically, the book presents a number of challenges to the film maker, notably the passages in italic script in which the narrator addresses his characters. These passages disappear in the film version, probably because they represented an insuperable problem. In the novel Enne 2 and Berta never meet, whereas in the film the love story occupies a substantial amount of the script. However, the aspect of the transformation from novel to film which is most interesting is the ending. The novel itself has a kind of double ending. In the first of these, trapped inside an apartment, Enne 2 waits stoically for his death at the hands of Cane Nero. The narrator offers to take him back to a day in his childhood and to Berta: '*Ma lui di sette anni, lo porto via. Non altro rimane, nella stanza, che un ordigno di morte: con due pistole in mano.*'[19] The book then comes to an end with an unnamed *operaio* having his first experience as a *gappista*, successfully shooting three enemy soldiers, but drawing back from killing a fourth. In the film version the second ending is closely reproduced, while the first ending presents some significant variations. Rather than waiting stoically for his death, Enne 2 leaps from the window of his apartment. His pursuers are unaware that he has shortly before attached a series of bombs to his body which, rather spectacularly, explode just as he hits the ground. This significant change has, I think, two linked explanations. In part its origins can be traced to what is undoubtedly one of the most famous and heroic of all Resistance deaths — that of Dante Di Nanni in Turin in 1944. Di Nanni's death soon became a key element in PCI propaganda during the war, but it was Giovanni Pesce's unforgettable description in *Senza tregua* which most captured the imagination of his (mostly young) readers, and which is reworked in Orsini's film. In Pesce's description Di Nanni throws himself to his death as follows:

> Adesso non c'è più niente da fare: allora Di Nanni afferra le sbarre della ringhiera e con uno sforzo disperato si leva in piedi aspettando la raffica. Gli spari invece cessano sul tetto, nella strada, dalle finestre delle case, si vedono apparire uno alla volta fascisti e tedeschi. Guardano il gappista che li aveva decimati e messi in fuga. Incerti e sconcertati, guardano il ragazzo coperto di sangue che li ha battuti. E non sparano. È in quell'attimo che Di Nanni si appoggia in avanti, premendo il ventre alla ringhiera e saluta col pugno alzato. Poi si getta di schianto con le braccia aperte nella strada stretta, piena di silenzio.[20]

Orsini therefore takes a number of elements from Pesce's description, but with the important added detail of the suicide bomb. The reasons for this crucial addition can be ascribed to the late 1970s climate. As I mentioned above, under the presidency of Sandro Pertini (elected shortly after the assassination of Aldo Moro) the fight against terrorism, left and right, assumed new dimensions. In particular Pertini and others fought hard to break down the connection which had been made between the violence of the Resistance period and the violence of the 1970s. Enne

2's suicide bomb at the end of the film offers a clear example of political violence for legitimate ends. The film version of *Uomini e no* is, therefore, not simply a film about the Resistance, but also a film about terrorism, and a film which distinguished Resistance violence from terrorist violence.

In addition to the texts by Calvino, Pavese, Viganò and Vittorini which were published in the 1940s, this period also sees the emergence of Beppe Fenoglio whose status as the greatest writer of the Resistance is by now firmly consolidated. Fenoglio's *Una questione privata* has twice been turned into a film for TV. The most recent version (1993), screened to coincide with the 50th anniversary of the Resistance, employed the services of the English actor Rupert Graves to play Milton, the protagonist caught up in a hopeless search to free his friend Giorgio and discover if he had had a relationship with the beautiful but ephemeral Fulvia. The TV version sticks very closely to the published version of *Una questione privata*, with no evidence of additions or other changes. Like other film versions which stick close to the original the value of this production was to really to repropose a literary text in a format which, arguably, is more accessible to the Italian public.[21]

All the novels and films discussed so far are characterised by their positive depiction of the Resistance movement and those who participated in it. The most consistent threat to this paradigm has come in the shape of the journalist Giampaolo Pansa. During the 1990s Pansa published a series of novels which suggested alternatives to the heroic Resistance narrative, emphasising (excessively in the views of many) the civil war characteristics which the historian Claudio Pavone had highlighted in his landmark 1991 study *Una guerra civile*.[22] Pansa's novels had some impact but it was only with the 2003 book *Il sangue dei vinti* that his 'revisionist' interpretations really hit the headlines and had a widespread impact. *Il sangue dei vinti* is an example of a kind of docufiction, in which Pansa and his female assistant set out to reveal the truth about the *resa dei conti* at the end of the war. The book is written in the form of a travelogue, with the two characters visiting various locations around Italy and describing the killings of Fascists which took place. At the end of the book Pansa's assistant reveals that she is the daughter of one of the members of the Volante Rossa, a group which carried out a series of post-war killings in Milan. *Il sangue dei vinti* has been followed by a number of similar publications, the most recent of which is the 2014 *Bella ciao. Controstoria della Resistenza*.[23]

Unlike the other literary texts discussed in this chapter, *Il sangue dei vinti* was turned into a film within a few years of its original publication. The film's director, Michele Soavi, is well-known for his role in maintaining the traditions of the Italian horror film. Soavi has collaborated with Dario Argento and his filmography includes the 1994 zombie comedy *Dellamorte Dellamore*, which stars Rupert Everett as a beleaguered cemetery keeper. Soavi's slightly dubious pedigree lies behind the play on words in Claudia Morgoglione's review in *La Repubblica*: 'Tutti gli orrori dei partigiani nel film più discusso del Festival'.[24] The festival in question was the 'International Film Festival' in Rome, championed by Gianni Alemanno, the right-wing mayor of Rome and son-in-law of a former leader of the neo-fascist MSI. The presence of the film at this event gave rise to not unexpected polemics. *Il sangue dei vinti* had been turned down by the 'rival' festival in Venice, and was given the honour of opening the festival followed by a public debate. During the debate, an increasingly animated Placido seems to have taken responsibility for defending the film, explaining that, like his father before him, he had no problem wearing a black shirt. Echoing Pansa's own ideology he was, he stated 'di sinistra', but had been unaware of a part of Italian history 'che non appare nei libri di storia e che bisogna conoscere senza reagire con emotività ideologica'.[25]

Pansa's 2003 novel has two protagonists, Pansa himself and the librarian called Livia Bianchi, who works at the National Library in Florence. The name is a rather unsubtle reference to the Resistance hero Dante Livio Bianco. He asks her to photocopy a book for him, which she refuses to do given copyright regulations and then offers him a coffee. Anyone who has ever studied in the National Library will realise straight away that this is clearly a work of fiction. In the film, whose script was co-written by Michele Soavi and Pansa, these two characters are replaced by individuals who, on the face of it, have nothing to do with the original novel.[26] Pansa becomes a detective figure in the shape of Franco Dogliani, played by Michele Placido, while the librarian is transformed into the character of Elisa, played by the then emerging Romanian-born Ana Caterina Morariu. The substitution of the journalist by a detective, and the replacement of the librarian by what would appear to be an academic raises a number of questions. In the film Dogliani shares some of the characteristics of the Pansa figure of the novel in that he acts as a guide for the young Elisa, who drives him to various locations in a Volkswagen Beetle. As in the book, both characters are involved in a shared quest for the truth — although what they are searching for in the film is rather different than was the case in the book. In the former, the two protagonists strive to reconstruct the history of the post-war killings during the course of a road trip. In the film the search is more about the tragedy which affects the lives of Dogliani and Elisa, and by extension all Italian families, during the climax of the war. Sensibly, the film discards the embarrassing hints of some kind of sexual chemistry between Pansa and Livia. So there are some basic similarities between the protagonists of the book and the film, but the differences are rather more striking. What might account for these quite radical transformations? There are a range of possible explanations. On the one hand, it could be suggested that the erasure of the Pansa figure is connected to a deliberate act of self-effacement. Pansa had placed himself at the centre of the novel and portrayed himself as a journalist-sage on an almost messianic mission to show Lidia and his readers what really happened at the end of the war. It could be — given the intense controversy created by the book and the inflammatory nature of Pansa himself — that it was thought wise to replace him with someone different. As a detective it could be argued that Dogliani is a rather more reliable figure than that of a journalist. Although it is fair to say that not all detectives in Italian *gialli* actually discover the truth, there is a feeling of trust amongst the viewing public that the detective is a reliable and dependable individual, sitting above the journalist in what we might describe as the epistemological hierarchy.

In this context it is also worth reflecting briefly on the status and career of

Michele Placido. In 1976 Placido played Tom in *L'Agnese va a morire*, as we have seen. It is unlikely that many contemporary viewers of *Il sangue dei vinti* were aware of Placido's previous involvement in the cinema of the Resistance; nevertheless it is striking that the actor's only previous appearance in a film of this genre was in a fine example of 1970s orthodoxy. In a way Placido is countercast as an occupant of the 'grey zone', an honest man without political views who tries to do his job, irrespective of the political situation. However, while only a few cognoscenti might have made a connection between the communist hero played by Placido in the 1970s, and the supposedly apolitical detective of 2008, many viewers would have spotted a more familiar link to Placido's earlier career, namely Corrado Cattani, the Mafia-hunting detective of the TV series *La Piovra*. Cattani's death in the fourth series of *La Piovra* remains one of the iconic moments of Italian television in the 1980s and still has the capacity to provoke horror and outrage today.[27] He remains one of Italy's best-known actors and has a special status on the Italian screen. His appearance in *Il sangue dei vinti* gave the production considerable lustre, a star element and a certain degree of kudos, but above all an actor associated with the search for truth, at all costs.

The film version of *Il sangue dei vinti* starts, not in the luminous surroundings of the National Library in Florence, but in complete darkness. Portentous music in a minor key reinforces the tone of complete mystery. Strange thudding noises are heard, as if from beyond the cinema screen, and then what can only be described as a 'breakthrough' occurs — a hole is punctured, we see broken bricks and a chink of light, followed by further thuds as a wrecking ball smashes its way through the screen which, we realise, is a wall, and we the viewers are 'inside' a building. The darkness of the cinema reflects the darkness of the room. The ham-fisted symbolism of these opening shots is relatively easy to decode. We, the cinema-goers, have been fed a diet of Resistance films which have kept us in total darkness — but now the wrecking ball of Giampaolo Pansa is going to smash through years of obfuscation and show us what really happened.

An unknown character enters the building with a torch, which soon illuminates a skeleton, while a caption informs the viewer that we are in the San Lorenzo area of Rome in the 1970s. At this point the scene cuts to a shot of Dogliani entering a building in Rome — perhaps a cinema or a lecture theatre — to watch black and white images which also appear on the screen before us. The images, given a semblance of authority by the appearance of the Istituto Luce symbol which appears in the top right of the screen that Dogliani is himself watching, depict executions, of individuals and of groups. It is not initially clear who are the victims, nor indeed the executioners, but a connection is made between the recently discovered corpse and a group awaiting execution whose hands are also tied by barbed wire, an obvious symbol of oppression. As Dogliani insouciantly watches the images, which include a woman whose head has been shaved being paraded around the streets by exultant partisans, some of whom wave the Italian flag decorated with the Savoy crest, there is a further cut which involves the addition of another timeframe. The scene is now inside a bus as a young woman writes in her diary. It is 19 July 1943 and she is on her way to Rome to spend her honeymoon, staying with her brother. Her husband sits beside her as the words 'tratta dall'opera *Il sangue dei vinti*' appear on the screen. The young woman cannot wait to see her brother, but she doubts that 'Francesco' will be able to meet them. Francesco, we deduce, is the character played by Placido who we see entering a flat where the bloodstained corpse of a woman in a blue dress, her hands tied with barbed wire, has been found (the skeleton in the earlier scene). In this scene Placido's hair, previously grey, is a lustrous (though not entirely convincing) brown. Further cuts suggest that the scenes involving the detective in the flat and the married couple are taking place simultaneously. It is at this point that the young couple become aware of American bombers heading to Rome. The images of the bombers appear to be documentary footage — they are in colour but nevertheless look like authentic images. The intercutting of fictional and documentary footage is most likely a reference to Rossellini's *Paisà*, which used this technique in order to give a fictional film an authentic gloss. While a reference to *Paisà* might be viewed as an act of homage to a canonical Resistance film, given Pansa's well-known iconoclasm it is more likely that the allusion is more a piece of criticism, suggesting that films like *Paisà* have contributed to a rhetorical vision of the Resistance which the current film is determined to cut through, or to judge by the opening frames, to smash.

The results of the bombing of San Lorenzo are twofold. Firstly, the young bride loses her husband when their bus is strafed, and decides as a consequence to enlist with the Fascist *ausiliarie*. Secondly, the evidence of the murder in the flat is covered up, with the body remaining interred until the 1970s demolition team inadvertently uncover her. In each case the people who are held responsible are the Allies and their bombs. It was the Allied bullets which killed Lucia's husband, leading to her decision to become an *ausiliaria*, and the Allied bombs which covered up the evidence from the flat, while destroying the lives of innocent families in the San Lorenzo area. This attribution of guilt represents an interesting departure for Pansa and a new development. In a sense he seems to be shifting the blame away from Italy and the Italians and placing it squarely on the shoulders of the Allies. Lucia's decision to join up is for the love of country as well as for her dead husband. Yet either way the spark is not a political one — the belief in Fascism — but rather a decision based on the interaction of the personal and the intimate with feelings of national pride and the need to maintain the honour of the nation following the outrage of the Allied bombing of Rome.

Lucia's decision to join the *ausiliarie* occurs at a relatively early point in the film, but by this stage viewers will have got their bearings. If they had read the novel *Il sangue dei vinti* they would have been entirely justified in asking themselves a simple question: what has all that has appeared on the screen so far got to do with the original novel? The book, as outlined earlier, does not deal at all with the events of 1943 but is instead confined to a relatively narrow period of history, the end of the war and the bloody settling of accounts. Why does the film version stretch the narrative to a much earlier point in the chronology of the war? Why include a Fascist *ausiliaria* in the plot? The answer to these questions, and others, lies in the choice of the name of Lucia for the widowed bride. The reference to *I promessi sposi* could not be clearer, although surprisingly only one of the press articles on the film makes the connection, and the review by that most intellectual of film critics, Paolo Mereghetti, makes no mention of a Manzonian intertext.[28] The transformation which takes place in the film is that of a move away from a book which claims to reveal the truth about the horrors of the *resa dei conti,* to a national epic which strives to reveal the colours and cadences of the Second World War in Italy, a civil war which tore families apart and in which the defeated were the real victims. As the film develops Dogliani slowly begins to understand and unravel the murder mystery. Several pages would be required to give anything like a meaningful account of what is an extremely convoluted plot. The victim is, so it seems initially, a prostitute and the identical twin of an actress (both played by Barbora Bobulova). However, as the narrative proceeds, Dogliani discovers that the actual victim was the actress, murdered by the prostitute sister. In a doubling reminiscent of Medardo in *Il visconte dimezzato* the actress is the bad sister, while the prostitute (a victim of the tragic circumstances of the Second World War) is the good sister. Given the Roman setting of the early stages of the film, it would seem reasonable to suspect that the figures of Romulus and Remus are being referred to. As such, the twin sisters could be interpreted as the twin souls of the new Italy whose reconstruction has been impeded by a failure to understand that they are essentially two sides of the same coin.

This is of course all rather hackneyed, but that is not the point. The film has a clear didactic objective and neither Pansa nor Soavi are concerned about subtleties, as will become even more evident as we look at the rest of the film. The theme of the doubling of the twin sisters is also reflected in the character of Lucia and her other brother Ettore Dogliani, played by Alessandro Preziosi. Ettore is a partisan with strong Communist beliefs who, naturally enough, disapproves of his sister's decision to join the opposition. Wholly predictably, their lives become increasingly entangled as the film progresses. In a key scene Ettore's partisans attack the barracks where Lucia and her fellow Fascists mount a spirited defence. Ettore sprays machine-gun fire through a top-floor window, failing to hit any of the Fascists, but his bullets rip through a map of Italy, half of which falls to the ground. No doubt a serious point is being made here — the Civil War tore Italy in two, but it is achieved in such a guileless fashion that it is difficult to take seriously. Lucia manages to escape from the barracks and holes up with another Fascist who snipes at partisans from a bell tower. Before their final defeat the sniper manages to shoot Ettore dead. The Resistance hero is covered in the tricolour flag while his Fascist sister who — it is clear — also fought for her country, is subjected to a range of tortures (including rape) and paraded around the streets in a ghoulish display of public execration and obloquy. Despite Franco's desperate attempts to rescue her she is executed. At the end of the film Elisa takes him to the place where she was buried, in a field next to a graveyard. The long grass which grows above her forgotten corpse is reminiscent of Pavese's *La luna e i falò,* and sure enough the voice-over recites the celebrated lines from *La casa in collina* in which Corrado muses on the victims of the Civil War.

The film of *Il sangue dei vinti* thus manages to do something which no other Resistance film had done — get Pavese's *La casa in collina* onto the screen.

In the various reworkings of Resistance novels which this chapter has analysed there is one common element which runs through all of them, with the exception of *Il sangue dei vinti*: the almost absolute fidelity to the original. There are some minor variations, but the Resistance novel would appear to be a kind of sacred object when it is placed into the reverential hands of film-makers, perhaps indicating that the fictional texts relating to this defining moment in twentieth-century history occupy a unique space in the development of Italian textual transformations.

Notes to Chapter 25

1. Italo Calvino, *Il sentiero dei nidi di ragno* (Turin: Einaudi, 1947).
2. Martin McLaughlin, *Italo Calvino* (Edinburgh: Edinburgh University Press, 1998), p. 19.
3. The Modena City Ramblers have, however, made a song out of the novel. Entitled *Il sentiero*, the song first appeared on the 2005 album *Appunti partigiani* and is more an act of homage to Calvino than an adaptation of the novel. The CD also contains a version of Calvino's own Resistance song *Oltre il ponte*, as well as *Il partigiano John*, a homage to Fenoglio.
4. The best analysis of these questions in the Italian context is Millicent Marcus's pioneering study *Filmmaking by the Book* (Baltimore: Johns Hopkins University Press, 1993).
5. Renata Viganò, *L'Agnese va a morire* (Turin: Einaudi, 1949); Elio Vittorini, *Uomini e no* (Milan: Bompiani, 1945); Giampaolo Pansa, *Il sangue dei vinti* (Milan: Sperling & Kupfer, 2003).
6. There is an interesting variation of this process in Rossellini's 1959 film *Il generale della Rovere*. The film is loosely based on Indro Montanelli's own experiences, which were turned into the script. Montanelli then went on to publish a novel, bearing the same title: Indro Montanelli, *Il generale della Rovere* (Milan: Rizzoli, 1959). In 2011 RAI produced a two-part mini-series based on Montanelli's book.
7. Aldo De Jaco, *Le quattro giornate di Napoli: la città insorge* (Rome: Editori Riuniti, 1953), Alcide Cervi, *I miei sette figli* (Rome: Edizioni di cultura sociale, 1955). The text of *I miei sette figli* was in fact a joint project involving the collaboration of *L'Unità* journalist Renato Nicolai who, it is likely, ghosted the book in its entirety. Versions of *I miei sette figli* published after 1956 are interesting, amongst other things, for the removal of references to Stalin. On this point see Philip Cooke, 'What does it matter if you die? The Seven Cervi Brothers', in *Assassinations and Murder in Modern Italy: Transformations in Society and Culture,* ed. by Stephen Gundle and Lucia Rinaldi (New York: Palgrave, 2007), pp. 33–44.
8. While an analysis of the phenomenon is outside the scope of this chapter, it is interesting to note how, in another form of textual transformation, there are numerous examples of 'readings' of selected passages of Resistance novels which have appeared in various media. For example, Radio 3 transmitted a series of 'Pagine — Le parole della Resistenza' in 1995, including a reading by Oreste Rizzini from *La casa in collina*: <http://www.teche.rai.it/2015/09/la-casa-in-collina-cesare-pavese-letto-da-oreste-rezzini/>. There are now many examples of such readings on YouTube.
9. Pavese's novel was originally published together with *Il carcere* in *Prima che il gallo canti* (Turin: Einaudi, 1949).
10. It is interesting to compare this long delay in Italy with two cases from the USA and France. John Steinbeck's novel *The Moon is Down* (New York: Viking, 1942), depicting the potential of Resistance in Northern Europe (and originally a two-act play), was made into a propaganda film the following year. Vercors's *Le Silence de la mer* (Paris: Editions de Minuit, 1942), on the other hand, was adapted into a film in 1949.
11. Squarzina had, in the late 1950s, written and directed one of the very few Resistance plays to have had any impact, *La romagnola* in *Teatro* (Bari: Laterza, 1959). For a discussion see Philip Cooke, *The Legacy of the Italian Resistance* (New York: Palgrave, 2011), pp. 80–81.

12. The novel in question is Giosé Rimanelli's *Tiro al piccione* (Turin: Einaudi, 1953).
13. *Matrimonio in brigata: le opere ed i giorni di Renata Viganò e Antonio Meluschi*, edited by E. Colombo (Bologna: Grafis, 1995), p. 188.
14. 'Montaldo dirigerà il film *L'Agnese va a morire*', *L'Unità*, 3 August 1975, p. 11.
15. 'Cominciano a Ravenna le riprese de "L'Agnese va a morire"', *L'Unità*, 10 January 1976, p. 9.
16. The film, first shown in 1975, was itself an adaptation of Ronconi's theatrical version of the *Furioso*.
17. David Ellwood, *L'alleato nemico* (Milan: Feltrinelli, 1977).
18. The film was premiered in the city of Naples and the showing coincided with the anniversary of the 'quattro giornate di Napoli'. It transpires that this initiative was taken by Maurizio Valenzi, the Communist mayor of Naples. See 'In anteprima mondiale "L'Agnese va a morire"', *L'Unità*, 27 September 1976, p. 5.
19. *Uomini e no*, p. 191 (italics in original).
20. Giovanni Pesce, *Senza tregua* (Milan: Feltrinelli, 1967), pp. 136–45.
21. Another film from the 1990s, Luchetti's *I piccoli maestri* (1997) is a case in point. The film version struggled to cope with the subtle irony of Meneghello's original, replacing it with rather hamfisted comedy. For a discussion of Luchetti's film and Guido Chiesa's excellent film version of *Il partigiano Johnny* see Cooke, *The Legacy*, pp. 188–89.
22. Claudio Pavone, *Una guerra civile: saggio storico sulla moralità nella Resistenza* (Turin: Bollati Boringhieri, 1991).
23. Giampaolo Pansa, *Bella ciao. Controstoria della Resistenza* (Milan: Rizzoli, 2014). For a much longer discussion of Pansa than is possible here see Cooke, *The Legacy*, and John Foot, *Italy's Divided Memory* (New York: Palgrave, 2009). More generally on the battle over the memory of the Resistance see Filippo Focardi, *La guerra della memoria. La Resistenza nel dibattito politico italiano dal 1945 a oggi* (Rome and Bari: Laterza, 2005).
24. Claudia Morgoglione, 'Tutti gli orrori dei partigiani nel film più discusso del Festival', *La Repubblica*, 26 October 2008.
25. 'Il sangue dei vinti non piace a destra', *La Stampa*, 27 October 2008.
26. At the time of writing the full-length version of the film was available to view on YouTube. It had been uploaded on 6 April 2016 by 'SEMPER FIDELIS A NOI', an individual whose avatar is Benito Mussolini. There are currently two comments 'Grazie Fratello, questo film è bellissimo! A Noi' and 'uno dei film più belli di tutti i tempi!'.
27. In the same year as his TV death (1989) Placido went on to stand as a Republican/liberal candidate in the European elections, garnering over 11,000 votes. Though not elected (Giorgio La Malfa won the seat) this was a rather better performance than two of his fellow candidates, Ernesto Galli Della Loggia and Bruno Zevi, who did not break through the 3000 mark. The 1989 elections were, as far as I know, Placido's only serious foray into politics.
28. Paolo Mereghetti, Review of *Il sangue dei vinti*, *Corriere della sera*, 1 November 2008. Morgoglione, 'Tutti gli orrori', describes Placido as 'un po' Don Abbondio un po' poliziotto esemplare'.

CHAPTER 26

Controtendenze narrative novecentesche: *La Storia Romanzo* di Elsa Morante

Franca Pellegrini

La Storia Romanzo.[1] *Uno scandalo che dura da diecimila anni* esce nel 1974. La Seconda Guerra Mondiale è ormai sullo sfondo del presente di molti e con essa gli echi della catastrofe e della miseria dell'Italia di quegli anni. I conflitti sembrano, però, ancora aperti in un'Italia che soffre una stagione di speranze e insieme di scontri ideologici post-Sessantotto, scontri che riaprono il dualismo destra-sinistra e che si concluderanno con gli anni del terrorismo nero e rosso. Gli intellettuali discutono sul futuro mentre il ventennio fascista pesa ancora sulla coscienza di molti. La parola-chiave a sinistra è impegno. La politica invade le scuole, le piazze, le fabbriche, la cultura, i giornali, l'editoria. Pasolini, Calvino, Eco, solo per citare i nomi più illustri, scrivono poesie, romanzi, saggi; sui quotidiani e sulle riviste si discute su come fare letteratura e il dibattito è aperto sulle scelte linguistiche da operare. Nel 1972 Calvino pubblica *Le città invisibili*, niente di più distante dal romanzo della Morante e dieci anni prima, nel 1962, era uscita l'*Opera aperta* di Eco. La letteratura è pervasa dalle linee dettate dal movimento '63 e il romanzo tradizionale sembra essere decaduto per sempre; si propongono alternative anche formali come ciclostili, volantini, manifesti.

In questo quadro decomposto, Elsa Morante scrive *La Storia*, un romanzo di stampo tradizionale a dispetto di ogni *diktat* ideologico, politico e letterario, e sceglie di pubblicarlo in edizione economica, ottenendo un grande successo editoriale: operazione anomala e straniante rispetto alle correnti del momento che riapre alla narrazione romanzesca. Così si esprime a proposito di quel periodo Romano Luperini nel 1999:

> La stagione dello sperimentalismo, affermatasi negli anni Sessanta, comincia a mostrare segni di esaurimento nel corso del decennio successivo. A metà degli anni Settanta, il successo della *Storia* della Morante — a scapito del contemporaneo e ben più complesso *Corporale*, con cui Volponi scrive il suo romanzo forse più sperimentale — denuncia già un'inversione di tendenza, aprendo la strada al ripristino del genere 'romanzo storico': pochi anni dopo, nel 1981[2], *Il nome della rosa* porterà a compimento tale rovesciamento, fornendogli l'avallo autorevole di uno dei maggiori teorici dello sperimentalismo neo-avanguardistico, Umberto Eco. Finita la stagione dell''opera aperta' si torna al 'romanzo chiuso'.[3]

Il romanzo *La Storia* procede con un andamento rigorosamente cronologico a cerchi concentrici: alcuni flashback sono presenti soprattutto nella prima parte, quando si raccontano le vicende della famiglia di Ida, che si intersecano con la scansione degli avvenimenti storici dal primo Novecento fino agli anni della Seconda Guerra Mondiale. La veridicità è data dalle pagine di Storia premesse a ciascun capitolo, ordinate dal '19★' (capitolo che fa da prologo della storia: dal 1900 al 1940), poi dal 1941 al 1947 (corpo centrale del testo) e dalla sezione finale, in parallelo con il primo capitolo, che reca il titolo '19★' ('....1948–1949–1950–1951' fino all'anno 1967), riportando soltanto gli avvenimenti storici seguiti alla Seconda Guerra Mondiale. La storia di Ida e della sua famiglia si è fermata, e la frase con cui si chiude il capitolo e il libro '..... e la Storia continua .....' (ST,[4] p. 656) è dimostrativa del fatto che a dispetto del nostro esserci e delle tribolazioni provocate dalla Storia, le nostre esistenze appaiono marginali e ininfluenti nel correre del tempo, divenendo centrali solo se poste all'attenzione del lettore. La vita non finisce con la morte dei protagonisti: Nino lascia un seme dietro di sé, una figlia, a conferma di un possibile futuro, come ribadisce l'epigrafe gramsciana: '«Tutti i semi sono falliti eccettuato uno, che non so cosa sia, ma che probabilmente è un fiore e non un'erbaccia». (Matricola n. 7047 della Casa Penale di Turi)'.[5] (ST, p. 657)

L'intero repertorio storiografico indica al lettore il background degli avvenimenti narrati che andranno a costruire il mosaico finale. L'operazione ha una sua logica stringente: personaggi ed eventi sono condizionati e definiti nel loro tempo. Non esiste vita fuori dalla Storia, sembra dire la Morante, non esiste Storia senza la vita dei singoli. Il secondo Novecento e il secolo a seguire hanno vissuto e continueranno a vivere di quel paradossale conflitto, che ha ucciso intere generazioni all'interno dei campi di sterminio, che ha distrutto città e paesi, che ha visto l'utilizzo della bomba atomica, che ha investito con un'ondata di odio e di razzismo popoli inermi, gettandoli nella desolazione della miseria, della fame e della morte. Non si piange allora sulla sorte di Ida o di Useppe o di Davide Segre, né di fascisti o di comunisti, si piange sull'umanità intera, capace di produrre una Storia difficilmente riconducibile al romanzesco, e per questo posta in premessa alla fiction, si piange sul farsi consapevoli di quanto quel periodo abbia condizionato la vita futura, la Storia, degli uomini. La grande Storia diviene elemento necessario, ineluttabile alla comprensione del mondo, ma solo se accompagnata dalla breve storia di Useppe, vissuto per la durata della guerra e finito con questa, simbolo di un'umanità che stenta a intravedere un futuro dopo la catastrofe mondiale. Nonostante la loro separazione fisica, il vero e il verosimile si intrecciano nel testo in modo indissolubile al fine di indagare le movenze dell'animo umano, per dare a chi legge in quel momento e sempre la visione di un universo intelligibile solo attraverso una lettura sincronica della Storia e delle storie. Al di fuori delle maglie della tradizione e della stessa scrittura dei suoi romanzi precedenti, la Morante costruisce un nuovo modello di romanzo: non un romanzo storico e neppure neorealista, ideologico o popolare.

E all'indomani della sua uscita *La Storia* scatena un acceso dibattito ideologico, in primis sulle pagine de *il manifesto*, per dilagare poi su altri quotidiani, settimanali e riviste specializzate.[6] Le critiche espresse nell'immediato da autorevoli maître à penser riguardo al romanzo di Elsa Morante sono impostate in prevalenza secondo una visione ideologico-politica sulla funzione della letteratura e sulla scelta del genere narrativo. Questo e altro si legge nell'articolo 'Contro il romanzone della Morante' a firma di Nanni Balestrini insieme a Elisabetta Rasy, Letizia Paolozzi e Umberto Silva: 'Di grandi scrittori reazionari corre voce ce ne siano ancora, certo però non pensavamo ci fosse ancora spazio per bamboleggianti nipotini di De Amicis'.[7]

È l'idea della fiumana di una Storia che tutto e tutti travolge, in specie le classi subalterne, a non essere accettabile dalla critica marxista dell'epoca. Tuttavia ciò che più colpisce nel leggere quelle recensioni è il rifiuto, per alcuni addirittura ostentato, di un confronto ravvicinato col testo: 'chi ne ha letto dieci righe, chi dieci pagine, chi un po' di più'.[8] È piuttosto, da gran parte degli intellettuali dell'epoca, una presa di posizione pro o contro i postulati ideologico-letterari che regolano la narrazione della *Storia*. Vittorio Saltini e Cesare Garboli si confrontano così sulle pagine de *l'Espresso*. Scrive Saltini:

> Il personaggio che nel romanzo ragiona, Davide Segre, mi sembra del tutto imporsi alla pretesa di ridurre le contraddizioni della storia 'borghese' al livello dei propri pensieri: è invece sintomatico che quest'unico ragionamento sia raffigurato come autodistruttivo, e che quest'anarchia non violenta si scateni in una sorprendente violenza su un soldato moribondo. La coscienza non vale; la natura è tutto.[9]

Ribatte Garboli:

> Allo stesso modo, Davide Segre, il personaggio-chiave della *Storia* (altro che svalutazione della coscienza) sfida coi suoi torturati discorsi da eroe drogato i poveri inebetiti radioascoltatori (tutti proletari) di una partita di calcio. Il romanzo diventa un richiamo disperato, un'azione 'politica'.[10]

È Natalia Ginzburg che con la sua recensione sul *Corriere della Sera* del 21 luglio 1974 getta luce su alcune questioni al centro del dibattito, e in particolare sul ritorno a un romanzo scritto per un lettore. Scrive la Ginzburg in apertura dell'articolo: '*La Storia* è un romanzo scritto *per gli altri*. Ora, da moltissimi anni, l'idea di un romanzo scritto *per gli altri* sembrava volata via dalla terra'.[11]

Di rimando Rossana Rossanda si esprime in modo irrimediabilmente duro nell'agosto del 1974:

> *La Storia* non solo non mi pare un libro felice, ma quello che più tradisce il limite della Morante. [...] Vender patate è meglio che vendere disperazione; non solo perché è più utile, oltre che coerente con i semplici valori cari alla Morante, ma perché è più lineare.[12]

Lo stesso Italo Calvino nell'articolo intitolato 'Allora Hugo disse alla Morante...' critica il romanzo per il suo gusto popolare un po' rétro:

> Il primo punto da discutere sul libro della Morante è se esso costituisce veramente una proposta di romanzo popolare d'oggi. Ciò che in questo libro più m'interessa è il ricorso al 'romanzesco' che vorrei avesse molto più sviluppo. [...] Mi basti dire che secondo me il vero termine di confronto è *I miserabili* (altra operazione volutamente 'fuori tempo') come modello di

summa del romanzesco popolare e di rapsodia dell'epos storico-sociale. La commozione è un ingrediente necessario di un'operazione di questo tipo, ma in Victor Hugo l'accettiamo proprio perché è espressa in termini apertamente melodrammatici.[13]

Se Calvino, pur criticandone l'aspetto pseudo-sentimentale, intravede la potenzialità narrativa del testo della Morante e si occupa dell'aspetto letterario del romanzo e non di quello rigorosamente ideologico, ponendo al centro della questione quel romanzesco, quell'epos che riemerge dalla cenere della neoavanguardia, dal canto suo Alberto Asor Rosa stronca non solo il libro della Morante, ma anche ogni sua possibile propaggine:

> Il pericolo è che la produzione ci inondi di romanzi riempiti di questi linguaggi spuri e inverecondi (nel senso, esattamente, che non hanno vergogna di usare qualsiasi mezzo pur di raggiungere l'effetto). Speriamo che gli scrittori resistano alla tentazione di seguire questo successo, — se sarà un successo — e soprattutto speriamo che le resistano gli editori.[14]

La Storia Romanzo (come recita il titolo voluto dall'autore) è de facto un'opera che, a dispetto dei critici degli anni Settanta, rinnova e reinterpreta il modo di narrare, riapre al racconto epico, al romanzesco, e ottiene il consenso del pubblico. Sappiamo che in quegli anni la destrutturazione del romanzo è il dettame letterario proposto dalla neoavanguardia, la Storia e le storie sono escluse dal panorama letterario. Non si narra, si specula intorno all'io e si decompone anche fisicamente il libro. Così si esprime Barilli su *Il Verri*:

> Che *La Storia* sia stata accolta da almeno una parte della critica (seppure la più facile e corriva) con insolite grida di esultanza, sta a indicare forse il punto più basso raggiunto in Italia dalla cultura attorno ai problemi del romanzo. La 'restaurazione' segna il movimento ultimo del pendolo, l'*establishment* può dimostrare di essersi ripreso tutto lo spazio che, tempo fa, aveva dovuto cedere ai suoi accusatori, sorti proprio dalle colonne di questa rivista e poi organizzati nella 'nuova avanguardia' e nel Gruppo '63.[15]

Il romanzo di successo è considerato funzionale a quel mondo capitalistico di cui l'*intellighenzia* neoavanguardista cerca proprio in quegli anni di sradicare i presupposti.

Per questo l'opera della Morante è presentata dalla critica coeva come una sorta di scandalosa inversione di marcia verso una narrazione ormai abusata, quella cioè che si serve di una storia, giocata sui sentimenti, sul dolore, sulle passioni di chi la attraversa, priva di quell'impasto politico-ideologico indispensabile per ritenerla un'opera di valore.

Si è contestato altresì alla Morante un neorealismo ritardato, fuori tempo massimo e non riuscito rispetto alla corrente letterario-cinematografica post-bellica, ma questo non sembra davvero l'intento della *Storia*. Così ribatte alla critica Natalia Ginzburg:

> Quelli che hanno detto che *La Storia* ha parentele con il neo-realismo, si sono sbagliati. Il neo-realismo vedeva la seconda guerra mondiale, e Roma in quegli anni, e la borsa nera, e le deportazioni degli ebrei, e il dopo-guerra, da vicino

e però in piccolo, su uno sfondo dai contorni duri e precisi, suggellati da rozze speranze. Qui, le medesime cose sono viste in una dimensione immensa e confusa, in profondità e nello stesso tempo come da lontananze sterminate, e non ci sono più tracce di quelle stesse rozze speranze.[16]

Come si vede, risulta difficile attribuire al romanzo *La Storia* un carattere neorealista, come ripropone, ancora nel 1981, Romano Luperini in *Il Novecento*: 'Si tratta di un'opera in cui rivive un populismo di ritorno, con conseguenti esiti di sapore neorealistico che stupiscono in una scrittrice che — per formazione e per gusto — al neorealismo non era certo riducibile'.[17]

Forse il racconto morantiano è l'insieme di molte etichette: un romanzo che abbraccia la tradizione precedente, la rielabora, la mischia senza pregiudizi e la restituisce in una forma narrativa impropria per quegli anni, ma in prospettiva capace di aprire a un nuovo modo di fare letteratura. La cifra stilistica diviene la complessità che annuncia un mondo nuovo, impossibile da leggere attraverso lenti manichee. Il mondo diviene universo, l'umanità vive nella Storia e nelle storie, il romanzo si fa voce, megafono di coloro che non hanno voce, la realtà è vista con i loro occhi, vissuta con le loro misere forze, con la semplicità di interpretazione di ciò che accade. È l'epopea degli ultimi, degli inermi, ma anche la tragedia dei forti, forti solo per attimi forse, in un capovolgimento di posizioni che nessuno salva e che nessuno può eludere. L'apertura del romanzo dimostra che non c'è esenzione dal soffrire lo scandalo della Storia: Gunther, il militare tedesco, che stupra Ida ne è esempio. Egli stesso è vittima della Storia, non è pietà per gli invasori quella che si legge nelle pagine del romanzo, ma una sorta di prologo illuminante per il prosieguo della lettura. Il soldato tedesco è il padre di Useppe, la Storia si ingarbuglia, 'non si snoda | come una catena | di anelli ininterrotta. | In ogni caso | molti anelli non tengono'.[18] È in questa complessità ibrida che risiede il centro motore del romanzo.

Il set in cui si sviluppa l'intera vicenda è Roma. La città eterna diviene parte, insieme ai suoi abitanti, della storia di Ida e dei suoi figli e della Storia di quegli anni. Si cammina per le vie e i quartieri romani, come San Lorenzo e il Testaccio, si respira l'aria delle borgate, come Pietralata ('Pietralata era una zona sterile di campagna all'estrema periferia di Roma, dove il regime fascista aveva istituito qualche anno prima una sorta di villaggio di esclusi, ossia di famiglie povere cacciate via d'autorità dalle loro vecchie residenze nel centro cittadino') (ST, p. 179), e si assiste alla catastrofe provocata dai bombardamenti, si tocca la miseria di una città ridotta in ginocchio, che sullo sfondo mantiene la sua bellezza antica. Neppure la Storia millenaria di Roma è sufficiente a fermare le aggressioni e le devastazioni prodotte dal conflitto: 'Ogni tanto, la notte, per la città risuonavano le sirene dell'allarme aereo; ma la gente a San Lorenzo se ne curava poco, persuasa che Roma non verrebbe mai colpita, per la protezione del Papa il quale difatti veniva soprannominato *la contraerea dell'Urbe*' (ST, p. 92). Pur tuttavia la presenza del Vaticano e del Papa non salveranno Roma.

La voce narrante entra in scena per brevi incisi: 'In città era stato ucciso un fascista e un comunicato delle forze di polizia della Città Aperta (tale era stata dichiarata Roma fin dall'agosto) minacciava provvedimenti gravi' (ST, p. 250), e solo per precisare, dall'alto, la condizione in cui versa la città eterna e i suoi abitanti alla fine del conflitto:

> Negli ultimi mesi dell'occupazione tedesca Roma prese l'aspetto di certe metropoli indiane dove solo gli avvoltoi si nutrono a sazietà e non esiste nessun censimento dei vivi e dei morti. [...] e la nube disastrosa dei bombardamenti, che attraversava di continuo tutto il territorio provinciale, calava sulla città un tendone di pestilenza e di terremoto. (ST, p. 324)

E infine per annunciarne la liberazione:

> La sera del 4 giugno, per la mancanza della luce elettrica, tutti si coricarono presto. Il Testaccio era calmo, gli Alleati entrarono a Roma. D'improvviso, si levò un grande clamore per le strade, come fosse Capodanno. Le finestre e i portoni si spalancarono, s'incominciarono a sciogliere le bandiere. Non c'erano più Tedeschi nella città. Dall'alto e dal basso si sentiva gridare: Viva la pace!! Viva l'America!! (ST, pp. 344–45)

Tuttavia, anche in questo caso, la città è parte della Storia e delle storie dei suoi protagonisti. Non è mai essa stessa protagonista: 'E a lei sembrava incredibile che in tutta l'enorme Roma non si rimediasse da riempire una pancia così piccola'. (ST, p. 329) Roma è funzionale al racconto. La descrizione non appartiene al narratore onnisciente, come il paesaggio del Lago di Como a Manzoni, appartiene a chi la vive quotidianamente. I quartieri sono vissuti, non descritti, le strade sono percorse da Ida, Useppe e Nino. La lingua è la loro, lo sguardo è il loro: 'Quanto poi alla città di Roma, Nino, personalmente, contestava l'idea di risparmiarla con riguardi speciali, esagerati. Su Roma, anzi, secondo lui, poco male se ci cascavano le bombe: visto che il massimo valore di Roma erano le rovine, Colosseo, Foro Traiano, eccetera'. (ST, p. 164)

Le visite di Ida nel quartiere ebraico, prima[19] e dopo[20] la deportazione, rendono conto dello stato delle cose del presente.

A fare da controcanto alla grigia e sofferta peregrinazione esistenziale di Ida per le vie di Roma è l'intesa e il viaggio fantasmagorico di Useppe con il cane Bella: 'Immediatamente, il cane volò su per la scala, e ne riportò giù un sandalo; poi rivolò, e ne riportò giù l'altro, con l'aria contenta di chi capisce tutto. Tale fu il primo incontro di Useppe con Bella'. (ST, p. 435), la loro convivenza: 'Così, da oggi furono in tre nella casa di Via Bodoni; e, da questo medesimo giorno, Useppe ebbe due madri' (ST, p. 474). I loro percorsi dalla città verso una campagna incontaminata rassicurano su un futuro contraddittorio, che dovrà prima o poi aprirsi su nuovi orizzonti: 'Non appena sbucati dal portone all'aria aperta, sùbito se li vedeva partire in corsa, scorribandando, zompando e scapriolando verso l'ignoto; e ai suoi richiami vociferanti, da lontano Bella in risposta premurosamente le abbaiava: «Tutto bene [...]»'. (ST, p. 495)

Con un andamento narrativo fiabesco, la Morante porta a spasso il bambino e il cane, attribuendo all'istinto di Bella il ruolo di guida:

> E oggi, per la prima volta, Useppe e Bella valicarono i loro confini soliti. Senza nemmeno accorgersene, cammina e cammina, superarono Via Marmorata,

seguendo tutta la lunghezza del Viale Ostiense; e raggiunta la Basilica di
San Paolo, presero a destra, dove Bella, chiamata da un odore inebriante,
incominciò a correre, seguìta da Useppe. (ST, p. 507)

I protagonisti del romanzo, 'l'arcipelago di miserabili' nella definizione di Balestrini,[21] sono scelti fra quella popolazione rappresentativa degli italiani del periodo. Ida è una maestra, viene da una famiglia medio-bassa del sud, rimane orfana e poi giovane vedova, trasferitasi a Roma, deve affrontare il periodo della guerra con i suoi soli e limitati strumenti. Non è un caso isolato nel panorama storico italiano dell'epoca, non è la diseredata verghiana e neppure l'eroina della Resistenza, ma rappresenta la semplice quotidianità dell'esistenza. Al centro del racconto dell'epica morantiana vive la famiglia Ramundo-Mancuso. Ida e i suoi figli, Nino e Useppe, costruiscono il polo di attrazione intorno al quale ruotano gli altri personaggi. È attraverso la loro vicenda che vediamo la deportazione degli ebrei del ghetto e conosciamo i Mille, Eppetondo, Davide Segre, Santina, Remo, Carulì, i Marrocco. Ecco l'umanità dello stanzone di Pietralata nella versione di Useppe:

> D'altra parte, Useppe aveva presto imparato i nomi di tutti quanti: Eppetondo (Giuseppe Secondo, ossia il Matto, ossia Cucchiarelli, il quale invero non era tondo per niente, anzi alquanto secco), Tole e Mémeco (Salvatore e Domenico, i due fratelli più anziani di Carulì) eccetera eccetera. [...] Senza dubbio, per lui non esistevano differenze né di età, né di bello e brutto, né di sesso, né sociali. Tole e Mémeco, erano, veramente, due giovanotti stortarelli e rincagnati, di professione incerta (borsari neri, oppure ladri, secondo i casi), ma per lui erano tali e quali a due fusti di Hollywood o a due patrizi d'alto rango. La sora Mercedes puzzava; ma lui, quando giocava a nascondarella, sceglieva a preferenza, come nascondiglio, la coperta che lei teneva sui ginocchi; e al momento di sparire là sotto, le mormorava in fretta in fretta, con aria complice: «Stà zitta, eh, stà zitta». (ST, pp. 185–86)

Ognuno di loro è vissuto da Ida, Useppe o Nino: attraverso la loro percezione e il loro sentire conosciamo un universo di uomini e donne che si muovono nella storia. Sono capitoli di un'odissea moderna: ogni incontro rappresenta un'occasione di conoscenza, e attraverso la vita degli altri i protagonisti prendono coscienza di ciò che a loro stessi sta capitando. Nello sguardo dei compagni di avventura vedono il proprio sguardo e comprendono la realtà circostante, decifrano l'atteggiamento umano di fronte agli eventi. Lo specchio introspettivo risiede nella reciprocità. Ida, come Useppe, non conosce la Storia del momento, non capisce la persecuzione degli ebrei, la vive e ne ha paura. È Davide l'unico consapevole del destino della sua gente e del suo. Tuttavia Davide è inserito *a latere* della storia dei Ramundo-Mancuso. Il dramma consapevole di Davide fa da contrappunto alla malattia inconsapevole di Useppe. La lucida lettura intellettuale del mondo non salva dalla tragedia, anzi la precipita. La fine parallela dei due disperati segna la volontà della Morante di avvicinare le esistenze umane al di là di età, estrazione sociale e raziocinio. Useppe non razionalizza, ma sente e percepisce la miseria e le atrocità che lo circondano. Useppe non viene informato della morte di Nino, ma avverte che Nino non tornerà. Sa che Nino è sparito per sempre dal suo mondo e il suo mondo sparisce pian piano, attraverso le crisi epilettiche che lo isolano dalla consapevolezza del dolore. È il dolore del mondo che si manifesta nella malattia di Useppe. Quando non ci sono crisi, Useppe è allegro e vitale, con la fantasia si costruisce uno spazio immaginario in parallelo a quello reale, unica salvezza alla miseria della sua fragile esistenza.

I due giovani, Nino e Davide, sembrano essere personaggi complementari nell'andamento del romanzo: 'La riapparizione di Carlo-Davide, come una staffetta, precedette di poco quella di Nino. Appena due giorni dopo, sul primo dopopranzo, Ninnarieddu si presentò a sua volta in casa Marrocco; e la sua visita fu l'opposto di quella di Davide, sebbene altrettanto breve'. (ST, p. 354)

Nino è la parte istintiva, viscerale della gioventù di allora, e forse di sempre, che assume atteggiamenti camaleontici nel corso dell'esistenza, adattandosi di volta in volta al mutare degli eventi: da fascista a partigiano e poi contrabbandiere. Per Nino tutto si può fare, tutto è possibile. Davide è la parte intellettuale, è la coscienza del mondo e delle ingiustizie perpetrate, portatore dei sensi di colpa per essere un sopravvissuto, per non aver potuto niente di fronte alla furia della Storia. Per Davide niente si può cambiare. Nino cavalca la Storia come la sua motocicletta, Davide ne rimane annichilito. L'anarchia di Davide non è la soluzione, ma la fuga verso una libertà irraggiungibile. Entrambi hanno segnato il loro destino: Nino muore vivendo, Davide di fatto è già morto mentre vive.

Il focus del testo, tuttavia, è posto sulla storia di una donna all'interno della Storia di un paese e di un mondo in guerra. *Lo scandalo che dura diecimila anni* è forse da leggersi in questa direzione: quanto la guerra modifichi le esistenze normali e le tramuti in esistenze disperate. Non esiste consolazione, perché l'unica consolazione di manzoniana memoria sarebbe credere nella possibilità di una redenzione. *I promessi sposi*, infatti, propongono un lieto fine e gli umili manzoniani riescono tramite la Provvidenza a portare a termine il loro disegno. Per i personaggi della Morante non esiste questa via e la conclusione del romanzo non lascia spazio a nessuna rivincita né terrena né ultraterrena. Iduzza sopravvive ai figli, ma non a se stessa, finendo pazza in un ospedale psichiatrico. E questo è il primo elemento consistente della narrazione. Il centro vero del romanzo è Ida, non Useppe, non Nino. Sono gli occhi di Ida che guardano il mondo decomposto, la marcescenza umana prodotta da un conflitto devastante. E con la vita di Ida si apre e si chiude il romanzo, che si sviluppa a cerchi concentrici a formare un gorgo che tutto sommerge. Così Ida è introdotta dalla Morante:

> La donna, di professione maestra elementare, si chiamava Ida Ramundo vedova Mancuso. Veramente, secondo l'intenzione dei suoi genitori, il suo primo nome doveva essere Aida. Ma, per un errore dell'impiegato, era stata iscritta all'anagrafe come Ida, detta Iduzza dal padre calabrese. [...] Ida era nata nel 1903, sotto il segno del Capricorno, che inclina all'industria, alle arti e alla profezia, ma anche, in certi casi, alla follia e alla stoltezza. (ST, p. 21)

Questa la descrizione della sua fine, con un 'io' che propone il narratore come parte attiva della vicenda. La Morante usa di norma una narrazione in terza persona, ma in particolari situazioni interviene l'io narrante, come per dar conto di una storia vissuta dal vero:

> Io credo, invero, che quella piccola figura senile, di cui taluno ricorda ancora il sorriso quieto nei cameroni deliranti dell'O.P., non sia durata nove e più anni se non per gli altri, ossia secondo il tempo degli altri. Uguale al transito di un riflesso che, dal suo punto irrisorio, si moltiplica in altri e altri specchi a distanza, quella che per noi fu una durata di nove anni, per lei fu appena il tempo di una pulsazione. (ST, p. 648)

Scrive la Ginzburg a proposito della scelta del narratore:

> La Storia è un romanzo scritto in terza persona. Un romanziere, oggi, della terza persona, ha paura come di una tigre. Egli sa che nella terza persona, nell'egli, si nasconde ogni specie di pericolo. Scrivendo 'io' si sente assai più sicuro, perché tutti i suoi limiti sono subito denunciati. Nella *Storia* l'io narrante esiste, ma si affaccia solo ogni tanto, e nello spazio di poche righe. L'io narrante è però, nella *Storia*, importantissimo, e non denuncia dei limiti, ma è invece il punto da cui viene contemplato il mondo. È un punto insieme altissimo e sotterraneo, dotato di uno sguardo che vede l'infinita estensione degli orizzonti e le infinite e minime rughe e crepe del suolo. Tale sguardo non conosce limiti, né in estensione, né in profondità.[22]

L'andamento della narrazione è costruito in modo circolare e ogni avvenimento è inserito sia nel macro-contesto storico del periodo sia nel micro-contesto della vita di una donna. Ida affronta il mondo e la Storia con una coscienza che mostra, solo a tratti, sprazzi di lucidità che emergono dalla sua esile figura in lotta per la vita, incapace di raggiungere il suo obiettivo di sopravvivenza.

La convergenza dello sguardo sul mondo della Morante con quello di Ida appare naturale in quanto sguardo femminile: la scrittrice sa calarsi nella profondità di sentire di una donna con mezzi cognitivi tanto limitati perché ciò che unisce la Morante a Ida è la percezione sensibile del mondo, quel livello di lettura della realtà e degli altri che non passa attraverso la sola razionalità, la cultura e la raffinatezza di pensiero; è l'intuizione del presente, gli affetti, la gioia e la paura che muovono le membra di Ida di giorno e di notte. Il corso della sua vita di stenti è modulato da emozioni, da stati d'animo e da un istinto, a tratti, primordiale.

A partire da questo presupposto, il libro si sviluppa su due piani di narrazione: lo sguardo consapevole del narratore onnisciente che dall'alto muove la storia e lo sguardo miope dei personaggi che dal basso avvertono la Storia, ma non la comprendono fino in fondo, rimanendo strettamente legati alla loro piccola storia personale. In questo dualismo, a tratti sapientemente intersecato, si dipana il racconto. Il lettore è lì, portato tanto a volare alto sulle ali della Storia (deportazioni, assassini di innocenti, bombardamenti, rastrellamenti, avanzate e contro avanzate) quanto a immergersi nel fantastico mondo del piccolo Useppe e in quello roboante di Nino, del semplice quotidiano di Ida e del farneticante, irrisolto elucubrare di Davide Segre. È questo l'aspetto più interessante ed epico della narrazione morantiana e quello più criticato al momento della sua uscita del romanzo: il fascino che costringe ad aprire e socchiudere gli occhi, a una visione dall'alto contestuale a quella dal basso: una visione razionale, logica e cronologica, e una visione empatica, fantastica, astorica.

La Morante costruisce così una partitura che ha un andamento doppio: la Storia è funzionale alle storie e viceversa. L'una non vive senza l'altra e la Storia non è protagonista assoluta del testo, ma ne fa parte, alla stessa altezza e con lo stesso valore della storia della povera Ida e del piccolo Useppe.

Useppe, Ida, Nino e gli altri non sono personaggi che aspirano a restituire in modo asettico la realtà di un mondo, sono piuttosto personaggi che esprimono il sentire, la profondità della sofferenza e della gioia che vengono loro offerti. Nino sembra sempre saper cogliere l'attimo e la sua fine non è determinata dalla guerra o dal sacrificio partigiano, ma dal contrabbando e da un banale incidente stradale in tempo di pace. Nino non è un eroe in senso tradizionale, legato al sacrificio per un ideale, Nino è un ragazzo di vent'anni, che cerca di respirare appieno la vita e si adatta al contesto in cui vive:

> La statura di Nino, in quell'anno [1943], s'era fatta molto più alta. E il disegno del suo corpo s'adattava a questa crescenza in un modo sbandato, cambiando senz'ordine né misura: con effetti di sproporzione e sgraziataggine, i quali, però, nella loro durata passeggera, gli davano un'altra grazia. Come se la forma della sua infanzia si rivoltasse, in una lotta drammatica, prima di cedere alla sua impazienza di crescere. (ST, p. 147)

Della vita di Nino cogliamo soltanto alcuni passaggi significativi, lo vediamo nel suo andirivieni frenetico, nel rapporto con il fratellino, con le donne, con gli amici, con i cani e in quello adolescenziale e contrastato con la madre. Ma quando entra in scena è una festa per tutti:

> Gli dispiacque sapere che Carlo-Davide era stato a cercarlo inutilmente; ma se ne rassegnò subito, con una scossa dei ricci, dicendo: «Lo rivedo a Napoli». E si spassò a raccontare barzellette, fischiò motivi di canzoni, e ogni momento sbottava a ridere come un fringuello. Tutti erano eccitati dalla sua presenza festosa. (ST, p. 354)

Esiste in lui una sorta di consapevolezza innata di dover lottare per vivere, proprio come i suoi cani, a cui è fortemente legato, ma senza mai disperazione, enfasi o distruzione. È positivo, vitale e pensa di essere pure immortale, incarnazione della gioventù di ogni tempo.

Useppe non è un personaggio strappalacrime. Useppe nasce da uno stupro di un soldato tedesco ai danni di Ida, indifesa e succube del suo stesso destino: 'Il corpo di Ida era rimasto inerte, come la sua coscienza: senz'altro movimento che un piccolo tremito dei muscoli e uno sguardo inerme di ripulsa estrema, come davanti a un mostro'. (ST, p. 68)

Useppe è il frutto della guerra, rappresenta la società derivante dal conflitto, nasce e vive la sua breve esistenza tutta all'interno delle sofferenze belliche che rappresenta *in toto* fin dal suo concepimento e dalla sua nascita:

> Il parto non fu lungo né difficile. Pareva che quella sconosciuta creatura si adoperasse a venire alla luce con le proprie forze, senza costare troppo dolore agli altri. [...] Era, difatti, proprio un *mascolillo*: cioè, un maschio, ma piccirillo, invero. [...] E dopo essersi affermato in quell'eroica impresa di venire al mondo aiutandosi da se stesso, non gli era rimasta nemmeno la voce per piangere. (ST, p. 95)

Per paradosso Useppe nella sua magrezza, solitudine e malattia riesce a comunicare la vita. Il suo rapporto con la natura e la trasfigurazione della realtà sono la sua salvezza fino a quando le atrocità dell'uomo non riusciranno a devastare completamente la sua anima. Questa la scena alla stazione di fronte al treno dei deportati:

> Il bambino stava tranquillo, rannicchiato sul suo braccio, col fianco sinistro contro il suo petto; ma teneva la testa girata a guardare il treno. In realtà, non s'era più mosso da quella posizione fino dal primo istante. E nello sporgersi a scrutarlo, lei lo vide che seguitava a fissare il treno con la faccina immobile, la bocca semiaperta, e gli occhi spalancati in uno sguardo indescrivibile di orrore. «Useppe...» lo chiamò a bassa voce. Useppe si rigirò al suo richiamo, però gli rimaneva negli occhi lo stesso sguardo fisso, che, pure all'incontrarsi col suo, non la interrogava. C'era, nell'orrore sterminato del suo sguardo, anche una paura, o piuttosto uno stupore attonito; ma era uno stupore che non domandava nessuna spiegazione. (ST, p. 246-47)

Useppe muore proprio come l'umanità stessa, l'*humanitas*, è morta dopo il Secondo conflitto mondiale nella visione della scrittrice.

Il realismo della Morante si perde presto nei sogni di Ida, nelle fantastiche visioni del bambino, nel suo colloquio intimo con gli animali, Blitz, Peppinello e Peppinella, Bella, e nella narrazione dall'alto e dal basso che il testo propone. Non è la fotografia aerea e un poco incolore del mondo dei subalterni quello raccontato dalla Morante, è la penetrazione di quel mondo, delle sue smagliature, delle sue incrinature profonde, intime, che ne mostrano le ferite emotive. Il narratore prende posizione dietro l'obiettivo e si sposta, dando conto delle diverse angolazioni della realtà, anche quelle più riposte, oniriche, psicologiche, annullando così il realismo *tout court*.

È un genere nuovo, un guazzabuglio di categorie critiche che spiazza e che affascina.

Il successo di pubblico ottenuto dal romanzo fin dalla sua uscita in libreria e l'argomento trattato contribuirono, inoltre, a suggerire la definizione di romanzo popolare. Ora questa categoria critica relegava il testo in uno scaffale di libri di facile consumo per tutti.

La Storia però male si propone come un feuilleton senza conseguenze di riflessione per il lettore, non solo per la sua mole (quasi 700 pagine), ma per argomento e struttura. È il soggetto trattato che sconsiglia di etichettarlo come un romanzo di facile successo perché popolare nei contenuti espressi, a meno che al termine popolare non si attribuisca un significato positivo. *La Storia* è un romanzo popolare perché parla appunto del popolo e al popolo. Gli eroi non sono cavalieri lancia in resta e neppure agiati borghesi che vivono il dramma della noia esistenziale, *La Storia* raccoglie le storie di molti Italiani, che negli anni Settanta ancora avevano negli occhi le sofferenze della Guerra e del dopoguerra, e di quelli nati dopo il conflitto che nel narrare familiare respiravano i residui di quel periodo. Per questo la storia di Ida viene condivisa anche da chi intellettuale non è, da chi impara nuove storie, da chi riflette su quelle storie e sulla Storia. Per questo la sua popolarità non può essere sovrapposta alla definizione di romanzo popolare. Non è e non vuole essere la rappresentazione melodrammatica di un periodo storico, è la messa in scena di quel periodo storico. E ha ragione Calvino a sostenere che alla *Storia* manca il lato melodrammatico dei *Miserabili*. L'intento della Morante sembra essere il suo contrario, rendere asciutto ed essenziale il racconto di una sofferenza, direi quasi ineluttabile: il dramma non risiede nel destino dei singoli, piuttosto nel rendere tangibile attraverso i singoli la tragedia di un intero mondo e in particolare di quello occidentale. È lungimirante la visione della Morante, non si limita allo spazio del racconto, ma costruisce prototipi di sofferenza, di un'umanità malata, di un mondo che si autodistrugge.

Potremmo registrare altre voci di critici che videro nella *Storia* un romanzo da contrastare per ragioni ideologiche, ma anche per la sua impostazione narrativa e per la sua immediata popolarità (da ricordare infatti che il libro vendette 100.000 copie in pochi mesi). Invece *La Storia* è un testo narrativo che apre, proprio in quegli anni, a una riflessione sul modo di fare e di intendere la letteratura in un rapporto stretto con il pubblico verso cui è diretto. L'aspetto popolare del libro, il suo successo, anticipa sia quello che sarà di lì a pochi anni il successo editoriale di altri romanzi, uno su tutti *Il nome della rosa*, ormai bestseller, sia l'espansione del mondo editoriale e il cambiamento di rotta culturale, anche in Italia.

Di fatto è a partire dagli anni Novanta,[23] a circa vent'anni dalla pubblicazione, che critici italiani e stranieri riprendono a discutere sul romanzo della Morante, rivedendo in buona parte il giudizio stilato all'indomani della sua uscita, ma soprattutto il testo viene studiato da angolazioni differenti. Si scopre così che la complessità del romanzo offre possibilità di interpretazioni critiche molteplici, dallo sguardo di genere alla lettura psicanalitica, politica, storica, ma anche linguistica e filologica; *La Storia* viene finalmente collocato nel suo alveo naturale: un romanzo di successo che a buon diritto può essere posto sullo scaffale dei testi di riferimento del Novecento letterario italiano. Una sorta di revisionismo critico che riconosce a *La Storia* di essere preludio 'alla ripresa della narratività poi esplosa nel decennio successivo',[24] come scrive nel 1998 Gino Tellini. A suggello della mutata prospettiva, Mario Barenghi nel 1999 afferma che 'la massima narratrice del Novecento italiano rimane Elsa Morante'.[25]

Con gli anni 2000, il riconoscimento sembra completarsi: Elsa è riabilitata dal mondo letterario e molte sono le manifestazioni (convegni e riconoscimenti pubblici) che la vedono protagonista.[26] La critica torna a scrivere anche del suo romanzo più contrastato e nel 2007 Alberto Casadei ribadisce: 'Elsa Morante, con *La Storia* [1974], [propone] un'opera che sia in partenza fruibile come bestseller popolare, e insieme come *novel* classico, nel quale le modalità realiste sono paragonabili a quelle impiegate da Tolstoj'.[27]

Sempre del 2007 è il saggio di Spinazzola 'Morante, la storia di Ida e Useppe' che propone una lettura della *Storia* in chiave femminile e matriarcale:

> Nessuna argomentazione c'è bisogno di elaborare in proposito, e neppure è il caso di spender parole di elogio per il comportamento della protagonista: il legame tra chi ha dato e chi ha ricevuto la vita ha un'evidenza organica anteriore a ogni ragionamento. L'esaltazione della femminilità nella figura di Ida trae forza proprio dall'insistenza con cui sono posti in risalto non i pregi ma i limiti di una personalità disastrosamente mediocre: a sublimarla è solo l'impegno direi

intransigente con cui assolve il compito di tutte le madri, ossia il sostegno della vita dei loro nati. Siamo nell'ambito di una istintività priva di qualsiasi rimando metafisico. Alla femmina spetta *naturaliter* un ruolo protettivo, oblativo, mentre al maschio inerisce un carattere aggressivo, prevaricatore.[28]

Il saggio conduce un'interpretazione contenutistico-testuale della *Storia*: la lente del critico è appoggiata sul testo e la tramatura viene esaminata nei suoi risvolti più celati. Ciononostante, nella sua complessa linearità, un romanzo come *La Storia* non sembra potersi risolvere nel dualismo maschile-femminile, poiché la struttura caleidoscopica e il personaggio poliedrico della stessa Ida non possono essere ricondotti a quell'unica lente, '*naturaliter*', dell'istinto materno.

Rimane il fatto, tuttavia, che con gli anni Duemila, il passaggio critico appare compiuto: il romanzo della Morante non è più osservato come un caso letterario, ma in relazione alla produzione narrativa italiana. *La Storia Romanzo* entra così nel canone del Novecento.

Notes to Chapter 26

1. La configurazione del titolo *La Storia Romanzo* rispecchia la volontà della Morante che in una lettera a Erich Linder, in occasione dell'uscita del libro in America, scrive: 'Mi hanno fatto notare che la copertina reca il titolo scritto così History: A novel [...] Ora bisogna togliere quei due punti, che falsano il titolo [...] Bisogna mantenere il titolo originale come d'accordo, ossia: history a novel' (Lettera del 18 Dicembre 1976), in Giovanna Rosa, *Il paradosso della «Storia Romanzo»*, in <https://air.unimi.it/retrieve/handle/2434/213919/260226/05_rosa%20Storia%20Perugia.pdf> [consultato il 15 Luglio 2015].
2. Così nel testo.
3. Romano Luperini, *Controtempo* (Napoli: Liguori, 1999), p. 157.
4. Si fa qui riferimento all'edizione: Elsa Morante, *La Storia Romanzo* (Torino: Einaudi, 1974), nel testo abbreviato ST.
5. Antonio Gramsci, 'Lettera n° 129: 3 giugno 1929: a Tatiana', in *Lettere dal carcere*, in <https://letteredalcarcere.wordpress.com/2010/04/26/lettera-n%C2%B0-129-3-giugno-1929-a-tatiana/> [consultato il 19 Luglio 2015].
6. Per una bibliografia completa degli scritti su Elsa Morante si rimanda a 'Scritti su Elsa Morante' <http://193.206.215.10/morante/studi.html> [consultato il 18 Luglio 2015]. Per dar conto del dibattito sul libro della Morante, si riporta di seguito una selezione degli articoli su *La Storia* usciti al momento della sua pubblicazione: Alberto Asor Rosa, 'Il linguaggio della pubblicità', *La fiera letteraria*, 40 (1974), 7–8; Luigi Baldacci, 'Il romanzo «pascoliano» di una nuova Elsa Morante', *Epoca*, 1241 (1974), 77; Nanni Balestrini [et al.], 'Contro il romanzone della Morante', *il manifesto*, 18 luglio 1974, 3; Renato Barilli, 'Elsa Morante, «La storia», Einaudi, Torino 1974', *Il Verri*, 5, 7 (1974), 105–10; Antonio Benetello, lettera da Padova a Oreste Del Buono', in 'Ma che storia questa *Storia*', *Linus*, 10 (1974), 12–13; Gianfranco Bettin, 'lettera da Marghera a Oreste del Buono', in 'Ma che storia questa *Storia*', *Linus*, 10 (1974), 17–18; Italo Calvino, 'Allora Hugo disse alla Morante', *l'Espresso*, 1 settembre 1974, 37–38; Cesare Cases, 'Un confronto con "Menzogna e sortilegio", in 'Il libro di Elsa Morante', *Quaderni piacentini*, 53–54 (1974), 177–91; Liana Cellerino, '«La storia» di Elsa Morante', *il manifesto*, 6 luglio 1974, 3; Goffredo Fofi, 'Alcuni appunti sul romanzo "La Storia"', *Ombre rosse*, 7 (1974), 90–94; Rina Gagliardi, 'La Morante non è marxista. E allora?', *il manifesto*, 19 luglio 1974, 3; Cesare Garboli, 'Pro e contro', *l'Espresso*, 11 agosto 1974, 37; Natalia Ginzburg, 'I personaggi di Elsa', *Corriere della Sera*, 21 luglio 1974, 12; Cosimo Ortesta, 'E. Morante, l'utopia che contamina e non redime', *il manifesto*, 31 luglio 1974, 4; Pier Paolo Pasolini, 'La gioia della vita la violenza della storia', *Tempo*, 30 (1974), 77–78; Pier Paolo Pasolini, 'Un'idea troppo facile nel mare sconfinato della storia', *Tempo*, 31 (1974), 75–76; Giovanni Raboni, 'Il libro di Elsa Morante', *Quaderni Piacentini*, 53–54 (1974), 174–76;

Franco Rella, '«La storia» un mediocre romanzo borghese, da criticare da un punto di vista marxista e proletario', *il manifesto*, 24 luglio 1974, 3; Rossana Rossanda, 'Una storia d'altri tempi', *il manifesto*, 7 agosto 1974, 3; Vittorio Saltini, 'Pro e contro', *l'Espresso*, 11 agosto 1974, 36–37; Bruno Schacherl, 'Il mito di Useppe e il romanzo popolare', *Rinascita*, 33 (1974), 19–20; Vittorio Spinazzola, 'Lo «scandalo» della storia', *l'Unità*, 21 luglio 1974, 3.

7. Balestrini, p. 3.
8. Balestrini, p. 3.
9. Saltini, p. 36.
10. Garboli, p. 37.
11. Ginzburg, p. 12.
12. Rossanda, p. 3.
13. Calvino, p. 37.
14. Asor Rosa, p. 8.
15. Barilli, p. 105.
16. Ginzburg, p. 12.
17. Romano Luperini, *Il Novecento* (Torino: Loescher, 1981), tomo 2, p. 677.
18. Eugenio Montale, 'La storia', in *L'opera in versi* (Torino: Einaudi, 1980), p. 315.
19. 'Finché da un giorno all'altro, lei che prima delle leggi razziali non aveva incontrato mai nessun ebreo fuori di Nora, seguendo una sua pista incongrua s'orientò a preferenza nella cerchia del Ghetto romano, verso le bancarelle e le botteghe di certi ebreucci ai quali ancora a quel tempo era permesso di seguitare nei loro poveri traffici di prima' (ST, p. 58).
20. 'Era un circuito più minuscolo d'ogni minuscolo villaggio, anche se dentro ci si affollavano, a famiglie di dieci per ogni stanzetta, migliaia di giudii. Ma oggi Ida ci si trascinava come in un labirinto enorme senza principio né fine; e per quanto lo girasse, ci si ritrovava sempre allo stesso punto' (ST, p. 338).
21. Balestrini, p. 3.
22. Ginzburg, p. 12.
23. Per gli anni Ottanta pochi sono gli interventi critici su *La Storia*, si dà conto di seguito perciò di una selezione bibliografica sulla riapertura del dibattito a partire dal 1990, escludendo gli articoli apparsi sui quotidiani: Ersilia Alessandrone Perona, '«La storia» di Elsa Morante ha vent'anni', *Il ponte*, 5 (1994), 93–96; Alfonso Berardinelli, 'Il sogno della cattedrale. Elsa Morante e il romanzo come archetipo', *Linea d'ombra*, 80 (1993), 45–52; Graziella Bernabò, *Come leggere La Storia di Elsa Morante* (Milano: Mursia, 1991); Susan Briziarelli, 'Cassandra's Daughters: Prophecy in Elsa Morante's «La Storia»', *Romance Languages Annual*, 3 (1991), 189–93; Mariane Brosse-Boisset, 'Elsa Morante et le réalisme', *Narrativa*, 1 (1992), 132–62; Rocco Capozzi, 'Elsa Morante: The Trauma of Possessive Love and Disillusionment', in *Contemporary Women Writers in Italy: A Modern Renaissance*, a cura di Santo L. Aricò (Amherst: University of Massachusetts, 1990), pp. 10–25; Elena Commisso, 'Recuperating the Distance from the Margins to the Centre: Elsa Morante's La storia, the stories that build history', *Romance Review*, 9 (1999), 19–32; Cristina Della Coletta, 'Elsa Morante's «La Storia»: Fiction and Women's History', *Romance Languages Annual*, 5 (1994), 194–99; Margherita Ganeri, 'Elsa Morante: La storia e il romanzo neostorico', *Allegoria*, n. s., 24 (1996), 179–85; Cesare Garboli, *Introduzione a La Storia* (Torino: Einaudi, 1995), pp. V-XXVI; Katja Liimatta, 'Feminism, Feminine Historiography and Elsa Morante's *La storia*', *Romance Languages Annual*, 1 (1998), 281–87; Stefania Lucamante, *Elsa Morante e l'eredità proustiana* (Fiesole: Cadmo, 1998); Stefania Lucamante, 'Il romanzo realista e il «necessario realismo» di Elsa Morante', *Il cristallo*, 3 (1995), 40–41; Pier Vincenzo Mengaldo, 'Elsa Morante', in *Storia della lingua italiana. Il Novecento* (Bologna: Il Mulino, 1994), pp. 161–67; «Per Elsa Morante», Atti del Convegno (Perugia 15–16 gennaio 1993) (Milano: Linea d'ombra, [1993]); Lucia Re, 'Utopian Longing and the Constraints of Racial and Sexual Difference in Elsa Morante's «La Storia»', *Italica*, 3 (1990), 361–75; Rita Sodi, 'Whose story? Literary borrowings in Elsa Morante's «La Storia»', *Lingua e stile*, 1 (1998), 141–53; *Vent'anni dopo La Storia: omaggio a Elsa Morante*, a cura di Concetta D'Angeli e Giacomo Magrini (Pisa: Giardini, 1995); Sharon L. Wood, 'The Deforming Mirror: Histories and Fictions in Elsa Morante (1912–85)', in *Italian Women's Writing 1860–1994* (London: Athlone, 1995), pp. 152–68.

24. Gino Tellini, *Il romanzo italiano dell'Ottocento e Novecento* (Milano: Bruno Mondadori, 1998), p. 466.
25. Mario Barenghi, *Oltre il Novecento. Appunti su un decennio di narrativa (1988–1998)* (Milano: Marcos y Marcos, 1999), p. 11.
26. Questa una selezione di bibliografia critica relativa agli anni Duemila: Mario Barenghi, 'Tutti i nomi di Useppe: saggio sui personaggi della «Storia» di Elsa Morante', *Studi novecenteschi*, 62 (2001), 369–89; Giovanna Bellini, *Morante e la scrittura femminile,* a cura di Maria Pia Miglio (Roma: Laterza, 2005); Marino Biondi, 'Romanzi nel tempo: bilanci di fine secolo', *Il cristallo*, suppl. al n. 1 (2004), 13–73; Simona Cives, 'Elsa Morante, *La Storia*: appunti sul paratesto del manoscritto', in *Le Identità giovanili raccontate nelle letterature del Novecento,* a cura di Carlo A. Augieri (Lecce: Manni, 2005), pp. 414–30; Ugo Dotti, 'Gli scrittori e la storia: da Silone a Elsa Morante', *Belfagor*, 2 (2003), 125–58; Daniel Mangano, '*La Storia* ovvero il mondo salvato da un ragazzino', *Narrativa*, 17 (2000), 101–16; Lydia M. Oram, 'Rape, Rapture and Revision: Visionary Imagery and Historical Reconstruction in Elsa Morante's *La storia*', *Forum italicum*, 2 (2003), 409–35; Hanna Serkowska, *Uscire da una camera delle favole: I romanzi di Elsa Morante* (Krakow: Rabid, 2002); *Le stanze di Elsa: dentro la scrittura di Elsa Morante: Biblioteca Nazionale Centrale di Roma, 27 aprile-3 giugno 2006,* a cura di Giuliana Zagra e Simonetta Buttò (Roma: Colombo, [2006]).
27. Alberto Casadei, *Stile e tradizione nel romanzo italiano contemporaneo* (Bologna: Il Mulino, 2007), p. 50.
28. Vittorio Spinazzola, 'Morante, la storia di Ida e Useppe', in *L'egemonia del romanzo* (Milano: Mondadori, 2007), pp. 287–329 (p. 290).

CHAPTER 27

❖

Fragments of (Urban) Space and (Human) Time: Gadda's Poetics (with Baudelaire and Benjamin)

Giuseppe Stellardi

The present contribution[1] has a dual focus: I will try to show why it is impossible to 'resolve the equation' of Carlo Emilio Gadda's writing into a recognizable formula consistent with contemporary poetics; but at the same time I will also attempt to highlight ways in which his art can be made to resonates profoundly in unexpected cultural contexts. The result will, I hope, be an encouragement towards an open, non-restrictive and non-solipsistic reading of one of the most exclusive and impenetrable writers of the twentieth century.

Almost the entire oeuvre of Gadda (1893–1973)[2] can be said to be dominated by fragmentariness. All the works published in book form by him before the Garzanti edition of *Quer pasticciaccio brutto de via Merulana* (1957: Gadda was then 64), that is: *La Madonna dei Filosofi* (1931), *Il castello di Udine* (1934), *Le meraviglie d'Italia* (1939), *Gli anni* (1943), *L'Adalgisa* (1943–1944) and *Novelle dal Ducato in fiamme* (1953)[3] are collections of more or less disparate texts of varying length, including some very short and obviously incomplete ones, often previously published in literary journals or other periodicals. These texts are frequently derived from different narrative 'cantieri' ('construction sites', to use an expression often employed by critics) corresponding to specific novelistic projects, or other horizons of writing (also non-fictional, for instance journalistic), internally connected by what Dante Isella (in his *Presentazione* of the Garzanti edition) accurately described as a 'sistema a vasi comunicanti' ('system of communicating vessels'), making it possible for the same or very similar materials to resurface, over the years, in different editorial contexts. Another useful metaphor — this time from the botanical realm — for looking at the deep shape of the whole of Gadda's production in those years is perhaps that of the *rhizome* (a horizontal structure of underground roots and shoots), especially as exploited in a philosophical and literary perspective by Gilles Deleuze and Félix Guattari in *Milles plateaux*.[4] Both metaphors suggest that all of Gadda's works, in their individual and multifarious manifestations, are but the epiphenomenic, fragmentary and incomplete trace of a dynamic and unstable mass or organism, existing at a deeper and more obscure level than that represented by the relatively chaotic sequence of ostensible publications. It should not be inferred, however, that what lies beneath, albeit invisible, is sufficiently homogeneous and systematic to explain and resolve what is visible on the surface.

There are, furthermore, good reasons to say that fragmentariness continues in Gadda even after the more tumultuous period of his production (from the late 1920s to the early 1940s), remaining a feature of his major novels, *La cognizione del dolore* and *Quer pasticciaccio brutto de via Merulana*, which some critics consider good examples (in more than one way, that is, both structurally and stylistically) of the 'unfinished'. This will not form part of my discussion on this occasion, but I had it in mind when I started by saying that almost the whole of this writer's work — with only few exceptions — could legitimately be seen as fragmentary.

We must now turn to the reasons for this state of fragmentariness. Two antithetical ones, the first negative and the second positive, can be (and have been) advanced:

(1) In a negative mode, it could be said that Gadda, quite simply, is the kind of writer who finds it very difficult to finish what he starts (or to 'resolve' magmatic inspiration into harmonious structure and accomplished form); this 'inability to complete', of course, could then be linked to either personal, psychological and in any case autobiographical issues, or to a broader (cultural and social) state of malaise, making it hard for the artist (and not just Gadda) to find the right circumstances and setting, conducive to full realization of any programmatic intentions.

(2) In a more positive perspective, one might refer to some of the poetics enjoying currency at the time, and likely to lend theoretical support to a practice of fragmentary writing: we can think of the 'poetica del frammento', or the so-called 'prosa d'arte', variously associated with influential periodicals such as *La Voce*, *La Ronda*, *Solaria*, and so on. It is interesting to note that, taking this line of thought to the extreme, some critics have gone so far as to speak, in relation to Gadda (and other European writers from a completely different background, such as Samuel Beckett and Louis-Ferdinand Céline) of an anticipated, precursory form of postmodernism.[5]

There is merit in both of these lines of reflection; a writer is always affected (but rarely fully determined) by personal history and environment. So, in the case of Gadda, it is perfectly legitimate to look both at biographical data and contemporary movements, trying to link them with his work; but it is almost invariably a fatal mistake to make too strong a connection between writing and 'determining factors' meant to explain and justify it. Likewise, taking the long-term perspective to look at possible links with and influences on later trends is fine, but the twin risks of anachronistic (con)fusion and forced assimilation must be avoided.

Therefore, whilst the hypotheses mentioned above deserve to be taken into account, I do not think they provide sufficient explanation for the peculiar state of fragmentariness of Gadda's production. In order to add some significant points to the analysis, I propose to take a very cursory look at the origins of Gadda's writing, and first of all at the years when, whilst reluctantly engaging in a career as an engineer (forced upon him by practical considerations and familial expectations), the young Milanese was hesitating between literature and philosophy in pursuit of his innermost aspirations.[6]

Apart from some abortive narrative attempts, the most significant piece of writing undertaken by Gadda prior to 1924 is his Great War diary, the *Giornale di guerra e di prigionia* (in SGF II); this, however, is not a narrative, critical or theoretical work, was never meant for publication, and came out (with significant albeit passive resistance on the part of the author) only in 1965.[7] The first serious attempt at narrative writing took place in 1924 when, on his return from Argentina, Gadda (with the intention of competing for a literary prize) set out to compose a novel provisionally entitled *Racconto italiano di ignoto del novecento*.[8] This was never finished and all that is left is a mass of plans, fragmentary drafts and methodological notes, contained in two manuscript notebooks, entitled by Gadda *Cahiers d'études*. Of all the remarkable wealth of information therein included on Gadda's early literary outlook, I wish to retain a fundamental point: the would-be writer is, at that moment, very clearly intent on composing a 'canonical' novel, that is, one based on models or poetics belonging to the previous century. His avowed influences are Manzoni, Flaubert, Balzac, Dostoevsky and other nineteenth-century realist writers; and he envisages a wide and well-structured narrative organism, linking character psychology with historical context in a dialectic whole, which at one point he describes following the well-trodden idealistic, Hegelian formula of thesis, antithesis and synthesis (re-named by him *la Norma*, *l'Abnorme* and *la Comprensione*) (RI, p. 415). This, of course, is not to say that there is nothing original in Gadda's ideas; but the main direction is certainly traditionalist rather than innovative.

A second, crucial moment in the development of Gadda's ideas is represented by the *Meditazione milanese*[9] of 1928, a philosophical work in the most canonical of all philosophical forms, the dialogue. Again, there is a great deal that is interesting in it at the level of detail, and some ideas can even be regarded as being considerably in advance of his own time, but nothing indicating a desire to be radically innovative in terms of methods and practices. From Plato, to Italian humanism and renaissance, to Leopardi, Gadda is modelling himself on a well-established tradition and not engaging in active subversion or experimentation.

On the surface, therefore, the young Gadda does not seem interested in radical innovation. At a more detailed level, however, his ideas and writing practice, in both RI and MM, from the very beginning start to move irresistibly in the direction of what I would describe as 'incontrollable complexity', two main aspects of which are the impossibility of closing any system (incompleteness), and the inherent inadequacy and fragmentariness of any linguistic expression. These, inevitably giving rise to chaotic proliferation, are the seeds of what will subsequently coagulate into Gadda's mature style; the open admiration for the Macaronic writers, or for what he sees as Shakespeare's 'baroque' style and thought (of which there are ample traces in Gadda from very early on, starting with the *Giornale*) are symptomatic of this opposite tendency.

It is interesting to look at Gadda's numerous non-fictional writings in this light, to expose the existence of an uninterrupted reflection on the modes and reasons of literary writing, in general, and of his own in particular. This is recorded in approximately fifty texts (essays, reviews or other interventions), of varying significance, published between the early 1920s and 1970; among these, the most important in the first decade — and therefore corresponding to the same period as RI and MM — are the review of his friend Ugo Betti's *Il re pensieroso* (1923); *Apologia manzoniana* (which is actually a fragment, published independently in 1927, from the *Cahier d'études* of 1924); *I viaggi la morte* (also published in 1927, and later chosen to provide the title for Gadda's most important collection of essays); and the essay *Le belle lettere e i contributi espressivi delle tecniche* (1929).[10] If one tries to identify the main tenets of Gadda's explicit aesthetic theory at the time, as it transpires from these contributions, I think the list would be as follows:

(1) simplicity and clarity in expression (against what he defines 'verbosa complicazione');
(2) privileged position assigned to ordinary language (the 'forme dell'uso');
(3) exaltation of the 'work well done';
(4) anti-individualism, anti-elitism, literature as expression of collective life and experience, of the common effort and endeavour of 'le genti';
(5) 'moral substance' regarded as indispensable validation criterion for literary creation;
(6) fundamental link between particular and universal in a sort of 'realistic symbolism', manifesting itself also in an ideally symphonic structure of the narrative work.

In this perspective Manzoni is quite openly the modern model, the father and avowed master ('scrittore degli scrittori', SGF I, p. 679); and Horace ('il potente poeta', p. 582) is the forefather.

But if we were tempted to extract from all this a poetics of sorts, the main problem would be that — as already suggested — these ideas are extensively contradicted not only by the parallel discourse on the 'complessità irriducibile' going on primarily in the unpublished texts (*Racconto* and *Meditazione*), but also by both the appearance and the substance of Gadda's subsequent fictional writing practice (which of course at this stage is still largely to come: the first volume published by Gadda is *La Madonna dei filosofi*, 1931, now in RR I). To put it bluntly, I do not think any reader would recognize the characteristics mentioned above as prominently present in Gadda's own style. This seems to indicate not so much a hypocritical stance on the part of the writer in his public utterances, but rather a fundamental discord in his own relationship with literature. In my opinion, as I shall try to show, this inherent conflict will remain unresolved until the end.

It could be hypothesised that, following these ambiguous beginnings in the twenties, a change of heart may have taken place, leading to a new, more 'open' and more coherent poetics. Among Gadda's numerous essays in the thirties and forties (and beyond), the following are particularly relevant in this perspective: *Meditazione breve circa il dire e il fare* (1936, published in 1937, SGF I, p. 444); *Postille a una analisi stilistica* (1937, p. 820); *Lingua letteraria e lingua dell'uso* (1941–42, p. 489); *Fatto personale... o quasi* (1947, p. 495); *Psicanalisi e letteratura* (1948, p. 455); *Come lavoro* (1949, p. 427); *Un'opinione sul neorealismo* (1950, p. 629); *Intervista al microfono* (1951,

p. 502); *Manzoni diviso in tre dal bisturi di Moravia* (1960, p. 1176); *L'Editore chiede venia del recupero chiamando in causa l'Autore*, attached to the edition in book form of *La cognizione del dolore* (1963, in RR I); up to the very last text, *Umanità degli umili*, published in 1970 (SGF I, p. 1224).

The analysis of these texts, however, shows that Gadda never explicitly retracts the 'traditionalist' starting positions of the twenties, although their incompatibility with the other side of his thought, as well with his own writing practice, will become more and more dramatically patent. His *stated* position can almost always be ascribed to a desire to pursue an organic and systematic form of literary production, where language and style are consistently rooted in social realities, and ethically motivated. This position is in his case, in terms of literary disposition, inherently conservative.

However, the increasingly dominant notions of deformation, baroque and 'maccheronea', the insistence on tensions and irreducible contrasts as essential modalities of representation, inexorably push Gadda's discourse in the direction of an idea of literature which is radically opposed to that represented by the never rejected Manzonian ideal. But that doesn't mean that he moves closer to any of the available contemporary poetics. It is interesting to look, in this light, at the reasons for Gadda's violent rejection of the dominant literary trend of the late forties, as expressed in *Un'opinione sul neorealismo* (1950, SGF I, p. 629): 'la poetica neorealistica riesce a un racconto astrutturale, granulare', since neorealist vision is restrictive (compared to the immense richness of reality itself). 'Le figure, talora, diventano simboli: e io aborro dal personaggio-simbolo, come aborro dal personaggio-araldo'. Neorealists, furthermore, display 'un umore tetro e talora dispettoso come di chi rivendichi qualcosa da qualcheduno e attenda giustizia, di chi si senta offeso, irritato' (p. 630). He also imputes to the neorealists the 'tremenda serietà del referto', and 'il tono asseverativo [...] che sbandisce a priori le meravigliose ambiguità di ogni umana cognizione'. 'Il fatto', he maintains, 'non è che il residuo fecale della storia'. Ultimately, 'un lettore di Kant non può credere in una realtà obbiettiva'. As always, Gadda's analysis is awowedly far from objective; interestingly, he describes his own 'naturali tendenze', present and past, as 'quelle di un romantico: di un romantico preso a calci dal destino, e dunque dalla realtà' (*ibidem*). Once more, it is in the past and within tradition that Gadda finds the fundamental components of his own identity.

This point can be generalized by stating that Gadda's stance in relation to all contemporary poetics (and not just neorealism) is never sympathetic. When mentioned, these are systematically criticized; neither futurism, nor any other avant-gardes or experimentalist aesthetics are ever cited in a positive light (modernism, of course, did not exist at the time within the Italian literary-critical vocabulary, and even subsequently struggled for a long time to become part of it). Whereas Gadda does not hesitate, time and again, to make himself the supporter — against the current — of antiquated models (Manzoni, Belli, dialect poetry, Romanticism): except, however, when these in his opinion tend to become fossilized, for instance, in manifestations of linguistic or ideological dogmatism (Manzoni), narcissism (Foscolo), or patriotism (Carducci), and so on.

In short, and to condense a detailed analysis that cannot be reproduced here for lack of space: the writings of the thirties and beyond, on the one hand, see the irruption of the 'thought of the complexity' which, in the previous decade, was relegated to the submerged continent of the unpublished materials; but, on the other hand — and paradoxically — these texts never cease to reaffirm the aspiration to simplicity which dominated the very origins of Gadda's relationship with literature. The contradiction becomes openly visible, now that, in works such as *La Madonna dei filosofi* (1931), *Il castello di Udine* (1934), and then *La cognizione del dolore* (1938–41 in *Letteratura*),[11] the dominant characteristics of Gadda's style (variously identified by critics as 'baroque', 'expressionistic', 'macaronic' and so on) are there for all to see, to the extent that the writer himself is forced to defend and embrace them, as he explicitly does in *L'Editore chiede venia del recupero chiamando in causa l'Autore* (1963; RR I, p. 759).

The complication in Gadda's more mature thought derives, therefore, not so much from the arrival and public manifestation of notions (such as complexity, impurity and tension) which were already abundantly attested in the (then) unpublished writings of the twenties (in particular in MM, and also in *Secondo libro della poetica*[12]), but from the relevance they acquire when, publically and polemically manifested, they are linked specifically to concrete examples of literary writing, and primarily his own. One can detect, furthermore, an increasingly dark and desperate tone, and a steadily decreasing willingness to take seriously the very idea of a poetics, which instead had not seemed impossible initially.

An important point to note is that the problems facing the writer are, in his own opinion, not only (or not principally) linguistic and stylistic; on the contrary, an intricate formal construction and variegated linguistic texture is, for Gadda, only the necessary correlative of a state of affairs preceding any elective deliberation at the level of presentation. The growing complexity, which is responsible for the theoretical *impasse*, derives essentially from two sources: on the one hand, the unfathomable depth of subjective identity: 'ognun di noi mi appare essere un groppo, o nodo, o groviglio, di rapporti fisici e metafisici' (*Come lavoro*, 1949, in SGF I, p. 428); on the other, the impact of objective reality: external facts 'sovvertono in misura orrenda [...] nobili costellazioni d'agganciamenti interni, dovuti all'operosità nativa dello spirito' (p. 429). Such thoughts were already (theoretically and emotionally) present to Gadda's reflection in the twenties (RI, MM); but now they become swollen and metamorphose from objects of enquiry into veritable tumours of the mind. To the extent that, Gadda concludes, 'non mi è dato affermare [...]. Una mano ignota, come di ferro, si sovrappone alla nostra mano bambina' (*ibid.*). The definitive failure of any theoretical or self-definitory attempt is inevitable: 'una mezza dozzina di verità' and 'due dozzine di mezze bugie' (p. 427) is, ironically, the best that the effort to clarify matters manages to produce. The passing of time is a crucial component of this increasingly pessimistic perspective, since maturity inescapably brings with it a loss of naivety: 'Altra è la maniera dei vent'anni, altro è lo scrittore a cinquanta' (p. 428).

Such assertions inexorably contradict the ideal of linguistic simplicity and expressive felicity that dominated the mind of the hopeful would-be writer twenty years before; but the crucial point is that the resulting 'deformation' is not, here at least (*Come lavoro*, 1949), positively embraced, as will instead be the case in *L'Editore chiede venia del recupero chiamando in causa l'Autore*, as the truthful mirror held up to reality, and therefore the means of positive heuristic advance, but rather suffered as the result of an oppressive imposition. The initially (and consistently) lyrical instinct, which mutates into a rational drive in the philosophical dialogue (MM) and is always the expression of a generous, socially communicative impulse, exhaust itself in the dead end of frustration and personal impotence. This was already and almost prophetically anticipated at the conclusion of the *Giornale di guerra e di prigionia*, on 31st December 1919: 'La mia vita è inutile, è quella d'un automa sopravvissuto a se stesso, che fa per inerzia alcune cose materiali, senza amore né fede' (SGF II, p. 867).

Gadda's deep beliefs and aspirations do not seem to have changed across the decades, and neither has his firm allegiance to the most unlikely (given the actual characteristics of his own style) of models, Alessandro Manzoni. His writing *practice*, however, proves firmly irreconcilable with those premises. It is obvious that Gadda's writing is not ascribable to any of the masters (from the nineteenth century or before) to which he habitually and deferentially refers; neither Manzoni, Horace, Virgil, Livy, Caesar, nor Belli, Porta or Folengo can provide adequate criteria to reflect or contain the writing practice of the Milanese. The examples that Gadda admires above all others (the expressive felicity and the 'potente sinfonia' of Manzoni or Balzac; art as direct translation, in Horace or Caesar, of fundamental ethical and social values) cannot be converted at a personal level into a viable poetics. The 'spastic', the 'macaronic', the mixed, the doubles, the baroque become necessary to give voice to a form of experience that is itself dominated by chaos and, therefore, irreducible to transparent and rational coordinates; this is, we could say, the Shakespearian face of Gadda's inspiration.[13] However, since the initial model is never explicitly abandoned, the inevitable result can only be irredeemable contradiction.

There is, as I have shown, substantial continuity concerning some crucial ideas, which however appear more and more dissociated from the actual practice of Gadda's own literary production. But even at the conceptual level things become increasingly complicated starting from the end of the twenties. If, on the one hand, Gadda's thought seems to accept a greater complexity of forms and modes (*Tendo al mio fine*, 1931, in RR I, p. 119), on the other the chimera of some unified and overarching poetics becomes more and more improbable, and in fact is more and more frequently the object of explicit denunciation.

Following a trajectory of increasing complexity, Gadda reaches an aporetical condition that — in spite of some polemical declarations — is more suffered than embraced (since it now corresponds to a painful and insurmountable reality, rather than a theoretical hypothesis or philosophical problem). A writer's life and his work, Gadda believes, are functions of unresolved tensions that cannot be managed rationally, or justified ethically; art for Gadda is fundamentally impulsive and ultimately ungovernable. A moral duty of truthfulness remains, but at this point truth is no longer the resolution of the particular into the universal: it has become an entirely subjective matter, and literary writing is at risk of exhausting itself in irrational invective, in revenge: 'Nella mia vita di "umiliato e offeso" la narrazione mi è apparsa, talvolta, lo strumento che mi avrebbe consentito di ristabilire la "mia" verità, il "mio" modo di vedere, cioè: lo strumento della rivendicazione contro gli oltraggi del destino e de' suoi umani proietti: lo strumento, in assoluto, del riscatto e della vendetta' (*Intervista al microfono*, in SGF I, p. 502).

Dismissed the original hope of a complete (and necessary) theoretical systematization within a wholly adequate context (reality, which by now has revealed itself as too vast and chaotic even to be surveyed, let alone understood), any imaginary poetics must be recognized as only the tip of a largely invisible and inaccessible iceberg: to isolate this tip as representing full meaning is tantamount to turning it into a fetish and betraying the truth.

Having said this, it is certainly possible (and useful) to establish parallels, to 'insert' a posteriori Gadda, provisionally and tentatively, within a larger frame of reference, for instance (as already anticipated) contemporary Modernism,[14] or even Postmodernism — a later context, which some of the writer's modes seem to anticipate.[15] But, at the same time, it is imperative to give a full account of the pressing and precise reasons making a global and satisfactory esthetico-theoretical systematization impossible and, in particular, impracticable from *within* the 'Gadda system'. Gadda's constant preoccupation to justify his own writing does not translate in a poetics, not even implicit, not even derived. Too contradictory are the native tendencies in relation to the harsh demands of reality, too complex is the frame of reference (language, life, world); nor can we say, on the other hand, that the awareness of unresolved complexity and permanent tension is sufficient to compose a poetics, not at least as Gadda would want it. The idea of complexity, in fact, constantly clashes with its own opposite, the never rejected idealization of literary architectures favouring clarity and simplicity. Unfortunately for our writer, it seems that nothing less than simplicity *and simultaneously* totality would have been sufficient to give him some semblance of happiness in his self-identification as a writer.

Even when Gadda becomes a published writer, in the 1930s, it is easy to see that — in spite of his practice of fragmentariness and his inability to accomplish the grand project that he had in mind — an instinct of totalization is still at work in his writing. This is symptomatically visible in the form of a dual tendency towards encyclopaedic completeness and systematic closure. Both have a philosophical as well as a literary application; in his thinking and his imagination, in the world that he describes and in the categories that he employs to understand it, Gadda strives for exhaustiveness. Both totalizing instincts, however, are defeated by a subject matter and writing practice that irresistibly tends to exceed the limits of the text, and by a style that is constantly unstable, unable to adhere to either encyclopaedic or systematic completeness.

In fact, on closer observation it turns out that the encyclopaedic element, rather than being complementary to the systematic one, is fighting against it: it is, paradoxically, precisely the accumulation of materials, ideas and linguistic means that prevents (systematically, one might say) the consolidation of a closed system. There are two clear symptoms to this syndrome: lists and notes. Gadda is a great practitioner of (especially comic) enumeration, and of rambling (or manic) annotation. Some of his footnotes (notably in *L'Adalgisa*) run into several pages of historical digression or scientific popularization, fracturing the compactness of the narrative and turning it into a (tendentially) all-encompassing encyclopaedia, whilst at the same time depriving it of structural stability and closure.[16]

The important point is this: the chaotic, unsystematic and ultimately fragmentary appearance of Gadda's text is the result not of his adhesion to some currently circulating or prophetically anticipated poetics, be it modernist, avant-garde, or pre-postmodernist, but rather the result of a permanently unresolved conflict between the ideal and the real. A victim of this conflict, Gadda is, in fact, bereft of poetics and lives his writing as an endless struggle, in a permanent state of tension between opposing forces.

I would now like to take a closer look at one specific example, and then take the analysis further. I have chosen *L'Adalgisa* because I think it functions particularly well as an illustration of the points made so far.

L'Adalgisa, published in 1943–44 (now in RR I), is a fragmentary book about a city, Milan; it contains ten texts of variable length, not all ostensibly connected to each other by a common thread. More precisely,[17] we can separate them in three groups: the first text is an isolated residue from the old *Racconto italiano di ignoto del novecento*; numbers 5 and 7 derive from the 'building site' of *La cognizione del dolore*; whilst the largest group, numbers 2, 3, 4, 6, 8, 9 and 10, belong thematically to the 'cantiere' of *L'Adalgisa* proper (and related projects). At a closer look, however, they all share common roots, presenting (as we shall see) different facets of a single, incomplete whole. The book is, therefore, an excellent example of the 'communicating vessels' (or rhizome) structure mentioned above; it brings together apparently unrelated narrative projects, without attempting to resolve at the superficial level the multiplicity of settings, styles and perspectives into a unified organism; it thereby exposes its own fragmentariness, whilst at the same time revealing a deeper interconnectedness of all the different strains of Gadda's writing in those years.

We could read *L'Adalgisa*, therefore, as a broken mirror reflecting images of a single object (we could tentatively call it 'reality') through a multiplicity of authorial perspectives, none of which can individually satisfy the voracious instinct of totalization that drives the act of writing. Completion is made impossible not only by the infinite complexity and detail of the object (which is simultaneously physical, psychological, social, historical, and so on) and the variety of modes and styles employed to its enumeration, but also by a significant and almost schizophrenic fracture in the authorial disposition towards it.

This becomes more clearly visible by separating the texts into two main groups: the world of *La Cognizione* and that of *L'Adalgisa* are one and the same (albeit thinly disguised, in *La Cognizione*, by an imaginary south-American setting), but they are observed through opposing lenses. In the world of *L'Adalgisa*, despite the very considerable presence of a component of social criticism addressed primarily to the Milanese bourgeoisie, the atmosphere is in the main nostalgic and inclusive (the marginally intra-diegetic narrator presents himself as part of an environment that has now disappeared, and that he remembers affectionately); in the world of *La Cognizione*, however, an attitude of destructive (and ultimately self-destructive) criticism reveals the protagonist as irreparably and antagonistically separated from a society that he detests. The problem is: those two worlds are the same one, the Milan and the Brianza of the '20s and '30s, its middle-class, its habits, its life; the ambiguous, *amore-odio* narratorial and authorial relationship to it is, in *L'Adalgisa*, more openly visible than anywhere else, thanks to the simultaneous presence and mixing in the same volume (but in different parts of it) of the two separate strains. For this reason *L'Adalgisa* is a crucial passage in Gadda's evolution; in it, Gadda's discordant relationship to his social environment (the sole real object of his art, albeit examined through antithetical, objective/subjective modes) is revealed with utmost clarity, perhaps for the last time. From then on, bitterness and destructive criticism will prevail, providing a sort of unifying (negative) emotional perspective to the rest of the writer's production.

I would now like to look more closely at what could be seen as the broader[18] context and object of *L'Adalgisa*: the city. To find a statement of the authorial sentiments for the city (which is at the same time a sort of poetic declaration of intent, clarifying the main psychological orientation of most, but not all, of the narrative) we must look deep into the folds of the text. It is at the end of a comic digression (on public toilets, of all things!), in the middle of the second chapter (RR I, p. 326), that we encounter — as is often the case in Gadda — a sudden change of object and register, from scatological to lyrical, culminating in a poetic citation in French: 'la forme d'une ville — change plus vite, hélas! que le cœur d'un mortel'. The passage is by Baudelaire and comes from 'Le Cygne', one of the poems of *Les Fleurs du mal*, and more precisely from the section entitled 'Tableaux Parisiens'. Bearing in mind that the subtitle of *L'Adalgisa* is 'Disegni di vita milanese', it becomes clear that the citation is far from accidental, signalling in fact some sort of deep proximity between Gadda's and Baudelaire's contemplation of their respective cities.

If *Le Cygne* can elicit a variety of symbolic, ideological and political interpretations, its primary object and tone are relatively easy to describe: the *dépaysement*, sense of non-belonging and impotence, the contrast between reality and memory, the sudden and painful awareness of the irredeemable passing of time, the vision of the changing city in a halo of decomposition and death. This is the meaning of Baudelaire's verse, certainly for Gadda; what attracts his attention in particular is the role of time, and its effect on space, more precisely on urban space. Another passage from *Le Cygne*, that Gadda does not quote but definitely has in mind, helps clarify this point: 'Paris change! mais rien dans ma mélancolie / N'a bougé! palais neufs, échafaudages, blocs, / Vieux faubourgs, tout pour moi devient allégorie, / Et mes chers souvenirs sont plus lourds que des rocs.'[19]

What is this universal 'allegory', which devours everything, transforming it into something else? It is none other than time itself. Every aspect of the city, under the gaze of the poet, acquires a non-literal meaning, becoming an allegory of the passing of time. The old ('vieux faubourgs') and the new ('palais neufs, échafaudages') are all signs of a single movement, now revealed in its funereal, destructive essence. What, in this perspective, is a city? Rather like a human face, it is physical space visibly worked by a linear time subtracted to cosmic circularity, stability or redemption, and therefore irredeemably affected by loss, and ultimately by death. The agent of this (de)realization, of this sudden awareness of time as death, is memory ('mes chers souvenirs').

Such is also Gadda's main disposition in *L'Adalgisa*: one of nostalgic regret for the inevitable passing of time, which destroys a world that certainly deserves to be criticized, even hated perhaps, but not forever to be submerged by oblivion, because the narrator is attached to it by a myriad affects and memories. Therefore, the main role of literature is to contrast time, vanquish death, and make that submerged world live on, forever. The opposite disposition (that of *La cognizione*) is also present, with its destructive desire for revenge and justice over a society inherently false, perverted, and perverting otherwise noble souls (this already was an explicit theme in *Racconto italiano*). The contrast is, therefore, ultimately insoluble, between, on the one hand, writing as *pietas* and even *caritas* and, on the other, writing as an act of impious and uncharitable vengeance.[20] It should be noted, however, that even the latter is an affirmation of life against time and death, the (significant) difference being in the focus: what literature wants to preserve from death is in one case (*Cognizione*) the oppressed life embodied in the revolt of an individual against injustice and ugliness, in the other (*Adalgisa*) the fragile life animating a world inexorably destined to oblivion.

The reference to Baudelaire, the perspective on a changing city and the notion of allegory facilitate the transition to the third and most unlikely name in my title. Baudelaire is, by far, the most often quoted author in one the great monuments to fragmentary writing in the whole of the twentieth century: Walter Benjamin's *Das Passagen-Werk*[21] is an enormous 'Zibaldone'[22] of thoughts and citations that (also precisely for its fragmentariness, intertextual substance, interdisciplinary outlook, posthumous status, genre ambiguity, and incompleteness) has acquired an iconic status in contemporary philosophy and literature. But what can the connection be between Benjamin and Gadda, two authors who knew nothing of one another?[23]

First of all, there is a structural similarity between the *Passagen-Werk* and the *Cahiers d'études* for the *Racconto italiano*, both preparatory works for a book that never materialized (in Benjamin's case, it would have been an *Urgeschichte* of the nineteenth century, seen through the prism of the city of Paris). Secondly, there is a similar contamination of literature and philosophy; Gadda's intellectual path shows very clearly the vital link, or even the coexistence, of artistic creation and thought, and so the gnoseological (or, as he often said, heuristic) value of literature. But more importantly, the Gadda of *L'Adalgisa* shares with Benjamin (and Baudelaire) a deeply negative 'sense of time' in relation to urban environment:

and specifically, the awareness of the destructive presence of death in the life and constant transformation of a metropolis.

Finally, it is also possible to establish interesting (albeit undoubtedly subtle) metaphorical links between Gadda's oeuvre and the vision emerging from the *Passagen*. And, first of all, let us recall the primary meaning of the word 'passage' in Benjamin's perspective; it refers to a physical feature of the Parisian urban environment, the *passage*, that is, a covered pathway penetrating inside a compact block of buildings, linking different parts of the city. The Parisian arcade (open to the public and housing commercial activities, but less visible and accessible — for instance to vehicles — than and from a street) creates a special, semi-private atmosphere; and it is itself the sign of a form of life that is disappearing and dying out.[24] The city transforms itself, but at a price — a slow but constant loss of forms of life that soon become, one after the other, inevitably forgotten. Gadda's *L'Adalgisa*, too, is partly pervaded by the gaze on a city that changes, leaving behind a wealth of human experience destined to oblivion — if writing doesn't save it. Those forms of life are intrinsically connected to urban and architectural spaces, which constitute the object of intense attention on the part of the Milanese writer, especially in *L'Adalgisa* (Milan) and *Quer pasticciaccio* (Rome); in both works the city is 'felt' in its phylogenetic and historical evolution, in its relentless stratification, which ends by crashing and forever obliterating the past that only a few decades (or centuries) before was inhabited by a living people in its day-to-day existence. Space devoured by time.[25]

The whole of Gadda's oeuvre can be seen as a vast *Passagen-Werk*, a metaphorical urban body connected by semi-secret passages, and fed internally by a circulatory system distributing the same blood to all parts, and externally by an ample and varied intertextual and ideal hinterland; and also a universe of building sites, active or abandoned, a textual city in perennial transformation and never finished, only temporarily and apparently arrested in one of its infinite, possible states by virtue of some editorial decision (or the irrevocable decree of death), but in truth never free from the process of constant addition and evolution dictated by the imperative of totalization, or by reality itself. In that sense, too, the body of Gadda's writings is a 'work of passages'.

L'Adalgisa points in the direction of the secret heart of this chthonian world. Like Baudelaire's 'Tableaux parisiens' and Benjamin's *Das Passagen-Werk*, it is (also) the diffracted image of a city. Not a *civitas Dei*, nor an ideal *polis*, but a *civitas hominis*, a human city subjected to the corrosion of time, but preserved from it by the most human of all human prerogatives: memory, care, writing.

It is within this broad context that I have sought to understand Gadda's fragmentary writing, releasing it from the fetters of pre-conceived ideological schemes, and making it available to resonate to a variety of different harmonics.

Notes to Chapter 27

1. A first, partial draft of this paper was presented at the conference on 'Thinking in fragments: Romanticism and beyond', convened by Michael Caesar at the University of Birmingham on 16–17 December 2010.
2. The complete works of Gadda are available in the edition in five volumes supervised by Dante Isella, from which I quote: *Romanzi e racconti*, vol. I, ed. by R. Rodondi and others (Milan: Garzanti, 1990), henceforth: RR I; *Romanzi e racconti*, vol. II, ed by R. Rodondi and others (Milan: Garzanti, 1989), henceforth: RR II; *Saggi giornali favole e altri scritti*, vol. I, ed. by L. Orlando and others (Milan: Garzanti, 1991), henceforth: SGF I; *Saggi giornali favole e altri scritti*, vol. II, ed. by L. Orlando and others (Milan: Garzanti, 1992), henceforth: SGF II; *Scritti vari e postumi*, ed. by A. Silvestri and others (Milan: Garzanti, 1993), henceforth: SVP.
3. Plus *Il primo libro delle Favole* (Venezia: Neri Pozza, 1952; now in SGF II), which — as a compilation of fables and aphorisms — is different in nature, but still inherently fragmentary.
4. Gilles Deleuze and Félix Guattari, *Milles plateaux* (Paris: Éditions de Minuit, 1980).
5. See, for instance, Norma Bouchard, *Céline, Gadda, Beckett: Experimental Writings of the 1930s* (Gainsville: University Press of Florida, 2000).
6. The part of this essay concerned with the evolution of Gadda's poetics is, by necessity, only a brief summary of findings that I have been publishing, over the years, in a monograph and several articles (see especially: Giuseppe Stellardi, *Gadda: miseria e grandezza della letteratura* (Florence: Cesati, 2006). In particular, the embryonic discussion of the novelist's non-fictional writings is further expounded through a more detailed analysis in an article forthcoming in a special issue on Gadda of *Cuadernos de Filología Italiana* ('«In nome di quale poetica?»: l'antipoetica di Gadda').
7. The text is incomplete, unfortunately, since a few of the notebooks went missing at the time of the Caporetto defeat.
8. Henceforth RI, in SVP.
9. Henceforth MM, in SVP.
10. All of these texts are now in SGF I.
11. All in RR I.
12. *Il secondo libro della Poetica*, ed. by Dante Isella, *I quaderni dell'ingegnere. Testi e studi gaddiani*, n. 2 (2003), 5–28.
13. Shakespeare's influence on Gadda is comparable to Manzoni's and deserves a separate treatment (I deal with some aspects of it in 'Hamlet's ghost: the re-writing of Shakespeare in C.E. Gadda', forthcoming). To complicate matters further, the two fundamental models (Manzoni and Shakespeare) are not mutually exclusive in Gadda's mind; on the contrary, it is probable that the former (himself an admirer of the English dramatist) played a significant part in the onset of Gadda's admiration for (and in his interpretation of) Shakespeare's work (see Roberto Bonci, *'La distanza intercorrente tra la noia e la poesia'. Carlo Emilio Gadda interprete di Shakespeare*, Tesi di laurea, Relatore Prof. A. Bertoni, Università di Bologna, anno accademico 2010–11, unpublished). The fact remains, however, that it would be difficult to 'reduce' the two greats to a single, unitary set of aesthetic criteria.
14. R. Donnarumma, *Gadda modernista* (Pisa: ETS, 2006).
15. N. Bouchard, *Céline, Gadda, Beckett,* in particular pp. 82–122.
16. Of course, Manzoni, too, makes abundant use of digressions; this elicits a range of interesting questions, which cannot be addressed here. See Olivia Santovetti, *Digression: A Narrative Strategy in the Italian Novel* (Berne: Lang, 2007).
17. Here I follow, for the essential, Guido Lucchini's summary in his 'Note al testo' (RR I, p. 839), to which I refer the reader for additional details.
18. But certainly not the only one: the book also gives ample room to the analysis of the two main characters (Adalgisa and Gonzalo), as well as several minor ones — not to speak of course of the many important digressions. This multiplicity of objects, too, contributes to deprive it of a unitary feel.

19. Ch. Baudelaire, *I fiori del male*, original French text and Italian translation by L. De Nardis (Milan: Feltrinelli, 1964), p. 160.
20. I am grateful to Peter Hainsworth for pointing out a possible, indirect Dantean connection: this particular polarity can, indeed, be identified as a constitutive tension in the *Divina commedia*.
21. Translated in English as *The Arcades Project* (Cambridge: Harvard University Press, 1999). *Passage*, in German, French and English, just like *passaggio* in Italian, also means excerpt, fragment; but this resonance is entirely lost in the English translation of the title of Benjamin's work.
22. It should be noted here that the conference on 'Thinking in fragments', where these ideas were first presented, was organized by the *Leopardi Centre* at Birmingham University, and sponsored by the AHRC as part of the *Zibaldone Project*. Leopardi's gigantic body of disparate reflections is perhaps the quintessential manifestation of fragmentary writing in the nineteenth century and its impact on the following century remains to be fully investigated.
23. It is not impossible (albeit unlikely) that Gadda — whose range of intellectual interests included contemporary thought, for instance psychoanalysis — may have become aware of Benjamin's work, but only much later in his life. There is, however, no reference to the German philosopher anywhere in the *Opere*.
24. See for instance Zola's *Thérèse Raquin* (1867), almost entirely set in a *passage* near the Seine. With reference to this novel, Benjamin writes: 'If this book really expounds something scientifically, then it's the death of the Paris arcades, the decay of a type of architecture. The book's atmosphere is saturated with the poisons of this process, and its people are destroyed by them' (*The Arcades Project*, p. 875). Zola is also, at the same time, the writer who describes the other side of the same coin, for instance the destruction — by the new, rampant capitalism of big commerce in alliance with the banks — of large swaths of the city to make room for the new *grands magasins*. See, for instance, *Au Bonheur des Dames* (1883).
25. An echo of the nostalgic mood present in *L'Adalgisa* can be found in an occasional piece of the following decade, *Quartieri suburbani* (1955, in SGF I, p. 1128), a text on the city that 'si dilata' and 'si estende': 'Superstiti agli evi, alle loro poetiche e alle loro cannonate, sono i poetici relitti, i romantici frantumi d'un passato ch'era già vano rimpiangere ai nostri anni' (p. 1138).

CHAPTER 28

Il mistero dei due anelli: una postilla sopra la natura del discorso letterario, da Virgilio a Calvino

Nicola Gardini

Caro Martin,
    vorrei tornare sul concetto di lacunosità, su cui tu e io abbiamo già avuto modo di confrontarci in più di un'occasione, anche in pubblico. Nel mio libro *Lacuna*, come sai, ho usato un approccio specificamente pratico, fissando lo sguardo sulle narrazioni — romanzi e racconti, compresa la *Commedia* dantesca: ho mostrato omissioni di varia natura ed entità e indicato che l'omettere partecipa in maniera sostanziale alla formazione del discorso e del senso; e analizzato stili, libri e generi che più di altri puntano alla rimozione di elementi necessari (parole, episodi, spiegazioni, perfino l'argomento); e ricostruito una retorica del lacunoso, che risalisse fino ai trattatisti antichi, schizzato momenti di una storia del lacunoso e trovato in pensatori moderni una giustificazione profondamente morale per l'omettere. Qui mi piacerebbe assumere un approccio teorico; lasciare, per così dire, il microscopio per il cannocchiale, o addirittura — se mi si permette l'esagerazione metaforica — il telescopio. A qualche esempio ricorrerò, naturalmente, ma la mia attenzione sarà rivolta non al caso individuale, non alla risposta particolare, ma al problema.
    Parlare di lacunosità significa fondamentalmente postulare una totalità; la totalità del dire. Mi spiego: si dice perché *c'è* o si presume che *ci sia* un 'tutto del dire', e se anche 'si dice poco', quel 'tutto' non decade, ma resta, anzi *deve* restare, o non si potrà neppure più riconoscere il poco. Ammettere le lacune entro l'orizzonte del discorso critico, prima ancora di riconoscerle all'interno di una scrittura, è già di per sé pensare necessaria e inevitabile la totalità. Che scrivendo la si manchi o la si sfiori appena attraverso il sogno, la nostalgia, un'epifania momentanea, non è questo che qui interessa.
    Il senso comune, d'altra parte, basta a provare che un tutto-Tutto è irrealizzabile in una qualunque unità spazio-temporale; qualcosa si sottrae sempre, qualcosa si potrà sempre aggiungere... L'importante qui è che la totalità è presupposta dall'atto stesso del dire; è un'ipotesi categorica, che si ricostituisce non appena se ne constata l'inattuabilità. Su questa ipotesi o — per citare Pascal — *scommessa* si crea la scrittura. Nessun fallimento, nessuna frustrazione, nessuna disfatta potrà

mai cancellarla o impedirla. Risorgerà sempre, sempre invocata; e sarà tanto più vera quanto più lontana e imprendibile. Anzi: la totalità si pone di per sé e può porsi solo come lontananza, il che, per opposizione, fa della scrittura solo parzialità e avvicinamento, cioè un continuo, perenne mancare. La pienezza, insomma, si realizza per esperienza del suo contrario. È intuizione; forma intellettuale e non sensibile. L'orrore della pagina bianca è sacro orrore del tutto — inaccessibile, tuttavia disponibile; i lamenti all'afasia valgono come inni all'esprimibilità totale.

Che cos'è questo 'tutto del dire'? Non è l'esaurimento di un discorso, la completezza di un ragionamento. È l'esaurimento di *tutti i discorsi* e di *tutti i ragionamenti*; è la verità ultima, è la spiegazione del mondo. La scrittura insegue la verità — o non è scrittura. Non *una* verità, *quella* verità: ma *la* verità. Solamente davanti a un'ipotesi di verità assoluta la scrittura — pur incarnandosi ogni volta in un'unica forma — può accettare la propria fatale insufficienza e continuare a esistere, a credere in sé, a sentirsi parte necessaria della vita.

Virgilio mostra molto bene questa dialettica all'inizio dell'*Eneide*, mettendo a confronto due diversi tipi di racconto: quello di Iopa e quello di Enea. Iopa, il poeta della corte cartaginese, alla fine del primo libro canta l'universo:

> Hic canit errantem lunam solisque labores,
> unde hominum genus et pecudes, unde imber et ignes,
> Arcturum pluviasque Hyadas geminosque Triones,
> quid tantum Oceano properent se tinguere soles
> hiberni vel quae tardis mora noctibus obstet. (*Eneide*, II. 742–46)[1]

> Egli canta la luna errante e le fatiche del sole,
> donde la razza degli uomini e gli animali, donde la pioggia e i fuochi,
> Arturo e le Iadi piovose e i due Carri,
> perché tanto si affrettino i soli a bagnarsi nell'Oceano
> d'inverno o quale indugio attardi le notti.

Se i modelli di Iopa sono il Demodoco e il Femio dell'*Odissea*, il tema astronomico è originale. Credo, infatti, che l'Orfeo delle *Argonautiche* (I, 494–511), indicato dai commentatori, non sia poi così rilevante, nonostante un paio di evidenti somiglianze. Penso ai percorsi del sole e della luna (I. 500), agli astri (ibid.), però assai generici nel testo greco, e agli animali (I. 502). Il canto di Iopa, in verità, deve molto di più a Omero. La descrizione dello scudo d'Achille comincia proprio con una descrizione astronomica (*Iliade*, XVIII. 483–86), che presenta già il sole e la luna, le Iadi, i due Carri e l'immersione nelle acque dell'Oceano. La stessa immagine 'solis labores' sembra derivata dall'aggettivo greco, riferito al sole, 'akamanta' (*Iliade*, XVIII. 484), dalla radice del verbo 'kamno', 'mi stanco' — anche se 'sole' e 'fatica' sono associati in un celebre verso di Mimnermo. (Da notare che lo scudo di Enea nell'ottavo dell'*Eneide*, pur essendo un doppione di quello di Achille, sarà esclusivamente dedicato alla futura storia di Roma; da notare anche l'espressione 'non enarrabile textum', al v. 626, con cui Virgilio designa la mirabile ekphrasis — una delle prime attestazioni della parola 'testo', tanto più suggestiva per la vicinanza di 'enarrabile'.)

E passiamo a Enea. All'inizio del secondo libro si mette a raccontare, su richiesta di Didone, la propria vicenda personale. Lo sguardo, anzi la voce si sposta dal cosmo alla storia:

> Infandum, regina, iubes renovare dolorem,
> Troianas ut opes et lamentabile regnum
> eruerint Danai, quaeque ipse miserrima vidi
> et quorum pars magna fui. quis talia fando
> Myrmidonum Dolopumve aut duri miles Ulixi
> temperet a lacrimis? et iam nox umida caelo
> praecipitat suadentque cadentia sidera somnos.
> sed si tantus amor casus cognoscere nostros
> et breviter Troiae supremum audire laborem,
> quamquam animus meminisse horret luctuque refugit,
> incipiam.
>
> Indicibile, regina, dolore tu esorti a rinnovare,
> come la potenza troiana e il miserevole regno
> i Danai abbiano travolto, e le cose tristi che io vidi
> e di cui fui parte grande. Chi dicendo tali eventi
> Mirmidone o Dolopo o soldato del duro Ulisse
> si asterrebbe dal pianto? E già l'umida notte dal cielo
> precipita e tramontando invitano al sonno le stelle.
> Ma se hai così tanto amore di apprendere i nostri casi,
> e brevemente di sentire l'ultimo travaglio di Troia,
> benché l'animo abbia orrore del ricordo e rifugga dal dolore,
> comincerò.

Iopa ha cantato i 'labores' del sole, Enea ora canta il 'laborem' estremo di Troia. Da notare in questo preambolo (che scimmiotta una vera e propria invocazione alla Musa) anche l'aggettivo 'in-fandum', 'non dicibile', 'non rappresentabile', e l'avverbio 'breviter': Enea pone il suo racconto sotto il segno della più costrittiva lacunosità. Di fatto, lo sentiremo parlare per ben due libri, dunque per un sesto dell'intero poema. Il suo racconto, però, non è che un frammento del cosmo; che cosa sono, infatti, due libri di fronte al tempo universale? La notte in cui avviene il racconto di Enea, tra l'altro, sta volgendo al termine, è già ora di dormire, come sottolinea lo stesso Enea, e dunque bisogna sbrigarsi, correre, tagliare. Nel racconto di Iopa, al contrario, le notti si attardano, non vogliono finire, e non devono essere riempite da alcun racconto. Sono, infatti, loro stesse il racconto, sono il tutto di tutti i racconti possibili. E Didone, che cerca di trascinare la notte per rimanere il più a lungo possibile in compagnia dello straniero, non è certo un'immagine di grandezza o di ordine celeste, bensì il contrario: un'umana condannata a morte, già un fantasma. Nella sua bocca che prega l'ospite di raccontare il destino di Troia il vocabolario di Iopa — quell'''errantem', pronunciato nella medesima posizione metrica (I. 756), ora non più in riferimento a un corpo celeste, ma umano — torna con involontaria, tragica autoironia. Si avverte l'eco di un rovesciamento anche nell'''aestas' con cui si chiude il libro (I. 756), se abbiamo ancora in mente gli 'invernali' soli di Iopa (I. 745–46).

Didone costringe il discorso ad abbassarsi dall'universo alla storia umana, dalle cause prime del tutto ('unde [...] unde [...]', I. 743) al principio dei mali di un gruppo di Troiani ('a prima [...] origine', I. 753). In verità, Didone costringe il discorso a fare quello che fanno tutti i discorsi umani: ridurre. Il canto di Iopa sta appunto lì, a ridosso del discorso di Enea, come garante e simbolo vivente della totalità con cui nessun discorso — e non necessariamente perché intervenga l'invito di una donna innamorata — arriverà mai a coincidere. Il poeta delle *Georgiche*, d'altronde, dove dichiara il proprio amore per le Muse, già contrappone l'ideale di un canto cosmico alla ventura pur consolante di cantare solo la campagna e gli dei agresti:

> Me vero primum dulces ante omnia Musae,
> quarum sacra fero ingenti percussus amore,
> accipiant caelique vias et sidera monstrent,
> defectus solis varios lunaeque labores;
> unde tremor terris, qua vi maria alta tumescant
> obicibus ruptis rursusque in se ipsa residant,
> quid tantum Oceano properent se tinguere soles
> hiberni, vel quae tardis mora noctibus obstet.
> sin has ne possim naturae accedere partis
> frigidus obstiterit circum praecordia sanguis,
> rura mihi et rigui placeant in vallibus amnes,
> flumina amem silvasque inglorius. o ubi campi
> Spercheosque et virginibus bacchata Lacaenis
> Taygeta! o qui me gelidis convallibus Haemi
> sistat, et ingenti ramorum protegat umbra!
> felix qui potuit rerum cognoscere causas
> atque metus omnis et inexorabile fatum
> subiecit pedibus strepitumque Acherontis avari:
> fortunatus et ille deos qui novit agrestis
> Panaque Siluanumque senem Nymphasque sorores. (*Georg.* II. 475–94)

> Ma me le Muse dolci più di tutto
> delle quali porto il rito scosso da amore potente
> accolgano e mostrino le vie del cielo e le stelle,
> le varie eclissi del sole e le fatiche della luna;
> donde i terremoti, per quale forza i mari si gonfino alti
> rotte le barriere e di nuovo in sé calino.
> Perché tanto si affrettino i soli a bagnarsi nell'Oceano
> d'inverno o quale indugio attardi le notti.
> Se però impedirà che io raggiunga queste parti della natura
> gelido intorno ai precordi il sangue
> mi piacciano la campagna e i fiumi che irrigano le valli,
> che io ami senza gloria i corsi d'acqua e le selve. O le piane
> e lo Spercheo e il Taigeto dove baccheggiano le vergini
> spartane! O nelle fresche convalli dell'Emo
> mi si collochi e protegga in una vasta ombra di rami!
> Felice chi ha potuto apprendere le cause di tutto
> E le paure e il fato inesorabile
> ha gettato sotto i piedi e lo strepito dell'avido Acheronte.
> Fortunato anche colui che conosce gli dei agresti,
> Pan e il vecchio Silvano e le Ninfe sorelle.

E si noti che un canto cosmico affiora già nelle stesse *Bucoliche*, in bocca a Sileno (VI. 31 sgg.), in contrasto con l'umiltà del prevalente registro pastorale.

Del passo georgico Iopa cita ben due versi e ne parafrasa un terzo. La cosa non deve passare per semplice autocitazione alessandrina. La ripresa di un passo così programmatico nel canto di Iopa indica la diffusiva vitalità di un paradigma: l'endiadi tutto/poco, l'alternanza che non vuole e non può risolversi tra ricerca filosofica e narrazione umana, tra cielo e terra. Iopa, insomma, incarna il narratore totalizzante che né il Virgilio delle *Georgiche* né quello stesso dell'*Eneide* riescono a essere (né tanto meno quello delle *Bucoliche*), e che pure andrà sempre presupposto. Non dimentichiamo che Iopa riprende la rappresentazione dello scudo di Achille e che di quella rappresentazione fu artefice un dio. Potremmo, generalizzando, dire che ogni racconto aspira a sovrapporsi a una sua controparte divina.

★ ★ ★ ★ ★

Lo spazio della lacuna — spazio intorno alla lacuna e lacuna stessa — resta, per difettivo che sia, un modello di mondo, un paradigma, un segnale, una promessa. Contiene escludendo, rinviando al di fuori di sé, e funziona appunto perché rinvia all'integrazione, non fa che proiettare il piccolo sullo schermo della grandezza massima e identificarlo con questa o considerarlo una rappresentazione di questa, ad infinitum. Viene in mente Plutarco. All'inizio del trattato sulla scomparsa degli oracoli leggiamo dello spartano Cleombroto, che è appena tornato dal tempio di Ammone e lì ha appreso dai sacerdoti che la lampada perenne brucia ogni anno meno olio. Ciò sembra indicare che gli anni si vanno accorciando. Demetrio ride di questa interpretazione: come si possono trarre conclusioni tanto grandi da una cosa tanto piccola, stabilire sull'osservazione di una lampada e non attraverso la matematica che l'universo ('tà sympanta', 410 C) sia mutato? Cleombroto ribatte che negare che le piccole cose siano indicazioni ('semeia', 410 D) di cose grandi ostacola il sapere: perché impedisce di riconoscere prove e pronostici di molti fenomeni. Nella difesa di Cleombroto troviamo pienamente rappresentato quel metodo indiziario (una vera e propria semiotica, per riprendere il termine del bravo spartano) attraverso cui da tempo immemorabile gli uomini costruiscono la conoscenza:[2] risalire dal frammento al corpo integro. Apprendere (il 'cognoscere' di Virgilio e, prima di lui, di Lucrezio) è *restaurare*: intravedere nel residuo la pienezza primordiale, nella caduta di Troia la struttura del firmamento.

Quello che c'è dice di più di ciò che sembra dire. Occorre usare attenzione, occorre leggere, non soltanto vedere, e ritornare continuamente al testo, cercarci di più ogni volta. Michel Foucault ha teorizzato questa idea di 'ritorno a...' nel celebre saggio sull'autore. Il suo 'ritorno a' è un nuovo modo di leggere i testi scientifici e matematici del passato; di scoprirvi mancanze che erano sfuggite a lungo e così di far avanzare il 'discorso' in direzioni inattese. A me pare che la nozione di 'ritorno a' si presti molto bene a descrivere la manchevolezza di qualunque testualità o scrittura:

> ce retour s'adresse à ce qui est présent dans le texte, plus précisément, on revient au texte même, au texte dans sa nudité, et, en même temps, pourtant, on revient à ce qui est marqué en creux, en absence, en lacunes dans le texte. On revient à un certain vide que l'oubli a esquivé ou masqué, qu'il a recouvert d'une fausse

ou d'une mauvaise plénitude et *le retour doit redécouvrir cette lacune et ce manque* [mio corsivo]; de là, le jeu perpétuel qui caractérise ces retours à l'instauration discursive — jeu qui consiste à dire d'un côté: cela y était, il suffisait de lire, tout s'y trouve, il fallait que les yeux soient bien fermés et les oreilles bien bouchées pour qu'on ne le voie ni ne l'entende; et, inversement: non, ce n'est point dans ce mot-ci, ni dans ce mot-là, aucun des mots visibles et lisibles ne dit ce qui est maintenant en question, il s'agit plutôt de ce qui est dit à travers les mots, dans leur espacement, dans la distance qui les sépare.[3]

Foucault in questo bellissimo brano indica due diverse forme del restauro: da una parte, una nuova comprensione di quel che c'è ('tout s'y trouve'); dall'altra, l'individuazione di qualcosa che non c'è nel testo ('aucun des mots visibles et lisibles ne dit ce qui est maintenant en question') ma che finalmente si intravede tra le pieghe delle parole. Due diverse modalità investigative, due forme di intelligenza: l'Edgar Allan Poe della lettera rubata, che è lì, sotto gli occhi di tutti, e va solo *individuata*, da una parte; il Poe della rue Morgue, dall'altra, ovvero l'inchiesta poliziesca vera e propria, che congiunge i frammenti e trae le conclusioni. La prima modalità è, se vogliamo, la più semplice; consiste in un'illuminazione. La seconda è complessa e prende tempo, è un ragionamento, come nel lavoro di Sherlock Holmes: richiede anzitutto che in certi elementi si riconoscano delle tracce, che non siano presi solo alla lettera, ma siano interpretati per 'altro' e se ne estragga così una seconda conoscenza, che porterà alla verità; richiede, poi, che le tracce formino un puzzle e che, quindi, all'interno di questo si individuino i contorni dei pezzi mancanti e che finalmente i vuoti siano riempiti. Di questa modalità mi sono occupato in un capitolo di *Lacuna*. Qui vorrei aggiungere un paio di esempi che illustrino la prima — quella delle due, forse, più affine al lavoro dell'interpretazione letteraria o all'arte della lettura. Come suggerisce la parola 'illuminazione' che ho usato poco sopra, il restauro avviene all'improvviso, magari dopo un girare a vuoto o perfino una voluta resistenza dell'interprete al manifestarsi della verità. Pensiamo a un passo come quello in cui l'Orlando ariostesco, nella foresta, trova le scritte di Medoro (*Orlando furioso*, XXIII. 106 sgg.). La situazione è archetipica: abbiamo un testo e abbiamo l'interprete. Tutto è scritto, tutto si trova lì, per dirla con Foucault. Eppure l'interprete non capisce; certo, non *vuole* capire, perché la verità fa male, perché è insopportabilmente doloroso scoprire che la donna amata se n'è andata con un altro. Però, a forza di 'tornare a', pur anche per costringerti a credere il contrario, la verità salta fuori; a un certo punto non puoi più scansarla.

Prendiamo adesso un esempio da Proust, in qualche modo assai simile. Albertine se n'è appena andata dalla casa di Marcel, dimenticando di prendere due anelli. Marcel, che riceve gli anelli da Françoise, crede che uno sia un regalo della zia e l'altro un regalo che Albertine stessa si sia fatta. Françoise, senza immaginare quale dolore infligga a Marcel, gli fa notare che gli anelli si assomigliano — dunque, conclude Marcel, devono essere venuti dalla stessa persona, e dunque Albertine ha mentito sulla loro provenienza e dunque deve aver ricevuto anche le attenzioni di altri. Insomma, ancora una volta Albertine si rivela traditrice e bugiarda. Anche nel passo di Proust, come nell'*Orlando furioso*, la verità salta fuori da una rilettura — qui, specificamente, di un'immagine incisa sul gioiello (d'altronde, nello stesso poema ariostesco Orlando comprende fino in fondo il senso del testo scritto sugli alberi solo quando l'oste gli mostra — proprio come Françoise fa con Marcel — il monile che Orlando stesso aveva donato ad Angelica). Sul mistero degli anelli di Albertine e sulla verità che contengono Proust compone un vero e proprio micro-romanzo. Quando scopriamo che cosa veramente significano anche noi lettori dobbiamo tornare indietro, dobbiamo rileggere i passi in cui Albertine ha parlato degli anelli a Marcel, e ritrovarci la verità che ci era sfuggita la prima volta. Vediamo i passi rilevanti. Si comincia con l'apparizione del primo anello:

> Elle [Albertine] avait aussi des choses qui ne venaient pas de moi, comme une belle bague d'or. J'y admirai les ailes éployées d'un aigle. 'C'est ma tante qui me l'a donnée, me dit-elle. Malgré tout elle est quelquefois gentille. Cela me vieillit parce qu'elle me l'a donnée pour mes vingt ans.'[4]

Un centinaio di pagine dopo compare il secondo:

> Elle ôta un instant son gant, soit pour toucher ma main, soit pour m'éblouir en me laissant voir à son petit doigt, à côté de celle donnée par Mme Bontemps, une bague où s'étendait la large et liquide nappe d'une claire feuille de rubis: 'Encore une nouvelle bague, Albertine. Votre tante est d'une générosité! — Non, celle-là ce n'est pas ma tante, dit-elle en riant. C'est moi qui l'ai achetée, comme, grâce à vous, je peux faire de grandes économies. Je ne sais même pas à qui elle a appartenu. Un voyageur qui n'avait pas d'argent la laissa au propriétaire d'un hôtel où j'étais descendue au Mans. Il ne savait qu'en faire et l'aurait vendue bien au-dessous de sa valeur. Mais elle était encore bien trop chère pour moi. Maintenant que, grâce à vous, je deviens une dame chic, je lui ai fait demander s'il l'avait encore. Et la voici. — Cela fait bien des bagues, Albertine. Où mettrez-vous celle que je vais vous donner? En tous cas, celle-ci est très jolie; je ne peux pas distinguer les ciselures autour du rubis, on dirait une tête d'homme grimaçante. Mais je n'ai pas une assez bonne vue. — Vous l'auriez meilleure que cela ne vous avancerait pas beaucoup. Je ne distingue pas non plus.'[5]

E si finisce con l'apocalisse, dove la verità è messa in bocca alla serva stessa, alla Françoise già tante volte comicizzata, ora presentata all'improvviso — con assai scarsa plausibilità se non vediamo in lei una pura funzione narrativa — grande esperta di oreficeria ed estimatrice sicura degli oggetti di valore:

> Je pris les bagues. 'Que Monsieur y fasse attention de ne pas les perdre, dit Françoise, on peut dire qu'elles sont belles! Je ne sais pas qui les lui a données, si c'est Monsieur ou un autre, mais je vois bien que c'est quelqu'un de riche et qui a du goût! — Ce n'est pas moi, répondis-je à Françoise, et d'ailleurs ce n'est pas de la même personne que viennent les deux, l'une lui a été donnée par sa tante et elle a acheté l'autre. — Pas de la même personne! s'écria Françoise, Monsieur veut rire, elles sont pareilles, sauf le rubis qu'on a ajouté sur l'une, il y a le même aigle sur les deux, les mêmes initiales à l'intérieur...' Je ne sais pas si Françoise sentait le mal qu'elle me faisait, mais elle commença à ébaucher un sourire qui ne quitta plus ses lèvres. 'Comment, le même aigle? Vous êtes folle. Sur celle qui n'a pas de rubis il y a bien un aigle, mais sur l'autre c'est une espèce de tête d'homme qui est ciselée. — Une tête d'homme? où Monsieur a vu ça? Rien qu'avec mes lorgnons j'ai tout de suite vu que c'était une des ailes de l'aigle; que Monsieur prenne sa loupe, il verra l'autre aile sur l'autre côté, la tête et le bec au

> milieu. On voit chaque plume. Ah! c'est un beau travail.' L'anxieux besoin de savoir si Albertine m'avait menti me fit oublier que j'aurais dû garder quelque dignité envers Françoise et lui refuser le plaisir méchant qu'elle avait, sinon à me torturer, du moins à nuire à mon amie. Je haletais tandis que Françoise allait chercher ma loupe, je la pris, je demandai à Françoise de me montrer l'aigle sur la bague au rubis, elle n'eut pas de peine à me faire reconnaître les ailes, stylisées de la même façon que dans l'autre bague, le relief de chaque plume, la tête. Elle me fit remarquer aussi des inscriptions semblables, auxquelles, il est vrai, d'autres étaient jointes dans la bague au rubis. Et à l'intérieur des deux le chiffre d'Albertine. 'Mais cela m'étonne que Monsieur ait eu besoin de tout cela pour voir que c'était la même bague, me dit Françoise. Même sans les regarder de près on sent bien la même façon, la même manière de plisser l'or, la même forme. Rien qu'à les apercevoir j'aurais juré qu'elles venaient du même endroit. Ça se reconnaît comme la cuisine d'une bonne cuisinière.'[6]

È interessante che a questo punto, pur davanti all'evidenza più incontestabile, Marcel, come Orlando, cerca di illudersi che le cose non stiano così, pensando che proprio la somiglianza del secondo anello abbia indotto Albertine ad acquistarlo. Presto, però, dovrà capitolare.

> Atterré, les deux bagues à la main, je regardais cet aigle impitoyable dont le bec me tenaillait le coeur, dont les ailes aux plumes en relief avaient emporté la confiance que je gardais dans mon amie, et sous les serres duquel mon esprit meurtri ne pouvait pas échapper un instant aux questions posées sans cesse relativement à cet inconnu dont l'aigle symbolisait sans doute le nom sans pourtant me le laisser lire, qu'elle avait aimé sans doute autrefois, et qu'elle avait revu sans doute il n'y avait pas longtemps, puisque c'est le jour si doux, si familial, de la promenade ensemble au Bois, que j'avais vu, pour la première fois, la seconde bague, celle où l'aigle avait l'air de tremper son bec dans la nappe de sang clair du rubis.[7]

La lettura è compiuta, la verità è apparsa: ma, com'è tipico di Proust, ecco che già si allontana. Se ormai è accertato che Albertine ha mentito, una nuova lacuna si spalanca: l'identità imprendibile del suo amante, svanito dietro il simbolo anche troppo simbolico del rapace.

★ ★ ★ ★ ★

Attraverso l'esempio di Ariosto e di Proust ci siamo spostati dalla prospettiva di chi racconta a quella di chi legge. In fondo, il problema è lo stesso. Anche chi legge presuppone, più o meno consapevolmente, una totalità che non è tutta in quel che legge. Anche il lettore è sempre impegnato a correre dal piano della terra a quello delle stelle, a dividersi tra Enea e Iopa. Sul lettore che cerca i pezzi mancanti Italo Calvino ha scritto una vera e propria favola, *Se una notte d'inverno un viaggiatore* (1979). Come vuole la favola, l'intralcio o il problema interiore è esternalizzato, e narrato nelle dimensioni spazio-temporali di un mondo presuntamente reale. Il lettore, dunque, si ritrova tra le mani davvero un libro monco, un libro lacunoso:

> [...] ti trovi davanti due pagine bianche.
> Resti attonito, contemplando quel bianco crudele come una ferita, quasi sperando che sia stato un abbacinamento della tua vista a proiettare una macchia

di luce sul libro, dalla quale a poco a poco tornerà ad affiorare il rettangolo zebrato di caratteri d'inchiostro. No, è davvero un candore intatto che regna sulle due facciate che si fronteggiano. Volti ancora pagina e trovi due facciate stampate come si deve. Continui a sfogliare il libro; due pagine bianche s'alternano a due pagine stampate. Bianche; stampate; bianche; stampate: così via fino alla fine. I fogli di stampa sono stati impressi da una parte sola; poi piegati e legati come fossero completi.

Ecco che questo romanzo così fittamente intessuto di sensazioni tutt'a un tratto ti si presenta squarciato da voragini senza fondo, come se la pretesa di rendere la pienezza vitale rivelasse il vuoto che c'è sotto.[8]

Alla lacuna fisica il lettore cerca prontamente di porre rimedio, tornando in libreria e chiedendo che la copia difettosa del libro sia sostituita con una buona. Siamo all'inizio di un'avventura metaforica o metaletteraria, la cui sostanza è chiaramente e definitivamente decifrata verso la fine (per bocca di un altro lettore):

> la lettura è un'operazione discontinua e frammentaria. O meglio: l'oggetto della lettura è una materia puntiforme e pulviscolare. Nella dilagante distesa della scrittura l'attenzione del lettore distingue dei segmenti minimi, accostamenti di parole, metafore, nessi sintattici, passaggi logici, peculiarità lessicali che si rivelano d'una densità di significato estremamente concentrata. Sono come le particelle elementari che compongono il nucleo dell'opera, attorno al quale ruota tutto il resto. Oppure come il vuoto al fondo d'un vortice, che aspira e inghiotte le correnti. È attraverso questi spiragli che, per lampi appena percettibili, si manifesta la verità che il libro può portare, la sua sostanza ultima. [...] Non devo distrarmi se non voglio trascurare qualche indizio prezioso. Ogni volta che m'imbatto in uno di questi grumi di significato devo continuare a scavare intorno per vedere se la pepita s'estende in un filone. Per questo la mia lettura non ha mai fine: leggo e rileggo ogni volta cercando la verifica d'una nuova scoperta tra le pieghe delle frasi.[9]

Se una notte d'inverno un viaggiatore indaga il tema del mancare anche in rapporto allo scrittore. L'ho detto poco sopra, il problema è lo stesso. Se lo scrittore ha più merito del lettore, è solo perché solleva per primo il problema, perché provoca la riflessione e la ricerca con una scrittura che ha spinto lui prima che chiunque altro al confronto con l'impossibile ma innegabile totalità. Calvino inventa lo scrittore cimmerio Ukko Ahti. Nella mitologia greca i cimmeri, lo sappiamo, abitavano ai confini settentrionali del mondo in una terra che sfumava nel regno della morte. Ukko Ahti è l'allegoria stessa dell'incompletezza. Il suo romanzo *Sporgendosi dalla costa scoscesa* naturalmente non è finito (come non lo è nessun libro della letteratura cimmeria),[10] e quel che dice possiamo considerarlo un vero e proprio inno alla lacunosità, perfino un tentativo di dare alla lacunosità una sistemazione teorica:

> Ci sono giorni in cui ogni cosa che vedo mi sembra carica di significati: messaggi che mi sarebbe difficile comunicare ad altri, definire, tradurre in parole, ma appunto perciò mi si presentano come decisivi. Sono annunci o presagi che riguardano me e il mondo insieme: e di me non gli avvenimenti esteriori dell'esistenza ma ciò che accade dentro, nel fondo; e del mondo non qualche fatto particolare ma il modo d'essere generale di tutto. Comprenderete dunque la mia difficoltà a parlarne, se non per accenni.[11]

> [...] non può esistere alcun vocabolario che traduca in parole il peso di oscure allusioni che incombe nelle cose. Vorrei che questo aleggiare di presentimenti di dubbi arrivasse a chi mi leggerà non come un ostacolo accidentale alla comprensione di ciò che scrivo ma come la sua sostanza stessa; e se il procedere dei miei pensieri apparirà sfuggente a chi cercherà di seguirlo partendo da abitudini mentali radicalmente mutate, l'importante è che gli venga trasmesso lo sforzo che sto compiendo per leggere tra le righe delle cose il senso elusivo di ciò che m'aspetta.[12]

Una visione del genere torna, molte pagine dopo, nel racconto giapponese:

> c'è sempre qualcosa d'essenziale che resta fuori dalla frase scritta, anzi, le cose che il romanzo non dice sono necessariamente più di quelle che dice, e solo un particolare riverbero di ciò che è scritto può dare l'illusione di stare leggendo anche il non scritto.[13]

Il narratore stesso interviene a dar man forte allo scrittore cimmerio, il cui testo il lettore sta ascoltando nella traduzione a prima vista del professor Uzzi-Tuzii, inframmezzata da commenti e divagazioni dotte:

> Ma quando ti sei convinto che al professore la filologia e l'erudizione stanno più a cuore di ciò che la storia racconta, t'accorgi che è vero il contrario: quell'involucro accademico serve solo per proteggere quanto il racconto dice e non dice, un suo afflato interiore sempre lì lì per disperdersi al contatto dell'aria, l'eco d'un sapere scomparso che si rivela nella penombra e nelle allusioni sottaciute.[14]

Qui Calvino si sta preoccupando di indicare — seppure en passant — un altro aspetto della lacunosità: la sottrazione semantica cui sono sempre più soggette le scritture man mano che passa il tempo. La spiegazione del professore non è vieto esercizio (anche se la sua scienza è confinata in uno spazio deserto), ma è operazione necessaria, e ci fa capire che la lettura è determinata storicamente; e dunque, se perde qualcosa, sarà anche per la crescente distanza tra la cronologia del lettore e quella di ciò che legge. Lo stesso professore, d'altra parte, sembra voler scansare qualunque sospetto di pedanteria quando, anziché difendere banalmente l'utilità del suo sapere, si mette nei panni di un qualunque lettore e pronuncia una difesa dell'assenza, più cimmeria che mai:

> Leggere [...] è sempre questo: c'è una cosa che è lì, una cosa fatta di scrittura, un oggetto solido, materiale, che non si può cambiare, e attraverso questa cosa ci si confronta con qualcos'altro che non è presente, qualcos'altro che fa parte del mondo immateriale, invisibile, perché è solo pensabile, immaginabile, o perché c'è stato e non c'è più, passato, perduto, irraggiungibile, nel paese dei morti...[15]

Riepiloghiamo: il vuoto è esperienza del lettore, dello scrittore, ed è sostanza stessa della scrittura, come ci insegnano tutti gli esempi citati. Ma Calvino ha in serbo un'ultima sconvolgente variazione del tema, proprio sul finire del libro: la scrittura è piena, è il mondo che è vuoto. La lacuna non sta nella pagina, bensì al di là, e se non ci fosse la pagina non ci sarebbe proprio niente, non avremmo alcun luogo in cui illuderci di vivere: 'dietro la pagina scritta c'è il nulla; il mondo esiste solo come artificio, finzione, malinteso, menzogna'.[16] Sembra, dopo tanti anni, ancora la poetica di Biagio, il narratore del *Barone rampante* (1957). Il suo lungo racconto si conclude proprio con un richiamo all'assenza del mondo. 'Ombrosa non c'è più.' Ma chissà se quel mondo è mai esistito veramente… Non è forse soltanto *scrittura*, quel garbuglio continuo di lettere, 'zeppo di cancellature, di rimandi, di sgorbi nervosi, di macchie, di lacune…'? Nello stesso passo — segno di una continuità e di una specularità che hanno usato gli anni come possibilità massima di sviluppo — ritroviamo l'aggettivo 'puntiforme' con cui abbiamo appena visto descritto in *Se una notte d'inverno un viaggiatore* l'atto della lettura.

Viene da domandarsi, per finire, se possa chiamarsi correttamente 'menzogna', come fa *Se una notte d'inverno un viaggiatore* nella parte conclusiva, quel che comunque non ha un termine positivo. Se fuori della pagina non si dà 'realtà' come *mentirla*? Non saranno tutte queste immagini, questi sostituti assoluti, questa casa di specchi in cui il vuoto si moltiplica da infinite prospettive il solo modo possibile della verità, il canto totale di Iopa, il nome irrecuperabile sugli anelli di Albertine?

Notes to Chapter 28

1. Si cita da Virgil, *Eclogues. Georgics. Aeneid: Books 1–6*, a cura di e trad. H. Rushton Fairclough, rev. G. P. Goold (Cambridge, MA: Harvard University Press, 1999).
2. Vedi Carlo Ginzburg, 'Spie', in *Miti emblemi spie* (Torino: Einaudi, 1986), pp. 158 e 209, e Nicola Gardini, *Lacuna* (Torino: Einaudi, 2014), pp. 144–67.
3. Michel Foucault, 'Qu'est-ce qu'un auteur?' (1969), in *Dits et écrits, 1954–1988*, a cura di Daniel Defert, François Ewald e Jacques Lagrange, 4 voll. (Parigi: Gallimard, 1994), I, 789–821 (p. 808).
4. Marcel Proust, *La Prisonnière*, a cura di Pierre-Edmond Robert (Parigi: Gallimard, 1988), p. 55.
5. Ibid., p. 155.
6. Marcel Proust, *Albertine disparue*, a cura di Anne Chevalier (Parigi, Gallimard, 1992), p. 46.
7. Ibid., p. 48.
8. Italo Calvino, *Se una notte d'inverno un viaggiatore* (Milano: Mondadori, 1994), p. 41.
9. Ibid., pp. 254–55.
10. Ibid., p. 69.
11. Ibid., pp. 52–53.
12. Ibid., pp. 59–60.
13. Ibid., p. 202.
14. Ibid., pp. 66–67.
15. Ibid., p. 70.
16. Ibid., p. 239.

A NOTE ON LEGENDA

Graham Nelson

When the history of Legenda is written, Martin McLaughlin will be one of its heroes. His sense, good cheer, honest reputation, and unfailing capacity to get along with people have carried the press through many scrapes. Though he is a master of the raised-eyebrows, whites-of-his-eyes look of astonishment, Martin has the great gift of never over-reacting. I have only once seen words fail him, when an absurdly unlucky seating plan at a conference dinner placed two highly combustible colleagues right next to each other in front of people we needed to impress with our smooth running. The event passed off happily, of course. In the life of a publishing house, all crises come to nothing except the last. Martin saw to it that we never came to our last.

The many times we frowned over memos or balance sheets in Martin's sunny office in Wellington Square merge into one in my memory. A wine fridge and a high-end bicycle would be concealed among the bookcases, in so far as you can conceal a bicycle. Proofs would cover the central table, proving not least that our wrangling was getting us somewhere. On screen, browser pages of Scottish League transfer news would be not quite hidden by spreadsheets and Calvino essays. (Martin could never have been happy as a Renaissance man: Alberti may have been in his prime, but the Football Act 1424 had prohibited the game in Scotland.) Once in a while, Martin would offer wicked, though always affectionate, impressions of our colleagues. Mrs Higden in *Our Mutual Friend* says of one of her boys that, when reading newspapers out loud, 'he do the Police in different voices'. When reading emails out loud, Martin do the Professors in different voices.

In its earliest years Legenda was a team project of working academics buying in support services as needed. Malcolm Bowie, our charismatic founder, had gathered a group of both senior colleagues and young Turks: Martin, along with Diego Zancani, Peter Hainsworth and David Robey, took care of the nascent Italian list. Organisation was informal, and the nameless post of sorter-out-of-Legenda (Legenda Muggins might have been a fitting title) rotated. Alison Finch, Kevin Hilliard, Helen Watanabe, Nicola Luckhurst and others all did turns. Tales of those young days, of the formative moments in that far smaller-scale operation, are already as much legend as history, like Book I of Livy.

It was Martin who succeeded Malcolm to be the next prime mover behind Legenda, chairing both the European Humanities Research Centre, the Oxford unit which then operated us, and also the Editorial Board. After the fruitful RAE-census years of 1999–2000, in which Legenda published an unprecedented 20 titles, Legenda was developing into an appreciable business. Martin was to steer it for nearly a decade, with Ritchie Robertson as his close colleague and de facto deputy, Ritchie taking the chair himself for two of those years. The post was then taken up by Colin Davis of Royal Holloway, who in turn gave many years to the enterprise, and led the press until 2016.

But it was Martin, more than anyone else, who oversaw the crucial 2004 transition. '2004' is the '1066' of Legenda, the one memorable date in its history. This was the year in which it was put on a proper commercial footing for the first time, and new investment came from a partnership between Maney Publishing, a commercial journal publisher, and the Modern Humanities Research Association, a learned society. Where once Legenda had put on surges of activity, now there was a continuous flow of publishing. Two hundred and fifty-one books were to appear under this partnership, ranging across every European language. A particular pleasure for Martin was the appearance of his daughter Mairi's volume on the sociolinguistics of French news coverage, in a series edited and selected by the Society for French Studies. Mairi took after her father in all respects except one: she handed in the manuscript on time. Martin has to date edited or co-edited no fewer than six collective Legenda volumes but, as with one of NASA's more ambitious manifests, each launch in turn occurred two years later than originally scheduled. These were nevertheless fine books, and were a testament to a belief which has run through Martin's whole career: the conviction that the Humanities are not one thing but many, that they are a collective undertaking, and that the well-spring of the Humanities is the willingness to participate.

INDEX

Acarisio, Alberto 174
Acciaiuoli, Pietro Antonio 103
Accolti, Bernardo 102, 105–06, 109–10
Age (Agenore Incrocci) 346
Aimée, Anouk 384
Alamanni, Luca 125–26
Alamanni, Luigi 102, 125
Alamanni, Vincenzo 126
Albergati, Francesco Capacelli 195
Alberti, Leon Battista xviii, xix, xxiv, 105, 152, 157,
    159–62, 165–69
Alemanno, Gianni 388
Allen, Allida 332
Altieri, Ferdinando 174
Alunno, Francesco 174
Amphion, myth of 5, 18, 138–39
Anselmi, Pierantonio 120
Antinori, Bastiano 119
Antiquario, Iacopo 100, 110
Antonelli, Giuseppe 71
Antoniano, Silvio 108
Apollonius of Rhodes 425
Aquilecchia, Giovanni 144
Archer, Thomas 164
Aretino, Pietro 176
Argento, Dario 388
Ariosto, Alfonso 76
Ariosto, Ludovico, *Orlando furioso* xxvi, 139–40, 294,
    429–31
    and Scott 205
    portrayal of power xxiii, 69–81
    use of Lucan xxiii, 83, 86–89
    use of Virgil 92
    use of, in language learning 176, 180, 181–82
Aristotle xviii, 11, 33, 109, 119, 121, 122, 124, 126, 129,
    141, 146, 216
    Aristotelian philosophy 143, 145, 146, 216, 234
Arlenio, Arnoldo 120, 124
Arnold, Matthew 375
Asor Rosa, Alberto 398
Audebert, Germain 117
Audebert, Nicolas 127
Augé, Marc 326

Bakhtin, Mikhail 273, 274
Baldelli, Pio 341
Baldi, Gian Vittorio 384
Ballarin, Alessandro 71
Balsamo, Jean 55, 57

Balzac, Honoré de 412, 416
Bandini, Fernando 304, 371
Bàrberi Squarotti, Giorgio 273
Barbi, Michele 40–43
Barbieri, Gaetano 204, 209, 212
Barenghi, Mario 406
Baretti, Giuseppe xxiv, 173–84, 194, 195
Barilli, Renato 398
Barnaby, Paul 209
Barolini, Teodolinda 353, 363
Baronio, Cesare 219
Barozzi, Jacopo, da Vignola 151
Barthes, Roland 317, 318
Bartoli, Cosimo 158, 159, 166
Bartolomeo Veneto 69–70
Barzini, Luigi 336
Batten, John Dickson xxv, 239–54
Batten, Mary 242, 253
Battista Mantovano 106
Baudelaire, Charles 374, 419–21
Bazzoni, Giambattista 207, 212
Beccaria, Gian Luigi 273, 282
Beckett, Samuel 411
Beckman, Karen 260–61
Belli, Giuseppe Gioachino 416
Bellini, Lorenzo 180
Bellucci, Novella 299
Belpoliti, Marco 310
Bembo, Bernardo 104
Bembo, Pietro 104–05, 176
Beniscelli, Alberto 192, 194
Benivieni, Lorenzo 118
Benjamin, Walter 420–21
Berchet, Giovanni 202, 203
Bergalli, Luisa 215
Bergman, Ingmar 385
Berman, Antoine 54
Bernasconi, Luca 378
Bersani, Leo 357–58
Bertolotti, Davide 201, 202, 211, 212
Bessi, Rosella 273
Betjeman, John 375
Bettarini, Rosanna 6
Betti, Ugo 413
Bianco, Dante Livio 389
Black, John Sutherland 241
Bobulova, Barbora 392
Boccaccio, Giovanni:
    and Lucan 33–36

and Sacchetti 47-48
Decameron xxiii, 25-37, 320; translations of xviii, xxiii, 52-66
   Fiammetta in Batten's illustrations 241
   use of, in language learning 173, 174, 176, 179-80, 186 n. 54
Boethius, myth of Orpheus 2, 8
Boiardo, Matteo Maria xxiii, 78, 79, 81, 176
Bolzoni, Lina 140
Bonsaver, Guido 294
Borges, Jorge Luis xx, 320, 327, 328
Borghini, Vincenzio 40-49
Borsieri, Pietro 202, 203, 206-07, 211
Bosco, Umberto 36
Bosisio, Paolo 195
Botterill, Steven 355
Bourciez, Jean 61
Bowie, Malcolm 435
Bracciolini, Poggio 162
Bramante, Donato 153, 154
Brambilla Ageno, Franca 40, 41, 45, 49 n. 3
Branca, Vittore 42
Brandolini, Aurelio Lippo 97-98, 103-05
Brandolini, Raffaele 105
Brénot, Pierre Laurent 61
Broé, Bon de 126
Brooker, Christopher 319
Brown, Donald 257
Brucker, Jacob 225
Bruno, Giordano xxiii, 136-47
Buckhurst, Lord *see* Sackville
Buffon, Georges-Louis Leclerc, comte de 303-05, 307
Buonarroti, Michelangelo 154, 156, 180, 186 n. 43
Bürger, Gottfried August 202-03
Burlington (Richard Boyle), Third Earl 160-61, 162, 163, 164-65, 166, 167
Bynum, Caroline 363
Byron, George Gordon Byron, Baron 200

Caesar, Julius xix, 27-29, 31, 85, 92, 416
Calcagnini, Celio 71, 76
Calvino, Esther ('Chichita') xxii, 288, 289
Calvino, Italo 348, 388, 395
   and Ariosto xix, 294
   and Morante 397-98, 406
   Il barone rampante 434; and Leopardi xxv, 299-312
   'Flirt' prima di battersi xxv, 287-97
   Perché leggere i classici 65-66
   reverse vision 271 n. 15
   Il sentiero dei nidi di ragno 287-89, 292, 293-97, 383-84
   Se una notte d'inverno un viaggiatore xxv, 315-28, 431-34
   Il visconte dimezzato 392
   see also intertextuality, McLaughlin
Caminer, Domenico 195
Caminer, Elisabetta 195
Campbell, Colen 160, 163, 165-66

Campbell, Roy 375, 378
Cappello, Bernardo 120
Capponi, Lorenzo 128
Carducci, Giosuè 414
Caro, Annibale 108, 177, 178
Carosone, Renato 346
Cary, Henry Francis 239-40
Casadei, Alberto 77, 273, 406
Castelnau, Michel de 136, 143, 147 n. 3
Castelvetro, Giacomo 173
Castelvetro, Ludovico 178
Castiglione, Baldassarre 76, 108-10
   use of, in language learning 176, 177, 179, 181, 182, 183
Castiglioni, Giovan Battista 174
Cecchi d'Amico, Suso 332-35, 338, 347
Celentano, Adriano 346-47
Céline, Louis-Ferdinand 411
Cellini, Benvenuto 99, 176
Cervi, Aldo 383
Cesarotti, Melchiorre 192
Cestaro, Gary 362, 363
Charles V 76-77, 80
Charlewood, John 139
Chasteigner, Louis 127
Chiari, Pietro 192, 193, 195
Chiesa, Guido 394 n. 21
Clandon Park 158, 160, 166-69
Coleridge, Samuel Taylor 199, 203, 210, 239, 377-78
Colquhoun, Archibald xx
Compagnon, Antoine 93
Conan Doyle, Arthur 269
Conte, Gian Biagio 85
Cori, Angelo Maria 175
Corneille, Thomas 188
Cornforth, John 167
Corsi, Iacopo 106
Corsi, Pietro 305
Cortellessa, Andrea 299
Cortese, Paolo 106
Courtier, Jean 127
Coutts, Angela Burdett 170
Cristoforo Fiorentino (l'Altissimo) 110
Croce, Benedetto 367
Cromaziano, Agatopisto 224-25, 228-30, 234
Cujas, Jacques 124
cummings, e. e. 375, 378
Cyril, St, of Alexandria 216-25, 227, 230-34

D'Alberti, Matteo 162
Daléchamps, Jacques 125
Damascius 218, 219, 221, 224
Damiani, Rolando 311, 312
Daniello, Bernardino 33
Dante Alighieri 105, 142, 146, 215-16, 232, 373, 381
   and Lucan 26-36
   and Petrarch 10, 13-14, 18
   and Virgil 29, 30, 36, 37, 86, 243-45, 251, 253

Batten's illustrations: Beatrice 241; to the *Inferno* xxv, 239-54
Paradiso and diffractive reading xxvi, 352-64
use of, in language learning 173, 174, 176
da Ponte, Lorenzo 189
Davies, Jack 332
Davila, Caterino 177, 178, 181
Davis, Colin 436
Davoli, Ninetto 385
D'Azeglio, Cesare 203, 223
Deakin, Michael 218-19
De Amicis, Edmondo 397
De Bosio, Gianfranco 384
Defauconpret, Auguste-Jean-Baptiste 203-04, 209, 211, 212
Dei, Benedetto 109
Dei, Riniero 118
De Jaco, Aldo 383
Del Bene, Bartolomeo 123-24
Deleuze, Gilles 410
Della Casa, Giovanni 176, 180
De Marchi, Pietro 379
Demeurisse, Henri 53, 61-65
De Sanctis, Francesco 193
De Sica, Vittorio 331, 338, 343
Desportes, Philippe 129
D'hulst, Lieven 53
dialects of Italy 45, 48, 182, 340, 370, 372, 375-80, 414
Di Breme, Ludovico 202, 215
Diderot, Denis 192, 302
Diedo, Pietro 104
Di Nanni, Dante 387
Di Siena, Gregorio 29
Donne, John 375, 378
Dorat, Jean 127, 128
Doré, Gustave 239-40, 247, 248, 253
Dorsan, Claude 124
Dostoevsky, Fyodor 412
Dovizi, Marco Antonio 126
Dubois, Nicholas 159, 162, 167

Eco, Umberto xx, xxi, xxix, 317, 319, 395
Ekberg, Anita 340, 344
Eliot, T. S. 371
Elizabeth I 145, 147, 173, 174
Ellwood, David 331, 386
emblems, Renaissance 93, 122, 139
Empson, William 375, 378
Epicuro, Marc'Antonio 142
Equicola, Mario 105-06
Erasmus, Desiderius 143
Este, Alfonso I d' 74-75
Este, Ippolito d' 69-74, 76
Estienne, Henri 120
Estienne, Robert 118
Eurydice, myth of 1-18
Everett, Rupert 388

Farnese, Alessandro 119-20
Faseolus, Johannes 120-21
Fausto, Sebastiano (Fausto da Longiano) 77-78
Fedele, Cassandra 97
Feinstein, Wiley 323
Felici, Lucio 299
Fellini, Federico xxv-xxvi, 331-32, 336-48
Fenoglio, Beppe xxv, 272-83, 295-97, 388
Finch, Alison 435
Firenzuola, Agnolo 176
Fitzwalter (Benjamin Mildmay), First Earl 169
Flaiano, Ennio 336, 338, 348
Flaubert, Gustave 412
Floriano da Rimini 7, 12
Florio, John 137, 138, 139, 145, 174
Foix, Paul de 126-27
Folengo, Teofilo 141, 416
Fondulo, Girolamo 118
Fortuna, Sara 360
Foscolo, Ugo 414
Foucault, Michel 428-29
Fracassi, Clemente 343
Fracastoro, Girolamo 180
Franciolini, Gianni 336
François I 75-77, 118
Friedman, John Block 10
Frye, Northrop 275
Fubini, Mario 78
Furneaux, Yvonne 344
Futurism *see* Marinetti

Gable, Clark xxv, 331, 332, 347
Gadda, Carlo Emilio xxvi, 410-21
Galaverni, Roberto 273
Galilei, Galileo 178
Gambier, Yves 54
Garboli, Cesare 397
Gardini, Nicola 295
Garzanti, Livio 273
Gathercole, Patricia M. 60, 61
George II 166-67
Gerard, John 164
Germi, Pietro 336
Gesualdo, Giovanni Andrea 3
Gherardini, Lorenzo 43
Giacomini, Pierantonio 121-22, 125, 128-30
Giannetto, Nella 103
Gibbs, James 165
Ginzburg, Natalia 397, 398-99, 403
Giorgi, Marino 74
Giovio, Paolo 98, 110
Giraldi, Flavio Antonio 101, 106
Giraldi, Lilio Gregorio 97-98, 101, 106, 109
Giudicetti, Gian Paolo 78, 79-80
Giustiniano, Lorenzo 180
Goldoni, Carlo xxiv, 187-97
Gondi, Albert 129
Gondi, Jean-Baptiste I 129

Gondi, Pierre 129–30
Gozzi, Carlo xxiv, 188–97
Graves, Rupert 388
Grayson, Cecil xvii, xix
Grazzini, Antonfrancesco 100
Greville, Fulke xxiii, 136, 137, 139, 143, 145, 146
Grey, Earl, Henry 163–64
Gryphius, Sebastian 117, 118
Guattari, Félix 410
Guicciardini, Francesco 111, 178
Guicciardini, Lodovico 101–03
Guj, Luisa 325
Gürçağlar, Şehnaz Tahir 53
Gwynne, Matthew 137

Hainsworth, Peter 15, 435
Hamilton, George 163
Haraway, Donna xxvi, 352
Hardy, Thomas 375
Harrold, Earl, Antony 163–64
Hébrard de Saint-Sulpice, Antoine 125, 127
Hegel, Georg Wilhelm Friedrich 274, 276, 283 n. 2, 412
Henri III 129–30
Hermans, Theo 66 n. 14
Hewlett, Maurice 241, 253
Hewlings, Richard 161
Hilliard, Kevin 435
Homer 5, 9, 10, 18, 105, 272, 277–82, 425
Hope, Thomas 241
Hopkins, Gerard Manley 375–76, 378, 379–80, 381
Hoquet, Thierry 305
Horace 105, 413, 416
Housman, A. E. 375
Hugo, Victor 397, 398
Hussey, Christopher 167
Hypatia of Alexandria xxiv, 215–35

Iamblichus 222, 234
improvisation, poetic xxiii, 97–112
intertextuality:
    Ariosto 86–89
    Benjamin 420
    Boccaccio 33–37
    Bruno 138
    Calvino 294, 318–20, 324, 327
    Dante 25–37, 353
    deforestation as image for 94 n. 3
    Fenoglio 272–83
    Gadda 421, 422 n. 13
    Machiavelli 110–11
    Medici, Lorenzo de' 110
    Meneghello 372–74
    Petrarch 7, 11, 13, 14, 110
    Poliziano xviii
    Il sangue dei vinti 392
    Tasso, Torquato 89–93
    in translations 52, 53, 57, 65
Isella, Dante 283 n. 5

Jenkins, Simon 167, 168, 170 n. 1
Johnson, Samuel 180, 181
Jones, Inigo 160, 167
Jossa, Stefano 77
Joyce, James 262
Juvarra, Filippo 164

Kent, William 165
Kermode, Frank 328
Kezich, Tullio 347
Kirkpatrick, Robin 355
Kristeva, Julia 320
Krzycki, Andrzej 106

lacunae:
    in manuscripts 42, 44, 45
    in narrative xxvi, 295, 424–34
Lady Margaret Hall, University of Oxford xxv, 242–43, 253
Lambin, Denys 121–22
Lancetti, Vincenzo 204
Landino, Cristoforo 105
language learning, Italian 173–84
Lanza, Mario 346
Larkin, Philip 375, 378
Lates, David Francesco 175
Lattuada, Alberto 336
Lauro, Vincenzo 124
Lawrence, D. H. 375
Lazzaro-Weis, Carol 315
Lears, Jackson 269–70
Legenda 435–36
Legh, Sir Peter 166, 167
Le Maçon, Antoine 52–53, 55–65
Le Nain de Tillemont, Sébastien 225
Leo X 97–98, 101, 105, 111
Leonardo da Vinci 99
Leoni, Antonio 161
Leoni, Giacomo xxiv, 157–70
Leoniceno, Niccolò 106
Leopardi, Adelaide 311
Leopardi, Carlo 311–12
Leopardi, Giacomo 381
    and Calvino xxv, 299–312
    and Scott xxiv, 209–10
Leopardi, Monaldo 301
Leopardi, Paolina 311–12
Lepschy, Giulio 375
Le Tourneur, Pierre 202
Letronne, Jean Antoine 224
L'Hospital, Michel de 123, 126
Linnell, John 241
Livy 416
logisieren 56, 60

Lomazzo, Gian Paolo 151
Lombardo Radice, Lucio 325
Long, Lynne 53
Loren, Sophia xxv, 331, 332, 335, 342–43, 344, 347
L'Orme, Philibert de 156
Loy, Nanni 383
Lucan xxiii, 25–37, 84–93
Luchetti, Daniele 394 n. 21
Luckhurst, Nicola 435
Lucretius 428
Lukács, György 206
Luperini, Romano 395, 399
Lyme Park 158, 166, 167–69

Machiavelli, Niccolò 105, 107–08, 110–11, 143, 178–79
McLaughlin, Mairi 436
McLaughlin, Martin xvii-xxii, xxviii-xxxii, 49, 160, 239, 435–36
    and Calvino 296, 318, 319, 383
    and imitation 8, 84, 110
    and Legenda 435–36
    and translation 52–53, 55, 57, 60, 64, 65
Maffei, Bernardino 120
Malerba, Luigi 319
Malte-Brun, Conrad 202, 211
Manfredi, Eustachio 178
Manni, Paola 47
Manuzio, Aldo 100, 110, 139
Manzoni, Alessandro:
    and Diodata Saluzzo xxiv, 215, 223, 230
    and Gadda 412–14, 416
    and Morante 400, 402
    and *Il sangue dei vinti* 391–92
    and Scott 203, 204, 210, 213 n. 19
Marguerite de France 123–24
Marguerite de Navarre 55
Marinetti, Filippo Tommaso xxv, 258, 259–62, 264, 265, 270
Marone, Andrea 98, 110
Márquez, Gabriel García 321
Marquis, Don 369
Martin, Joseph 204, 212
Martone, Mario 312
Mastroianni, Marcello 340
Mattoli, Mario 346
Medea, myth of 86, 87–89, 90, 95 n. 13
Medici, Catherine de' 123, 124, 126, 128
Medici, Lorenzo de' 100, 101–02, 103, 105, 110, 111
    Selve 113 n. 15
Mei, Girolamo 119–20
Melato, Mariangela 384
memory, use of, in improvisation 109
Menegatti, Marialucia 69–70
Meneghello, Luigi:
    I piccoli maestri 394 n. 21
    poetry and translation xxvi, 367–81
Mereghetti, Paolo 392

Messina, Marguerite 58
Michelangelo di Bernardino 101
Milanini, Claudio 292
Milano, Paolo 273
Milton, John 180
Mini, Paolo 125
Mirabeau, Honoré-Gabriel Riquetti, comte de 58, 60, 65
Moevs, Christian 355
Molière 188
Molina, Tirso de 188, 189
Mondo, Lorenzo 283 n. 5
Montaigne, Michel de 99
Montaldo, Giuliano 384–85
Montale, Eugenio:
    and chance xxv, 258, 262–65, 270
    and Meneghello 370, 372, 373, 377
    'Upupa' 304
Montanelli, Indro 393 n. 6
Monti, Vincenzo 200
Morani, Aurelio 99
Morante, Elsa:
    and diffractive reading xxvi, 352, 360–61, 363
    La Storia Romanzo xxvi, 395–407
Morariu, Caterina 389
Morel, Frédéric II 122–23, 125, 127
Moretti, Franco 270 n. 4, 274
Moretti, Walter 77
Morgoglione, Claudia 388
Moro, Aldo 387
Morra, Rosario 372
Morricone, Ennio 386
Mouren, Raphaële 117
Mozart, Wolfgang Amadeus 189
Muñiz Muñiz, Maria de la Nieves 273
Muratori, Lodovico 222, 234
Muret, Marc-Antoine 130
Musgrave, George xxv, 240–42
Mussato, Albertino 10
Muti, Ornella 385

Najemy, John 111
Nassar, Eugene Paul 242
Navagero, Andrea 177, 178
Nerli, Neri de' 52, 57
Nero, Franco 384
New, Edmund Hort 241
Nutt, David 254

Onslow, Thomas, Second Earl 158
Oriolo, Filippo 99
Orpheus, myth of xxii-xxiii, 1–18, 425
Orsini, Valentino 384, 386–87
Ossian 203
Ottonaio, Francesco 124
Ovid 85, 86, 107
    myth of Orpheus 1–4, 7–9, 13, 23 n. 47

Owen, Wilfred 375
Ozell, John 159

Pacchioni, Federico 336
Padoan, Giorgio 28
Palermo, Evangelista 174
Palermo, Massimo 47
Palladio, Andrea xxiv, 156, 157, 159–68
Pallock, Frederick 240
Pansa, Giampaolo xxvi, 383, 388–92
Paolini, Marco 375
Parker, Edward Adams 242
Parks, Tim xx
Partisans *see* Resistance
Pascal, Blaise 424
Pasolini, Pier Paolo xxvi, 352, 356–58, 360, 361, 363, 385, 395
Pavese, Cesare 283, 299, 384, 388, 392–93
Pavone, Claudio 388
Pedullà, Gabriele 273, 296
Pedullà, Walter 273
Pellegrini, Ernestina 374–75
Pellegrini, Glauco 384
Pepys, Samuel 199–200
Perloff, Marjorie 259
Perna, Pietro 121
Pertile, Lino 355
Pertini, Sandro 387
Pertwee, Michael 332
Peruzzi, Baldassarre 150, 152, 153
Pesce, Giovanni 387
Petrarch (Petrarca), Francesco xix, 110, 162
    and Dante 10, 13-14, 18
    and *fabula* of Eurydice and Orpheus xxii–xxiii, 1-18
    Bucolicum carmen 8, 10, 11-12
    epystolae 7, 12-14, 17, 18
    forms of the Canzoniere 5, 6, 15, 16, 20 n. 22
    Laura 1-6, 12, 16-18; in Batten's illustrations 241
    Parthenias 7-12, 14, 18
    translation of Griselda tale 52, 54
    use of Ovid 110
    use of, in language learning 173, 174, 176
Philostorgius 218
Picart, Bernard 159
Pinelli, Tullio 336, 337, 348
Pirandello, Luigi xxv, 265–70
Pivano, Ferdinanda 348
Placido, Michele 385, 389–91, 394 n. 27
Plautus 110
Plotinus 222, 225, 229–31, 234, 327
Plutarch 428
Poe, Edgar Allan 429
Poliziano, Agnolo xviii, 105
Polo, Marco xx
Ponti, Carlo 335, 342
Porro, Girolamo 181
Porta, Carlo 416
Prete, Antonio 299, 308

Preziosi, Alessandro 392
Proust, Marcel xxvi, 429–31, 434
Puccini, Gianni 383
Pulci, Luigi 111
Puppi, Lionello 161
Pym, Anthony 54

Querno, Camillo 97, 101
Quintilian 109

Radcliffe, Ann 200
Ragusa, Olga 202
Rajna, Pio 77, 80
Ramus, Petrus 121
Raphael (Raffaello Sanzio) 71–72, 150, 153, 178
Rascel, Renato 346
Redi, Francesco 178
Resistance, in World War II 272–73, 275, 282–83, 287–97, 383–93, 401, 402, 404
Ricci, Sebastiano 159
Rigoni, Mario Andrea 304, 308
Robertson, Ritchie 436
Robey, David 435
romantic, *romantico* xxiv, 191, 199–210, 215, 230, 245, 262, 414
romanzesco 89, 90, 92, 96 n. 21, 200, 202, 203, 204, 206–09, 396, 397–98
Ronsard, Pierre de 128
Rose, Jack 332, 334–35
Rosi, Francesco 341
Rossanda, Rossana 397
Rossellini, Roberto 336, 337, 391, 393 n. 6
Rota, Nino 346
Rothstein, Marian 55
Roville, Guillaume 130
Rowland, Ingrid 146–47
Rucellai, Annibale 124–25
Rucellai, Carlo 124
Ruscelli, Girolamo 108, 110, 181
Rusconi, Carlo xxiv, 207–09, 212

Sabatier de Castres, Antoine 52–53, 58–65
Sacchetti, Franco xxiii, 40–49
Sacchi, Antonio 190
Sackville, Thomas (Lord Buckhurst) 137–38, 142
Saltini, Vittorio 397
Saluzzo, Diodata xxiv, 215–17, 219, 221–35
Salvini, Antonmaria 178
Sannazaro, Iacopo 106
Sansovino, Francesco 97
Sansovino, Jacopo 154
Sanudo, Marino 103–05
Sasso, Panfilo 109
Sassoon, Siegfried 375
Satta Flores, Stefano 385
Scaliger, Joseph 117, 127, 128
Scannapieco, Anna 195
Scawen, Thomas 166

Scawen, Sir William 158, 166
Scharf, George, Jr 240–41
Schlegel, August Wilhelm 201, 202, 211
Schlesinger, Adolph Martin 207–08
Schnapp, Jeffrey 260–61
Scott, Walter, translation of Waverley novels xxiv, 199–212
Serlio, Sebastiano xxiv, 150–56
Shakespeare, William 194, 196, 202, 207, 375, 378, 380, 412, 416, 422 n. 13
Shavelson, Melville xxv-xxvi, 331–35, 336, 337, 338, 341–48
Sidney, Sir Philip 144
Signoret, Simone 385
Simintendi, Arrigo 37 n. 2
Simon, Richard 217
Soavi, Michele 388, 389, 392
Socrates Scholasticus 218, 219
Soncini, Virginio 203–04, 206, 209, 212
Southerden, Francesca 310–11
Speroni, Sperone 176
Spinazzola, Vittorio 406–07
Squarzini, Luigi 384
Staël, Madame de (Anne-Louise-Germaine) 201, 202, 212
Statius 86
Steinbeck, John 393 n. 10
Steno (Stefano Vanzina) 331, 338, 346, 348
Stimato, Gerarda 74
Styles, Benjamin 164
Swift, Jonathan 193
Swineshead, Richard 141, 145
Synesius of Cyrene 218, 219

Tansillo, Luigi 142
Tasso, Torquato, *Gerusalemme liberata*:
    use of Dante 86, 91, 92
    use of Lucan xxiii, 83, 85, 89–93
    use of Ovid 92
    use of Virgil 86, 90, 91, 92
    use of, in language learning 176, 180
Taverna, Stefano 114 n. 39
Tellini, Gino 406
Thomas, Dylan 375
Thomas, Edward 375
Thomas, William 173, 174
Thulin, Ingrid 385
Toland, John 216–35
Toledo, Eleonora de 123
Tommaseo, Niccolò 28, 204
Toscano, Giovanni Matteo 125, 127, 130
Tournes, Jean II de 122
translation:
    literal 183–84
    retranslation xxiii, xxiv, 52–66, 159
    taxonomies 53–55
    see also Boccaccio, intertextuality, McLaughlin, Meneghello, Petrarch, Scott

Traquair, Phoebe 241
Trissino, Gian Giorgio 177, 179
Trotter, David 262, 265
Turnèbe, Adrien 120–21

Ubaldini, Lelio 127–28
Ugolini, Baccio 105, 106
Ungaretti, Giuseppe 373–74, 379

Valeriano, Pierio 98
Van Order, Thomas 350, 351
Varchi, Benedetto 108, 110
Vasari, Giorgio 99, 153–54
Vascosan, Michel 123
Venturi, Roberto 126
Vercors (Jean Bruller) 393 n. 10
Verri, Pietro 195
Vettori, Francesco 107, 110, 118
Vettori, Paolo 111
Vettori, Piero xxiii, 117–30
Viganò, Renata xxvi, 383, 384, 386, 388
Vignola *see* Barozzi
Virgil 101, 416
    Aeneid 34, 77, 84, 85, 86, 90, 91, 138, 139, 143, 278–81, 353, 425–28, 431, 434
    and Dante 28, 29, 30, 37, 142, 143, 215, 216; in Batten's illustrations 243, 245, 247, 248, 251, 253
    myth of Orpheus 1–2, 4, 5, 8–10, 15, 18
Visconti, Ermes 203
Visconti, Luchino 385
Vitruvius 151, 152, 153, 155
Vittorini, Elio 299, 383, 384, 387–88
Volonté, Gian Maria 384

Wadham College, University of Oxford xxiii, 43
Ware, Isaac 160, 166
Warner, Marina 191
Watanabe, Helen 435
Weaver, William xx
Weiss, Beno 322, 323
Westman, Robert 145
Wittkower, Rudolf 159, 165–66
Wren, Christopher 159, 160, 167
Wrest Park 163–64

Yeats, W. B. 375, 378–79

Zancani, Diego 435
Zanotti, Giampiero 178
Zappi, Faustina Maratti 215
Zatti, Sergio 86, 89
Zerbinati, Paolo 73
Zironi, Giuseppina 81
Zola, Émile 423 n. 24
Zorzi, Ludovico 194
Zuliani, Luca 111

www.ingramcontent.com/pod-product-compliance
Lightning Source LLC
Chambersburg PA
CBHW080048190426
43201CB00036B/2274